R R Angerstein's Illustrated Travel Diary 1753–1755

Industry in England and Wales from a Swedish perspective

This portrait of Reinhold Rücker Angerstein hangs in the boardroom of Jernkontoret in Stockholm. The text reads: 'Reinhold Gustafsson Angerstein, Assessor in the Royal Mining Council and Director of heavy forging for the nation. Born 1718. Died 1760.' Note that the patronymic appears as his second name rather than his mother's family name, Rücker, which was more often used.

R R Angerstein's Illustrated Travel Diary 1753–1755

Industry in England and Wales from a Swedish perspective

translated by Torsten and Peter Berg

with an introduction by Professor Marilyn Palmer

Science Museum

Published 2001

British Library Cataloguing-in-Publication Data
A catalogue record for this publication is available from the British Library.

Set from QuarkXpress in Postscript Monotype Plantin by
Jerry Fowler
Printed in Great Britain by the Cromwell Press
Cover design by Jerry Fowler

ISBN 1 900747 24 3

Science Museum, Exhibition Road, London SW7 2DD
http://www.nmsi.ac.uk

Contents

Angerstein's journeys in England and Wales, 1753–1755

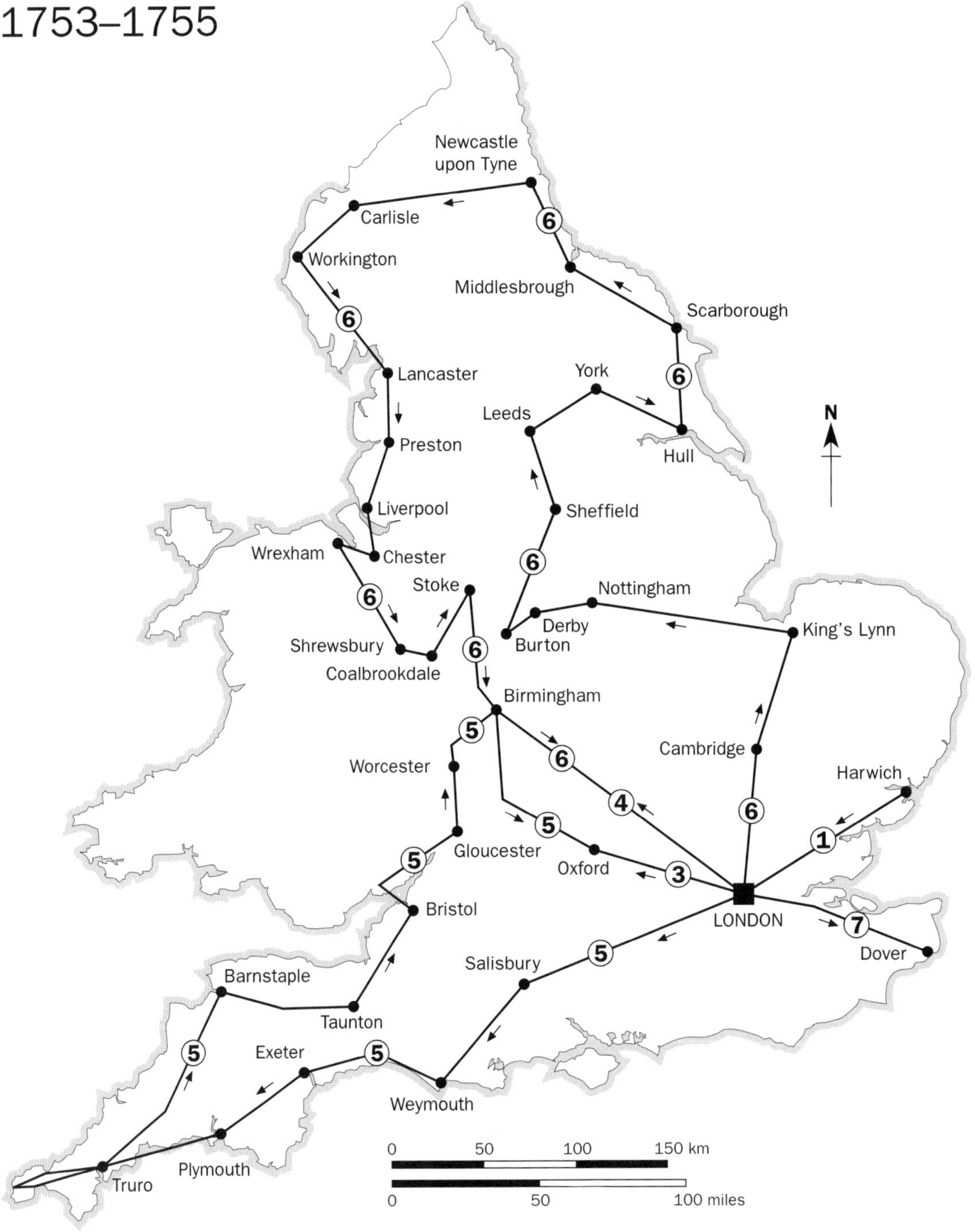

Places visited

Volume 1

1 15 September 1753. Harwich, Colchester, London.

2 22 September 1753. London, Isleworth, Windsor, Kensington, London.

3 3 October 1753. London, Uxbridge, High Wycombe, Oxford, Blenheim, Oxford, Woodstock, Oxford (23 October), Hounslow, London.

4 3 April 1754. London, Uxbridge, Aylesbury, Winslow, Buckingham, Banbury, Warwick, Birmingham (6 April), Aston (7 April), Bromford, Snowhill (8 April), Wednesbury (10 April), Bilston, Wolverhampton (11 April).

5 30 April 1754. London, Windsor, Stockbridge, Salisbury (1 May), Wilton, Stonehenge, Blandford, Spetisbury, Middleton, Dorchester (5 May), Weymouth, Portland (6 May), Abbotsbury (8 May), Bridport, Exeter, Newton Abbot, Totnes (11 May), Dartmouth, Modbury (12 May), Kingsbridge, Modbury, Plymouth (13 May), Looe (14 May), Fowey, St Austell (15 May), Grampound, Truro, St Agnes, Redruth (20 June), Cambourne, Penzance, Treen, Lands End, St Just, Marazion (23 June), Helston, Penryn, Falmouth, Truro (28 May), St Columb, Bodmin (29 May), Launceston, Holsworthy, Bideford, Barnstaple, South Molton, Tiverton, Wellington, Taunton, Glastonbury, Wells, Wookey Hole, Bristol, Hotwells, Woolland, Publowe, Warmley, Keynsham, Crews Hole (25 June), Durdham Common (25 June), Caerleon, Newport, Abercarn, Pontypool, Usk, Monmouth, Redbrook, Coleford, Mitcheldean, Flaxley, Gloucester, Upton, Worcester, Droitwich, Bewdley, Lower Milton, Kidderminster, Stourbridge, Dudley, Bilston, Wilden, Worcester, Pershore, Evesham, Moreton-in-the-Marsh, Oxford, High Wycombe, Uxbridge, London.

Volume 2

6 27 July 1754. London, Bow, Stratford, Epping, Bishops Stortford, Cambridge, Huntingdon, St Ives, Downham, Boston, Kings Lynn, Sleaford, Newark, Nottingham, Bulwell, Basford, Derby, Burton, Belper, Denby, Crich, Matlock, Winster, Chatsworth, Chesterfield, Sheffield, Chapeltown, Barnsley, Clifton, Wortley, Wakefield, Leeds, York, Beverley, Hull, Beverley, Scarborough, Irton, Osgodby, Whitby, Sandsend, Staithes, Guisborough, Stockton, Darlington, Middleton Tyas, Durham, Sunderland, Shields, Tynemouth, Newcastle, Teams, Swalwell, Winlaton, Blackhall Mill, Shotley Bridge, Chopwell, Derwentcote, Gibside, Benton, Newburn, Hexham, Carlisle, Maryport, Workington, Clifton, Whitehaven, Egremont, Borrowdale, Ulverston, Penny Bridge, Spark Bridge, Garstang, Poulton le Fylde, Preston, Wigan, Chowbent, Prescot, Liverpool, Warrington, Northwich, Chester, Holywell, Wrexham, Ellesmere, Shrewsbury, Coalbrookdale, Newport, Eccleshall, Newcastle under Lyme, Bilston, Wednesbury, Stowe, Winslow, Wendover, London.

7 23 January 1755. London, Crayford, Dartford, Rochester, Canterbury, Dover (29 January).

Acknowledgements

Translation of the diaries recounting Angerstein's journeys in England and Wales was to have been the crowning achievement of Torsten Berg's lifelong interest in industrial history. The idea came in about 1970, from Richard Smith and Stanley Chapman of Nottingham University, and I feel certain that my father would have wished to thank them most warmly for introducing him to this project, which came to dominate his later years. He would also have been grateful for much help and encouragement from fellow members of the Newcomen Society and the Historical Metallurgy Society, for which voluminous correspondence remains as testimony.

Alas, my father did not live to complete the translation. After his death in 1978 I took up the work, very hesitantly at first but, with the help of experts in many different fields, who have been astonishingly generous with their time, the task is done. The list of those who have helped is a long one.

In Sweden, first of all, I have to express deep gratitude to Marianne Fornander for all her help and encouragement, coupled with boundless admiration for her herculean task of transcribing all eight volumes of the diaries. Svante Lindkvist also helped with problems of palaeography and technical terms. At Jernkontoret, I have to thank the late Wilhelm Ekman, who made the original promise of financial help, Marie Nisser, representing the Mining History Committee, who found time for Angerstein in her busy life as professor at the Royal Technical Institute, and, not least, Yngve Axelsson, the endlessly patient Jernkontoret librarian.

I also wish to record here my formal thanks to the current management of Jernkontoret for their grant of funds towards publication and for permission to make use of copies of the illustrations.

Back in England, the late Kenneth Barraclough and Justin Brooke (who has recently completed a translation of the Kalmeter diaries) gave detailed advice on major sections of the translation. Many others, too numerous to list, helped in smaller ways on technical matters. Jeremy Russell gave advice on birds and Arthur Keaveney had to give Angerstein a rather low mark for his Latin.

I was delighted when Marilyn Palmer agreed to write the introduction and am most grateful for the enthusiasm she has shown for the subject.

On a more practical note, I have to thank Pamela Cotterill, Jennifer Jackson and Lucy Ross for turning poor carbon copies, scraps of hand-written manuscript and long out-of-date word-processing disks covering difficult material into a polished typescript.

At the Science Museum, I shall be forever grateful to Ela Ginalska for taking on the project. The Museum's Curator of Mechanical Engineering, Michael Wright, acting as technical editor, went far beyond the call of duty in making many useful suggestions and additions to the notes. Thanks also to Louise Wilson, who took the material through to the design stage, to her successor Lawrence Ahlemeyer and to Jerry Fowler, the designer.

Finally, just as my father would have wished to thank my mother, Gerky, for all her patient help and encouragement, I wish to thank my wife, Mary, for her wise advice and many suggestions for improving the text, not to mention her unfailing support over all these years.

Peter Berg
Canterbury, 2001

Introduction

The publication in English of the illustrated travel diaries of Reinhold Rücker Angerstein has been long awaited by those interested in the industrial development of Britain in the eighteenth century. Their value was first stressed in Sven Rydberg's extensive study of the journeys made by Swedes to England,[1] which was brought to the notice of British historians by Alan Birch,[2] who had himself studied parts of Angerstein's journals in the Jernkontoret in Stockholm. Michael Flinn provided an even more tantalising glimpse of their content in 1958,[3] and the English translation in 1992 of Karl-Gustaf Hildebrand's *Swedish Iron* included some of Angerstein's vignettes of British blast furnaces.[4] Although the translation of these valuable diaries from Swedish was begun many years ago, it is not until now that Peter Berg has succeeded in completing what his father had begun; the Science Museum has made his work available in an excellent illustrated edition. A treat is in store for all those who open its pages, not only to read the informative text but also to delight in Angerstein's evocative drawings.

Peter Berg's introduction places Angerstein firmly in the ranks of all those from the Swedish state institutions concerned with the regulation of the iron industry, the Bergscollegium and the Jernkontoret. He also explains the concern of the Swedes with the threats to their supremacy as the main exporters of bar iron to Britain during the eighteenth century, both from other iron-producing countries such as Russia and America, and from technical innovations within the British iron industry itself. It is therefore not surprising that a fair proportion of the 900 pages of the diary is devoted to the iron trade: Angerstein notes the proportion of Swedish iron compared to that from other countries in all the ports he visited, and also the comparative prices. He was also concerned to learn about the reputation of Swedish iron, particularly the important Öregrund iron from the Dannemora mines, which was regarded as the best for steel manufacture: he was pleased to note that this was in use in most of the steelworks he visited, such as Crowley's works at Swalwell and the Derwentcote cementation furnace, both near Newcastle.

Angerstein made a point of visiting as many blast furnaces as he could in the course of his travels, but at the great majority of them he found that charcoal was still in use for smelting, despite the claimed shortage of wood for charcoal burning. He says, somewhat disparagingly, that this is entirely due to unsatisfactory forestry: 'If the inhabitants became so thrifty that they would plant new trees wherever an old one had been felled, and replenish the hedgerows with fast-growing trees, there would be good reason to believe that there would be no more complaints about lack of charcoal for the blast furnaces and forges of England.' Insufficient research has been carried out on charcoal supply to British furnaces, but what has been done would, in fact, suggest that woodland management was taken seriously by ironmasters and their charcoal suppliers, and it may have been the cost of the quantity of labour needed to produce charcoal that was the main reason for the attempts being made to replace it as a fuel.[5,6] Only at Clifton furnace near Workington and the Coalbrookdale furnaces did he find evidence of coke-smelting, although he was not permitted entry into the former. He was pleased to note that, despite many experiments, the iron from these furnaces did not produce satisfactory bar iron and was used for castings. His observations bear out the now widely accepted view that the use of coke for iron smelting spread only slowly in the first half of the eighteenth century. As Philip Riden has pointed out, the output of charcoal-smelted iron in 1750 was probably greater than ever before.[7]

Angerstein travelled in Britain at a time when many technological innovations had already taken place, such as Newcomen's atmospheric engine, Darby's use of coke for iron smelting, water-powered silk-throwing and Kay's flying shuttle in the woollen industry. But many great advances were still to come: for example Watt's improvement of the Newcomen engine, Henry Cort's puddling process and Arkwright's water-powered machinery that slowly transformed textile production into a factory industry. He was therefore seeing a picture of England and Wales in a state of slow transition, with some exciting developments which he and many of his contemporaries were keen to visit, but also the continuity of craft and domestic production: the nailers of Belper and the Black Country, the spinning of hemp and flax by women and children in Exeter, the 'old women who had long tobacco pipes clamped in their mouths' as they spun wool and knitted stockings in Pershore. He was careful to record it all, the traditional alongside the innovative, which is what makes his diaries such a useful sequel to Daniel Defoe's observations 30 years earlier. Like Defoe, he makes clear the pattern of regional specialisation, which had characterised Britain from the late seventeenth century onwards. Hops were grown in Kent, stockings knitted in the East Midlands and Worcestershire, carpets were woven in Kidderminster and Wilton, buttons, buckles, tea trays and snuff boxes came from the Black Country and Birmingham. He notes that the inhabitants of Shrewsbury made iron window frames, an early sign of the versatility of local ironmasters, who were later to revolutionise building construction with the use of iron beams and columns. It is a surprisingly familiar Britain that springs from the pages of Angerstein's diaries.

Especially valuable, now that towns are dominated by commercial and retail ventures, are his accounts of their industrial diversity in the middle of the eighteenth century. In Exeter he viewed fulling mills, cloth presses, flour mills, a malt kiln and numerous iron manufactories. The townscape of Bristol was dominated by 15 glass furnaces, but he also saw soap and salt-boilers, factories for the manufacture of pipes, turpentine, lamp-black and pigments for water-colours, a lead smelter and lead shot works, as well as numerous brass and zinc works close to the town, the latter belonging to William Champion.[8,9] Liverpool, as well as being 'one of the most flourishing ports in England', boasted five sugar factories, 10 potteries for earthenware or so-called Delft ware, six factories for tobacco pipes, four glass houses, ten tobacco factories, two anchor forges, four salt pans, a sailcloth factory and a large number of saddlers and shoemakers working on goods for export. Nottingham echoed to 'the thumping and squeaking of the stocking frames, which can be heard all the time, encouraging the people to be diligent and industrious'. The workers produced more than 20,000 pairs of stockings a week and built the frames themselves. The inhabitants of Derby, 'a pleasant and well-situated town', had dammed the River Derwent and its tributaries to drive many mills for both silk manufacture and the rolling and slitting of iron, while the town also boasted renowned porcelain and white-ware works. These urban industries are familiar, and some evidence often survives in the form of adapted buildings, archaeological sites or museums, but Angerstein brings home the bustling activity that characterised eighteenth-century towns.

His fascination with mechanical devices is evident in both the diaries and the illustrations that accompany them. He had only been in London for a day when he went to view the water-pumping machinery situated below London Bridge, and his drawing is also a valuable record of the buildings on the bridge itself. He seems to have been largely unfamiliar with the wire, mesh-covered boulters used for sieving flour in corn mills, which he describes at mills in both Uxbridge and Newcastle.
He provides excellent drawings of the wooden lantern gears that were replaced by cast-iron bevel gears in most mills in the nineteenth century. He also described and illustrated the unique, if somewhat ineffective, spark machine devised by Carlyle Spedding of Whitehaven to provide light with less risk of explosion from firedamp. At the same time, however, he was conscious of the people who worked on the industrial sites that he visited, and it is possible to deduce something about the size of the workforce in particular industries, the gender balance and the use of child labour from his diaries. He often lists the numbers employed, together with their wages: there were six workers at Aston furnace near Birmingham who were paid 3s 17d per ton (the furnace produced 17 tons a week), while six workers operated the nine furnaces at Mr Taylor's brass works, also near Birmingham, and were paid 9s per week. He noted near Bridport how, 'in all small houses and cottages that I travelled past, both in the town and in the surrounding countryside, all women were occupied spinning hemp and making fishing nets'. Meanwhile young boys were employed to scutch the hemp using what he describes as stamps: they 'had to be very quick as otherwise their hands might be smashed'. More than 40 people were employed making flowers and figures in the Derby porcelain works, while over a thousand worked at the pin factory in Gloucester. In Cornwall, he found, most of the men were miners, while

children and young women were occupied in the stream works and on the dressing floors. Women and young girls in Wednesbury, on the other hand, were busy painting, glazing and enamel-firing snuffboxes, while the inventor of a screw-cutting machine in the same town had profited from his invention because 'both women and children can do the work without knowing anything else than how to turn the crank forwards and backwards'. Unskilled labour of this kind was there to be exploited. Such details are invaluable in providing information about occupations in this period, well before standardised parish register or census data are available.

Despite his primary interest in industry, Angerstein observed and noted different agricultural practices in the course of his travels. His visit was made before the great flurry of parliamentary enclosure towards the end of the century, and his comments on open-field agriculture in the Midlands are particularly interesting. On his way from Warwick to Birmingham, he commented on the large flocks of sheep grazing on common land which, except near cultivated areas, were allowed to wander without supervision because 'there are no wolves here' – a different situation from Sweden! Elsewhere he observed the farming of rabbits on the common land, watched over by warreners to prevent their theft, and in the West Midlands he even noted a watchman's hut on a sandy heath. North of Aylesbury, he both recorded and illustrated the S-shaped strips about 12 feet wide, characteristic of fields ploughed by large teams of oxen or horses which had to be directed at an angle to the headland in order to be turned. In early April 1754, he observed and drew a five-horse team in line pulling a plough near Warwick, while nearby a farmer was seen driving a horse that pulled a flattened bunch of tree branches to spread out the manure left by the cattle that had been grazing on it. He was told that the fields were left fallow every third year, during which time they were fertilised both with dung and lime, the latter being spread on top of the former and ploughed in when the weather was fine. Then, when the field was sown with wheat at Michaelmas time, it gave an abundant crop. In south-west England, where limestone was rare, it had to be imported, together with the coal to burn it, from south Wales and then burnt in large kilns near the coast. He also noticed that seashells were also collected and crushed as substitutes for burnt lime. His diaries give a good idea of the extent of lime-burning in England and the importance of burnt lime in the agricultural economy of the time. In Kent, he noted the extent of hop cultivation, providing an illustration of the poles stacked together awaiting use, while he commented several times on the use of staddle stones to raise hay and straw stacks off the ground.

He was, of course, even more interested in industrial than agricultural landscapes. His visit to the south-west of England in May 1754 provides us with an invaluable picture of tin streaming and copper working at a time when the landscape was not dominated by steam-engine houses, as it became towards the end of the century. The first Newcomen engine had been introduced into Cornwall in about 1710[10] and Angerstein would have been familiar with it from the published accounts by his fellow countryman, Marten Triewald, who had constructed a similar engine at Dannemora in Sweden, which came into blast in 1728.[11] He certainly saw some of them working at St Austell, Redruth and Carn Brea, and he commented on the existence of two, with a third under construction, at North Downs near Chacewater; the new one had a cylinder of 69 inches diameter. Surprisingly, though, he illustrated none of them, perhaps indicating that the typical features of the landscape at that time were the horse whims and waterwheels, which figure more largely in his pages. He visited some copper mines on the seashore near St Just (presumably Levant or Botallack), which he was told were discovered 60 or 70 years ago by a German, and certainly his drawing of a horse-whim enclosed in a wigwam-shaped hut is very reminiscent of German illustrations of this period. In the neighbourhood of St Austell, he saw numerous tin-streaming sites and includes a drawing of a water-powered stamping wheel and a series of rectangular buddles that echoes the well-known one by William Pryce made in 1778.[12] His many drawings of rectangular buddles are an extremely useful record of the dressing of tin, lead and copper before the early nineteenth century introduction of the circular 'Cornish' buddle which superseded them in many areas.[13] On Bodmin Moor, too, he commented on all the tin-streamers working in the valleys, as well as the remains of old stream works; he also noted old, abandoned mines while viewing the lead and zinc district of the Mendips. One of his most evocative drawings is that of abandoned horse-whims scattered across the landscape below the town of Wednesbury. Certainly, he was not only interested in innovative technology.

Angerstein was equally prolific in providing illustrations of buildings and of the towns that he visited. He captures the dominance over their respective towns of the castle at Launceston and of St Mary's Abbey at Whitby; the extent of shipping in the harbours of Lancaster and Bideford; the bridge at Newcastle separating the keels of the upper Tyne from the sea-going vessels below it. The staithes used to deliver coal to boats from the steep banks of the Tyne are also illustrated, together with a delightful vignette of a coal wagon on a downward slope, with its attendant sitting on the shafts to slow its progress. Similarly, he drew a gravity incline delivering coal down the steep slope of the River Severn to waiting boats, although his diary records that, on the occasion he viewed it, the winding man in his drum house at the top of the incline let the speed increase too much and the wagons were smashed to bits! The drawings he provides of kilns and furnaces are invaluable, since all too often we are left with only a ground plan revealed by excavation or, at best, a ruinous superstructure. There are numerous illustrations of lime kilns, reverberatory furnaces, pottery kilns and glass furnaces: a series of drawings of glass furnaces at Bristol are particularly valuable, illustrating the furnaces themselves (made of Stourbridge clay) inside their brick-built hovel, which he says is 70 to 80 feet in height. Of the iron blast furnaces he describes, he illustrates seven of them: Aston, Abercarn, Flaxley, Chapeltown, Maryport, Clifton and Coalbrookdale – the two latter have coking heaps alongside. Whereas we now generally see only the stone or brick-built furnace stack, Angerstein was able to record the ancillary buildings around the stack, which at Aston and Chapeltown seem to have been of wooden construction as they were in Sweden. Most of the drawings indicate the position of the waterwheel driving the bellows, while those of Abercarn near Pontypool and Flaxley in the Forest of Dean have wonderfully detailed depictions of the charging, blowing and tapping arrangements, illustrating the structure over the furnace throat which so rarely survives.
His drawings of the interiors of forges and tinplate works give some indication of the layout of the different components: that of Bromford Forge near Birmingham illustrates three hearths, two finery hearths and the other a chafery, together with water-powered bellows and forging hammer. Such details are very difficult to recover from excavated evidence, as has been found, for example, in archaeological work carried out on several forges in Cumbria.[14] Finally, his illustrations give a good idea of the relationship of one building to another and also of their topographical setting. The Abercarn furnace is situated at the bottom of a slope to facilitate charging, while the kilns for roasting the iron ore are at a higher level. Angerstein's drawing of the Coalbrookdale works shows the two furnaces, one of the mill ponds, the steam engine for pumping water back up to the Upper Pool and the large early Georgian houses of Rosehill House and Dale House on the slope above the pond.

This is the joy of Angerstein's diary for the industrial archaeologist. The sites one has known and cherished for a long time suddenly come alive in his pages. The Derwentcote cementation furnace in Northumberland and Wortley Top Forge near Sheffield are in production; the Five Towns are dominated by pottery kilns; the waterwheel of the Derby silk mill is turning 97,000 spindles; the mines of Redruth and Chacewater are producing large quantities of copper and tin. The itineraries he followed were largely directed by his interests in mining and iron production, and inevitably there are many other places one wishes he had had the opportunity to comment on and illustrate. The slate quarries of North Wales, the lead-mining districts of the Peak District and the cloth-producing areas of Wiltshire and Gloucestershire are just a few examples. But this is sheer greed: the diaries are a rich feast as they stand, and will be a much-quoted source of information for economic and social historians and industrial archaeologists for many years to come.

Marilyn Palmer
Professor of Industrial Archaeology and
Head of the School of Archaeological Studies,
Leicester University

Notes and references

1 Rydberg, S, *Svenska Studieresor till England under Frihetstiden* (Uppsala: 1951).
2 Birch, A, 'Foreign observers of the British iron industry during the eighteenth century', *Journal of Economic History*, XXV (1955), pp. 23–33.
3 Flinn, M W, 'The travel diaries of Swedish engineers of the eighteenth century as sources of technological history', *Transactions of the Newcomen Society*, XXX (1957–58, 1958–59), pp. 95–109.
4 Hildebrand, K-G, *Swedish Iron in the Seventeenth and Eighteenth Centuries*, first published in Swedish 1986–87, translated into English by Austin, P B (Stockholm: Jernkontorets Bergshistoriska Utskott, 1992).
5 Crossley, D, 'The supply of charcoal to blast furnaces in Britain', *The Importance of Ironmaking: Technical Innovation and Social Change*, papers presented at a conference in Norberg, Sweden, 1995 (Stockholm: Jernkontorets Bergshistoriska Utskott, 1995), pp. 367–374.
6 Bowden, M (ed.), *Furness Iron* (English Heritage, 2000).
7 Riden, P, *A Gazetteer of Charcoal-fired Blast Furnaces in Great Britain in Use Since 1660*, 2nd edn (Cardiff: Merton Priory Press, 1993), p.6.
8 Day, J, *Bristol Brass: the History of the Industry* (Newton Abbot: David & Charles, 1973).
9 Day, J and Tylecote, R F (eds), *The Industrial Revolution in Metals* (London, Institute of Metals, 1991).
10 Rolt, L T C and Allen, J S, *The Steam Engine of Thomas Newcomen* (Landmark Publishing, 1977, first reprint 1997), pp. 44–5.
11 Hildebrand, K-G, *Swedish Iron in the Seventeenth and Eighteenth Centuries*, first published in Swedish 1986–87, translated into English by Austin, P B (Stockholm: Jernkontorets Bergshistoriska Utskott, 1992), p.80.
12 Pryce, W, *Mineralogia Cornubiensis* (1778), plate v, facing p.232.
13 Palmer, M and Neaverson, P, 'Nineteenth century tin and lead dressing: a comparative study of the field evidence', *Industrial Archaeology Review*, XII (1), (1989), pp. 20–39.
14 Bowden, M (ed.), *Furness Iron* (English Heritage, 2000), pp. 67–76.

Background and biography

The crowning achievement of the life of Reinhold Rücker Angerstein was undoubtedly the diary of his travels through Europe, which gives an unparalleled picture of Western industrial development in the middle of the eighteenth century. The eight magnificent volumes in the archives of Jernkontoret, the Swedish Steel Producers' Association, together with the fine portrait (reproduced here as the frontispiece) which hangs in the boardroom, form fitting monuments to the man and his work. Angerstein, however, was by no means the only Swedish traveller engaged in what we would now call industrial espionage and, before relating the details of his life, we should consider why this activity was so important for Sweden at that time.

Earlier than the seventeenth century there were few contacts between Sweden and England. Students and others from Sweden who travelled abroad generally went directly south to the great cultural centres of the continent. England and Scotland lay off the beaten track, and hardly anyone went that way unless obliged to do so. After the middle of the seventeenth century, however, the situation changed considerably: England had become one of the great powers of Europe, with a leading cultural role. Of particular interest was that the country had become the most important in industry and technology, a position it was to retain for more than 200 years. Rapid industrial development brought with it a large increase in consumption of bar iron that could not be satisfied by domestic production. In fact, production in England dropped by half during the seventeenth century because of lack of availability of charcoal at reasonable prices. Sweden was the only country which had the resources to expand iron production to meet this increased demand, and there can be no doubt that it was the shortage of charcoal in England that led in turn to the almost explosive growth of bar iron production in Sweden during the 1600s. Exports grew sevenfold and Britain was by far the largest potential export market at the time.

Table 1, with figures drawn mainly from Heckscher's *An Economic History of Sweden*,[1] illustrates this point. From the table it can be deduced how important export of bar iron to Great Britain was for the economy of Sweden. Furthermore, the value of bar iron exports during the 1750s was no less than 74 per cent of the value of all goods exported from Sweden, and 44 per cent of the value of all goods exported to Great Britain. It is not surprising, therefore, that the Swedish authorities were extremely interested in following developments in Britain, fearing that other countries might increase their iron production to the point at which they could represent serious competition for Sweden. This happened, in fact, towards the end of the eighteenth century, though mainly as a result of the Swedish policy of restricting production and maintaining high prices in order to conserve timber stocks. British demand for iron increased steadily and, since Sweden was unable to supply adequate quantities, the field was left free for other countries. It was chiefly Russia that took the opportunity of entering this large market, and from 1767 its share was greater than Sweden's. This remained the case for most years until the end of the century.

Table 1 Export of bar iron from Sweden

Year	***Total export*** (ton/year)	***Export to Great Britain*** (ton/year)	***% of Swedish export***	***% of British import***
1600	4250	0	0	0
1699	*c.* 30,000	15,300	50.1	80
1750–59 average	41,200	24,500	59.5	64
1790–99 average	46,000	24,500	51.2	40

Figures include Scotland and Ireland.

Sweden was also particularly concerned about potential exports from the American colonies, but these never materialised.

Much more serious was the threat posed by the potential use of mineral coal in iron smelting instead of charcoal. There were virtually unlimited reserves of coal in Britain, and it was much cheaper than charcoal. Attempts had been made as early as the seventeenth century to solve the difficult technological problems posed by the change to coal, and news of these attempts had reached Sweden. At first it was mainly diplomats who provided this type of information, but later, travellers with knowledge of industry were sent at the Swedish government's expense and were expected to write reports on their return home. Between 1692 and the beginning of the nineteenth century, around twenty such 'industrial spies' are known to have visited Britain. Many of them wrote rather sketchy accounts of their travels, and some even limited themselves to short letters; unfortunately, the great Christofer Polhem was one of this latter category. Up to now, only four of the journals have been published: those of Ferrner, Geisler, Broling and Svedenstierna. The first of these contains little technical detail, nor does Svedenstierna have much to offer in this direction. Geisler's journal is rather short, but contains a great deal of interesting material, and was published in Sweden some years ago, edited by Torsten Althin.[2] Broling's book is well known and includes much technological information, particularly on iron-working.

The remainder of the Swedish travel journals rest unpublished in various Swedish archives. It has now, however, been recognised that these documents probably represent the best available sources of information on British industry, and in particular the iron industry, in the eighteenth century. In England, industry was largely free from government interference, with none of the institutions which existed in Sweden, such as the Mining Council (Bergscollegium) or the Society of Ironmasters, now the Swedish Steel Producers' Association (Jernkontoret), which kept extensive records, largely maintained up to the present day. It was clearly not in the industrial proprietor's best interest to publicise details of his manufacturing methods and processes, so the observations contained in the Swedish journals are often unique and of great value. Other countries did, in fact, send industrial investigators to Britain, although on a much more limited scale, presumably because no other country was so dependent on its exports there as was Sweden.

Reinhold Rücker Angerstein's diary of his visit to England and Wales during the 1750s consists of about 150,000 words and no fewer than 360 pages of illustrations taken from sketches by the author. This diary has a claim to be regarded as the most interesting of them all for a number of reasons: the breadth of the author's interests; his detailed descriptions of processes and equipment; and perhaps most of all, because of the many illustrations, which often give unique pictures of operations and machinery.

Angerstein's great-grandfather[3] was a German ironmaster who moved to Sweden in 1639 and soon acquired shareholdings in various ironworks in the province of Dalecarlia, including Vikmanshyttan and Turbobruk. It was at Vikmanshyttan that Reinhold Rücker Angerstein was born, on 25 October 1718. His parents were the mill owner Gustaf Angerstein and his wife Anna, daughter of a rich merchant in the town of Hedemora. R R Angerstein's education followed the usual pattern for the sons of well-to-do ironmasters: university at Uppsala and then, at 20, *auscultant* at Bergscollegium. Promotion appears to have come slowly: not until 1744 was he given an official position as clerk, then in 1747 he became secretary in the taxation office. It seems possible that he was spending altogether too much time helping to run the family ironworks, since his father had died in 1734, or else that he was indulging too freely in the good life open to a rich young man in the capital city. He would clearly have been a good match but, for reasons that we will never know, he did not marry.

In 1749, Angerstein decided to go on an extended duty tour of the Continent and Great Britain. He was given instructions to guide him in his studies by both the Mining and Trade Councils, who with Jernkontoret also provided financial support, although this was far less than needed to cover the full costs. His route lay via Denmark to Germany, Carinthia, Hungary, Italy, France, Spain, Portugal and Holland, and then to England, where he landed at Harwich on 16 September 1753. He remained in England and Wales until the beginning of 1755. Scotland was omitted, presumably because industry there was still in its infancy.

Angerstein arrived in London on 17 September and remained there until April 1754, apart from a three-week visit to Oxford, where the various magnificent colleges made a profound impression on him. It seems likely that the main reason for his long stay in London was to improve his knowledge of English, although there was also much to see in the industrial area: porcelain factories, iron foundries, smithies and workshops for instruments and other articles of iron and steel, as well as chemical factories. He also visited the Royal Mint and the waterworks at Chelsea with its steam engines, as well as the usual tourist attractions. He made useful acquaintances in the Swedish colony which helped in the planning of his journeys, including merchants such as Charles and Andrew Lindegren, who provided him with letters of introduction to their business contacts and arranged for him to be able to draw money along his route.

By the beginning of April, Angerstein's preparations were complete, and from then until the end of the year he was travelling virtually the whole time, making detailed studies of all the important industrial areas. One notable exception was Sheffield, where he stayed less than 24 hours, making only a short report about a pocket-knife factory. It appears that he showed rather too much interest in Huntsman's Crucible Steel Works and was invited to leave the town as quickly as possible. Angerstein never made any bones about using all possible means, legal or otherwise, of getting to see what he wanted, and there are several accounts of his being thrown out of workshops where he had no permission to be.

Angerstein was very interested in geology and mining, and has much to say about the coal mines he saw in many places, as well as the tin and copper mines in Devon and Cornwall. He also had the opportunity of seeing various mines for lead, zinc and iron ore, although this last was mainly mined in association with coal.

It was Angerstein's view that Sweden did not have much to learn from England on the subject of iron production, although he reported that the Darbys at Coalbrookdale were producing excellent pig iron for casting using coke. Coke iron was still rather more expensive than charcoal iron, in spite of high charcoal prices and, moreover, it could not be used for bar iron. It was only towards the end of the century that coke iron became cheaper through more efficient coking and use of larger blast furnaces with more powerful blowing. The problem of making good bar iron with mineral coal was not fully solved until Henry Cort's invention of the puddling process in 1784. English ironworks used a type of Walloon process, and Angerstein reports that mineral coal was used almost everywhere in fining hearths, except for the very best quality iron. At ironworks in the north of England, he found that fuel costs for fining with mineral coal were 6s per ton of iron, and with charcoal £3 15s. He observes in a number of places that charcoal was very expensive in England and cost between 10 and 15 times as much as in Sweden.

This was undoubtedly the reason why ironworks in the province of Värmland in the year 1754 could sell ordinary bar iron for £9 15s per ton ex-works at a good profit. The same iron cost buyers in the English provinces around £18. English ironworks sold their iron at about the same price, with only a modest profit in most cases. In other words, the English production costs were roughly twice those in Sweden.

Wooden bellows of the type introduced to Sweden from Germany during the 1600s were never widely used in Britain but, at a bar forge in northern England, Angerstein saw the first cylinder blowing engine in the country, and probably in the world. It was built in 1748, and had two cast-iron cylinders, 690 mm in diameter and 1370 mm long. During the latter part of the century, the old leather bellows were soon superseded by the new type of blower.

Angerstein was, of course, very interested in rolling mills, and he was able to visit many rolling and slitting mills, used mainly in the production of nail rod and iron bands. Many of the latter were exported to the wine-producing countries of southern Europe, especially Portugal. He had a special reason to study tin-plate production, as the firm Jennings and Finlay had asked him to find out why the tin-plate works they had built in Sweden at Johannesfors, modelled on an English works, failed to give satisfactory results. Angerstein was also able to study in detail the rolling and tinning of thin plate at Pontypool in south Wales, where the owner, Major John Hanbury, was a pioneer in this field. As early as 1697, rolling of black iron plate was being carried out on a commercial basis, but tin-plating was not successful until 1728. By the middle of the century, knowledge of Hanbury's equipment and techniques had spread over the whole country, and at least ten new tin-plate works had been built, of which Angerstein saw eight. He describes both the machinery and the process in great detail, and his report is the earliest known account of rolling mills and rolling-mill technology.

Grooved rolling mills are not mentioned at all by Angerstein, although an English patent on a design of this type was granted at the end of the 1600s, and further patents appeared during the first half of the eighteenth century. A fully practical and commercially viable design for a grooved rolling mill first appeared in 1783, when Henry Cort obtained his well-known patent.

Throughout his journeys Angerstein kept himself informed about ruling prices for iron and about consumers' views on the quality of the various types of iron available. Swedish bar iron was always stamped with a mark indicating origin, and Angerstein also notes Russian and American stamps (see Appendix 2). The Swedish Dannemora or Öregrund iron was regarded as the very best for steel making, and the best stamp, Leufsta, and those for the subsidiary works at Carlholm, Åkerby and Österby, as well as Strömsberg and Ullfors, commanded a premium of two or three pounds per ton. Moreover, Swedish iron was considered to be stronger, harder and tougher than iron from other countries. It also had better wear and corrosion resistance, and was generally neither cold- nor hot-short, so was used for horseshoes and nails, wheel tyres, anchors and salt-pan plates, as well as for any complicated blacksmith's work which required any great degree of accuracy.

The softer English iron was used for rolling plate and was also preferred for nails. Iron produced in England, Russia and Spain was preferred for band iron and iron fabrication in general. There are a number of questions here for a metallurgist which would be worth closer examination.

Our traveller could see in many places that foundry technique was very advanced in England, particularly at Coalbrookdale, where he was impressed by the large steam-engine cylinders he saw being made. The cast hammer-heads and anvils which were used in English bar iron forges were, according to Angerstein, very durable and cheap, but could not at that time be made in Sweden. He also studied wire-drawing shops and gives some interesting information on these.

Angerstein was especially impressed by the way in which iron fabrication was organised in Birmingham and at other places. He saw, for example, how forging and welding were carried out by one workshop, filing by another, grinding by a third and finally polishing by a fourth. Each workman carried out just one step in the production process and developed great skill and speed, which in turn resulted in low costs. He was also full of admiration for Crowley's large ironware factories in the Newcastle district, the largest in Europe. Over a thousand workers were employed at these factories, and the annual consumption of iron was 2700 tons, 450 tons of which they produced themselves, the rest coming from Sweden and Russia (1700 and 550 tons respectively).

Coal mines in the Newcastle area were studied carefully, with special attention paid to the many railroads with horse-drawn wagons which transported the coal to the River Tyne. The largest of these was the so-called Tanfield line, which was 15 km long and over which more than 200,000 tons of coal were moved annually.

Other industries looked at by Angerstein included production of alum, glass, ceramics, paper, salt, textiles and agricultural products.

At the beginning of 1755, Angerstein was ready to leave England, and on 29 January he took the packet-boat from Dover to Calais and continued through Belgium and Holland, making further studies. He returned to Sweden in the middle of the year after six years abroad. The journey clearly improved Angerstein's prospects of promotion, since in his absence in 1752 he was appointed *vice fiskal* at Bergscollegium, and the following year Director for heavy iron fabrication. This was a consultative post at Jernkontoret, which required Angerstein to promote and develop production of bar iron and steel, as well as forging and related processes, and equipment such as furnaces, hammers and rolling mills. Finally, in 1756, he was given the honorary title of 'extraordinary assessor' at Bergscollegium. His position at Jernkontoret was a very demanding one, and he was obliged to spend much of his time travelling around the country. At the same time he must have been working on the completion of his travel diaries.

Angerstein's inherited shares in Vikmanshyttan and Turbobruk must also have required a good deal of attention. These were sold in 1759, although since 1757 he had owned Vira sword works, where he had plans to establish a roll foundry with a reverberatory furnace on British lines. He also had plans to reorganise the old blade and scythe smithy along the lines of the modern factory operation he had seen abroad, but in this he encountered strong opposition from the smiths. One can imagine that in the course of time he would have won them over to his ideas, particularly since he had strong support from the authorities, but all this came to an end with his death on 5 January 1760. The cause of his death is not known, but the probate documents mention that he had been ill for some time, and this is probably the reason why, two weeks before his death, he sold Vira to his brother-in-law, the rich Archbishop Samuel Troilius.

At the time of Angerstein's death, only a start had been made on the enormous task of transcribing his diaries: two bound volumes (of the final total of eight) were ready and a third lacked only the illustrations. The Board of Jernkontoret obviously valued this material, not least, one assumes, because they helped to finance the journeys, and arrangements were made to complete the work. Responsibility for copying the text was given to an official of the Bergscollegium, and the drawings were entrusted to an engineer with an artistic bent. At a meeting of the Board of Jernkontoret on 31 January 1765 it was reported that the work was complete. The fair copy has remained in the library there ever since. Some of the original working documents have, however, been placed in the Swedish State Archives. These include two of the original twenty pocket daybooks for England and Wales (the rest are lost), an intermediate edited transcript and a couple of rough notebooks, as well as an account book covering the first months in London.[4]

Reinhold Rücker Angerstein's untimely death at the age of only 41 was undoubtedly a grievous loss to Swedish industry, as no-one carried through the ideas he brought home from his travels. Others were to follow in his footsteps, but none of them had his unique combination of vision and a strong practical bent, together with ownership of suitable enterprises in which to apply his knowledge and talents.

Notes and references

1 Heckscher, E F, trans. Ohlin, *An Economic History of Sweden* (Harvard, 1954).

2 Althin, T, 'Erich Geisler och hans utländska resa', *Med Hammare och Fackla,* 26 (1971).

3 Another member of the same family is thought to have been the ancestor of the London merchant John Julius Angerstein, whose pictures formed the nucleus of the National Gallery.

4 One of the pages from the notebook for 3 December 1753 and the corresponding page from the fair copy are shown on pages xx and xxi. Details of all the documents are given in Appendix 1.

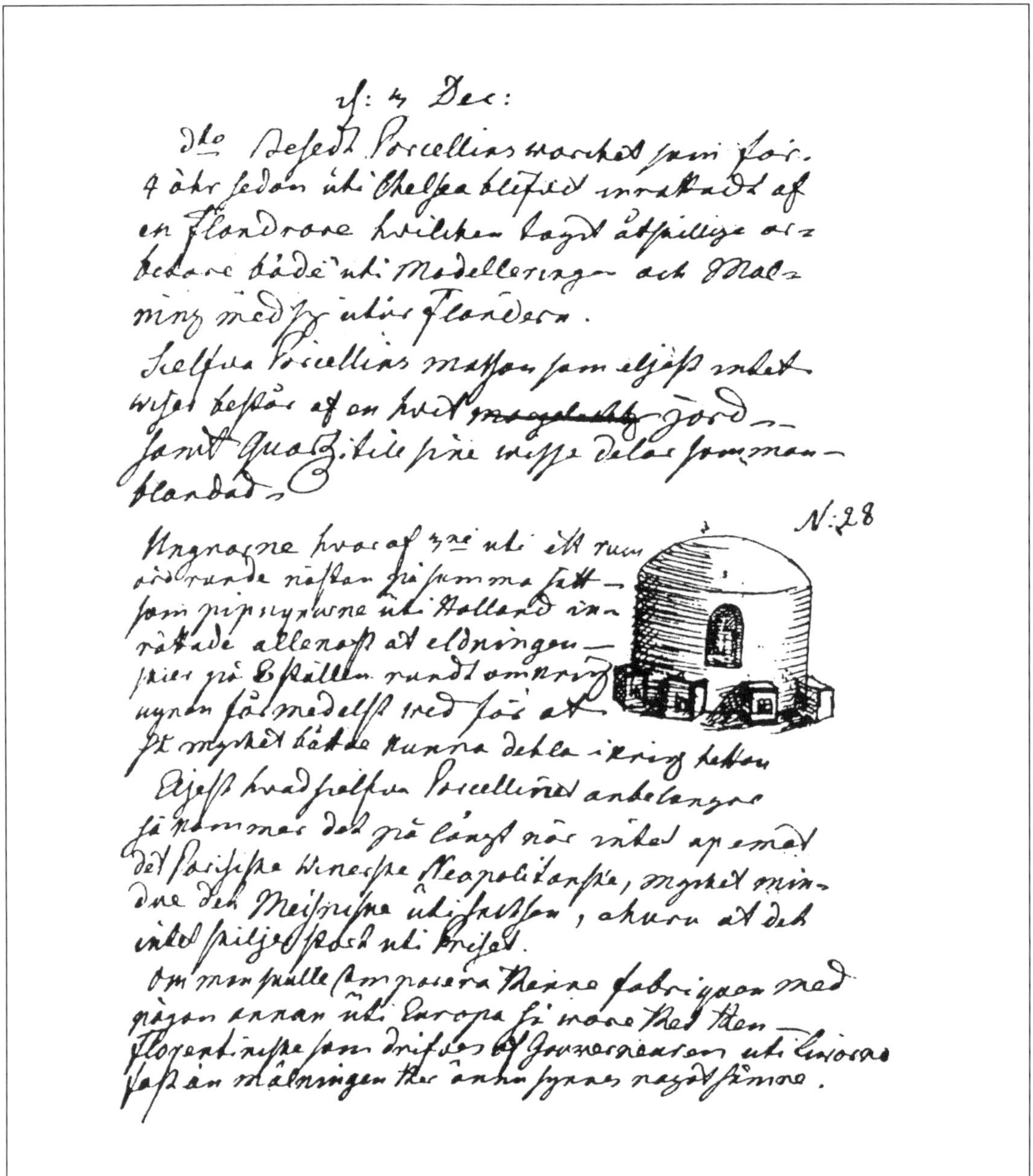
d: 4 Dec:
Dito besedt Porcellins warcket som för
4 åhr sedan uti Chelsea blifwit inrättadt af
en Flandrare hwilken tagit åtskillige ar-
betare både uti Modelleringen och Mål-
ning med sig utur Flandern.
Sielfwa Porcellins massan som eljest intet
wises består af en hwit ~~magnetisk~~ jord
samt Quartz. till sine wisse delar samman-
blandad
N:28
Ugnarne hwaraf 3ne uti ett rum
ordrande nästan på samma sätt
som pipmakarne uti Holland in-
rättade allenast at eldningen
sker på 8 ställen rundt omkring
ugnen samt medelst wed för at
få mycket bättre kunna hetta i kring
Eljest hwad sielfwa Porcellinet anbelangar
så kommer det på långt när intet up emot
det Parisiska Wienerska Neapolitanska, mycket min-
dre det Meissniska utifrån, ehuru at det
intet skiljer stort uti Priset.
Om man skulle comparera theras fabriquer med
någon annan uti Europa så wore thet then
Florentinska som drifwes af Gouverneuren uti Livorno
fast än målningen ther ännu synes något sämre.

Pocket notebook page describing a visit to the Chelsea porcelain factory on 3 December 1753; approximately actual size (Riksarkivet, Stockholm).

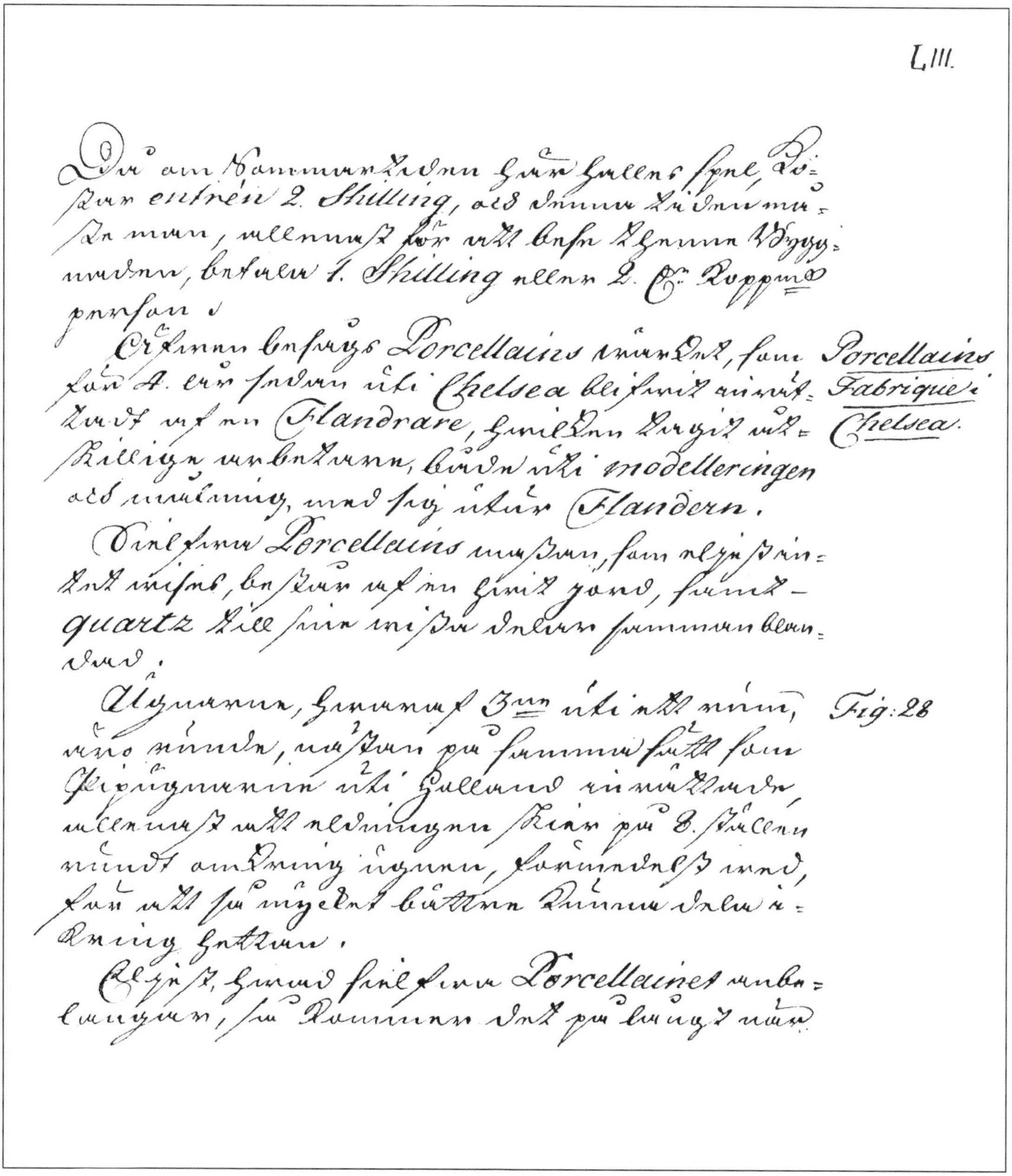

Page LIII from Volume 1 of the bound fair copy manuscript, including the visit to the porcelain factory; somewhat reduced. An enlarged version of the sketch of the kiln appears as Fig. 28 on the facing page (Jernkontoret, Stockholm). See pages 22 and 23.

Weights, measures and currency

The following conversions may be useful, though the figures were subject to local variation and should be treated with caution:

Linear measure	1 famn = 3 alnar = 178 cm
	1 aln = 2 fot = 59 cm
	1 Swedish mile = *c.* 6 English miles
	1 English mile = 1.6 km
Weights	1 skeppund (viktualievikt) = 20 lispund = 170 kg
	1 lispund = 20 skålpund = 8.5 kg
Volume measure	1 tunna = 2 spann = 147 litre (stricken measure)
	1 kanna = 2 stop = 4 kvarter = 1.3 litre
Currency	1 daler kopparmynt = 4 mark = 32 öre
	£1 sterling = *c.* 40 daler kopparmynt
	£1 sterling = 20s = 240d
	1s = 12d.

Volume 1

Latin pagination

Page numbers from the fair copy are shown in the margin.

Journey 1 Harwich to London

15 September 1753. Harwich, Colchester, London.

Fig. 1 Island of Goree

The passage from Holland to England

At nine o'clock in the morning of 15 September
I 1753, I boarded the packet boat at
Hellevoetsluis in Holland to sail from there to
England. A clear sky, pleasant weather and a
desirable breeze enlivened my senses, and made
my entire company happy. A beneficial wind
filled our sails, the shore disappeared out of
sight, and we continued our voyage with such
speed that already at four o'clock in the
afternoon the Island of Goree [Fig. 1] came
into view.

A high tower of stone has been erected on
this island as a landmark and on the other side,
on the left, there is also a beacon. All through II
the night we were pushed forward by a very
good wind, and as early as half past three in the
morning we sighted the English coast with its
lighthouse.

On 16 September, which was a Sunday, we happily lowered our sails in the harbour of Harwich [Fig. 2a]. Here we were immediately saluted by several sloops, loaded with customs officers who, when we left the ship, went so far

Fig. 2a Harwich harbour

Fig. 2b Harwich town

in their official zeal as to search us right down to the bare skin.

The harbour of Harwich appeared to be fairly good, but the town itself is both small and very insignificant [Fig. 2b]. Most of the houses are old and dilapidated, made of wood, and those that are built of brick are small and
III unimposing. The signs for the taverns, or inns and public houses, hang in a gallows placed right across or in the middle of the street. A gaol, or a kind of lock-up, was made of thick wooden grids, so that one could look through them, and the stocks were placed on the roof so that the criminal could easily be seen.

The journey to Colchester and the character of the countryside

The journey continued from here in a chaise with two horses, to Colchester, a distance of 24 English miles. The cost was 16 shillings, with 2 shillings in tips. The countryside was slightly hilly and everywhere cultivated with fields and meadows, and in a number of places planted with turnips. Instead of wooden fences, a ditch is dug along the roadside and the earth thrown
IV up to form a bank at the edge of the field, planted with bushes. The blackberries that grow so profusely in Spain were common on the banks. If the soil was sandy, chalk and dark-grey clay or marl had been carted onto the fields.

Colchester town

I rested overnight in Colchester, with my travelling companions, a Dutch Count by the name of Vassau and his Countess. Colchester is a fairly large but not very impressive town, located on a hill, with a small river called the Colne running below it. The people in this place earn their livelihood from sheep farming, preparation of wool, and in factories for light woollen and silk fabrics. The town is otherwise best known for its delicious oysters which are
harvested in a bay of the sea a few English miles V
away.

The journey to London

On 17 September I paid the post-chaise from Harwich to Colchester 16 shillings and hired another one to London, a distance of 51 English miles, for 2 guineas or 42 shillings. On this road I passed through the towns of Witham, Springfield, Ingatestone and Romford, all of them insignificant and small. At seven o'clock in the evening I arrived in London, where I parted company with Count Vassau and went to the lodgings with Mr Heinicken that had been booked for me by Mr Lindegren.[1]

On 18 September in the morning I took a walk down to the Thames beside the Tower in order to enquire about the ship from Holland carrying my luggage, but it had not yet arrived.

Water-pumping works in London

On 19 September I went to see the water-
pumping works under London Bridge [Fig. 3], VI
which consisted of five large undershot water wheels, driven when the tide is going out and standing still when it is coming in. The pipes used for the cylinders, and to convey the water under pressure to the streets, are in some cases

Fig. 3 Water-pumping machinery under London Bridge

Fig. 4 Westminster Bridge

made of cast iron and in some cases of lead, but the teeth of the gear wheels and the staves of the lantern pinions were cast of iron.[2]

Equilibrist

After dinner I went to a theatre outside the City where they were showing a pantomime and a man swinging and balancing on a rope. This balancing act was the best of its kind one could ever hope to see. He balanced on a swinging steel-wire cable, with a straw on his nose which he tossed back and forth to his forehead, chin, head, shoulders, etc. and with various tobacco pipes, one of which he placed on a round, broken-off piece of tubing put over his nose.
On the swinging cable he also juggled with VII
three apples, and with his sword held on the edge of a wine-glass.

Westminster Bridge

On 20 September I took a trip by boat up the Thames to the new bridge [Fig. 4] and St James's Park. The bridge is ....[3] long and consists of 14 arches, all made of dressed stone.

Promenade

In the evening I went to St James's Park to look at the many people promenading there.

Notes and references

1 Mr Anders Lindegren, one of two Swedish brothers who were merchants in London.
2 A very early reference to the use of iron for the gear teeth of millwork. Only two of the five wheels are shown, each driving four pumps.
3 Length omitted in MS.

Journey 2 London to Windsor

22 September 1753. London, Isleworth, Windsor, Kensington, London.

Fig. 5 Brickyards at Isleworth

Journey to Mr Lindegren's farm

In the morning of 22 September I started out on a trip to Mr Lindegren's farm, which is located five English miles beyond Windsor, my companions being Mr Lindegren himself, Mr von Plomgren[4] and Doctor Rothman.[5] Outside London in a large open space there were several gallows with robbers, here called 'Highwaymen', hung in iron cages. Further on, in a similar space, we saw several battalions of cavalry being drilled. They were well equipped.

Nature of open spaces

From the open spaces there is a clear view for miles to the west over a plain covered with heather or bracken. The former is cut and dried together with the thick turf overlaying the sand and clayey gravel of the region, and then used as fuel in the country and in the surrounding small towns. The bracken is also dried and stacked for use as bedding for cattle, which improves and augments the manure.

Brickyards at Isleworth

Some miles outside London, by a place called 'Eisensmith'[6] there are a number of brickyards [Fig. 5] with kilns fired with heather turf. The bricks were moulded on the banks of the Thames, and the sand screened from gravel found in the fields not far from there. The trip continued through Windsor Park, which is well stocked with deer, and past the mansion of the 'Master of the Chase', now occupied by the Duke of Cumberland.

Stacking of fodder

In this country hay and straw are stored in stacks [Fig. 6] which are never pulled down, but cut off piece by piece with sickles. The type of sickle used for removing hay and straw from the stacks is illustrated by the accompanying Figure.[7] At six o'clock in the evening I arrived

Fig. 6 Stacking of fodder

at Mr Lindegren's farm, which he rents from a farmer, and where his wife spends the summer.

Mineral well

On 23 September in the morning I travelled by carriage to a mineral well, located two miles from the Duke of Cumberland's Mansion, which in summertime is used for various maladies, but the vitriol content of the water is not very high. A short distance away, the Duke of Cumberland had recently built a summerhouse on a hilltop from which there is a wide outlook over open fields. One can also see the tower of Westminster Abbey in London, which
X is 18 miles distant. A fair-sized piece of land nearby is planted with pine and spruce, but it is hard work to eradicate the bracken which grew there before. The Duke has created a small lake[8] just below here by making a dam across a little valley. It is just over one English mile long, but not very wide.

Fig. 7 Mandarin's yacht

Mandarin's yacht

On the lake a mandarin's yacht [Fig. 7] has been built near the outlet where a cascade of water has also been provided. From the lake we travelled to the Duke's palace and passed an obelisk 60 or so feet high and built of the same kind of white sandstone as the summerhouse.

Obelisk at Duke of Cumberland's estate

This obelisk [Fig. 8] can be seen from all the rooms of the Duke's private apartments, towering over everything else.

Fig. 8 Obelisk

Fig. 9 Windsor town and castle

Duke of Cumberland's palace and curiosities

Arriving at the palace, which is not particularly remarkable so far as the architecture is concerned, we saw in two small enclosures a number of foreign animals, especially tigers and lions, musk-rats, porcupines, and American bears, which have been described in Swedish
XI scientific papers by Doctor Linnaeus. Outside the
gates there were large eagles instead of watch-dogs. In the stables were some beautiful English 'perforce'[9] horses and two arabs. The rooms were mostly furnished with pieces of copper.[10] In one chamber, we noted all kinds of foreign clothes for men and women.

After dinner at three o'clock we arrived home, and towards the evening went for a walk with the ladies.

Windsor, town and royal castle

On 24 September at three o'clock in the morning, I travelled from Mr Lindegren's house to Windsor [Fig. 9], a small town on top of a hill, where there is a royal palace and citadel as well as a beautiful cathedral, governed by a chapter of canons. The location of the castle is very beautiful and pleasant owing to the long views in every direction, and to the river
Thames, which flows past just below. XII

We first looked at the chapel, which is built of dressed stone, very like the stone used in Bordeaux and Rouen in France. It is whitish and soft. The church is built in the Gothic style of architecture. The ceiling vaults are very flat and are incomparably lovely [Fig. 10]. In the choir there is an organ, and a beautiful altar-piece in form of a painting depicting the Last Supper. There are also goodly chairs for the Canons, at that moment occupied by their wives.

In the small side chapels we saw some epitaphs, amongst them one of the Duke of ....[11] Outside the church there is another chapel which is no longer kept in repair. Through the broken windows we could see a handsome painting in the ceiling, and it was said that in Catholic times this church had been dedicated to a saint.

The palace is close by. It is fairly large and built around three sides of a quadrangle. Across

Fig. 10 St George's Chapel

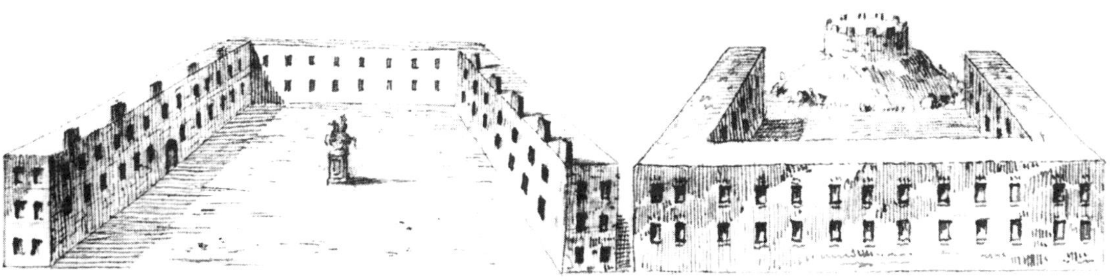

Fig. 11 Windsor Castle

XIII the open side there is a round citadel or keep on a high mound [Fig.11]. In the middle of the quadrangle stands a bronze equestrian stature of Charles II, paid for by a private citizen.
The rooms inside are mostly hung with Gobelin tapestry, and amongst many fine pictures there are some by Michelangelo and some by Snyders and others of the great masters. In one chamber one sees 14 portraits of the 'beauties' of Charles II. St George's Chapel is decorated with paintings by Verrio Neapolitano. His picture of King Edward taking the French King John and his son Philip prisoners is considered a masterpiece. In St George's Hall, Charles XI 'Rex Suecorum' is painted sitting on his horse.[12]
In the entrance hall below hang the antlers of a moose with a span of 6 feet 9 inches. However attractive the location of this castle may be, and
XIV however beautiful the buildings would be with only a small amount spent on repairs, the royal Hanoverian family will not go there because of the many memorials commemorating the Stuarts.

Manuring of fields

On the way home I noticed that the farmland is fertilised with burnt lime and chalk, mixed with refuse, ashes and other rubbish thrown out of the houses, as well as with dirt collected from the roads.

Fig. 12 Cage for horses

Farrier's shops

In Windsor, 'Eisensmith' [Isleworth] and some other smaller places through which the road took us, there were a number of farrier's workshops, and it was observed that the shoes were made wider than in other places. Swedish iron was used. At each workshop there was a kind of cage to hold unruly horses with one foot tied to a crossbar [Fig. 12].

Kensington summer palace

About three miles from London we went past Kensington, a small summer palace, where the King stays over the summer. XV

Marylebone pleasure gardens

Upon arrival in St James's Park, we alighted from the carriage and went to Marylebone to see the amusements put on here for the last time this year, consisting of music, illuminations and fireworks. The entrance fee was 1 shilling and 6 pence. Poles carrying illuminated lanterns of blown glass bordered the walks around the rotunda [Fig.13]. A large number of people were to be seen here, particularly young women and girls, who tried to charm the men present with their clothes and the way they walked. The music was nothing special, and the singing consisted largely of English arias. This lasted until ten o'clock, when a small fireworks display was set off, after which we went home.

XVI

Visits and walks

On the 26 September, I called on Mr Secretary Weynantz and Captain Gyllenspetz.[13]
Afterwards I took a walk in St James's Park and viewed the Royal Palace, a poor and irregular building. At noon I went to the Royal Exchange and called on Mr Ellicot, the clockmaker,[14] and then had my dinner at home at three o'clock,

Fig. 13 Marylebone pleasure gardens

the usual time in London. In the afternoon I wrote and dispatched mail to Messrs Grill and Christopher[15] in Amsterdam.

Types of iron

On 27 September, the morning was spent in the weigh-house, where I inspected iron from Russia and America. The former was mostly 3 inches wide and ½ inch thick, and the latter 2 inches flat and 1 inch square and stamped ***UNION***.[16] According to the evidence of several broken bars, this iron was cold-short.

Before leaving the weigh-house, all iron is stamped with a crown which avoids any further duty being charged within ten English miles of
XVII London. This was decreed by an Act of Parliament, which aims to counteract any prejudice that the English iron mills, whose products are supposed to be the equal of the American iron in quality, might meet if the trade were completely free.

New acquaintances

During dinner at the Royal Exchange, I met several Swedes, amongst them Mr Falker and Magister Ingerman, and several jewellers and artisans, and amongst them also Mr Seel[17] who has built a works for making vitriol a few miles from London. The raw material is pyrites, gathered from the seashore. For further information refer to Harveck.[18] I dined with Messrs Spalding and Brander,[19] and in the evening joined a party at a tavern.

London Bridge

On 28 September I had a look at London XVIII
Bridge, upon which houses have been built here and there along its length. It is not a particularly pleasant place because of the great amount of dirt that one sees there. This is a common fault in the City of London, owing to the dense traffic of large carts and wagons. It is nevertheless possible to walk freely along the sides of the street, behind the posts that divide them from the carriageway. In the evening I enjoyed good company in a tavern.

The Monument

On 29 September I viewed the Monument [Fig. 14] near London, built after the Great Fire in 1666, which started at this point, having been instigated by the Catholics to curb the Reformation. The height of the Monument is 202 feet and it is built of dressed stone in a similar way to the columns of Augustus and Trajan in Rome, although these are not of the same immense height and size as the
Monument. Mr Noring, Pastor of the Swedish XIX
Church,[20] who had recently inherited £30,000 from Victorin, the iron merchant,[21] had asked me to dine with him and I was regaled most magnificently.

Greenwich hospital

30 September. I travelled to Greenwich hospital where I marvelled at the splendid architecture of the building housing old and crippled sailors. In a large hall there were beautiful paintings both in the ceiling and on the walls which,

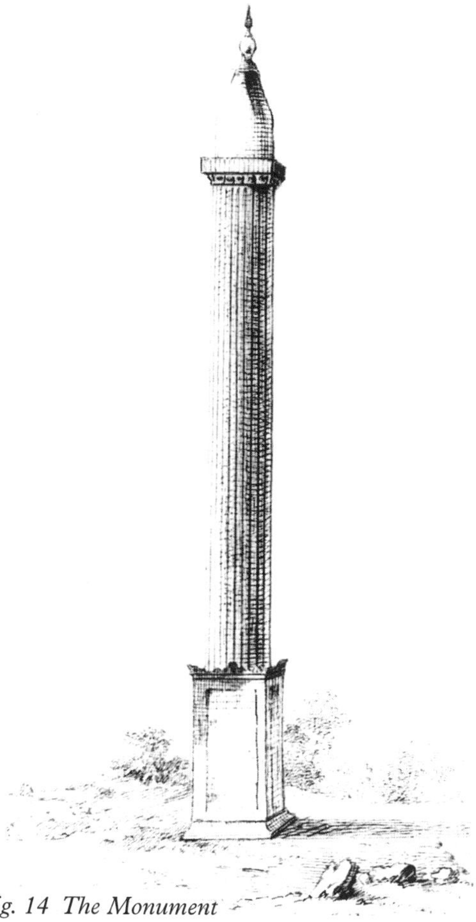

Fig. 14 The Monument

however, could not come under the heading masterpieces, notwithstanding that a whole book has been printed about them. There is a superabundance of deer in the park, which has a splendid prospect of the Thames. We dined with a tanner living a few miles away and returned to London towards the evening.

1 October. I took a walk in the park and made enquiries about living accommodation for the time when I return from my forthcoming journey to Oxford. XX

Factories along the Thames

Travelling home to the Royal Exchange by boat, a distance of two English miles, I saw, on the south bank of the Thames, iron foundries, a factory making white lead, glass-works, etc, which I intend visiting when I come back.

2 October. I ordered a carriage for the journey to Oxford, where I hope to learn English with more success than in London, where there are too many Swedes. At dinner in the Royal Exchange I said farewell to many friends, and afterwards dispatched mail.

English comedy

In the evening I attended a comedy, which was well acted. There was also a follow-on play, a kind of opera in English, but according to the Italian taste.

Notes and references

4 Mr von Plomgren, Swedish businessman, temporarily resident in London.

5 John Gabriel Rothman, born 1721, died 1772, Swedish Doctor of Medicine, author and politician who lived in England for a number of years during the 1750s.

6 Probably Isleworth, although Hammersmith is also a possibility, though that seems too close to London to fit RRA's account.

7 The sickle is not shown.

8 Virginia Water.

9 Sic: the German word for hunting on horses is 'parforcejagd' so this must be a reference to hunters.

10 Sic: may be a copyist's error.

11 Missing in MS.

12 Charles XI of Sweden's Queen, Ulrika Eleonora, was the sister of Prince George, husband of Queen Anne of England. Their father was King Frederick III of Denmark.

13 The former was Swedish Chargé d'Affaires in London 1748–58. The latter was probably a member of his staff.

14 John Ellicot, sometime Master of the Clockmakers' Company.

15 Swedish merchants.

16 The Union Iron Works, Hunterdon County, New Jersey was located about 50 miles due west from the southern tip of Manhattan Island.

17 Swedish chemist and manufacturer living in England.

18 RRA's note, not clear to whom or what he is referring.

19 Prominent Swedish merchants living in London.

20 Pastor of the Swedish Church in London 1748–61.

21 Lars Victorin, prominent and well-to-do Swedish merchant, living in London during the first half of the eighteenth century. Pastor Noring was Victorin's nephew and married to Anders Lindegren's daughter.

Journey 3 London to Oxford

3 October 1753. London, Uxbridge, High Wycombe, Oxford, Blenheim, Oxford, Woodstock, Oxford (23 October), Hounslow, London.

Journey from London to Oxford

On 3 October 1753 at nine o'clock in the morning I left London by hired carriage costing 3 guineas. Outside the city I saw the place of
XXI execution where every month several people are hanged. Along the sides a kind of amphitheatre had been built for the spectators.

Uxbridge, small town and flour mill

I dined in Uxbridge, a small town not noteworthy for anything but a flour and sifting mill seen there. It was of a very special design as far as the sifting is concerned, which is carried out by rotation as shown by Fig. 15. The letter A[22] denotes the sieve, which is covered with gauze and enclosed in a wooden box, so that the flour is not lost as dust. The sieve is driven by gearing from the shaft of the water wheel. Also driven by the wheel, but on the other side of the millstones, is a machine to lift the sacks. The shaft serving as a cable drum is provided with a face gear, driven by the lantern pinion on the millstone shaft. Moving the shaft axially when the sacks have been hoisted up disengages the gears. The same machine, but in a more
XXII perfected version, can be seen in Newcastle and also in the windmills of Holland.

High Wycombe, town and flour mill

I stayed overnight at High Wycombe, which is located 32 miles from London and 25 from Oxford. Soldiers were billeted here, increasing the population beyond the normal. To run a number of sifting mills from one water wheel, they use ropes driven by a drum or flat pulley on the wheel shaft and driving other pulleys, that in their turn power the sifting machines. This is similar to the way strings are employed on a spinning wheel.

Iron ochre

On 4 October, a few miles from Oxford, we passed several pits, in which a yellow iron ochre was being dug, as well as a dark-brown iron ore, that was put in small heaps by the roadside to
be used for repairs. XXII

In a small hut in the field we found some women and men who were sorting the ochre and making it into a paste resembling red lead. This was formed in square moulds into thin cakes, which were dried prior to being sold.

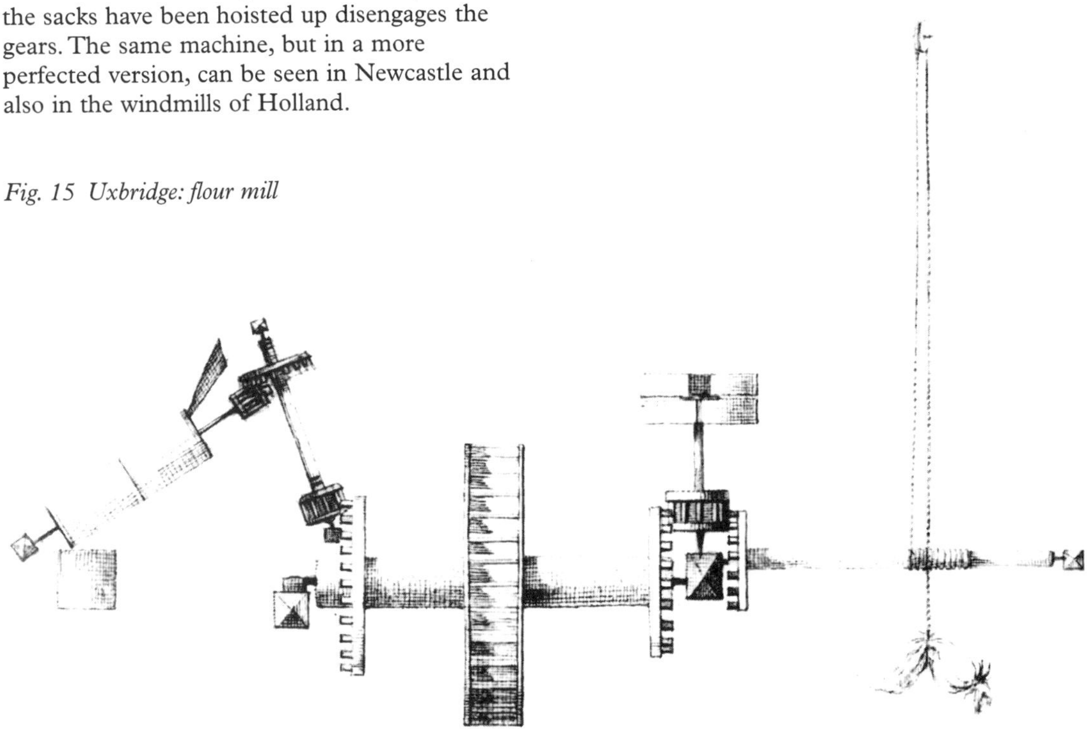

Fig. 15 Uxbridge: flour mill

Fig. 16 Queens College

The city of Oxford, university and its colleges

At one o'clock I arrived in Oxford, in olden times called Oxon, which, owing to the many colleges and other public institutions, is a very splendid university. Here I called on Mr Sibthorpe, Professor of Botany, to whom I had a letter of recommendation from Pastor Noring, and he showed me the Botanical Garden, which is well laid out and particularly remarkable for its lovely yew hedges. There were also both German and Swedish spruce trees and pines and cedars growing in the garden. On 5 October I saw some of the colleges, of which there are no
XXIV fewer than 20, each more magnificent in its architecture and equipment than the last.

Fig. 16 gives a good idea of what the buildings of Queens College look like from the High Street, where it is situated. At the back there is another large, square building with a garden beside it. The foundation of the college goes back to the year 1340, and the founder was Philippa, the Queen of Edward III. Since then it has been enlarged by several monarchs, until finally Joseph Williamson completed the building, and in his will endowed it with an income of £6000. In addition, a number of others have given books and large sums of money. Beside the College there still stands an old building which was the residence of King Henry IV whilst he studied here. The members
XXV of the college are 16 fellows, two chaplains, eight taberders, 16 scholars, two clerks and 40 exhibitioners, as well as masters, bachelors, gentleman commoners and other students.

6 October. Besides Queens College there are 19 others in Oxford, which are just as resplendent and large, indeed some are even larger and grander. Amongst these there is every reason to count All Souls College, which has superb Gothic buildings, a beautiful library and a lovely garden. The library is 90 yards long, and was built at the instigation of Colonel Codrington. A marble statue of him stands in the middle, and in addition, a number of benefactors and learned men who have been connected with the college are seen in half-length portraits above the bookshelves. £6000 was donated for the building of the library, and £4000 for the purchase of books. A large collection of books was also given. In this college there are a warden, 40 fellows, two chaplains and nine clerks. The buildings of Christ Church College are still larger. The work on them was started by Cardinal Wolsey in 1638 and completed in 1665.[23] Two marble statues of Dr. Fell stand opposite one another above the entrance, and in the quadrangle, which is very large, there is a fountain with a statue of Mercury above it. The dining room, or hall, is considered to be one of the largest in Oxford. The cathedral also serves as chapel for the College, and has admirable stained-glass windows. The whole of this large building is occupied by four canons, and each of them has a pretty garden with his apartment. Next to it is the so-called Peckwater Court, new and modern, including a magnificent library, in the
Corinthian order, 76 yards in length, not quite XXVI
complete. Canterbury Court, Chaplains Court, Court of Grammar School, Corpus Christi and Merton Colleges are in the immediate neighbourhood, and are large and splendid buildings with fine gardens.

Fig. 17 shows a new building at Magdalen College which is pleasantly situated in a

Fig. 17 New building, Magdalen College

beautiful park and is 116 yards long. The old college beside it is built around a quadrangle in which there are many heiroglyphic statues. King Henry II originally founded this college as a hospital. Later it was altered to a college.
Its members are one president, 40 fellows, 30 demis, ditto divinity lecturers, schoolmasters and usher, four chaplains, one organist, eight clerks, 16 choristers and altogether 108 students. The hospital was dedicated to St John
XXVII the Baptist. His day is still celebrated with a sermon from a stone pulpit outside the chapel, and with many other Catholic ceremonies, which still to a great extent are retained by the colleges even though they are members of the Church of England. Besides the colleges already mentioned, there are also Balliol, Brasenose, Exeter, Jesus, Lincoln, Oriel, Pembroke, Trinity, University and Wadham, all large and extensive, but in particular St John's and New College are unsurpassed, both in respect of buildings and of gardens, libraries and other arrangements.
In addition, there are five halls, which also have good buildings, but differ from the colleges in that they are not incorporated into the University. The students living in the halls must,

Fig. 18 Clarendon's printing-works

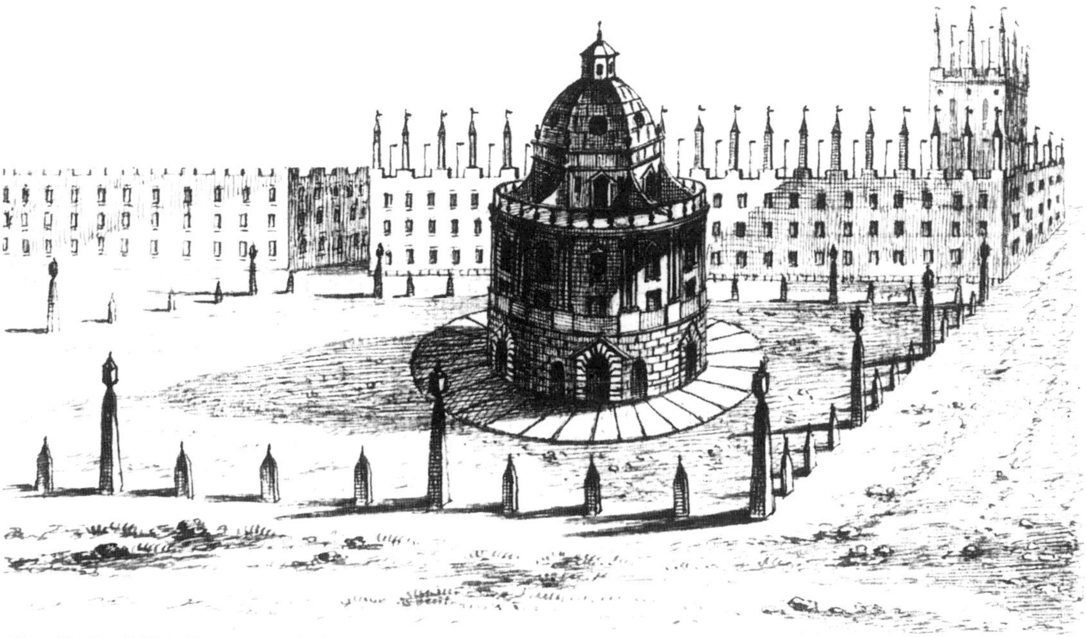

Fig. 19 Radcliffe Camera and Square

however, take an oath to obey all the statutes
XXIX and customs established there and decreed by
the chancellor.

On 7 October, I visited the printing-works, founded by Lord Clarendon in 1711. The building was erected in the Doric order, and on top of it are the nine Muses, and over the doorway facing the courtyard behind, a statue of Lord Clarendon.

From the 8th to the 12th I was occupied virtually every day viewing various colleges and other beautiful buildings, amongst them particularly the Public Academy or School, the Academic Theatre, the Ashmolean Museum and the Radcliffe Library, of which Fig. 19 gives an approximate picture.

Half of this building cost £40,000[24] and salaries, wages and purchases of books amount to £450 per annum. Radcliffe was a Doctor of Medicine at Oxford and a student there in his youth. The building has only recently been completed and so far there are no books in it. Apart from the Radcliffe Library, the foremost public library is the Bodleian, which is filled
XXX with a number of old books and manuscripts.

On 12 October I saw the Bodleian Library, adjacent to the Old Schools, but in its own building. It is filled with a great number of books, fastened with iron chains. The picture gallery is of considerable size and mainly filled with portraits of benefactors of the University. The medallion cabinet is also sizeable. In the centre of the floor stands a bronze stature of the Duke of Bedford, one of the most prominent benefactors. Besides the portraits, there are other paintings worth mention, particularly sea pictures and fleets of ships. In the natural history cabinet one sees many skeletons of animals and fish, and also petrifactions, and snakes and insects in spirits of wine, and various
other old rarities. The Sheldonian cabinet of XXXI
antiquities is filled with antique Greek inscriptions and also contains some marble busts and two fine rune-stones.[25] The theatre is semicircular in shape and has a beautiful painting on the ceiling. The roof is so constructed that it is self-supporting, without pillars.[26] In this room, which is used for solemn ceremonies, there are books all along the walls and a throne for the chancellor, whose installation takes place here.

Blenheim Palace

13 October. Blenheim is located six English miles from Oxford and was built at the expense of Parliament. It is most gloriously decorated, with beautiful original paintings by Rubens, Raphael, Rembrandt and Snyders, and also with the loveliest Gobelin tapestries depicting the Duke of Marlborough's victories. The library is
superb and built just like the Imperial Library XXXII
in Vienna.

The Palace contains a marble stature of Queen Anne, in whose reign it was built. In the entrance hall one sees four bronze statues, that are copies of the finest antique ones in the gallery in Florence. Upstairs are some marble statues, not quite so good. Above the great doors leading from the entrance hall, stands a white marble bust of the Duke of Marlborough.

Thirteen hundred paces from the Palace one sees a column 140 feet high with a statue of the Duke at the top. On three of the sides of the column, three different Acts of Parliament have been engraved, all concerning the gift to the Duke of Marlborough and all his descendants, heir after heir, in perpetuity. Woodstock belongs to the domains and also the whole of the large park and estate with all the income therefrom, and in addition, another £5,000 from Parliament.

On the side of the column facing the Palace XXXI
one finds the story of the Duke of Marlborough's life and exploits.

14 October. The distance from the Palace to the column is 1300 paces, and the bridge is 200 feet long, but the arch has a span of 80 feet. The column was erected in 1723 by the Duke of Marlborough's widow, as stated by the inscription above the first entrance known as the Great Arch.

Oxford, city and river

15 October. I took a walk to the west side of Oxford where I viewed flour mills, the town wharf, and several boats provided with cabins that can travel 50 English miles up the river to Gloucestershire. Here are an old stone bridge and the remains of an ancient fort with a high tower.

16 October. On the south side I viewed the
bridge across the river[27] and the pressure pump XXX
that supplies water to a number of places in the town, particularly to Christchurch College where there is a fountain.

Church service

On 21 October I visited several churches and colleges and took part in the service of the Church of England when Holy Communion was administered. This was carried out in the following way: the communicants sat around the choir and the priest gave them the bread

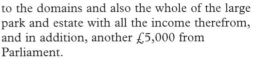

Fig. 20 Column at Blenheim

Fig. 21 Park at Blenheim

and then carried the chalice to each person, who took it in his hands and drank of the wine. The words of administration are repeated each time that the wine and bread are served.

Woodstock, iron and steel factories

On 22 October I took a trip to Woodstock to gather further information about the steel factories located there. The principal articles made here are watch-chains, watch-keys, buckles, toe-buckles, buckles for men's shirtfronts, corkscrews, nutcrackers, buttons etc.
XXXV There are no more than three masters here, each with two or three workers. The names of the masters are Grantham, Medcalf and George Eldridge. A fourth, by name of Edward Staunton, moved to Oxford a short time ago. The price of watch-chains is 1½ to 3 guineas; watch-keys cost from 6 to 10 shillings. Corkscrews are 4, 6 to 8 shillings for the plain ones, though decorated ones cost as much as one-and-a-half guineas.

Shoe buckles cost half to 1 guinea, but 2 guineas if decorated with cut steel. Garter buckles are 1 guinea and neck-tie buckles, the same. Most of the work on articles of this type is carried out when the material is still in the form of soft iron. Subsequently it is packed in paste and case-hardened. After that the parts are finally assembled and polished. Parts that are very thin and minute, for example the smallest links and screws for watch-chains, are made of steel from the start and are generally not hardened, or if they should be, they are
tempered to restore the strength and toughness. XXXVI

During the processing care is taken to complete all work as far as possible before the case-hardening takes place, and that includes much of the polishing, which makes the final polishing operation so much easier. When making 'diamante' items, the steel diamonds are screwed into place and the whole object completed before being taken apart again for case-hardening and polishing, after which it is finally assembled.

To make it possible to polish small pieces, they are screwed into a pin, mounted on a handle which, when in use, is supported by a wooden beam. The paste used for the case-hardening is made by charring old leather until

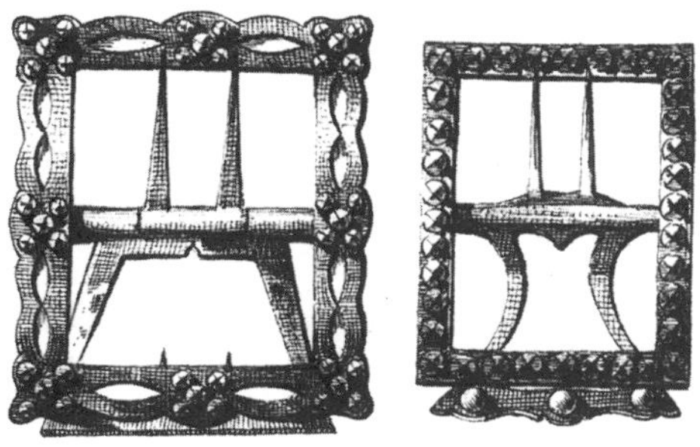

Fig. 22 Shoe buckles

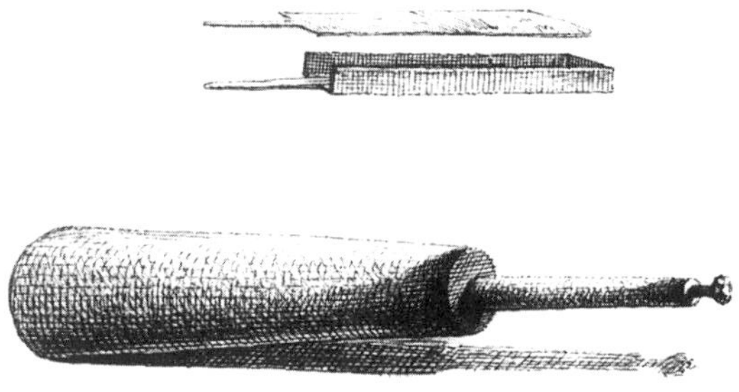

Fig. 23 Handle for polishing small articles; box for case-hardening

it can be pulverised in a mortar, after which it is mixed with brine or urine. The following is another and better mixture: 'Cows or horse hufs and sheeps horn burnt till thy will, pound in a
XXXVII Mortar, mixt with a little salt and urine or Brine, makes the best Hardning'.[28] When the articles are ready for case-hardening, they are placed in an iron box and covered with the paste. The packed box is covered with an iron lid and placed in the hearth, in which the fire has been blown up to a high temperature. The lid is made with a little handle (see Fig. 23), so that it can be lifted up for checking the heat inside. The temperature has reached its proper level when the black material of the paste is white-red all over. The box is then removed from the fire and the contents thrown into a cauldron full of water. A sample piece, dimensioned in accordance with the articles in the bath, is also placed in the box and subsequently fractured to show how far the hardening has penetrated, if it has gone too far
or not far enough. XXX

Small screws and other similar items that might warp are placed on top of the hot box for tempering and then thrown into oil, which gives them toughness. For the polishing, white whetstone from the Levant and oil is first used, then emery mixed with oil, and finally, tin oxide with good spirits. The emery and the tin oxide are applied with special wooden sticks, but the last polishing is carried out by rubbing with the palm of the hand and fine tin oxide. I was told that it requires two weeks' work for one person to make a pair of buckles costing 2 guineas.

Journey from Oxford by post-chaise

23 October. In the morning I left Oxford by post-chaise and travelled 50 English miles from nine o'clock in the morning until half-past six in
the evening. This distance equals eight Swedish XXX
miles.[29]

Fares are generally 9 pence per English mile or 18 'styver',[30] but I used a new company charging 6 pence per mile. However, for every 12 or 14 miles, 1 shilling or 12 pence must be paid in tips to the post-boy.

A post-chaise is very light and usually fitted with steel springs at the back. Two people can sit inside and up front one can hand a travelling bag or small trunk. It is pulled by two horses, one of which stands between the shafts and the other one, ridden by the post-boy, stands on the left-hand side and pulls by means of leather straps. The right-hand shaft of the post-chaise is bent outward so that both horses can stand in front of the vehicle and not as in France, Spain, Italy etc., where only one horse or mule stands in front and the other one, ridden by the post-
boy, on the side, outside the shafts. The result is XL
that the chaise is not pulled so efficiently, as is the case when the English system is used. From the road we saw Windsor Castle on the right,

Fig. 24 Post-chaise

Fig. 25 *Hounslow and farriers workshops*

two miles distant, and St Peter's College, which lies below it.[31] We then passed through three small towns where there was a little activity. Overnight I stayed in Hounslow, ten miles from London, because I feared that I might be robbed by some highwayman in the evening. A little food, a bed and tea for two people cost 10 shillings here or '20 daler kopparmynt'.

24 October. In Hounslow I saw two farriers workshops and enquired about the price of Swedish iron and was told that it cost 22 shillings for 100 English pounds. The horse-shoes sell for 6 pence each but are very wide and heavy. Their hearths do not have copes or chimney-stacks over them, but only a hole in the wall behind them for the smoke. In some places this arrangement drew out the smoke from the mineral coal used very well, especially in clear weather. XLI

On the way between Hounslow and London there were a number of brickyards with kilns, some of which were similar to those described on 22 September, but in another place bricks were fired without kilns. A pile of green bricks was built 15 feet high, 44 feet wide and 180 feet long, traversed by small flues 4 feet apart. The whole stack was covered with clay to conserve the heat and fires were made in the flues with mineral coal and peat. The clayey sand found in the neighbourhood is moulded to bricks without previous mixing. During the drying these bricks are covered with straw mats against rain, and also at night as is done in Holland. XLII

London

I arrived in London at 12 o'clock noon and went to Mr Koppenholtz in Suffolk Street, Westminster.

25 October. I went around to various places in the City and Westminster in order to find comfortable lodgings, which Mr von Plomgren had already found at 15 shillings per week and moved into towards the evening. Since my old lodgings in Suffolk Street were paid for a week in advance, I stayed there for the time being.

Fig. 26 *Brickyards*

Theatre in London

27 October. I stayed at home, because it rained, but in the evening I went to Covent Garden Theatre where an excellent tragedy was performed. The follow-on play was a
XLIII pantomime called *Harlequins Sorcerer*, which consisted mainly of many changes of scenery together with funny tricks and sudden imbroglios that really could amaze a spectator. The theatre at Covent Garden is not really very large, but just the same it holds more than 800 people. The tickets cost from 1 shilling to 5 shillings.

Swedish and Danish churches

28 October. In the morning, I visited the Danish and Swedish churches, both located in a part of London known as Tower Hamlets, which is east of the Tower. The two churches are practically the same size and design, but the Danish is, nevertheless, the most attractive of them, both in regard to location, the building itself and the ornaments inside.[32]

Theatre in London

On 29 October, at noon I was at the Royal Exchange and then dined in Westminster with several compatriots. Towards the evening we visited Drury Lane Theatre, where a tragedy
XLIV called *Venus Preserved* was being acted. The performers were so proficient that it would be difficult to find their equals. Everything is portrayed so true to life that it is virtually impossible for the spectator to believe that he is seeing a play.

Iron-producers' warehouses

30 October. I was at the Exchange at noon and in the afternoon in some warehouses belonging to iron-manufacturing firms, to compare work from different towns and to obtain information about prices.

In the evening I was at the theatre in Drury Lane and saw *Anglais à Paris*, which is a reply to *Française à Londres*.

Mr Brander's natural history cabinet

On 1 November I saw Mr Brander's collection of fossils and petrifications at his home, mainly mussels, shells and also coral, bones and teeth.
XLV The most curious of these items was a piece of elephant's tusk, and two of its molars, found in Devonshire here in England, deep down in the earth.[33]

A short voyage

5 November. I was invited on board a ship by a Swedish captain and treated to stockfish, salt meat and other ship's fare. I was soaked by rain both coming and going, and since tips and the charges for hire of coaches and boats were quite high, I paid dearly for my treat.

Washing of cotton cloth

On 6 November I walked across St James's Bridge[34] and viewed a glass-works making bottles, and a washhouse for cotton cloth. In the latter, the washing was carried out by passing the piece of cloth over a roller, cranked by hand, and in and out of a bath of soap-suds kept warm in a copper cauldron beneath the roller.

Lord Mayor's show in London

On 9 November I visited a timber merchant together with Mr Lindegren and saw the Lord Mayor's procession going up the Thames to
Westminster in boats with a splendid display of *XLVI*
pageantry, including waving streamers and firing guns. The oath is taken in Westminster Hall and the members of the courts sitting in the Hall are invited to the Lord Mayor's banquet and ball. From there the two Lord Mayors, the old one and the one taking over from him, walk a little way down the Thames and then continue by carriage with a large procession of all the guilds. Amongst them the butchers had their peculiar band playing by beating butcher's knives with shin bones of oxen, the two being tuned to produce notes, resulting in a kind of music. The procession entered the Guildhall surrounded by a fearsomely large mob that cheered the new Lord Mayor and hissed the old one. Moreover, the windows of the latter's carriage were broken, although some people were of the opinion that this had been done accidentally by his own followers, hired to walk by the side of the carriage, cheering loudly, thereby preventing the hissing of the dissatisfied mob from being
heard. *XLVI*

The banquet was served in the Guildhall, to which a great number of people had been invited by tickets that had to be given up at the entrance. The number of guests in several large halls was so great that that there was hardly room to turn around, from which one can conclude how much space there was for dancing. This feast, at which one was offered tea, wine and other regalement, if one could only get at it, lasted until the morning of the second day.

The King's birthday with reception and ball

The 10th day of November, the King's birthday, was inaugurated by the firing of guns in St James's Park. At noon there was a large reception at the Court with very many distinguished people in the most exquisite clothes and the ladies bedecked with priceless jewels. The King entered the audience chamber about one o'clock, and walked back and forth in
VIII the room talking to a number of the ladies. The Prince of Wales did the same, but the other Princes and Princesses stood quite still as long as the King was present. In the evening, there was a large ball at the palace. I saw The Beggar's Opera at the theatre in Covent Garden, which only serves to encourage highwaymen and robbers.

Blacksmiths' shops

13 and 14 November. I viewed blacksmiths' shops and workshops for grinding and polishing.

Session of Parliament

15 November. I saw the Houses of Parliament in Westminster and the Opening of Parliament, and also heard the King's speech to the House of Lords and the House of Commons, and the Duke of Newcastle's proposal to revoke the bill concerning the naturalisation of the Jews.

On 17 November, I started to attend Dr King's classes in physics.[35]

20 November. I heard the debate in Parliament on the Jewish Naturalisation Act,
LIX during which the Lord Chancellor and Lord Temple spoke for and against.

Theatre in London

On 22 November I was occupied with describing and making notes on the trade with Senigallia and Ancona in Italy. In the evening I saw Harlequin's Sorcerer at Covent Garden, which owing to its many sudden changes of scenery was the most amazing performance of its kind that I have ever seen.

Glass polishing

On 23 and 24 November, I continued my notes on the Italian trade, after which I viewed some workshops for the grinding and polishing of glass. On Saturday evening I attended Dr King's lecture on Physics.

Zinzendorf church

On 25 November in the Zinzendorf church[36] I heard the Count's son-in-law, Baron Watervill, preach. I could not detect any particular difference from the Lutheran creed, except, possibly, that he never mentioned any other person of the Holy Trinity than the second,
using the names 'the Saviour', 'the Lamb', etc. L

Iron weighing and prices

26 November. I saw the balances for weighing iron, which stand in various private yards along the Thames. Mr Herford, who for 30 years was Mr Victorin's partner, gave me the following information about the price of iron:

Gothenburg iron £16 per ton
Stockholm iron £17 per ton
Öregrund iron £19 per ton

Russian iron is made into hoop-iron here in England, in lengths from 5 feet to 20 feet. The Russian iron now fetches the same figure as that from Gothenburg. Of the former there is quite a large quantity standing in the weigh-house at the moment. It is all of large dimension and fairly well forged. Some of it is of good quality and made from good raw material, especially that from Siberia, stamped 'Old Russian Sabel'.

Steel prices

In Bristol, blister steel is made from Öregrund LI
iron and sold without forging, just as it comes from the cementation furnaces, for £28 to £30. 'German steel'[37] made in this country costs £50 to £56.

Tower of London: Arsenal, Crown Jewels and Mint

On 27 November I saw the Tower of London containing the Arsenal, with cannon for the artillery and small arms for the infantry, the latter mostly new and sufficient for about 50,000 men. They are very well arranged, in good condition and provided with brass fittings. There were pieces of ordnance of various kinds, such as mortars, guns with multiple bores, a cannon made of wood, strongly banded with iron, and a gun made of wrought iron.[38] The Crown Jewels were shown in another building. There were many of them, very precious and kept behind an iron grille. The Mint was also

Fig. 27 Stamp for coin

shown to us, but at the time of our visit only halfpennies were being coined.

The invention shown by Fig. 27 was the
LII same as the one I saw in Paris, namely a screw
with leaden balls fixed to it in order to increase the power.

Steel factories
On 28, 29 and 30 November I saw some small steel factories, and also visited Parliament.

Steam engine at Chelsea
3 December. I went to Chelsea and saw the steam engine that pumps water for Westminster.

Ranelagh Gardens
I also saw the Ranelagh Gardens and the Rotunda, where music is performed in the summer. This amphitheatre is built of wood, plastered outside and with the same treatment given to the ceiling inside. There are boxes all around the inside where one can listen to the music and also partake of food and drink and enjoy other amusements. For the orchestra there is an especially large box with an organ, and in the middle of the room, a bar serving tea, coffee and chocolate. The amphitheatre is 200 feet in diameter. The garden is very well planned, with a
LIII number of summerhouses, benches, ponds, etc.

In summertime, when there is music, the entrance fee is 2 shillings, but this time of the year one has to pay a shilling, or a two-daler copper coin per person, just to see the building.

Chelsea porcelain factory
The porcelain factory was also viewed. It was established in Chelsea four years ago by a man from Flanders, who brought with him a number of workers, both modellers and painters.[39]

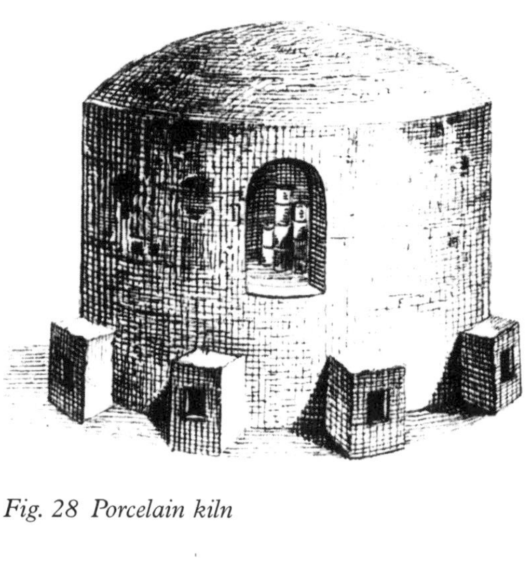

Fig. 28 Porcelain kiln

The clay, which normally is not shown [to visitors], consists of a white earth and quartz, mixed together in certain proportions.

The kilns, of which there are three in one workshop, are round and designed in practically the same way as the clay-pipe kilns in Holland, except that they are fired with wood in eight places around the periphery in order to distribute the heat so much better. As far as the products are concerned, they do not, by a long
LIV way, compare with those from Paris, Vienna or Naples, and even less with those made at Meissen in Saxony, although there is little difference in price. If one should compare the Chelsea factory with another in Europe, it would be one in Florence, which is run by the governor of Livorno, although the painting there appears somewhat inferior to that of Chelsea.

Zinzendorf's mansion

I also looked at the mansion of the Moravian Archbishop, Count von Zinzendorf, which he recently built, apparently without any lack of either money or good taste. Nevertheless, I have heard that the Moravians went bankrupt with debts of £170,000, for which sum their factories and his mansion have been mortgaged to settle the bankruptcy.

Natural history collection

On the way home I had a look at the curiosities exhibited in a coffee house. They comprised a
LV number of foreign animals and birds preserved in spirits of wine and several small objects from America and other places, also a painting of an Egyptian mountain rat and some specimens of ore from America.

The Botanical Garden in London

The Botanical Garden belonging to the Society of Apothecaries in London had four small orangeries and many foreign trees and plants. In the middle of the Garden there is a small statue of Mr Sloane,[40] who gave this establishment for the benefit of the public.

Mr King's physics lectures

4 December. I moved to Mr King's house. He gives public instruction in physics, and lives in Duke's Court.

5 December. I was occupied with some experiments in physics, and on 6 December in the morning made further physical experiments.

Session of Parliament

At noontime I heard a new bill concerning the prevention of the cattle disease being discussed in the House of Commons.

7 and 8 December I was also in Parliament. LVI

Moravian sermon

9 December. I heard Spangenberg preach in the Moravian Chapel. Amongst other topics he mentioned the old Lutherans, to whom the Moravians consider themselves to belong.

Iron weigh-house and various types of iron and steel

10 December. Went to the weigh-house and inspected all the different kinds of iron that I could find there, especially the American. Most of it was forged to 1-inch-square bars and generally red-short. In addition some bars were cold-short. The Russian iron was similar, although some stamps were quite cold-short, but most of it was made of good and ductile material, and, according to what I was told, made in Siberia. There was no Spanish iron in the weigh-house and it was said that little or none of it has arrived here since the war.[41] Similarly, there was no English iron, only ploughshares and a few small lots of salt-pans. There was a considerable quantity of salt-pans, made in Southwark in London. LVII

Steel is made from Swedish iron in the neighbourhood of Bristol, and is called blister steel, and also from a kind of German iron which is considered very good. The master, who started this works 30 years ago, had first offered to go to Sweden, but when he was not accepted, he was received here by Mr Herford's brothers. Large shipments of steel come here from Holland as well. This is made in Remscheid[42] and each different grade of steel is used for its own particular purpose. There was a small shipment of pig iron or cast iron from America, which is used by iron founders around London, and serves to mix with cold-short iron, because it has a tendency to be red-short. In every port all old guns that can be found are bought up LVIII
and Swedish ones are reputed to afford the best iron available. Pig iron is sold by the hundredweight, which costs 12 shillings, or 9 shillings for an inferior product. One hundredweight equals 112 English pounds, or 120 Swedish pounds.[43] Three hundred Skeppund of iron weighs 39 tons 16 to 17 hundredweight.[44] Twenty cwt. is one ton.[45]

Mr King's lecture

13 December. I heard Mr King's lecture on physics, during which he expressed the opinion that amber is exuded from the roots of poplars.

Testing of steel for magnets

I had arranged to have German and English steel tested for magnets and found the English to be the better, but a piece of steel from the Anchor Mill in Remscheid was also good. After dinner I visited Mr Ellicot and went with him to the Royal Society.

Iron foundries at Southwark

LIX On 14 December I travelled to Southwark to see the iron foundry there. In Fig. 29, **a** is the hole through which the molten iron is ladled out and poured into the moulds. Alternatively it runs out at **d**, when a large cauldron or cylinder is to be cast. **b** marks the opening through which old cannon are charged to be melted down, but when balls and other small pieces of iron are used, they are charged through opening **a**. Letter **c** marks the door through which coal is shovelled in. Consumption thereof is 20 'Lorne' per day and 200 'Lorne' per year.[46] **e** is a grate, through which the coal ash falls. The chimney must be tall so as to produce a strong draft. Melting a sufficient quantity of iron of $1\frac{1}{2}$ tons of castings takes two to three hours, according to what we were told.

Here are cast all kinds of plates, panels and other parts for stoves and hob-grates.

Garden rollers [see Fig. 30]
Naves for large carriage wheels *LX*
Bombs and cannon balls
Rolls for iron-rolling mills
Weights
Pots and cauldrons
Flat-irons
Grates and grills
Fences

The axles of the garden rollers are supported by wrought-iron brackets fitting into slots cast into the ends of the rollers. For cannon-balls, weights and other rough work, the moulds are made in loose sand, but for more particular work, such as pots and cauldrons, the moulds are made in flasks, the same as in Holland.

It is often necessary to use two or three or more separate flasks for one mould, which are subsequently put together as shown by the drawing Fig. 31. To ensure that it is possible to separate the flasks, without breaking off parts of *LXI* the mould, the top surface of the sand in the flask is sprinkled with powdered brick, before another flask is added. The sand for the moulds consists of fine white quartz that goes red after having been used a few times. Before a new melt starts, the furnace is cleaned out very thoroughly and all surfaces covered with fine sand, which prevents the iron from sticking to them. The furnace is built of brick from Oxford,

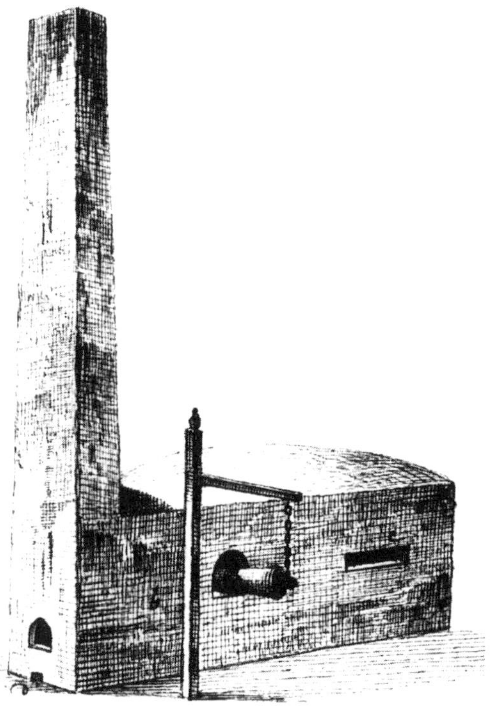

Fig. 29 Furnace for melting iron scrap

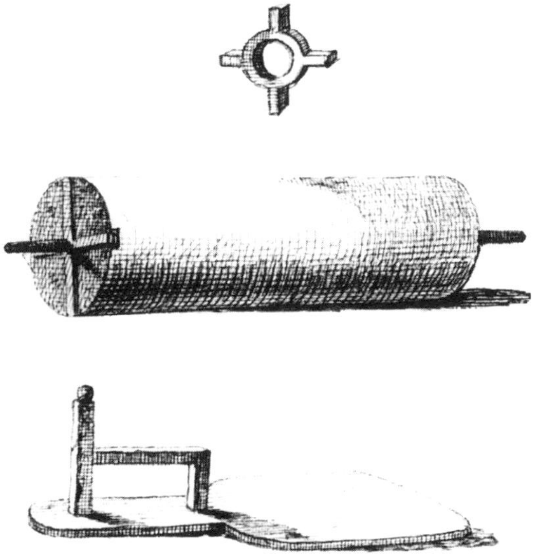

Fig. 30 Garden roller and boot scraper

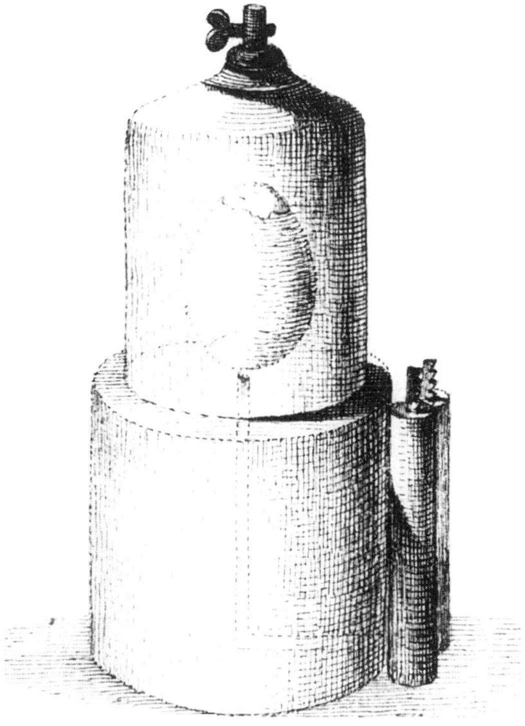

Fig. 32 Mr King's experiment

each brick 9 inches long and 3 inches thick. In such a foundry there are five workers, three for making the moulds and the other two for taking care of the firing of the furnace and the melting.

Session of Parliament

15 December. In Parliament I heard a bill being discussed which concerned the steps to be taken in order to prevent the cattle sickness.

Mr King's experiment

In the evening, during Mr King's physics lecture, an experiment [Fig. 32] was carried out with the air-pump, which concerned the air bubble located at one end of an egg. In a vacuum this bubble expands so much that both the white and the yolk are forced out through a hole previously made at the other end. The purpose of the air bubble appears to be to provide the chicken with air. But it is also necessary for the preservation of the egg itself, because in old eggs that have gone bad, one can ascertain that there is little or no air in the bubble. If an egg is painted with egg white outside to close the pores, it should be possible to keep it for several years without deterioration.

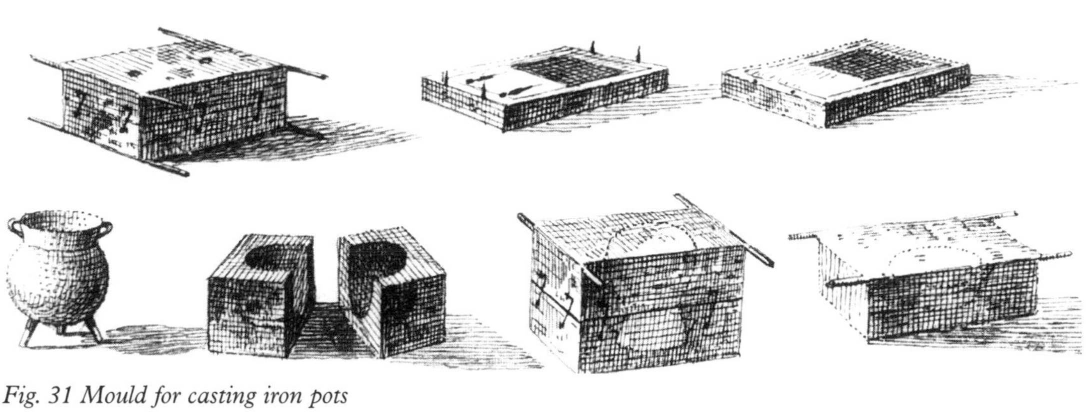

Fig. 31 Mould for casting iron pots

Notes and references

22 Neither letter A nor wooden box shown in the drawing.

23 Dates erroneous: founded in 1532.

24 Not clear why only 'half' is specified.

25 The collections to which RRA refers were probably those of Elias Ashmole, housed in what is now known as the Old Ashmolean Building, completed in 1683.

26 Designed by Sir Christopher Wren.

27 Folly Bridge, from which St Aldate's rises steeply, past Christchurch, to Carfax at the town centre, suggesting that the 'pressure pump' must have worked against a considerable head of water.

28 RRA gives this recipe in English, probably copied – or miscopied – from a written source.

29 A Swedish mile – still in use in common parlance – is equivalent to ten kilometres or roughly six-and-a-quarter English miles.

30 Swedish coin of which there were nominally 10.66 to one daler copper-coin.

31 Eton College.

32 The Danish Church – built 1696 and abandoned and replaced by a church in Outer Drive, Regents Park – and the Swedish Church – built 1728, abandoned 1911 and replaced by a new one in Harcourt Street, W1 – were located in Wellclose Square and Swedenberg Square in Stepney, E1.

33 Gustaf Brander was a well-to-do Swedish merchant in London who was also very interested in Natural History, and a member of the Royal Society.

34 Westminster Bridge.

35 Dr Erasmus King was the most active lecturer on natural philosophy in London between 1747 and 1753, lecturing in his 'Experiment Room' at his house in Duke's Court.

36 The Moravian Chapel in Fetter Lane. The leader of the Moravians was Count Nicholas von Zinzendorf.

37 Probably steel from Blackhall Mill, owned by a German émigré (q.v.), although this could also be a technical term.

38 The pieces of ordnance described were almost certainly historical curiosities.

39 This is probably a reference to Nicolas Sprimont, who came from Liège, the only remaining founding partner by RRA's time, though it is thought that the factory was established rather earlier than he suggests, possibly as much as ten years before his visit. See Savage, G, *Porcelain through the Ages*, 2nd edn (Penguin, 1963).

40 The garden was established by the Apothecaries in 1673 and Sir Hans Sloane presented them with the freehold of the land in 1721. It is now known as the Chelsea Physic Garden.

41 The War of the Austrian Succession, 1741–48.

42 Town in Germany, known for its manufacture of cutlery, hand-tools, etc.

43 The old Swedish pound or 'skålpund' was equivalent to 425 g.

44 It is not immediately obvious why 300 skeppund appears here. There were, however, several different kinds of 'skeppund', and if the most usual one, 'skeppund viktualievikt', equivalent to 170 kg, is taken, 300 skeppund would amount to 50 tons 2 cwt. It appears, though, that RRA was using the 'skeppund stapelstadsvikt', widely used for export business, although the correct figure would be just over 40 tons 3 cwt.

45 RRA writes this sentence in English.

46 The word 'lorne' is written out in the manuscript as if it were an English word, though such a measure cannot be traced. Coal was usually measured in 'loads' at this time, and it is possible that RRA was thinking of the German word 'lore' meaning 'cart'. In any case, 20 per day and 200 per annum implies only working ten days a year. Two thousand per annum would make more sense.

Volume 1

Arabic pagination

Page numbers from the fair copy are shown in the margin.

Journey 4 London to Wolverhampton

3 April 1754. London, Uxbridge, Aylesbury, Winslow, Buckingham, Banbury, Warwick, Birmingham (6 April), Aston (7 April), Bromford, Snowhill (8 April), Wednesbury (10 April), Bilston, Wolverhampton (11 April).

Fig. 1 Tobacco-pipe factory

Tobacco-pipe factory

1 On 3 April 1754, I left London and just outside the town I viewed a tobacco-pipe factory [Fig.1] with a kiln fired with coal. In it, old pipes from the tavern were heated to burn out the dirt in them so that they can be used again as new.

Fig. 2 St Thomas's Church

I also saw St Thomas's Church [Fig. 2], which has an obelisk on the roof.[1] On the 4th, I travelled to Uxbridge, which is 15 miles from London. On the way there are a number of small towns of little or no interest and the same is the case between Uxbridge and Little Missenden.

Fields with flint and chalk

Between Missenden and Aylesbury there were 2
several fields full of flints, but the people told me that little or no chalk is added because the ground is full of it; on the other hand, it was observed between Aylesbury and Buckingham, where there was little or no flint, that the fields were fertilised with chalk. At Winslow and near it a kind of soft limestone was quarried and used for road mending. It was full of petrifications, all more or less destroyed.

The gates were made as shown by Fig. 3. The upright on the side of the hinges was bent at the top and connected to the upright on the other side by means of a diagonal cross-bar.

The fields were divided into curved strips 12 feet wide, as shown by Fig. 4.

Fig. 3 Field gates

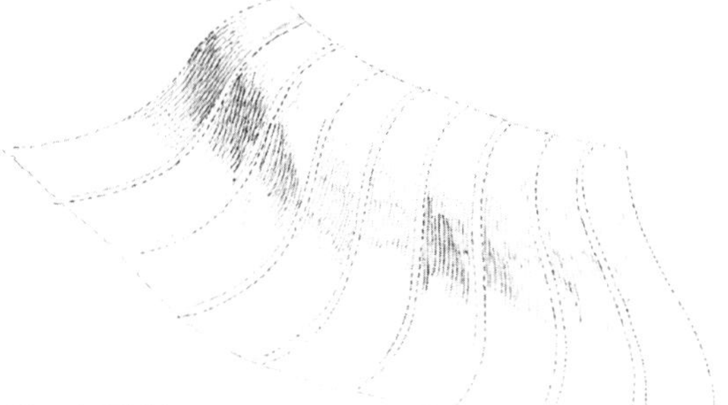

Fig. 4 Fields

Figs. 6 and 7 Rooks and Farmhouses

At Winslow I passed an arched brick kiln [Fig. 5] in which lime also was burnt from a bluish limestone.

Gardens at Stowe

I arrived in Buckingham so late in the evening that it was impossible to view Stowe, which belongs to Lord Cobham and is reputed to have the most beautiful garden in the whole of England. Past Buckingham flows a small stream
3 on which there is a mill.

Fig. 5 Brick kiln

Rooks

5 April. I observed at various farmhouses groves of tall trees, full of rooks' nests [Figs. 6 and 7]. At some there were as many as a hundred. These birds are here completely black and only differ from ravens in sound and size. They are good for the fields and meadows because they eat worms and other vermin that spoil both corn and grass.

Farmhouses

In the houses of farmers or peasants, there are 4
brick-built seats on each side of the fireplace, and on the same side as the door a settle, half built up with brick, and so high that it prevents draughts, as shown by Fig. 8.

Hay and straw stacks

The haystacks [Figs. 9 and 10] were either round, of smaller diameter at the bottom than at the top, or square. The straw stacks were supported by small stone posts 18 inches high, which in their turn carried a small stone tabletop. On this were laid poles on which the stacks were built. The whole arrangement can be seen in Figs 9 and 10.

Fig. 8 Farmhouse interior

Duke of Argyll's palace

At Addington between Winslow and Buckingham is situated the splendid estate belonging to the Duke of Argyll. The palace and the walls around the park are built of greyish brick, made in this locality.

Types of stone

Between Buckingham and Banbury the earth is red and the stone found there contains iron and is full of petrifications. The church and houses of Banbury are built of this stone. It is thought that this stone was first deposited in the sea in the form of clay, then metamorphosed to a flint and subsequently to chalk, and finally, by the action of an iron compound, to its present state. It may still be subjected to many changes. 5

At Warwick there is a free stone, consisting of a light-coloured sandstone, similar to one found around Bordeaux and in several other places in

Figs. 9 and 10 Details of stacks

Fig. 11 Warwick Castle

France. Further on we came upon a sandy heath showing where the sandstone had originated.

Warwick Castle [Fig. 11]

In Warwick I saw the Castle which is very old and has a beautiful view. Nowadays it belongs to the Lord Brooke who is supposed to have an annual income of £22,000. He is at present in Paris. Here I was shown a giant's breastplate weighting 52 pounds, his helmet weighting 50 pounds, and his sword weighing 14 pounds. This giant was said to have been a soldier at Warwick, and that he had killed a giant from Denmark during his last fight.

Hedges and thatched roofs

Instead of hedges, a kind of juniper tree called gorse that has thick and sharp thorns and
yellow flowers was planted in some places. 6
This grows abundantly in Spain.

In order to avoid building expensive roofs for farm sheds, the upright posts support a grid of poles on which small tree branches are placed, which in their turn support a covering of straw.

Fig. 12 Farm shed with thatched roof

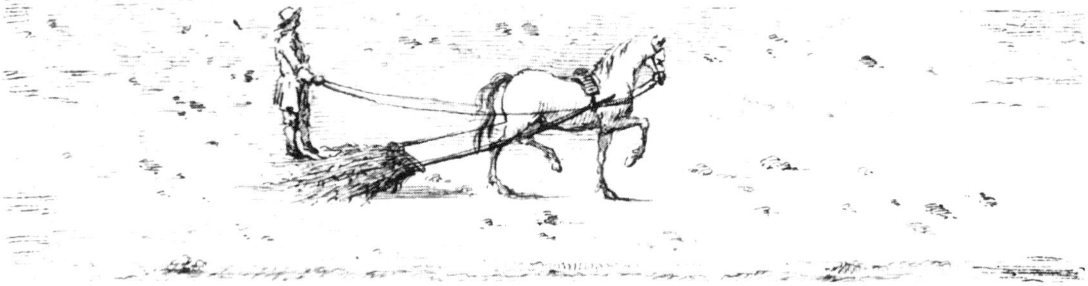

Fig. 13 Manure spreading using branches

Working of fields
A farmer was seen driving a horse that pulled a flattened bunch of tree branches across his field to spread out the manure left by the cattle [Fig. 13]. The fields were ploughed with three to five horses pulling one plough, which also required two people, one to steer it and one to drive the horses, which were harnessed in a single row, one in front of the other as is common with heavy goods-wagons [Fig. 14].

of grass. If there are any cultivated fields nearby that have to be protected, there are shepherds to keep the sheep away from them. Otherwise they are all alone and not looked after by anybody. This can be done without endangering the animals because there are no wolves here, and the foxes do not do any harm, except possibly to the small lambs. These stay out with the other sheep both day and night even in quite frosty weather.

Fig. 14 Ploughing team with five horses in line

In some places the fields are raised like garden beds, with little or no headland, in other places a width of 12 feet was raised and then 12 were quite flat and ploughed for grass, as one
7 can see in the annexed drawing 15.

Grazing sheep
During the whole of this day's travel great numbers of sheep were seen grazing on common land that was generally full of tussocks

City of Birmingham: parliamentary election
From Warwick to Birmingham the distance is 21 English miles and from London to Birmingham 114 miles. I arrived in this city at eight o'clock in the evening and was dismayed to find all inns full of drunken blacksmiths and other artisans. My surprise, however, vanished soon enough when I found out that an election
of Members of Parliament was in progress. 8

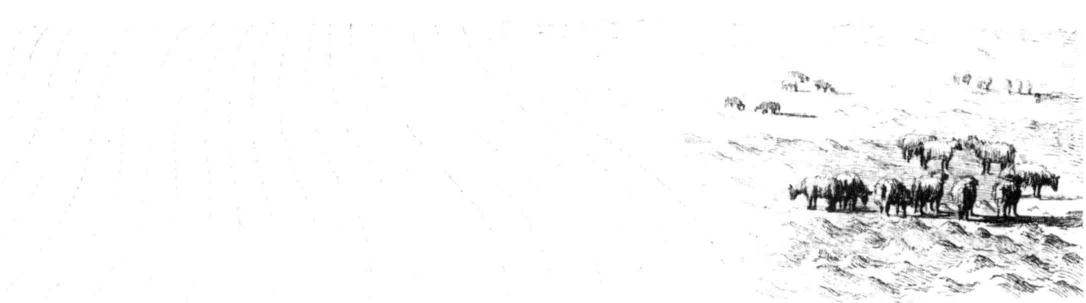

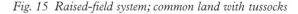

Fig. 15 Raised-field system; common land with tussocks

Wine and punch are generally freely available on these occasions, not only in the town where the election is going to be held, but also in the neighbouring towns and in places quite far away. There are many artisans living in the town who have served their seven-year apprenticeship in Coventry. By doing this they acquire lifelong rights to vote in parliamentary elections in Coventry, irrespective of where they may choose to live. At the beginning of 1754 the subject of parliamentary elections and the question of what could be done to prevent disorder resulting from the distribution of free beverages at such occasions was seriously discussed. But however strongly the question was raised and supported by some English patriots, nothing was done.

Type foundry

The 6th, in the morning, I went to Mr Baskerville who lives just outside town, to see his type-foundry and factory for tea-trays and other household goods made from thin iron sheet. The type is cast in a mould that is held in 9
one hand and can be opened and shut very quickly. The metal, which is ladled into it, consists of lead, arsenic and regulus of antimony.[2] At the same time as the metal enters the mould, in which one letter at a time is cast, a rapid movement is made by the hand holding the mould, which increases the pressure at the bottom, where the actual letter is formed.

Tea-tray factory

In the tea-tray factory, semi-finished sheets from Bristol were pickled, scoured, dried and primed and varnished, and then painted with birds of all kinds, some pictures and flower arrangements. Such a tray is sold at a half to 2 guineas according to size and quality of painting.[3]

Aston blast furnace

The Aston iron furnace [Fig. 16], where ore is smelted to yield iron, is located a mile from the town. It is built in the same way as the furnaces in Hanover and in most parts of Germany. The height is 24 feet, the opening at the top is 2 feet square, and the shaft widens downward

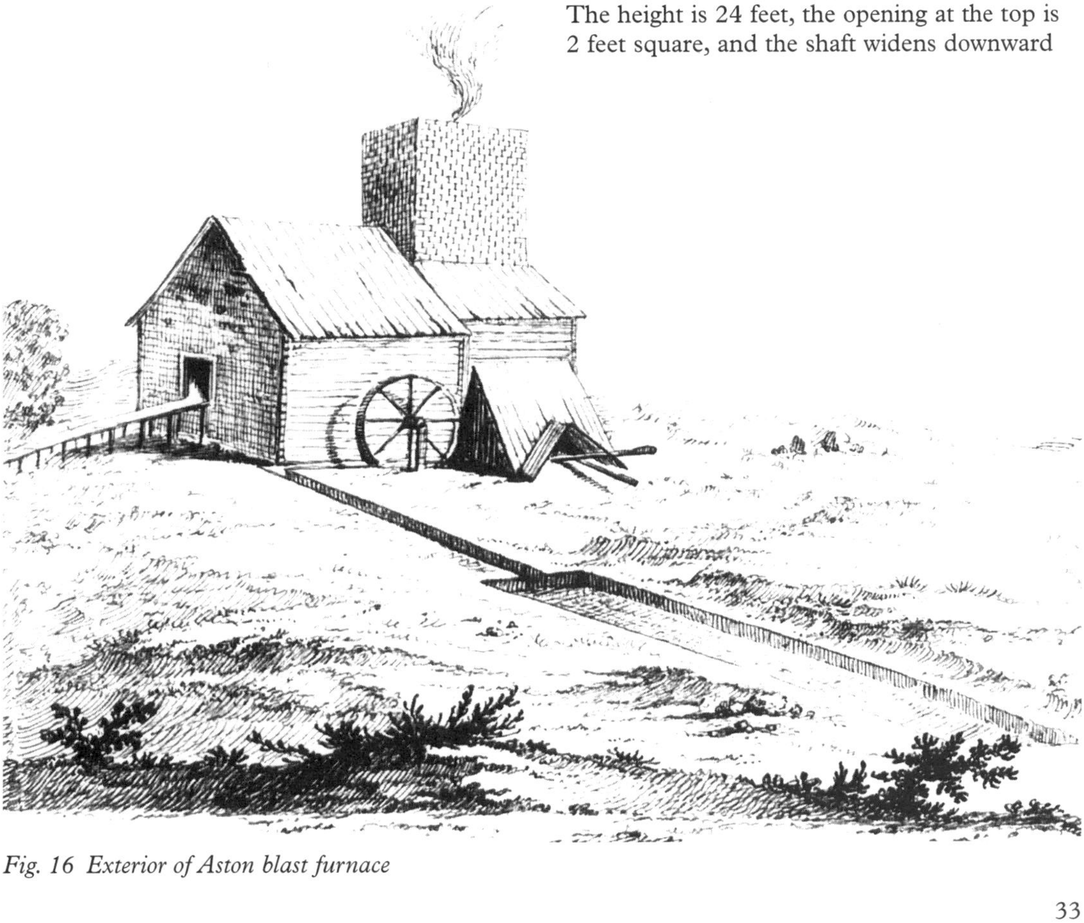

Fig. 16 Exterior of Aston blast furnace

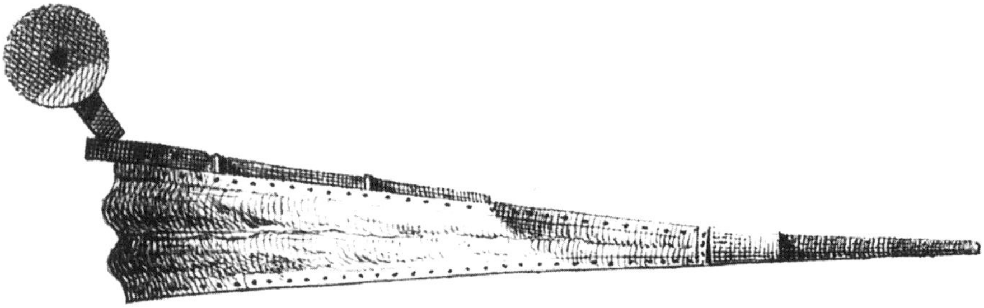

Fig. 17a Bellows

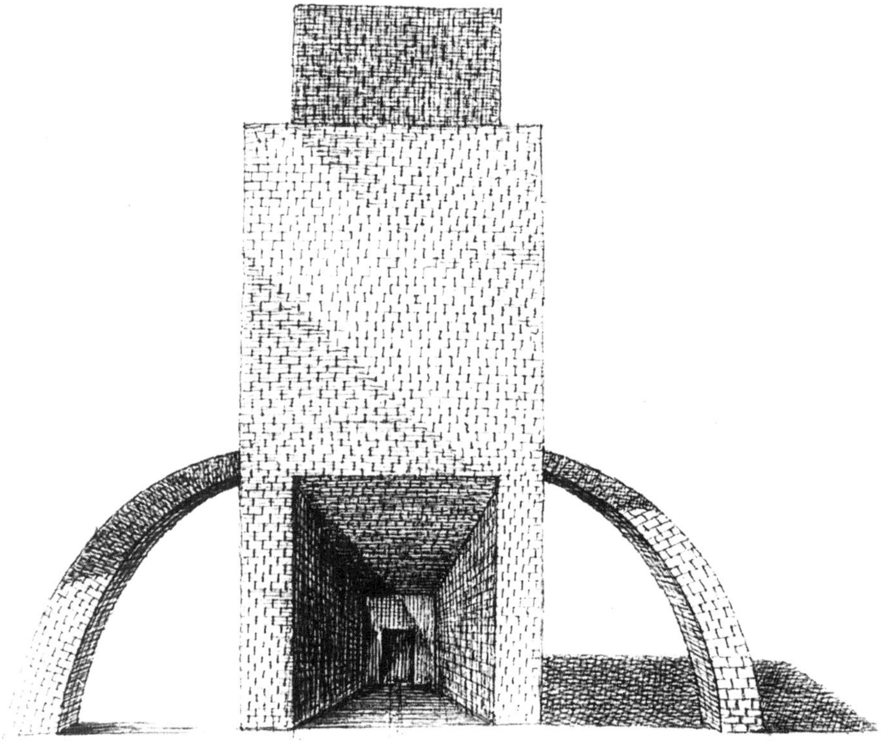

Fig. 17b Details of Aston furnace

until the bosh is reached and then contracts to
10 the hearth, which is shaped like a parallelogram. Charcoal made from oak, ash and birch is used here and the wood is purchased by the cord, which is 8 feet long, 4 feet wide and 4 feet high, and costs 13 to 14 shillings. The ore is obtained from the coal mines six-and-a-half English miles away. It looks like a blue clay that has hardened and contains remains of twigs. Seventeen tons a week can be made here. There are six workers at the furnace, who are paid 3 shillings [per week] and 17 pence per ton [of iron] and produce 17 tons per week. The furnace is charged every half-hour with six measures of coal, 36 inches long by 4½ inches wide, and nine measures of ore 18 inches long .....[4] Four 'Bird' [sic][5] or dozen measures of coal per 24 hours.

The bellows were made of leather, 18 feet long, and cost new between £60 and £70 [Fig. 17a]. The cam [on the drive shaft] consisted of a large piece of wood that could be moved back and forth in case the alignment
between bellows and shaft varied. 11

The overshot water wheel was 21 feet in diameter and constructed in the Swedish manner with closed buckets. The furnace itself was built of brick with flying buttresses at two corners [Fig. 17b].[6] During its last blast the furnace worked for three years except for 11 days.

Fig. 18 Plane-iron

Fig. 20 Punch block for button manufacture

Iron and steel fabricators
I also visited a number of manufacturers to see how they carried out their work, particularly as far as iron and steel are concerned.

Gunsmiths
In the gun-making trade there were works that welded the tubes for the barrels by hand with the help of dies. As soon as the welding was completed, the pipe was heated to an even cherry-red and planed with a long plane-iron, in which teeth had been filed and sharpened as shown by drawing 18. The pipe is then sent to a water-driven mill for boring. The operation is paid for by the piece. It is then polished, first with a square drill and a piece of oak, painted with oil, attached to the side of the drill.
The proper high polish is obtained by using the same piece of oak and fine emery [Fig. 19].

Die and punch factory
I also saw a works where punches and dies for the button factories were made. Steel was only used inside one end with iron around it. These punches and dies were made with the aid of master punches and dies and were rounded with a concave hammer or die. The tools were subsequently sent to the engravers to be engraved with all kinds of shapes and patterns. Fig. 20 shows the block of iron in which the punches are fitted.

File cutting
File cutting is here carried out in the same way as in Steiermark [Austria] and Schmalkalden [Germany], with the exception that the files are ground before this operation. To prevent

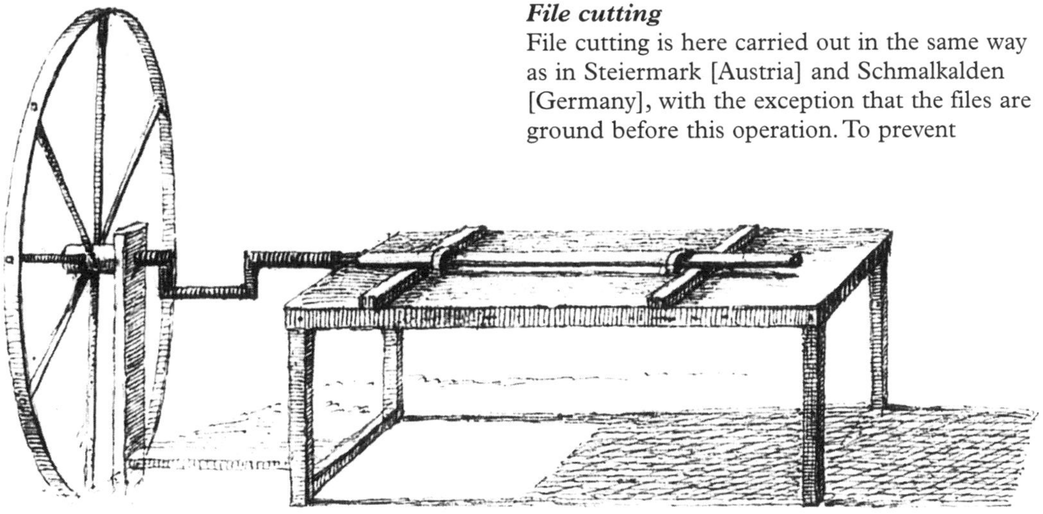

Fig. 19 Polishing bench

Fig. 21 Bromford Forge – general view

damage to the underside of the files during
13 cutting, lead is placed under them and they are held to the anvil by a frame placed over them.

Churches

7 April was a Sunday, and I visited the churches, of which there are three belonging to the Church of England as well as various meeting houses for Presbyterians and Quakers.

Iron foundry

I also saw the iron-melting furnace and how the pouring was done and how they cast slabs, hammerheads and anvils for forges, etc. For all of this, wooden patterns and sand moulds were used. The only thing to be pointed out in this connection is that pulverised brick flour was strewn over the sand surfaces to make the mould smoother and the casting better. After dinner I met some button manufacturers in Mr Baskerville's home. All of them took a jaundiced view of strangers because they were quite jealous of their machines and workers.[7]

Bromford Forge

In the morning of the 8th I went to Bromford
14 Forge, which is located three-and-a-half English miles from Birmingham, see drawing no. 21, and is provided with water by the river 'Edsborsen' which flows past and partly through the town.[8] In the forge, which was built of wood, the hammer and its drive and other equipment were the same as in Sweden. There were three hearths in operation, two of them finery hearths using charcoal, and the third a chafery hearth heated with mineral coal. It required two hours to make a bloom weighing 1¼ cwt. The weekly production was 7 tons, and last year the total production amounted to 340 tons. The wages were 99s.6d, which is divided between ten people. The finers, numbering six, get 10s.6d each, and the four hammerment 9 shillings each.[9] The iron made here is cold-short. The works belong to Messrs Knight and Spooner, who also own the blast furnace that lies on the other side of Birmingham, to the west.

Nail smithies

On the way to Bromford I saw several nail 15
factories, where there were generally four smiths for each small hearth.

Rabbits

On the way I encountered a large number of rabbits that had dug their holes on a sandy heath. Here stood a watchman's hut, indicating that they belonged to a farmer in some village in the neighbourhood.

Rolling mill and thimble machines

8 April. On the way back from Bromford, I saw Mr Taylor's rolling mill for brass and copper

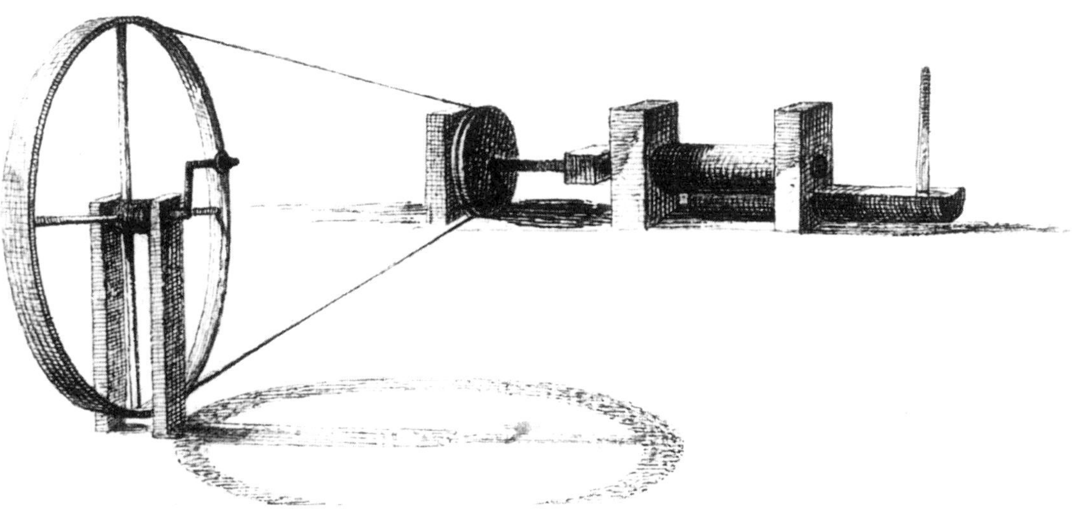

Fig. 22 Grinding of rolls

sheets to be used by the button factory. There were a number of small rolling mills and also, on the top floor, some machines for the manufacture of thimbles, not in use at the time. This equipment is, however, supposed to be so ingenious that it can produce 20 gross per day with the assistance of six people.

I also saw here a machine for cleaning and grinding rolls, which was very clever. The invention consisted of placing under the roll a piece of wood hollowed out on top to fit the
16 curvature of the roll and which could be moved back and forth axially by a workman whilst the roll was rotated. This man was also continuously busy smearing oil and emery or hard sand on the wood. See drawing no. 22.

Gun-barrel boring and welding

A little way nearer town there was a works for boring gun barrels, but there was nothing new to be seen. The workman had to push the barrel back and forth with the aid of an iron bar. He was provided with a hose of leather that gave water for cooling the barrels. In the same place there was a forge for the welding of tubes for the gun barrels. All the work was done by hand. In the anvil there were 13 dies of various sizes and forging was carried out in a certain rhythm and 'music'. When the pipe was welded it was heated in another hearth and then planed with a planing iron, 4 feet long. At the middle of this there were 26 notches cut and sharpened, all within a distance of 13 inches. There were also rolling mills for copper and brass sheets,
17 used for boxes and other items manufactured in the same place, but behind closed doors. In some of the rolling mills both rolls were driven by one water wheel by means of gears. See drawing no. 23.[10]

The foreman of the mill himself repaired rolls with holes in the surface by hammering in rivets and filing away the protruding parts. The housings for the rolls were cast in two parts that were fixed to a heavy oak plank, as shown by drawing no. 24.

Steel furnace [also includes two iron stamps]

On my way back to Birmingham, I viewed a steel furnace at Snowhill, see drawing no. 25. It contained three boxes or pots, holding

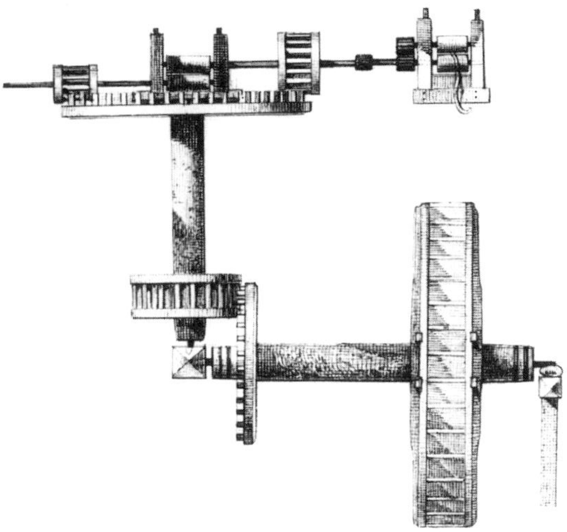

Fig. 23 Rolling mill gear train

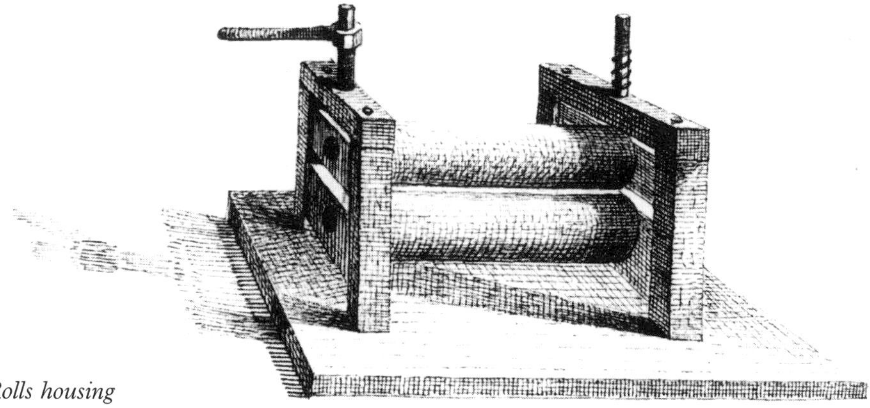

Fig. 24 Rolls housing

altogether 7 tons of iron packed in cementation mixture. The heating goes on for six days and uses 16 tons of coal. The workers were paid 9 shillings to 10 shillings per week. Only Öregrund iron is used here. It comes from Bristol and was said to cost £22 per ton.
18 The Russian iron has been tried but does not produce such good steel, and the English is quite useless for the purpose. The steel is sold for £28 per ton. There was also another steel furnace here, having only one fireplace and two boxes.

Fig. 25 Steel furnace and iron stamps[11]

Button factory

Just below the steel furnace there was a button factory, to which I gained access with the assistance of the owner of the steel works. I saw here the casting, stamping, turning, polishing and scouring carried out very quickly and deftly, mostly with aid of the lathes, the spindles of which are split to hold the loop of the button. The owner of the works then came in and started to berate the workers for letting me in. I did not wish to become involved in any trouble with him, so I went on my way.

Brass-works

The brass-works, see drawing no. 26, lies the
other side of the town and belongs to Mr Turner 19
and consists of nine furnaces with three built together in each of three separate buildings.[12] The furnaces are heated with mineral coal, of which 15 tons is used for each furnace, and melting lasting ten hours. Each furnace holds nine pots, 14 inches high and 9 inches diameter at the top. Each pot is charged with 41 pounds of copper and 50 pounds of calamine, mixed with [char]coal. During charging I observed that a handful of coal and calamine was first placed on the bottom of the pot, then came the mixture, which was packed in tightly, followed by about a pound of copper in small pieces, and finally again coal and calamine without copper, covering the top. This procedure was said to lengthen the life of the pot both at the top and the bottom. The result of one charge was 75 pounds of brass, with a value of £4.10s per
cwt.[13] The calamine comes from Derbyshire, 20
40 miles from Birmingham and 12 miles the other side of Derby, but the copper is brought from Wales. The foreman's wages were 14 shillings and those of the labourers 9 shillings

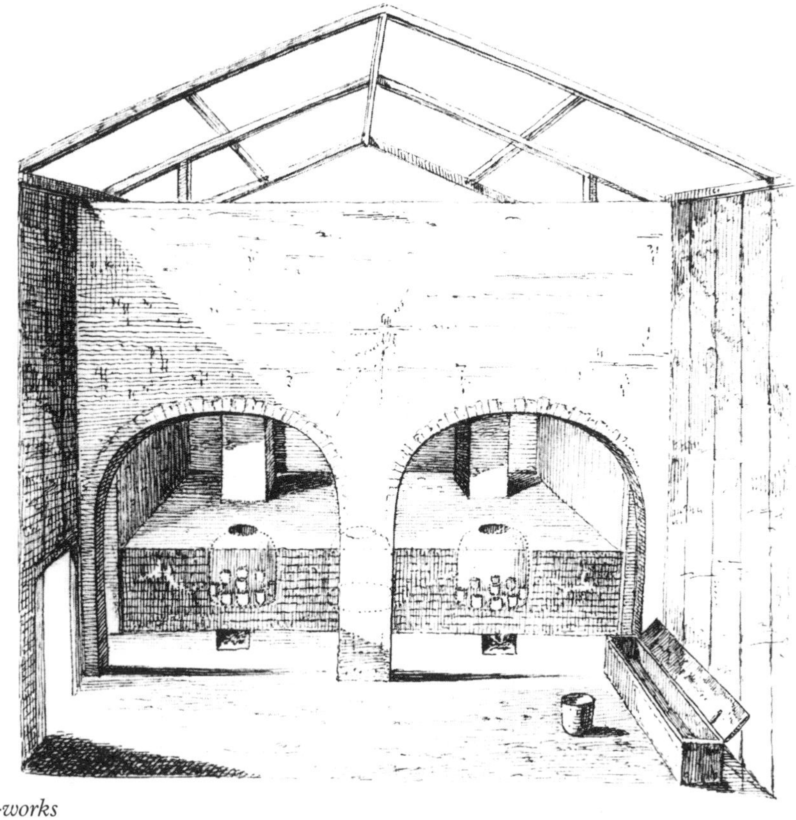

Fig. 26 Brass-works

per week. There are six workers for the nine furnaces and casting takes place twice every 24 hours. The yearly production amounts to 300 tons. The price of the copper is 12d per pound and of the brass 10d per pound.

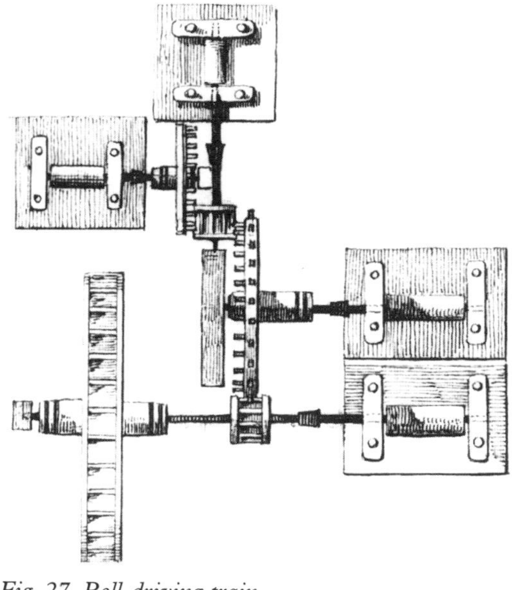

Fig. 27 Roll-driving train

Rolling mill

9 April. I walked two English miles south of Birmingham to look at a rolling mill for sheets for boxes and narrow sheets of copper and silver plated tin to be used for the manufacture of buttons. This mill is not shown to strangers, but due to the recommendation of a file-cutter, whom I had taken with me as company, I was let in. This upset the owner when he arrived a little while later, and he loudly upbraided both the workers and the file-cutter. One of the workers asked me for a halfpenny, which he rolled out to a length of 30 inches.[14] Another one was rolled to three times its diameter,
without losing its text, figures or picture. *21*

Otherwise there was nothing special to be seen at these works except that one water wheel drove four stands. These were arranged in several directions as shown by Fig. 27.[15]

Grinding mill

From the rolling mill I went to a grinding mill belonging to the same owners, where axes, hoes, saw blades, files and other rougher types of edge tools were ground on two large stones. The mill is water driven and to increase the speed of the stones as much as possible, the power was

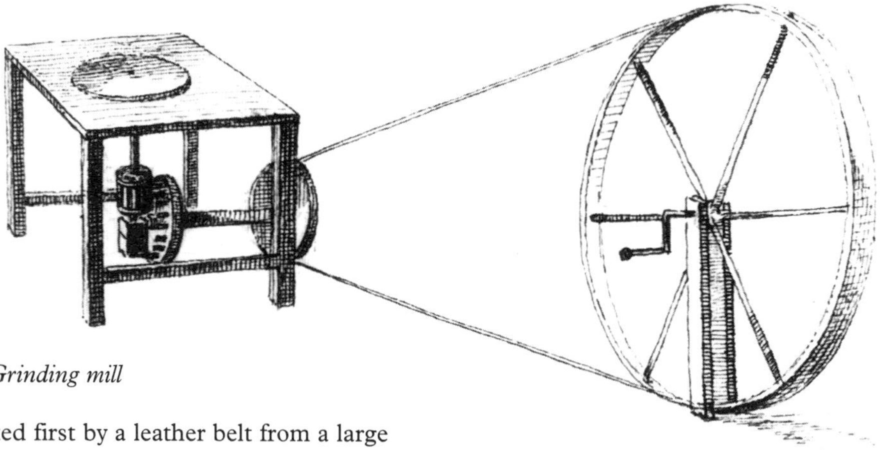

Fig. 28 Grinding mill

transmitted first by a leather belt from a large pulley to a smaller one and by a large trundle driving a smaller lantern pinion. By this arrangement the stones rotate eight to ten times
22 faster than the water wheel. See Fig. 28.[16]

A little more than a mile from here lies Mr Richardson's grinding mill, which is designed in the same way as the one previously described, but instead of two grinding stones, there are eight and sometimes nine driven by one water wheel. When more than one grinding stone is to be used, no greater preparations are required than the placing of further belts over the wide pulley. The periphery of this pulley is made up of slats. The stones are made of red sandstone, quarried five or six miles away. The real advantage of this method of grinding was partly due to the position of the grinder, who sat more or less above the stone and thus could use his strength and weight on the objects he was grinding, and partly due to various implements of wood used to support thin and small articles. For a saw blade, for example, an

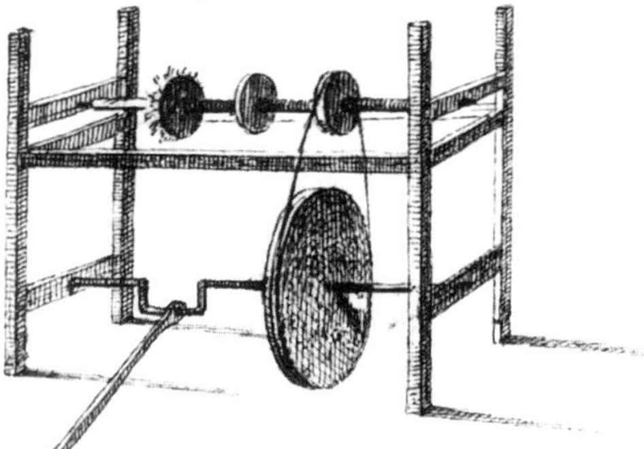

Fig. 29 Polishing machine[18]

oak board is employed to press a major part of 23
it against the stone. For sword blades and knives, similar pieces of wood, designed according to the particular application, were also used. Small boys had been given work suitable for their strength. They had to scour and grind small files and knives. Those who were more grown up were occupied with sword blades, kitchen knives and other similar objects, and the largest with axes, large files, saw blades, sickles, etc. Wages were paid according to the amount of work involved and each article had its own figure or price. One of the large rasps or files cost one halfpenny in wages to the grinder.

Prices of files

The payment for grinding one large Rubber[17] is one penny.

For the cutting of large files the payment is 24
2d to 3d and the latter sell for 6d per pound.

Files of 3 pounds cost 2s.

Ditto of 2 pounds cost 3s.

Small files from 1½d to 9d.

From 1½d to 9d, the price always increases by increments of ½d but from 6d it goes to 9d.

Candlesticks cost 10s.6d.

Ditto with snuffers 18s.

Snuffers 4s.

Stand 6s.

Silver plated spurs 7s.

Polishing of steel

In Birmingham I also saw a number of other works, in which I observed how cleverly they polished small articles of steel, using discs of tin

Fig. 30 Horse gin[20]

and emery, working in the same way as the grinders. Brushes mounted on a spindle were also used. The spindle was driven by a water wheel or by a hand-driven crank working horizontally, as shown in drawing no. 29.

Observations on factories

Although I had to use many tricks and much effort before I could get to see everything I wished to, I observed in a number of factories
25 that I visited that each worker had his individual and specialised work to do. Some were occupied with filing, others with punching, polishing, grinding, final cleaning and so on.

Soldering of silver on iron

Soldering of silver onto iron for spurs and buckles is a type of work which has not been known for long, but which is now quite common in Birmingham.[19] The iron object must first be completed and filed clean. Then a thin sheet of silver is placed over it and tied on firmly with iron wire. The thickness of the silver depends on how long the article is expected to last. Silver solder is placed around the edges of the sheet and the whole package is transferred to a coal fire for heating to soldering temperature. Subsequently the work is filed and punched according to certain patterns, with punches especially made for the purpose. Spurs are filed smooth and polished. Buckles are sold
26 for 3s.6d to 5s, and spurs for 5s to 9s a pair.

Wednesbury coal mines

10 April. I travelled to Wednesbury, which is located eight miles from Birmingham, where the rich coal mines start that supply the forges and manufactories of the whole district with coal and fire. I went down into 'Becker's' mine, which is located just before the town and is 52 yards deep. From the surface to the first heading the depth is 27 yards, and then follows one yard of a black, broken-up slate called 'clunch' or shale, then a 6-foot seam of coal called thin coal, followed by 10 yards of clunch and finally the great coal seam, which is 10 yards thick and is called thick coal. It is also found in other places 11, 12 to 13 yards thick. The shaft was round and the upper part of it, which passed through clayey gravel, was lined with brick. The mine was worked according to

Fig. 31/1 Horse gin and engine house

the 'holing' or undercutting method – see drawing no. 30.

The miners first removed the lowest part of
27 the seam and then worked upwards splitting off large blocks of coal as they moved along. Small pieces of coal falling during the mining operations, and which as far as quality is concerned are just as good as the larger ones, are left in the mine, because it is too much trouble raising them to the surface and transporting them. Below the coal seams there is generally iron stone, a kind of iron ore that has the colour of bluish clay and many traces of roots, petrifactions and shells.

A horse gin with one horse was employed for winding [Fig. 31/1]. The coal was raised in square wicker baskets holding 3 cwt, a quantity which was sold at the pithead for 6d. In Birmingham, six miles away, the price was 5½d per cwt. The transport from the mine either uses wagons carrying 3 tons, pulled by six horses or donkeys, harnessed one in front of the
28 other in a single file.

Nineteen people were employed in the mine and were paid 2 shillings for 12 hours work. From this mine there was access to another one, just as large and working the same seams. The two collieries together owned a steam engine for pumping. It had a cylinder 38 inches in diameter. The piston could exert a total thrust of 14.095 centner[21] because the pressure on each square inch would be 9 pounds. The pumps were 12 inches in diameter and the valves made according to a new invention, which consists of covering the valve flaps on both sides with sheet iron, the package being held together by screws. This design increased the life of the leather and gave it better resistance to the pressure of water and air. See drawing no. 31/2.

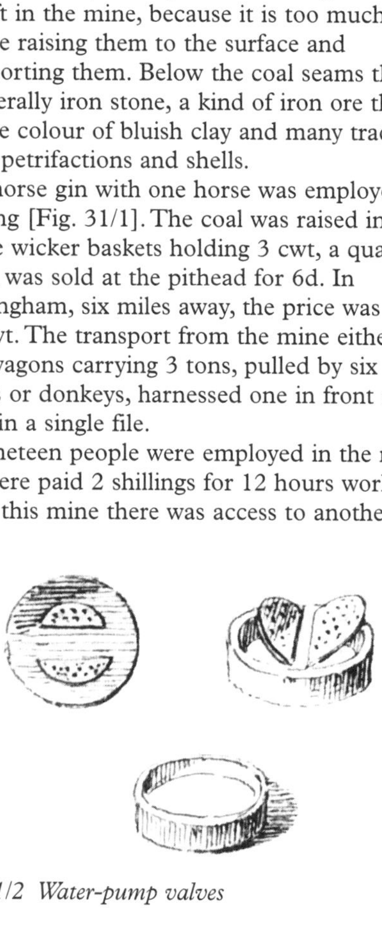

Fig. 31/2 Water-pump valves

Iron mine

A short distance beyond Wednesbury there was
an iron mine 16 yards deep. 29

The seam is 12 inches to 18 inches thick, and consists of a blue, clay-like kind of rock, that is heavy and rich in iron. The ore is sold per 'blume', which is a pile 5 feet long, 6 feet 6 inches wide and 1 foot 6 inches high and costs 10s.6d.

From Wednesbury I went across a very large plain, where I saw numerous abandoned coal mines. Also on the way to Bilston, which is two miles from Wednesbury, I saw a number of coal mines, some of them still being worked (drawing no. 32). Some of them were equipped with steam engines.

The town of Bilston and its factories

Bilston is a town that consists mainly of factories for metal boxes and other cast and punched work which comes under the heading 'Toy ware' or 'Quincaillerie'.[22] I viewed one or two of these works, where the people were
occupied with the making of paste gems and 30
enamelled work to be incorporated into boxes

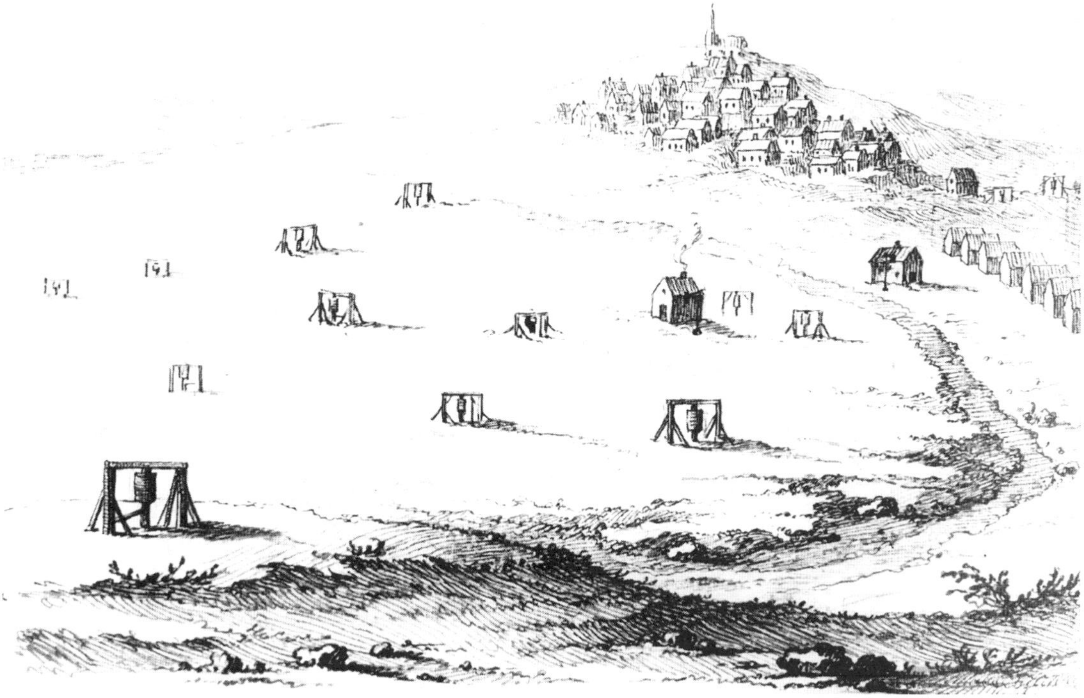

Fig. 32 Coal mines near Wednesbury

and watch chains and with the filing and carving of mother-of-pearl. Of this ware, I was shown a set of tea caddies and boxes, which cost 60 guineas. For purchases of half-a-dozen or a dozen of these items a discount of 15 per cent is allowed.

Wolverhampton town and factories

On my arrival in Wolverhampton, here called Hampton, I found a large number of people busy with buying and selling, and was told that a market was generally held here twice a week, on Wednesdays and Saturdays, and that on the former day particularly many artisans and merchants were present. This soon became obvious to me, because I had hardly entered my room at the inn, before scores of smiths came in to offer their wares for sale. Included in these were nails, tools, locks, hinges, key-rings,
31 buckles, corkscrews, watch-chains, flat-irons,
crimping-irons, sugar axes, snuffers and other similar goods in iron and steel which fetch a good price. Amongst the merchants staying at the same inn as myself, I noticed a Quaker, who was recognisable because of his flat hat without buttons. This merchant bought a large quantity of the above-mentioned goods and it was observed that he most of the time got a better price than strangers, because he always took the seller aside to close the deal and settle the payment.

Towards evening I took a walk in the town, which has a diameter of about one English mile and is provided with a goodly number of well-built houses of brick. On the outskirts of the
town, where most of the artisans live, there are 32
also many wretched hovels, which clearly show that also in this place the worker is left with the bones, whereas the merchant takes the meat for himself. The church is quite large, built of sandstone and located in the centre of the town [Fig. 33]. Half of it is Gothic and, according to custom in this country, built with the tower in the east [sic]. At a later date it has been enlarged by adding to the east end and as a result the tower now stands in the middle. The same thing had been observed at a number of other churches in this region. In the churchyard stands a pillar that formerly supported a Catholic saint, but in the time of Cromwell the statue was pulled down, as was the case with all other idolatrous effigies of this kind. In the town there was also a school built in modern style and very
attractive, but dirty both inside and outside. 33

Retting of flax

In a meadow outside the town, flax was spread out on the ground, and I was told that it was

Fig. 33 Wolverhampton parish church

placed there to be retted and bleached.
The same thing was seen in a number of other places, which indicates that, at least in England, it is easier to do this work in the spring than in the autumn as in most other countries.

Notes on iron and steel factories at Wolverhampton

The main reason why the manufacturers in Wolverhampton can undersell the iron and steel products of other manufacturing towns is the great help that they get with the work from women and children, who do most of the polishing, screwing of parts together and other such finicky work requiring more time than skill. As far as filing and forging are concerned, this work is done by the master and journeyman, but just the same, one also sees
34 small boys occupied with filing. Stones, discs and brushes are used for polishing here, in the same way as described under the heading 'Birmingham'.

Buckle manufacture

On 11 April I visited a number of workshops and observed their customary working methods. In the manufacture of buckles [Fig. 34/1–10] I saw that some were occupied in forging the hook and the spike, others in filing them and others in assembling them in the ring.
The buckle ring itself has its own workman, after which another files and polishes. All of these special tasks have their own way of being carried out. In forging the hook, the sheet metal is first hammered out and then formed as is shown in Fig. 1 of drawing 34, and bent together as in Fig. 2, heated, soldered and
stamped as in Fig. 3; the tools are shown in 35
Fig. 1. In the position where the hole is to be there is a narrow raised part on the anvil, as is shown in Fig. 4, and for hollowing out, the stamp is used, [see] Figs 5 and 6.

In the manufacture of the buckle spike, the same work is carried out, but it is filed out in the middle and sold by the smiths in the form shown in Fig. 7. For large spikes, a depression is used to round the shanks, and to make the part to be filed out thinner, see Fig. 8. Another workshop forges the ring for the buckle, which to begin with is bent into a ring and welded together as in letter (a) of Fig. 9, and then made square on the point of the anvil, Fig. 10, and sold for 6 pence. Hooks and buckle-spikes were 5½ pence per dozen.

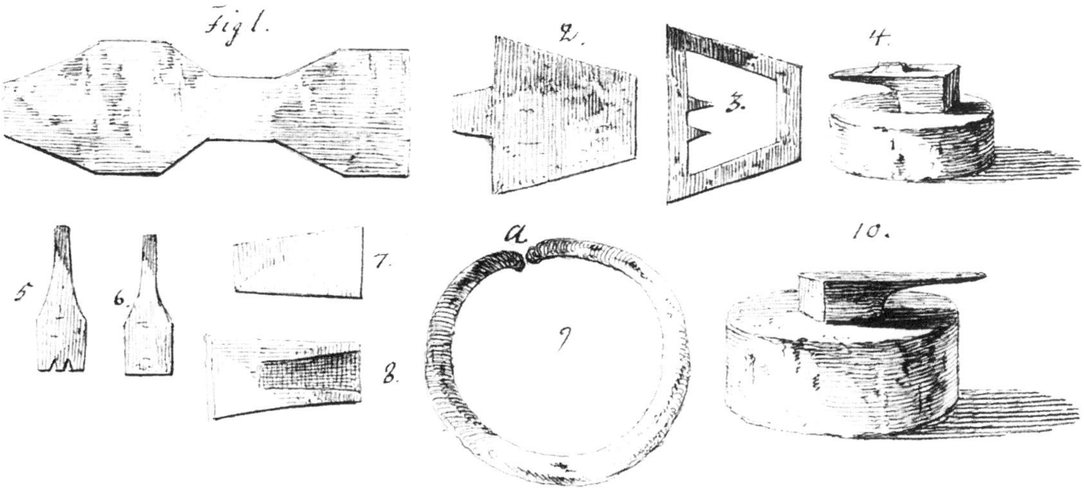

Fig. 34/1–10 Buckle manufacture

Coal mines

On the way from Wolverhampton I passed a number of coalmines that here were 20 yards deep, but the coal seam was only 7 feet thick.
36 Thus the workings have not proceeded farther than to the top seam, which in Wednesbury is called the 'thincoal'. In some shafts that were being sunk, there was first a clayey gravel 5 to 6 yards thick, then a white sandstone-like rock down to 12 yards, followed by the so-called 'clunch' and finally the coal. Between Bilston and Wednesbury on the large plain, where the thick seam has been exhausted many years ago, there were several small shafts sunk down to the 'thincoal' seam, which here is only 2 to 3 feet thick, in order to remove the iron ore lying above it.

Iron ore in coal mines

This ironstone is the same kind that is found in other places in this district below the thincoal, and occasionally under the thick coal seam. The colour is bluish and shows it was originally a blue clay, which later became impregnated
37 with a large quantity of iron particles.

I raked through some of the heaps of iron ore, which are evenly spread out in squares about 18 inches high, and found a number of petrifactions and impressions of trees, twigs, pine-needles and cones, and amongst them also some shells.

Discourse on coal seams

The reason for this mixture cannot be anything else than a great flood of water, which pulled down enormous forests of coniferous and other trees, and in due course swept them into a bay of the ocean where they remained until the pores of the wood filled with water – making it heavy enough to sink. The large mass of trees has subsequently become covered with clay and sand to a considerable height. After very many years, and after the changes to which the earth
is subject from time to time, the water receded 38
from the ocean bay and the deposits in it became dry. The enclosed vegetable matter had then gained freedom to follow its own nature, which is to decay, ferment and burn. But the burning and charring took place under a cover of gravel and rock 20, 30, and up to 40 yards thick. The particles which one generally sees disappearing into the air during burning could therefore not be expelled and were forced to remain within their allotted veins or limits. Coal, pitch, oil, rubber, resin and tar, which during burning are separated, each from the other, are combined together to a seam called mineral coal.

In spite of the violent movements to which this mass of vegetable matter was subjected during this time of burning and charring, which
perhaps caused many of the earthquakes that 39
have occurred, one finds that the coal practically everywhere lies according to such an orderly pattern that one can hardly believe it possible that the theory which I have put forward is correct. All the lines in the coal, which I first thought were fine cracks, are horizontal in the seam and one never finds them inclined, unless the seam itself is similarly inclined. If the seam

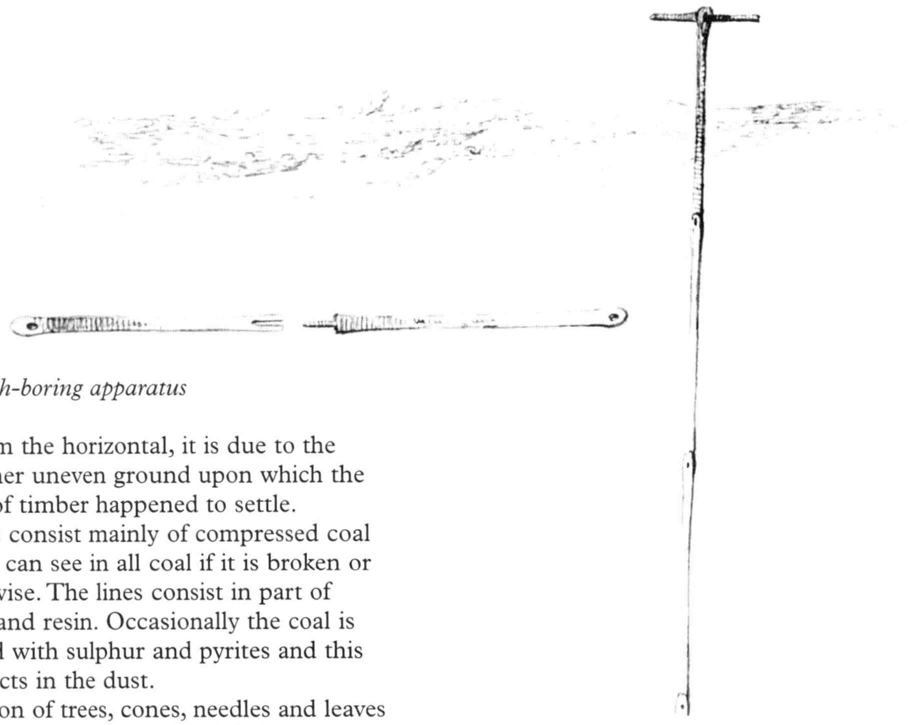

Fig. 35 Earth-boring apparatus

deviates from the horizontal, it is due to the hills and other uneven ground upon which the great mass of timber happened to settle.

The lines consist mainly of compressed coal dust, as one can see in all coal if it is broken or split lengthwise. The lines consist in part of dried pitch and resin. Occasionally the coal is impregnated with sulphur and pyrites and this mostly collects in the dust.

40 Petrifaction of trees, cones, needles and leaves that occur in the clay immediately below and above the coal seams confirm my theory, but also show that the fallen trees could not have been floating in the water very long before they were sunk by being covered by some heavy material. Otherwise neither needles nor cones could still have been attached to the trees, as was in fact the case. The clay adjoining the coal seam is called 'clunch' and is black and impregnated with smoke and in it there is no vegetable matter, although there are signs that there might be. As soon as the clay begins to take on a bluish colour one finds that it is impregnated with iron and also contains great quantities of vegetable matter, some of it not petrified. In this iron ore I have also found some shells mixed with the fossils of vegetable origin which shows that the
41 ocean bay into which the timber was driven had at some time, both before and after this great event, been calm enough to allow shellfish to breed and the water to deposit the sediment. Subsequently, sand-banks were thrown up on top, which in due course became the sandstone now lying above the coal. The shingle and clayey gravel covers everything else with the exception of some black soil at the very top. It is considered that the shingle and gravel are partly produced by the waves of the ocean, particularly in places near the shore, and partly by the general progress of nature and other growth promoted by the combined action of the four elements on our globe.

Earth-boring apparatus

To find coal seams, holes are bored with a 42
boring apparatus, right down to 80 yards depth. The bore or auger is made in many sections that can be pushed together, one into the other. See drawing no. 35. The last section is hollow so that samples of soil can be brought up with it

Fig. 36 Melting of iron filings

Fig. 37 Chimney stacks built over coal shafts

and inspected to determine their nature. Another end section is fitted with a steel bit so that it can cut through stone or any other hard material with which it may come into contact. The auger is half-an-inch thick. The workers are paid 4 pence per pound of soil brought up.

Melting of iron filings

In a forge I observed melting and forging of iron filings. The filings were first washed in water and then squeezed into the shape of balls which were placed in a red-hot furnace (see drawing no. 36) to produce a crust all round them. Subsequently they were heated further in blacksmiths' hearths
43 and forged by hand as required.

This iron is considered to be the best that can be had in this district and is particularly in demand by manufacturers of watch-chains and buckles.

Iron and steel manufactories in Bilston and Wednesbury

In every village, house and farm on the road between Wolverhampton and Wednesbury, one found a smith's workshop making buckles, rings, locks and nails. In one farmhouse between Bilston and Wolverhampton there was a factory for snuff-boxes and other enamelled work, where a large number of women were employed in preparing the enamel, dipping the copper sheets and painting. They were also occupied in firing and tempering the enamel, which took place in a kiln equipped with a muffle. The kiln had to be watched carefully to ensure that the flame from the coal did not reach the enamel objects. Later on I saw a
factory making the same things in Wednesbury 44
and there are also a large number of them in Bilston. The boxes fetch good prices when sold, according to the quality of the painting. A discount of 15 per cent is allowed if one takes a dozen or more.

Remarks concerning coal mines

On 12 April, I went down to the old coal-mining field and saw some places where the coal had caught fire a few years ago and where the fire is still burning. Of the fires there was

now nothing to be seen but the smoke emerging from chimney stacks built over some of the shafts in order to draw it to particular places and to prevent the fire from spreading (drawing no. 37). In some heaps of iron ore, taken from the thincoal seam, I found a number of petrifactions similar to wood, roots and shells, which were quite obvious, as well as two stones containing something that looked much like
45 pine cones, which were not petrified, but only broken, and enclosed in the clay-like rock and preserved from decay for, perhaps, many hundreds of years.

Forging of nails

In a forge close by, I obtained information about the price of nails and wages paid for their manufacture. Twenty-two-pound 'Sharp', $3\frac{1}{4}$ inches long, are sold for 5 shillings per 1000. The labour cost, not including the iron, is 16 pence per 1000. Ditto 14-pound 'Sharp', just over $1\frac{1}{2}$ inches long, are sold for 3 shillings 7 pence per 1000 and the wages paid are 4 shillings per 1000.[23]

Iron, cut into rods by the slitting mill, cost £20 per ton.

In a village on the other side of the coal field called Darlaston there were very many nailers
46 and also workmen specialising in other products such as buckles, fire-irons and gunlocks etc.

Fig. 38 Furnace for filings

Gunlocks

Gunlocks are made here and sold for five, eight and up to 16 shillings each. The most inferior ones are sold to America for 1 shilling and 6 pence. Two miles east of Wednesbury I viewed an iron-works comprising melting furnace and hammer for iron filings, rolling mill, gun factory and saw-blade factory.

Iron filings and small pieces of iron cut off during the gun-making process were put into crucibles that were placed in a reverberatory furnace (see drawing no. 38) in order to fuse the contents together.[24] The resulting lump of iron was removed from the pot and forged. The blast for one of the chafery hearths was conveyed from the bellows in lead pipes more than four fathoms long. The bellows were driven by one of the water-wheels for the rolling mill. The buckets of the hammer wheel were made of iron plate and parts of them had corroded away 47
completely. It was said that the corrosion took place after poisonous water from coal mines had been led to the wheel through a canal.

Rolling mill

The rolling mill was not now in operation, but was built in the same way as the one in Birmingham as illustrated by drawing no. 39 [letters missing], with rolls on one side and a slitting mill on the other side at a distance of 8 feet. The rolling mill is driven by two water wheels which also, by means of gears, drive the slitting mill. One of the wheels, standing in the middle of the forge, drove two rolls. The roll-stand already described (letter A) was used for rolling the iron before it was taken to the slitting mill, but the rolls on the other side (letter C) which were 30 inches long, were designed for the rolling of flats.

Turning of rolls 48

I happened to be shown how the rolls were turned, for which purpose a hardened and sharp-cornered piece of steel was used. Its size is indicated by Fig. 40. After the roll had been duly placed in position [in the rolling-mill stand] a heavy iron bar was put in front of it [on the base plate] and fastened to the mill housings. Some pieces of iron were placed inside this bar to fill the space between it and the roll. See drawing no. 40. Finally, the piece of steel was placed next to the roll, touching it with its uppermost edge. When the water wheel was started the steel did its job and removed all

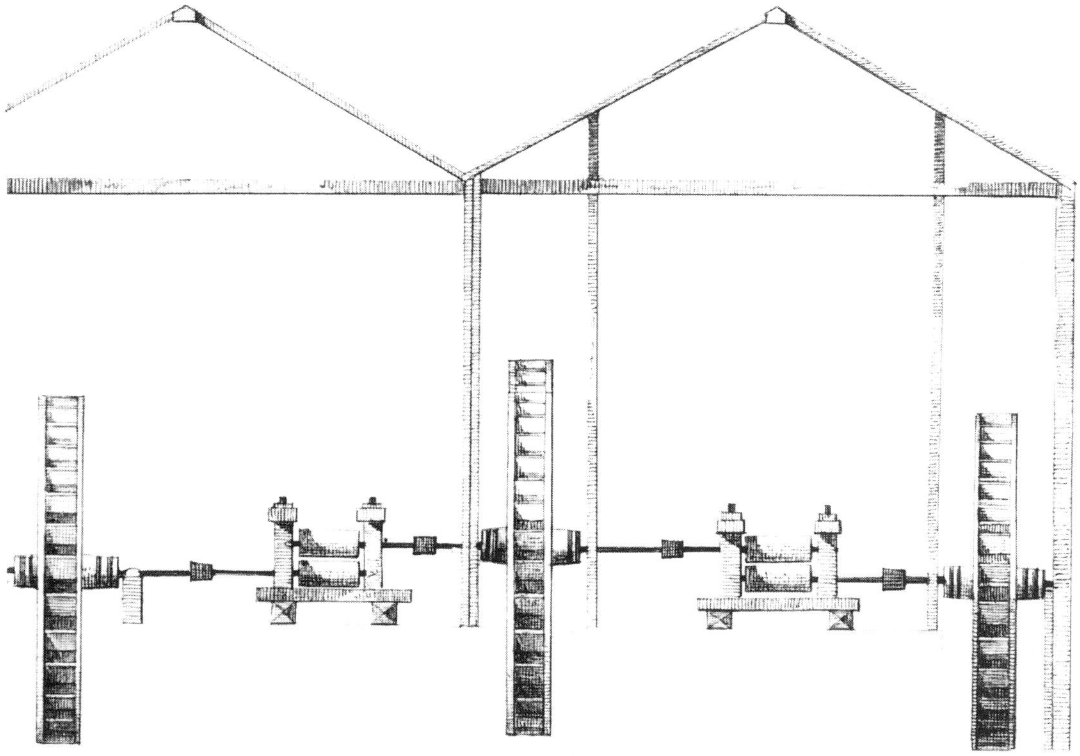

Fig. 39 Rolling mill

unevenness from the surface of the roll. Nevertheless, a workman always had to be present to tighten the steel against the roll by means of a wedge, and to turn the steel when one edge had become dull, which happened quite frequently. Each piece of steel could be used in four positions, or in eight if it were accurately square. It should be noted that if
49 steel with too heavy [a] cross section were used, it would not become sufficiently hard. In this way the turning continued along the whole of the roll, including the part that goes inside the wobbler box, until the entire roll surface had been turned smooth.

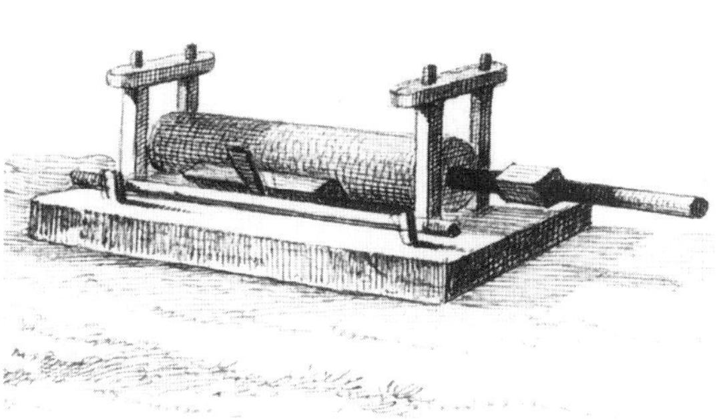

Fig. 40 Method of turning rolls

At Messrs Crowley's warehouse in Greenwich, the large sugar-rolls were turned by a machine driven by a horse. A workman held the point of a hardened steel bar supported by a cross bar against the roll surface. This is the usual way of carrying out the turning operation. On the road from Birmingham to Bromford, I saw rolls being scoured by sand with a machine built especially for this purpose, described under the date 8 April.

Gun forging and boring

Under the same roof as the rolling mills were two hearths for gun forging. In other places, the plate [for the gun barrels] was forged to specified width and thickness, which is a quite difficult job. Here the rolling mills were used instead, which made the work very easy and
fast. The welding was carried out by hand, after 50
which the barrels were reheated in another hearth and then planed with an iron, which has also been described under the date of 8 April. In addition to this gun barrel forge there were also two others in the neighbourhood, all belonging to Mr Willits. The boring was powered by a water wheel and carried out on a

bench as already described under 8 April. These works were occasionally stopped by lack of water, and in order to overcome this disadvantage the owner built a Dutch windmill of brick, which is said to have cost a large sum of money. It had, so far, never been used because the English are not so familiar with
51 windmills. Willits was willing to spend a considerable sum of money to learn of a way of taking in the sails without stopping the mill, because the stopping is very inconvenient and also dangerous in view of the position of the mill just above the water [Fig. 41].

A little way down the stream he had built a brick mill for boring, but in spite of the considerable sums expended, it had never been perfected so that it could do the work for which it was intended. These two buildings were generally called 'Mr Willits' Folly' by the people living in the district.

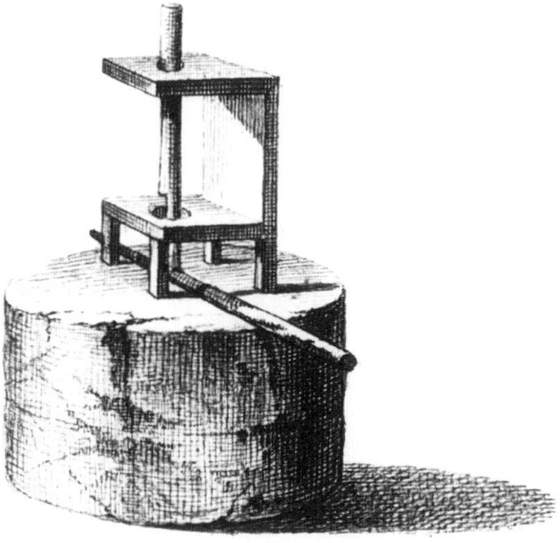

Fig. 42 Blade punch

Factory for saw blades

In one workshop I saw a machine for cutting saw blades. To operate it, one man must hold the blade whilst another one hits the punch with a small sledgehammer. As soon as the first piece has been punched out the blade is placed in a mounting which ensures that all the teeth are evenly distributed along the length of the blade. 52

The iron bar lying under the machine serves to lift the punch up again after each blow. For each type of saw a different machine is

Fig. 41 Wind and water mills

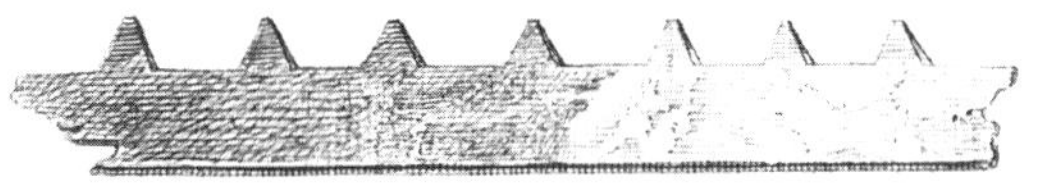

Fig. 43 Saw blade

required, because the size of teeth increases with the size of the saw blade. The width and shape of the teeth of the blade that was being made in my presence are shown by drawing no. 43.

A hand saw 2 feet long costs 4s.6d, but large blades cost 2 shillings per foot, and saws of 7 feet in length, 15 shillings.

On the way to Wednesbury, I passed a number of workshops for saw blades and also a separate forge where the blades were forged by hand, three skilled men working at each anvil.

Gun locks

Gun-lock smiths living in the neighbourhood sold the simplest locks at 1s.6d a piece, but the
53 reasonably passable ones for 5 shillings. If you order them of good quality you can have them for 8 shillings to 15 shillings, according to the smiths. The simple locks are mainly exported to the colonies.

Remarks on pine cones

On my return to Wednesbury I observed two pine trees standing by the houses. My guide told me that the pine cones are gathered up and kept in the houses where they predict the weather, because they are said to close up when the weather is going to turn to rain, and open again when it is going to be clear and dry.

Smoke-driven spit jack

The inn where I lodged had a spit jack driven by the smoke and draught in the chimney stack. I have seen such an apparatus before in the Papal State in Italy, although the design was somewhat different from the present one, which was nearly flat, whereas the one in Italy protruded into the chimney in the shape of a
54 snake-like spiral, as shown by drawing no. 44.

A machine of this kind costs 2 guineas to buy, and is kept in operation by the maker, including oil and maintenance, for 3 shillings a year.

Gun stocks

On 13 April I saw the workshop of a maker of gun stocks and admired the dexterity of a journeyman who could use the axe both to the left and to the right. The butts being manufactured were made of juniper wood,[25] intended for rifles to be sent to the colonies.

Screw machine

The stock-maker, Mr Brown, had invented a machine for cutting screws and making screw-cutting dies, which were considered to have many advantages. The die consists of two pieces of steel, of which one is fitted to a bar mounted on the table of the machine, and the other to a

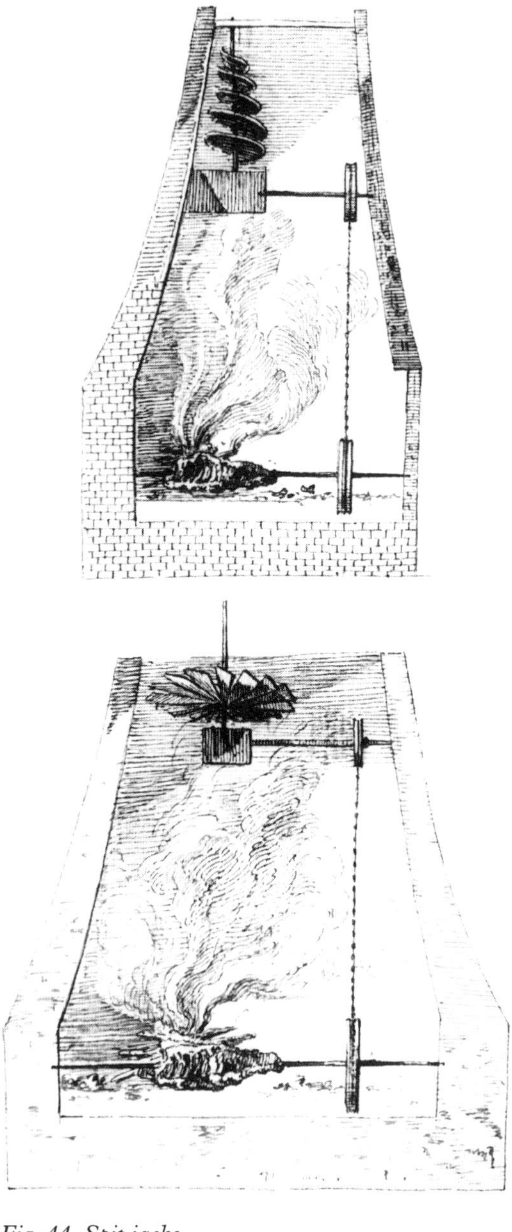

Fig. 44 Spit jacks

lever behind to the bar, as shown in detail on drawing no. 45. The screw-blank is clamped to the end of the cranked shaft and placed between the two halves of the die, and a weight
55 is hung on the end of the lever to press them together much more firmly. The crank is then turned backwards and forwards until the screw is finished. To make the dies one must use a hardened screw, and the two parts of the die must be in the unhardened state, but after the thread has been cut they are fully hardened. If one has a number of dies [of different sizes] it is possible to turn various kinds of screws on the same machine. However, for very large screws a larger machine would be required. The owner was willing to sell the know-how for 50 guineas. He claimed that this would be very profitable because both women and children can do the work without knowing anything else than how to turn the crank backwards and forwards.

Factory for boxes and wagon springs

56 I was then shown a factory for enamelled snuffboxes which had been started in Wednesbury some years before. Mostly women and young girls were employed here, busy with painting, glazing, firing of enamel and other work. One could buy here a pretty enamelled snuffbox for 2s.6d, and larger ones, according to the size, for 4, 5, 6 to 8 shillings. If one bought half-a-dozen at one time, a discount of 2s.6d in the pound was allowed. The same man who owned the box factory had also started a factory for carriage springs, which are made of steel,

Fig. 46 Wagon spring

and according to various designs and patterns, see drawing no. 46. They are sold by weight and the price is $7\frac{1}{2}$d to 8d per pound.

Coal mine, remarks on its age

On 14 April I went down into a coal mine that had recently been opened up. The seam had been found at a depth of 9 yards with the assistance of earth boring. When the miners had worked the seam a short time they broke into an old coal mine, which was so much more surprising as this locality was covered by very old oak trees, and there was no sign of any shaft or other means of access. See drawing no. 47. 57
It makes no difference in what time or during whose reign this mine was worked, because a few hundred or thousand years more or less do not matter, since the fireclay and cement that has been deposited over everything by water to a height of $1\frac{1}{2}$ to 2 inches shows that a very long time has passed from the time it was worked. From the way the mine had been

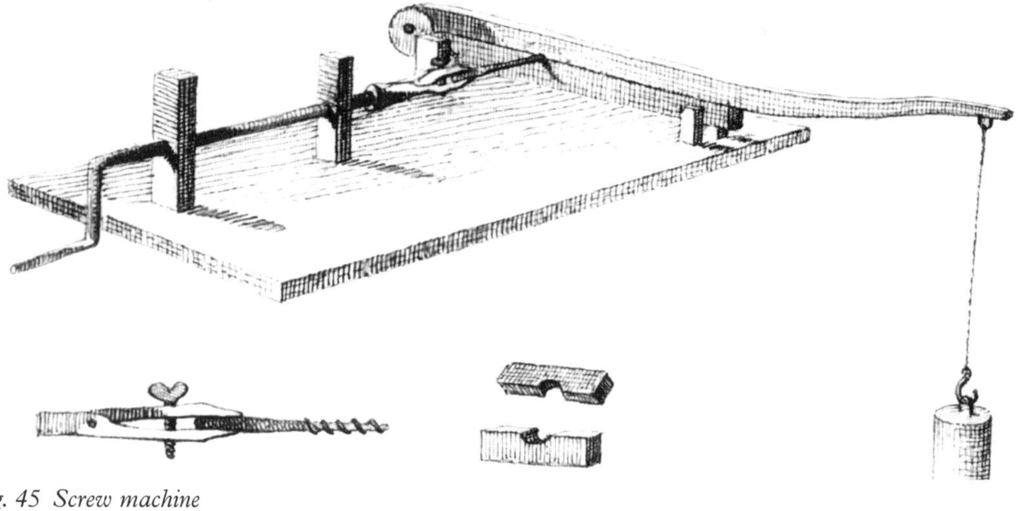

Fig. 45 Screw machine

Fig. 47 Old coal mine

worked, so that it had not collapsed, one can judge that the miners of that day had more skill and took more care with their work than those living today. Every five fathoms, a pillar of coal a yard square had been left, and one could walk between them, as under the vaults of a church.[26] But I also observed at all parts of the workings that the slippery clay permitted me to reach, that no more than half of the thickness of the seam had been removed, even if one included the roof which contained 2 feet to 2 feet 6 inches of coal. It therefore appears very probable that another similar mine was worked below the one I was in, in order to avoid making the pillars too high, and perhaps also in view of the ventilation, which will be shown in time. I would estimate the age of this mine to be two to three thousand years, because in the Pyrenees one finds silver mines which were worked in the same way in the days when Hannibal was living. Below a vault, which was somewhat larger than the rest, I saw the trunk of a birch tree that had been used as a support. It had rotted away completely inside, although the bark still looked to be quite fresh. Instead of the great care with
59 which the mines were worked in the old days, one now observes in the mining industry a great deal of carelessness and lack of forethought. This is particularly apparent in this district, where everything that can be reached is removed, which makes the mines unsafe, and often causes the miners to lose their lives.

I now took the road through Birmingham back to London. During the trip I saw the slitting mill in Birmingham, that has been described in connection with my second visit to Birmingham together with Mr Plomgren.

Price of iron

Note: in Birmingham the price of Swedish bar iron is £19.10s per ton. It is ordered from Sweden via Bristol, and the yearly consumption is said to be as much as 2000 tons. Transport from Bristol to Bewdley costs 12s per ton, and from Bewdley to Birmingham 12s 6d.

Abstract from a letter to Messrs Finlay and Jennings[27] regarding rolling and tinning of iron sheet in England, dated 19 July 1754:

Sheet-iron rolling and tinning in England

In reply to the second, third and fourth questions concerning the iron used for the folding of sheets for tinplate in England, it is made in Pontypool or at other iron-works in Wales and Lancashire where sheets are rolled. In the blast furnaces, a red and loose iron ore mined in Lancashire, which is similar to the Biscayan, is generally mixed with other ore. The refining and forging of the iron is carried out according to the French method used in Roslagen.[28] Great care is taken to ensure that the product is free from defects both internally and on the surface. The ends of the bars are therefore not suitable for this purpose. Redshort iron, in particular, is useless for the rolling of sheets for tinplate. All other kinds can be used, although they may be more or less suitable depending on how soft and ductile they are. I should think that pig iron from Grangärde,[29] with the addition of pig iron from the Öregrund district,[30] would produce wrought iron that would be just right for this requirement in Sweden.

The reply to your questions 5, 6, 13 and 16 is that the tin bar, the raw material for this

tinplate rolling, is forged to the greatest length possible and then, without reheating, cut up into short pieces, equal in length to the width of the sheets to be rolled. For example, a tin plate $10\frac{1}{4}$ inches wide and $13\frac{1}{2}$ inches long requires a tin bar $10\frac{1}{2}$ inches long, 4 inches to $4\frac{1}{6}$ inches wide and $\frac{1}{2}$ inch thick. A plate $12\frac{1}{4}$ inches wide and $16\frac{1}{4}$ inches long requires the bar to be 13 inches to $13\frac{1}{6}$ inches long, $4\frac{1}{4}$ inches wide and $\frac{1}{2}$ inch to $\frac{7}{8}$ inch thick.
The tin bar is heated eight times before the rolling is completed to final size. It always enters the rolling mill 'broad-side on' and after the initial heating it passes eight times through the rolls which are screwed down a little after each pass. If the plate reaches a length of twice its width during this heat, which, however, does not happen very often, it is doubled and after a second heating given another five to six passes. The plate also passes through the rolls the same number of times after the third and fourth heatings, and is then again doubled, resulting in a pack of four plates. The quadruple pack is subjected to two more cycles of reheating and rolling before it is divided into two, which are then doubled. These two separate packs of four plates each are twice again reheated and rolled until the correct length is reached. In this way the short tin bar mentioned to begin with is rolled out to eight plates, which are
63 subsequently trimmed to size in the usual way.

In reply to the seventh question, I remind you that the rolls should be in proportion to the plate that is going to be folded. The length of the roll-face should not exceed the width of the plate by more than 2 or 3 inches because otherwise the stress on the rolling necks will be too high and cause premature breakages.

Fig. 48 Reverberatory furnace

In regard to the 8th, 9th and 10th questions, which concern the material for the rolls and the method of casting them, the following should be observed: the rolls should be cast of re-melted iron, preferably pig iron suitable for making wrought iron for conversion to blister steel. The melting should be carried out in a reverberatory furnace, see drawing no. 48. In London and Bristol, English pig iron and old cannon are used, but the rolls would be better if Öregrund pig iron or other good Swedish pig iron were employed, because this iron has greater strength
and hardness than the aforementioned. 64

The mould for the rolls is made of clay, supported with iron at the sides, so that the clay can be rammed down hard. See drawing no. 49.

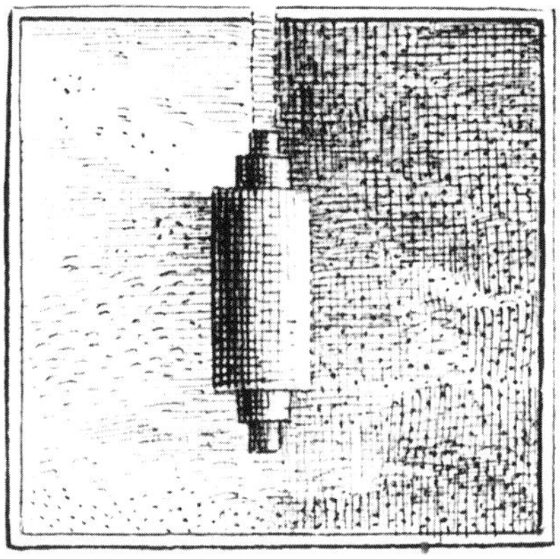

Fig. 49 Mould for rolls

The iron flows into the mould through a 12-inch-deep hole at letter 'f' [missing] in order to increase the pressure and thus obtain a denser iron.

When the casting is completed the roll is turned by means of a square piece of steel, the edge of which is forced against the roll by wedges. See drawing no. 50.

Before the roll can be placed in the roll-stand for turning, the roll-necks must be turned. For this purpose holes are punched in the ends of the roll so that it can rotate on two centres as shown by drawings 51 and 52. The power for the rotation is provided by the water wheel through a train of cast gears.[31] A roll 16 inches
in length generally has a diameter of $11\frac{1}{2}$ 65
inches to 12 inches before turning has taken

Fig. 50 Turning of rolls

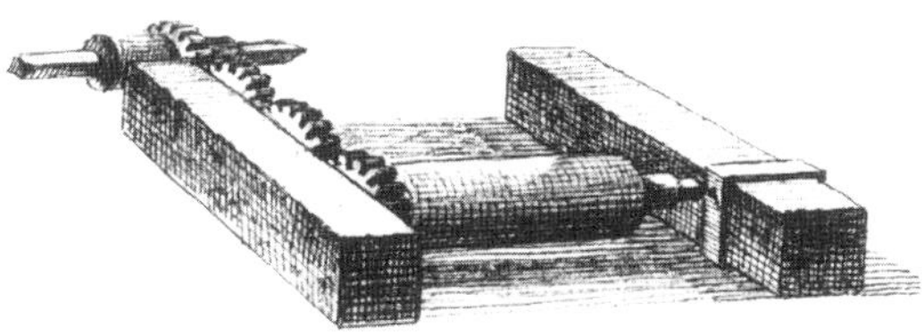

Fig. 51 Lathe gear-train

Fig. 52 Cast gear-wheel

place, and 11 inches afterwards. The necks are 5 inches long and 3½ inches smaller in diameter than the body of the roll. One of the roll-necks is extended and worked to a four-inch-square cross-section which serves to connect the roll to the water-wheel shaft (which has a similar square cross-section) by means of a cast-iron coupling or wobbler-box which is slid over the two. This wobbler-box has an internal cross-section of 4 inches square. See drawings no. 53 and 54.

A stand of rolls requires four chocks, four roll-neck bearings, four uprights or posts with their threaded portion, four screw-down nuts, and two spanners. I have seen chocks of both greater and lesser size than the ones I sent home, but those were of convenient length and suitable for use with both small and large rolls. The thickness from the outside edge to the hole is 2½ inches, the diameter of the hole is 4½ inches and the distance between the holes is 15 inches. See drawing no. 55.

The bearings proper for the roll-necks rest in the recesses in the chocks, and are generally made of non-ferrous metal, the strength of which is adapted to suit the rolls. This is shown by drawing no. 55.

The uprights or posts shown by drawing no. 56 are of forged iron 4 feet long and 4 inches in diameter, with a loop at the bottom through which a bar is placed to keep the post in position. At the top there is a threaded part. A nut of non-ferrous metal belongs to each post, and each housing is provided with two

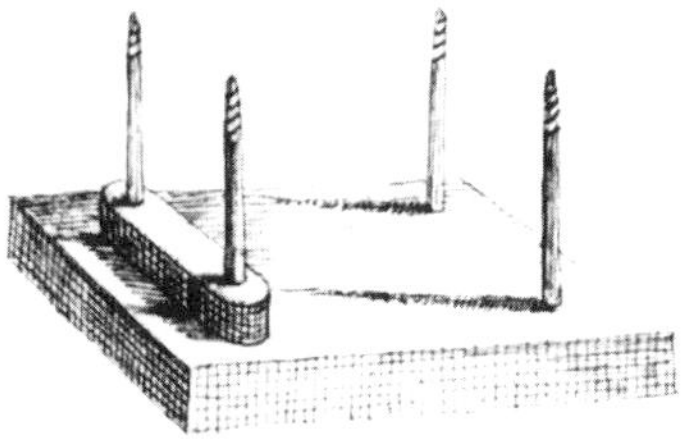

Fig. 53 Details of roll mountings

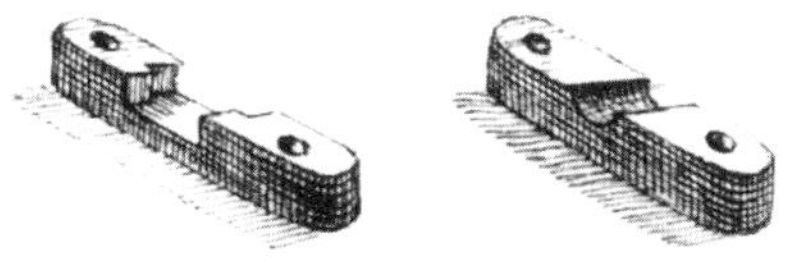

Fig. 55 Roll bearings

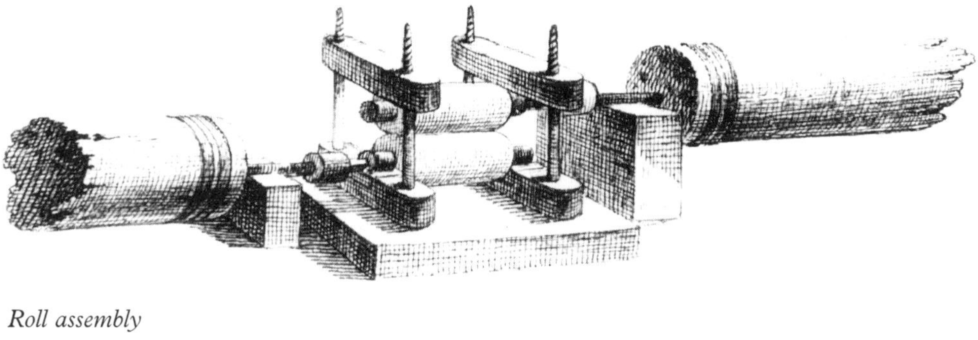

Fig. 54 Roll assembly

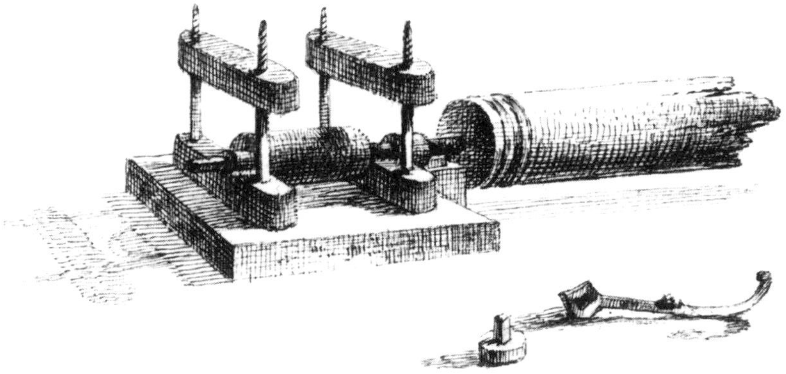

Fig. 56 Roll mountings and spanner

spanners as shown by the above-mentioned drawing.

The bed for the rolling-mill stand is generally 12 inches thick, see drawing no. 57, and made up of an oak beam 9 inches thick covered by an iron plate 2 inches thick. In addition, cast-iron
67 wobbler-boxes are also needed, such as shown by drawing no. 57.

They are 9 inches long and 10 inches in diameter and their purpose is to connect the water-wheel shaft with the wobbler of the roll. Two are required for a sheet-rolling mill driven by two water wheels rotating in opposite directions. A sheet or tinplate rolling mill consists of one stand only and can produce 2650 to 2970 pounds per week or three boxes of 225 plates each per day. There are three workers: a roller, a catcher, and a heater. The two former do the work on the mill, and the heater takes care of the reheating furnace.

The furnace is built of Stourbridge brick, which can best withstand the heat. Internally it is 5 feet long, 1 foot 8 inches wide, and 1 foot 8 inches high. It is fired with mineral coal that is shovelled directly into the furnace, the bottom of which consists of an iron grating. This lets the air through, thus creating a draught.
See drawing no. 58. 68

Charcoal would be more suitable for this purpose, and in a reverberatory furnace, such as I have described previously, it would also be possible to use sticks and twigs to begin with. Twenty-eight to 30 tin bars are charged into the furnace and from these are rolled enough plates to fill a box of 225. As soon as all rolling on the first heat has been completed, the rolling is stopped to allow the rolls to cool and to reheat the plates. During this time one of the workers is occupied with doubling of the plates, another with recharging of the furnace with fuel and iron, and the third with shearing the plates to size. From the rolling mill the plates are taken to the annealing room where they are annealed and allowed to cool in order to make the iron soft and pliable for the removal of flaws and of

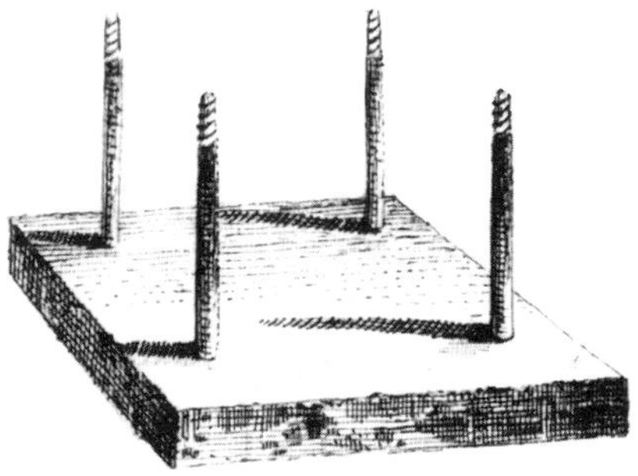

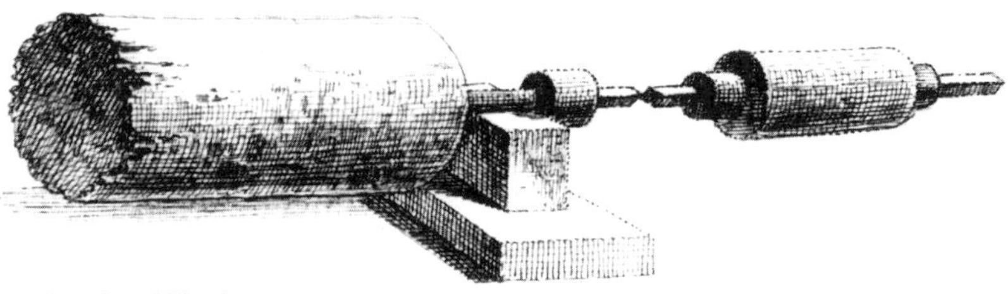

Fig. 57 Roll bed and wobbler-box

Fig. 58 Reheating furnace

69 scale, which during the rolling, adheres very firmly to the plate surface. Three to four people are occupied with this work. When their task has been carefully completed, the cold plates are put through another rolling mill to be levelled and smoothed. They are then for 24 hours put into the 'lees', which at this place is made of lukewarm water and wheat bran. The preparation of the lees takes place in long wooden troughs that are so deep that the plates can be placed in them on edge. Vaults or warm rooms are not used here as they commonly are in Saxony. When the plates are removed from the lees they are scoured with a little sand and rinsed in clean water, in which they remain until they can be dipped into the tin pots. The
70 tinning is a special process which is similar to that used in Saxony. The pots in which the tinning takes place are cast of iron, the first being $18\frac{1}{2}$ inches long and deep and 4 inches wide. The second pot can be somewhat smaller, but the third is only 1 inch deep inside.

See drawing no. 59. Eighty plates are put into the first pot and cooked for an hour before they are removed. In the second pot, the plates are dipped one at a time, and then placed on edge in a rack made of iron. From there, a third worker dips them into the third pot, which is only done in order to melt off the thick coating of tin which sticks to the lower edge of the plates. The firing must take place in a little furnace and the pots must be fired separately,
71 because the first and last pot require higher heat than the middle one, which serves to give the plates lustre. In the first pot some works use half resin and half tallow to melt on top of the tin, but in the other only tallow is used. As soon as the plates have gone through the tinning process they are cleaned, hot as they are, with wheat-bran and a bunch of tow. Finally they are packed in their boxes, which contain 225 single plates or 100 double and weight $1\frac{1}{4}$ cwt or 140 English pounds. For each box holding 100 plates, it is expected that 14 pounds of tin are used.[32] The corresponding figure for the consumption of tallow is 6 pounds, which generally is not taken into account in this area.

Fig. 59 Tinning pots and furnaces

The wages of the workers are:

1st for rolling	15½d per box
2nd for pickling and scouring	11d per box
3rd for annealing and scraping	6d per box
4th for tinning	8d per box
5th for polishing with wheat-bran	2d per box
Total	3s.6½ d.

Tinplate delivered at Bristol:

Box	Dimension	Price per box
Single tin 1/3 x no. 1	10¼ x 13½ inches	15s
Single tin 1/3 x no. 2	10 inches bare x 13¼ inches	49s
Single tin 1/3 x no. 3	9¾ inches bare x 13 inches bare	47s

Of the above-mentioned plates, one box holds 225 sheets or plates.

Double tin	12½ inches x 16¼ inches	50s
Double tin x alone		52s

Of these, one box holds 100 plates.

The distance from Pontypool to Caerleon is eight miles and the cartage 6s.6d per ton. From there the plate is carried to Bristol by ships owned by the iron-works proprietors. Mineral coal is cheap in this place because there are many coal seams in the neighbourhood, but charcoal which is used in the blast-furnace and the forge costs 'between four and five 'plåtar' per stig'.[33]

One ton of pig iron costs £7 here, and the
bar iron now costs between £16 and £17 and 73
sells for £20.10s per ton.

(End of the letter dated 19 July 1754 to Messrs Finlay and Jennings).

Notes and references

1 Possibly St Thomas's, Portman Square, though the square itself was first laid out in 1761.

2 Commercially pure metallic antimony.

3 The description of the work in the factory makes it clear that the sheets were purchased from Bristol, cut to size and with the edges beaded and, since the first operation was pickling for descaling, they must have been delivered in the black condition.

4 Dotted gap in MS.

5 'Bird' – written in English – must be RRA's version of 'burden' or load of charcoal.

6 The illustration shows the buttresses placed in the middle of two opposing sides of the furnace.

7 Enticing skilled workers to move to foreign countries was quite common at this time and RRA was not above trying this himself.

8 RRA may have meant Edgbaston, though Bromford Forge was, in fact, on the River Rea.

9 These figures are not entirely consistent, but may refer to a week when the production was less than normal.

10 Fig. 23 contains puzzling features. The stand of rolls on the left appears to rest on the large trundle wheel without any other support, though it may have been a convention of the time that fixed framing was not shown. Furthermore, as the gearing is depicted, the lower roll of this stand would have nearly twice the speed of the upper. Again, the proportions in the sketch may not have been accurate.

11 The iron stamps in Fig. 25 must have been on the Swedish bar iron RRA found at Snowhill. EOE has not been identified; 'arrow under circle' may be Finnån or Afdala.

12 According to Joan Day, *Bristol Brass: the History of the Industry*, (Newton Abbot: David & Charles, 1973), p.101, this was the works in Coleshill Street established in about 1740.

13 In making brass, the calamine (zinc carbonate) is reduced chemically to zinc metal, losing weight as the gases are driven off, and besides this an appreciable weight of zinc metal is lost by sublimation and burning; on the other hand, very

little of the copper is lost. So, with the figures given for the charge and yield, the resulting brass would be about 46 per cent zinc, an improbably high figure. If, on the other hand, the charge were 50 lb copper, 41 lb calamine (reversing the figures noted) and charcoal, yielding 75 lb brass, the zinc content would be about 33 per cent, much more plausible. It is also possible that RRA overlooked the addition of scrap brass, a common practice.

14 This would have reduced the thickness to about 0.002 inch.

15 In this drawing there is no provision made for driving both rolls and one must assume that only the bottom rolls were driven, which was not uncommon with sheet mills of early type. The two stands on the right might seem to be set up for tandem rolling but they will, of course, run in opposite directions.

16 Fig. 28 shows the large wheel fitted with a hand crank so as to appear to be man-powered, though the link to a water wheel may be omitted for simplicity.

17 A large coarse file.

18 The scale of the machine is not obvious, but the 'hand-driven crank' looks more like a treadle jointed to the floor.

19 The process described is close-plating, which had a long history before RRA's time.

20 Does not match text, but is another version of Fig. 31/1.

21 The centner was equivalent to 100 to 120 lb so RRA's figure seems to be wrong by a factor of ten. Calculation suggests that it should be about 10,200 lb which would be ample to cope with the pump-load of around 7500 lb.

22 Small metal goods.

23 These figures are exactly as given in the MS, though something must be wrong.

24 RRA certainly uses the Swedish word for 'melting' in the heading in the margin of page 42, although he makes it clear that the heating only produced a crust and did not actually melt the metal. On page 46 above RRA again used the same Swedish word, which this time is translated as 'fuse', probably more correct. In the latter page no mention is made of casting, so we may conclude that the metal was not melted in the pots. In any case, it is unlikely that in 1754 the art of making crucibles for melting wrought iron was known. The main reason for using crucibles was, no doubt, to keep the iron from oxidising too much. The process described was a partial welding together or the iron scrap, which was completed under the hammer.

25 This may seem an unusual choice of timber, but it may be that juniper was particularly resistant to pests or conditions of high humidity found in the colonies.

26 Such wide spacing of the pillars seems unlikely, even if borne out by the drawing.

27 Robert Finlay and Francis Jennings, the former a Scot and the latter from Ireland, settled in Stockholm during the first half of the eighteenth century. For a number of years in the middle of the century, their firm was the largest merchant-house in Sweden and also the largest exporter of iron. They also owned a number of iron-works, including Johannesberg, where an attempt was made in 1749 to set up a tinplate mill. This was designed by Samuel Schröderstierna, who had studied the design and operation of such a mill in Shropshire, but it was never very successful and was abandoned in about 1765. Unfortunately, Schröderstierna's notes appear not to have been preserved.

28 This method was known as the Walloon process in Sweden, and produced the best-quality Swedish wrought iron. The majority of the Walloon mills were located in the province of Uppland, north of Stockholm. In England this iron was often referred to as 'Öregrund iron' after the port in the Roslagen district from which it was shipped.

29 An iron-making district about 120 miles NW of Stockholm.

30 This observation would only apply to Sweden, where the export of this pig iron was strictly prohibited until the middle of the nineteenth century.

31 This train of gears appears to serve the purpose of bridging the distance between the water-wheel shaft and the position where the 'lathe' could be located.

32 This would correspond to a coating thickness of 0.0013 inches, roughly ten times thicker than modern practice. No tin losses have been taken into account, but there is no reason to suppose that they were very large.

33 The 'plåt' was a Swedish coin equivalent to three shillings, and the 'stig' a variable measure of volume for charcoal, usually amounting to 5¼ cubic yards. In Sweden at this time, charcoal from the forests owned by the iron works cost less than one plåt per stig.

Journey 5a London to Plymouth

30 April 1754. London, Windsor, Stockbridge, Salisbury (1 May), Wilton, Stonehenge, Blandford, Spetisbury, Middleton, Dorchester (5 May), Weymouth, Portland (6 May), Abbotsbury (8 May), Bridport, Exeter, Newton Abbot, Totnes (11 May), Dartmouth, Modbury (12 May), Kingsbridge, Modbury, Plymouth (13 May).

Journey from London to Salisbury

On the last day of April at 11 o'clock at night, I left London by the 'Flying Machine', which goes to Salisbury. As the day dawned, we passed the Thames on a wooden bridge built across the river with arches and much half-timbering.[34] I passed Windsor Park and saw the Duke of Cumberland's obelisk, the dam with the waterfall, a yacht for sailing, and the Mandarin Bark which is built entirely according to the taste of the Chinese. I also saw an observatory built a little distance away on a hill from which there is an excellent view over the bare slopes and smooth fields or commons that one finds in this locality. I travelled many miles across sandy heathland where only heather and a little dry grass grow. Occasionally one saw gibbets in the fields, where highwaymen or brigands had been hanged, enclosed in cages so that their bodies may remain hanging as long as possible to provide an example to other licentious
74 characters. Just the same, this does not carry much weight in England, where people do not mind dying a few years early if they can live well as long as their lives last.

Oak plantations

On the way to Salisbury, 36 miles from London between the villages 'Yostom', Barkham, Turges, and the market place 'Tharoboro', there were a number of large plantations of oak trees on the commons that appeared to be 30 to 40 years old judging from the size of the trees. All the oaks were planted at a distance of 16 feet from each other and so regularly, that in many places one could walk between them as if through an avenue. If the people in other parts of England where there are such large commons were to follow this example and plant trees, there would
75 be enough wood within a generation to supply charcoal to all the iron-works that cannot use mineral coal. This, however, will never happen, because the inhabitants are more interested in their sheep-breeding and in having sufficient grazing for their cattle. Considering the excellence of their wool manufactures, this gives them just as good a living, particularly as long as they can buy the raw materials for their own iron and steel fabricating industries cheaply from Sweden and Russia.

The plain fields appeared again between 'Steventon' and Stockbridge, where a great number of tumuli were to be seen, as is the case all over 'Southamptonshire' on all plains and treeless hills. This is shown in detail in drawing no. 60.[35]

Salisbury and its factories

I arrived in Salisbury at five in the afternoon.
It is located on a long meadow by the river 76
Sarum. By means of dams the inhabitants have running water in canals along every street. The most remarkable sight in this place is the great Cathedral with its beautiful stone-built tower. Otherwise there are not many buildings or houses that make a show. There are here half a dozen knife- and scissors-smiths, who are famous for their excellent work. There are also one or two gunsmiths and makers of carriage springs, and some looms for flannel and light cloth.

Scissors factory

The production of scissors is very superior, but they also know how to charge very well for it. One can have pairs of scissors from 1s 6d each, up to 4 guineas, which is eight 'Ducats' [in Swedish money]. Their scissors are made from large pieces of steel that nowadays come from Messrs Crowley's works in Newcastle, but
formerly came from Holland. 77

This steel is well worked and is what they call a 'mild steel'[36] which facilitates the manufacturing operations and prevents the finished article from warping after hardening. Regarding the manufacture of this type of steel, see under Newcastle and Blackhall Mill.

Iron and steel prices

On 1 May 1754, on my journey to Salisbury and Cornwall, at a distance of 39 miles from London, I ascertained the following prices for iron and steel. The stamp ***RD***[37] cost £30 and

Fig. 60 and Fig. 61 Salisbury and its factories

can be transported on the river Thames to within 14 miles of Salisbury.[38] Iron 'Gratheb'[39] [cost] £20 and are used for gun barrels. Cast steel is 2s.6d per pound, but is not used very much. Shear steel from Crowleys works in Newcastle cost 56 shillings per cwt or 6d per pound and is used for scissors and knives, etc. Mild German steel is £60 per ton. The carriage by sea cost 6d and by land 9d, or together 25 shillings per ton. William Berger, Coach-
78 spring Maker, sells coach springs for 1 shilling per pound. A spring for a chaise weighs 31½ pounds, the length is 2 feet 6 inches, the width 2⅜ inches and the thickness 1½ inches. Blister steel is too hard for carriage springs. Iron coming to Salisbury is transported from London and first taken [by ship] to Redbridge[40] and thence overland 20 miles. The carriage is 25 shillings. 'Basche Rose' 19d Newcastle.[41]

In Plymouth, the price of Swedish iron in small quantities is £21, of English £20. The consumption is as much as 50 tons [per year]. Another man told me that he bought the stamps ***EL***[42] and ***M+***[43] for £18 to £19. In Bridport, the consumption of Swedish iron is ten to 50 tons, and the price £20 to £21. In Axminster, the price was also £20 to £21 and here the quantity used rises to 50 or 60 tons. In Honiton, Swedish iron fetched up to £21, and the usage was 60 to 70 tons. In Exeter, 450 tons of iron are consumed yearly, thereof 250 tons Spanish, 150 tons Swedish, and 50 tons English. 79
The purchase price is £17.10s for Swedish, £17 for Spanish, and £17 to £17.10s for English. The Spanish iron is used for horseshoes and is forged hot. Swedish iron 4½ inches wide and ½ inch thick is used for presses, and 12 inches by ½ inch for scythes. The price [to the smith] is £19 to £20 per ton.

Outside the town there are a number of smiths who make scythes from Swedish iron and Newcastle steel. The ironmongers in Exeter are: Mr Smith, who sells up to 150 tons, but who had travelled to Topsham to receive Spanish iron; Mr Nicholas Black, ditto; Mr 'Bahsen', ditto; Mr 'Oierns'. Raw material for screws of mixed Swedish, Spanish and English iron cost 10d per pound [or £93 per ton]. The Spanish iron is somewhat redshort and the Swedish and English are hard, but mixed together they make a good and strong iron. The Spanish iron is sometimes rather uneven. 80

Earl of Pembroke's estate, Wilton House

On 2 May I travelled, accompanied by two ladies, three miles from Salisbury to Wilton House, which belongs to the Earl of Pembroke. Several arms of the rivers Nadder and Wylye, with clear running water, flow through the grounds making the region very attractive and pleasant. The mansion itself is rather old fashioned, but it contains many rare and costly things. There are many urns, statues, busts and bas-reliefs of marble. There are also columns of granite, tables of porphyry, 'groit', verd-antique and Roman diaspore. These antiques, about which a whole book has been written, were collected by the predecessor to the present Earl, who during his journeys in Greece, Egypt and Italy with infinite expenses and trouble acquired them and brought them here.

81 The nose of a statue of Apollo found in Athens covered with iron ochre, had been dyed to a reddish rusty colour, but it was nevertheless just as beautiful and of superb workmanship. A small bas-relief of mosaic was also said to have been found amongst the ruins of Greece. Well-preserved columns of red and bluish granite had been found in Alexandria or further up in Egypt. The gentleman was so anxious to collect antiques and other rare and uncommon things during his travels that he was the cause of a decree issued in Rome, forbidding the export of antiques from then on. There are also a considerable number of paintings, no less rare and costly, among which a family group by Van Dyck, that takes up the whole end of a large gallery, is worth seeing.

The garden is laid out according to a wild, but nevertheless superb, taste and there are
82 several water channels and a large pool with a cascade of water falling down below a summer-house. There is also a cold bath. On a rocky mound stands Marcus Aurelius, a copy of the statue on the Capitol in Rome. The intention is also to erect a temple here according to the way they were built by the Druids, of which the remains may be seen at Stonehenge.

Carpet manufacture at Wilton

In the town, which lies quite close, the Earl has established a factory for Turkish carpets, and very beautiful ones are made here. The process of weaving flowers and figures in various colours is the same as for brocade, with the difference that the woollen yarn is placed immediately over rods and then cut as with velvet. In Salisbury there are also some workshops for woollen cloth, particularly flannel and thin Turkish cloth.

The whole of this neighbourhood is particularly noteworthy for its sheep-breeding
83 and within a six miles radius of Salisbury more than 100,000 sheep graze.

Remains of Old Sarum

Old Sarum, or Sorbi Dunum, lies two miles from Salisbury and was a very ancient British town, of which now only a few entrenchments are visible. Nevertheless, the plot of land itself maintains the right to elect two Members of Parliament.

Discourse on ancient monuments and Stonehenge

We travelled ten miles north from Salisbury over hilly heaths that are hardly cultivated at all and are covered with very many tumuli.
The famous Stonehenge [Fig. 62], which without doubt is the remains of some temple used by the ancient Britons, is visible at several miles distance, but the nearer one comes, the more astonished one is at the colossal size of the construction. See drawing no. 62. The structure itself was circular with an [outside] diameter of 108 feet and consisted of three rings, one
outside the other in form of a colonnade. 84
The innermost circle consisted of 30 upright stones, 30 feet long, 6 feet wide and 3 feet thick. Between them there was a space of 4 feet. The thickness of the stones decreased a little towards the top. The part that is below ground has a rougher finish than the part above the ground. On top of the upright stones, lintels are placed that are made of such large and massive slabs of stone that they cover the distance between the uprights and half the width of two of them. It should be observed that the uprights are provided with two tenons on the top surface which look like half an egg. The lintels have corresponding mortice-holes on the underside. This system of joining holds the structure together very strongly.

The outside circle used to comprise 60 stones, 30 uprights and 30 lintels. Of the former, 17 are still standing and 11 of these still
have their lintels in position. One of the 85
uprights has fallen halfway over and is leaning against an edge of the inner circle. Another six are lying on the ground, some in one piece and some broken. Twenty-two stones are thus missing, and have no doubt long ago been removed by thoughtless people. The method used was probably to saw them on the spot into pieces that could then be used for buildings and other purposes. The outer circle was located a little more than 8 feet from the middle one and was made up of 40 smaller stones. These stones are made of granite, but the others of a

Fig. 62 Stonehenge

somewhat coarse, but nevertheless white, marble, which in Italy goes under the name of Greek Marble. This stone is said to be found 16 miles away in the upper part of Wiltshire. There is good reason to doubt this because in such a case one would see the stone used for the buildings. In the middle of the temple there is an altar of refractory stone, which could withstand the heat of the many sacrifices that perhaps daily were performed on it. Altogether
86 there were 100 upright stones and 40 lintels, of which the whole temple was assembled.

Dr Stukeley has written a book in folio about these remains,[44] in which he puts forward a number of theories concerning their age and building, which he claims to have traced to the time of the Phoenicians or the invasion of Egypt by Cambyses. He destroyed the heathen temples there and drove away the priests, who then supposedly fled to England and became master builders, as if the ancient inhabitants of this country without them would have had no idea of religion, divine service, or the building of temples.

As far as the chronology of the remains is concerned, the Mosaic history of the age of the world compels him [Dr Stukeley] not to go further back than to the time when the Phoenicians flourished. There is good reason to believe that they traded with the people along 87
the English coast both in tin and iron. But if the aforesaid author had studied the ruins of Rome, Greece, Egypt, etc., about which one has reliable information as to their time of flourishing, it should readily have been apparent that here [at Stonehenge] a much greater antiquity could be glimpsed. I am convinced that he would then have placed Stonehenge first in order of antiquity, both because of the very special architecture and way of building, and because of the deep holes that time has corroded into an otherwise very firm and durable marble. It can also be assumed that the Britons had tin and iron-works a long time before the Phoenicians arrived, otherwise there would have been no reason for the trade between them that is known to have existed. Furthermore, it is not probable that the Phoenicians, more than any other people, were born with the gift of smelling out minerals (with
the exception, however, of certain Germans). 88

The above-mentioned Doctor wishes to prove his conjectures with another hypothesis, namely: the magnetic needle changes its declination from time to time, and according to a table that he has made, the variation from the

true meridian was six to seven degrees east in the time of Cambyses. The Doctor claims this to be principal alignment of the temple, including the altar and the entrance. He also claims that this alignment is now within seven degrees of a line determined by the rising and setting of the sun (at midsummer). If the author had studied natural history more closely, which indisputably gives us the most reliable proof of the chronology and age of the world, he would readily have been able to appreciate the result of the many changes caused by the submersion of the land in the sea from time to time from the infinite number of layers that exist down in the
89 earth of all kinds of shells, petrifactions, carbonised trees and other very curious miscellania. He would also understand that the movements of the poles of the Earth can most simply and naturally be traced back to the centrifugal force which necessarily must alter after each change taking place on Earth, be it ever so small. Such an event must also displace our midday alignment, and if astronomical observations were sufficiently accurate and reliable, we would not lack evidence or proof either concerning this or the obscure and puzzling questions regarding chronology and many other upheavals that have taken place on our globe.

Blandford, its factories and sights

On 3 May I went from Salisbury to Blandford, which was burnt down 20 years ago. It has now been rebuilt very well, and has a small manufacture of cotton stockings. The inhabitants were
just then holding their Carnival, which consisted 90
of various spectacles that drew people from adjacent places. The festivities started on 1 May with a horse race that continued the following day. During these two days the horses ran for a total distribution of prize money amounting to 500 guineas. On the last day, the attractions were cockfighting and 'Chockelplay'. At the cockfighting each one of the bird owners put up 10 guineas in addition to what may have passed privately between other people. The Chockelplay took place in the afternoon. It is fencing with sticks, and taken so seriously that skulls are sometimes fractured. The winner is the one who first draws blood from his opponent. The game can go on for a long time owing to the skill of the fencers in fending off the blows with another smaller stick equipped with hilt and hand protection of rope. See drawing no. 63.

At this game 10 guineas were also paid, and 91
the competitors who won were separately recompensed with 2 or 3 guineas each, according to skill and courage. There were so many farmworkers and craftsmen here this time, who all wanted to join in, with blows from the sticks and bleeding wounds, that the game went on until it was dark.

Gentleman's house

On 4 May I took a walk up the river Stour that flows past Blandford, and came to a beautiful house of a gentleman, who had erected two pillars, see drawing no. 64, further up towards the highway that runs to Salisbury. These pillars were built partly of flint and partly of calcite

Fig. 63 Fencing with sticks

Fig. 64 Pillars near Blandford

crystals found in a chalk pit not far away. Fifty cavalry men quartered in Blandford had selected this place for the training of their horses. In the meadow I observed that they had dug a pit for the manure, which had been
92 carted out, to accelerate the decay.

The gates could be opened both ways and always fell back to the latch and closed it by themselves. This is due to the special design of the hinges, which can be seen in drawing no. 65a. **a** consists of a strong hook and eye, which alone carries the weight of the gate. **b** comprises two spikes. The head of one of them has two semicircular recesses on the edge. The head of the second spike has been shaped into two prongs that match the recesses of the first. The recessed spike is driven into the post and the other one into the gate itself so that they fit together. When opened, the gate will consequently always slope inwards, regardless of the direction of opening. **c** is the latch itself, which falls into a rectangular recess in the head of a spike driven into the appropriate post, this is letter **c:d**.

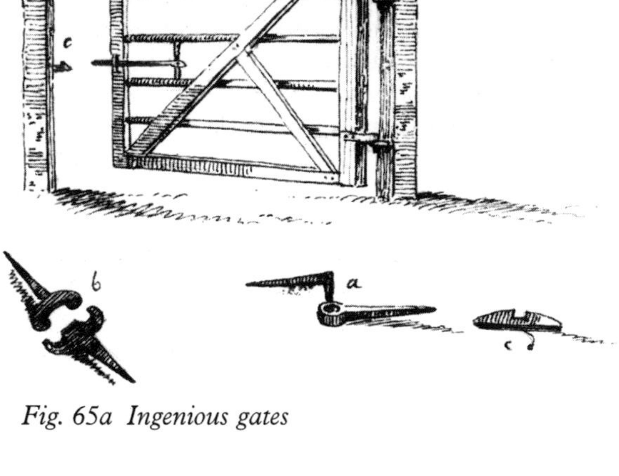

Fig. 65a Ingenious gates

A little way further up in the district there was a flourmill driven by ordinary lantern pinions and, just above it, a fulling mill for chamois leather.

Transformation of flint into chalk

Even further up there was a chalk pit, from which chalk was taken to lime kilns, and here it was possible to see very clearly the destruction
of the flint and how it gradually progressed until 93
the stone became soft and white like chalk.

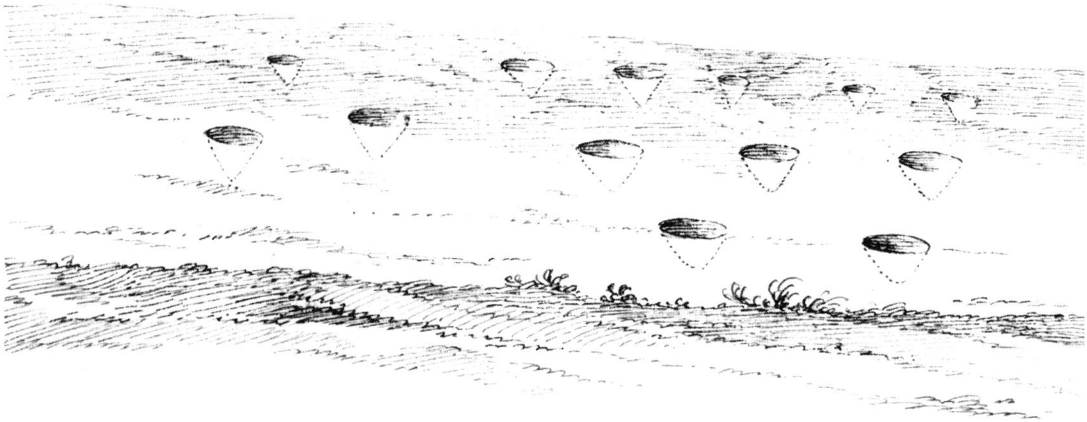

Fig. 65b Old iron mines

Petrifications

I also found some pieces of belemnite or coral. It was not possible to decide which, because these fossils had been subjected to such great changes, having been embedded in clay for a very long time, then during another aeon hardened to flint, and finally destroyed and transformed into chalk. Here lay a fallen oak 16 feet in diameter. In 6 inches I counted 40 rings, and its age was thus more than 1000 years.

Old iron mines

I left Blandford in the morning and went to Spetisbury, which is a few miles off the road to Dorchester. In the fields there one can see for a distance of several miles, innumerable pits that are now covered with grass inside [Fig. 65b]. In olden times these pits were iron mines which,
94 according to tradition, were worked by the ancient Britons in the days when the Phoenicians traded with the Dorset coast. Most of the pits are situated on the southern slope, and in the surrounding fields one finds solidified iron ochre that is heavy and rich in metal. One can conclude that the mines were worked underground in the same way that nowadays is employed in Perigord and Alsace-Lorraine in France.

Tumuli

All fields that I passed were filled with tumuli, common all over this part of the country.

Wool spinning

In the village of Middleton all the women were occupied with the spinning of wool. This work was carried out with a spindle driven to rotate on its shaft by a cord, in its turn put in motion by a lightweight wheel, in the same way as is usual in spinning mills for cotton.

Town of Dorchester and antiquities of the district

Dorchester has been a British fortress and it still 95
has some remains of old earthworks and walls. Parts of the former are now planted with trees, making them into beautiful promenades. Outside the town there is an amphitheatre which has been shaped from a bank of earth, and is supposed to have been made in the time of Claudius Neronius, when Julius Agricola had his encampment nearby. On a high hill two miles from here, one sees earthworks and encampments of unrivalled size.[45] They consist of three embankments and the same number of ditches, 80 to 100 feet deep. This clearly proves that the Romans both feared and respected the race of people that inhabited Britain in their time. Nearer to the town lies an encampment made by the Danes, but it is not so strongly built or as large as the one described above.

This town is known for Dorchester Beer which, however, is not only brewed here, but also at various places around the county.
There is a considerable trade in this beer both 96
with Ireland and with foreign places.

Sheep farming

Otherwise, sheep farming is the main employment in this district, and it enables the people to make a considerable income with the least trouble, because each sheep brings in 5s to 6s per year. One thousand sheep would provide a farmer with £250 to £300. This business, which in 150 years has grown so considerably in

Fig. 66 Burning of chalk to lime

Dorchester and the surrounding countryside, is said to be the reason for the decrease of the population and of cultivation of the land. This is because very much land that formerly was ploughed is now only used for sheep grazing and requires no more than one-tenth of the labour force that was previously fully employed in arable farming. But it should be noted in this
97 connection that the population, which has decreased in one place due to the new type of husbandry, has increased so much more abundantly in other parts of the land where woollen mills have been set up so that, on an average, the country has derived benefit from the change. The region has a surplus of grain, and the manure produced in the sheepfolds results in a much more abundant supply from a small piece of land that could previously be grown on a far larger one.

Burning of chalk to lime

On 5 May, on the road to Weymouth, which is eight miles from Dorchester, I saw the burning of chalk to lime. The kiln, shown in drawing no. 66, was built in the chalk pit itself, and was conical in shape and about 12 feet high.[46] The chalk is piled up inside in such a way that it permits the heat to rise. The pile is covered
with a mixture of crushed chalk (and water) in 98
which airholes are made with a stick. The kiln is fired with mineral coal for two days and the lime produced is rather weak. In the chalk pit I saw a number of pieces of stone, that resembled roots and other vegetable matter, and which had not been so quickly reduced to chalk from their acquired flint hardness as the material surrounding them.

Discourse on stone quarries

Further on I noticed a quarry where the rock consisted mainly of limestone. On some of the strata there were large quantities of small, petrified shells, that had not been transformed to the same extent as the petrifications found in the chalk pit. From this it may be concluded that the rock had been metamorphosed directly
from clay into limestone without having 99
previously passed through the stages of having been flint and chalk. What appeared peculiar in this quarry was that under 6 inches of top soil and 1 foot of clay, a seam of gypsum 1 to 2 inches thick had been formed. Below this followed another 1 foot of clay, after which the rock commenced and continued to 12 feet depth, beyond which the quarrying had not proceeded. See drawing no. 67.

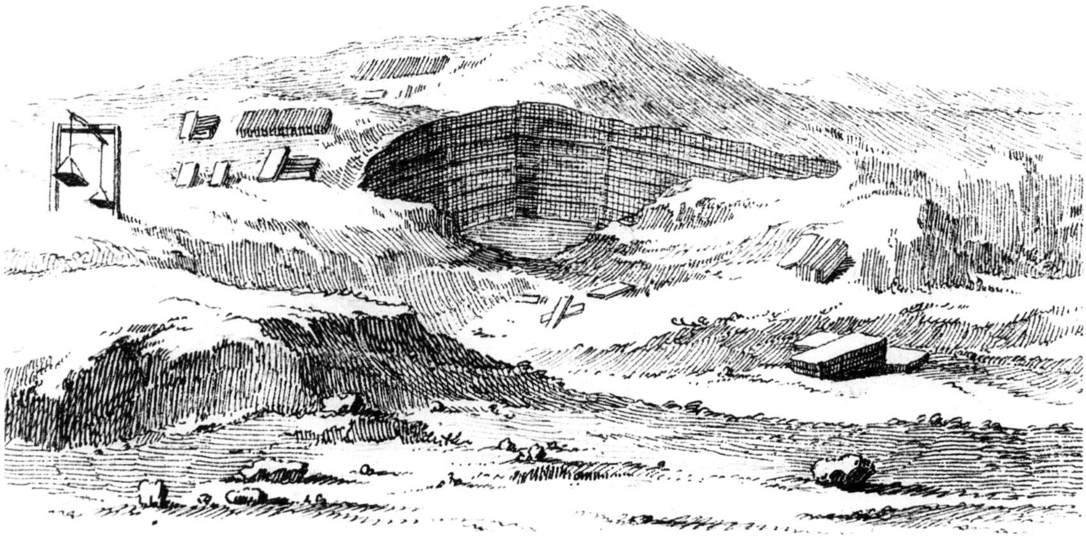

Fig. 67 Limestone quarry

Between the different layers of limestone I observed that there was always clay, 1 inch or a little less in thickness. This indicates that each layer or seam contains its own special factor, promoting the process of petrifying. As far as the streak of gypsum is concerned, it was clearly apparent that it had crystallised in the clay itself either by the transformation of the clay to gypsum, or by the gradual growing of the crystals, which had the shape of inverted arrowheads as shown by drawing no. 68a.

100 The formation of the crystals had in due course raised the overlying clay and topsoil, and this seems to be the most probable explanation.

There was now no work going on at the quarry, but I did see a weighing machine, which made me understand that the stone slabs produced here are sold by weight.

Town of Weymouth

One first begins to see Weymouth, the sea beyond it and Portland, from the top of the smooth and treeless hills a few miles away.

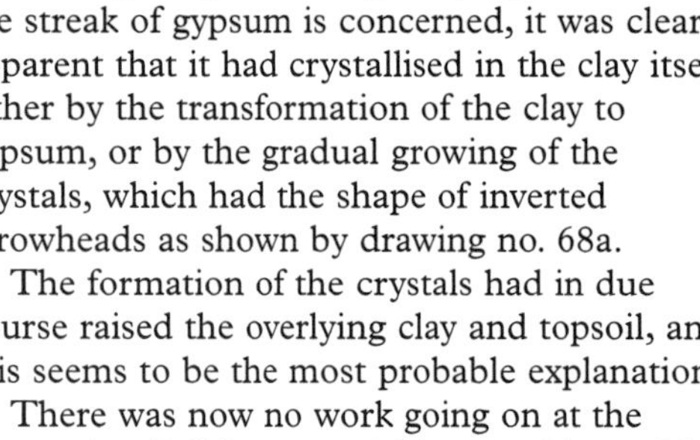

Fig. 68a Gypsum stratum

The harbour in Weymouth is small, but good and secure, and sufficient for 50 ships and more. The ships here are employed in the transport of the malt, beer, oysters, wool, etc. that are the products of this district. The town itself is now very insignificant, but one can understand that it was formerly more important because it still elects four Members of Parliament, the same number as London. *101*

Weymouth harbour and the types of rock in the neighbourhood

The attached drawing no. 68b shows the harbour of Weymouth and the inlet to it, which is a river providing anchorage that is from 160 feet to 180 or 200 feet wide. Inside the harbour there is also a vast bay where ships go in wintertime. This would make the most wonderful harbour if it only were deep enough for large ships.

The top of the rocky peninsula jutting out into the sea at Weymouth consists of a sandy clay that has become hard. The hardness increases the nearer one comes to the sea, and when the seashore is reached the cover consists mainly of limestone. All of the rock is full of oysters, shells, coral balls, ammonites and belemnites.

It should also be noted that in the top layer of the soft and sandy clay there had been large quantities of interlaced roots of seaweed, which had left their imprints after the metamorphosis.

When they have been lying for some time on *102*
the seashore these imprints also become as hard as stone. There were so many petrified oysters

Fig. 68b Weymouth harbour

on the shore, that I picked 40 lb of them in little over half an hour. Some of these were of great size and had both shells intact.

Cold baths at Weymouth

The bay of the sea that lies east of Weymouth has a very clayey bottom, uncomfortable for persons who might wish to take cold baths. Wagons have therefore been constructed carrying huts made of boards, capable of carrying seven or eight people, who are driven out into the water, where they can enter the sea by means of steps and get out again, without being crowded or seen from the shore. This costs 1 shilling per person.

Portland

In the morning of 6 May I went to Portland, 103
see drawing no. 69, which lies four miles from Weymouth and which is only separated from the mainland by a river that one crosses by ferry. One then meets a long neck of land consisting of shingle that stretches for 12 miles north from Portland. This neck of land or beach is remarkable for its length, height and narrowness, as well as for the fact that it is solely made up of small shingle. In wintertime and in stormy weather this makes such a loud rattle and clatter that it can be heard up in the country many miles away. It is difficult to ride a horse up to the top of this beach, not only

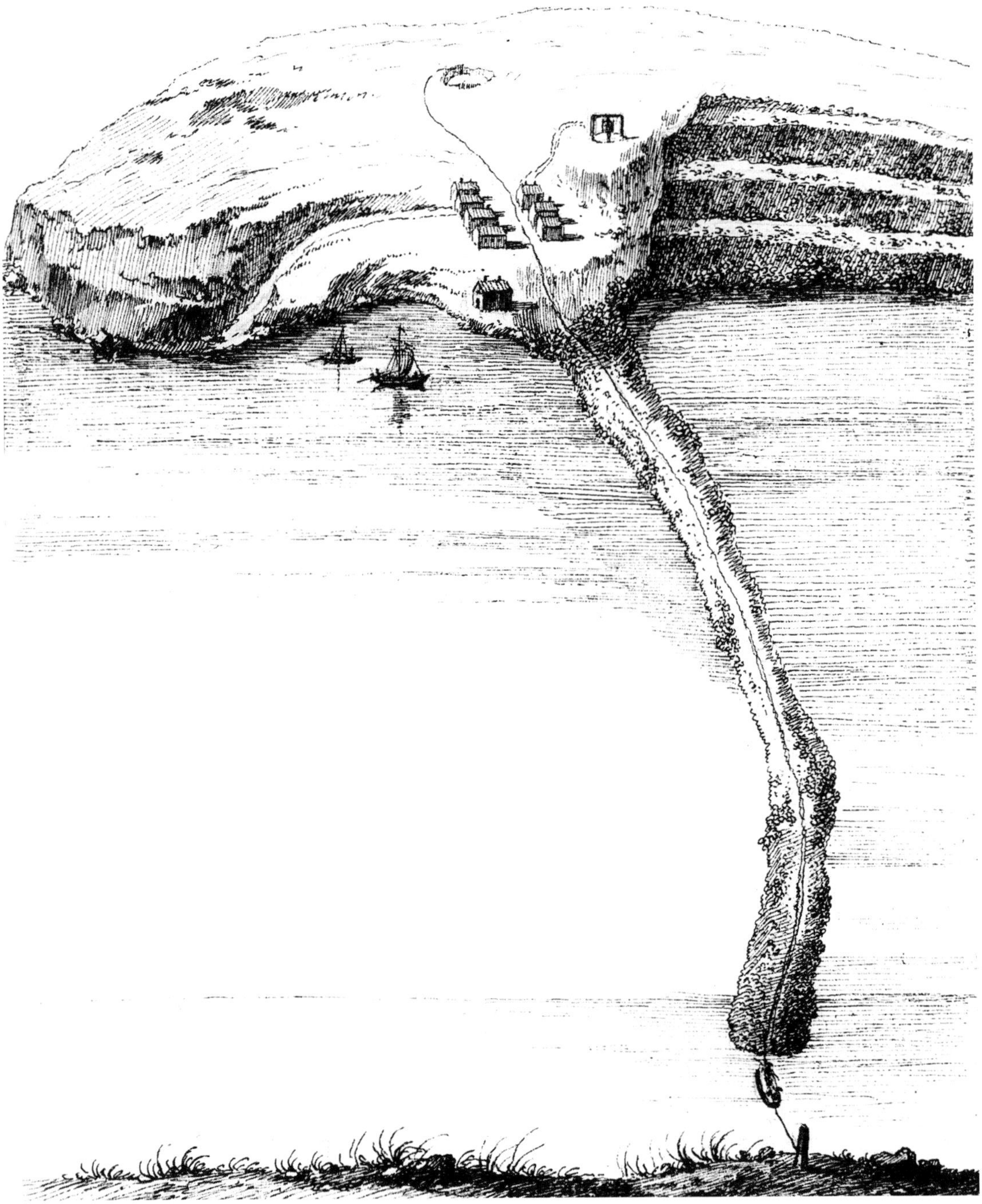

Fig. 69 Portland

because it is very steep, but particularly because the rounded shingle gives away under the horse's hoofs, which sink down deeper than in sand. On reaching the top, one sees on the side of the beach that faces the sea three banks of
104 shingle, one above the other, which look like entrenchments. The highest one has been thrown up by the waves during a very violent storm. The middle one is of the height normally reached by the sea in wintertime, and the lowest one was now being subjected to the action of the waves. The observations regarding the

growth of the sand and shingle at the seashore that I made two years ago at Sete in Languedoc were confirmed here, and the evidence was so much more impressive because I was told that some 400 feet from the shore the seabed consists of a blue clay suitable for anchorage. It follows that the shingle cannot have come from the bed of the sea, but must have been generated by the strong movements of the water against the shore. The tides have also contributed by alternately wetting and drying
105 the particles that already have started to form themselves into stone or crystals. One should furthermore not forget the increased attraction between the homogeneous particles in accordance with the growing weight of the grains of sand or the pebbles of shingle. According to these principles, the pebbles should grow ad infinitum, but in the superabundance of shingle there was seldom a pebble or stone that had reached the size of a fist. This, also, has its definite reasons: the larger the weight of a pebble of shingle, the greater the friction between the individual pieces, and this is sufficient to keep them to a certain size as long as they are pushed back and forth by the waves. As can be seen, when they happen to lie still in the surging waves, there is nothing to prevent them from growing and increasing. One can also observe this in rivers that are not too rapid. 106

Quarries and trades at Portland

The Island of Portland is considered to have a circumference of no more than nine miles, which from time to time becomes smaller because the shore falls into the sea and is submerged. This is caused by clayey rock of which the whole of the island consists, and by the various long strata of flint and the chalk-like limestone above it, which we shall have the opportunity of discussing further on.

Fig. 70a Rock strata at quarries[47]

The quarries yield the so-called freestone, a soft and chalk-like type of limestone, suitable for building purposes, that is sold in London, Holland, Denmark and other places, and which is the basis of the main industry and trade of this locality. The inhabitants are indeed in addition possessed of both fields and meadows which now, however, have been considerably diminished due to the large stone quarries that have been worked for 200 years. See the
107 attached drawing no. 70a.

Letter **a** is the uppermost layer, consisting of black topsoil, that further down becomes brownish and mixed with slabs of stone, which have been part of the uppermost stratum of clay, deposited by the water before the big change took place and the island rose from the bottom of the sea.

Letter **b** is a stratum of freestone $1\frac{1}{2}$ feet to 2 feet thick, and everywhere impregnated with seashells, bivalves and other fossils.

Letter **c** is a seam of good freestone which does not contain so many of the so-called screw shells.

Letter **d** also consists of a freestone layer 8 feet thick and of good quality. It contains some shells and occasionally ammonites.

Letter **e** is also an 8-foot stratum of freestone containing some petrifications, amongst them ammonites with a diameter of 2 feet and more. During my visit I arranged to have one with a diameter of 22 inches cut out.

Letter **f** consists of a dense and hard flint, that looks quite dark or black.

Letter **g** is flint and limestone mixed.

Letters **h** to **n** are similar to **g**.

The attached drawing no. 70b shows Portland from the south-west.

First there are 2 feet of soil and slabs of stone. (See drawing no. 71.) Then 2 feet to $2\frac{1}{2}$ feet of soft limestone with fossils, mostly screws. Ditto, a somewhat harder stone, 8 feet thick, which a mixture of fossils consisting of bivalves, ammonites, etc. Ditto, stone with
smaller fossils, that make it more compact. It is 109
also 8 feet thick. Ditto, freestone of good quality and properties, which is generally 8 feet to 9 feet thick. Below it there is a seam of dense flint, 4 feet to 5 feet thick. Then came alternate layers of flint and limestone, sometimes mixed together in one seam. The total thickness is 50 feet to 60 feet. Then, finally, underneath follows a bluish-grey clay which continues down to the level of the sea and is between 80 feet

Fig. 70b Portland from south-west

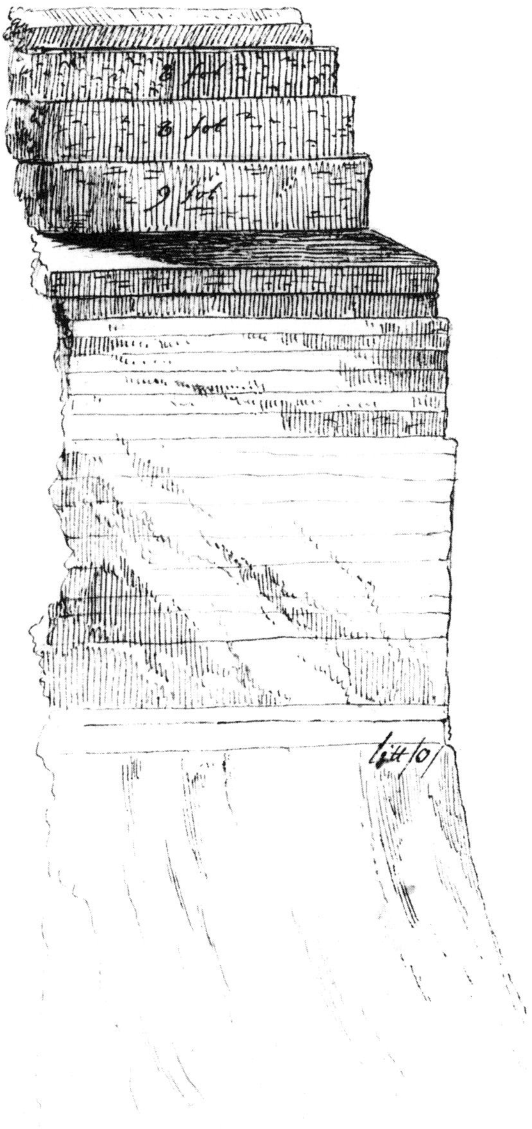

Fig. 71 Strata at Portland, south-west

and 90 feet thick. The total height of the coastal rocks at this place is about 180 feet. A light blue clay begins at letter 'o' and continues in layers of such diverse colours that they can be distinguished from each other from a distance.
110 Some of these clay formations, especially those at the top, have already been partly metamorphosed to flint, of which one finds pieces of considerable hardness. However they cannot be called flint until they have reached the degree of hardness that has given them their name. In those seams that have already been subjected to the flint transformation, one finds that the flint has been dissolved and replaced by a greyish chalk, which in time hardens and assumes the nature of limestone. It would have reached this state already immediately after the transformation, but not to the degree it achieves later on, when it has become increasingly hard due to being saturated with the lime-containing solution of salt.

The people who work on the freestone get paid 6d for every 4 square feet,[48] the Crown gets 7d and the landowner 3d. 111

At the beginning of my description of Portland it was mentioned that the area of the island decreased because the rocks keep falling into the sea. See drawing no. 72. Clear proof of this is the Church at Portland, which is considered to be very antique and maybe 1000 years old. It was without doubt built on firm and secure ground, but is now ready to topple over. The same applies to many rocks nearby, which also are prepared to travel to visit their home and their mother, the sea, where they originated. Two months ago the walls of the church bulged considerably. Some of the pillars have fallen down and the wooden benches have been broken in many places. The graves have been opened by a large crack that portends the complete downfall of the entire building. 112

There are also many signs indicating that some of the cliffs on this side [of the island] will before long sink down into the depths of the sea. The cause of all of this is the clayey foundation of the island, which, when eaten away by the waves, leaves the overhanging mass without support, so that the building erected on it must inevitably slide downwards and fall. This does not, however, happen very often, so that sometimes one or more centuries have passed without any significant parts [of the island] having come to such an end. In some places one can nevertheless see a number of these rock falls that as yet have not been completely covered by the sea. These have left plain indications of the great quantities that have fallen on each occasion. 113

On 8 May I travelled from Weymouth out along the coast to a little place called Abbotsbury, where there was previously a very fine monastery, the ruins of which can still be seen. One of the churches is even now well-preserved, and used as a barn for threshing, certainly the most splendid I have seen in that line. A small brook forms a little lake near the sea shore, and here one can see a great number

Fig. 72 Church at Portland

of swans belonging to a gentleman's family, which employs people solely for the purpose of looking after them. I counted up to 120 swans.

Bridport town

The road continued along the Abbotsbury brook until we approached Bridport, which is such a good-sized town that it elects two members of Parliament and has a large trade in cordage, sailcloth and fishing gear. In all small houses and cottages that I travelled past, both in
114 the town and in the surrounding countryside, all women were occupied spinning hemp and making fishing nets.

At a flourmill I saw a machine for scutching of hemp, as shown by drawing no. 73. Two boys were employed to turn the bunches of hemp between every blow of the stamp. Each boy had two stamps to look after, which gave him plenty to do. They had to be very quick as otherwise their hands might be smashed.

Exeter Cathedral

On 9 May I viewed the cathedral in Exeter, which is 280 feet long and 64 feet wide. It has two towers and a number of antique monuments in Gothic style. At the end of the choir in the so-called Chapel of St Mary, there is a library. The chapter and the choir meet for prayers three times a day. There is an organ to
accompany the singing. The verger intimated to 115
me that it was forbidden to enter the church wearing spurs because the long cassocks worn by the members of the chapter had occasionally been damaged by such instruments. Before the chapter had ended I hurried outside and up in the tower, where finally my heels believed that the spurs would be unable to touch the long robes. Here there was a magnificent view, and one could see the whole town lying low down by the river, and the country rising in rounded hills that were all green now and all around embellished with hedges and trees. On the side of town where the river flows towards the sea, one could see the towns of Topsham and Exmouth and the sea itself.

The superb view can be seen not only from the tower, but also from the ramparts built by the side of the castle. These ramparts have now been made into pleasant promenades after
having served as defences for this always- 116
populous town over several thousand years.

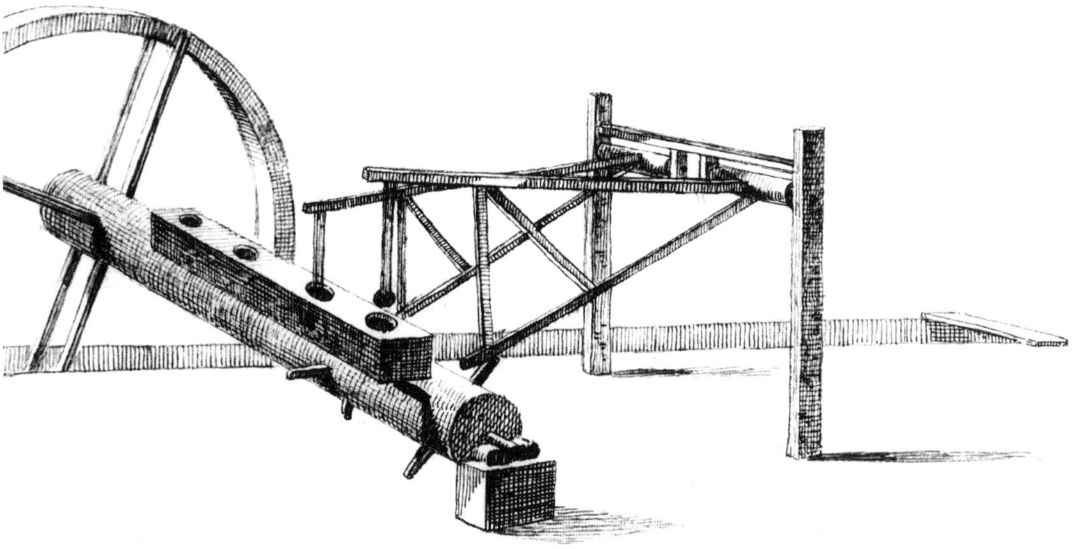

Fig. 73 Machine for scutching hemp

Its antiquity is partly proven by the fact that it has been known by no fewer than nine different names. The ancient Britons called it 'Pen-Caer' or 'Caer Eke', the Romans named it 'Augusto', Ptolemy called it 'Isca', Antoninus said 'Isca Domniorum', the Saxons 'Exanchester', then it became 'Monketown', and finally Exeter.

The town of Exeter and its woollen manufactories

The main means of livelihood in this town at the present time are the manufactories for 'Droguettes', Serges, 'Durays', 'Shaloons', Plushes and other light woollen cloths, that keep the whole of the district occupied. These goods are subsequently sold on the market days in Exeter twice a week, to be dyed and pressed. By the river Exe there were a number of fulling mills busy with pounding, washing and drying. The feet or stocks of the fulling mills are not as sharp-cornered as the ones I have seen previously. Before the cloth is placed in the mills
117 it is soaped and sprinkled with urine. When this operation has been completed, the woollen cloth is again placed in the fulling mill, see drawing no. 74, to be pounded and washed, after which it is fastened to frames for drying. With their many different colours they contribute to the beautiful view from the promenades, in addition to the other attractive sights.

Besides these water-driven mills, there is by the river Exe a machine for pumping water to the higher parts of the town. This is constructed in the same way as the pump under London Bridge. There is an old but fairly large stone bridge over the river, and not far below it the ships arrive after having passed through five locks recently built in the canal dug between Topsham and Exeter. The distance between the two is only three miles. All goods passing through this canal must pay 2s 6d per ton, but the harbour of Exeter is otherwise free from 118
dues of any kind.

Towards evening I took a walk to see the weirs that have been built at two places in the

Fig. 74 Detail of fulling mill

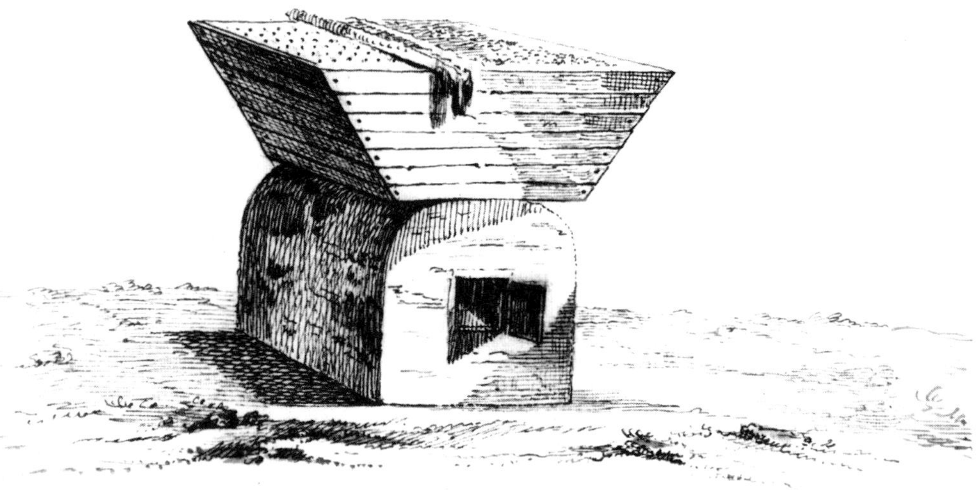

Fig. 75 Newly-invented malt kiln

river Exe to divert the water to the fulling mills, the water pump and a flourmill. I also viewed a new malt-kiln, recently invented by a stonemason from Plymouth. See drawing no. 75.

Above a small furnace, a large box of planks is built that is much wider at the top than at the bottom. Across it, nearly at the top, some stout iron bars are placed that support slabs of slate through which holes have been drilled at very close intervals, thus permitting the heat to rise. The slate is covered by a blanket of hair on which the malt to be dried is spread. The process is readily completed in 24 hours with a saving on coal of one-third. Welsh mineral coal costs 21s per 12 bushels, but Newcastle coal
119 fetches only 14s in this place.

However, the first mentioned is much more suitable as it does not produce any smoke. The malting took place in the same room, and went on for 12 days.

Gunsmiths

I visited three gunsmiths who were busy repairing shotguns and other firearms, and they told me that for new orders they use Spanish iron, which is tougher and more reliable than either Swedish or English.

Remarks on English women

During my walk I saw a number of the women of this town whose beauty certainly surpassed that which otherwise is common in England, although the English fair sex, just the same, generally excels that of many other nations in this respect.

Spinning of hemp and flax

Some poor women were here occupied with spinning of hemp and flax, see drawing no. 76. They used the same method as a rope-yard, the only difference being that the yarn was much
finer and that two strands were spun at the 120
same time, one with each hand. A little child, three to four years old, amused itself by cranking the wheel and by winding the yarn on to a reel. Both kinds of yarn are used for sacks. This spinning can earn the worker 6d per day.

Iron manufactories: iron prices in Exeter and comparison between different kinds

On 10 May a number of blacksmith's shops were viewed, making screws for presses, gratings, roasting-jacks, fire-pokers, etc. My main purpose in making these visits was to find out the price of iron and the reputation of the different kinds of iron available here, originating from Spain, Sweden, Russia and England. For screws, Spanish, Swedish and English iron is mixed together, which results in a tough and strong product. The Swedish iron is considered best for the spades that are made in various places in the surrounding countryside. Horseshoes must be made of Spanish iron, but
they are here forged hot and do not last very 121
long, which pleases the farriers. For nails and other forgings that have to last, the Swedish iron is considered best, owing to its strength and durability. Spanish is used for gun-barrels and English for bars in gratings and for other similar purposes where it does not have to be worked very much and where it is not subjected to

Fig. 76 Spinning of hemp and flax

heavy stress. Most of the smiths agreed that the price of iron at the present time is 18s per cwt for the Swedish and 19s for the Spanish. Screws for presses sell for 10d per pound and spades for 8d to 10d per pound.

To obtain an even more reliable knowledge of the iron trade in Exeter, I visited some ironmongers, of which there are four in the
122 town dealing in bar iron, namely, Mr Smith, Mr Black, 'Johan Bagsen' and Mr 'Ovins'. I made a summary of the information obtained and the following figures represent averages:

Swedish iron with Gothenburg Stamps[49] now costs	£17.0s.0d
Cost of loading the ship in London etc	2s.6d
Freight to Topsham	5s.0d
Cost of passing the canal from Topsham to Exeter	2s.0d
Unloading, etc	6d
Total	£17.10s.0d

The shipping costs for Russian iron, which is only found in very small quantities in Exeter, are the same, but the price is 10s less. English iron sells at the same price as the Swedish, but very little of it is used. Spanish iron, of which most is consumed, is higher in prices than all the rest. At the present time, one cantar of the heaviest iron which is 3 inches wide and 1 inch thick cost 80 real in Bilbao;[50] 3 inches by ½ inch, 90 real; and the ordinary flat and
square, 96 real. 123

On average, these figures represent 88 real for 155 lb English weight or, per cwt, 65 reals or 30 Daler Coppercoin, which is the same as 15s or £15 per ton. The freight comes to 10s per ton. The better quality iron from San Sebastian will cost £18 per ton.

Expenses in London:	
Shipping 'Wadfred & Co.'	2s.6d
(Some [shippers] charge 3s.6d for this.)	
Freight	5s.0d
Canal charges 'passing the work'	2s.0d
Ditto, unloading	6d
Total	10s.0d

Iron of the following stamps: ***Lx***[51] ***oo***[52] ***EL***[53] 4½ inches wide, ¾ inch thick for presses, costs £17.10s in London, and the same price applies to 3½ inches × ¾ inch for shovels, and 1½ × inches ½ inch for scythes.

Mr Smith, who nowadays sells more iron than anybody else, stated that some time ago he

bought 2 tons of the stamp ***W***[54] 7 inches wide, $\frac{3}{4}$ inch thick and 5 feet long, which he
124 considered to be Öregrund iron, for £15.5s per ton, but for $1\frac{3}{4}$ inches × $\frac{5}{8}$ inch × 8 feet long of stamp ***HOS***[55] he paid in London £17. It was intended for tyres. Ditto $3\frac{1}{2}$ inches for spades was purchased for the same price. The stamps ***IS***,[56] ***IL***,[57] ***X***[58] from Gothenburg cost £16.10s, ditto ***GC***[59] cost £13 and ***Stenback***[60] ditto £17.

OPS[61] from Gothenburg is considered a good stamp: 2 inches square from Bilbao there costs £18, ditto 3 inches wide and 1 inch thick and very badly forged cost the same, but if it is somewhat more carefully worked, it fetches £20.5s to £21.12s. It is desirable to keep the length to 8 feet, taking into consideration the transportation and the possibility of storing it in an upright position. The total consumption was said to be between 300 and 400 tons.

Before the war most of the demand was satisfied by Spanish iron, but due to the present difficulties in obtaining it, the consumers have become so used to Swedish and Russian iron
that they now must take half their purchases 125
from these countries. They have especially found the Swedish iron of particular stamps better and cheaper than the Spanish. Mr Smith thought that the total demand in Exeter does not exceed 330 to 340 tons [per year], of which 200 tons was said to come from Spain.

In a number of places I had made efforts to get in to see how cloth is pressed, a process for which Exeter is renowned. See drawing no. 78a. I never succeeded, however, until I gave Mr Smith, who is an ironmonger, the addresses of Mr Lindegren in London, and of the Burgomaster of Stockholm, Mr Plomgren, in case he should like to deal directly with them. Mr Smith assured a friend of his, upon his honour, that I had nothing to do with the trade in or manufacture of woollen cloth. After this I was allowed to view a works of considerable
size, consisting of 16 presses, each one costing 126
about £50.

Pressing was carried out in two stages. First, with the aid of a furnace, according to the old method [built into the base of the press]. An iron plate 3 inches thick was placed on top of the furnace and heated with coal during the pressing operation. Enough paper was placed between the cloth and the plate to ensure that there was no danger that the cloth would be burnt. When the cloth has been heated through

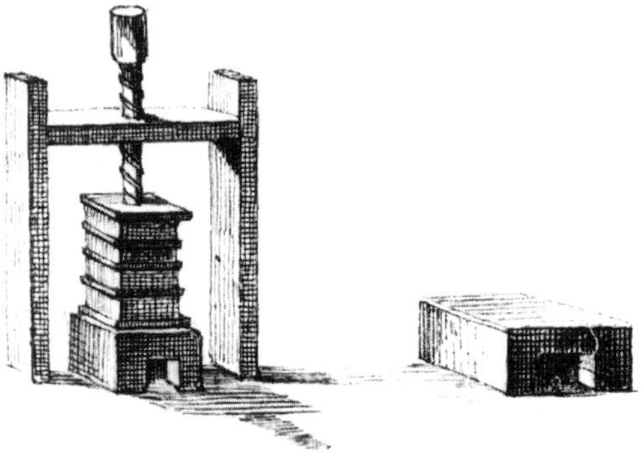

Fig. 78a Cloth presses (heated)

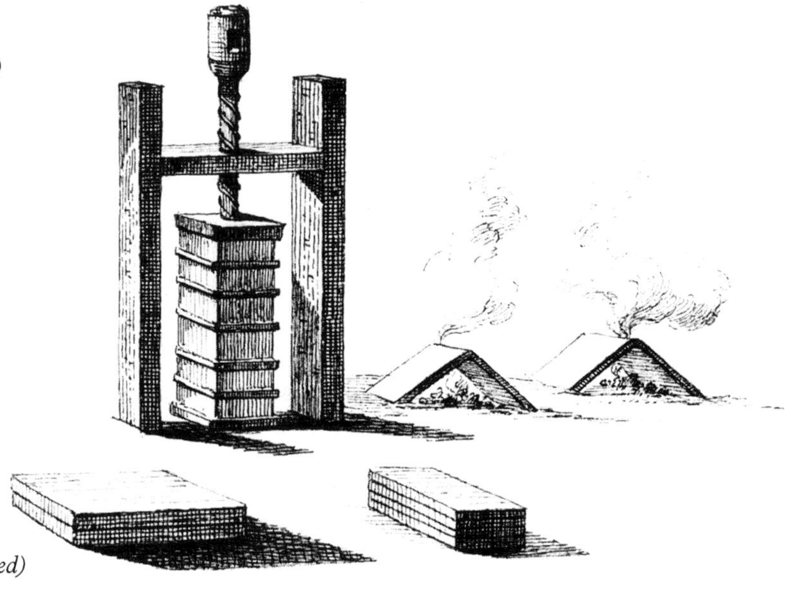

Fig. 78b Cloth presses (unheated)

Fig. 77 Exeter, Topsham and Exmouth

in this way, it is taken out and placed in a second press to be cooled. This second press was made in the same way [as the first] except that it was not provided with a furnace. Instead, a preheated slab of iron 3/4 inch thick, was placed between each piece. The slabs were preheated with heather. Each piece was pressed twice hot and once cold, first in a larger press and then in a smaller one. The whole of the
127 process for one piece of 'shalloon' or 'druggett' costs 4 to 5 shillings. The canvas in which it is wrapped is painted and costs 13 pence. The presses are illustrated by drawing no. 78b.

I then travelled by post [chaise] from Exeter and was thoroughly soaked on the way to Newton Abbot, a distance of about 15 miles. We passed a town[62] from which there was a view for many miles over the surrounding countryside and the towns of Exeter, Topsham and Exmouth. See drawing no. 77.

No forests were to be seen, only the well-cultivated land with its enclosures of green hedges consisting of oak and other trees, which would come in handy as fuel in wintertime, not least because the smiths otherwise used coal from Newcastle.

Newton Abbot, town and woollens manufactories

In Newton Abbot I saw the weaving of 'shalloons', 'longette' etc. at which the workers were fast and dextrous. A piece 32 yards long and nearly a yard wide was completed in two days, for which the worker was paid 2s.9d.

Fig. 79 Weaving reeds and wool washing

128 A weaver told me that a 'landlord' in this neighbourhood had goods worth several thousands of pounds in stock and would not offer them for sale until the price had become higher.

The women were busy weaving, the father made reeds, and the mother ...[63] of yarn, that were made the same way as nets by tying over a round iron rod and under and over a lath of wood. See drawing no.79. The weaver's reeds were made of reeds, cut by means of a machine, and the yarns that they were tied with had been pulled through a paste made of whale-oil and resin. One man told me that during the war they had to make weaver's reeds of iron because no reed was available. The iron reeds are very durable but not good for the reed-making trade as they hardly ever wear out.

The washing of the wool was here carried out by a little brook. The wool was first placed in hot water and stirred around with a wooden fork for a little while, and then taken up and the 129
water squeezed out by hand. Afterwards about half a pound at a time of the wool was thrown into a wickerwork basket standing in the brook. When it has been washed and the fibres well disentangled by means of an iron fork, the wool is taken up again, made into rolls and placed in an oven for drying. See drawing no. 80.

The payment for washing 20 lb is 3d. The kettles containing the warm water in which the wool was first placed were made of brass. The twisting of the wool was performed on the same kind of 'machine' that is used for silk.

Totnes, town and wool manufactories

In the evening I arrived in Totnes, which is about 22 miles from Exeter. Here I viewed the carding of the wool, carried out in the same way as in Leyden in Holland. The combs are made of double iron spikes and are warmed in a small oven fired with coal. The wool, previously oiled,

Fig. 80 Wool drying and combing

130 is placed on the combs and pulled out to long slivers that are rolled up for further use and spinning.

On 11 May I walked around to see the sights of Totnes, which is pleasantly situated on a steep hill by the river Dart, and has a very old castle at the top end of the town. See drawing no. 81. Here there was recently a battle royal for two seats in Parliament, and the people were rather pleased that it was now over and done with.

As far as manufacturing is concerned, the same work is done as in Exeter and in the whole of the surrounding district. Markets are also held here on certain days, when the manufactured goods can be sold. Subsequently they are washed and pressed in the same way as in Exeter. The mill contains two pairs of fulling-stocks, the first to stamp in the soap and urine,
131 and the second for washing it out by means of water that is run into the stocks during the pounding. See drawing no. 82a.

Tanneries

The preparation of leather was only viewed in one place, and I saw how the fleshy side was cut off with a knife specially made for this purpose. The hides were then worked between wooden rods set in a tree stump. See drawing no. 82b. I also saw here a cow of extraordinary size, with an udder that appeared to hold six or seven gallons of milk.

Iron prices and iron trade

The ironmongers here were 'Mr Rule', 'Mr Tope', the postmaster, 'Mr Silsorte' and 'Mr Doger'. Nearly all of them agreed that the sale of iron in this place did not exceed 70 to 80 tons per year, which was mainly used for horseshoes. For this purpose the Spanish iron is considered the best. But since there was now a scarcity of it, I asked a farrier why the Swedish iron could not be used just as well. He answered that horseshoes of Swedish iron are more 132
durable, and hence less profitable for the makers. The price of Swedish and Russian iron is now 20s and of the Spanish when available, 21s per cwt. The ironmonger told me that they pay 17s in London [for Swedish and Russian iron] and for the Spanish, which comes from Weymouth, 18s and 19s. The English is the same as the Swedish, and some of this, coming from Bristol, is used. The ironmongers purchase all their iron from 'Richard Reinhold',[64] a Quaker who lives in Bristol but comes here twice a year to collect payments due and to take new orders.

In the neighbourhood of Totnes a type of granite called Moorstone is quarried, and by the river there were some blocks ready for shipment.

Fig. 81 Totnes

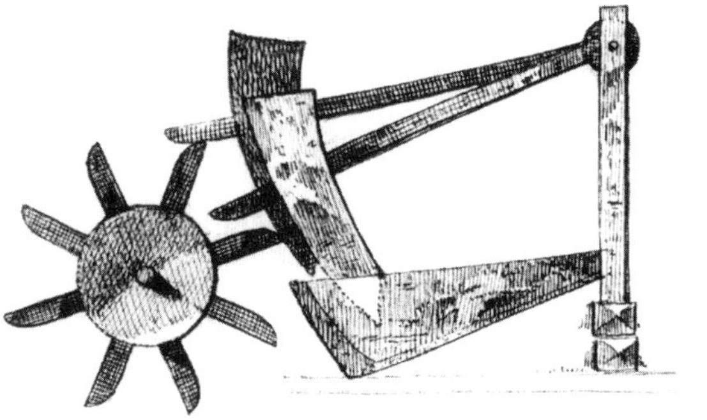

Fig. 82a Fulling mill

Fig. 82b Treatment of hides: tannery knife and preparation block

The town of Dartmouth, its fisheries, trade and shipping

After dinner I travelled to Dartmouth, see drawing no. 83, which lies ten miles from Totnes
and has an excellent harbour at the outlet of the 133
River Dart. There were only 12 ships in the harbour, but I was told that when all the ships that already had sailed for Newfoundland and the fisheries, commonly between 50 and 60, return from their expedition, the harbour and the neighbourhood generally look much more impressive.

'Mr Arsos. Holdwerst' is the most prominent shipowner and he alone is said to fit out eight to ten ships for America. On return these ships take their cargoes of fish directly to Portugal, Spain, France and Italy. This fleet commonly sails late in February or in March and returns in November. In addition to the sailors and those who are hired to take care of the fishing, each ship is compelled to have on board two
farmhands who have not made any voyage 134
before, and one who has been along once previously. This is done in order to make more men accustomed to the sea. Ships that do not carry the requisite number of novices do not have the right to select the best places according to the order in which they arrive in America.

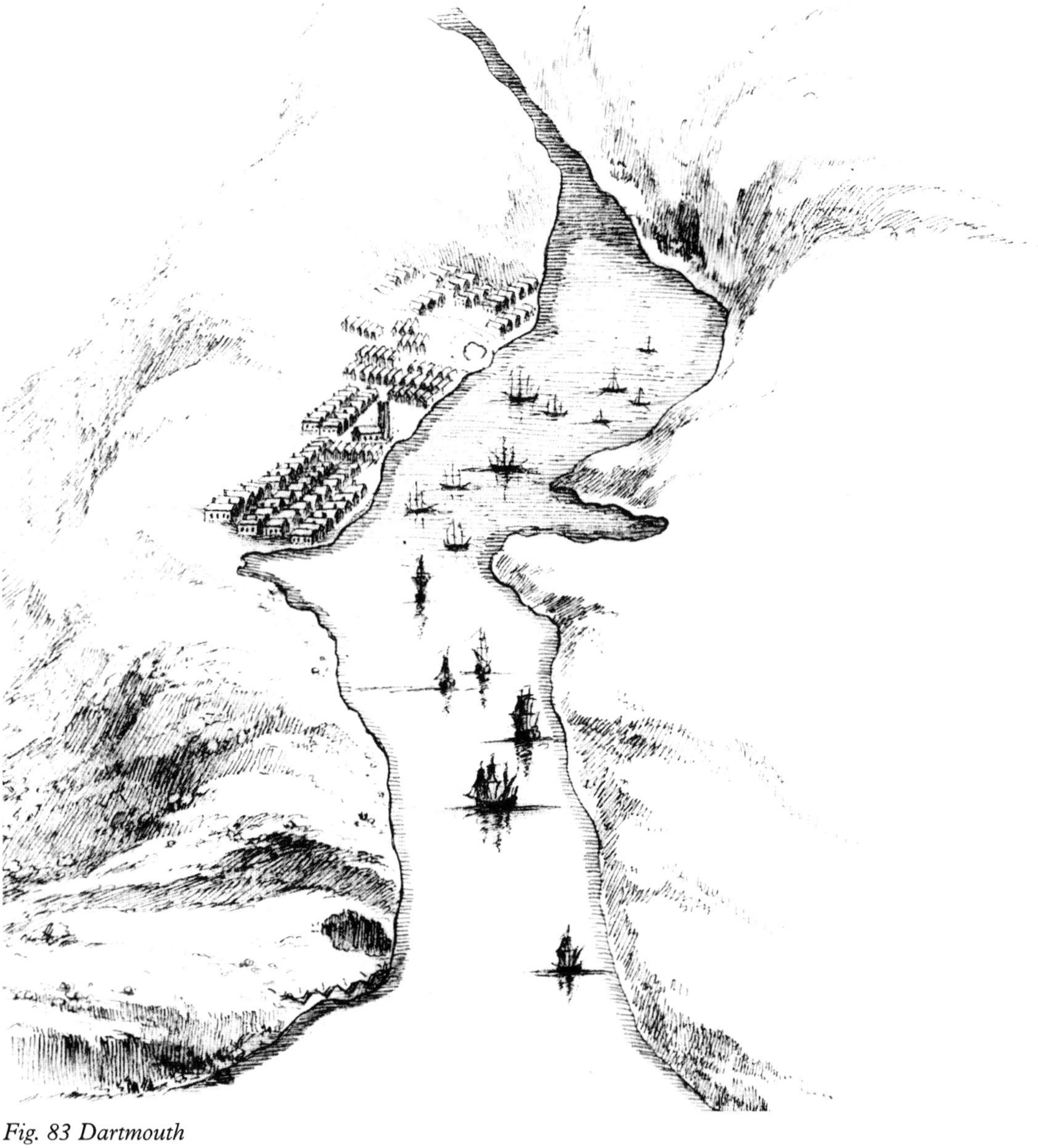

Fig. 83 Dartmouth

In addition, it happens that many hundreds or thousands of people travel on the ships as passengers to seek their fortune as fisherman along the coast and who, in due course, sell their wares to the highest bidder. The large ships fish on the sandbanks that are 90 English miles off the coast. This trade creates an infinite number of sailors for the English nation, which in addition to the large profits that it brings, constitutes a great advantage for a country that
135 especially has to defend itself at sea.

Iron gun-carriages

On the way to the castle, which lies a little way from the town by the mouth of the river Dart, I observed a battery of 12- and 18-pounder guns and noticed that the carriages were provided with cast-iron wheels having treads 3 inches wide. Treads and hubs were connected by means of an integrally cast, rather thin, disc in which holes had been made to form spokes. The diameter of front wheels was 21 inches and of the back one, 18 inches. See drawing no. 84.

Fig. 84 Iron gun-carriages

Types of rock
The whole of this district with mountains and hills consists of slate that dips south into this way: /////. In some places there are pockets of limestone and this is burnt in a large kiln between Dartmouth and the Castle. See drawing no. 85.

Modbury town and serge manufacture
On 12 May in the morning, I travelled from Dartmouth to Modbury, in which town it is estimated that there are 700 weavers of serge. However, it is not remarkable for anything else. Serge of many kinds is made here, and after being fulled and scoured it is sent to London, where it is subsequently dyed, pressed and 13
finished. 'Mr Pering' alone has more than 100 looms.

Slate quarries at Kingsbridge
In Modbury I was told about a slate quarry in Kingsbridge that was supposed to be 300 feet deep and quarried in a very curious way. Therefore I betook myself there, more than eight miles back and forth, but found that this much talked about quarry was not more than 50 feet deep. The road down goes down round the periphery, and it has two water pumps. See drawing no. 86. The slate at Dartmouth, and also at other slate quarries seen on the way from there, dipped south, but in this quarry it was practically perpendicular, with only very little dip south. Below the quarry at the foot of the hill, an adit had been started for the purpose of drainage and to facilitate the transport of the slate, which now requires winding. The slate was cut 9 inches high and 7 inches wide, of which

Fig. 85 Lime kiln

Fig. 86 Slate quarries at Kingsbridge

1000 pieces are sold for 21s. The yearly sales
137 amount to between 700 and 800 guineas. Most of the production goes to Holland and the carriage is 10s per 1000. Here there are also other similar quarries in the neighbourhood, that provide work for Kingsbridge with cargoes and cartage, although the town also is known for its woollen manufactures, particularly the making of serge. It also has a harbour where ships can enter at spring tides.

Notes regarding the genesis of slate

On the way from Kingsbridge to Modbury, I observed how the slate had become solid through some kind of crystallisation which, however, does not take place above water, because it is likely that this kind of rock is destroyed when it lies next to the soil without being constantly wet. It thus appears most probable that slate is a product of the sea and is formed by rapid crystallisation of precipitated
138 cement into thin and steep plates. In this process it is hardly possible for shells or other products of the sea to become enclosed in the slate, and it is a fact that they are not found in slate if it dips steeply. It is said that in addition to veins of quartz, small pieces or balls of pyrites are the only heterogeneous material occasionally found in it.

Limestone quarries and lime burning

Between Modbury and Plympton, and also nearer to Plymouth, a number of large lime kilns were seen. See drawing no. 87. The stone burned in this place is a marble with red and green veins that occurs here and there in slate hills. It is so fissured at the surface that it cannot be used for fireplace ornaments or for other large articles. The lime is partly used for building in the district, for example, to hold roofing slate in place. In the towns hereabouts, the houses often have both roofs and walls covered with it. The lime is also used to improve
the fields, being mixed with a red clay. 139

The town of Plymouth, its fortress and iron trade

On the13th day of May, I viewed the harbour of Plymouth, which is quite good for small ships, but so shallow that they sit on the clayey bottom

Fig. 87 Lime kilns

when the water is low. See drawing no. 88.

The citadel appeared very massive according to the standards of fortification of a hundred years ago, when the art of laying explosive mines was not so well developed. Today it would soon be blown up, however hard the marble hill is upon which it stands. The trade carried on in this town is mostly in fish products and in woollen manufactures, and has very little to do with iron. The reason for this is that the iron consumed at the dock, the royal shipyard and the anchor forge is bought in London and sent directly to the dock. Owing to
140 this system they sometimes get more than they know how to make use of. Mr Fox told me that he recently bought a few tons of heavy Gothenburg iron from the dock and paid £16 per ton although Swedish iron, according to unanimous statement by other ironmongers, is said to fetch £17.5s to £17.10s in London at the present time, to which must be added 5s to 6s for freight to Plymouth. Mr Reinholtz,[65] 'Ditto Hanbury, Robert and Aring',[66] 'Ditto Johns and Company' in Bristol, generally supply the whole of this district with iron and as a rule come here twice a year to collect payments for the last deliveries and to obtain new orders, as well as to make a note of everybody's requirements. The iron that these ironmongers sell here and in the whole of the surrounding country is partly Swedish, partly English and
very little Russian. 141

There are others who order the Spanish iron from Bilbao and San Sebastian, which now has become so scarce that not a single bar can be found in Plymouth or in the small surrounding towns. The result has been great grumbling on the part of the blacksmiths, and especially the farriers who consume most of it. Just the same, the grumbling gradually dies down as they have time to get used to the Swedish or English iron which, according to what I was told by an anchor smith, are better than the Spanish in regard to resistance both to wear and rust. Iron of these types loses less through scaling during forging than the Spanish, of which the loss is 20 lb per cwt whereas the Swedish does not lose more than 14 lb. The English iron is, after all, not quite as good as the Gothenburg iron, but just the same the smiths say that it is tolerable

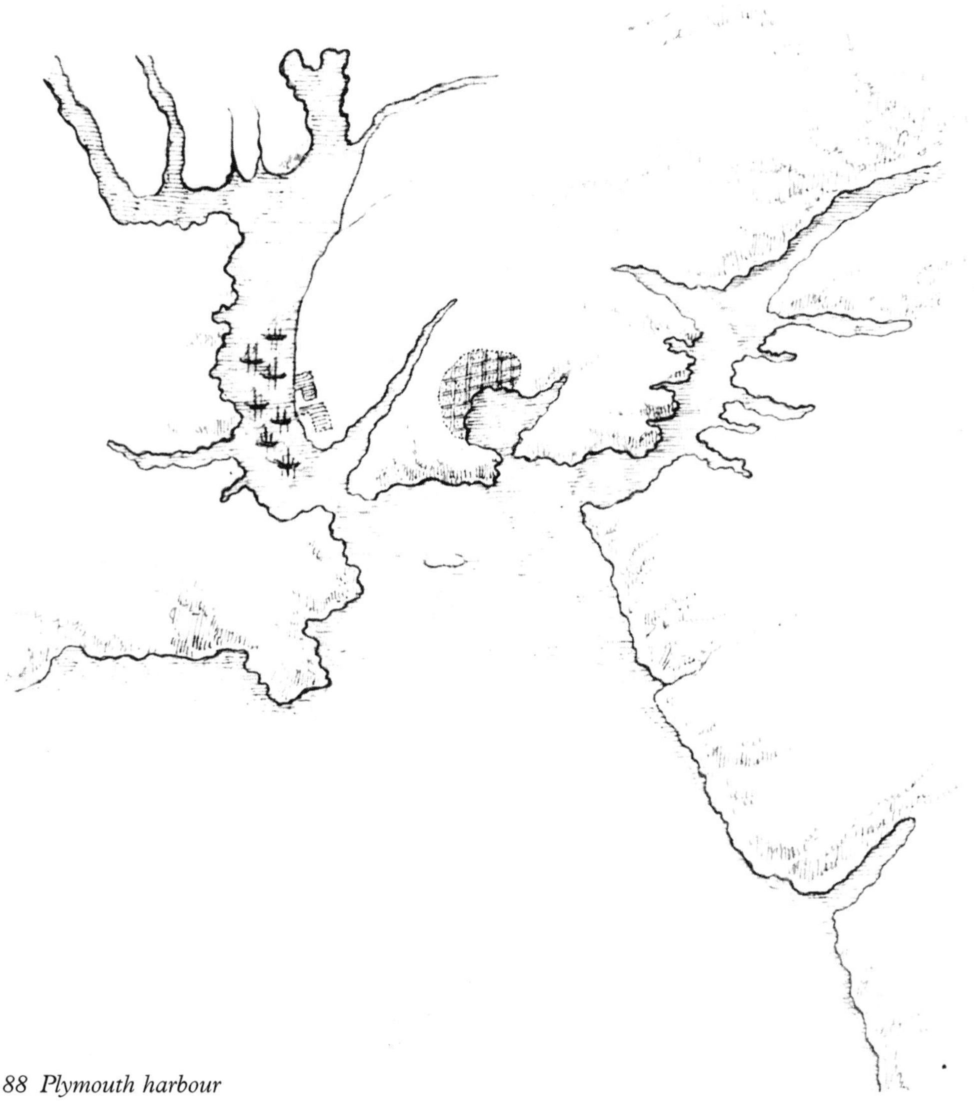

Fig. 88 Plymouth harbour

142 and pay 19s per cwt or £19 per ton, whether it is the one kind or the other. If the trade in Swedish iron were free, and the iron supplied was not of the worst kind, the consumption thereof would not fail to increase, but it is now, on the contrary, decreasing. The reason is that the iron merchants who supply this part of the country themselves own iron-works above Bristol. They are in the first place concerned with the sale of their own production, and supplement it afterwards with Swedish iron.

The latest delivery of Spanish iron was retailed at 21s. According to what I was told by Mr Nichols, the price in San Sebastian is now 90 and 96 reals for the best, but the last shipment from Bilbao cost 82. Another of the merchants, by the name of 'Mr Trichs', said that the Spanish iron nowadays costs £18.10s to 143
£18.19s in San Sebastian and that the freight from there amounts to 10s per ton. 'Mr Mousette', who also trades in iron, was of the opinion that he could sell Spanish iron for 23s if he only had any of it.

As far as the consumption of iron in Plymouth is concerned, all the ironmongers agreed that it cannot be more than 100 tons or thereabouts per year. Of this, at least a third, if not half, is Spanish iron when it is available. It has, however, for several years begun to become scarce. The reason for this is partly the

increase in the manufacture of finished iron products in Biscay and Guipuzcoa, and partly the increased sales to America, since forges with smaller hammers have been built around San
144 Sebastian making it possible to forge to many sizes that previously could not be produced by the heavy and clumsy hammers otherwise found everywhere in Biscay. I was also told that some iron arrives from Norway as ballast in their ships, loaded with timber, planks, pitch and tar. Swedish ships also bring beams, spars and boards to Plymouth, but the Norwegian timber is considered better, particularly 'halfbottom boards'[67] because the surface of the Norwegian ones is removed before sawing.

Russian iron 3 inches wide and 3 inches thick is in demand because when it is split the size is just right for forging to horseshoes. It is the same with the Spanish iron. The Russian 'Spiaggio' 3 inches by ¼ inch is used for tyres,
145 but the sales in this part of the country are small because no wagons are used, most of the transport being handled by packhorses, owing to the many steep hills and mountains with which Cornwall is well supplied. Some time ago a Danish ship anchored in the roadstead of Plymouth. It was loaded with sacks, cocoa, hides and other goods, and had come from Saint Thomas in the West Indies.[68]

Trade in Plymouth

The main trade of Plymouth, in addition to fishing and the Newfoundland business, is in light woollen cloth of many kinds, most of which is owned by 'Mr Minion', a Frenchman.

The Plymouth dock and other admiralty installations

The dock, shown by drawing no. 89a, is located two English miles from Plymouth, nearly by the outlet of the river Tamar, and has an excellent harbour surrounded by mountains on all sides. Here are three docks and a large pool for ships' timber, all quarried out of a hill of slate. 146

The first dock [Fig. 89a] can hold two of the largest warships, one behind the other, but in the second one there is room for even more ships. I was told that the timber pool is also soon to be converted into a dock when the pool, which serves the purpose of storing the timber in water, will be moved further out. The boards are here preserved by being subjected to fumes from tar-water in the same way as in Holland. By the side of one of the canals there was a building, which I presumed was for the purpose of heating the tar-water.

Each kind of board or type of small timber used for shipbuilding was stored in its own shed, and each one of these was provided with a label showing the size and type of material it contained, the year of purchase and the source.

Most of the wood had come from Danzig 147
and Prussia, and I saw no label announcing that any timber had arrived from Sweden.

The ships' and anchor forge [Fig. 89b] consisted of three different rooms that together contained 32 hearths and very many workmen under one roof. The iron used here was Swedish of a number of good stamps, but I was told that some Spanish iron was used as well for anchors and placed in the middle of the bar as a core.

Fig. 89a Plymouth dock

Fig. 89b The ships' and anchor forge

A little distance away from the dockyard was the gunyard, also quarried from a hill of slate. In it were large numbers of iron guns, all with the name of their ship written on them. The arsenal for firearms and other ships' accessories is a pretty building on one side of
48 the gunyard. Pine trees and roses are now being planted in front of the ponds, where previously hedges were growing.

At the top of the yard of the first dock, there is a large, long building for the Admiralty officials. There were between 30 and 40 warships in the harbour, but only one of them, called the *Northumberland*, was rigged. She was decked out with wimples and discharging her guns in honour of a noble gentleman who had just boarded her.

Notes and references

34 This must have been the celebrated wooden bridge at Walton.
35 This should, apparently, have shown some of the countryside around Salisbury, but this is missing.
36 At this time 'mild steel' probably meant a steel with a carbon content in the lower range of steel produced by the blister method, around 0.5 per cent.
37 Rottnedal (Värmland).
38 The Thames is at no point nearer than 43 miles from Salisbury. The '14 miles' may refer to the River Avon, although the Avon Navigation was abandoned about 1730.
39 This may mean scrap-iron grate bars, although these are likely to have been cast iron.
40 At the top of Southampton Water.
41 The nature of 'Bache Rose' has not been deciphered.
42 Didrikshammare.
43 Ås or Åltersta forge in the province of Gästrikland.
44 William Stukeley, *Stonehenge* (1740).
45 Maiden Castle.
46 A rectangular kiln is shown in the drawing.
47 Two drawings numbered 70, the second of which appears to be another view of Portland.
48 Clearly 'square feet' in the MS, but should perhaps be 'cubic feet'.
49 No iron, of course, was made in Gothenburg. This was the shipping port for much Swedish iron, especially from the province of Värmland.
50 The 'cantar' was equivalent to 155 lb and the Spanish 'real' was worth about $2\frac{1}{2}$d at this time.
51 Västanfors (Västmanland).
52 Österbybruk (Uppland).
53 Didrikshammare.
54 Tunafors (Södermanland), strictly speaking not Öregrund iron.
55 Gravendal, Strömsdal, Thyfors (Dalarna).
56 Krontorp (Värmland).
57 Bjurbäck, Aminnefors, Storfors (Värmland).

58 Smedjebacken (Värmland).

59 Uncertain – 'crowned GG' was the stamp of Molkom (Värmland).

60 Harg (Uppland), known in Sheffield as 'STEINBUCK'.

61 Björneborg (Värmland).

62 There is nothing that can be described as a town between Exeter and Newton Abbot, but the view appears to be that from Harcombe Moor.

63 Blank in MS.

64 Most likely Richard Reynolds, father of the Richard Reynolds (1735–1816) who was a partner of Abraham Darby.

65 See note re p.132 of MS.

66 Probably 'Hanbury, Roberts and Allen, Merchants in Bristol' as written out in an English hand in one of RRA's notebooks.

67 From the old Swedish term 'halvbottenbrädor'. These boards measured 13 × 1¾ inches.

68 At this time a Danish colony.

Journey 5b Plymouth to Bristol

Plymouth, Looe (14 May), Fowey, St Austell (15 May), Grampound, Truro, St Agnes, Redruth (20 June), Cambourne, Penzance, Treen, Lands End, St Just, Marazion (23 June), Helston, Penryn, Falmouth, Truro (28 May), St Columb, Bodmin (29 May), Launceston, Holsworthy, Bideford, Barnstaple, South Molton, Tiverton, Wellington, Taunton, Glastonbury, Wells, Wookey Hole, Bristol.

The journey from Plymouth

On 14 May in the morning I left Plymouth and
crossed the Sound, which is half a mile wide, by
ferry. The villages 'Stora Tause' and Millbroke
149 are hardly worth mentioning, but by the side of
the road, across Little Sound, lies the King's
brewhouse which belongs to the dock and is
said to be of the largest in the country.

Looe, a small harbour

Looe has a small harbour at the mouth of a river and a few batteries of guns for defensive purposes, but is otherwise a rather poor and miserable place between two rocky hills.
A gunsmith who had settled there told me that Swedish iron is the best for gun barrels, and totally rejected the Spanish, both in regard to strength and in regard to its lasting qualities during prolonged use.

Here one follows the coast, sometimes on top of steep cliffs and at other times on the sand below, and occasionally even in the sea when the tide is high.

Fowey, a harbour and its trade in iron and other goods

Fowey, illustrated by drawing no. 90/91, is the next harbour one meets and is located eight miles from Looe.

From Plymouth one pays for 30 miles
according to the stage tariff commonly used in
this district. 150

Figs. 90/91 Fowey

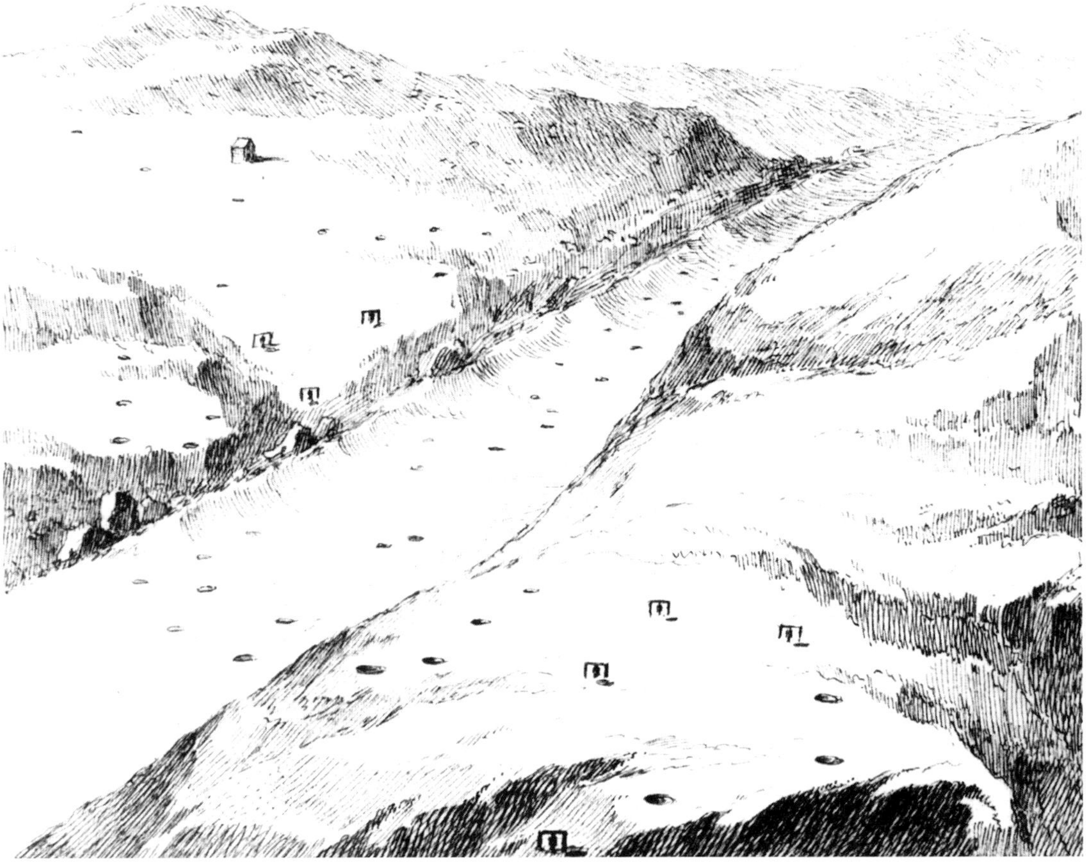

Fig. 92 Tin mines at St Austell

The harbour is reckoned to be excellent, and lies at the outlet of a river between two high hills. The town is built on both sides of the river. The main trade carried on here is pilchard fishing, which is said to be very good at certain times. Some tin also arrives from the direction of Liskeard, and from abroad are imported Norwegian boards, beams and spars, tar, hemp and iron. The iron used to come from Bilbao and San Sebastian in Biscay, and Guipuzcoa, but has now become so scarce that none of it is for sale.

Mr Reynolds from Bristol, who travels all around this part of the country three times a year to take orders for iron and collect payments, in the same way as the merchants from Västergotland in Sweden do with their goods, also supplies this town with Swedish,
151 English and Russian iron, partly from Bristol and partly from London. The latest price paid for ordinary Gothenburg stamps was £17.10s per ton, not including freight, which generally amounts to 10s or 11s. 'Mr Tax' is an iron merchant here, and he told me that the total consumption could not be more than 80 tons per year, including Spanish iron.

St Austell, a small town

In the evening I arrived in St Austell, which is located eight miles from Fowey, and is a small country town where now great preparations were being made for .....[69]

Tin mines at St Austell

On 15 May I went to see the extensive tin mines located two miles the other side of St Austell on both sides of a valley, as shown by drawing no. 92.[70] They consist of a number of parallel veins that run straight across the valley and up the hills on either side and sometimes happen to come together. The mines on the western side are the richest, and here two steam 15
engines have been installed by Mr Lemon, but they do not have sufficient capacity to take all

the water away, and the work in the mines has to stop for a couple of months during the wettest period. At the mines they were occupied with pumping out the water, and at a number of places along the small stream that flowed by, with the stamping and washing of ore that was contaminated with other types of rock.
The aforementioned veins or lodes of tin were vertical and of varying width, from the thickness of string to several inches. When it happens that the two lodes meet, the width can reach a foot or more of pure mineral or 'lod' as the ore is called here. On the eastern side there were other mine owners[71] working a number of shafts, and they were now also employed in
153 pumping out water and with repairs to the shafts. The lodes are much poorer here and have to a great extent been metamorphosed into a yellow copper ore,[72] which is separated from the tin as far as possible and sent to Bristol for smelting, because no-one in this area understands the smelting of copper ore, nor is it possible to start this type of industry here owing to the lack of forests. The parts of the ore that cannot be cleanly separated are crushed and washed out to recover the tin. During the washing it is also possible to recover some copper, which in the form of ore is lighter than tin ore. The country rock at these mines is of light colour and silvery appearance, but the veins are surrounded by quartz, that occasionally has formed pretty crystals, here called Cornwall diamonds. The deepest of the mines is about
30 fathoms, but they had driven an adit at the 154
bottom of the valley, which at a further depth of five fathoms drains the water from them.
This adit is also of incomparable assistance to the washing works, because with its help they can provide a head of water from the stream wherever they like.

On the way back I saw a large number of the tin-streaming works that have been started in every place where water is available. The main occupation of the people here is to drive adits or to cut leats, to convey the water as far as possible and to obtain higher heads of water for the washing. See drawing no. 93a. When the people in the valleys were working in an adit

Fig. 93a Cutting leats

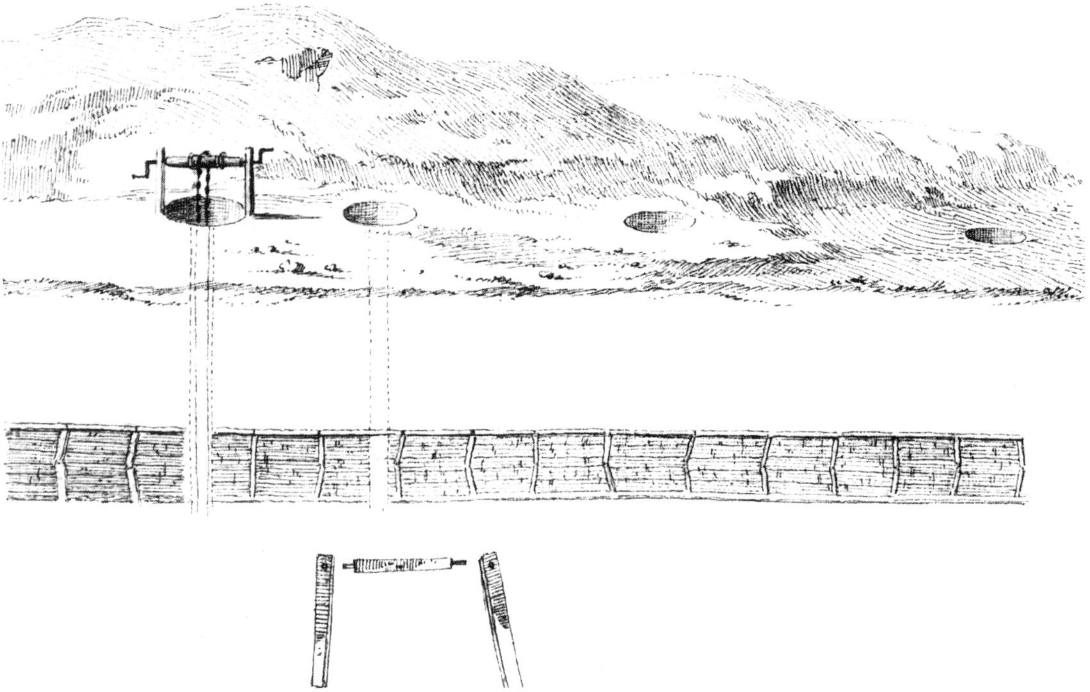

Fig. 93b Details of adit construction

that was not too deep, they used the old-fashioned rag-and-chain pump to remove the water. For the timbering of the adits, Norwegian timber is used and any ends of planks that can be found. Before carrying out the actual
timbering, they compress both roof and sides of
the tunnel with wedges to make any soft and
loose earth more firm and to prevent it from 155
collapsing before the timbering is completed.
See drawing no. 93b.

Fig. 94 Tin streaming

Fig. 95 Stamping mill and buddles

At the first stage of washing in the wash pit, a grate 3 feet long, made of iron, is placed at a steep angle under the flow of water, so that all gravel and other stones roll down it, while only the sand falls through, which is immediately suitable for further washing. See drawing no. 94.

All large stones and shingle obtained during the first washing of the sand and earth are used to make walls at the sides of the pits, and also in the middle of them, thus providing more room for the water and making the stream as deep as possible at all points. The larger pockets of tin ore, sometimes found under the overburden, are dug out and placed directly on the grating
156 whilst the washing is in progress.

The workers are so familiar with the colour of the tin ore that hardly any of it can escape their keen eyes and attention. The lumps of ore that are mixed with quartz or other kinds of rock are thrown aside and piled up for stamping. Everything that is won in the mines, except pieces of pure tin ore, also goes to the stamping mill, which generally consists of a small water wheel driving three stamps. One end of the stamp trough is made up of a piece of finely-perforated iron sheet, through which all the crushed material has to pass. Nothing can get out of the trough that is not fine enough to pass this sieve and is thus suitable for washing. See drawing no. 95.

The first washing that takes place after stamping is carried out in a wooden box sunk into the earth to a depth of 2 feet to 2 feet 6 inches, constructed in such a manner that the
water can run out through a channel at one 157
end.[73]

The crushed ore is placed in a box above the upper end of the buddle, and water is made to flow over it evenly and continuously. A boy with an iron shovel makes furrows in the ore that are filled in, but remade again and again, until all the pulp has been washed away. The richest parts stay in the buddle, but the lighter parts are flushed out through the opening at the lower end. See drawing no. 96.

Each time the box becomes empty, the lightest portion of the ore in the buddle below it is swept away with the aid of a small broom. The process is repeated until the buddle is full of washed ore, which is then divided into three parts, removed separately with a shovel.
The third part, farthest away from the head of

Fig. 96a Buddle details (version one)

the buddle, which is the lightest, is taken to a frame to be washed again as described below. The second part, in the middle of the buddle, is
158 washed again in the same way as before.
The third part, nearest to the inlet, is good washed ore, which is placed in the calcining furnace and finally cleaned up with the aid of a kieve[74] and a sieve. The next washing of the poorest ore takes place on a frame suspended on trunions, so that it can be turned upside-down and cleaned between each washing operation. All this work is done by small boys.

Calcining of tin ore

Calcining is the next process to which the tin ore is subjected, and it is carried out in a reverberatory furnace fired with pit coal from Wales. The time required for the calcining cannot be determined in advance because the dressed ore may contain more or less sulphur and other impurities, but the colour of the ore and the smoke shows when it is completed. When the calcining is finished the ore is again
washed in sieves and is then ready for smelting. 159
For the final dressing, the ore is placed in a

Fig. 96b Buddle details (version two)

smooth trough and the red colour that has appeared during the calcining is washed off. See drawing no. 97.

If a 'Venturer' carries out dressing for his own account, he sells the ore, when sufficiently washed,[75] for 21s.6d per 66 lb to the people carrying out the smelting. If he washes the ore for the account of someone else, he must pay a sixth of each pound [of ore] to the landowner,[76] and may not work without his permission or without having been granted a licence or mining-claim by his steward. The water costs 30s per year or more according to the circumstances, and this payment is made to the person from whom the water is obtained.

Tin smelting

The smelting at St Austell and some other places in Cornwall is effected by means of charcoal in a building known as a blowing house. On the other hand, the smelting carried
160 out in Truro and in most other places is carried out with coal in a smelting house equipped with reverberatory furnaces. The furnace shown by drawing no. 98 is built practically the same way as the ones at the tin smelters in Saxony, but is somewhat smaller. Leather bellows supply the blast and the smoke goes out through the side to a masonry flue 80 feet to 100 feet long, leading to a vaulted tower, standing between 24 feet and 32 feet higher than the smelting furnace. The tin that is carried away with the smoke belongs to the person who maintains the blowing house, and he gets no other remuneration for letting his furnace. The furnace is 4 feet high and 1 foot 9 inches square, and built of long slabs of grey rock that here is called moorstone and is obtained at the top of the hills. It is not, however, particularly heat-resistant. This moorstone is also used to make moulds for the blocks of tin, and is specially quarried and shaped for this purpose.

Old tin mines

In the afternoon, I went to another side of 161
St Austell, where there were also some tin mines that had now been closed owing to too much water or because the lodes had ceased to produce a sufficient quantity of mineral to make the work profitable. An adit or level, which will be about a mile long, is now being driven to one of these mines. The type of rock here is not so hard that it is difficult to work, but it is so firm that no timbering is required. In this district timbering is quite expensive, as most of the wood that is used has to be purchased in Norway and shipped to England.

Fig. 97 Calcining oven and dressing tubs

Fig. 98 Tin-smelting furnace

In another hill I saw some old mines that for a short time had yielded large quantities of rich tin ore, but soon had become exhausted. The tin lode, which occurred in a coarse grey rock, had been found when a tin-streaming
162 works was started in a little stream that flows through this place.

Remarks on the genesis of tin ore lodes

On inspection of this type of grey rock, one could clearly see that it had been crystallising at the same time as the tin lodes, before they were disturbed [by the mining operations]. It was still possible to see in many places where it had been covered by earth, how the grains of quartz and the feldspar crystals were in the process of being formed, and how they increased in hardness and strength with the depth below the surface. On careful examination, one can find the marks of half the mineral veins at the beginning of crystal formation, which here takes place under a cover of a foot-thick layer of sandy and clayey gravel. This vein could not have failed to become both deeper and richer through the increase in height of the rock, if it had only been left undisturbed for a few thousand of years. It is also most probable that it could still grow and become enriched if time would give it 163
back its bed-quilt and forcing-house again, which were taken away and destroyed when the earth was removed. It has been observed that where the stream workings are very rich, the solid tin lodes do not last long. This indicates that the country rock itself has been dislocated

during the formation of the crystals and has not become stabilised.

Gold in dressed tin ore

Between St Austell and Lostwithiel grains of gold are found in tin-streaming works and occasionally stones containing veins of gold. I saw samples of both in St Austell as well as at Mr Rosewarne's smelting house at Truro. In England, a private person is not allowed to work a gold mine because this is a royal prerogative, which now is in the possession of a gentleman in London. Nevertheless, I was told that the miners, who lived in the neighbourhood where
164 the gold occurs, had become wealthy within a few years, because they pick out the largest grains during the washing of the ore and sell them to the smelting houses, which in their turn sell to the goldsmiths in London.

Cockfighting

16 May. There are no horse races in this county, but instead they have cockfighting associated with great festivities, and this took place in St Austell on this day. On the day before, the cocks that are going to fight are each numbered, described and weighed. The owners, who are generally present at such a delicate and serious operation, are so meticulous that even the weight of the feathers is considered critical. For this reason, the tail, wings and feathers are cut off in advance up to the neck, or even right up to the comb, which itself has been cut off some time before. There are special people, called
165 cock-feeders, who take care of this, and feed the cocks with eggs and other invigorating food to increase their courage and strength.

The cockfighting was held in a small amphitheatre called the Cock Pit, specially built for the purpose. In the middle of the floor there was a small raised place covered with green turf where the duels actually took place. The tower bell was rung to announce the time when the games were to start, and the spectators collected in the Cock Pit after paying an entrance fee for the day of 1s. The cocks were carried in racks, with their feet tied together so that they could not hurt themselves with the long spurs of steel that were fastened to their feet, and the fight began as soon as they were freed and had reached the turf. Nobody in this place brings any cock to the pit without betting £5 on it.
166 When gaming, this means 5 guineas. Occasionally during the fighting it happens that, in addition, £20 to £30 is staked on each side, not counting what the spectators bet between themselves. This betting is accompanied by tremendous noise and shouting. Sometimes the fights come to an end fairly quickly because one of the cocks has been stabbed in the temple by a steel spur. Sometimes the fight goes on up to half an hour before one of them is slain. When the battle lasts a long time the cocks get so tired that they often fall down unconscious. They are, however, not allowed to lie on the ground for longer than it takes for one of the cock-feeders to count to ten, when they are put on their feet and set upon each other again. As soon as one of the cocks has fallen down dead, the bets are paid either in cash or by charging to the account between the betting parties.

When the fighting is over for the day the 167
accounts are settled, and there might be 15, 20 or 30 of them. In this way, three days are spent at the fights, and the nights are wasted on sumptuous entertaining, dancing, cards and dice. Everyone amuses himself as best he can, but the persons who gain most pleasure and assured profit are the landlords of the inns and pubs, who on these occasions raise the prices of their food and an innocent traveller has to suffer for it.

Truro

Truro, shown in drawing no. 99, lies 12 miles from St Austell and halfway between them is Grampound, where there is some woollen-manufacturing business.

Woollen manufacture at Grampound

I saw here one man controlling all the different operations involved in the manufacture of cloth and shalloons. He carried out the scouring, combing and spinning of the wool, and the weaving, fulling, dyeing and pressing of the cloth. Although this man knew how to organise everything and how to instruct his children and
work people in the various processes, he was not 168
too high and mighty to travel around the country selling his products. And to earn a few shillings with his horses, he did not mind acting as my postillion to Truro.

Tin mines at Polgooth

On the way from St Austell, I passed the mines at Polgooth, and a number of other shafts and stream-works by the little streams. Nearer to Grampound and Truro no tin mines were seen.

Fig. 99 Truro

The town of Truro and tin-smelting works
Truro is situated between hills, which here are covered with earth and grass for grazing in the same way as almost everywhere in this country. Two small rivers flow through the town and the harbour is reached by the tide so that ships of 150 tons can enter it, although they sit dry in the mud when the water recedes again. Large quantities of tin ore mined within nine to
169 12 miles of Truro are brought to the town in sacks on horseback, and smelted in the blowing houses. One of these is situated just outside the town and has eight furnaces, and the other a mile away, with ten furnaces all under one roof. The smelting furnaces are of the reverberatory type and fired with coal from Newcastle and Wales. The attached drawing no. 100 shows their design.

The internal length, not including the fire grate, is 8 feet and the width varies from 2 feet 6 inches to 4 feet, the widest part being nearest to the grate, which is placed at one end of the furnace. The metal is tapped at one side and the hearth slopes in this direction. The door for tapping is marked with the letter 'A' [missing] on the drawing. The [internal] height is 1 foot. 400 to 500 lb of tin ore are charged at a time and placed in layers alternating with layers of powdered coal of a kind that comes from Wales and is called culm.[77] The smelting takes six hours and the metal is tapped into an iron ladle, from which it is poured into moulds of granite
170 holding 50 lb. The tin that has been melted once is not sufficiently pure and ductile, and must be refined a second time. The aforementioned blocks are placed in the furnace and as soon as they have had time to melt the metal is tapped into the usual large moulds that produce blocks of 300 lb in weight. These are subsequently stamped and sent to Truro. On arrival in Truro the blocks are weighed,

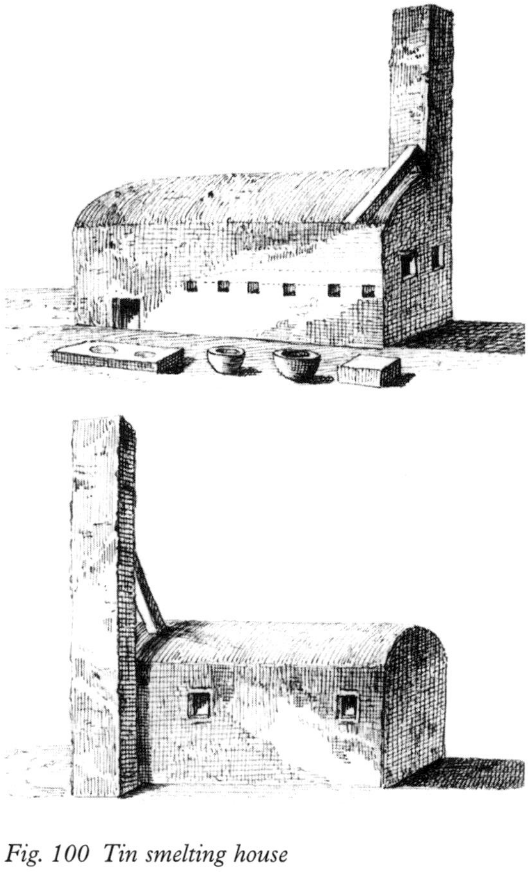

Fig. 100 Tin smelting house

Fig. 101a St Agnes

numbered, assayed and stamped, which costs…[78] The King's duty is 4s per cwt.[79] One cwt or 112 lb is sold for £3.8s.2d, and a ton for £72. When the tin ore arrives at the smelting house it has already been assayed and paid for according to the tin content, or 13 lb of tin metal for 20 lb of ore, but occasionally more or less, depending on how rich the washed ore
171 is. All ore is brought on horseback to the furnaces in sacks, and the content of tin is not estimated according to weight, but expressed as the amount that each sack yields. The blocks of tin weighing 300 lb are also carried away from the smelting furnace by pack-horses, one block on each horse, resting on sticks placed over the saddle.

The tin mines of St Agnes

On 18 May I visited St Agnes, which can be seen in drawing no. 101a. It is located on the northern sea coast eight miles from Truro, and is only a village around a church, but known for the many and rich tin mines that have been worked virtually all around it. The foremost of these mines is called Polberro and belongs to Mr Donnithorne. It has been worked so carelessly that a part of it fell in some time ago. Quite a few cliffs appear ready to take the same
172 trip, as may be seen better on the attached drawing no. 102.

The mine is now 60 fathoms deep from the surface and goes down to 20 fathoms below sea

Fig. 101b Timbered mine shaft

level. The tin lode itself strikes east–west and dips south or inland, which is all shown in the above-mentioned drawings. The main lode is generally 3 feet to 4 feet wide, but when it meets other smaller lodes, which has happened, the total width may increase to 12 feet or 16 feet. Including crushers and dressers there are 250 workers at this mine. For mining a fathom in depth and the same in width the payment is 57s and it has happened that this has produced £600 obtained from a cubic fathom. In some places the levels or adits are timbered with Norwegian beams and boards, of which 173
ordinary logs cost 9d to 10d for each foot [see Fig. 101b]. Mr Donnithorne paid the mineral owner dues of £1200 for last year, which is one-twelfth of the whole production, and this amounted to £14,400. In the last quarter, 200 blocks of tin were delivered, weighing 300 lb each.

19 May. This mine was worked some 60 years ago, but was abandoned due to lack of water to drive the pumps. However, the lode

Fig. 102 Cliffs at St Agnes

was not very rich or large at that time. Mr Donnithorne has since repaired an old leat cut into the side of the mountain and has thus obtained water for a pump wheel placed down in the mine, but is now no longer adequate to drain the deeper parts of the mine. He is
174 therefore considering the construction of a new leat, making it possible to install another pump wheel. This could also be done with the present leat, because from its level the water has a fall of no less than 90 feet, whereas the diameter of the existing wheel is only 20 feet. I suggested that a water pressure engine should be installed here, which should be incomparably useful and would not cost very much.[80] But a person who does not have sense enough to realise that a 90-foot waterfall might be used for more than one wheel of 20 feet diameter could not be expected to deal with much more difficult matters. The main objection to this proposal was the instability of the leat and the cliffs overhanging the sea, visibly leaning towards a fall. See drawing no. 103.

However, all this could be avoided by a new
175 perpendicular shaft, or by an adit from the leat to the winding shaft, which is located at quite a distance from the sea shore and could last several hundred years before the sea eats it away.

The other mines located both east and west of Polberro are worked partly for tin and partly for copper. Mixed with these metals there are also black cupriferous mispickels and cobalt [sic], which however, are not recognised or put to any use. The lodes worked in the above-mentioned mines are so numerous that the local people do not know the exact number. According to an estimate there should be 12 to 15 within a diameter of one English mile that have been exposed and worked at various places along their length.

On 20 May I travelled from St Agnes to Redruth, a distance of eight Cornish miles, which are considerably longer than English. 17
The road continued across a large plain that was uninhabited and where there were no mines, although some exploratory pits were seen here and there, and also ancient burial mounds.

Tin mines in the neighbourhood of Redruth

Two miles north-east of Redruth I entered a mining district which stretched for two miles from the plain, striking east and west, and worked by innumerable holes and shafts. Most of it was now flooded, which generally happens in wintertime. They were, nonetheless, busy

Fig. 103 Cliffs at Polperro

with the installation of a new fire engine in addition to the old one and the water engines[81] erected below ground in the adits. The main lode itself consists of a yellow copper ore, but there is also grey copper ore underneath.[82] Further towards the east, a number of lodes appear that are worked both for copper and tin. The lodes are in some places 8 feet to 10 feet wide and sometimes only a couple of inches. They are generally perpendicular, in a soft granite. Drawing no. 104 shows this mining district. Some of the mines are 210 feet deep, and have adits 60 feet to 90 feet long.
The district is called North Downs.

Redruth, a small town
Having arrived in Redruth, which is an insignificant little place, as most Cornish towns are, I walked a mile west of it where the church is located, below a mountain called Carn Brea. In ancient times there was a castle there, and fortifications. See drawing no. 105.

A large stone peculiarly placed on top of
178 other slabs of stone is said to have been a place of sacrifice, but the holes that were worn into it clearly showed that this stone had been used for grinding flour. The same kind of stone is still used for mill stones and one of these, newly cut, was lying beside it. The castle, the design of which is shown in the previous drawing [no. 104], is very ancient, but nonetheless appears to have been built during a much later period than the fortifications that enclose the space around it, about 200 feet in diameter. As shown by the deterioration of the ramparts and the cliffs themselves, these were several thousand years old. Here there was a wide outlook over both seas, the one on the north side and the one on the south side, and also over Penzance, which is located 16 miles away to the west. See drawing no. 105. To the north of here, at a distance of three to four miles, a number of copper smelters
could be seen, and in the east, the extensive 179
mining district on the other side of Redruth.
In the valley where the church is located, there were many stamps and buddles for tin. On the southern slope of the hill there were also the remains of old dressing floors, and a recently

Fig. 104 North Downs mining district

started mine, in which there is a good hope of finding tin ore. The shaft went through rock rich in hornblende, although the upper part of the mountain consisted of granite.

In Redruth there is some trade in iron for the needs of the mines, which so far have obtained most of it from Redruth [sic].[83] 'Mr John. Hoschen' has until now obtained his iron and stamp-heads from Bristol, but he accepted from me the address of Mr Lindegren in London. The price of iron is 20s to 21s. The stamp heads from Bristol cost £24 per cwt, but the ones made here of foreign iron cost £28. When they are worn out the smiths take them back and pay
180 14s per cwt. Stamp heads cast in Bristol with forged brackets cost 20s. The largest stamp heads are 14 inches high, 10 inches wide and 7 inches thick. Good iron for rock drills cost 30s.

Copper mines in the neighbourhood of Redruth

From Redruth I went to the copper mines north of Carn Brea, where a number of lodes are worked. Pool, one and a half miles from Redruth, has four lodes, 6 inches to 3 feet in thickness, that strike east and west, on which 11 shafts have been sunk, some to a depth of 270 feet. There is also a fire engine and an adit at the 150-feet level. Two hundred people work above and below ground here, and 2100 lb of ore, or one ton, fetches ten to 30 guineas. The total sales amount to 200 tons per year.
The mines are worked by Squire Praed and 18
Mr Abel Angove. Bullen Garden is two and a half miles from Redruth. The lode strikes east–west and is 9 feet to 10 feet wide and 40 feet deep. The adit is at the 18-feet level and contains three water wheels. The ore is yellow and grey and sells for £6 to £13 per ton. The mine belongs to Messrs Johns and George. Wheal Gerry copper lode is 3 feet to 4 feet thick, and dips slightly north. The mines are 27 fathoms deep and there is an adit at the 19-fathom level, which joins another adit driven to an old copper mine on the same lode called Wheal Kitty. See drawing no. 106.

The ore is yellow and black and is sold for £6 to £13 or £14 [per ton]. There are 16 workers here and the mine belongs to Mr Tom Harris. Tresavean copper mine is located two and a half miles north-east of Redruth. The lode strikes east and west. Five years ago this mine

Fig. 105 Ruins near Redruth

82 started to yield such abundant quantities of yellow and grey copper ore – here called 'ore' – that the 'Lord of the Fees' or the mineral lord sometimes received as his share £140 [worth of ore] per month.

In many places I observed that when shafts were being sunk either for exploration or for the ventilation of adits, a funnel made of boards, according to drawing no. 107, was turned against the wind to convey fresh air through a wooden tube reaching right to the bottom, to the miners working there. Fresh air is often scarce even at modest depths.

Dolcoath copper mine belongs to Mr Johns and partners. It has a large number of shafts, a fire engine and three water wheels. The lode strikes east and west, the same as the aforementioned, and dips a few degrees north.

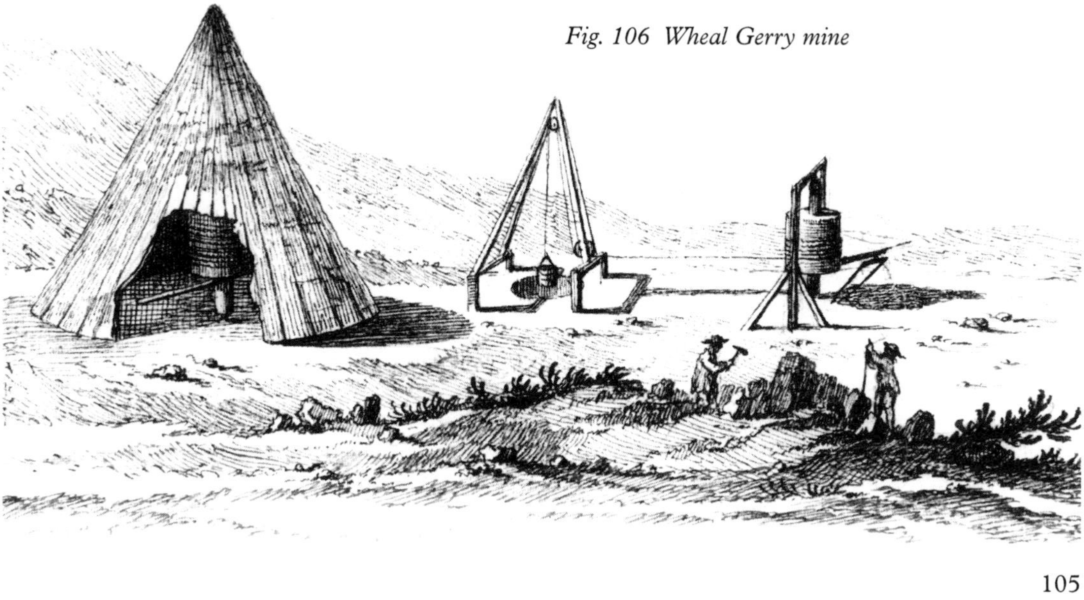

Fig. 106 Wheal Gerry mine

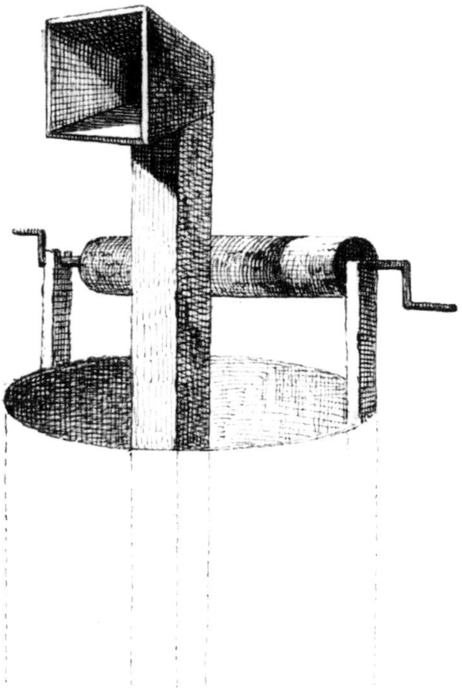

Fig. 107 Ventilation of mine shafts

It is 80 fathoms deep in some places and has an adit at the 30-fathom level. There is an
183 abundant supply of ore, both yellow and black, which is sold for £6 to £16 per ton.

Copper smelting furnaces

In the Parish of Camborne, three and a half miles from Redruth, there is a copper smelting mill belonging to Mr Robert Severin, who here smelts the ore to a matte and then sends it to his copper-works in Wales, 20 miles beyond Bristol, called Redbrook.[84] The furnace is built in practically the same way as the calcining or roasting furnaces for tin ore. It is 7 feet long, 5 feet wide and 7 inches to 12 inches high. The height over the fire grate is 18 inches. The fireplace is as long as the furnace is wide, and its width is 21 inches. The chimney-stack stands at the front by the outlet end, where the slag is raked out. The tap-hole is on the side facing the yard. The slag is put into moulds of iron 18 inches long and 9 inches wide and 9 inches deep, and then used for building. For this purpose it is matchless both in respect of colour and durability. All buildings belonging
184 to the mill were built of this material.

The furnace is fired with Welsh coal, and some of this is also placed with the ore.

In the neighbourhood were also a number of stamps and dressing-floors for tin ore coming both from stream-works and from the above-mentioned copper lodes, which also contained small veins of tin.

After stamping and dressing, the ore that is contaminated with sulphur and copper must be calcined or roasted. For this purpose roasting furnaces were built in three places along the road. They have a hole at the top for the charging of the ore and another little hole at the bottom for raking it out after it has been sufficiently roasted. The roasting requires more or less time according to how heavily the ore is contaminated. It takes from 12 to 18 and 24 hours. Each charge of ore weights six hundredweight. The furnace operator is paid
18d per charge. 18

The furnace is 6 feet long and 4 feet 6 inches wide internally. 'a' is the charging hole for the ore, 'b' is the hole for raking the ore down when the roasting is finished. 'c' is the opening for stirring the ore with an iron rake. 'd' is the opening for the smoke. 'e' is the fireplace where the coal is placed on iron grating bars. 'f' is the hole that is opened to take out the ore that has been raked down into the hole 'b'. See drawing no. 108. This kind of works is known as a Burning House [sic] and generally has two roasting furnaces, operated by one man.

Tin-smelting furnaces

At Rose an Grouse, two miles from Penzance, there was a smelting-house for tin with five reverberatory furnaces, not working now. It belongs to Mr George Blewett. One-and-a half miles on the other side of Penzance there are four such furnaces and they were also shut down. They were built in the same way as the
ones in Truro. Forty years ago there were 18
blowing houses [sic] here.

The town of Penzance and its trade

Penzance, shown by drawing no. 109, is a pretty market town, but not very large, on a bay of the ocean on the southern side of Cornwall 10 miles from Lands End. Fish, tin and copper ore are the main goods that are exported from here. The imports are wood, iron, steel, hemp, grain, coal and other necessities both of food and clothing, for which the demand is good, because the inhabitants of this district direct their aims and endeavours so firmly towards the underground treasures, that for their sake they

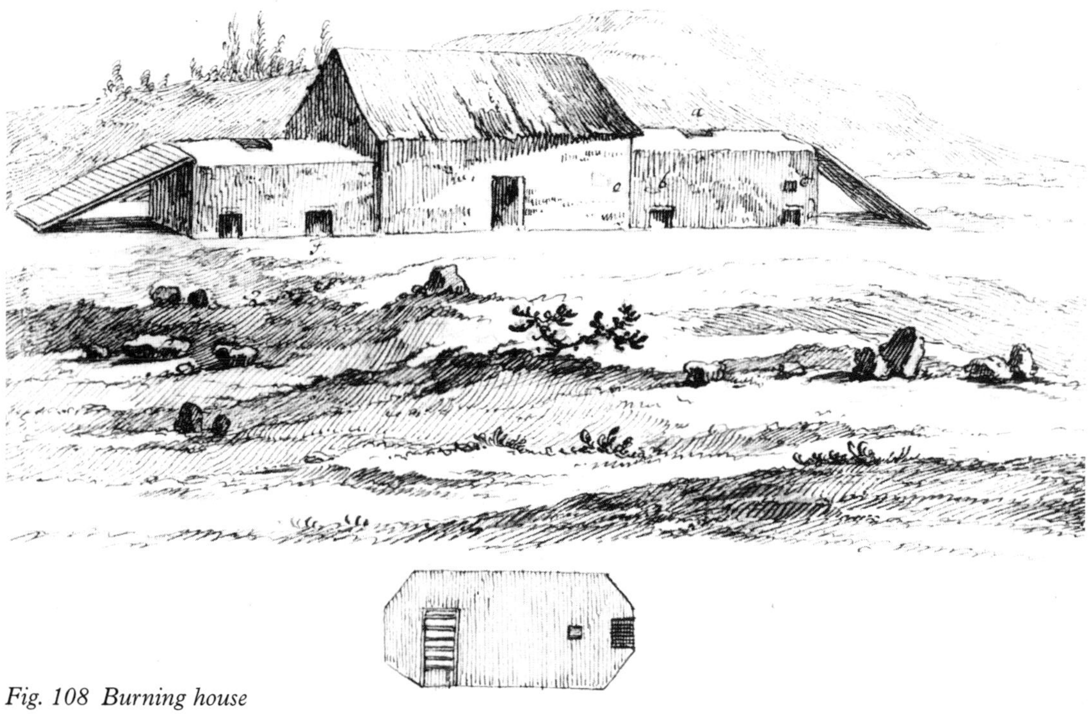

Fig. 108 Burning house

forget both fields and meadows, stock-raising, handicrafts and the making of articles of clothing and other commodities.

A ship from Arendal in Norway had just arrived when I came to Penzance, and it was loaded with beams and boards, which here are known collectively as timber. Beams, logs or spars are paid by the square foot,[85] of which 50 now cost 30s or 7d per foot. Boards 5 feet long, 8 inches wide and 1 inch thick cost 4 guineas per 100. Mr Johns' brother and partner travelled to Arendal last year with a Norwegian ship and is now expected back with the load of timber that he has purchased. Mr Johns also trades in iron but his entire yearly turnover does not exceed 40 to 50 tons. On the other hand it is said that Mr Blewett in Market Jew[86] each year sells between 2 and 300 tons of iron, of which Swedish is the smallest part, because in this place they complain about its brittleness. In addition it is dearer, both as far as the purchase price and the freight are concerned,
88 than the Russian, which is shipped here instead of ballast. The same could also be done from Sweden, if one could only compete with the Norwegians in regard to price in the timber trade. Selected timber and boards should not be sent to this place, because most of it is used for timbering in the mines and similar purposes.

In the same harbour there was a whale (see drawing no. 110) recently captured, 15 feet long. It was found dead and floating in the water a few miles out in the sea. The head was about a third of the whole length and the tongue fairly large. It had no teeth in the mouth, but instead a stiff bristle around the jaw. The nose was pointed at the front and the tail had no fins. The entrails were very full and blown out, the flesh coarse and covered with blubber, two fingers thick, which now was being
removed for boiling to whale oil. Some of the 189
mariners told me that it was a small kind of whale called a Blower, which spouts water when it sees a ship.

New tin mine

On 22 May I travelled with Mr Beard a few miles to the coast of the sea to inspect a tin lode that had been discovered a few months ago on his land in the steep slope down to the shore. The lode was from 8 inches to 1½ feet thick, and had already been subjected to a considerable amount of working, by means of a number of shafts sunk along it to the depths of 6 to 8 to 10 fathoms. No stamping and dressing had been carried out and none of the ore had been sold, so that it was not possible to know what the profit might turn out to be. 'The Lord

Fig. 109 Penzance

of the Ground'[87] has negotiated 1s.6d, but had still not decided if he was going to permit his best meadowland to be laid waste for the sake
190 of this work that might bring him little reward.

Standing stones and ancient monuments

The trip continued three miles westwards to the neighbourhood of St Buryan, where there was a circle of standing stones, said to have been a Druidical place of sacrifice, as shown by the adjoining drawing no. 111. At letter 'A' there are 6 feet between the stones and to the right of this entrance there are ten stones and only one that has fallen. Opposite the entrance on the other side of the circle there is an open space of 18 feet between the stones, and it looks as if one stone from there had been removed, which in its day had been the twentieth stone, because ordinarily there is a gap of 8 feet between the stones except at the entrance, and when the width of the stone is added, it is just 18 feet. The height of the stones above ground is 4 feet and the thickness 15 inches. In the Cornish language these stones are called 'Dons Mein'
which means Dancing Stones or Dance 191
Stones.[88] About 600 yards to the north there are two standing stones about 200 yards from each other, and to the north-west, about

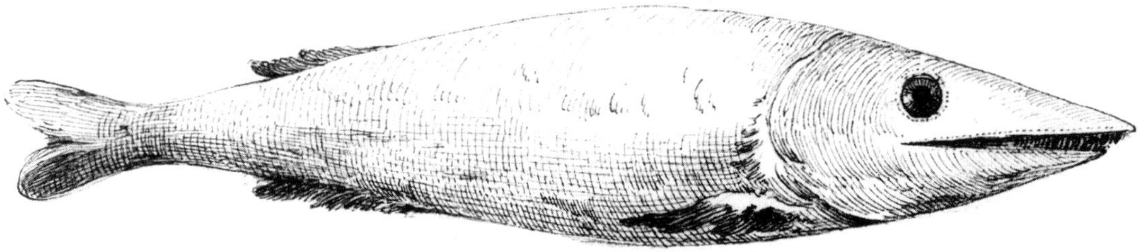

Fig. 110 Whale

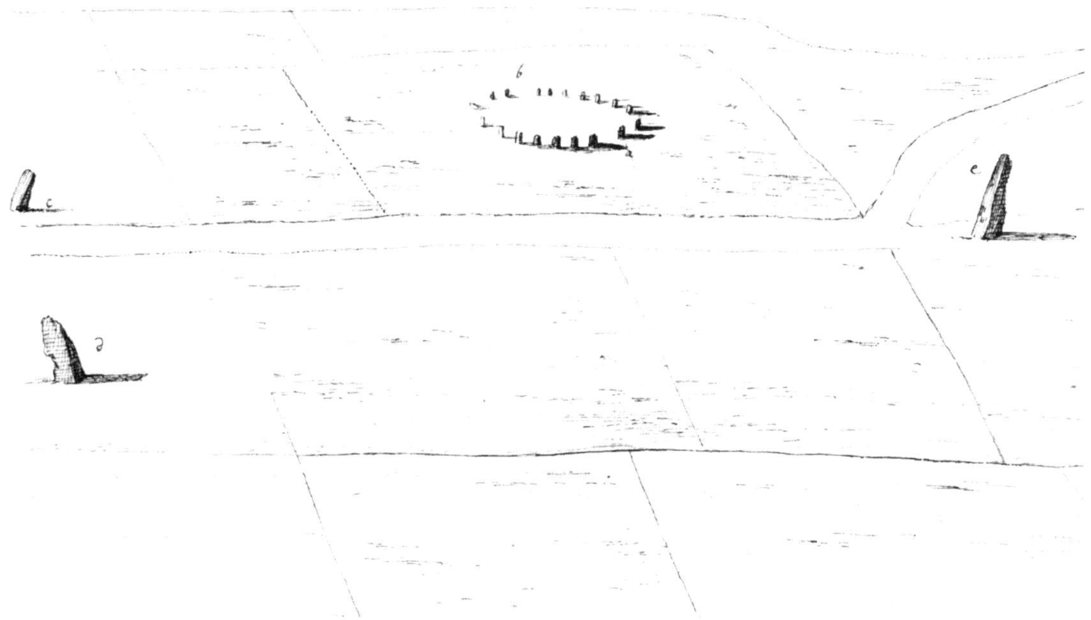

Fig. 111 Standing stones

100 yards distant, another stone 8 feet to 10 feet high above ground. According to an old tale told by the peasants, the two first-mentioned stones whistle, the third plays and the 19 dance when they hear the cock crow. Such a story, told to some simple-minded persons simply to pass the time, could have been the origin of the name Dancing Stones. I dare say that dancing was practised at the sacrifices and worship of the Ancient Britons, and one can be sure that this lured many more people, including youngsters, to come to church than the traditional worship of our days, even if one bends one's knees and puts on a mien of solemnity and devotion. The Children of Israel
192 sang and danced around the Golden Calf. David did the same in front of the Ark. Many Eastern people dance whilst they praise and glorify the works of their gods. The priests of the Turks whirl around in their mosques. The Catholics walk two by two in processions and sing, although rather too slowly for dancing.

Enclosed pastures

From here I took the road to the south-west towards the sea, and passed many enclosed pastures and meadows that had a standing stone in the middle for the horses and cattle to rub themselves against.

Granite used in building

All the stones encountered here are granite or grey stone, which in this district is so abundant that all the buildings and houses are built of it.

Remarks on the decrease of population

The people were now employed partly with the ploughing of fallow fields, of which there were
very many here, partly with the piling of turf for 193
burning to fertiliser, and partly with the collection of heather and furze for fuel. Wherever a stream flowed there were remains of old tin stream-works, and many ruins of buildings showing that the place had a larger population 100 years ago than now. This may have been caused by the American colonies to some extent, because many English people go there for the sake of the fisheries and never return.

Treen Castle, an ancient monument

By the seashore lies the so-called Treen Castle, illustrated by drawing no. 112, which shows its antiquity by the fact that the massive walls of granite masonry, through the ages, have melted away and become so ruinous that there is hardly anything left of them. The cliffs further out on the point, have, no doubt, many times in the past been used for defensive purposes and were once built upon.

Fig. 112 Treen Castle

194 ***Remarks regarding the metamorphosis of stones and rocks***

It is not, however, only the works of man that here have been subject to transformation due to the corrosion of time, but also the bedrock itself, nature's solid creation, has in its turn been forced to submit to natural laws. The most remarkable thing that is shown to visitors here is a stone 16 feet long, 9 feet wide and 6 feet high and well rounded, which rests on a high rock, so well-balanced that it can be rocked back and forth with one hand, as can be plainly seen. The reason for this is none other than the one previously put forward regarding the destruction of the rock. One can with pardonable assurance state that not only this particular stone, but many thousands of others
195 lying here and there on these cliffs for long ages, were once attached to the bedrock, part of one single mass.

In its maturity, this mass started to crack and to break down, as the waves of the ocean and the rain deprived it of the soil that gives it food and protection. This can clearly be learned from studying the cracks, which further down were closed up, but at the surface, so corroded by time and air that they were several feet wide in some places.

We continued southwards along the coast to Land's End, which consists of many high cliffs, from which the Isles of Scilly, lying 50 to 60 miles off the coast, [sic][89] can be seen in clear weather. There is an old legend that these islands were once connected with the mainland. I am very willing to agree with this, as I believe that the ancient inhabitants of this country
worked there in tin mines on the neck of land 196
between them, thereby facilitating the breaking-through of the sea, which in any case continuously eats itself into the Cornish coast.

Notes on the age of the Cornish tin mines

It is true that one does not see many signs of old mining operations here, but nevertheless it has been proved by classical authors, such as Herodotus, Polybius, Strabo and others, that the Phoenicians were already trading in tin on the coast 3000 years ago.

The tin mining here cannot have been [newly] started at this time and must already have been brought to efficient operation. Daily experience shows perfectly well how slow the

development of new ideas is. According to opinion nowadays accepted by the learned world, the old inhabitants of the northern countries were simple and stupid, so the development of all new inventions must have been sluggish and slow in ancient times. Consequently, when we now it takes a hundred years to consider the development of a small
197 trifle to reasonable perfection, we must perhaps leave them a thousand years and more to bring their tin industry, and maybe also other minerals works, into production.

St Just, a village known for beautiful women

A little to the north of Land's End, one comes to a church village called St Just, known for its beautiful women and for many mines, working both tin and copper. I had no time to spend in enjoying myself watching the fair sex, who, according to English custom, keep away from the men, and not much time even to look at the other marvels.

Tin mines at St Just

There are a large number of tin mines three to four miles on either side of St Just.[90] The lodes that are worked strike east and west, and are surrounded by granite rich in quartz. In some
198 places, and particularly where two lodes meet, the mines are rich, but in between, rather meagre and impoverished.

Copper mines at St Just

The copper mines are just by the seashore (see drawing no. 113) and were discovered 60 or 70 years ago by a German, who worked them for a short time. The inhabitants of Cornwall thus learned to know copper ore and its value, and it is now so much in vogue that the copper ore soon will bring in just as much as the tin. During the last year, ore from the copper mines of Cornwall to a total value of £120,000 was despatched to Bristol and Wales, whereas the production of tin during the same year has not reached a higher figure than £160,000. There are two copper mines here, about half a mile apart, the lodes of which are vertical and strike south-east and north-west. The former is 3 feet to 4 feet thick and has fairly rich ore consisting of yellow and blue copper pyrites in coarse mica
199 and hornblende. The other lode also produces yellow copper pyrites but, in addition, chalcocite or copperglance in pockets. It has been worked into the steep slope of the cliffs by the seashore and down to 40 feet below the water-level, which makes it rather difficult and water-logged.

An attempt has been made to prevent this by means of a flat-rod driven by a water-wheel, conveyed in a launder built and supported on the side of the sea-cliffs.

Tin mines

On the way back, three to four miles from St Just, there was a large number of shafts sunk on tin lodes, but the ore seen there appeared rather poor and was dispersed in granite rich in mica.

Cultivation of fields and meadows in Cornwall

The people were occupied with their turf fires, producing fertiliser for fields and meadows, of which there are very few in this locality, because everybody is very keen to get work in the mines and on the dressing-floors. The rural culture has, therefore, become mismanaged and neglected, which does the country much more harm and causes a much greater loss than the 200
profit that in many places can be produced by the mines.

Market Jew, a market town[91]

The 23rd day of May I travelled three miles from Penzance to Market Jew, which is located by a hill called Cornish Mount[92] in the village, and has a greater trade and business than Penzance, all due to a top-merchant [sic], who lives there and whose name is Mr Blewett.
I visited him to talk about the iron trade, which in this place is mainly with Spain, Bristol and St Petersburg, owing to the convenient transport arrangements that have been mentioned before.

Helston, a country town

From Market Jew, I took the road to Helston, which is a country town three miles from the sea. Nevertheless, it has quite a large trade and the surrounding country is very pleasant owing to its location between two valleys and on a 201
little river called the Cober.

Tin mines and horse whim

On the way there we passed a number of mines that were no longer in operation. On the way from Helston to Penryn we did, however, come

Fig. 113 Copper mines at St Just

across some tin mines that were being worked, and at one of them there was a horse-whim of special design.

Penryn, a market town

I arrived in Penryn on 24 May. It is located between two small rivers, two miles up from Falmouth and is a neat little market town, which has the same advantage as Truro, that ships can come up there on the rising tide, but there is, nevertheless, not as much business here. Mr 'Pell' and Mr 'Borcher' are the most important merchants in this place, but do not do very much in iron.

Falmouth, a market town

Falmouth has an excellent harbour and trade with Portugal, which latter is strongly supported by the packet boat that sails from here to Lisbon every month. Three East Indiamen had recently arrived and the people in the country
202 and the towns were all doing their utmost to smuggle in from the ships tea, silk cloth and other goods subject to high duty. However, they often failed when the watchful Customs Officers caught them. A Mr Dobbs is the most prominent merchant here and he also imports some iron, but it is a small quantity compared with that sold in Truro, which is imported by Mr Lemon from Russia, Sweden and Spain.

Fertilising of fields and meadows with sand from seashells

In the harbour of Falmouth, near St Mawes Castle, a kind of sand was taken up that consists of crushed seashells and is used in this locality to fertilise fields and meadows, which it does very successfully. Its colour is grey as ash. With this sand they fertilise fields that are going to be used either for sowing wheat or other corn, and its effect is sufficient for four years of crops and
203 six to seven years of grazing before the soil requires attention again. For a Cornish field with an area of 160 square yards, each yard 9 square feet, 300 sacks or horse-loads of the above-mentioned sand are used. If they have to travel a long way to collect the sand, 100 sacks or less may be enough. This type of sand or marle is suitable for every kind of soil.

Acquaintance with Mr Emys

On 25 May I left Falmouth and went to Mr Emys' house, which lies two miles from Penryn. I was very well received and given specimens of native copper and seaweed, which is a kind of grass that grows along the seashore and shows many beautiful colours. It is collected from the coast near here and is prepared by placing on paper or under glass. However, it must be carefully protected from the sun and
204 must not be exposed to the air too much, otherwise the colour will pale after a time. Together with Mr Emys I travelled to see Mr Lemon's house, which he is building nearby at great cost. On the way to Truro I inspected tin-smelting furnaces located near the town, and was present at assays, which have to be made against payment for everyone bringing in parcels of tin ore.

Acquaintanceship with Mr Lemon

The 26 May I dined with Mr Lemon and, after dinner, we went by sloop four miles down the river to Tregothnan, which belongs to Lord Falmouth's estate. Here we were shown a specimen of native copper, shaped as illustrated by Fig. no. 114 [missing],[93] consisting of solid metal and chalcocite, with a total weight of
60 lb. Originally this weighed 180 lb, but part 205
of it has been sent to the Royal Society. This copper specimen was found in a copper mine called Wheal Fire, five miles from Helston, that is no longer worked.

Several copper mines in one district

On 27 May I visited a copper mine called Bullen Garden, located 13 miles from Truro and three miles from Redruth, together with Mr Rosewarne. This mine was missed when I travelled through Redruth on 20 May, owing to a mistake by my guide. The lode strikes east and west and is 10 feet wide. It dips slightly south and lies in a hornstone rock spar mixed in with a coarse granite veined with spar. This formation runs east and west and cuts through the whole country. The mine is located about 2000 feet from Carn Brea Hill and has been worked to a depth of 47 fathoms. It is provided with two
water wheels placed in an adit at the 18-fathom 206
level. The adit is 100 fathoms long; 80 to 100 people work in the mine and produce 600 to 700 tons of ore a month, with an estimated value of £6 to £8 per ton. The ore is a yellow chalcopyrite interspersed with grey ore.

The Entral copper mine is very near to Bullen Garden, but it works another parallel lode, which is 2 to 3 feet wide and has the same dip and strike as the other. The ore is yellow and blue[94] and is sold for £19 per ton and the yearly production is 40 tons.

Pool, Roskear and Tolgarrick mines, which are in the same district as the aforementioned,
and Trewan and North Downs mines, two miles 207
further east, are operated by one company. They have two fire engines, and another one with a cylinder 69 inches in diameter is being built. There are four lodes here that generally yield tin down to a depth of 15 fathoms, but then suddenly copper, which has already been followed down to 60 fathoms in some places. The ore is here sold for £10 to £12 per ton, and when all the fire engines are started it is expected that it will be possible to employ up to several thousand workers and that the

production of copper will increase considerably.

Chasewater is the latest mine to be started in the eastern part of this district. Like the aforementioned, it has yielded a rich copper ore, which here is sold for £8 to £10 per ton. Every month some 500 to 600 tons of copper ore are raised, and sometimes 700 tons. In this mine, too, the ore is mixed with tin deep down, but at the top there was only tin as is common
208 in this district. There are two water-engines in one shaft here, that are barely sufficient to keep the mine free from water, especially during the winter, because it is low-lying and attracts water from other smaller mines between Chasewater and North Downs. These are worked by other owners who also enjoy the benefits of the fire engine, without contributing anything to it.

This mine has now been worked down to some 60 fathoms and the lode dips much more to the south than is the case anywhere else in Cornwall.

In this extensive district there has been no further mining to the east until one reaches St Austell, about which information is given in the entry for 14 May. About 40 miles from there in the same direction lies the so-called Dartmoor in Devonshire, where the Ancient
209 Britons several thousand years ago had their stream-works. The very considerable remains of these, which can still be seen, are the subject of wonderment in our time.

Tin and copper mining district west of Redruth

West of Redruth lies a district consisting of tin and copper mines that have been opened up in many places towards Penzance. Some years back they yielded large quantities of ores of both kinds, but now they have been abandoned because the ore failed with increasing depth, and the high cost of pumping out the water began to exceed the proceeds from the sale of ore. It was at one of these mines that Mr Lemon founded his prosperity, because he was able to make £25,000 in a short time. From having been a miner, he started to become so prosperous that he is now considered to be worth six million daler kopparmynt.

On the other side of Penzance, three miles
210 further west, a tin lode has been found by the sea-shore, from six to 12 inches wide, which strikes in the same direction as that mentioned above in Redruth. This has been exposed in several places, but does not show promise of yielding such rich and plentiful ore as the former.

Tin and copper district in St Just, west of Redruth

Further on towards Land's End lies the parish of St Just, where there are many tin lodes being worked in a kind of granite. Nevertheless, they are located too near the northern side of the country to be included in the Redruth district, and belong better with another district north of Redruth where the rich tin mines of St Agnes have been put into operation. Amongst them is Polperro, mentioned under the date 18 May which is located in the cliffs just by the seashore. Last year it produced 800 blocks of tin, worth £14,400. The same district has also been extended to the east, towards St Columb, where there are both copper and iron mines 211
stretching a mile further north.

In the above-mentioned tin-mining district in St Just there are two copper lodes that are worked in the steep slope of the cliffs down to the sea. One of these was discovered about 50 years ago by a German, who started to mine it. This was the beginning of copper mining in this country.[95] Previously this kind of ore had either been disregarded or separated from the tin ore and discarded in the same way as are today 'Witebade', black blende and mundic.[96] These names now refer to arsenic, iron pyrites and cobalt ore that never have been used here for any good purpose, but have been thrown on the waste heap as unknown and worthless metals. These lodes strike north-north-east and south-south-west.

Tin ore district at Helston, south of Redruth

South of Redruth yet another district has been 212
opened up at Helston. It consists of many parallel tin lodes, of which nowadays only a few are being worked. These are producing fairly satisfactorily, but have previously had a better reputation. This district strikes east and west and can thus only continue a few miles on either side of Helston before it sinks below Falmouth Bay in the east or below the sea at 'Pengevenion Point'[97] in the west. The part of the district that has been worked only stretches about two miles north of the town of Helston.

Remarks about the older mines

It does not appear unlikely that the lodes of the aforementioned districts, such as these by

Redruth and St Agnes, are the same ones that strike across Dartmoor, which lies 45 to 50 miles away. On Dartmoor there are, even now, substantial remains to be seen of the works of the ancients. These are thought to have been
213 stream-works, as there are no shafts or proper
mines. One should, however, also consider the old lead mines above the town of Wells in Somersetshire. These were all worked to deep levels by means of narrow shafts of which nothing else remains than small, conical pits. This gives one reason to believe that the old tin mines worked on Dartmoor in ancient times may have been destroyed in the same way and hidden from our eyes by the changes brought about over the years.

Old and new tin-smelting processes

As far as the smelting process of the ancients is concerned, it is thought that they did not take much trouble with it. A hole 6 to 8 feet deep was dug in the ground, filled with charcoal on top of which the black tin was placed, and set alight. This gradually melted the tin, which collected at the bottom, where it remained until
214 the smelting was completed.

This lump of tin was then broken up by means of wedges to facilitate transport and to bring it up from the furnace pit. Such pits are reported to exist in many places both in Cornwall and Devonshire, where there have been old stream-works. Their use for tin smelting is said to be proved by grains and pieces of melted tin that can be found when the earth around them is washed.

In later times, and as long as charcoal was available, blowing houses were used for smelting the dressed tin, and these are still in use at St Austell and at Lostwithiel. The new method, employing pit coal and reverberatory furnaces, as described under the date 17 May in Truro, has not generally been used in this country for longer that 40 years.

Nevertheless, it has been found to be more advantageous, both in respect of the consumption of coal and other costs of the smelting operation, and of the much shorter
215 time required for smelting.

In this connection, it is to be noted that the tin smelted from its ore in a blowing house with charcoal is purer and more malleable than tin smelted by the same method in a reverberatory furnace. The price of blowing-house tin is therefore always 8s per cwt higher than that made by the new method. Nonetheless, blowing house tin is always more in demand and is sold more quickly.

Stamping charges and duties on the copper and tin industries

When the tin has been smelted in its furnaces and poured into a granite mould to make a block of 300 lb in weight, it is taken to the nearest coinage town, of which there are five, namely Truro, Liskeard, Helston, Lostwithiel and Penzance. Here the blocks are stamped and numbered, after first having been assayed to determine their tin content and quality.

In addition to coinage stamp and number, two other stamps are generally placed on the blocks, namely the stamp and number of the owner, making a total of four stamps, not
including the weight, which also is stamped in. 216

The washed tin ore is generally paid for in tin metal or money in accordance with the current price for the metal. Four shillings per ton of tin are paid in duty to the Prince of Wales, who is also Prince of Cornwall and the same to the King for coinage, 3s.2d per 100 lb of 'Postgrath' to obtain four coinages a year, instead of three as hitherto. The mines pay one-sixth in duty to the 'Lord of the land' or to the landlord of the copper and one-third of the tin. When a tin mine is started on land belonging to the Prince a duty of one-fifteenth is paid, and the same to the owner of the ground one-fourteenth part, which altogether amounts to one-third part; but for copper nothing is paid.[98]

Fire engine

In the North Downs copper mines, mentioned
under 27 May, the partners pay the contractors 217
for the fire engine one-fifth of all ore raised during the first seven years. Thereafter the engine will belong to the partnership without further payments. The cylinder of the above-mentioned engine is 69 inches in diameter. The boiler or kettle is 15 feet in diameter, 30 feet high and weighs 6 tons. It is made of iron plates.[99]

The tin mine called Truan lies in the North Downs area and has four parallel lodes within a distance of 120 feet. Like the whole area, they strike east and west and dip south 2 feet in 6 feet. The fire engine draws up eight to ten hogsheads of water per minute.[100] It is estimated that 600 people can be put to work in this mine and that the monthly production will

be 1000 tons of copper ore, worth £6 to £10 or
218 £11 per ton.

The journey from Truro

The 28th. In the morning I packed my specimens of ore, and one cask and a chest of these were left with Mr Rosewarne to be dispatched to Mr Lindegren in London. I then set off with post-horses for St Columb, 12 English miles from Truro. The road crosses many rounded hills, most of which are cultivated in this locality. An occasional little common is seen, overgrown with yellow flowering gorse, which looks very much like juniper bushes.

Abandoned mines

Near St Columb I passed some mines that had been worked many years ago. From the appearance of the heaps of stone seen around there, I concluded that they had been looking for tin, but actually found yellow copper ore, which they at that time did not know how to use. It would still be possible to pick out a lot of
219 it from the waste heaps. These mines have lodes which strike east and west, and according to the geography of this part of the country it looks as if these lodes belong to the same district as St Agnes, already mentioned under 27 May.

St Michel, a village

In St Michel,[101] on the way to St Columb, which is nothing but a miserable village although it calls itself a town and sends two members to Parliament, I saw flagstaffs and banners hung up for three candidates. The postillion told me that there had been here such terrible revelling and drinking for two weeks that most of the inhabitants had ruined their health.

St Columb

St Columb is not of any greater importance although it does possess a few more buildings than St Michel, and today there was held here a curious meeting accompanied with 'bumpers' or the emptying of full tankards. Many of the red-faced clerics, who had been informed that I had
220 some knowledge of minerals and had travelled such a long way to visit the mines in Cornwall, invited me to partake of their punch-bowls. They showed me two kinds of ore that had been dug up three miles from here, from lodes 10 feet to 15 feet thick striking north-east and south-west. They believed that the ore samples contained silver or cobalt, and told me that Mr Bishop, who lived a mile away, was supposed to have stoneware plates, painted with [a pigment made from this ore].

Iron ore lode

I immediately betook myself there accompanied by an apothecary, who was very sure of his tale about the cobalt. However, I found that the colour was violet, instead of blue as it should have been, and that the alleged cobalt ore was a blue iron ore, attracted by the magnet after it had been roasted. The other one, which was supposed to be silver bearing, was a blue-grey iron ore with small, shining specks. It was slightly attracted by the magnet, even before roasting. This is a very rare phenomenon
outside Sweden, and has influenced an English 221
writer of history to call it lode stone or magnet stone. I can hardly doubt that a good iron could be made from these ores, but it is fortunate for Sweden and other 'Kingdoms of Iron' that the ore lodes are located in a country without forests and also some miles from the coast, which makes the transport to Wales or Scotland difficult and expensive.

Bodmin, a country town

I continued my trip from St Columb to Bodmin, 13 miles to the east, which is an extensive and, according to Cornish standards, fairly considerable town. They were now having the biggest market of the year, the main activity being the sale of cattle.

Grazing for oxen and sheep

The surrounding country provides a great supply of cattle, because the extensive moors or wastelands lying between Bodmin and
Launceston afford grazing that is particularly 222
good for oxen. They are let out at the beginning of the month of March and remain there, without further surveillance, until the end of the month of December. Only the tail is marked with some particular colour so that the owner can recognise them again, when they are brought in at the end of the year. During the three months that the animals are kept inside, they are fed on corn-straw. The sheep are treated in the same way, but they are allowed to stay out the whole year on the commons, which do not have any forests or wild animals that could cause them harm. The sheep are not even given the small amount of care of being taken in winter-

Fig. 115 Quoit

time, except when too much snow falls, which, however, very seldom occurs. On such occasions they are fed on the green leaves of ivy that grows by stone walls and around the oaks.
223 The sheep are shorn in the month of July, so that the wool has time to grow again before winter and cold returns. It is reckoned that each ewe produces an income of 5 to 6 shillings per year. In addition it reproduces its own kind without any expense for the owner, and provides the farmer with meat and milk if he so desires.

Ancient monument

On the road to Bodmin, not far from St Columb, I was shown four standing stones, with another one lying on top of them, all of considerable size. They consisted of a dark marble and are thought to have been used in a dim and distant past as an altar for sacrifices. This and similar structures are known as quoits in the Cornish language, which has fallen into disuse. The height of the standing stones above ground was 8 feet to 9 feet, the width 4 feet and the thickness 1½ feet. The structure is nowadays rather misshapen and leaning over, as can be seen clearly in the attached drawing no. 115.

A few miles from here, by the side of
Bodmin Moor, there are also said to be stones, 224
set in three circles, one outside the other. The stones are 4 feet to 6 feet high, and the inner circle is the highest and in this respect the structure shows some similarity to the 'stone-mountains' near Salisbury,[102] which has been a kind of temple and place of sacrifice for the former British inhabitants. These stones are called the Hurlers.

Tin streaming

In many places where the land was low-lying and where water was available, one saw the people busy in their stream or tin-washing works, which gives them a livelihood even if the work is

Fig. 116 Inn-keeper

quite wet and hard. The tin ore that is obtained in this locality is sold in Lostwithiel or Truro.

Publican of unusual girth

For a pot of cider the postillion showed me an inn-keeper who is supposed to be the heaviest in England just now. I was convinced that few could compete with him as far as fatness is concerned, although his height was not out of 22.
the ordinary. See drawing no.116

Large plain with road markers

On 29 May I set out from Bodmin in the morning for Launceston across the long moor

Fig. 117 Road-markers

Fig. 118/119 Launceston and Newport

or wasteland which is reckoned to be a distance of 22 miles. An occasional house, however, was to be seen from the road.

To guide travellers in misty weather, the people hereabouts have at times been conscientious and have erected high stones of granite (see drawing no. 117). Some of these were well worked and had water-filled ditches all round, as a hindrance to thoughtless people who might want to damage them. These standing stones and road-markers, shown by drawing 117, also serve the purpose of providing something for the cattle to rub themselves against, particularly the oxen, of which very many graze here. Otherwise there are no stones or trees on these hills and plains.

Old abandoned stream-works

226 Wherever a river or brook flows in the valleys, considerable remains of old stream-works can be seen, and in one place a number of shafts sunk along a line striking east and west. Most of these had fallen in, but nevertheless did not appear as old as the stream-works, which look as if time had simply melted them down.
The waste heaps consist nowadays mainly of earth and sand, although it is known from the experience of later times that earth and sand are washed away by water and that nothing but gravel of various sizes is thrown on the heaps.

In these rounded hills and wastelands the river Tamar has its source.[103] It separates Cornwall and Devonshire and flows into the sea at Plymouth.

Launceston, a town and its suburb Newport

Launceston (see drawing no. 118) was a border fortress built in the days when the Princes or Earls ruled Cornwall, and remains of the castle can still be seen. At that time it was called 'Castle Terrible'. Newport (see drawing no. 119)
is a suburb of Launceston, but nevertheless it 227
has the right to send two members to Parliament, just the same as Launceston.

Members of Parliament

The distribution of the seats is here rather peculiar, the same as in so many other places in Cornwall, because sometimes quite sizeable towns have no members whereas some other contemptible little village has the right to elect two. The County of Cornwall elects altogether 44 members, who all are of the same opinion as the King.[104]

The County of Devonshire

On leaving Launceston I also left Cornwall and entered the County of Devonshire, which on this side is more mountainous than Cornwall.

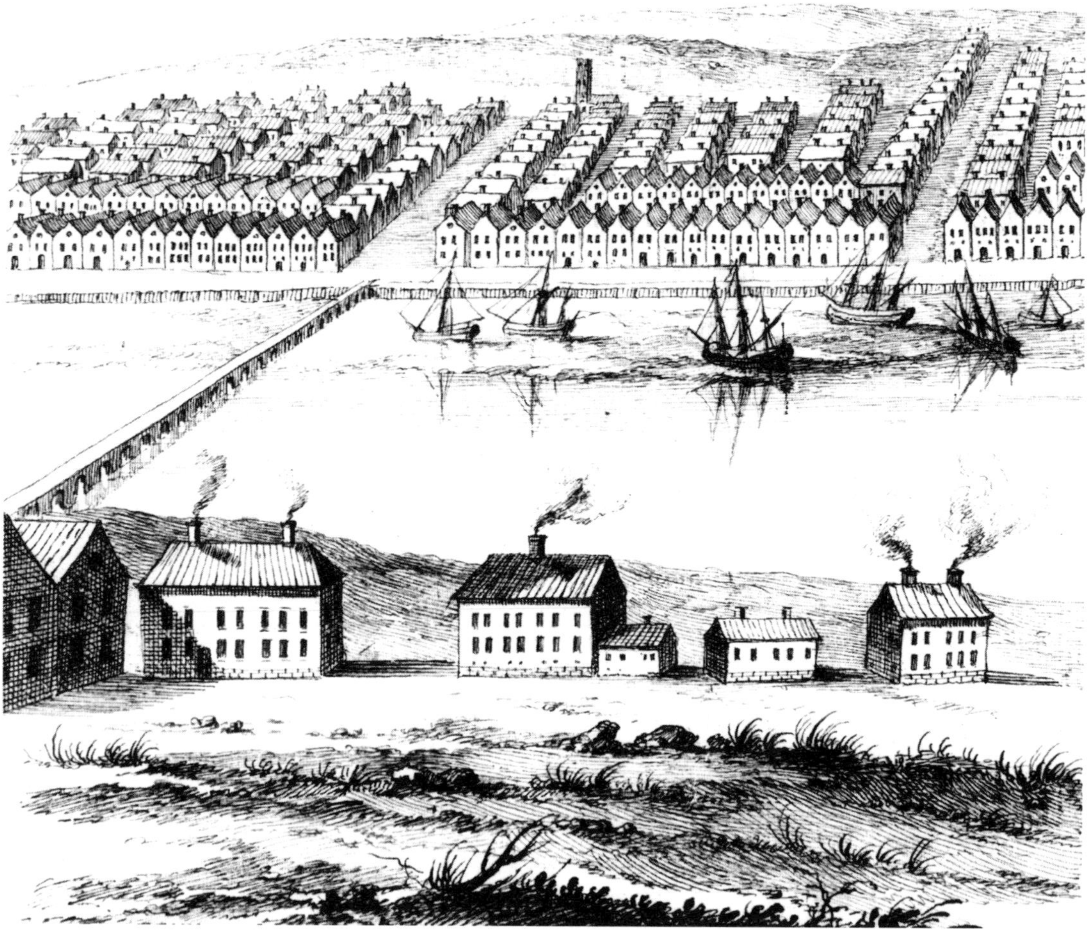

Fig. 120 Bideford

But the mountains are rounded and covered with earth, so that Dartmoor and other wastelands that are found there could very well be cultivated if there were only enough people in the country.

Holsworthy, a market town

The first town that I met in this province was Holsworthy, which lies 14 miles north of Launceston and is a large and important market
228 town, although it does not have the right to send members to Parliament. Neither has it been given consideration in any of the English travel books.

Sources of livelihood in Cornwall and Devonshire

As soon as one leaves Cornwall one sees the people doing other kinds of work. In Cornwall, most of the men are miners, and children and young women are occupied in the stream-works and on the dressing-floors. In Devonshire, on the other hand, one sees the spinning wheel, hears the looms banging and notices many other occupations connected with woollen manufacture.

Bideford, a seaport, its fisheries and trade in iron

Bideford (see drawing no. 120) is a seaport town that has a fairly good harbour at the outlet of a small river. It is located 19 miles from Holsworthy. Fishing is their main business, and a number of ships voyage to America and the Mediterranean. There is an anchor-forge here that uses 50 to 60 tons of iron yearly, mostly from Bilbao and Bristol. The latter consists of
English, Swedish and German ranges of sizes, 229
which here are sold at one price, £17.10s to £18 per ton, whilst the Spanish fetches £19.

Fig. 121/122 Barnstaple

Retailed, this iron gives a profit of 10s or more, according to the circumstances. William Ellis in Appledore, at the mouth of the river, is a wholesale iron merchant here. When the tide is out the ships are left sitting on the bottom, which consists of a light-coloured clay. The same thing happens in all ports at the outlet of rivers, in Cornwall as well as on the coasts of Devonshire. The bridge [across the river] is of stone and has 24 arches. The design is otherwise not remarkable. See drawing no. 120.

Barnstaple, a town and its manufactures

The 30th. Barnstaple (see drawing no. 121/122) lies eight miles from Bideford on a small river and can be reached by ships at high water. The town is well built and has a considerable trade in woollen manufactures made in the
230 surrounding countryside, and also, to some extent, in the town itself. A tannery and workshop for the preparation of sheepskin was also established here some time ago.

The iron trade in Barnstaple is not very large and most of the iron is supplied by Mr Robert Hanbury, a Quaker from Bristol, who supplies English, Swedish and Russian products. The consumption may reach 60 to 70 tons per year. Some small lots of Spanish iron are sometimes fetched from Bilbao, once a year generally, but I was told that there is nowadays none to be had. The price of the abovementioned makes is now £18.10s and £19 per ton. Mr Andrew, 'Mr Pasma' and William Rowe are the iron merchants here.

South Molton, a manufacturing town

From Barnstaple I took the road to South Molton, which is a considerable and populous manufacturing town, in which large quantities of 'Sallons', 'Plush', 'Bays', 'Tammy' and 'Pladt' are made, that are transported to Barnstaple for shipment.

Tiverton, a town and its school

Tiverton is located 19 miles from South Molton
and is considered to be the most beautiful and 231
populous town in Devonshire next to Exeter. Two rivers, the Exe and the Lowman meet here, and stone bridges over them were built a long time ago. In addition to the woollen manufacturers that are the usual business in Devonshire, the town also derives great benefits from the 'Free School' or 'University', which was founded by a cloth merchant here, and attracts a large part of the youth of the county.[105] In the River Exe there are large numbers of salmon and trout. During the course of 130 years this town has burnt down three times, but is, nevertheless, now quite well built up again.

Whetstone quarry

On the road between Tiverton and Wellington, a distance of 12 miles, I got into the company of

a farmer, who with eight horses had transported whetstone to Barnstaple, which he quarries on
232 his land six miles from Tiverton.

The advantages of limestone in agriculture

From this farmer I obtained information about the advantages of using limestone in farming. Most of the farmers in Devonshire use this instead of manure, however expensive and rare it is, in some places, particularly around Barnstaple, where they are compelled to obtain the raw limestone from Wales as well as the coal to burn it with. They then have to burn it in large kilns. One sack of burnt lime, two of which might make one barrel, are sold in this locality for 7d. A piece of land that requires one bushel of seed-corn, needs four such sacks. The lime is not spread on the fields immediately after burning, but is mixed with two-thirds parts of clay or other soil placed in alternate layers with the lime to make a heap out in the open. This mixing generally takes place in the month
233 of May and the heap is not disturbed until August when the lot is spread over a field as the harvest is carted in. Subsequently the fields will yield wheat for two years and barley the third. This fertiliser is reckoned to be best for layered or cold soil, but not suitable for sandy earth, unless it has previously been mixed with clay. If the lime were spread on the field during ploughing and sowing, immediately, without being mixed with earth and allowed to mature in the air, which is successfully done in Limousin and 'Basit' in France, it was considered that it would burn the seed. However, it is more likely that during the time it is lying in the heap mixed with the soil, it will attract further salts from the air and thus become more productive.

Remarks about red earth

Near Tiverton the red earth that was previously noticed in the neighbourhood of Exeter began to appear. This soil is incomparably light and spongy, and where it sweeps across the country
234 like a river it makes it fertile and lovely beyond description. One could easily be persuaded that Paradise had been moved here from Damascus in Asia. Many ages ago that was also such a pleasant and fertile land that some Orientals living in those parts invented the fable that Man himself, as the noblest and most precious of all earthly creatures, had originated there. But, as everything in this world is subject to decay and change, even this bliss could not forever be tied to one place. The earth gradually started to change its nature and instead of the red and highly fertile soil, a barren quartz sand slowly crept in, and by degrees gained predominance. The descendants, therefore, had reason to doubt whether the land they lived on was the same as that which in the days of their
forefathers had been so abundantly fruitful. 235

Spain is also a country that proves my theories regarding this subject, because it nowadays has so many sand-heaths and so much wasteland, whereas it is known from history that in olden times it was cultivated to a far greater extent. One never hears that the inhabitants suffered famine during the Punic Wars or that there was any lack of provisions during the many visits that often were made by Carthaginians and Romans.

Goose husbandry and its profitability

Between Tiverton and Wellington there were some small commons, upon which not only horses and cattle grazed, but also large numbers of flocks of geese. I was told that the latter give the inhabitants in these parts considerable profit although they do not work or give any care and attention to them. Their mature geese hatch many eggs, sometimes 20 and more, and are subsequently always careful to take their young to the grazing and back home again without anybody looking after them. A nearly fully grown
young goose sells for 18 pence in Tiverton, 236
which is three daler copper coin. Speaking of geese, I remember having seen, both here and in Cornwall, a quill through the two nostrils of the geese. This prevents them from crawling through the hedges and from flying over fencing and damaging fields and meadows.

Taunton, beautiful countryside and industrious people

31 [May]. Taunton (see drawing no. 123) is located in the middle of the lovely country that I have just described, and is not only populous but large and important. It lies in the most fertile and paradisiacal country and is still populated by industrious and hard-working people. Such industry was not heard of once throughout the Old Testament. The story of Adam and Eve tells us that they did not even have enough energy to provide themselves with clothes, let alone to sow and reap, but
they were driven out from paradise into a 237
barren land.

Fig. 123 Vale of Taunton

Woollens manufacture in Taunton
The manufacture of woollens is the main occupation that is followed here, and one sees persons of both sexes, from eight to 80 years old, engaged in the preparation of wool, spinning, weaving, dyeing, pressing, etc.
The best kinds of cloth generally made here are 'Sagathies', 'Duroys' and others. They are as a rule sold in Exeter. There are 1160 looms working here and a university for Quakers.

King's Sedge Moor, a large plain
The road continued across wide low-lying plains nearly all the way to Wells, which is 30 miles from Taunton. One could clearly see from the black peat soil, which is much in evidence everywhere on this plain, that it had been marshland and previously lake or sea. Now, owing to its fertility, it had reached a stage where it is suitable for breeding bullocks. It has lush grazing for innumerable horses and cattle.

Fig. 124/125 Wells and Glastonbury

In one or two places the plain had been drained
238 by ditches in the manner of the Dutch.

On the large plain, called King's Sedge Moor, there are two hills on which churches were built in Catholic times, and their ruins can be seen from far away.

Glastonbury, an old monastery

Glastonbury (see drawing no. 124) lies on one of the hills, and has been a most remarkable monastery, renowned for many miracles. Arthur, who was one of the kings of the Saxons, is thought to be buried here.

The town of Wells, its Cathedral and stocking factories

Wells (see drawing no. 125), a small but beautiful town, is only four miles from Glastonbury and has a lovely Cathedral, which is supposed to have been founded by King Ina, but later rebuilt in the Gothic style of architecture. The Cathedral still has a fairly large income and many clerics, who officiate at the services and belong to the choir. Here are 27 prebendaries, 19 canons, a dean, a chancellor, a precentor and three archdeacons. The Bishop's Palace is very old but magnificently constructed, and provided with
both embankments and a moat. 239

In this town large quantities of stockings are manufactured and the womenfolk here always have their knitting at hand, even when walking in the street, just as in the province of Dalecarlia in Sweden.

Mendip Hills

Above the town rise the Mendip Hills, where in former days there were many lead and zinc mines, but I first took the road towards the north-west to see the well-known cave called the Wookey Hole.

Wookey Hole, a cave

Wookey Hole (see drawing no. 126) is located two miles from the town of Wells, in the precipitous slope of a limestone mountain called the Mendip Hills, where a spring gushes forth. It is uncertain if the spring was the cause of the cave, or if the cave was the cause of the spring, or if the cave was made by human hand, thus uncovering the spring in this place where it still has its source. There are also other holes and

Fig. 126 Wookey Hole

Fig. 127 Old mines

caves in the slope of the limestone mountain, and each one of them in its time and its turn
240 has been a spring.

Undoubtedly there have been many more of them up above, although the erosion of the water has lowered the water level, thus causing the caves to be abandoned and destroyed many ages ago.

What does give one reason to believe that this cave is the work of humans is the fact that there are innumerable holes and pits on top of the mountains above it, which are remains of the mining activities of the ancient people. It appears therefore probable that the Ancient Britons drove adits from the valley to carry away the water from their mines, as there is no water right down to the level of the spring or the entrance to the adit. The entrance to the cave is a letter 'A' (Fig. 126) and from there one comes to a number of large, vaulted chambers with loose material dumped in them, closely resembling a badly worked mine. One also walks down some stone steps until one reaches the same level as the outlet of the water, Letter 'B'.

241 Below the vaults there is dripping water in many places, which forms stalactites, or a kind of limy marble of various shapes. As the visitor walks past, the people who rent the cave point them out and mention their names in a singing dialect.

Paper mill

A little way from the cave or the outlet of the water there is a paper mill, driven by the same water. It is provided with knives in the Dutch manner and, owing to the clear water available, the paper that is made here is considered the whitest in England. From the cave, where one is presented with some stones against payment of a penny, I took the road up the hill, which is quite high. On top there is a large plain where a horse race is held most years in the month of April.

Old and abandoned lead and zinc mines

As I advanced further on the plain, I noticed more pits and my guide told me that they were
old mines, of which some were still in operation 242
and were viewed by me (see drawing no. 127). These mines are all worked for lead, but with it there is always calamine, which seems to originate from the destruction of the lead. At each one of these lead-mines there was a narrow shaft sunk to a depth of 30, 40 to 60 yards. When they reach a fair depth in the rock, a crosscut, striking north and south, is driven to find the lead lodes, which generally strike east and west or north-east and south-west. The lodes referred to are mostly vertical, but sometimes dipping south or near the vertical. They are 8 inches, 12 inches to 18 inches thick and also increase to considerable thickness when two lodes happen to meet. It often occurs that the miners come upon the workings of the ancients, which are said to be so narrow that in
some places it is impossible to squeeze in. 243
This gives the people reason to believe that the former inhabitants of the country were of much

Fig. 128 Washing of lead ore

smaller stature than the present. The solution to the mystery is that these mines and their crosscuts, that were worked a very long time ago, have become narrower through deposition of limestone from the lime-containing water.

The ore is raised in small buckets by means of a hand-winch, and then dumped and screened. The fines are washed in a low buddle as shown by the attached drawing no. 128. The clean ore is sold for £8.8s per ton and calamine, always obtained with the lead, for £4.4s per ton. Most of the lead mines are said to be along the road to Bath and they are all worked by the farmers in the locality. There are supposed to be more than 30 of the mines.
244 All mines within two miles of Wookey Hole are free from water, right down to the level of the stream leaving the cave.

The hills around here consist of a greyish kind of limestone. There is now nothing left of the workings of the ancients except a large number of pits spread around the field over a distance of several miles. The lead ore mined here is a coarse, cubical galena that also contains some silver. The calamine lies on the side of the lead vein, and occurs as a red earth or a light grey crystalline mass that resembles some types of limestone and is generally coated with yellow zinc ochre.

Smelting of lead and zinc ores

The lead ore is sold in Bristol and smelted at Hotwells in reverberatory furnaces, specially designed for the purpose, which will be described later on. There are also lead furnaces at the copper-works four miles from Bristol. The calamine is used partly by the brass-works
around Bristol, and partly for the zinc-smelting 245
works established at Warmley by Mr Champion several years ago, but still kept very secret. Nevertheless, a similar zinc-smelting process has recently been started at the new copper-smelting works belonging to Mr Williams and his partners, and it is encroaching upon Mr Champion's to some extent. In this country nobody worries about such a thing, because everybody is free to establish any kind of works that they wish.

Notes and references

69 Missing in MS.

70 These were undoubtedly the mines in the Polgooth Valley, although this is not mentioned by name. It is known that in 1741 Polgooth was one of only three mines in Cornwall rich enough to have a steam engine. See Barton, D B, *A Historical Survey of the Mines and Mineral Railways of East Cornwall and Devon* (1964), p.10.

71 RRA writes 'mine owners', but according to Justin Brooke (private communication), there is considerable confusion in Cornwall, even today, as to what constitutes the ownership of a mine. It can mean the owner of the minerals in the ground, or mineral owner; the lessee of the mine; or a shareholder (also known as an adventurer) or person who holds shares in a partnership working a mine.

72 Chalcopyrite.

73 Generally known as a buddle.

74 Box filled with water.

75 Known as 'black tin'.

76 Strictly speaking, the mineral owner.

77 Anthracite that will pass through a screen with one-eighth-inch holes, according to Chambers Technical Dictionary (1947 edn.).

78 Information missing in MS, but Justin Brooke states that this would have been 2s per block of 300 lb.

79 This would have been the Duke of Cornwall's coinage fee, at 4s per Cornish Stannary hundredweight of 120 lb.

80 RRA would probably have known about water-pressure engines from his travels on the Continent. They were certainly used in Cornwall around 1800, according to D B Barton in *A History of Tin Mining and Smelting in Cornwall* (1967), p.38.

81 Literal translation: these could either be water wheels or water-pressure engines.

82 Chalcopyrite and chalcocite, respectively.

83 Should probably be Bristol.

84 In fact in Gloucestershire, on the east bank of the River Wye.

85 More likely, cubic foot.

86 A member of the well-known family from that village, now known as Marazion.

87 The mineral lord.

88 Now known as the Merry Maidens.

89 More like 25 to 30 miles.

90 These mines were in what is now known as the Botallack-Pendeen district, which extends along the coast from Aire Point in the south to Morvah in the north. The best known were Botallack, Levant and Geevor.

91 Now known as Marazion.

92 The prominent feature here is St Michaels Mount, an island in the bay. There may have been an error in transcription.

93 Missing from MS.

94 Azurite or chessylite.

95 Copper mining actually began in Cornwall about 1583 (Justin Brooke, private communication).

96 'Witebade' has not been identified; black blende was probably zinc sulphide; mundic was either mispickel or iron pyrites.

97 Not identified.

98 RRA's figures of taxes paid on tin are at variance with the facts. No fee was payable to the King; post-groats were charged at two of the four quarterly coinages. Dues of about one-sixth were payable on copper to the mineral owner. Dues on both copper and tin were generally paid in kind; they began to be paid in cash on copper about 1725 (Justin Brooke, *ibid.*)
The paragraph should read:
'Black tin is generally paid for in tin metal. Four shillings per hundredweight are paid in duty to the Duke of Cornwall. Post-groats are paid at two coinages of the four held each year.
The mines pay one-sixth in duty to the mineral owner on copper and one-third on tin. When a tin mine is started on bounded land belonging to the Duke of Cornwall, dues of one-fifteenth are paid to the bounders or owners of the ground, which altogether amounts to one-third part. For copper, nothing is paid.'

99 These dimensions seem improbably large and the proportions unusual. At six tons total weight, the plates would only be about one-eighth of an inch thick and the structure would be likely to buckle under its own weight. These boilers were commonly in the shape of circular haystacks, with the height more nearly equal to the diameter. It is possible that RRA over-estimated the size of the part hidden by brickwork.

100 Approximately 500 gallons per minute.

101 The old name for Mitchell.

102 Stonehenge.

103 The true source is not far from Hartland Point on the north coast, but one or two tributaries rise on Bodmin Moor.

104 On what subject is not clear: this is a literal translation.

105 Blundell's School.

Journey 5c Bristol to Pontypool

Bristol, Hotwells, Woolland, Publowe, Warmley, Keynsham, Crews Hole (25 June), Durdham Common (25 June), Caerleon, Newport, Abercarn, Pontypool.

The town of Bristol, its trade and shipping

1 June. Bristol is located by two small rivers four miles from the sea, but it has such high tides, which can rise and fall up to 30 feet or 32 feet, that the largest ships can go up into the canals enclosing the city on three sides. This advantage, together with the fact that in times of war, ships bound for Bristol do not have to pass the French
246 coast, made this place a very long time ago a large and powerful commercial city, competing with London both in business and wealth. They trade with every place on earth and are also in a position to sell the goods that are brought back as return freight. They can obtain in the country enough goods to keep their ships occupied continuously, some of it in the form of their own manufactures, such as copper, brass, lead, iron and glass. The Shipping and Trading Company for Guinea is here reckoned to be amongst the most advantageous, and it gives them very large markets for all kinds of manufactures. In addition there is also the American Trade that brings back pig iron, tar, tobacco and other raw materials.

Bristol prices in force, June 1754

Iron pots, large and small, per ton	£13.0s.0d
English bar-iron	£17.0s.0d
247 Ditto	£18.0s.0d
225 sheets of tinplate in a box size 13$\frac{3}{4}$" × 10$\frac{3}{4}$"	£2.12s.6d
Ditto Black, 1" smaller	£2.11s.6d
Tar from Carolina 'Brill'[106] weighs 256 lb	7s.6d
Note: 'Mr Bantz'[107] gets for import:	
Iron stamps for ore dressing per ton in Cornwall	£1.3s.6d
Anvils and hammers, ground per lb	15d
Copper in lumps, ditto	12d
Spelter	8d
For 1 ton iron from Bristol to Bewdley is paid in carriage per load	5s.0d

Mr 'Joh. Cly Spoon' is an agent in Bewdley, and for 1$\frac{1}{4}$ cwt nails from Bewdley to Bristol the carriage is 4d and the same amount from Bewdley to Birmingham.

The City is mighty large, but not very remarkable as far as buildings are concerned, with the exception of Queen's Square, College Green, Royal Exchange etc. The most important thing is that the merchants here enjoy the great 248
advantage of having their warehouses and offices right by the quayside.

Iron foundries in Bristol

In Bristol there are four iron foundries that mainly cast pots and other small castings in sand. The principal foundry belongs to Mr Hillhouse and Co., who also own a forge where anvils, hammers, ships requisites and small anchors are made. Iron pots, cast here, are sold for £13 per ton. The cast iron used here comes partly from America and partly from Lancashire, but most of it is purchased from Holland and other places in the form of old cannon etc, that cost £6 to £7 per ton.

Glass furnaces and factories for bottles in Bristol

Amongst the manufactories in this town are glass factories, including some for bottles with 249
furnaces as shown by drawing no. 129 [letters missing]. Altogether, there are 15 of them, but not all are in operation. Inside, the furnace is built like any other glass furnace (Letter 'A') with calcining furnaces on the side (Letter 'B'). The work is done with four crucibles or pots, two on each side, opposite each other. (Letter 'C'). The other two sides that cross are the fire-places or opening 'D', to throw in the coal that rests on thick two-inch-square iron bars. (Letter 'E'). The furnace proper is vaulted underneath, like an adit, with two openings (Letter 'F') on each side, to provide draft for the furnace and the fireplaces. The high and lower wall around the glass furnace, and designated by letter 'G', only serves as a chimney stack and to carry away the smoke. It is generally 70 feet to 80 feet high and made of brick masonry. The glass-furnace proper is built of brick made of Stourbridge Clay, 2 feet long 5 feet wide and 6 inches thick and which cost 2s.6d each, smaller ones 1s to 2s. 250

Instead of sand, the Stourbridge clay is mixed with crushed and ground bricks that have

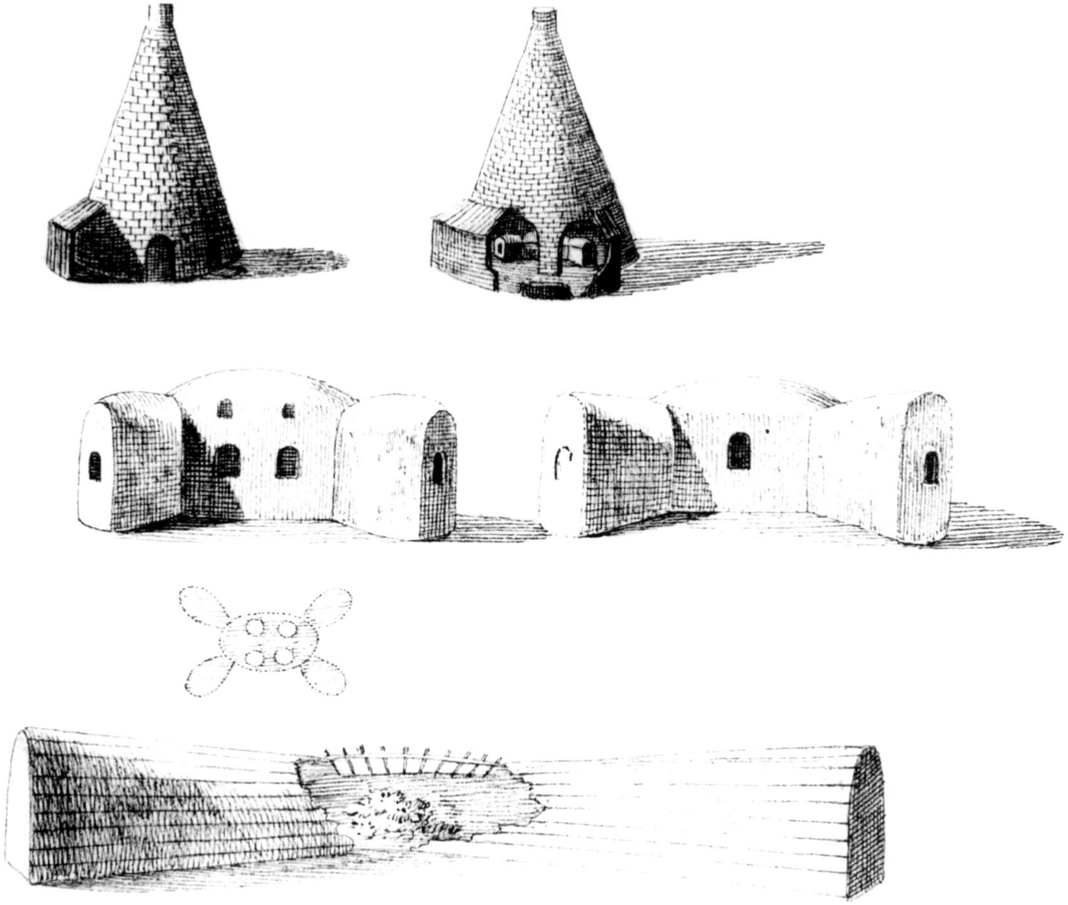

Fig. 129 Bottle factory furnaces

already been used in glass furnaces. It is, however, generally necessary to throw away the outside parts that have been glazed, otherwise they could act as a flux for the whole of the brick. For the grinding of the used brick a kind of oil mill is used, consisting of a horizontal stone with a vertical one rolling on top of it, as shown in the attached drawing no. 130.
The upper stone is always provided with a cast-iron tyre, $1\frac{1}{2}$ inches thick and of the same width as the rim of the wheel, in order to prevent wear of the rim itself.

For the manufacture of glass bottles the following is used:
(1) Sea sand, as ordinarily found on the seashore.
(2) Soap ash, or potash, which is extracted from wood, with some limestone added.
251 (3) 'Shrope', a bluish iron slag.
(4) Kelp, a kind of soda or barilla, burnt from seaweed in Wales. This is quite salty on the tongue, and serves as a flux for the other ingredients.
(5) Limestone is also used.
(6) Old bottles.

The sea sand, the soap ash and the kelp must first be mixed in the arches or vaults (which are designated by Letter 'b') See drawing no. 129. [letters missing] for 10, 12 to 13 hours. They are then put into the glass pots in their correct proportions together with iron slag. The pots must always be kept red hot in their furnaces so that they do not expand too quickly and crack when put into the glass furnace proper.
The iron slag, which contains some iron, is very bad for the pots because the iron generally eats into them.

To remove the pots from the glass furnace
and put them back again an iron trolley is used, 252
designed as shown in the attached drawing no. 131. One hundredweight of glass is charged into each pot and measured by the Customs

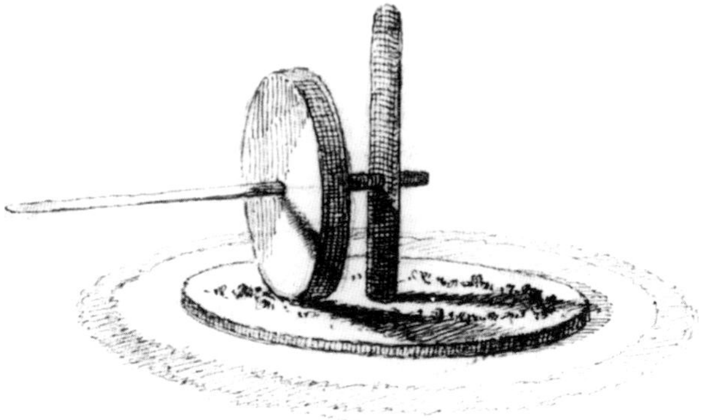

Fig. 130 Brick-crushing mill

Fig. 131 Iron trolley

Officer with an iron rod. For this the Government is paid 2s.4d.

At each glass furnace there are four master glass-blowers, two on each side of the hearth, paid 25s per week.
Ditto four workmen paid 18s per week.
Ditto four workmen 15s per week.
Ditto four workmen 10s per week.
Ditto four workmen 4s per week.

A week's work is called a furnace.
One furnace of work on both sides is 240 dozen bottles, and anything produced above this figure is paid for extra.

240 dozen bottles are called a complement.
One sack of coal, or three bushels, costs 7d here, 1½ to 2 tons of pit coal are burnt per day.
Each dozen bottles sells for 20d.
253 Ditto for name or brand 4d.

If the bottles are exported, the duty is refunded, which is called getting a drawback. This only amounts to 14d per dozen.

In Bristol there are now only five glass furnaces for window glass in operation, but a number that are idle. In addition to the above-mentioned glass furnaces for bottles there are three that make window glass. The design is virtually the same as that of the preceding, with the exception that on each side of the furnace there is a smaller and a larger hole, in which the blown bulb of glass is placed for reheating when it has cooled off. A hole is then made in the end of the bulb, which is placed against the flaming fire that is kept going in another smaller furnace, with a large, round opening as shown by attached drawing no. 132. The blowpipe to which the bulb is fixed is placed in an iron hook and rotated, with the bubble in front of the fire
254 when the glass, due to the rotation or the so-called centrifugal force, becomes flatter and

Fig. 132 Window-glass furnace

flatter and yields and expands to a round disc 4 feet to 4 feet 6 inches in diameter. This disc is subsequently placed in the cooling ovens to be cooled for several days. Afterwards it is cut into two and packed in baskets, here called crates. Each crate holds 24 halves, namely: 12 halves with the thick centre that was fitted to the blowpipe, which are called 'bullseyes' and the 12 others are called 'small halves'. A crate generally weighs 111 to 115 lb. There are four factories for white glass in Bristol and the furnaces are built in the same way as the ones already mentioned, although without calcining kilns on the side. All firing is done with pit coal. The composition of the glass is potash, soda or kelp, fine pearl-sand from the Isle of Wight, red lead, white arsenic and saltpetre, but the proportions are a secret that they did not wish
255 to disclose.

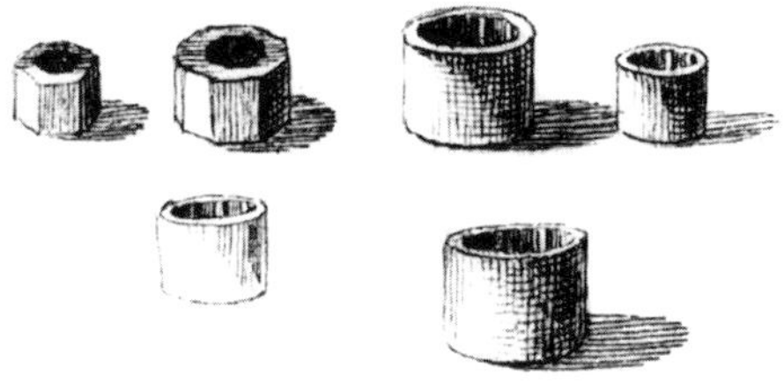

Fig. 133 Glass pots

The duty on this glass is paid in the same way, according to the weight, ascertained by measuring in pots, as described in connection with window glass. The amount of the duty is 9s.4d per hundredweight. The glasses here are made in every shape and fashion, with or without bubbles and twists in the stem, and are sold by the piece, and the workmen are paid by the complement. The pots are illustrated in drawing no. 133. An ordinary wineglass with twists in the stem costs 4d.

Soap-boilers at Bristol

In the city of Bristol there are also many soap-boilers, who buy their potash from Wales and Danzig and the tallow from Ireland. The ordinary white soap sells for 56s per 100. The ash used by soap-makers is mixed with lime, before it is subjected to leaching. The residue after leaching
256 is sold to the bottle glass furnaces.

Salt-boilers at Bristol

In addition there are four salt-boilers, who buy rock-salt from Lancashire and Liverpool and pay £7.5s per ton. It is subsequently dissolved in water in wooden vats, to which the water is supplied by a horse-driven pump. Then it is boiled in large, iron salt-pans, 8 feet long, 5 feet wide and 1½ feet deep, that simmer for ten to 12 hours before the crystallisation starts, when the fire is dampened down. At the start of the boiling, ox-blood and a few egg whites are added, which are said to cause precipitation and separation of the impurities from the salt. The salt coming from here is very fine and completely white. It is sold at 10s for two bushels or 100 lb in weight. Salt for salting down fish and meat must be boiled very slowly and simmered for four days, whereas the boiling process already described can be carried out in one day. If boiled too quickly, the salt would not be so coarse and form such large crystals as this
use requires. 257

Factories for pipes, turpentine, lamp-black and other goods at Bristol

There are a large number of pipe factories that obtain their clay from Wales, the Isle of Wight and Poole in Dorset. There are also resin distillers, producing distilled turpentine oil. Lamp-black is burnt, all of which is carried out at St James or the western part of Bristol. The resin secreted by spruce and fir trees in Carolina and New York is called turpentine and costs 6s.6d per hundredweight. But the spirits of turpentine that is distilled from it sells for 36s per hundredweight. Rosin is the residue after the distillation and it sells for 9s per hundredweight, and black rosin for 8s. For each barrel of turpentine resin, brought over from America, the Government pays a bounty for 'encouragement' of 1s.6d but for the tar, 3½ to 4s per barrel. When it gets to Bristol it is sold for 7s.6d per barrel.

The Swedish and Norwegian tar is
considered to be better and to have more body 258
and a better smell, but cannot be sold at the same price as the American.

At the same factory they also make pigments for watercolours. These are ground by perpendicular millstones, (see drawing no. 134 [missing from MS]), that were formerly used in a Spanish snuff factory, now shut down, since the Scottish snuff has become popular. This happened during the war and was said to be the result of a rumour spread around that the Spaniards had put poison in the snuff to kill Englishmen.

Fig. 135 Hotwells Spa

'Venetian Red' is made from a red iron ore and sells for 14s.6d per hundredweight.
'Spanish Brown' is made from brown iron ore and sold for 4s to 5s per hundredweight.
'Yellow Ochre' is made from iron ochre and sells for 4s to 5s per hundredweight.
'Lomlach' is sold for 10s to 20s.
259 'English Finch' is a yellow colour made from a gravel called wadwax,[108] which poor women collect for small payment. When the pigment has been extracted by leaching it is filled into skins and sold at 32s per hundredweight.

This considerable factory, which occupies virtually the two sides of an entire street in the city of Bristol, belongs to 'Mr Vetter' of St James.

Hotwells Spa

Hotwells Spa or 'St Vincentz Rock', which is shown by the attached drawing no. 135, is located two miles from Bristol, between high hills, on the banks of the River Avon, which all ships to or from Bristol must pass. This Spa is not very old, but nevertheless, a number of houses and lodgings have been built, and their number increases year by year as more and more people go there. The waters of Hotwell are lukewarm and contain dissolved lime or salt as
can be seen when tartaric acid is added, which 260
gives the solution a milky colour that can be clarified again by sulphuric acid. This water is supposed to have the special quality of keeping better in bottles than any other. A large quantity of it is, therefore, sent to America and all over Europe, which gives the glass-houses in Bristol a considerable turnover and advantage. Each dozen bottles filled with Hotwell water costs 1s and that amounts to a large sum of money brought in every year. Those who come here to use the well pay a subscription of 5s in the pump-room, and already, at the beginning of the season, there were 50 subscribers.

Mill for pottery glaze

Opposite Hotwell, across the river lies a mill, (see drawing no. 136) for the stamping and grinding of glazing for pottery. It is driven by another spring, which gushes forth at the foot of the beetling limestone crag on that side in the
same way as the Hotwell spring does on the 261
opposite bank. However, this mill only has a head of water twice in 24 hours, when the water in the river is low.[109]

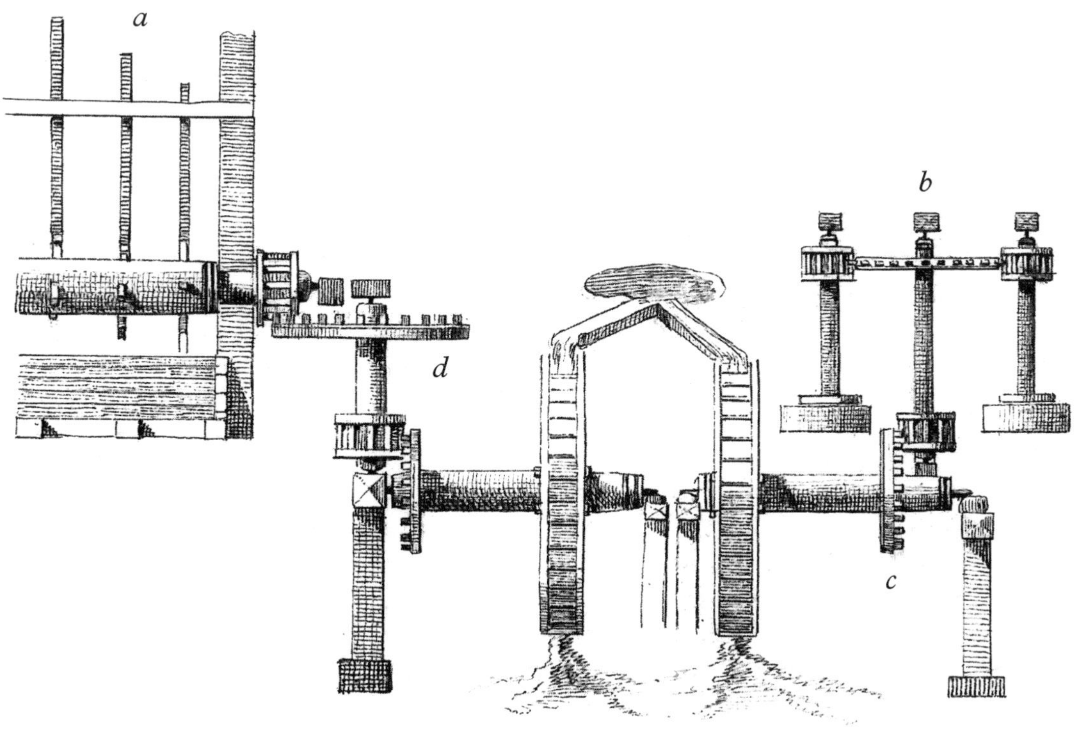

Fig. 136 Stamp- and stone-drive trains (letters added)

Pottery glaze

The glaze is prepared in the following way: lead and tin are burnt to ash in a reverberatory furnace and then melted together with quartz sand. The product is a white glass, which is red in spots after the melting but becomes white when it is stamped and ground.

The design of stamps and the mills is shown by the aforementioned drawing no. 136, letters 'a' and 'b'.[110] The trundle wheel 'c' drives six pairs of stones and the trundle wheel 'd', six pairs of stones in addition to the stamps. After stamping, the glass is ground in a tub full of water. The man who lives here and supervises
262 the grinding is paid 7s per week and has a cold bath as well, which is also of some value to him.[111] The mill belongs to 'Mr Franco' who has a glass furnace near the Church of St Mary Redcliffe, where this mixture is turned into glass.

Lead Smelter

A stone's throw further up on the bank of Bristol's river lies a lead smelting-house, where galena is smelted in a reverberatory furnace belonging to Mr .....[112] The furnace is built according to the attached drawing no. 137. It is 8 feet square, not including the fireplace. The height outside is 7 feet and the bottom is covered with Stourbridge clay, as is the whole interior of the furnace. The hearth is deepest at the centre and here the lead collects, as it melts around the sides where the flame is hottest. *263A*[113]

As soon as a part of the lead has been melted and has collected in the hearth, it is removed and kept warm in an iron crucible by means of a coal fire below it. The removal of the lead takes place a number of times during the smelting of a ton of galena, which is the quantity generally charged.

The smelting of seven-and-a-half 'skeppund' or one ton of galena usually takes ten to 11 hours. One ton of galena yields from six to nine hundredweight lead.[114] Ten tons of galena are smelted per week. One furnace is run by four workmen, two master-smelters and two furnace hands. Twenty bushels of pit coal are required for each smelting and possibly more, because nobody keeps any accurate account of it. The coal here costs 9d per sack, which is one horse-load. The lead is cast in iron moulds, as shown by Fig. no. 138a, which hold 128 lb lead, *263B*
weighed on a balance during the pouring.

Fig. 137 Reverberatory furnace in lead smelter

Lead shot is sold for 17s.6d per hundredweight and large quantities of it are made in Bristol.

Refining of lead containing silver

At the works here described, there are two smelting furnaces, but only one working now. At the Crew's Hole copper-works, there are another two furnaces, but neither of them is working owing to shortage of ore. When there is silver in the galena, it is recovered from the lead by refining in a small refining hearth with bellows on one side [see Fig. 138b]. The hearth proper consists of a round kettle of iron that
264 can be taken out to be lined with bone ash and then be put back in again. The diameter of the hearth is only 15 inches. The refining hearth is not being used nowadays because the ore obtained from the Mendip Hills is too poor in silver to make its recovery a paying proposition.

Rolling of tinplate

The Woolland sheet- or tinplate mill lies five miles to the west of Bristol[115] and belongs to Mr Palmer and Co.[116]

This mill is furnished with rolling mills constructed in the usual way, though somewhat large in proportion to the size of the sheets made here. One size is $14\frac{3}{32}$ inches long and $10\frac{1}{8}$ inches wide, another is $14\frac{1}{4}$ inches long and $10\frac{1}{2}$ inches wide. The mills are shown in the attached drawing no. 139. They also had here the measurements of another kind of sheet, of which nothing has been made so far. This is 17 inches long and 12 inches wide and is

Fig. 138a Lead casting

Fig. 138b Lead-refining hearth

265 reckoned as a 'double' compared with the others.

In two stands of rolls, 3000 boxes or small chests can be made of the above-mentioned tin plates.[117] Each box holds 225 sheets or plates and weighs one-and-a-quarter hundredweight or 140 English pounds. The best part of 200 tons of iron is consumed per year. For this purpose nothing but the highest quality English iron from Wales [sic] is used. This iron is forged into bars 4½ inches wide and half-an-inch thick and 10 feet long or more. The longer they are, the smaller is the loss through the defects to which the end pieces are susceptible. The shearing of the bars is done by a shear that is forced up by a cam driven by the water wheel. The sheared length is 10 inches.[118] These sheared bars are first charged into a mill-furnace to be heated. The furnace is
266 constructed according to the attached drawing no. 139 and is 4 feet wide, and 6 feet long, not including the fire grate, which is in the back. Each stand of rolls requires one furnace for heating. The heated bars pass through the rolls seven to eight times, and after each pass the rolls are screwed tighter together. The screwing down is done by one of the men at the stand, when the other one catches the sheet on the opposite side, passing it back above the top roll to go through the mill a second time, and so on.

When the first heat has been lost, the sheets are again put in the furnace for reheating, and when they are taken out they are doubled and pass through the rolls again a few times. The third time they are quadrupled, but the fourth time two sheets are separated from the other two only to be doubled again[119] and once again quadrupled. The result is that a piece of iron
14 inches long, 4½ inches wide and 1 inch 267
thick is rolled into eight sheets 14 inches long and 10½ inches wide, not counting the jagged edges, which are cut off. Specially made patterns of iron are used to mark out the final size of the sheets, which are cut accordingly.

After the sheets have been cut, they are heated again and then put into the lees, which is an acid water, prepared from wheat-bran. The latter costs 7d to 8d per bushel here.

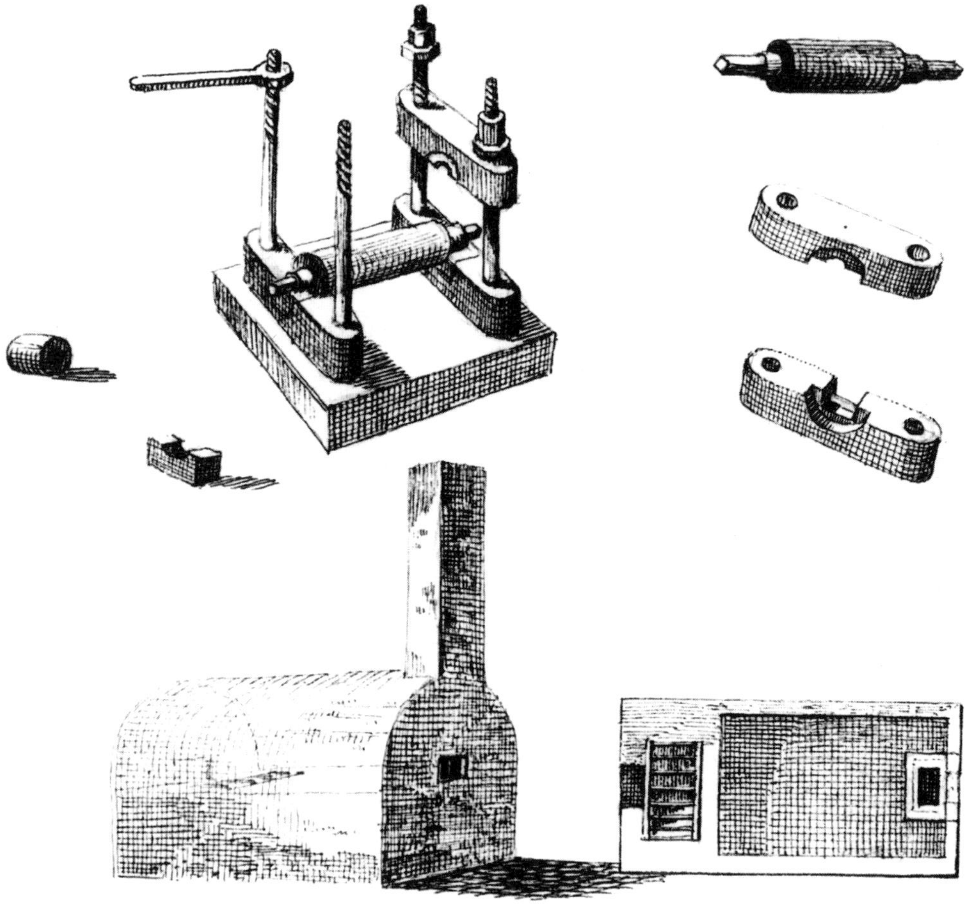

Fig. 139 Tinplate mills

The bran is placed in wooden tubs that stand above the heating furnaces, and water is poured on top. The mixture is allowed to go sour for three to four days, before the sheets are put into it. The sheets are generally allowed to soak in the lees for 24 hours and are then taken up and scoured and thrown into clean water until they are to be tinned, when they are put into the large kettle, filled with molten tin and grease
268 or tallow.

When the sheets are put in the kettle the tallow must be cooled with a little water, because otherwise too much cold material would enter it, as generally 75, 80 to 100 sheets go in at the same time.[120] The sheets are allowed to remain in the kettle one-and-a-half hours but, if the sheets are bad,[121] longer time is required up to two-and-a-half hours. When this operation is complete, the sheets are taken up from the kettle and placed on a grid, which can be seen in greater detail in drawing no. 140.[122]

Another workman takes them from there and dips them in the kettle, which has now been cooled down to a lower temperature for the polishing, and puts them back on the grid again. From there they are taken by a third man, to be dipped in a small trough [with molten tin] an inch deep to remove the thick tin on the edge of the sheets. They are afterwards scoured with wheat-bran, and packed in boxes for sale. The workers here were paid by the
week, because the mill is still new and not quite 26
finished. The rolling master gets 14s and his assistant, 8s to 10s per week.

Forge for copper sheet and deep kettles
All the iron used for this rolling is English.
A short distance above the tinplate rolling mill described in the foregoing lies Publowe copper forge belonging to Mr Percival[123] and Co. Copper plates for large distillation vessels etc are forged here and sold for 15d per pound and

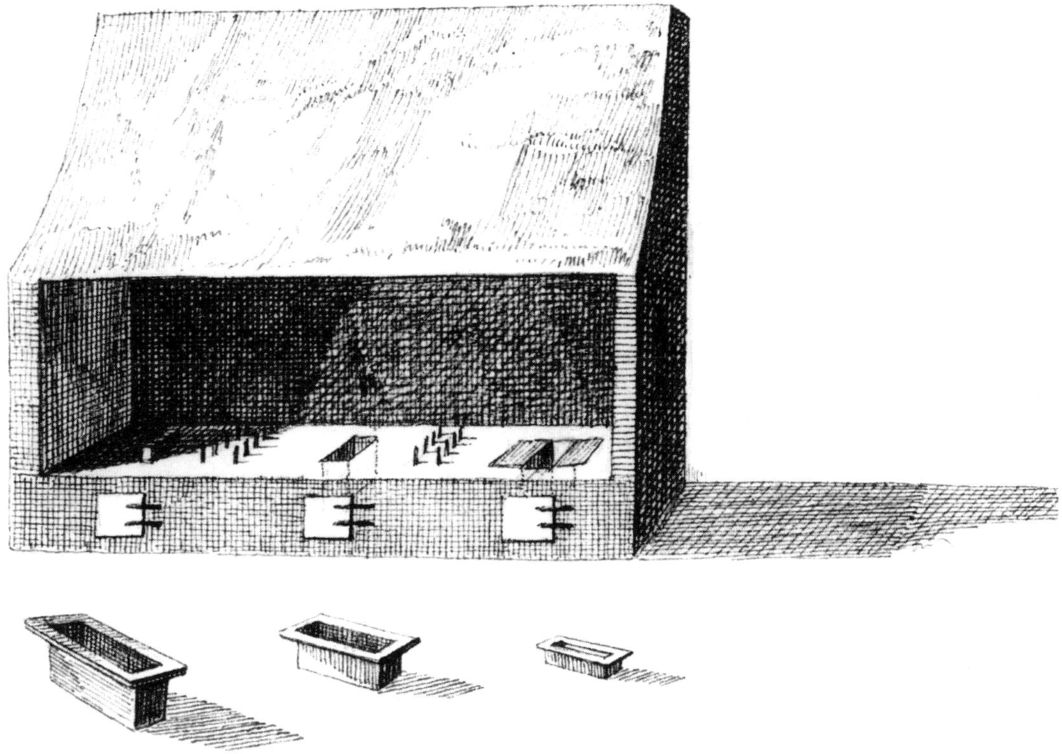

Fig. 140 Tinning furnace and kettles

some for 18d. On a level with this forge is another one with small hammers for deep kettles.

Forge for brass kettles

A little way below the tinplate rolling mill, on the same stream, lies Bye Mill,[124] a battery-works for brass kettles belonging to the 'Great Brass Co.'.[125] Copper in small lumps or bars
270 costs 12d per pound and £105 to £112 per ton.

Brick and Tile Yard

On the western side of Bristol, just outside the city, there are a number of brickyards (see drawing no. 141), where roofing tiles and bricks for the building trade are made of a clay found on the site and taken up from ponds. After the clay has been mixed and kneaded it is made into squares by placing the mould 'b',[126] which is an open frame, over 'a', and packing it with clay. The excess is cut off with a steel wire, fitted to a bow 'c'. The squares must then be partly dried before they can be bent to shape with the aid of another mould 'd'. The tiles are subsequently placed on shelves for drying and finally in the kiln for burning. Four people can make 750 tiles per day, for which the senior man is paid 2s, the next person 20d, the third and fourth 18d and 14d. Total costs for burning and everything else are said to amount to 11s.

One thousand pantiles or roofing tiles are 271
sold for 50 shillings, and 38,000 can be burnt at a time in one kiln. The burning takes five days and requires eight wagons of small coal, each wagon estimated to cost 17s.6d. Ordinary bricks cost 3s.6d in labour per 1000, not including expenses in connection taking up of the clay and burning. They are sold for 22s per 1000 and 33,000 can be burnt each time, requiring five to six days.

Warmley copper and brass-works

Warmley copper-works (see drawing no. 142) is located five miles south of Bristol,[127] and belongs to Mr Champion & Compagnie.
There are 15 copper-smelting furnaces in operation.
Ditto 12 brass furnaces.
Ditto four spelter or zinc furnaces.
Ditto one battery mill or forge with small hammers for kettles.
Ditto rolling mill to make sheets for kettles. 272
Ditto one rolling and slitting mill for brass wire.

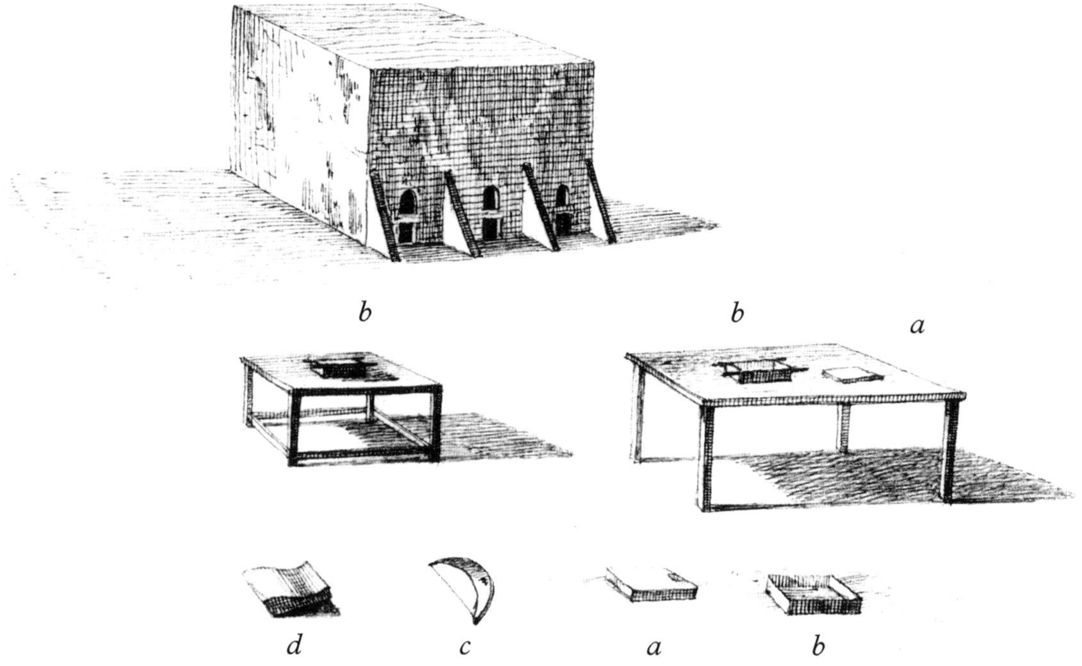

Fig. 141 Kiln and moulds (letters added)

The most curious thing about this mill is that it is driven by water, pumped to a height of 18 feet by a fire engine, and discharged into a large pond or reservoir, from which it flows to the water wheels and then back to the fire engine to be pumped up again.[128] Mr Champion told me that this fire engine cost £2000 to build and install and that in addition it requires £300 worth of maintenance every year.

Mr Champion's clerk or book-keeper said that the works uses 5000 bushels of coal every week, which, because they have their own coal mines, only costs three Swedish 'styfwer' per bushel.

The copper furnaces at Warmley are all built according to the same design as shown by drawing no. 143a. The length is 6 feet, not
273 including the fire-grate, which is 18 inches wide.

The width is 4 feet, where the hearth is widest. The furnace is 2 feet high above the fire grate and 8 inches at the other end by the chimney, in order to force the flame down on the ore or other material to be melted.

The ore is charged from above, through a small hole, which is closed by a brick when not in use. Each charge consists of four hundred-weight of ore and the operation is continued until the furnace hearth, which is 4½ inches to 6 inches deep and slopes inwards towards the tap-hole, is full of metal. The slag is raked off frequently between each new charge, and this continues until the ore that was charged last has been melted down. The smelting process requires six to eight hours before the furnace is full, but the time differs considerably depending on the quality and metal content of the ore. Nothing is added to the ore coming from
Cornwall, but when they have a very slow- 274
melting ore, some burnt lime is shovelled in with it. However, with each charge a few pieces of copper slag are in any case thrown in. They float on the smelted mass until they become liquid. Depending on the metal content, the ore must be re-smelted many times, generally seven to eight, and sometimes five, and sometimes only two, especially when they have copper ore from New York in America, which is said to be very rich, but rather scarce. When the workers are asked how many times the ore is melted before it becomes pure copper, the answer is 20 times.

Brass-works

By the town of Keynsham, five miles from Bristol on the way to Bath, there are two specially-built brass-works, belonging to the
Bristol Brass Wire Co. comprising rolling and 275

Fig. 142 Fire-engine house and water pump

slitting mills for brass wire, and rolling mills for large brass sheets for Guinea pans and kettles, as shown by attached drawing no. 144. There is also a wire drawing mill for brass wire here.

The annealing furnaces are fired with wood, but the ones for sheets are fired with pit coal, placed in two narrow fireplaces on either side of the hearth, as shown by attached drawing no. 145.

In addition to this works, in the building on which no expense has been spared, a short distance further up by the Bristol river, or the river that comes from Bath, there is a battery-works, with a number of small hammers in three buildings. All the hammers are driven by gear wheels, with cogs of wood inserted into cast rings, as shown by drawing no. 146.[130] Such a wooden cog is said sometimes to last several months. At one end of the town of Keynsham there is another battery mill consisting of only four hammers and an 275B annealing furnace.[131]

On the road between Keynsham and Bath there is yet another, comprising three workshops and 12 hammers. Only one mile from Bath there is still another one.[132]

Steel-works

At the end of Keynsham, next to the brass battery mill, lies a steel-works, with furnaces and one hammer for forging. The steel here is made from Öregrund and other Swedish iron.

Fig. 143a Copper furnaces: exterior and plan

Spanish, English and Russian iron is also used. The proprietor who owns this works converts iron for the merchants in Bristol against payment per ton. For the converting to blister steel, the payment is £2 per ton. If it is also forged to bars, £1 extra has to be paid. All the Spanish iron that is converted here has to be forged to bars because otherwise it could not be
276 sold. The sales price is £26 to £27 per ton for the forged bars. The 'Steel-master', to whom this works belonged, had recently died, and when I arrived the widow soon appeared. She was so big and fat that she could have concealed the whole steel furnace, where at that moment iron was being loaded into its coffins, with crushed coal in between the bars, and fire sand on top.

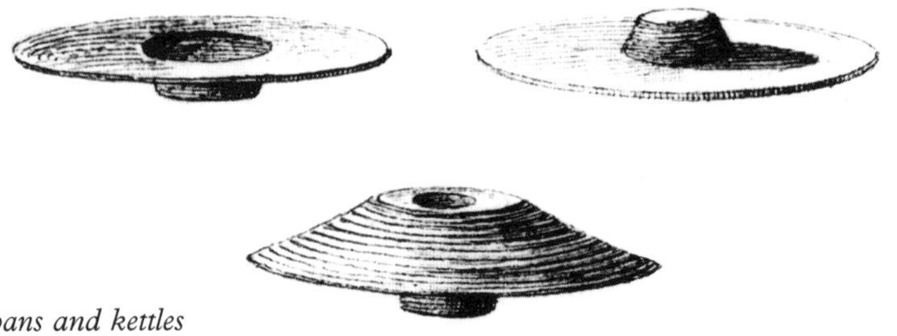

Fig. 144 Guinea pans and kettles

Fig. 145 Annealing furnace

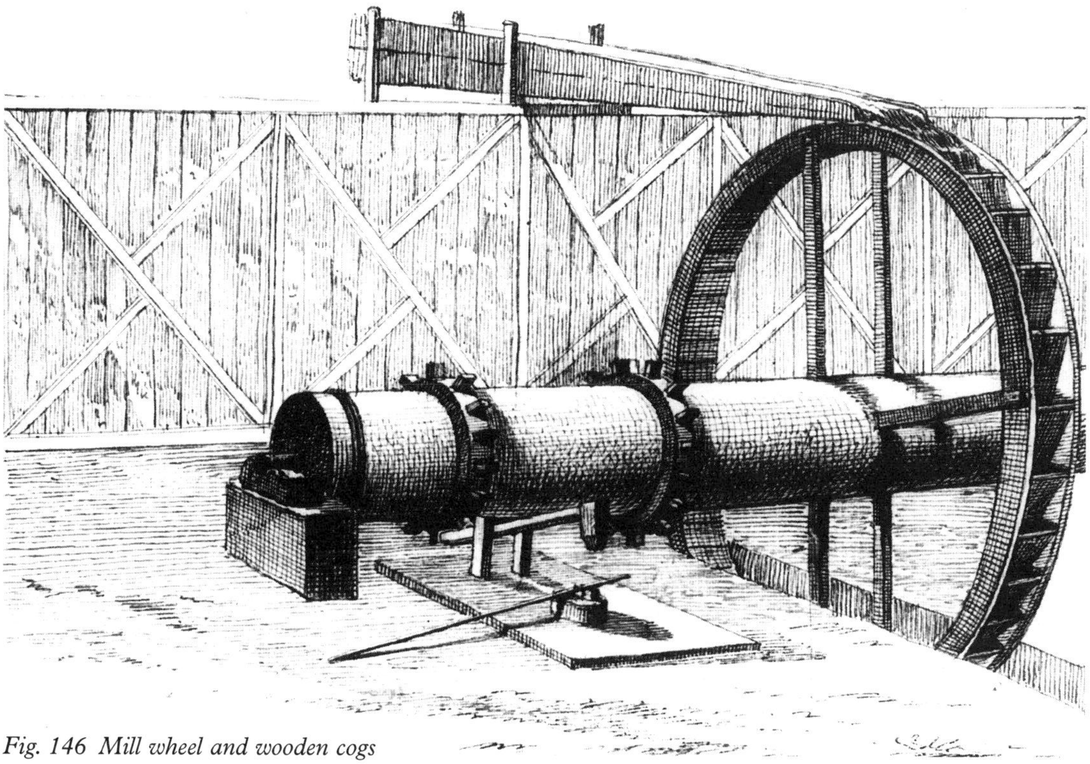

Fig. 146 Mill wheel and wooden cogs

Coal mine

I also viewed a coal pit on the way to Crew's Hole copper mill, which is shown by the attached drawing no. 147. The shaft, into which one descends on a rope half-an-inch in diameter, was 168 feet deep and lined with stone masonry at the top where the rock was not firm enough. Like all the shafts in this locality, it had the shape of a square with
277 rounded corners.

I was told that there are a number of coal seams here, one below the other, although all of them are not so thick that it would pay to work them. The thickest seam on this side [of Bristol] is 3 feet, sometimes a little more, but other times also less. It generally dips south, but nevertheless it does happen at times that it dips in some other direction or is horizontal or perpendicular, although not for any great distance.

Remarks on the origin of coal seams

The coal here, as has also been observed in other places, derives its origin from forests thrown down by over-flowing seas. When the seas receded, the wood, after many aeons of time, started to ferment and caught fire and became carbonised under its cover of earth. During this process the bituminous parts became agglomerated and separated from the
pure carbon and now generally occur dispersed 278
at random in the coal seam. They have since become harder and harder, through other

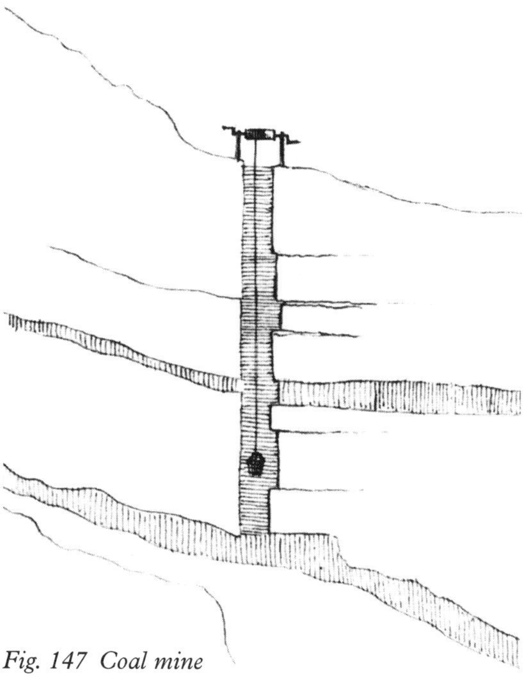

Fig. 147 Coal mine

Fig. 148 Crew's Hole copper-works

material that has been added, such as further bituminous and sulphur-like matter, and through mineralisation. The added matter has, due to its similarity to this combustible mass, been more attracted to it than any other kind of mineral or salt.[133]

The workings in the coal mines are supported by thin posts of oak or spruce that is bought by weight and costs 12 to 18 shillings per ton. One sack of coal holds three bushels, weighs 200 to 250 lb and sells for 6d to 7d retail. To glass houses and smelting furnaces, the small coal is sold for 3d to 4d per bushel. The lightest coal is the best because it contains less heterogeneous matter. The landlord is paid one-eighth of the sales price, and as the mine becomes exhausted, the people who own it will have to make the land level again. I was told
279 that in this mine there is very little water, although it is partly located under the river. Nevertheless there is a fire engine to keep out what little water that they do have.

Crew's Hole copper-works

The copper-works at Crew's Hole lies two miles south of Bristol,[134] besides the river that comes from Bath. It is shown in drawing no. 148. There are no fewer than 49 copper-smelting furnaces in operation here, and at the new copper-works half a mile further up,[135] there are another 17 furnaces, or a total of 66, all belonging to a large partnership called 'The Brass Wire Company'.

The smelting process has already been described in connection with the Warmley copper-works. I only observed here that when two or three smeltings have been made and the matte starts to appear, they do not let it run out and form one large mass, but make small box-like moulds in front of the tap-hole. These are assembled from iron plates, as shown in drawing
no. 143b, in the same way as for cast iron.[136] 280

The refining is here done in the same way as at Vauxhall in London, in reverberatory furnaces, constructed like the other smelting

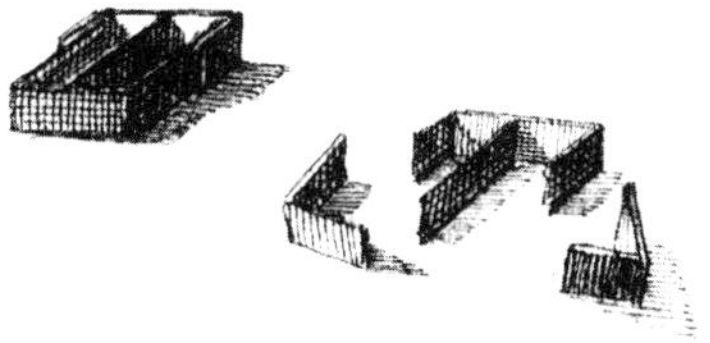

Fig. 143b Moulds for copper

furnaces, but so that the depth of molten copper in the hearth is more uniform. The man who tends the furnace is paid 10 shillings per week, but there are also others, getting 15 to 18 shillings.

Lead-smelting furnaces
At the new copper-works there are also two recently-built lead furnaces that were not in operation owing to shortage of ore. The process and furnace design have already been described under Hotwell.

Spelter- or zinc-smelting furnace
Here there is also a spelter furnace made to the design invented by Mr Champion and put into operation at the Warmley works as long as 15 to 18 years ago. The furnace, shown by drawing no. 149, is built just like a glass furnace and is fired in the same way with pit coal, as is commonly done in this locality. 281

The zinc ore is first calcined or roasted slightly, then as much of it as possible is picked out by hand and the rest sieved to remove the galena. The ore is finally dried and placed in crucibles together with coal. The crucibles are made of Stourbridge clay, with holes in the bottom. The crucibles are sealed at the top so

Fig. 149 Spelter furnace

that the metal must go down through the holes at the bottom, to which 6-foot-long pipes are attached leading down to another room below the furnace. The spelter metal drips down through pipes into buckets of water placed under them. However, since the buckets are placed 10 feet lower down and the metal is of such a nature that it evaporates as soon as it is molten, a considerable quantity of it disappears into the air, which makes the smelting less profitable and also makes the work difficult and unhealthy for the smelters. The pipes leading from the crucibles should go down into a room
282 with water and water vapour.

This would not only make the noxious smoke disappear, but also recover a substantial quantity of spelter that now flies away into the air.

Hay-making and stacking

On the way from Crew's Hole and new copper mills to Baptist Mills, I passed several meadows where the people were busy haymaking. This is done in the same way as in Sweden, including mowing, spreading, drying, raking and placing into rows, with the exception that there all the hay is stacked and tramped down thoroughly. When the stack, shown in the attached drawing no. 150, is completed, it is raked outside so that the hay is smoothed and slopes downward. The stack is undercut to a height of about 2 feet, 6 inches so that the base has a smaller diameter than the rest, thus eliminating any drip on the base. When the stack is made, brushwood and branches from a tree or two are placed beneath so that the hay will not touch
283 the ground and rot.

Rope-making and sailcloth factory

Near the city there were several rope-walks, where rope yarn was spun by women. On this side of the city there was also a sail-cloth factory in which all the work with the weaving etc was done by men. There were also brickyards, which have been mentioned before.

Baptist Mills brass-works

Baptist Mills is located to the south-west, one and a half miles from Bristol. It has 48 brass furnaces, and belongs to the Bristol Brass Wire Co. There are two kinds of brass made here, namely: Arco and Brass [proper].[137]

For Arco, 40 lb of copper and 60 lb of calamine are charged, producing 78 lb of arco. Ditto, of 40 lb copper and 56 lb of calamine, 89 lb of arco is obtained.
This kind of brass is used for castings.

To make Brass, the following charge is used:
11 lb of arco
18 lb of scrap brass
30 lb of granulated copper of best quality
56 lb of calamine or gallmey which makes 89 lb 284
of brass.

This is cast in stone moulds and cut into five pieces. These are then rolled, slit and drawn to wire.

Calamine roasting and milling

The furnaces are continuously in operation and I was told that in some places the fire has not been out for several years. The brass is cast twice a day or 11 times a week. No work is done on Sunday, but the furnace fires are kept going and metal is charged although the draught is damped down. The calamine or gallmey used at this works comes partly from Wales, partly from the Mendip Hills in Somerset, and partly from Flintshire. The last mentioned is considered the best. For one ton of calamine £3 to £3.10s is paid. It is first calcined in double kilns for four hours, and then crushed

Fig. 150 Haystack

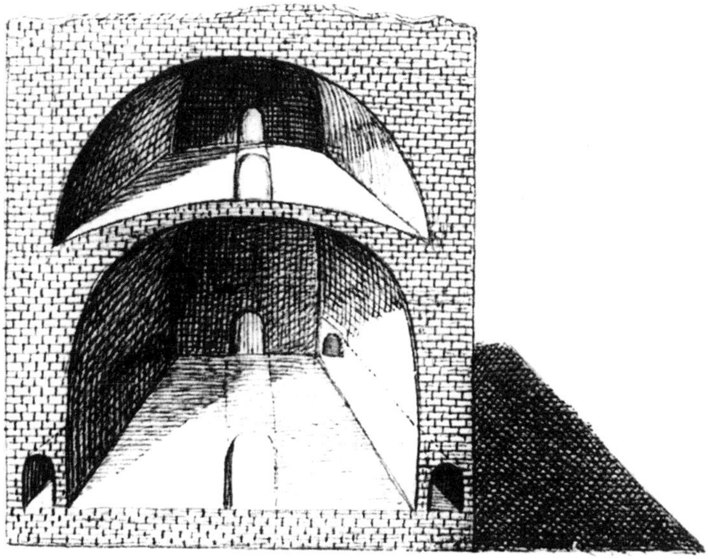

Fig. 151 Calamine kiln

and separated from the lead that it contains,
285 ground, and returned to the kilns for drying.

See drawing no. 151. Here were two mills for grinding the calamine, driven by water. A windmill of brick was also being built for this purpose, because the grinding is slow.

Workshops for repair of brass kettles and dishes

In addition to the brass furnaces, the calamine mills and the calcining kilns, there are also some workshops here for the repair of brass dishes and kettles that during hammering have become holed or cracked. These defects are repaired by soldering and insertion of new pieces and it is all so neatly done that it cannot be seen when the articles have been turned. Most of the workers come from Aix la Chapelle in the Duchy of Jülich.

The largest dishes that are sent to Guinea are 4 feet in diameter and the smaller, 1 foot, and there are in addition 50 to 60 various sizes in
286 between.[138] It was said that of this article alone, Guinea uses 80 to 90 tons per year. The negroes are supposed to use the large dishes when they wash or when they coat themselves with ointments to become even blacker.

Lime-burning

Lime kilns, as illustrated by drawing no. 152a, are found all around the city near the river. The limestone that is burnt in them comes from cliffs of Hotwells, two miles below the city by the navigation channel. The stones are broken into pieces of uniform and suitable size. The kiln is first charged with coal, which is kindled into a good fire, then one or two layers of stone, followed by coal and stone again repeatedly, as rapidly as the fire has time to burn right up to the top of the kiln, which is generally 12 feet to 15 feet high. When the kiln has been filled in this way and the contents start to sink together somewhat, the lime stones at the bottom are pulled out and more is added at
the top of both stone and coal. The kiln is kept 287
in operation continuously, and the people have the same occupation every day. They charge new limestone and coal at the top, and pull out the burnt product at the bottom and slake it. At the Crew's Hole copper mill there was a lime kiln built of masonry in slag dump. There were workers who sorted the fine parts from the lumps of slag and placed it in layers between the limestone, with a little of coal added. The mixture could be ignited and burned as well as pure coal. The fines contain a good deal of coal ash that has fallen through the grates of the copper furnaces and this must be removed and the fires moistened before they will burn. One bushel of burnt lime sells for 3 pence. It is packed in barrels and sent all over the country for mortar and fertiliser.

Pipe factory

In Bristol there are very many factories for tobacco pipes, but they do not make very good

Fig. 152a Lime kiln[139]

288 ones, which to some extent is due to the clay, but is also due to the fact that the smoking of tobacco is not popular amongst Englishmen of rank. It is generally a pastime for the common people and old hags, whom one sees with pipes always hanging from their mouths. One gross of pipes of the poorest kind is sold for 10 pence. Ditto, longer pipes for 14 [pence]. Ditto, best quality, 9 inches long, for 2 shillings. Concerning the last mentioned, I was told that the cost of clay that comes from Barnstaple in Devonshire, together with wages, oil etc comes to 14 pence per gross, one gross reckoned to be twelve dozen. Of these pipes, huge batches are sent to the American Colonies. The kiln was as has been described before in my notes from London.

Soap-boilers in Bristol 289

There are also a number of soap-boilers in Bristol, obtaining their potash from Wales, tallow from Ireland, now costing £42 per ton, and oil from Spain and Portugal. Liquid or solid soap made with olive oil and called Spanish soap, is sold for 58 shillings per cwt. Ditto, soap made of tallow is sold for

Fig. 152b The New Passage across the Severn

54 shillings per cwt. In order to improve the appearance of the latter they mix in squirts of indigo, making it look like blue-veined marble.

Journey from Bristol via the New Passage

On 24 June, St John's or Midsummer's Day,[140] I travelled from Bristol to Wales. I arrived in the afternoon at New Passage, ten miles from Bristol on the River Severn, which in this place ought to be known as a bay of the ocean as it is four miles wide [Fig. 152b]. On the way to New
290 Passage I passed through Clifton Down located on the hill above Hotwells Spa. It has a number of attractive summerhouses, with which the inhabitants of Bristol have embellished this place.

Durdham Common

The road continued across a common called Durdham Down, where there was a magnificent prospect out towards the sea and King Roads, where ships enter the Bristol River from the Severn. Many of the spa visitors promenaded on this common, some in carriages and others on horseback. A masonry wall has just been built at the top of the steep slope down to the river, which makes this promenade safer and more pleasant. Towards autumn a horse race is held upon the common, and it was said that there is a great influx of spectators both from Bristol and from other towns and villages many miles away.

Freemasons Lodge

On my arrival at the Severn, I met a number of travellers who were waiting for passage, but the 291
ship could not sail due to the winds that had lasted for two days and still kept the waves surging. There was also a Lodge of Freemasons from Bristol, who had assembled to celebrate the day in the traditional way. Before long I was introduced into this worthy and amusing company, which made the day short and pleasant in this otherwise dull and lonely place.

Passage across the Severn

On 25 June wind and rain that made themselves heard throughout the night did not hold out any promise of a speedy and safe passage. However, towards dinnertime, when the tide had started to flow out against the wind and the waves, the captain decided to take the risk. More than

20 horses and an even greater number of passengers, as many as there was room for, were crammed into the ship. Another ship, belonging to the opposite side, had to return empty, as it was not allowed to take cargo or passengers
292 from our side.

The horses were so unruly during the crossing that it seemed that the ship would fly apart. This caused her to spring a leak and the waves washed over her. Passengers screamed and wailed, the sailors were hampered by the overcrowding, quite at a loss as to what to do, and complete confusion reigned. We all expected a catastrophe at any moment. This fear continued until we approached land and could with great joy jump onto the rocks to dispel the anxiety that had filled us all with consternation.

Assault of the sea upon terra firma

Having arrived at the other side of the water at the ferry station, which is in Wales, an old man showed me how the waves eat into terra firma, and told me that in his youth he had cut corn in a place that now is a rock 10 feet out in the water.

Remarks about ebb and flood

Ebb and flood are here so strong that the water falls and rises between 50 feet and 60 feet every
293 12 hours. There are five hours of ebb, when all the water runs out, and another seven hours of flood when it comes streaming back again. These changing movements of the water are longest and strongest when there is a spring tide, which occurs at Full Moon, or when the attractions of the Sun and the Moon on the Earth act together. This happens when they are placed on one each side of the Earth, all three on one straight line. The result is that the united forces pull the water on either side of the Earth which, considering the natural equilibrium that all things created are endowed with, has the same effect on the sea as if the attraction of these bodies, namely the Sun and the Moon, on the Earth were united on one side, which can be demonstrated by experimental physics.

Iron forge at Caerleon

On 25 June I continued my trip in the afternoon in the company of two Quakers, Mr Roberts and
Mr Williams, to Caerleon, which means a town 294
for a Roman legion. It is located eight miles from the Severn on a navigable river.

Mr Roberts has recently built a forge with three hearths, a little way from the town. We went to see it, and it is shown in drawing no. 153.

The frame of the hammer was built of brick.

The breast-shot wheels for the bellows and hammer and their buckets were designed according to Spanish or Biscayan practice. Nevertheless, the head of water here is high enough to permit the use of over-shot wheels, but they would not be more advantageous in this case when the wheels run at high speed, because it is more difficult for the water to escape from the deep buckets that one must employ on over-

Fig. 153 Breast-shot wheel and hammer

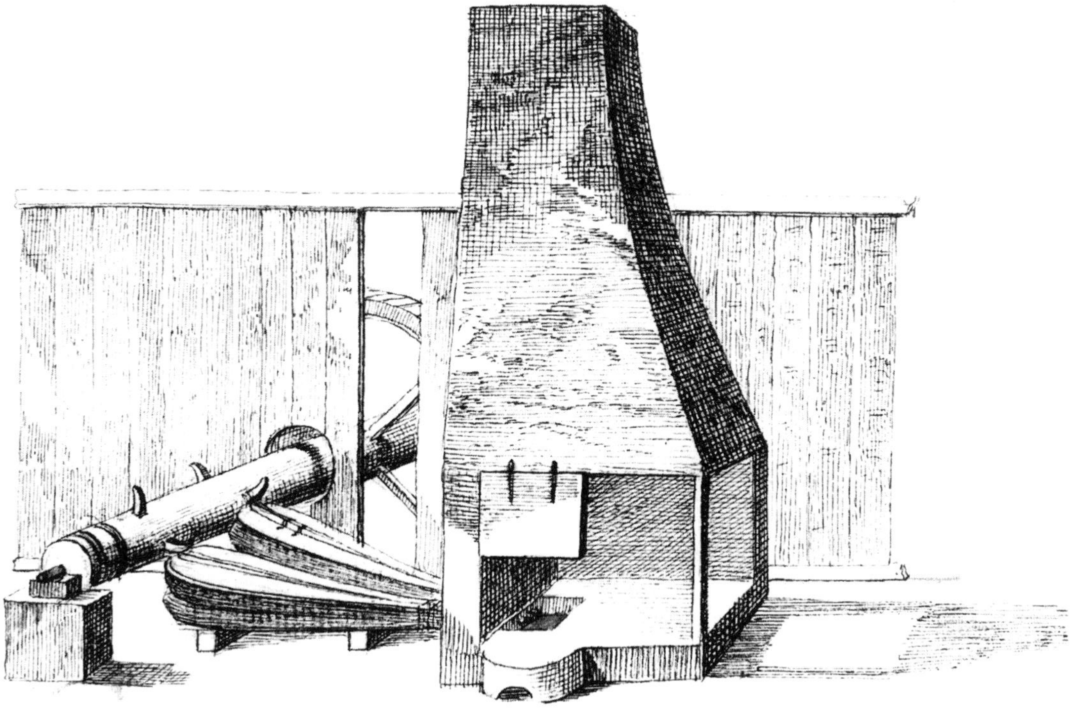

Fig. 154a Finery hearth

shot wheels, than to leave the shallow and open buckets on a breast-shot wheel.

The three hearths were divided in such a way that two were used for the melting of the iron and called finery hearths, while the third, on the
295 other hand, was only used for forging the bars and called a chafery hearth.

The finery hearths are made of cast-iron slabs, 2 feet long, 15 inches wide and 6 inches to 6½ inches deep below the tuyere, which was forged of wrought-iron.

The chafery is larger across, so that it is possible to place in it, side by side, four lumps of iron as they come from the finery hearths, drawn out in the middle to a length of 1 foot, 6 inches or 2 feet as shown in the attached drawing no. 154a.[141] Across the end of the chafery hearth there is an upright slab of iron, which serves to keep the coal together and heaped up high [Fig.154b]. This gives a more intense heat. Both kinds of hearths use nothing but charcoal, which mostly is made in this locality from oak, lime, beech, etc. Sometimes birch and other deciduous trees are mixed in. Charcoal is very expensive here, because in the neighbourhood, for several miles around, there
296 are no other trees than those planted in the hedges surrounding the fields and meadows.

Calculation of the price of the iron

Pig iron per ton £6.	4 tons = £24.
Two-and-a-half loads of coal per ton @ 36s per load.	Three times = £13.10s.0d.
Wages per ton 19s 6d.	For 3 tons = £2.18s.6d.
Total	£40.8s.6d.
Carriage to Caerleon 8s	= £1.4s.0d.
Ditto by sea to Bristol, 2s.6d per ton	= 7s.6d.
The cost of bar-iron in Bristol, not including interest on the building cost, manager's salary, etc.	
Grand Total	= £42.0s.0d.
This amounts to £14.13s.4d. per ton.[142]	
Ditto interest on the cost of the land occupied by the forge and on the buildings cost	= £1.10s.0d.
Total	= £16.3s.4d.

One load of coal here costs 36 shillings. A load consists of 12 horse loads and each horse load is a sack, which should fill a coal-measure 3 feet square and 20 inches deep.[143] 297

In the refinery the workers are allowed 18 horse loads, or one-and-a-half loads of coal per ton of iron. At the chafery, 12 sacks or one load

Fig. 154a Chafery hearth

of coal is allowed per ton of iron. The total consumption of coal is thus two-and-a-half loads, or £5.8s.0d.[144] Three men work at each refinery hearth, or six altogether, paid 10s 6d per ton. Two refinery hearths can produce 6 tons of iron per week and the same 6 tons can be forged to bars in the chafery, if only there is sufficient water. At this forge water is sometimes scarce, particularly when the weather is very dry. The pig iron used at this forge is made at Abercarn, which lies further away from the sea, 18 English or three Swedish miles from
298 Caerleon. It is brought here on horseback and the transport costs 8 shillings per ton. The pig iron is in the form of slabs 2 feet, 3 inches to 2 feet, 6 inches long and 6 inches wide at the middle. They are nowadays reckoned to cost £6 per ton at the furnace. 26½ cwt of pig iron or one-and-three-quarters[145] tons is allowed per ton of bar-iron, but the finers told me that they do not need quite so much when the pig iron is of good quality. For each bloom or loop, three-quarters of a hundredweight or 84 lb of pig iron is used and 20 loops are made per 24 hours.

Town of Newport

From Caerleon we travelled eight miles[146] further to a small town called Newport, see drawing no. 155, which is located on a navigable river, eight or ten miles[147] from the Severn. Here, close by the river, are the beautiful ruins of a castle that was the residence of one of the Welsh barons who was once absolute ruler of this country.

Mineral coal in the river

As soon as the tide goes out a number of poor
people appear to pick mineral coal from the 299
bottom of the river just above the bridge. However frequently they come back there is always something for them hidden in the ordinary shingle that the river has carried with it from the hills above, which contain an abundance of coal seams.

Heaps of iron slag

On this side of the town there were also some pits by the bank of the river where old iron slag was dug up for re-melting in the blast furnaces, reputedly producing a good iron.

Lead mines

On the road between Newport and Abercarn there were two lead mines. Neither of them was very rich or particularly remarkable in any other respect.

Fig. 155 Newport

Fig. 156 Coal mines near Newport

Fig. 157 Abercarn blast furnace: exterior

Coal mines near Newport

I also saw a number of coal workings on two high mountains, where I was told there were three seams above each other, dipping sometimes south and sometimes north up to 2 feet in 6 feet.[148] These seams are found at depths of 42 feet to 60 feet and 90 feet. Sometimes the overlying rock is thicker, but the seams are at the same distance from each other.

The deepest seam is generally the thickest, being 3 feet to 4 feet deep, but the others 1½ feet to 2 feet and the top one sometimes not more than a suggestion of a seam. I heard the statement made that there is no lead lode in this locality except in limestone, and no coal seams where there are limestone quarries. The coal seams, as shown by drawing no. 156, are generally covered by sandstone and clay slate and next to the coal, petrified wood and impressions of other vegetable matter. By a high mountain shown on the drawing, on which there are coal mines, it was observed that in the middle of the slope there was a coal mine and a kiln for burning lime. This reveals that limestone can be found below coal seams, but not above, as has already been noted. In the valleys between the mountains there are some woods of deciduous trees that already were in poor condition because too many trees have been felled, although the iron-works in the neighbourhood have not been in operation for more than three years. The woods consist of oak, plane, birch, etc and are first felled and placed in piles[149] for drying for some time. Subsequently it is sold to the forge-masters, who take care of the charcoal burning.
The wood is sold according to 'worst' which is a pile 4 feet long, ...wide, and 4 feet high, and costs 4 shillings.[150] Sixteen 'worst' are stacked on end to make the stack and in the middle a pole is placed.

When the stack has been completed and covered, the pole is removed and a fire is set in the hole to start the burning. The stack is first covered with twigs and small tree-branches on the outside and then finally with turf.
The diameter is generally 8 feet to 10 feet and the burning takes eight to nine days.

Abercarn iron-works

Abercarn[151] is located eight miles from Newport, and here an iron-works was started three years ago by some ironmongers and Quakers from Bristol, Mr Hanbury and Mr Roberts and other partners, who also own
302 Caerleon forge that has just been described. The works consists of a blast furnace, a forge with three hearths, a tilt-hammer to draw down bars for iron and steel wire and a wire-mill. The outside of the blast furnace building is shown in the attached drawing no. 157.

It is so well placed by the side of a precipitous cliff, that neither coal nor ore has to be lifted, but can be pushed in a wheelbarrow directly from the coal storage heap or the roasting kilns onto the charging floor of the furnace. The kilns are also placed so that the ore can be tipped directly into them from the sacks on the backs of horses and then withdrawn at the level of the furnace top. All the work in connection with smelting is thus arranged so that Nature gives as much assistance as possible and little manual labour is required. The height of the furnace from the
hearth to the top was 24 feet according to what 303
I was told, but it looked to me to be 2 feet to 3 feet more. The top aperture, or the throat, into which the raw materials are charged is nearly square, being 21 inches in the direction of the blast and about 22 inches across it. This cross-section does not alter until 6 feet down, below which it becomes octagonal or round with a diameter five to six times larger than the width of the throat. When the bosh is reached, the diameter again decreases and the cross-section reverts to rectangular 5 feet above the bottom of the hearth, which below the blast is 2 feet long, 1 foot 6 inches wide and 1 foot deep. (See drawings no. 158a and b).

The original shape of the hearth does not last very long because as soon as the campaign has started, both the cross-section and the depth are enlarged to a rounded oval [sic], which after a few weeks of operation often contains five to six times as much iron as it did to begin with. The masonry lining of the furnace consists of a red and quartz-like sandstone which is soft, but was said to
withstand the heat fairly well. 304

At this blast furnace, three kinds of iron ore are used. One looks like a blue clay and lies either below or above some of the coal seams. It has impressions of tree roots etc, the same as the Wednesbury ore. The second kind is more black in colour and splits easily into thin flat layers, but looks like soap-stone. The third kind is a light-coloured clay that is hard and similar to iron inside, but quite soft and powdery where there are clefts and fissures.

This ore is brought on horseback from a distance of several miles, and each sack or horse

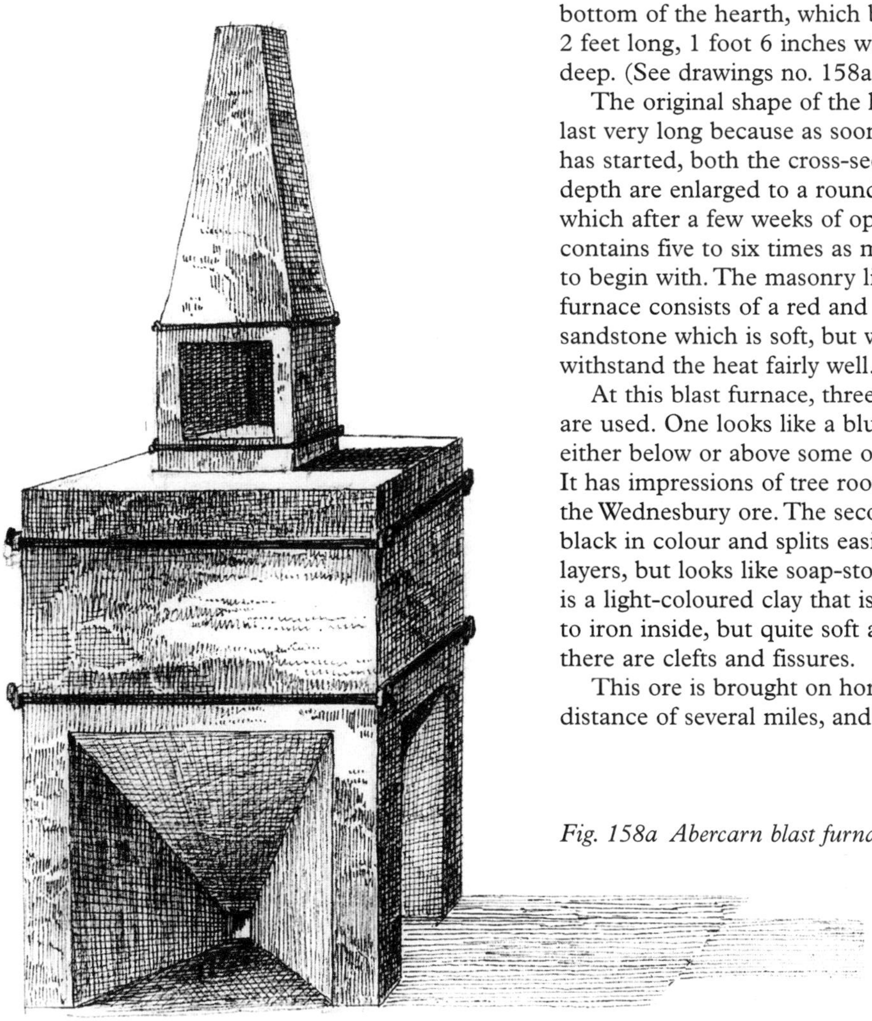

Fig. 158a Abercarn blast furnace

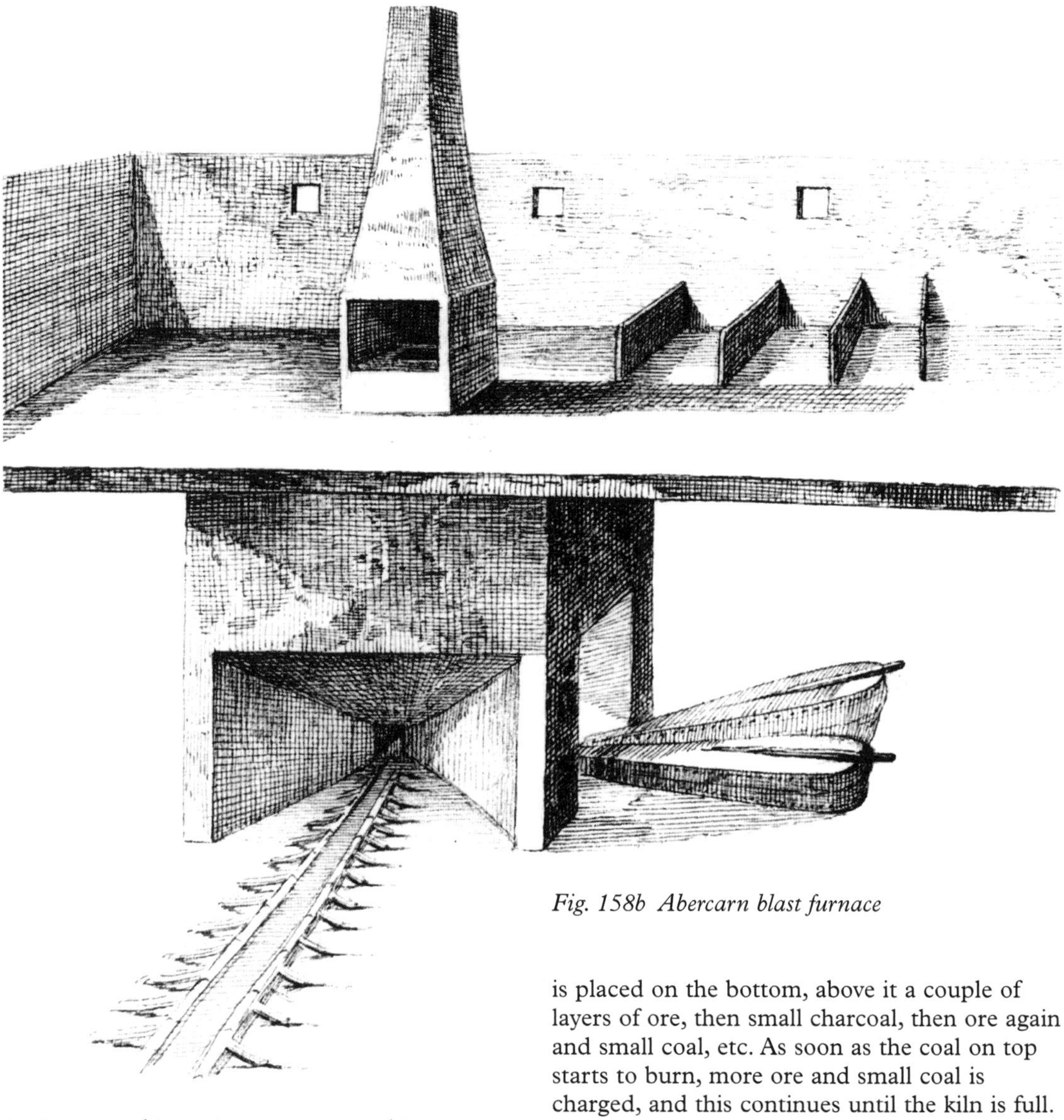

Fig. 158b Abercarn blast furnace

load costs 13½d and weighs about 1½ cwt or 168 lb and more if it is rich. For every two sacks, another two have to be given free of charge. This furnace also uses small additions of Lancaster ore that comes by sea from Liverpool
305 and costs shillings per ton including freight and other costs. The same ore is used at Bristol for the manufacture of red pigment or so-called Spanish Brown. It is more or less comparable to the ore from the Biscay, which produces the soft iron.

Drawing no. 157 showing the blast furnace at Abercarn also shows the roasting kilns to the left on the same level as the top of the furnace. The roasting is carried out in the same way as is usual for burning lime, namely, some dry wood is placed on the bottom, above it a couple of layers of ore, then small charcoal, then ore again and small coal, etc. As soon as the coal on top starts to burn, more ore and small coal is charged, and this continues until the kiln is full. The kilns are 10 feet high, the diameter at the bottom is 2 feet 6 inches and at the top 9 feet. When there is no more fire at the bottom the ore is raked out through three openings. As the charge sinks down at the top, the kiln is charged 306
again so that it keeps burning as long as the furnace is in blast. Thirty-four horse loads of coal are required to fill the furnace. One horse load should be equal to a measure 1 foot 6 inches square and 2 feet 6 inches deep, and costs 3 shillings. This was at the beginning of the campaign and, each half-hour, eight pans or measures of coal, six of ore and one of limestone were charged. The coal measure was 3 feet long and 1 foot 6 inches wide, and the ore measure 1 foot 6 inches long and 9 inches

Fig. 159 Abercarn: straining hammer, zig-zag iron, iron wreaths and hearth

wide, and the ore measure 1 foot 6 inches long and 9 inches to 1 foot wide.[152] The furnace is tapped twice in 24 hours, but as the campaign advances and the hearth becomes larger, the iron is held for 24 hours, so that it becomes purer and performs better during the fining process. When the furnace is in full swing, the production can reach 18 to 20 tons per week, or
307 3 tons for each tapping.

At the furnace there are four workers,[153] two on top who get 7 shillings per week, and two below who get 8 shillings each per week. The latter are paid in addition by the ton for castings, which sometimes can bring them in as much as the weekly wage. One ton of iron is reckoned to cost £6 at the furnace. The forge lies by another little river about half a mile from the blast furnace, and is not different from the one at Caerleon, already described.

In this country they do not know the art of making wooden bellows,[154] which consequently are not used either at the furnaces or the forges. Instead, they use leather bellows made of thick sole-leather. The bellows run fairly fast in the forge but are slowed down a little when the smelting is nearing completion. The resulting product is here called a loop, and weighs
308 between 76 and 84 lb.

The weekly production is 18 to 20 loops.[155] Forge slag is used as a flux. The hammer and the anvil are of cast iron and made in moulds of sand, as is also the case with gudgeon pins and blocks, and cams for the wheels driving the bellows. They have recently started to strengthen the hammer-shaft with strong iron bars placed both on top and underneath, which makes them last much longer than they commonly have done before. The springboard is also made much longer than previously so that the hammerhead proper strikes it, which causes less distortion. See drawing no. 159.[156]

A little way below the forge, but by the same stream, there is a straining hammer[157] and a mill for iron wire or so-called steel wire. The straining hammer draws the iron down to between $\frac{1}{2}$ inch and $\frac{5}{16}$ inch square and 10 feet in length, bent in zig-zag and rolled into rings of 'wreath-iron'[158] that can be placed 309
inside a hollow water wheel to be rolled around and scoured with iron slag (see Fig. 160a).[160] When the scouring is completed, the rolled-up iron rings are thrown into a pond where they are left for three to four weeks to become rusty in the water, after which they go through the draw plates a couple of times.[161] Subsequently they are annealed, scoured and rusted again as described above. This is repeated a third time before the iron becomes reasonably fine. The second time it is thrown into the pond it remains twelve to fifteen days, and the third time only eight days. As far as the straining hammer is concerned, there was nothing

Fig. 160a Abercarn: scouring drum wheel [159]

noteworthy except that the stool on which the hammer-man sat during the forging was mounted on rollers and could be pushed back as the bar got longer during the drawing down. The wire mill was built in the same way as a mill for brass wire, but here a very hard and dense steel is required for the draw plates.
310 This is imported from Holland and costs 1 shilling per pound and sometimes 18 pence. Three-quarters of the draw plate is of iron and it is steeled only on the outside edge where the fine holes are to be punched through. Sixteen kinds of iron wire are made here and sold by the bundle or by ring at 19 to 36 shillings. A ring weighs six stones and a stone is $10\frac{1}{2}$ lb,[162] consequently a ring weighs 63 lb.

Notes and references

106 Not identified.
107 Probably a Bristol merchant.
108 A mineral containing manganese.
109 When the tide is out.
110 Letters missing in MS.
111 Possibly this means the use of the spring for bathing.
112 Name missing in MS.
113 Two pages numbered 263 in MS.
114 The theoretical yield from pure galena is 86.6 per cent or about 17 cwt per ton. The very low yield noted by RRA indicates that the ore was very impure and that the losses of lead in the smelting process were high.
115 In fact about seven miles to the south-east.
116 Joan Day, author of *Bristol Brass*, says that at this time a number of partners are mentioned in the deeds, including one Richard Palmer. Woolland was originally a grist mill but was converted to tinplate rolling in the 1730s which continued until the 1780s (private communication).
117 This must be the annual production.
118 On the following page the sheared bars are said to be 14 inches long, which is more likely to be correct.
119 In order to do this, one end would have to be cut off.
120 The purpose of cooling the tallow with water is not clear.
121 It is not explained what caused the sheets to be considered bad. Most trouble in tinning was due to the surface not being clean, but it would not become cleaner by standing in the tinning kettle for an extra hour.
122 No gratings are shown on the drawing.
123 Joseph Percival of Bristol, according to Buchanan and Cossons, *Industrial Archaeology of the Bristol Region* (1969), p.119.
124 This must have been Baptist Mill.
125 Probably the Bristol Brass Wire Company.
126 Letters missing in MS have been replaced.
127 Warmley lies nearly due east of Bristol.
128 A description of a 'returning engine', a widespread way of using a pumping engine with a water wheel to afford rotative motion before the rotative steam engine was developed in the 1780s.
129 Two pages numbered 275 in MS.
130 RRA refers to 'gear wheels' and 'cogs' but it is clear from Fig. 146 that he is drawing attention to the use of wooden tappets set in cast-iron rings to raise the hammer tails, a remarkable arrangement at this date.
131 Probably Saltford – see Buchanan and Cossons, *op.cit.*, pp.115–127.
132 Probably Weston – as above.
133 These speculations are, of course, very much at variance with modern views, but appear to reflect opinions of geologists of the time.
134 In fact, three miles to the east.
135 This may be the Conham works, where copper smelting began in 1696.
136 The plates were probably also cast iron.
137 The figures given below are suspect. In the first case, the theoretical yield of brass from 40 lb copper and 60 lb calamine is about 70 lb if absolutely all the calamine is reduced to zinc and there are no losses, so the quoted figure of 78 lb would represent a product with a zinc content close to 50 per cent. The second case is even less likely. The third case makes more sense, but the zinc content is still over 40 per cent. Holtzapffel, writing 100 years later, gives 'Bristol brass' as 16 copper to six zinc (27 per cent zinc) and 'common brass' as 16 to eight (33 per cent zinc), and it is generally accepted that it is hard to produce a brass with a higher proportion of zinc than this when using the cementation process, which is what is described here. See also MS p.19.
138 The reason why so many sizes were made is that the dishes were nested for export, to save space on shipboard.
139 There are two drawings numbered 152.
140 The feast of John the Baptist, six months from Christmas, celebrated as Midsummer's Day in Sweden.
141 The 'lumps of iron' shown are clearly in the form of what are known as 'anconies', the products of forging a bloom in the finery. The ends are usually of rough square section, finished to the final shape of the bar in the chafery.
142 This calculation must be regarded as approximate as RRA allows one-third wastage, and in fact 3 × £14.13s.4d = £44, so an extra 13s.4d has crept in.
143 Presumably 'load' means a wagon load. A measure of the dimensions given would have a volume of 15 cubic feet or 11.7 bushels.
144 Again, an error has crept in: 2.5 × 36s = £4.10s.
145 In fact, one-and-a-third tons.
146 The actual distance is only a couple of miles.
147 The distance along the Usk to the Severn is not more than four miles.
148 A dip of 18 degrees.

149 RRA uses the Swedish word 'stavrum' for the piles, a measure for a heap of wood 2'4" × 2'4" × 9'9".

150 This measure has not been identified, neither in Swedish nor in English, though it may be related to the German words 'Wurst' in the sense of 'roll' or 'Wulst' meaning 'wreath', hence 'cord'. If the missing dimension is four feet, it could be a local word for 'cord'.

151 According to H R Schubert, *History of the British Iron and Steel Industry* (1957), p.366, the Abercarn furnace was erected on a tributary of the River Ebbw in about 1576. Forges and wire works were added, and continued in operation until the middle of the nineteenth century.

152 Unfortunately the depth has been omitted, so that it is not possible to calculate the volumes of the two measures. The measure was probably, as in Sweden, in the form of a box shovel with the front end open. With this implement it would be possible to take a roughly-measured quantity of ore or limestone from the storage bins by the furnace throat. The bins can be seen in drawing 158b. Charcoal would not have been stored on the bridge because of the danger of fire, but would be brought in as required for each charge from storage houses at some distance from the furnace.

153 There must have been four workers on each of the two shifts.

154 On the Continent and in northern Europe wooden bellows came into use during the eighteenth century, but in England this stage of development was generally omitted, and leather bellows were superseded by cylindrical cast-iron blowing engines.

155 This corresponds to 1370 to 1680 lb per week, per hearth.

156 The drawing does not show any springboard, but it is a trip-hammer.

157 H R Schubert, *op. cit.*, p.296 says that 'the straining hammer was evidently introduced from Germany, where it was known as the "reckhammer". It was a tail hammer, much lighter than the usual power hammer of the forge and accordingly striking much faster'. See also William Rees, *Industry before the Industrial Revolution* (1968), p.608 ff.

158 RRA uses the Swedish word 'kransjärn', literally translated as 'wreath iron'. The rings shown in drawing no. 159 certainly do resemble wreaths, but the term has not been encountered elsewhere. The zig-zag form could have been a consequence of drawing the iron down under a hammer with a narrow peen (consistent with the light weight, suggested above).

159 Two drawings are numbered 160: the scouring wheel, which we have labelled 160a, and 160b, an illustration of what may be the kilns used for roasting ore at Abercarn or Pontypool. There is no reference in the text.

160 The device described is a tumbling barrel directly water-driven by means of paddles attached to the periphery. There must have been a door to allow access to the interior though this is not shown in the drawing. This ingenious design has not, as far as we know, been described elsewhere.

161 The procedure described, of first scouring the iron and *then* steeping it to let it rust, then putting it through the drawplate without further cleaning, seems surprising.

162 This 10½ lb stone might be a local variant of the more usual 14 lb stone.

Journey 5d Pontypool to London

Pontypool, Usk, Monmouth, Redbrook, Coleford, Mitcheldean, Flaxley, Gloucester, Upton, Worcester, Droitwich, Bewdley, Lower Milton, Kidderminster, Stourbridge, Dudley, Bilston, Wilden, Worcester, Pershore, Evesham, Moreton-in-the-Marsh, Oxford, High Wycombe, Uxbridge, London.

Iron mines and blast furnace near Pontypool

Towards the evening I started my trip to Pontypool, which lies seven miles from Abercarn. The road goes through deep valleys and the mountains on either side are very steep, but covered nevertheless with grass. Near Pontypool there were some deciduous woods in the valleys. One-and-a-half miles from the town the iron mines could be seen in the precipitous slope of a mountain and there were also a number of coal mines working in the same place.

The blast furnace[163] is half a mile from the
311 mines and one mile from Pontypool.
The campaign was now in its sixth month. The design is similar to that at Abercarn: all the blast furnaces in this part of the country are built in this way, as if cast in the same mould. The furnace is tapped twice in 24 hours and produces 1½ tons each time, or 21 tons per week, although I was told that the output occasionally exceeds this figure. The coal here costs 2s.6d a horse load, but four years back the price was only 2s.0d. Two keepers are paid 8 shillings each per week, and two [get] 7 shillings. Other workmen occupied with roasting etc are paid 5 to 6 shillings per week.

The roasting is here carried out in the same way as already described in connection with Abercarn. This method of roasting has also been discussed under the heading 'Lime-burning at
Bristol'. It only differs from the latter in that for 312
burning lime, mineral coal is used between the layers of stone, whereas for iron ore, only small charcoal is employed, sieved from the charcoal used in the blast furnace. The application of mineral coal to roasting or iron-smelting is avoided at all costs because it makes the iron brittle and generally of poor quality, or as people in this locality who are experienced in these matters say, 'the iron is poisoned.'

Summary of costs for the iron-making at Pontypool[164]

The pig iron is reckoned to cost	£6 per ton.	
26 cwt costs	£7.10s.0d.	
Two-and-a-half loads mineral coal [sic][165] @ 30s per load	£3.15s.0d.	
Wages, per ton	19s.0d.	
Carriage to Caerleon	8s.0d.	
Total	£12.12s.0d.	
Expenses for building and maintenance	£1.0s.0d.	
Manager's remuneration	5s.0d.	313
Grand total	£13.17s.0d.	

Fig. 160b Roasting ovens at Pontypool [not identified in text]

Fig. 161 Water wheel at Pontypool

The town of Pontypool

27 June. Pontypool is a town of little importance and only worth mentioning because of its iron-works and its mills for rolling and tinning sheets and wire drawing, all in the hands of one owner, namely Mr R Hanbury, the present Member of Parliament for this county. Mr Hanbury's house is well built and lies in a deer park on the side of the river on which iron-works have been erected, although they are at some distance from the house.

Pontypool: forge, rolling, slitting and tinplate-works

The blast furnace has already been described on the way from Abercarn and lies one-and-a-half miles from Pontypool. The forge is provided with three finery hearths occupying nine people, namely three for each hearth, who are paid 10 shillings per ton and fine and forge to anconies 10½ tons per week. These hearths consume two-and-a-half dozen horse loads of coal, that nowadays costs 2s.6d a load. 314

A little farther down there is another forge with three chafery hearths that are only used for drawing down the iron. Each hearth employs three people, who get 9 shillings per ton in wages. At this forge the iron is drawn down to bars of the sizes required as raw material for the rolling and wire mills. Otherwise there is nothing noteworthy, except what has already been reported at Caerleon and Abercarn. Nevertheless, it might be considered remarkable that the water driving the wheels flows out of

the bottom of the pond through a pipe which then bends upwards by the wheel and takes the water to the same level as that in the millpond. The water then flows out onto the undershot wheel paddles. See drawing no. 161.[166]
The advantage of this arrangement is that the
315 wheels can be kept going as long as there is any water in the pond, which would not be possible if a flume leading from the top part of the dam were to be used to convey the water to the wheel. Otherwise there is nothing particularly advanced in this idea that could not just as well be achieved by means of an ordinary water trough. In the last-mentioned forge there was a rolling and slitting mill, until recently used for rolling and cutting the rods for the wire mill. Since these slit rods have not proved as satisfactory for wire-drawing as the ones hammered down by the tilt hammer, slitting of wire rods has been discontinued and the rolling and slitting mill is used instead to cut nail rods, which are consumed in the district. They are sold for 18s.6d per cwt or £18 per ton.

A little way farther down there is a shear to cut the iron for the sheet- and plate-rolling, see drawing no. 162. It was an extraordinary sight
316 to see an iron bar 6 inches wide and one inch thick being cut with this machine as easily as a fingernail with a pair of scissors. The same waterwheel also operated a kind of machine for rolls, provided with gears.[167] The roll is placed in ordinary roll housings and turned by means of a piece of steel that is wedged in against the direction of rotation. The roll-turning was not now in operation, but I was told that one of the largest rolls, used for black sheets, can be finished to perfection in four to five days by this method. Rolls have also been taken here with broken necks, on which new necks have been turned so that they can be used again, because rolls are particularly expensive in this place as they cannot be cast at the blast furnace in Pontypool, but must be ordered from the foundries in Bristol.

There are three rolling mills for sheets and 317
plate here, namely: two tinplate and one for large black sheets or plate. The mill-stands are made in the usual way as already described at Woolland near Bristol. The only thing to be noted here was that the body of the tinplate rolls did not exceed 14 inches in length and 11 inches or 12 inches in diameter after turning. The rolls for the large sheets or black plates had a body 26 inches long and a diameter of 11, 12 to 14 inches. They are driven by two water wheels running in opposite directions.

The furnace in which the sheets are heated is shown by drawing no. 163 and built of [brick made from] Stourbridge clay in order to withstand the fire so much the better. Inside it is only 18 inches to 20 inches wide, 5 feet long
and 2 feet high. The bottom consists of a cast- 318
iron grate to provide an even draught throughout. The furnace is fired with pit coal that is thrown in through the opening shown by Fig. 1 in drawing no. 163.

At the lower tinplate mill, a reverberatory furnace has been built where the coal is charged into the back end, as shown by Fig. 2, drawing no. 163 but, as the other way of heating the sheets is used in two places, it gives one reason to believe that it is better. At the rolling mills for tinplate, the opening through which the sheets are charged into the furnace for heating is only 12 inches or 13 inches square, but at the larger mill the opening is 26 inches high, but only 8 inches wide. When the sheets or, at the beginning of the rolling, the cut bars have been placed in the furnace, the aperture is closed by a sheet to keep the heat in. The short pieces of bar that are rolled to tinplate are 4 inches to
$4\frac{3}{16}$ inches wide, $\frac{1}{2}$ inch thick and $10\frac{1}{2}$ inches 319

Fig. 162 Shearing-mill details

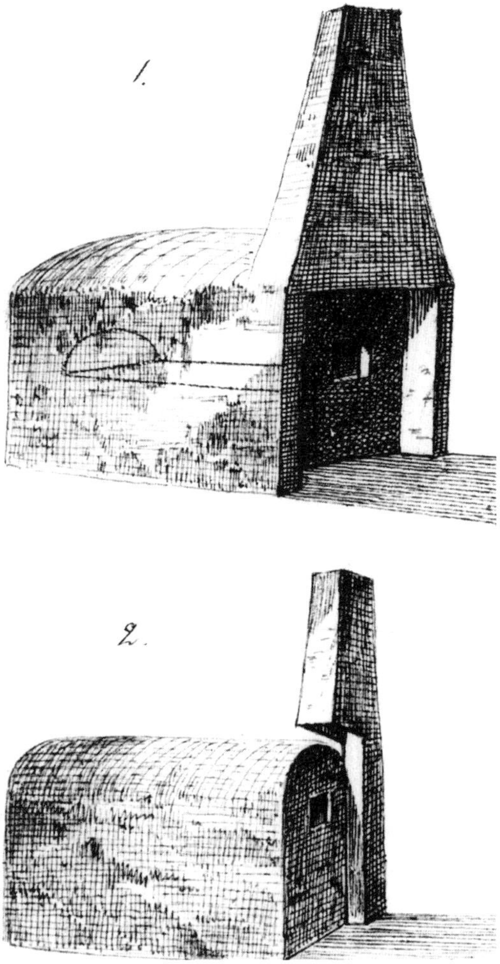

Fig. 163, nos. 1 and 2 Furnaces for tinplate

long. Ditto, 13 inches to $13\frac{3}{16}$ inches long and $4\frac{1}{2}$ inches wide and $\frac{1}{2}$ inch thick. From these stumps, sheets of 10 inches to $10\frac{1}{3}$ inches width and 13 inches to $13\frac{1}{2}$ inches width are rolled, the off-cuts not included. Another type of sheet, $9\frac{3}{4}$ inches wide and 13 inches long, is also sold, as well as double sheets up to $12\frac{1}{7}$ inches wide and $16\frac{1}{7}$ inches long. The bars forged for the black sheets should be 6 inches wide, 1 inch thick and 22 inches to 24 inches long. When the iron stumps have been heated in the furnace, they are taken out with a long-handled pair of tongs by the man in charge of the furnace and handed to the roller one at a time. The roller passes the bar-stump through the mill broadside on and it is received by another man on the opposite side, who passes it back again,[168] and so on, up to eight times on
one heat. The sheet that has been rolled to a 320
length of 1 foot in this way is put aside and the rolling continues similarly with another bar and so on until 20 or nearly 30 bars have passed through the rolls. The men then stop the rolling for a little while, both to have a rest and to let the rolls cool down in the air, because water would immediately cause them to crack. Whilst the rolls cool off, the workers are occupied with shearing of completed sheets and doubling and quadrupling of other sheets for further rolling as will be described further on. The sheets that already have been rolled on the first heat are reheated the second time and rolled again in the same way as described above, passing through the rollers five times on this heat. They are then
doubled and given five passes after a third 321
heating.

The sheets for tinning have, after this rolling, grown so much in length that they can be quadrupled. The next time four sheets, or one sheet quadrupled, is passed through the rollers, so that it is further elongated, so that it can be doubled. This is done by separating the sheets from each other two and two, so that they can be doubled again as just described to four sheets that are given five to six passes, or in two heats, until they reach their correct length. This completes the whole process as far as the rolling is concerned. The result is eight sheets rolled from one short bar, as described at the beginning. Three workers can roll one ton of sheets for tinning per week, and are paid $15\frac{1}{2}$d for each box of 225 sheets. The wages paid for
the rolling of the large sheets as they come from 322
the mill are 3 pence per pound. The rolling process is the same except that the sheets are doubled once and are rolled out in several heats from a piece of iron 22 inches to 24 inches long, 6 inches wide and 1 inch thick, to a width of 24 inches and a double length of 3 feet or a total of 6 feet.

When the sheets to be tinned have been rolled to final dimensions, they have to be annealed and have slivers and other surface defects removed, and be pickled and scoured before they are in a fit state to receive the tin coating. This is carried out in the same way as already described at Woollard.

Just as there are two rolling mills for tinplate at Pontypool, there is also a double workshop for the tinning. I was told that they there produce 1500 boxes per year of tinplate, but
that 2000 boxes could very well be made. 323

The wages are:

1. For rolling, per box	15½d
2. Annealing	11d
3. Pickling and scouring	6d
4. Tinning	8d
5. Polishing with wheat brass	2d
	3s.6½d

Tinplate delivered in Bristol

Single tin 1/3 × no. 1, dimension 10¼" × 13½", price per box 51s
Single tin 1/3 × no. 2, dimension 10" × 13¼", price per box 49s
Single tin 1/3 × no. 111, dimension 9¾" × 13", price per box 47s
One box of the above mentioned plates contains 225 plate.
Double Tin 12¼" × 12¼" 50s
In Swedish measurements 13" × 17"
One Box of Commons 8×8 Jaggones.[169]
Double Tin X alone 50s
Boxes contain 100 plates or sheets

From Pontypool to Caerleon the distance is reckoned to be eight miles and carriage costs 6s.6d per ton. From Caerleon the sheets or
324 plates are sent by ship to Bristol, which costs[170] ... per box.[171]

Wire mill at Pontypool

Of the works at Pontypool, the straining hammer for wire rods and the wire mill remain to be mentioned. The latter has four heavy gripping tongs and six lighter draw benches above, where the wire is drawn by winding it onto small vertical drums, all six of which were driven by the same gear wheel. Each one of the drums can be stopped individually for adjustments etc by being lifted out of the coupling by means of a lever. But as these appliances do not differ from the ones generally found in a mechanised wire mill, and the rest of the iron-wire processing already has been described at Abercarn, it is considered unnecessary to say anything about it here.

Secrecy at Pontypool Works

In connection with Pontypool there is nothing further to be mentioned except that everything is kept very secret and that all strangers are forbidden to approach the works. Anybody who intends viewing them must be prepared to use
325 every possible means of achieving his wish. I did not fail this time, but in the end I was caught by the implacable proprietor himself and was forced to witness the castigation of the workmen who let me in. In addition I had to listen to a torrent of abuse in broken French for which I, however, paid him back in his own coin as well as I could. Amongst other things, I told him that he did not have to be so afraid of showing strangers his methods of manufacturing, which in any case had originated in Liège and were brought to England from there. Just the same, it cannot be denied that the design of rolling mills has been considerably improved in England, particularly when they are compared with the ones in Liège and Namur where the rolling of sheets is unknown and not even considered possible.

Sheet-metal fabrication in Pontypool

In Pontypool there are two brothers by the
name of Edward and Thomas Allgood, who 326
from black sheets fabricate bread baskets, tea trays, snuff boxes, and various kinds of sheet-metal work that is cut and embossed in rings,[172] and then scoured, dried, varnished and painted in the same way as at Mr Baskerville's factory in Birmingham. An ordinary snuffbox with a golden flower painted on it is sold for 2 shillings, and a smaller version for 18 pence. Tea trays cost from 4 shillings to 18 shillings, etc.

Nail-forging in Pontypool

Here there were also seven nail forges, working only to supply the requirements of the surrounding part of the country as they were unable to compete with nails from Birmingham or Bristol. Nevertheless, practically all towns around here have some 'nail shops' which always have plenty of work.

'2 lb of abnails'[173] weigh 2 lb per 1000
Small nails or tacks cost 7d per 1000 in wages
and are sold by the master, who has to pay 327
for workshop, iron, coal and tools, 16d per 1000.
'3 lb of abnails': wages 9d per 1000. Of these, 8000 can be made per week.
'4 lb of abnails': wages 12d, sales price 18d; 1500 to 2000 made per day.
Threepenny nails: weigh 3 lb per 1000. Wages 10½d. 1500 to 2000 can be forged per day.
Four-penny nails: weigh 6 lb per 1000. Wages 12d.

Sixpenny nails: weigh 7 or 9 lb per 1000.
Wages 14d.
Eight-penny nails: weigh 12 lb per 1000.
Wages 18d.
Ten-penny nails: weigh 18 lb no. 14[174] per 1000.
Wages 20d, sales price 4s.
Twelve-penny nails: weigh 20 lb per 1000.
Wages 24d.

The iron costs 2d per pound. Four hands consume two loads of coal per week, costing 7d per load. The journeymen hire themselves lodgings, two meals per day and laundry for 3s per week. The food consists of meat, bread, salad and 'table-beer', so they should be well satisfied.

From Pontypool I travelled on 28 June
328 through Usk to Monmouth, a distance of 18 miles, through a beautiful and flat country, now badly damaged by a hail storm that eight days ago was swept across the countryside here by a north-westerly wind.

Usk, a small hamlet

Usk is an insignificant little hamlet and the livelihood of the population is farming and some spinning of wool.

Monmouth town

Monmouth has a better reputation and also an attractive town hall, a new church and a large bridge across the river, which is navigable and provides some business for the town in the form of trade with Bristol, in addition to farming.

Iron-works near Monmouth

Half a mile from the town there is an iron-works[175] that nowadays belongs to Mr Daniel,[176] a Quaker and ironmonger in Bristol. The works comprises two forges, one with three finery hearths and one hammer for reheating and drawing down to bars the iron smelted in the
329 finery hearths and forged only to anconies. At both forges nothing but charcoal is used which according to what the workers told me, costs 4s.6d per horse load. For each ton of iron the finery uses 15, and the chafery seven horse loads. Nine men work at the finery hearths, namely three for each hearth, and they can smelt and forge to anconies $8\frac{1}{2}$ to 9 tons per week and are paid 10s.9d per ton. Twenty loops are made per 24 hours, and each loop weighs 84 lb. For one ton of bar-iron $26\frac{1}{4}$ cwt of pig iron is used, or from 4 tons of pig iron, approximately 3 tons of bar-iron is obtained. If the pig iron is good, the yield is better.

Four people work at the two chafery hearths, but on day shift only, and draw down to bars the wrought iron made in the finery hearths.
They are paid 9 shillings per ton. 330

The bar-iron made here is sent to Bristol by ship, and is mainly sold in Devonshire and Cornwall, where these iron merchants have their customers. The pig iron consumed at the Monmouth forges is purchased partly in Bristol and partly from the furnaces in the locality. The former is American iron that nowadays costs £6, £7 to £10 per ton, and is said to be of very poor quality, but sometimes good enough according to what the finers and hammer men told me. The price of iron smelted at the blast furnaces in the locality is now £7 per ton, and occasionally slightly more.

Cost summary for the bar iron

4 tons pig iron @ £7	£28.0s.0d	
22 horse loads charcoal @ 4s.6d per ton	£14.17s.0d	
Ditto wages per ton, 19s.9d.	£2.19s.3d	
For 3 tons, total	£45.16s.3d	331

One ton of bar iron will thus cost £15.5s.5d. In this connection it should be remembered that at this works gains are made both on 'over coal'[177] and 'over iron' when the quality of the pig iron is good. The profit due to 'over coal' seems to have been taken into consideration already because at other forges in England 30 horse loads of coal are allowed per ton of bar iron. The finers and hammer men could not have had accurate information about the price of charcoal because the wood in the Forest of Dean is sold by the Crown Commissioners. Subsequently the purchaser has to pay for cutting, charcoal burning and transport costs and, irrespective of how high the expenses are in this locality, a horse load of charcoal cannot cost more than 2s.6d, or at the very most 3s. Assuming that 3s is the correct price per horse load, the figure calculated above is high by 22 times 1s.6d, or £1.13. If this amount is deducted from the total of £15.5s we arrive at a
true figure of £13.12s.5d. 332

To this amount we have to add the cost of transportation, building, repairs, and the salary of a manager, etc so that the total cost in Bristol will amount to at least £16. The sales price at
the moment is £18. 333

Redbrook copper-works

28 June. Redbrook is located on the Monmouth river,[178] four miles[179] from the town of Monmouth. It consists of two copper smelting works. The first one comes to[180] belongs to Messrs Jackson & Swan and has 14 smelting furnaces, not being used for the time being. The other one belongs to 'London's Copper Compagnie'[181] and consists of 36 furnaces, all with natural draught and arranged for smelting with pit coal. All of these were working.

The copper ore used here comes mainly from Cornwall, and the cost of transportation is only 7 to 8 shillings per ton. Some grey and yellow copper ore also comes from County Kerry in Ireland and the purchase price is £15 to £20 per ton, depending on the quality. The furnaces are designed in the same way as the ones already
334 described at Bristol, only with the difference that here a cast-iron box is provided on top of the furnace into which the charge is shovelled [see Fig. 164].

The box has a hole in the bottom that fits the hole in the arched roof of the furnace through which it is charged. To rich ore that does not contain sulphur they add some crushed pit coal for the first [stage of] smelting. The roasting furnaces are twice as large as the smelting furnaces and have four doors to make it easier to stir the ore with a rake. The ore has previously been broken and ground or crushed by means of a millstone running on edge. These are the same as the ones used for the preparation of snuff in Spain and Portugal, and have already often been mentioned by me in other places. The production of copper at these works is estimated to amount to 250 tons per year, which is refined, forged and rolled, partly here and partly at other works. For the latter purpose it is first sent to London where the warehouse is, and from there sent out to be
worked up and fabricated for various purposes. 335
There is also a copper refinery belonging to the same company in Vauxhall by London, which has been mentioned in the foregoing under the heading 'London'. At this works there are also hammers for copper and rolling mills, where the copper is rolled to plates for different applications. These are sold for 12, to 14, to 16 pence per pound according to the finish of the sheet.[182] The wages were 1 shilling per day.

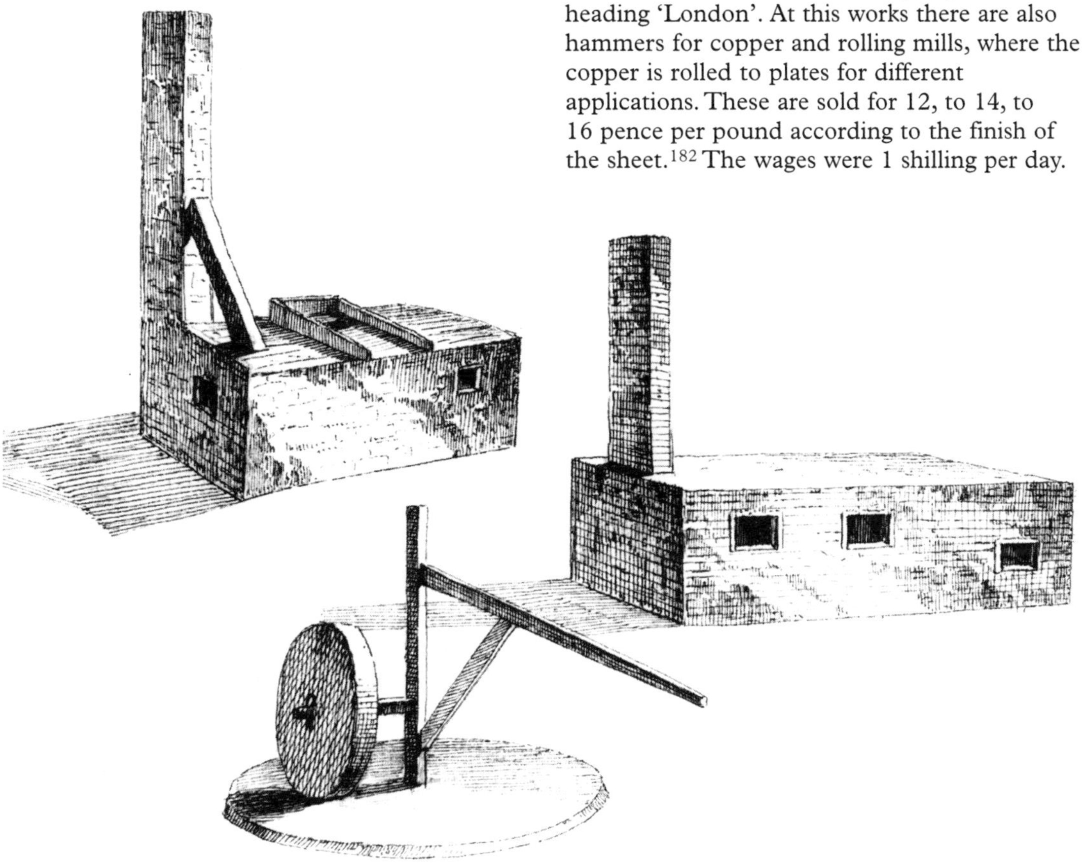

Fig. 164 Furnaces and ore-crushing at Redbrook

Redbrook blast furnace

Redbrook blast furnace is located a mile from the copper works and belongs to Mr Pitt,[183] who produces 16 to 17 tons per week. The furnace is tapped once every 24 hours. The ore is obtained four miles from here, above Coleford, and costs 8 shillings per ton, two loads making 1 ton. Copper cinder or burnt pyrites from the Forest of Dean cost 5 shillings. Twelve horse loads of coal are called a load, which costs 30 shillings and the consumption amounts to 30 loads per week. Two keepers are paid in wages 16 shillings
336 per week, two chargers get ten and labourers 7 shillings. The iron costs £5 at the furnace and sells for £7.

List of the various items of cost for the pig iron produced at Redbrook.

In a week 30 dozen loads of coal @ 30s	£45.0s.0d
Ditto, 40 tons of iron ore @ 8s per ton	£16.0s.0d
Ditto, 12 tons of cinder @ 5s	£3.0s.0d
Ditto, Limestone 5½ tons @ 3s	16s.6d
Ditto, wages to four people	£2.12s.0d
Cost of leasing the land, building costs, manager's salary etc.	£4.10s.0d
Cost of blowing in furnace	£1.0s.0d
Total	£72.18s.6d

The production is generally 16 tons of pig iron per week and each ton consequently costs
337 £4.11s.1½d at the furnace.

Lord Gage's estate

A mile further up lies Lord Gage's seat on a high hill. It is well built and has a splendid view, but is badly maintained. It is called 'High Meadow'.

The town of Coleford

I continued through the town of Coleford, which is located close by the Forest of Dean and one mile past it to the west.

Iron mines near Coleford

I encountered the iron mines of the forest, of which there are a great number all along the whole plain. Most of them however must already have been emptied of ore in ancient times. The ore dips south but does not form any regular lodes, but occurs in pockets that are mined. The ore, here called 'brush',[184] consists of a limestone rock impregnated with glassy nodules of limonite, blue-grey in colour. There is also the red, earthy iron ore that is similar to the Biscayan and here called red ochre.

Nowadays no more of the latter is mined than that which is shipped to Holland for the production of 'Spanish Brown'. The total 33
production is no more than 40 tons per year, which sells for 36 shillings per ton.

Spanish Brown, a pigment

In Rotterdam there was no factory for Spanish Brown, but there is one in Bristol that I have already described and I believe that the red ochre is shipped from here to Bristol.[185]

The Forest of Dean, a wood

From the iron mines of Coleford I travelled through the Forest of Dean, which is estimated to have a diameter of eight miles and a circumference of 30 miles. Most of it belongs to the Crown and it is the Crown that maintains a staff of foresters to take care of the deer, of which there are very many, and also to mark out and sell wood to the owners of blast furnaces and forges in the locality. These gentlemen subsequently arrange to have it burnt to charcoal themselves. Every year in August the shooting of deer in this forest is free, but 1 guinea tax has to be paid for each stag. Anyone who owns land in the neighbourhood is free to shoot any deer that stray onto his property, and if they are injured 33
they may be pursued on Crown lands. Every year some parts of the forest are reserved for charcoal burning, and the wood sold by the cord, which is 4 feet high, 8 feet long and 3 feet wide. Nowadays a cord costs 8, 9, 10 to 11 shillings according to the quality of the wood. Oak is always the most expensive. In this forest there are only deciduous trees, such as oak, beech, ash, etc and also some clumps of birch, although only in a few places. Parts of the forest in private possession appeared to be in poor condition, but on Crown land there were still considerable quantities of wood, which, made into charcoal in the usual way, should last for many a long year. 34

Nevertheless it was observed that the forest in this part of the country does not grow particularly well although the soil is fairly good. The landscape is dominated by small hills.

Charcoal-burning

The burning of the wood to charcoal is carried out in the same way as already described under

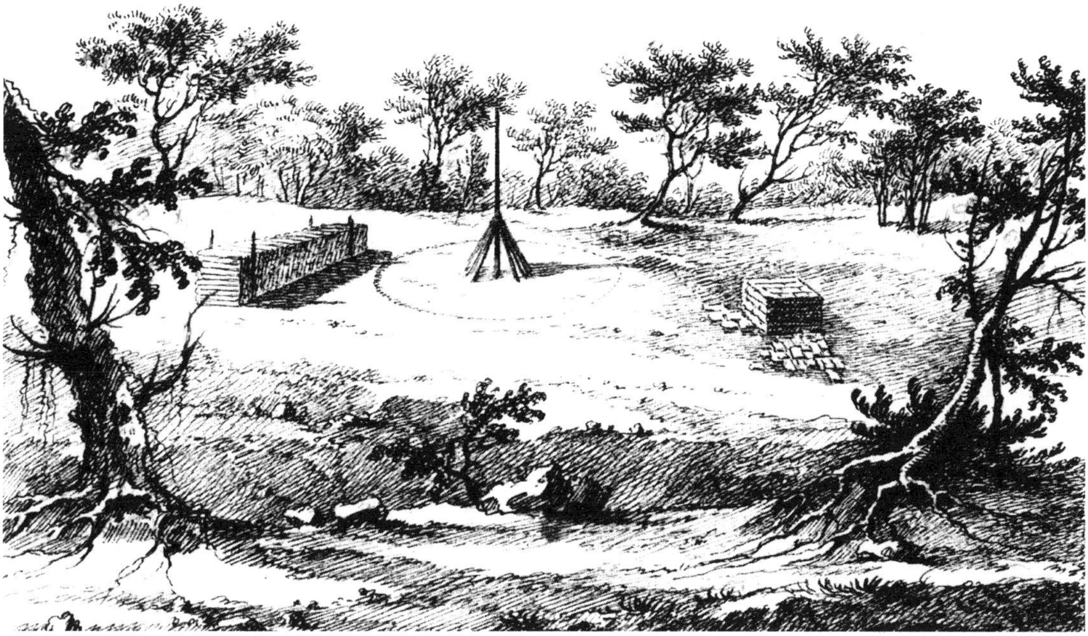

Fig. 165 Charcoal-burning

Abercarn. The actual work is done by the so-called 'Colliers', who throughout the year do nothing else. To make a stack, seven, eight to ten cords of wood were required and the charring took eight, ten or 12 days and nights. The stacks were usually covered with sods [Fig. 165]. The wages for the charcoal burning are paid by the cord and amount to 1s.6d. The payment for the felling of the trees and stacking in cords is also made by the cord and the amount is 2s.4½d.

Coal seams and mines

Under the whole of this district there is a coal seam 60 feet, 90 feet or 120 feet below ground, that is worked in many places. Nevertheless it is generally not more than 1 foot 6 inches or 2 feet thick and very occasionally 4 feet to 5 feet.
341 The coal is otherwise inflammable and suitable for the purpose of heating, although it sometimes contains pyrites. In the coal, fine particles of charcoal can quite clearly be seen, which indicate the origin of this coal seam. The miners told me that the seam dips towards the Forest of Dean in practically all places around it, and does not have a constant degree of dip. The coal sells for 6 pence per horse load at the mine.

Machine for pumping water

At one of the mines, where there was a great deal of water, I saw a pump as shown in drawing no. 166. To speed up the pumping, the crank was driven by gear wheels. However, since the water was not raised much more than 1 foot, the people had gone to much trouble and expense for nothing.

Transport from the Forest of Dean

Carriage for coal and ore collected from the Forest of Dean costs 1 shilling per load (of 12 sacks) and mile. Thus the payment for carrying 342
one load a distance of eight miles is 8 shillings, which is expensive. The high cost is due to an agreement made by the people in this neighbourhood that nobody is allowed to work as a carrier unless he has four horses, and nobody is allowed to keep horses unless he has acquired the 'Liberty of the Forest'.[186] To do this he has to first work for a year and a day in some mine belonging to the Forest of Dean. The local iron-masters have often complained about these self-assumed rights, but without gaining anything thereby.

Large hailstones

All the places that I have passed through yesterday and today showed lamentable evidence of the terrible storm and large hailstones that struck the neighbourhood on the 14th of this month. In the forest it beat all corn and grass down to the ground, killed chickens, lambs and other small creatures, and suddenly

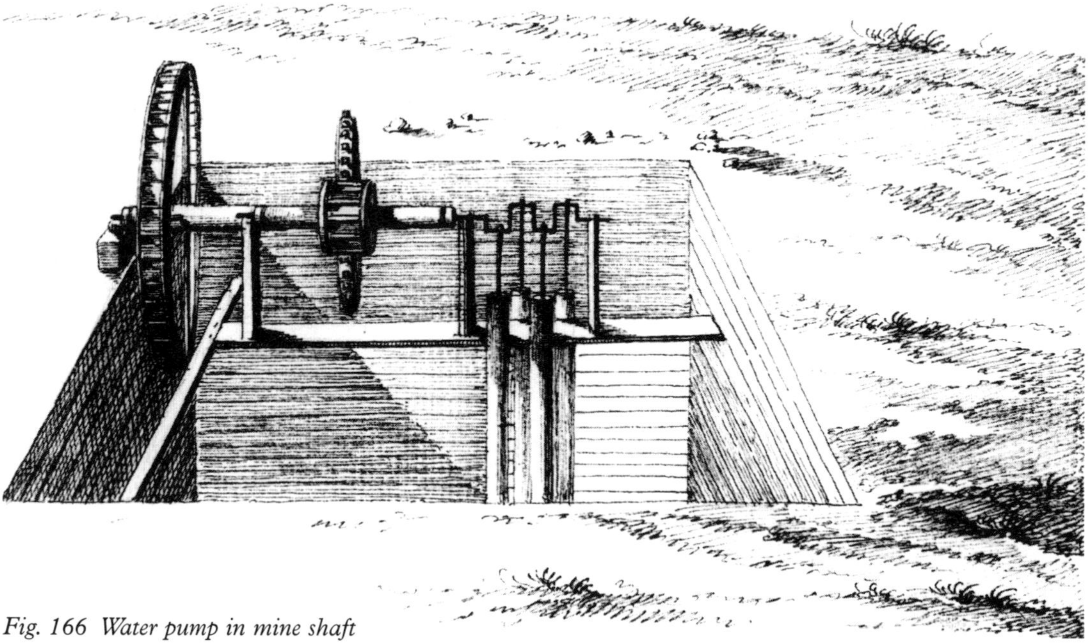

Fig. 166 Water pump in mine shaft

caused such a flood of water that a whole forge
343 with heaps of coal and other appurtenances was completed ruined and swept away. The forge was located in this district and belonged to Mr Pitt.[187] The hailstones were said to have been 4 inches, 5 inches to 6 inches in circumference, and one man from the forest tried to make people believe that he had seen slabs of ice one inch long, 6 inches wide and 2 inches thick which must have fallen from the sky, because neither before nor after the hailstorm had the temperature been low enough to cause the hailstones to freeze together on the ground.

St Michael Dean, a small town

St Michael Dean[188] is a small town with a pretty church that has a pointed tower of dressed stone.

Slag heaps

The whole of this hamlet is built on old heaps of slag or cinder which is now dug up and sold to the blast furnaces in the locality, where it is made into pig iron which is said to be of good quality and tough. One load of cinder weighs 1½ tons and is sold for 7s.6d at Flaxley, which
344 is located three miles from here. Nobody knows how long these ironworks have been in existence, but the people around here have deluded themselves into believing that the Danes worked here during their invasions many centuries ago, and this may have happened in some places. But if one takes into consideration the large quantities of such slag that still remain in the Forest of Dean, it appears that the work connected with their production would have been much too large for the Danes and sufficient for long periods of time before their arrival.

Stone quarries

By the side of the forest, not far from Dean,[189] there are a number of large quarries where a sandstone-like slate is obtained that is used for the lining of blast furnaces, for floors, for the paving of streets, and for grindstones.
The preparation of the slate for these purposes provides a living for many people who live in huts that they have built for themselves right inside the quarries.

Abandoned mines

Near Mitcheldean there are also extensive mines that were worked for iron ore in ancient times and are nowadays called 'Bloomery Works'. It is possible to travel all day through these
underground caverns without reaching the end. 34

Iron mines

At Mitcheldean there are furthermore some new iron mines, but at the surface the ore is not of any great value. This ore is bluish, but not of the kind that attracts the magnet.

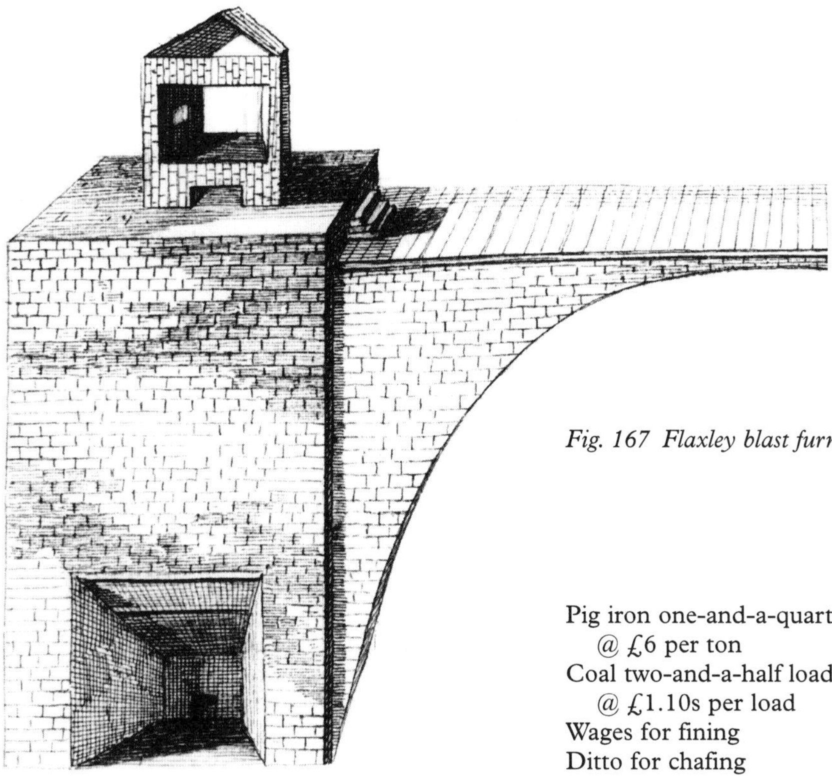

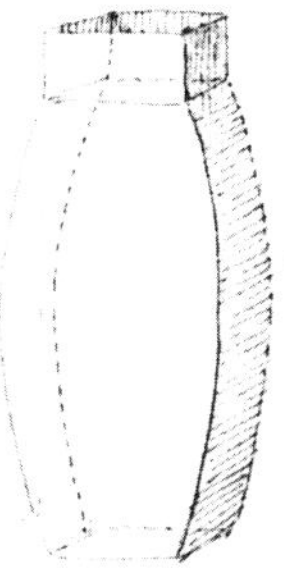

Fig. 167 Flaxley blast furnace

Pig iron one-and-a-quarter ton @ £6 per ton	£7.10s.0d
Coal two-and-a-half loads @ £1.10s per load	£3.15s.0d
Wages for fining	10s.0d
Ditto for chafing	9s.0d
Total	£12.4s.0d

Paper mill

On the way from Mitcheldean to Flaxley on 29 June I came across a paper mill,[190] driven by water, and a beating engine constructed in the Dutch way,[191] and owned by Mr Foley.[192] Here a quire is considered to be 24 sheets of paper and there are 20 quires to a ream which, according to the quality of the paper, is sold for
346 6, 8, 10, 12, 14 shillings to 21 or 25 shillings.

Flaxley forges

The uppermost Flaxley Forge consists of one finery hearth where the production does not reach a higher figure than 2 tons per week. If the finers carry out the process with clean coal[193] they are paid 10 shillings a ton as usual, but if small coal with much fines called 'Cray' is used, they are paid 12s.6d. It is estimated that for one ton of iron, two-and-a-half loads or two-and-a-half dozen horse loads are required, costing £1.10s per dozen. Twenty-six cwt of pig iron are provided for each ton of bar-iron. Eighteen horse loads of coal are used for the fining and 12 for the chafing, which amounts to a total of two-and-a-half dozen.

To this amount must be added the cost of buildings, interest on the capital employed, the
salary of the manager or clerk, rent for the land 347
occupied by the mill, etc. Only two people work at this forge and are there from morning to night, producing 14 loops a day, each loop weighing from ½ to ¾ cwt. Half a mile further down, there is another similar forge with one hearth, and still further down along the brook, a chafery or forge where three workers carry out the forging of the bars. Owing to lack of water it has been necessary to divide the works into three separate forges. At the lowest forge as much iron is drawn down to bars as can be fined in the other two, which amounts to about 5 tons per week, but the water shortage occasionally compels the chafery to shut down.

Flaxley blast furnace

Flaxley blast furnace [Fig. 167] is situated between the two lower forges and built in the
same way as the one in Redbrook, which already 348
has been described. The weekly production of pig iron is 12, 14 to 20 or 22 tons, for which 32 to 40 loads of coal, costing 30s per load are

used. Of the grey ore that is called 'Brush', 12 bushels are charged, costing 6 shillings per dozen and, of the cinder, two dozen. One dozen cinder weigh as much as two dozen grey ore and cost 7 shillings a dozen. Bushel measures for cinder ore are 9 inches deep and 21 inches in diameter, and a bushel measure for grey ore is 9 inches deep but only 16 inches in diameter. Six 'bey'[194] crowned bushels and six 'bey' struck bushels are considered to make up a dozen.

Mr Colchester's estate

On the way from Flaxley to Gloucester, which is a distance of ten miles computed or 13 miles measured,[195] I came upon a beautiful gentleman's seat which was being built at Westbury and belongs to Mr Colchester. Above the entrance there was a carved coat of arms with the motto 'Super Aetera Virtus'.[196] The garden was well planned with a number of
349 ponds. In the middle of one of them there is a statue of Neptune.

Malt kiln and mill

In the nearby village I saw a kiln and a mill for malt. The kiln is constructed with a furnace of the same kind as the one described under 'Exeter', but instead of being made of stones with holes in them, the floor covered with cloth on which the malt is placed was built of bricks provided with holes. These bricks were made in Stourbridge. 'Colm',[197] which is coke made from mineral coal, is used for the drying.

The mill was made of steel, which is usual in England, and was similar to a horizontal coffee mill. Both the barrel and the roller were provided with spiral grooves as shown in drawing no. 168. To increase the speed of rotation the mill was driven by a larger wheel actuating a smaller one by means of a rope-drive. The malt was sold for 4s a bushel.

Bean fields and apple orchards

Along the road there were many fields planted with beans and meadows with apple orchards
that serve the cider pressing. 350

In this district an abundance of cider is made, partly consumed here and partly sent to Bristol for export to foreign countries.

The city of Gloucester and its pin factory

Gloucester is a considerable town and it has a large cathedral built in the Gothic style. It is well situated by a branch of the Severn which here is divided into three arms, but further up and lower down they unite again. Small ships can go up to Gloucester and even further up the Severn to Bewdley, where there is a shipping centre for Staffordshire. Nowadays the most interesting sight in Gloucester is the pin factory, where more than a thousand people are said to be employed. The brass wire is straightened by

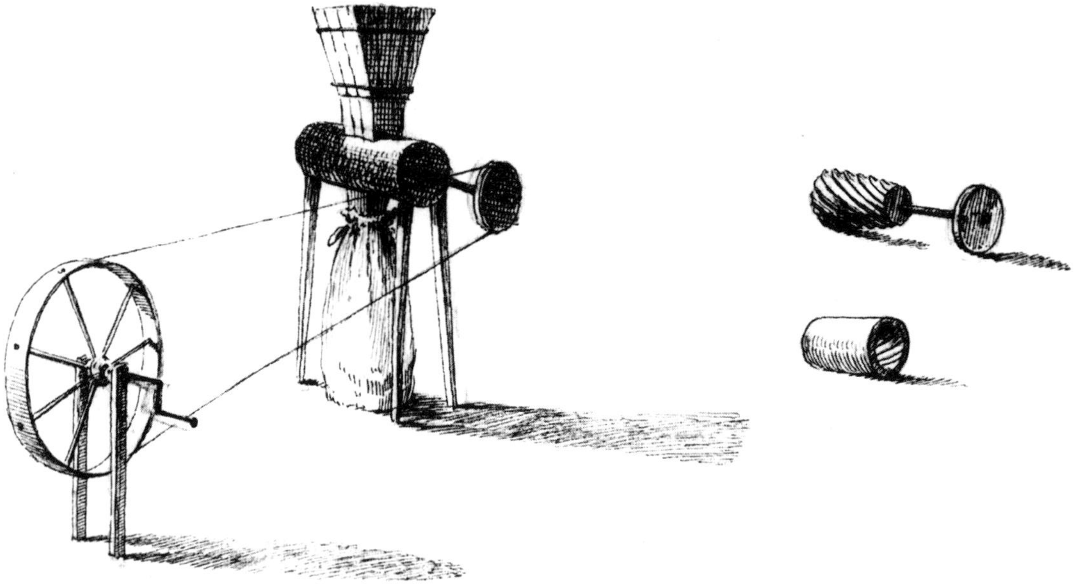

Fig. 168 Malt mill

being threaded and pulled through upright steel pins, which causes it to lose its tendency to roll itself up into rings. This wire is subsequently cut into rods 18 inches long, and then into the various lengths required for pins. These are
351 afterwards ground, or more correctly, filed by means of a wheel of steel provided with cut teeth. The head is pressed on to the stem by a foot-operated press. The pins are then placed in drums and polished by rolling the drums around. Finally they are put into a cauldron with crude cream of tartar or argot and granulated tin and boiled for some hours.[198]
In the pin-making trade the production of blanks for the pinheads is a special branch involving the winding of brass wire onto a rod. The operator takes 50 to 60 turns of the spiral thus formed in his hand at a time and cuts them off to form the blanks. He can handle 15 lb per day. The women and girls in the town are mostly occupied with pressing these blanks onto the stems to form the heads. They are paid ten to 11 shillings per 50 lb of pins, and the work can be done in 12 to 14 days without special effort. The worker who cuts the pinhead blanks gets 2d per pound and can produce 15 lb per day.

Mr Pitt, a great iron master

Mr Pitt[199] owns many iron works in Wales and
352 Gloucester, and has a warehouse in Gloucester that is managed by his brother. I was told that iron is now sold for £20 per ton and that very little Swedish iron is sold in this place.

Production and consumption of iron in England

It was also said that the consumption of iron in England is 45,000 tons per year, of which 16,000 tons are produced in the country.

Scythes

A type of scythe 3 feet 6 inches long, coming from Stourbridge and called a 'Harwoad' scythe, is sold for 3s.6d each.

Raisin wine

In Gloucester and in many other places further up in the country, a large quantity of wine is made from Spanish raisins. It sells for ...[200] per pint.

Highwaymen

Towards evening I travelled from Gloucester to Upton, which is about 16 miles away, and passed across a large common or outlying land where, shortly before, a merchant coming from Gloucester market was robbed of 19 guineas by three highwaymen. However, they had been polite enough to give him back his watch.

Oak plantations and their protection

In some places there were plantations of oaks
with the trees provided with a covering of twigs 353
and small branches to protect the trunks against being damaged by sheep and cattle that graze on this large common in great numbers.

Abandoned copper mine

On the way I had on the left hand side, towards Wales, a view of a large mountain called 'Thownenhill'[201] where some years ago a copper mine was found, though nothing further has been heard about it being worked.

Upton, a town

Upton is a pleasant little place situated by the Severn, with a strong stone bridge [Fig. 169]. The inhabitants of the town make their living mainly by trading with the surrounding countryside, which they can do so much better because all ships from Gloucester and Bristol must pass Upton on the way to Bewdley, Worcester, Shrewsbury, etc. On the other side of the river there are some brick kilns and the clay is found in the same place. The road leading from Upton to Worcester is pleasantly located by the river Severn.

The city of Worcester and its factories for gloves and porcelain

On 30 June I travelled from Upton to Worcester,
which is nine miles. Worcester is called a city 354
and is a fairly large town adorned with many beautiful buildings, amongst which the Cathedral, a large Gothic edifice, and the Town Hall are particularly outstanding [Fig. 170]. The latter has been built in recent years and the front is decorated with a number of statues including Queen Elizabeth and the Kings Charles I and II. This city was some time ago very famous for its manufacture of fine cloth. Since the foremost leaders of this industry passed away and left behind them considerable fortunes, their heirs have succumbed to idleness and conceit, with the result that the factories have gradually declined, so that nowadays little
is heard of them. Instead, the making of gloves 355
has grown from a small beginning to such a large

Fig. 169 Upton

trade and manufacturing industry that more than a thousand households get their livelihood from it. Gloves from Worcester are now reckoned to be the best and finest in England. Glove-making comprises very many processes i.e.[202]

1st	The skins arrive at the 'skinners'.
2nd	Dressing 'in the pits'.
3rd	'Porer', 'Zach. Washbins' and 'Poren'.
4th	The 'cutter' is paid 8d to 10d per dozen.
5th	'Stropper' and 'sewer', per dozen 2s.
6th	'Flapper' and 'Valte'.
7th	'Peinter' who sews the gloves on the outside gets 3d to 15d per dozen.
8th	'Dyer' and 'Colourer' gets 6d to 12d per dozen.
9th	The 'finisher' gets 12 to 16d per dozen.

The best, fine 'women's kid' gloves sell for 18, 20 and 22 and 24 shillings a dozen.

The porcelain factory was founded some years ago by some merchants in the city and has been so successful that nowadays more than a
356 hundred people are employed there.
The porcelain made here appears attractive enough and the workers are well advanced in the art of modelling, but the painting is of a lower standard. The raw material for the porcelain is a mixture of quartz and ashes of burnt bone, and some proportion of pulverised glass is also said to be added. The kilns are built in the same way as those at Chelsea, near London, which already have been described. Otherwise they are here, as at all other places where similar factories have been started, extremely jealous of their processes and a stranger must be prepared to use many cunning ruses and also have good introductions before he can find out what they are.

'Witz'[203] *salt wells and boiling*

4 July. Droitwich is located eight miles from Worcester on the River Salwarpe and is renowned for its abundant salt-springs, over which at various times five shafts or wells have
been sunk to a depth of 180 feet before the 357
spring was reached. However, the supply of salt water is now more than sufficient so that more of it runs to waste than is used for salt-boiling. The reason for the waste is the very high tax that has been imposed on salt and makes the work of the salt boiler less profitable. The digging of salt wells started many years ago, but the salt content of the water was not very high until the great spring 2½ inches in diameter was struck. Nowadays there are 30 salt pans here producing between 9 and 10 tons of salt per week, but the production ceases in wintertime because there is not sufficient sale. These works pay £52,000 a year duty to the Government, which equals more than two million daler copper coin. To boil a pan of salt requires 12 cwt of coal costing
7d to 8d each. 358

Twelve to 13 pans are boiled per week, each pan yielding 46 bushels of salt, and three bushels weigh 112 lb. The excise duty is 3s.1d per bushel, and the salt is sold for 3s.5d. The wages for the salt boiler are 1s per pan. The ground rent or the rent paid to the owner of the well is £10 per year. At the end of each week the

Fig. 170 Worcester

unusable salt that has settled on the bottom and is called 'Peichins' is removed, and thrown away in the river. It generally amounts to about 3 cwt. Any small holes or leaks that appear in the bottom of the pan are stopped with a paste of lime and saltwater. At the end of the boiling the brine is clarified by the addition of two egg whites and a little resin.

The same fires that heat the salt pans also dry the salt, the hot gases and smoke being led through masonry pipes and channels right around the drying rooms and finally to a
359 chimney standing in the middle of the floor, as shown in detail in drawing no. 171. Hammered plates for salt pans are preferred to rolled ones, because the former are reputed to stand up longer to corrosion and cost 27s a cwt. Bar iron costs 20s and 21s. The plates must be 10 inches to 11 inches wide and 1½, 2, 3 and 4 feet long.

Between the salt works and Bewdley the distance is said to be eight miles,[204] but the road is deep in mud and very difficult on the vast and treeless heaths.

Preparation of fern ash

Near Milton[205] and Bewdley I saw large numbers of poor women with children, who collected and burnt fresh ferns.[206] Inquiries established that this was done to recover the ash, which was considered to be unsurpassed for washing clothes. After the ferns are burnt, the ash is mixed with water and made into balls that are placed on an open coal fire or in the kitchen grate to be thoroughly burnt, after
which they are ready for use and sold for one 360
penny for five or six balls of 2½ inches diameter. The ferns should be wet when burnt otherwise they will not yield ash. This ash is called fernash and many people in this locality make a living out of collecting it.

Rabbit warrens and rabbit-catching

On the commons here great numbers of rabbits were seen that had dug so many holes in the ground that it was dangerous to ride by the side of the road where the horse could stumble in one of the gaps and fall. Although there is such an abundance of rabbits, they are owned by somebody, and so-called 'warreners' watch over them and see to it that they are not taken away by strangers. However, it is quite a job to catch them, as they are very quick on their feet and hide away in their underground passages.
To catch the rabbits, the warreners first let loose a little dog that chases them into their holes,
and then a little animal called a ferret is let into 361

Fig. 171 Salt pan

the holes after them. Small nets about 1 foot square and provided with draw strings are then placed over the holes, and the strings tied to sticks stuck into the ground. When the rabbits see the ferret, which is much smaller than they are themselves, they are so scared of him that they immediately flee out of the holes. When they try to pass the little net covering the way out of their lair, the string pulls it together and the rabbits lie there imprisoned inside it. They are then killed by a blow with the edge of the hand. Occasionally it happens that the above-mentioned ferret drives the rabbits into a blind hole. The warrener then has to listen carefully to hear approximately where the ferret is so that he can dig it out, because the enmity between the two different kinds of animals is so great that the ferret will not leave the rabbits so long as they are in the hole in front of him, but keeps
362 gnawing their behinds.

Lower Milton iron-works

Towards evening I arrived at Lower Milton, which is an iron-works consisting of three hammers and four hearths and located in Worcestershire. It belongs to Mr Knight, who also has another iron-works a little way further up, by Upper Milton.[207] In addition he owns many other works in the district. Six hearths fine 18 tons a week, when all goes well, and this is drawn down to bars by three other hammers and hearths. The production of these two works probably amounts to 800 tons per year, and the pig iron is obtained from Lancashire and Wales, and also to some extent from America. The coal comes down the Severn from Shropshire 20 miles away. The wages are the usual, 10s per ton in the finery and 9s in the chafery, or a total of 19s. In the chafery hearths mineral coal is used, but otherwise charcoal. The price of the
iron is £20.10s per ton. 363

They were now using American pig iron of the stamp ***PRINCIPIUM***[208] for their wrought-iron production. This stamp is easy to work but the product is always cold short. It is slit by a slitting mill and sold to the nailers for £22.10s per ton.

Bewdley town and port

Bewdley is a small place, but business there is quite good, due to the harbour, which serves the manufacturing towns Birmingham, Wolverhampton, Stourbridge, Dudley, Wednesbury, etc, all located in Staffordshire. In this county there are many manufacturers of nails and other articles of steel and iron, as well as of copper and brass, such as boxes and similar fine work. A great deal of this is shipped down the Severn to Bristol. Large quantities of Swedish and German[209] iron and other goods are carried as return cargo to be worked up to steel, or in the slitting mills to rods for the

364 nailers and also for other purposes, for which the iron from these countries is particularly suitable. Nearly 2000 tons of foreign iron is estimated to pass through Stourport every year, and it is imported from St Petersburg and Sweden by Messrs Spooner and Knight and by Lloyd etc in Birmingham. Mr Finch of Dudley, who is a large-nail merchant, also imports a small quantity.

From Bewdley to Birmingham the carriage cost for iron is 12s to 16s per ton. For manufactured goods from Birmingham to Bewdley the charge is 20s per ton. From Bristol to Bewdley by river costs 5s per ton.

Iron prices

Pig iron from Lancashire nowadays costs £7.10s; from Mr Knight's works £7; from America £6.10s; of the best quality, £7. The merchants in Bristol and Birmingham and other towns have their warehouses in Bewdley.
365 Mr Pelton's representative is Mr Carteret. Mr Spooner's is called John Con. Mr 'Cariks', ironmonger in Bewdley did not now have any Swedish iron in stock.

Kidderminster, town and carpet factories

Kidderminster, three-and-a-half miles from Bewdley, is a small town famous for its carpets or Turkish rugs and its factories for tapestry, that had their origins at Wilton near Salisbury, although from the very beginning these articles were imported from Flanders. This carpet is woven in the same way as flowered velvet, only with the difference that velvet is made entirely of silk, whereas the warp of the carpet is linen and the weft is woollen yarn of divers colours. The latter is cut with a knife along the wires that are woven into the cloth just as in the making of velvet. In the town there are now 60 carpet looms, one master weaver of cloth with three looms, and one with two looms for women's
366 aprons.

The carpet is 27 inches wide and the price per yard of 3 feet is 5s. Two yards can be completed per day and the wages for the weaving are 1s per yard. Mr 'Pisal' alone keeps 32 carpet looms working.

Braidwaters steel-works

On the way to Stourbridge, which lies seven miles from Kidderminster, I visited Braidwaters steel-works, consisting of two furnaces which, however, are not in use at the same time, as when one is cooling down, the other is at full heat. The steel is made from Öregrund iron, of which the stamp ***L*** [210] is considered the best, next come ***Double Bullet***, ***OO***,[211] ***G***,[212] ***CDG***,[213] etc, but other good Swedish stamps are also used at a pinch, as well as Russian, though these never produce steel of as perfect quality steel as the first-mentioned Öregrund stamp. There was now some building going on at the works and the furnaces were made to the same capacity and dimensions as commonly used in London. 367

A hammer to forge steel for special purposes also belonged to this works and, for the reheating, there was a specially designed furnace [sic]. The iron stamped ***L***[214] costs £23 per ton. The conversion to steel costs £1 to £2.10s and the profit on the conversion is £2.[215] The price of first-quality steel, namely blister steel,[216] is £28; second quality is £27, and forged steel costs £32 to £33 per ton. For the cementation, only crushed charcoal made from oak is used, as well as coarse charcoal breeze, which is packed into the chests and then covered with fine sand.

Plating hammer for saw blades

A little further up there was a plating hammer for large saw blades, forged of steel.

Stourbridge town and industry

Stourbridge is famous in the first place for the nail-making that is carried out all around the neighbourhood, and in the second place for the 368
glass works, producing drinking glasses, window glass and bottles, of which there are now eleven in operation in the area. Stourbridge clay, which is so well known because of its great heat resistance, also comes from here. In addition there is in the district an abundance of coal seams and a number of mines for working them.

Forging of nails at Stourbridge

A nailer can work up two bundles of slit iron per week, with a total weight of 1 cwt which gives him an income of 1s.6d.[217] Two such bundles now cost 22s or £22 per ton. This has recently been increased by £1.10s per ton by Messrs Knight and Spooner who in this country increase the price of iron as they please, which gives the workers, who do not get any more for their labour, reason to groan and be angry. They recently sent a fiery cross to Mr Knight at Wolverley, threatening to pull down the house

369 that he recently has had built, which cost him £5000, unless he agreed to sell iron at the old price. Due to this message, Mr Knight was compelled to have a guard around his house with loaded guns and cannons for two weeks, until the excitement cooled down but, in spite of this, the price remained the same.

There is no Swedish iron in this area now, let alone any Russian, and the result is that these gentlemen who own most of the iron-works around here can take the opportunity of increasing the price of their wares. The price of nails was noted down at Dudley. In this district, within a diameter of 18 miles, 9000 tons of iron per year are slit in slitting mills and most of it is used for nail-making. Even more would be consumed if there were not a shortage of foreign iron, which the above-mentioned iron-masters exploit on purpose to secure the sale of
370 their own poor and cold-short iron.

Nail-making in Wednesbury

In Wednesbury, two miles from Bilston, there are also many nailers, and also in Darlaston.

Glass-works at Stourbridge

The glass-works at Stourbridge are arranged in the same way as the ones in Bristol that already have been described. Mr Rogers has two glass houses close by the town, one making drinking glasses of various kinds, and the other, window glass and bottles. For white glass, the crucibles, which come from the Isle of Wight, are charged with soda, potash, red lead, arsenic, some safflower,[218] and waste glass. Safflower is also used for window glass to give it a bluish colour. This glass is made by blowing and swinging, and a pit is provided to facilitate the work. When the bubble becomes long and large enough, it is touched with a wet iron bar at the lower end so that the thick bottom cracks and
371 can be knocked off. The bubble is again placed in the furnace for further heating and touched with the edge of the wetted iron bar, which causes it to crack on one side. Subsequently it is once more placed in the furnace, and finally flattened out and cut off.

It was said that the two glass-works together paid the Government £2500 in excise duty. The duty is paid according to the volume or weight of glass that is in the crucibles, which is measured by the customs officer for each batch with the aid of an iron rod.[219] The weight is then calculated in the way already mentioned together with the price of glass in the section
about Bristol. 372

Fire clay at Stourbridge

The Stourbridge clay is dug up half a mile from the town and looks bluish as long as it is wet, but whitens to a light-grey colour as soon as it has had time to dry. Immediately above this seam there is another one of ordinary clay, used for making bricks, and above that lies a seam of coal which is, in turn, covered by hard rock. However, in some places where there are outcrops of coal, the rock is not to be seen. The fire clay feels very smooth and slippery between the fingers, but nevertheless it has to be ground and sieved before it can be used for bricks and other products that must be fire-resistant [Fig. 172].

In the making of crucibles or pots for glass, the ground clay is mixed with some finely ground bricks or old, used pots. The latter material must first be very carefully separated
from the glassy pieces that stick to it that would 373
give the vessel, which otherwise stands up very well to the fire, a lower melting point and poorer lasting qualities.

Bricks made of this fire-clay are sold for 25s per thousand, and the common ordinary bricks for 11s per thousand. The wages are 4s per thousand. A special brick, thicker at one end, is made for furnace arches and sold at 2s.6d per hundred. In addition to bricks, crucibles and the like, great quantities of clay are sent by wagon to Bewdley, the carriage amounting to 5s or 6s per ton. From Bewdley it is shipped to Bristol and other places in England by water. The cost of freight to Bristol is also 5s per ton, and the clay is sold there for 27s and 28s per ton. Half a mile further down the valley a new clay mine 48 feet deep was being opened. During the sinking of the winding shaft, two new coal seams have been found, one a foot
thick and the other 18 inches. 374

Works at Stourbridge

The coal seam now being worked lies below the latter. During the removal of the earth at the surface, a third seam was found above the clay, and in the rocky hill beside the valley there is said to be a fourth. At this mine a water-driven pump has been installed [Fig. 173].

Factory for frying pans

Close by stood a forge that makes iron sheets for frying pans, which are finished in

Fig. 172 Crushing, drying and kiln at Stourbridge

Stourbridge. The wages for forging the sheets for the pans are 2s.6d per cwt. After the sheets have been forged roughly to shape, they are taken to Stourbridge and hammered by hand to a certain size. They are then placed in an iron mortar or mould, eight or nine in a pile, and hammered down with a heavy pestle to form the sides. This machine was invented here, but its performance has not been as good as planned.
375 Therefore the method used in Stourbridge itself, as well as in Birmingham and Coalbrookdale, is to hammer the sheets down into a conical die as shown in drawing no. 174. If a large pan is to be made, the die is filled with iron scrapings and filings, and these are removed in proportion to the smaller sizes that one wishes to produce.[220] The wages are 5s per cwt and the finished product is sold for 28s per cwt. This factory belongs to William Allen.

Stock- and gun-lock factory at Stourbridge

Stock locks or gun locks are also made by some masters in Stourbridge and sell for between 4s and 30s per dozen. Those 9 inches long are the cheapest, namely 4s; 10 inches long 6s; 12 inches long, 12s; 13 inches long, 16s; and 15 inches long, 30s. Gunlocks, double bridle,
sell for 5s to 7s and 12s; 'water pan and bolt' for 376
14s; three-quarter bridle, 2s.6d; single bridle 3s.6d; common trading 1s; trading fine, 1s.3d; half bridle, 1s.10d. Cloth shears cost 16 pence a pound.

Field and meadow fertilising

Where the earth is sandy, lime mixed with dung is used as fertiliser for the fields in this district. Lime and soil mixed together are sprinkled on grassy banks immediately after sowing, and garden beds are given the same treatment.

Fern ash

In the whole neighbourhood ferns are burnt to ash which is made into balls and said to be better for washing linen than soap.

Coal mines

Between Stourbridge and Dudley, which is a distance of five measured miles, there are a very many coal mines, and also fire engines for drawing out the water. Most of the coal seams lie at a depth of 150 feet to 180 feet and are in
some places 11 yards or 31 feet thick. 377

Fig. 173 Clay and coal mine at Stourbridge

Occasionally one finds two seams, one above the other, and these are not so thick. On the plain nearer to Dudley there are many coal mines worked by Lord Ward who lives in the vicinity. Below the coal seam there is iron ore in the same way as in Wednesbury. In Wednesbury, which is four miles from here, several houses are reported to have fallen into the coal mines that have been worked beneath the town without proper supporting pillars.

Dudley Castle

Dudley has an old castle belonging to Lord Ward that was destroyed by fire some years ago [see Fig. 175].

Limestone quarry with fossils

The hill on which it was built consists of three strata of limestone dipping south and containing many fossils of shells, particularly the so-called screws, small crustacea, bivalves, etc.

The limestone strata here are being quarried
378 very industriously, and the stone is burnt to lime down in the quarries and sold to the surrounding countryside as fertiliser for the fields.

Fall of wagon and horses

A carter who arrived yesterday to load lime drove his team carelessly and lost six horses and a wagon. The wagon had turned over into a quarry and pulled the horses down with it, one by one. As is always the case here, they were hitched one in front of the other in a single row. The loss is reckoned to be £100. In desperation the carter wanted to follow his team, but was prevented by another man.

Nail and other iron factories in and around Dudley

The main occupation in Dudley and the surrounding district is the forging of nails. In addition there are many factories and workshops for iron manufactures, such as malt-

Fig. 174 Pan-forming machine

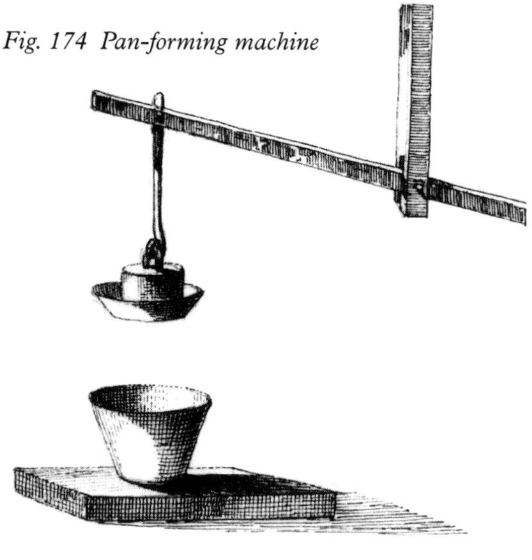

Fig. 175 Dudley Castle

and coffee-mills, hinges for doors and caskets,
axes, and other large-edge tools, screw-vices,
379 horse-locks, etc. The prices of nails are shown
by the list below.

Clout nails, 2½ lb	14½d per 1000
Ditto 3 lb	2s per 1000
20 penny nails, 30 lb or 3d per pound	7–8s per 1000

Note: 100 nails, that is six score, or 120 nails.[221]

6 lb of nails, 175 nails per pound	2s.0d per 1000
4 lb of nails, four-penny lb 15 score nails	1s.6d per 1000
3 lb of nails, three-penny lb	1s.3d per 1000
2 lb of nails, two-penny lb	1s.0d per 1000
7 lb of nails, sixpenny lb	2s.3d per 1000
8 lb of nails, sixpenny lb	2s.5½d per 1000
9 lb of nails	2s.9d per 1000
10 lb of nails	2s.11½d per 1000
12 lb of nails	3s.5d per 1000
13 lb of nails	3s.8d per 1000
14 lb of nails	3s.11d per 1000
15 lb of nails	4s.2d per 1000
16 lb of nails	4s.5d per 1000
17 lb of nails	4s.8d per 1000
18 lb of nails	4s.11d per 1000
380 20 lb of nails	5s.3½d per 1000

For larger sizes than 20 [penny] nails, the wages are 1d per pound, and the sales price 3½d per pound.

Iron is now paid for by the bundle, which weighs 60 lb and costs 11s or £22 per ton. The slitting does not cost more than 15s per ton, but 1 cwt is reckoned to be lost during the heating, so that one ton of iron for which £20.10s is paid, actually in this way will cost £22 per ton and a little more.[222]

Horse locks are sold per dozen for 17s to 30s according to quality and size. 'Gott' locks sell for 8s a dozen.

Corn mills, 7 inches diameter sell for 1 guinea
Corn mills, 9½ inches diameter sell for £2
Corn mills, 10 inches diameter sell for £3
Coffee mills sell for 4s to 10s.

Flat bars for mills, made of Swedish iron, cost £26 per ton for the best quality.

Hinges 18 inches long, cost 3s, ditto 12s per
dozen. 381

Screw vices between 18 and 100 lb in weight sell for 5d per pound, 4 lb in weight for 4s; 5 lb in weight for 4s.6d; 6 lb in weight, 5s; 7 lb in weight, 5s.6d; 8 lb in weight, 16s.

'Witthans', an edge toolmaker, sells axes for 5d per pound, house carpenters' axes for 17d each, ships carpenters' for 20d, Coopers' for 20d.

James Knight 'Veiser' asks 5½d per pound for vices free in Dudley.

Cradley ironworks

From Dudley I took the road to Cradley forge which belongs to Mr Croft of Birmingham.

There is also a blast furnace here that was not in blast now, but I viewed a hammer with a reverberatory furnace and a hearth for reworking scrap iron. The wages were 15s per ton and the weekly production 2 to 3 tons. The furnace and process have already been described before at Wednesbury. There was also
382 a forge with two hearths for fining of pig iron with charcoal. The production amounts to between 4 and 5 tons a week and the wages are 10s. The same pig iron is also used at another forge further down the river. The slitting mill was not in operation, but I observed that the rolls had a diameter of 11 inches and the slitting discs were 12 inches with an overlap of one inch. The mill was driven by two water wheels. The annual production amounts to 700 tons, although in a week 20 to 25 tons can be slit.

Woods

Between Cradley and Birmingham I travelled through a forest that might have been three to four miles long and a quarter mile wide. It consisted of oaks and other deciduous trees. A cord of wood is 4 feet high, 8 feet long and 4 feet wide and costs 11, 12, and up to 14s. A cord 6 feet long, 4 feet high and 4 feet wide costs 11 to 12s. Two cords make a load of
383 charcoal. Note: eight to 12 sacks make a load, and one sack holds eight bushels. The wages for burning the coal are 3s to 4s per load. Mr Knight pays for carriage to the forge 4½d per sack, or a penny a mile. The wood costs 11s per cord not including wages that amount to 2s a cord for cutting and 4½d per cording.

Grinding mill for scythes

Not far from Cradley there was a grinding mill where scythes are ground for 20d and 22d a dozen. A scythe costs from 2s to 2s.2d or 2s.3d.

Aston blast furnace

The blast furnace at Aston near Birmingham, which was described during my previous stay in this district, produces 17 tons a week with a consumption of 28 to 30 tons of charcoal.

Various ironworks on the River Stour

The following works are located on the River Stour, not counting corn mills, namely: Cradley forge, mill and furnace; Stourbridge plating forge; Whittington forge; Turton mill; Hyde mill; Cookley forge; 'Haberley' forge;
Wilden; 'Mylord' forge; 'Pinehall'; 'Pinehall 38
mill'; Witton two forges; 'Minigen' two forges; 'Prestar' wire mill.[223]

Birmingham, a manufacturing town

Birmingham is the principal town for fabrication of iron, steel and brass and also for making divers finer articles and quincaillerie.

Rolling and slitting mill

I viewed the slitting mill belonging to Mr L Laid, which handles 17 tons a week of Swedish iron, or 600 tons per year. The charge for slitting of iron is 16s per ton, and for steel 30s. Thirty tons per day[224] can be slit and the wages amount to 8s or 9s per week [each] for two people.

Horseshoe nails are stamped with wooden stamps, driven by a wheel with a donkey walking in it, and finally by a crank, and then

Fig. 176 Stamping mill for horseshoe nails

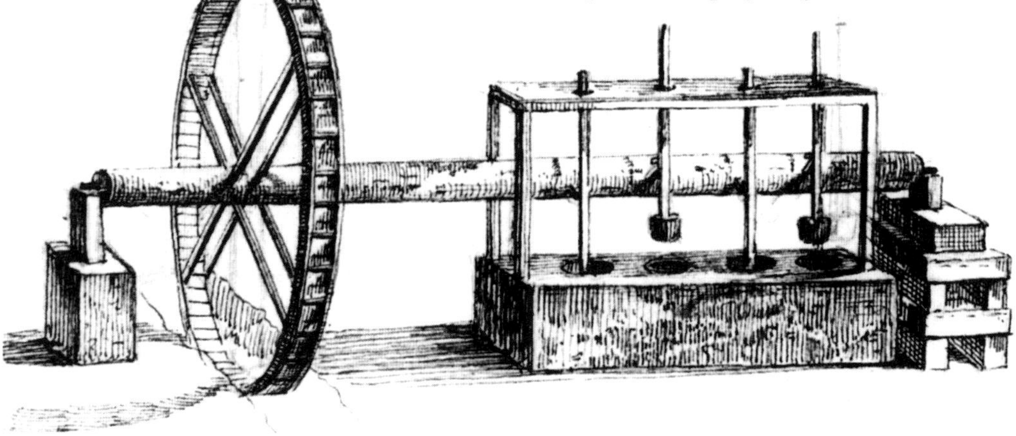

put together, rubbed, polished and pressed [Fig. 176, water driven].

Iron and steel prices, consumption transport costs

Prices of iron and steel: Öregrund iron is assumed to fetch £22. Ditto Stockholm iron £18.10s to £19 per ton. Blister steel £27 to
385 £28 per ton. German steel intended for edge tools, £48 per ton. Mr Spooner imports 1000 tons of iron, Mr Elaid 800 tons, and makes himself 270 tons, Mr ....[225] also imports 300 tons, and Mr Finch in Dudley, 500 tons.

The river Trent is 18 miles distant from Birmingham and carriage by wagon costs 9d per cwt but for all other goods than bar iron, 1s. From Trent to Bristol the charge is 18d per cwt. One cord of wood 8 feet long, 4 feet high and 4 feet wide costs 14s to 15s. Iron sheets for tea trays are from 27s to 31s per cwt.

Steel-works

I also saw Mr Kittle's steel furnace where the stamp ***L***[226] and other Öregrund iron is converted, but the price was not known because the iron is obtained from Mr Spooner who is a good friend of Mr Kittle's. The price of the steel was here £28 per ton. At this works, located in the town of Birmingham, there are two furnaces of which one is always fired and in operation. There was iron in stock for cementation and the
386 stamps were the following: ***L OO :P:*** [227] which are considered the best for steel. ***CDG SWV HSG***[228] rank next in the order of quality. The stamp ***L crowned***[229] is considered good for gunlocks and springs.

Locksmiths between Stafford and Wolverhampton

On the road between Stafford and Wolverhampton there are many locksmiths, who live in miserable hovels and deliver their products to Wolverhampton every Wednesday, which is the market day. Stock locks from 5 inches to 16 inches cost from 3s.6d to 36s a dozen. Casket locks 1 inch to 2 inches square are sold for 3s.6d to 36s a dozen. Hinges are priced at 6d per pound.

Wolverhampton: prices and consumption of iron

Wolverhampton: the ironmongers Messrs Jervis, Corsen and Son, import 100 tons of foreign or Swedish iron. The price was £22 per ton with six months credit. Slit English iron costs £22 per ton. Iron for 'bushes'[230] made from old 'Holland iron' is sold for 23s per cwt. Swedish
iron comes to Bridgnorth, ten miles away by 387
road. Carriage costs 10s a ton. Iron from Bristol by water costs 20d per cwt. Swedish 'Clair iron'[231] for candle-snuffers and other polished work, costs 21s per ton. Ditto for horse shoes and tyre iron 20s or 21s. On the road to Wednesbury: axes cost 56d per pound; spades are sold for 2s to 3s each.

Gunlock prices at Bilston[232]

Bilston: Gunlocks, common 'Traidel' 15d each. Lock in 'rest', $6\frac{1}{2}$d to 7d. Wages for filing of above-mentioned locks, 6d to 7d.

Gunlock prices at Wednesbury

Wednesbury: Mr Burchard charges for musket locks, 14d. Small 'corst', $12\frac{1}{2}$d. Trading, bought a sample of it, 14d. Double three-quarters, 3s.9d. Double 'Credlock', 5s. Ditto $4\frac{1}{2}$, 6s to 7s each. Ditto gunlocks at another gunsmith. Small 'colst' 12d. Musket ditto 14d. 'Traiding fans', 4d. Best ditto, 20d. Half bridle 24d; three-quarters ditto 2s.2d. 'Solid pans'
three-quarters bridle, 2s.6d. Ditto 3s. 388

Waterpans, 6s.6d. Waterpans ditto, 8s. Bolt double bridle, 6s.6d. Ditto 8s. Ditto 9s. Waterpan and bolt, 10s.6d. Waterpan and bolt, ditto 12s.6d.

Blade and button factories in Birmingham

The largest factories for buttons are Mr Taylor's, who has 600 people working for him, and Messrs Alcock and 'Chuchsen' who are considered to employ more workers and make 4000 gross a week.

Wilden forge

On the way to London I viewed Wilden forge located by the River Stour in Worcestershire and belonging to Lord Foley. Here are two hammers, three finery and one chafery hearths, and the production is ten to $11\frac{1}{2}$ tons a week. $471\frac{3}{4}$ tons were made in the year 1753. The hammer
weighs 7 cwt. 389

One ton of iron requires one-and-a-half loads of charcoal. The chafery hearth uses pit coal. The wages for the fining are 9s.6d. During the year 1753 the price of iron was £19 per ton, but it was raised to £20.10s at the beginning of 1754. Slit iron costs £22 per ton. 'Overiron', made by the finers and chafers when they produce more than 20 cwt of bar iron from 26 cwt of pig iron, is rewarded by double wages.

Tinplate mill at Wilden

At Wilden there is also a mill for rolling and tinning sheets, of which 40 to 50 boxes are made per week. Each box contains 225 tin plates, sold for 50s. At the tinning, tallow and resin are used. One box requires 14 lb of tin. On the whole, the process is the same as the one at Pontypool, with the exception that the plates are put through a stand of rolls after
390 tinning to make them smooth. I passed through Upper and Lower Witton with forges belonging to Mr Knight, already described on the trip from Wales to Birmingham.

Ironworks on the River Stour

Most of the forges on the River Stour obtain their pig iron from Lancashire, Wales and America. The price of pig iron is now £7 for Welsh, £7.10s for Lancastrian, and £6.10s to £7 for American, not including carriage, which is not so expensive because it is often possible to ship the iron by sea and then up the River Severn to Bewdley.

Prices of wood and charcoal

One cord of wood 4 feet high, 8 feet long and 4 feet wide costs 10s to 14s, cutting and cording included, which otherwise cost 2s.4$\frac{1}{2}$d. Nine cords of wood are placed in a pit or stack, that yields four to five loads of charcoal. One-and-three-quarter cords generally produce a load of coal, which here is counted as eight sacks, although it is the same
391 measure as 12 sacks in other places. The wages of the charcoal burner are 3s.6d per load and the stack is charred in ten to 12 days. Carriage costs 1s per load and mile, so that a man who carried eight sacks on three horses for six miles gets 6s.

Between Wilden and Worcester the road passed over a common that was planted with oak, ash and beech. I also went through Worcester, which already has been described on the trip from Wales to Stourbridge.

'Amersham' town[233]

Six miles from Worcester lies Pershore on the river Avon, which is navigable all the way to Warwick. This is a very great advantage for the whole of this district, having regard to the ease with which iron and other heavy goods are transported up the country from Bristol, with grain and cheese going back in return.

Pershore town and wool-spinning

Pershore is also on the Warwick River Avon, where there is an abundance of fruit trees,
particularly pears and cherries. The business of 39
this town is mainly spinning of wool and knitting of stockings. All the old women had long tobacco pipes clamped in their mouths as they worked.

Old wheat stacks

Here there were a number of wheat-straw stacks that were said to be five to six years old and still not threshed.

Evesham town and stocking-knitting

Evesham is also on the pretty little River Avon, over which there is here a beautiful stone bridge. Knitting of stockings and horticulture are the main occupations in this place.
Two churches here stand close together and nearby a superb tower has been built where their combined bells are hung.

Agriculture

The fields were ploughed with diagonal furrows as previously noted on the trip from Birmingham to London. The ploughs used were
fitted with small iron wheels underneath. 39

Lime kilns

Moreton in the Marsh is located near a high hill where there are many lime kilns that are fully occupied with supplying the surrounding countryside with its requirements of lime for the fields and for the building of houses. Flints began to appear near Blenheim and Woodstock, and chalk a few miles further on.

Chalk as fertiliser

On some kinds of soil unburnt chalk acts as fertiliser, but for soil of a colder nature it must be burnt. Blenheim, Woodstock and Oxford were described on the journey to Oxford.

Crystallisation of stone strata

At the sandstone quarries outside Oxford, it was observed how the strata of stone had crystallised in the same way as described at Nottingham.

Beech forest

In the neighbourhood of West Wycombe there is a splendid beech forest, that supplies London with wood for the glass-works and for other purposes on special occasions.

Lace-making at High Wycombe

High Wycombe is famous for lace-making,
394 which occupies the women in this place.

Wire mill and paper mills

A few miles down the river there is a wire mill and 20 paper mills, one after the other.

Clupton wire mill

Clupton wire mill is 25 miles from London and belongs to Mr 'Berck'. Twenty different kinds of iron wire are made here, of which the coarsest sells for 20s and the finest for 45s a bundle, weighing 62 lb. The yearly production is 1500 bundles. The iron comes from Wales and is made of pig iron smelted from the grey ore and cinders that are found in the Forest of Dean. Swedish iron was said to be too uneven for iron wire, soft and hard in the same bar. Cast steel[234] for the draw plates comes from Germany and costs 56s per cwt. The process is otherwise the same as described in Wales and Pontypool.

Fences and gates

Near Uxbridge, which lies by the River Colne,
all of the fences and gates of the so-called 395
'China Theatre' are of the design shown in drawing no. 177.

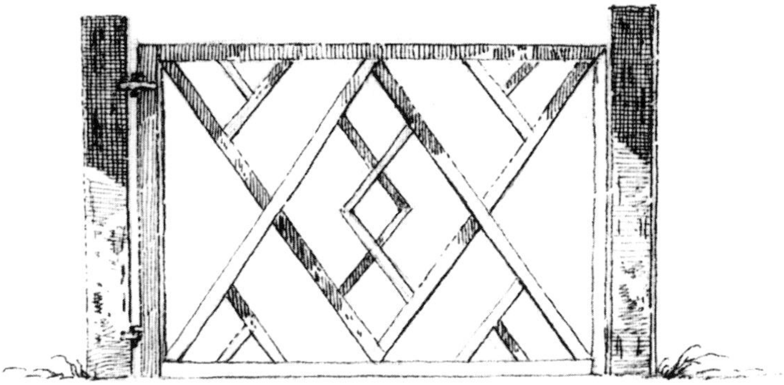

Fig. 177 Gate near Uxbridge

Notes and references

163 Trosnant or Old Furnace, west of Pontypool.

164 This must refer to costs for making wrought-iron bars.

165 This should obviously have been 'charcoal' – *vide* comments in previous paragraph. In some places mineral coal was used in chafery hearths, but never for fining.

166 Fig. 161 seems to show the pipe rising in the form of a siphon, definitely higher than would be needed to lay water onto an undershot wheel. It is possible that the height of the orifice could be adjusted, keeping it below the level of the water behind the dam.

167 Cf. MS p.64.

168 The sheets are passed back above the top roll.

169 It is not clear what is meant by this line, and it is most likely that RRA has made mistakes in copying a price list.

170 Figure omitted.

171 This information on tinplate production corresponds fairly closely to that given in the letter to Messrs Finlay and Jennings MS pp. 60–73 and RRA's observations at Woollard.

172 Literal translation; probably refers to 'raised ware'.

173 A supposedly English word in the MS; probably 'hobnails'.

174 It is not clear what 'no. 14' indicates.

175 This works was known as Monmouth Forge and appears to have been located just outside the town on the River Monnow – see William Rees, *Industry before the Industrial Revolution*, pp.341–2.

176 Thomas Daniel the Elder, prominent iron merchant and iron master in Bristol

177 'Over coal' and 'over iron' are literal translations from the Swedish. It was customary in Sweden

at this time to encourage the workers in the forges by an incentive scheme involving definite allocations of pig iron and charcoal for each unit of finished product. The quantities of raw materials allocated were determined so that it was possible for competent workers to make substantial savings, so that iron and coal were left over from their allocations. This 'over iron' and 'over coal' was in effect sold back to the proprietor at a price profitable to both parties. If, on the other hand, more raw materials were used than allowed for as a result of incompetence or carelessness on the part of the workers, this had to be paid back.

178 Located on the River Wye.

179 About two-and-a-half miles.

180 The Upper Copper Works.

181 The Lower Copper Works belonged at this time to the English Copper Company; see William Rees, *op.cit.,* p.501.

182 RRA calls the product o the rolling mill 'plate' in one place and then 'sheet' a couple of lines later. The mill probably rolled both, but at this time there was no clear distinction between the two.

183 According to Cyril Hart, *The Industrial History of Dean*, pp. 96–7, there were two blast furnaces at Redbrook. The 'lower furnace having come to an end, the Gage family built on or near the same site a new furnace which was let by Lord Gage on 29 September 1742, with two forges at Lydbrook, to Rowland Pytt. William Rees *op.cit.* p.305 states that Rowland Pitt, of Gloucester and Tintern, was active in industry in the Aberavon and Neath districts.

184 According to Cyril Hart *op.cit.* p.241, brush is a massive or stalactitic haematite with little or no gangue.

185 RRA had spent some time in Holland and was obviously inclined to doubt the information he was given about export to that country.

186 A reference to the rights and privileges of the Free Miners.

187 Probably one of the forges at Lydbrook leased by Rowland Pitt from Lord Gage.

188 Now Mitcheldean.

189 Probably Ruardean. According to Cyril Hart *op.cit.* p.300, there were in 1787 20 quarries in Ruardean Walk.

190 This must have been Guns Mill, converted from an iron furnace at some time between 1732 and 1743.

191 Known as a 'Hollander'.

192 No doubt a member of the well-known Worcestershire family.

193 Charcoal free from fines.

194 The word 'bey', neither English nor Swedish in this context, may be a copyist's error.

195 This probably means 'as the crow flies' and 'actual distance by road', in which case the distances quoted are reasonably correct.

196 'Virtue above the skies'.

197 RRA probably means 'culm' which is anthracite slack.

198 This process deposits a thin coating of tin onto the pins.

199 This must be the same Rowland Pitt or Pytt referred to on MS p.335.

200 Price missing.

201 This must have been part of the Malvern Hills, but it has not been possible to identify the exact location.

202 The terms are given in the MS as English, but the spelling is doubtful.

203 Droitwich

204 About 12 miles.

205 A village now part of Stourport.

206 Probably bracken.

207 According to William Rees *op.cit.* p.327, the forges at Milton and the other iron-works seem to have been acquired by Richard Knight from the Foley partners, probably before Knight's own entry into the partnership in 1707. Richard Knight died in 1707 so, at the time of RRA's visit, the works would have belonged to his sons or grandsons.

208 Principio Forge was built in 1723–4, the first in Maryland, and was for many years the leading American iron company, active until the Revolution.

209 In view of what is said below, it seems likely that RRA means Russian iron rather than German. This could be a copyist's error as the two words are similar in Swedish: Ryskt and Tyskt.

210 Leufsta forge (Uppland), established in 1566 or possibly earlier, was one of the largest iron-works in Sweden for many years, finally closed down in 1926.

211 Österbybruk (Uppland).

212 Gimo forge (Uppland), established in 1615 and closed in 1946.

213 Not identified.

214 Leufsta (Uppland).

215 RRA states that the best-quality iron costs £23 and with the cost of conversion up to a maximum of £2.10s, the cost of the best quality steel is thus £25.10s. The price is stated to be £28, giving a profit of £2.10s, which accords reasonably well with the stated profit figure of £2 for conversion.

216 Probably all cementation steel would have been known as blister steel.
217 This must be the daily income, which would give the worker a weekly wage of nine shillings, similar to the wages of other workers encountered.
218 The word used in the MS certainly appears to be 'safflower' but it is doubtful whether a vegetable dye would survive molten glass temperature.
219 The iron rod was used to measure the depth of the melt and, since the horizontal dimensions of the pot were known, the depth gave the volume and hence weight.
220 In this way the diameter of the die above the filling could be made to match the required diameter of the bottom of the pan.
221 Something appears to be missing here.
222 The correct figure is £21 12s.
223 Works with names in inverted commas have not been identified.
224 The figure of 30 tons per day must be a mistake in transcription: three tons per day would agree with the iron consumption figures.
225 Missing from MS.
226 Leufsta.
227 Leufsta; Österby; Carlholm-Åkerby.
228 Unidentified; Stålboga (Södermanland, established 1641, closed 1881); Fredriksberg-Annefors (founded 1721, closed 1890 and 1896).
229 Unidentified.
230 Written out as an English word in MS; probably bushes for wooden cart and carriage wheels.
231 This quality has not been encountered before; also, the price must be 'per cwt'.
232 The information on gunlock prices must have been taken from price lists. RRA's versions of the English terms are fairly approximate and require further research.
233 This must be Pershore and the duplication of information must be a transcription error.
234 This is a surprisingly early mention of cast steel of German origin.

Volume 2

Arabic pagination

Page numbers from the fair copy are shown in the margin.

Journey 6a London to Sheffield

27 July 1754. London, Bow, Stratford, Epping, Bishops Stortford, Cambridge, Huntingdon, St Ives, Downham, Boston, Kings Lynn, Sleaford, Newark, Nottingham, Bulwell, Basford, Derby, Burton, Belper, Denby, Crich, Matlock, Winster, Chatsworth, Chesterfield, Sheffield.

1 ***The journey from London***

On 27 July [1754] I started my journey from London and took the road to Cambridge. I stopped 3 miles from London at a town called Bow, where a porcelain factory has been established, but I was not able to view it at this time because the owner was away, and no-one is allowed in without his permission.[1]

Kilns burning lime for fertiliser

In the neighbourhood of the porcelain works, here known as the china house, there were a number of lime kilns, constructed in the same way as often described before. The lime is made by burning a mixture of chalk and pitcoal. The lime is taken out from the bottom when it is burnt, but great care has to be taken to keep the kiln full at all times, as it is difficult to light the fire again if it should go out.

The lime is mainly used as fertiliser and is
2 mixed with soil, dug up by the side of the road, and with dung. To begin with the materials are placed in layers on top of each other, but are later mixed by shovelling so as to be ready for carting out to the fields by Michaelmas.

Stratford, a small town with a steam engine

Stratford is also a small town, joined together with Bow, but not remarkable for anything but a steam engine which is kept in continuous operation pumping the pure spring water found here through pipes and channels to London.

Two pumps raise the water to a height of about 10 feet and from there it is conveyed under pressure through another pipe to a reservoir placed in a 60-foot-high tower above the steam engine. From this reservoir the water flows by gravity through pipes of oak to all places where it is used.

Summer palaces around London

Eight to 10 miles from London one sees many
3 beautiful residences and manor houses or so-called Gentlemen's Seats, mainly built to provide recreation during the summer, but not occupied in the winter.

Forest at the town of Epping

Near Epping, a town of little importance, one travels through a forest 3 or 4 miles in diameter, consisting of oak, elm, ash, lime and other broad-leaved trees. Since there are no mines or bar-iron forges in this neighbourhood, the wood is used for building half-timbered houses, with the interstices filled with wattle-and-daub. It is

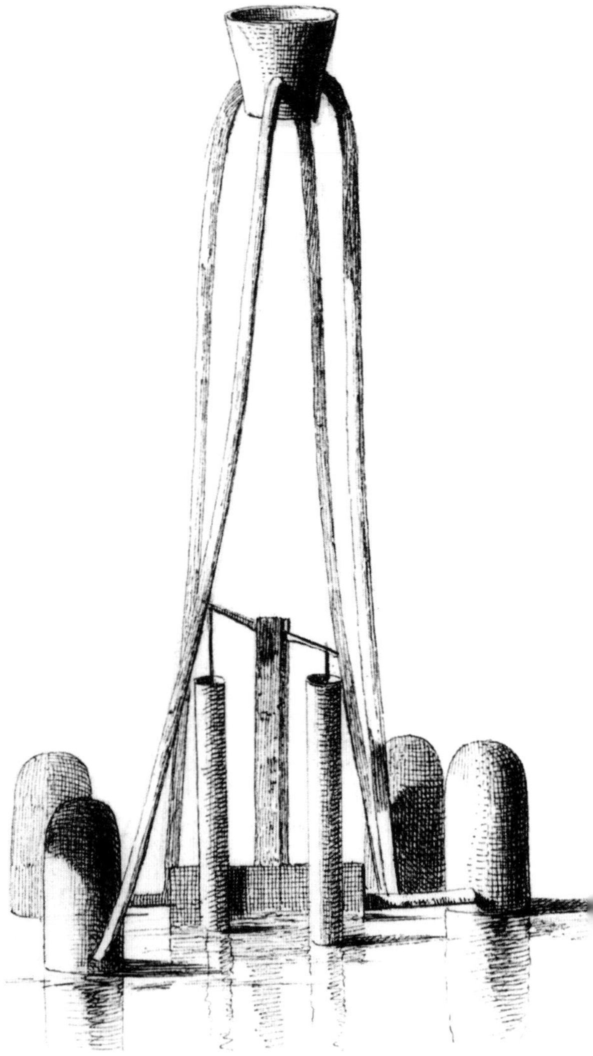

Fig. 178 Water pumps at Stratford [2]

also sawn into planks and employed for making wooden pipes and various tools and articles for household use.

Houses of inferior kind

Houses in this district belonging to people of medium rank are also constructed with half timbering, but the wattle is covered with a mixture of lime and sand, decorated with all sorts of figures on the outside.[3] Along this road I also saw one or two houses with gables of
4 brick, although otherwise they were half timbered [Fig. 179].

Houses of the better kind

Houses in these parts classified as Gentlemen's Seats are built of brick, of which great quantities are made along the road and in other places nearby. The clay that is used is of the ordinary kind, abundant in Sweden. It would be better employed there for this purpose, making houses fireproof, rather than being allowed to lie unprofitably, often harmful to agriculture.

Fertilisers for farms

The farmers in this district are very industrious in collecting dung for their fields and meadows. It is generally placed by the highway and mixed with the topsoil obtained beside it. The topsoil is first thrown over the dung-heap, but in due course the two materials are mixed by being moved a short distance by shovelling. In this operation care is taken to lift soil and dung
together straight from the bottom. 5

If the soil that is to be treated with this fertiliser is of a cold nature, that is, consisting of clay or sand, some lime made by burning chalk, which occurs in various places nearby, is mixed in. It is said in this district that lime is of no benefit for 'hot' soil, i.e. rich black soil. The fertiliser is spread on the fields at Michaelmas time.

Hockerill and Bishops Stortford, small towns with maltings

'Acrell' and 'Bishopswood' are adjoining small towns.[4] Their employment and business is mainly connected with agriculture and malting. Four shillings per eight bushels has to be paid in Excise Duty to the Crown when the malt is placed in the malthouse, where it is kept moist for two days. It is sold for $2\frac{1}{2}$ shillings per bushel and, if it is exported, a refund is
obtained for the duty. 6

Twisting machine for woollen yarn

At Hockerill I viewed a twisting machine for woollen yarn, constructed in the same way as machines for twisting silk. In it four strands were twisted together for the knitting of stockings, which in this part of the country is carried out to satisfy household requirements. The twisted woollen yarn is sold for $2\frac{1}{2}$ pence per ounce or 3 shillings and 4 pence per pound.

Fig. 179 Half-timbered house

Cambridge and the characteristics of the countryside

28th June. The distance from Hockerill to Cambridge is 26 miles, and the countryside between them is fairly flat and well cultivated. It was sown partly with wheat, partly with barley and partly with rye, and the latter was now already ripe. In this part of the country, rye is used for bread, both by itself and mixed with wheat, which otherwise is unusual in England.

Five or 6 miles from Cambridge the spires of 'Kings Chapel' started to appear.[5] Owing to its incomparably beautiful design, it is considered
7 to be one of the masterpieces of Europe, even if it is in the Gothic style.

Huntingdon horse-racing and cock-fighting

On the 29th at noon I went from Cambridge to Huntingdon, a distance of 16 miles, to see the horse-racing that started then and lasted four days.

The Marquis of Huntingdon's brown horse 'Antelope' won the 90-guinea prize this day in a race with Mr Vernon's bay gelding, not counting what was won in bets between the two parties. Afterwards, several horses raced for a saddle. The meadow where the horse-racing takes place is quite flat and smooth, and is located just outside Huntingdon. On it the track has been laid out in the shape of a 3-mile loop, which the above-mentioned horses ran round as fast as they could three times, all in less than a quarter of an hour.

There were large numbers of spectators, many of them ladies, both in carriages and on horseback, all in a frenzy to gratify their desire
8 to bet on one horse or the other. As 'Antelope' had already won at Huntingdon and Newmarket races, the betting was 2 to 5, or 3 to 7 guineas, and I heard many people here who hardly had clothes on their backs loudly shouting 7 guineas.

The next day, which was a Tuesday, there was cock-fighting in the morning, and in the afternoon three horses ran for £50. Each of them carried a jockey weighing 8 stone 7 lb, each stone being 14 lb.

On Wednesday the cock-fighting continued. In the afternoon, the above-mentioned Marquis of Huntingdon challenged his horse against a new horse anyone dared to race against him, as long as it had never previously run for a prize. This was with the proviso that the Marquis be allowed to purchase any winner amongst the unknown horses for £20.

On Thursday there was cock-fighting again, and a horse-race between the Duke of Cumberland and four other lords. The horses were six-year-olds and had to carry 11 stone
7 lb or more. The old horses, here called 'aged', 9
carry 12 stone.

The town of St Ives, its business and iron trade

The difficulty of finding quarters in Huntingdon at this time, and the high cost, induced me to go to St Ives, 5 miles further down by the same river.[6] This town does the same kind of business as Huntingdon, consisting of trading and shipping by river from King Lynn, situated 40 miles down river by the sea.

The iron consumed in these places all comes by water from Kings Lynn, where a group of merchants has gained control of the trade after paying, as I was told, Mr Finch of Cambridge £1000 to stay out of it.

Nonetheless, two of Mr Finch's relations in Cambridge are still importing up to 150 tons per annum, supplied by Messrs Finlay & Jennings.[7]

The price of iron in these towns nowadays varies between £19 and £20, according to
circumstances and terms of credit. 10

Downham and its trade in butter

30th. From St Ives one walks on the edge of a canal[8] dug through low-lying land to Downham, some 20 miles distant. This road is very pleasant in the summer, especially now, when very many people were busy making hay in the extensive meadows.

By the canal bank there were cottages every half-mile or so where large quantities of butter are made during the summer. Some is made by churning, and some by heating the milk whilst it is being agitated and the butter squeezed together by hand.

The butter made in this low-lying part of the country, about 30 miles in diameter, is sent to Downham market every Saturday. At this time of year more than 2000 firkins of butter a week arrive here and are subsequently sent to London.

One firkin of butter contains four stone or 56 lb and sells for 22 shillings at this time of
year, but in April it fetches 30 and at 11
Michaelmas 22 shillings.

Fig. 180 Method of cutting peat

Cutting of peat
In these wet meadows large quantities of peat are cut, sold for 2½ shillings per hundred. The cutting is carried out by means of a spade, as in drawing no. 180, producing pieces of uniform size, 8 inches in length with a cross-section three to 3½ inches square. The turves are subsequently put in piles for drying, with open spaces between to permit air circulation [Fig. 180].

Windmills for raising water
Here windmills, built in the same way as in Holland, are used to raise the water from the low-lying land, which is separated from the canal by banks thrown up on either side. The ebb is clearly perceptible in the canal. The boats that ply up and down the canal are towed by horses.

Fishing for eels
People on board during the trip amuse themselves by spearing eels with a fishing spear, stuck down into the mud as frequently as
12 possible. If a fish is struck, it is brought up by the spear, which is barbed.

Cranes
Many cranes were seen here, because there is plenty of food for them in the form of fish that swim into the water meadows when the water is high in the canals.[9]

King's Lynn, its harbour and trade in iron
Lynn Regis is situated at the mouth of the River Ouse, and has a convenient harbour. Ships of all sizes can enter it on the spring tides, but between these, entry is limited to medium-size vessels, of which the town itself owns a considerable number. If all ships, large and small, are included, the fleet amounts to 150 sails.

The many navigable rivers and canals in the country above Lynn give this place much trade and business. This consists particularly of shipment of corn, wool, butter etc as well as importation of iron, planks, timber, tar, hemp, coal, wine and other necessities that the country
is unable to produce for itself. 13

A so-called bounty of 5 shillings is paid by the Government for every eight bushels of wheat exported; for rye, the bounty is 3½ shillings and for barley and malt, 2½ shillings. According to the customs rolls, the total bounty paid in 1750 was £33,000; in 1751, £24,000; in 1752, £19,000 and £8000 in 1753. The decrease in exports over the last few years is due to a falling-off in demand from abroad and consequent lowering of the price, causing farmers to keep their corn in storage until demand and prices increase.

In addition to large quantities of planks and timber consumed for general purposes in the populous districts trading with Lynn, the method of protecting the banks of the rivers from falling in that is in use here, and illustrated by Fig. 181, has contributed materially towards increasing the consumption, because it employs very substantial amounts of timber at Lynn alone.

Wool is not exported, but is shipped from
14 here to other provinces in England where the manufactories are located, most going to Leeds in Yorkshire.

One tod[10] of wool, which is 28 English pounds, now costs 13 shillings and 6 pence for the shortest and finest, and ten to 11 shillings for the long.

The butter is mostly shipped to London, and for this reason Downham, 3 miles up river from Lynn,[11] is called 'London Market'.

Of the foreign nations that trade here, the Norwegians are the most diligent, with their boards and, to some extent, tar. Last year, 29 ships from Norway unloaded their cargo in this harbour. From Sweden, only nine ships arrived with iron, not counting iron that had been fetched by English ships. According to the customs rolls for 1752, 824 tons of Swedish iron and 74 tons of Russian iron were imported. For 1753, it is supposed that the imports will amount to about 1200 tons. For the year 1751,
15 the iron imports from Sweden were 1437 tons and from Russia ten tons.

The trade in iron is now in the hands of a company of wealthy merchants in Lynn, in which Messrs 'Hagg', Allen, 'Thixen', 'Aldamin', Robinson, Hague, Swan etc are partners. Messrs Clark and 'Adlersen', of whom the first-mentioned has been in Sweden several times, have also previously imported some iron but, since the Company has influenced all buyers to deal with it exclusively, they have been unable to continue this business.

Mr Finch in Cambridge has also been a large importer of iron, but the company has bought him out, as some say for £1000 and others say for £2000. His nephews, Charles and Jonathan Finch in Cambridge, have nonetheless imported 120 tons.

Nowadays the price of iron in this town is £17 per ton for cash and £17½ for three
16 months' credit, £17.15s for six months and £18.5s to £18.10s for 12 months. The Company cannot increase the price as much as they would wish as long as Mr Clark still has some iron in stock and, by keeping their prices low, they hope that he will become tired of the business. He told me that he would be willing to give it up if he could sell the quantity of iron that he now has in stock, amounting to about 80 tons, for £17 [per ton].

In addition to being troubled by the above-mentioned smaller merchants, the Company is greatly inconvenienced by the proximity of Hull. When the price starts to rise at Lynn, merchants in Hull often send iron over to Lynn to be sold.

The warehouses in Lynn are conveniently located and fairly well stocked with iron, about 150 tons as far as I could judge by eye, and this in spite of the fact that nothing had yet been imported this year. Lynn has no export of iron,
as all imports are consumed by the adjoining 17
provinces, which are Northamptonshire, Huntingdonshire, Bedfordshire, Cambridgeshire, Rutlandshire, parts of Lincolnshire and Nottinghamshire and the greater part of Norfolk.

As far as Norwich and Yarmouth are concerned, they have regular connections with Sweden themselves and together import about 600 tons of iron in a year.

Mr 'Aldred' of Norwich imports about 160 tons from Mr Beckman in Gothenburg.[12]

Mr 'Folwer'[13] in Yarmouth buys 150 tons from Stockholm in addition to what he imports from Hull. In addition to iron, some boards and tar are also imported in Swedish ships. Timber, hemp and tar also come from Vyborg and other Russian ports.

The merchants of Lynn intend to establish shipping connections with America for the export of fabricated iron products and the import of tar, sugar etc.

Nature of the countryside

Taking the shortest road from Lynn to 18
Lincolnshire, one first takes the ferry across the river[14] and then has to pass twice over the so-called 'Wash', where one must watch the time to make sure that the tide is out. At other times it is impossible to get past because of the depth and width of the water. When there is a spring tide, it covers large areas of the low-lying land, where in 40 miles or more, no rise or hill is to be seen except some banks which have been thrown up as protection against the sea, or small mounds on which windmills stand.

Horse-race

In a small town in this district where I had intended to stay overnight, there had been a horse-race during the day, and all the inns were

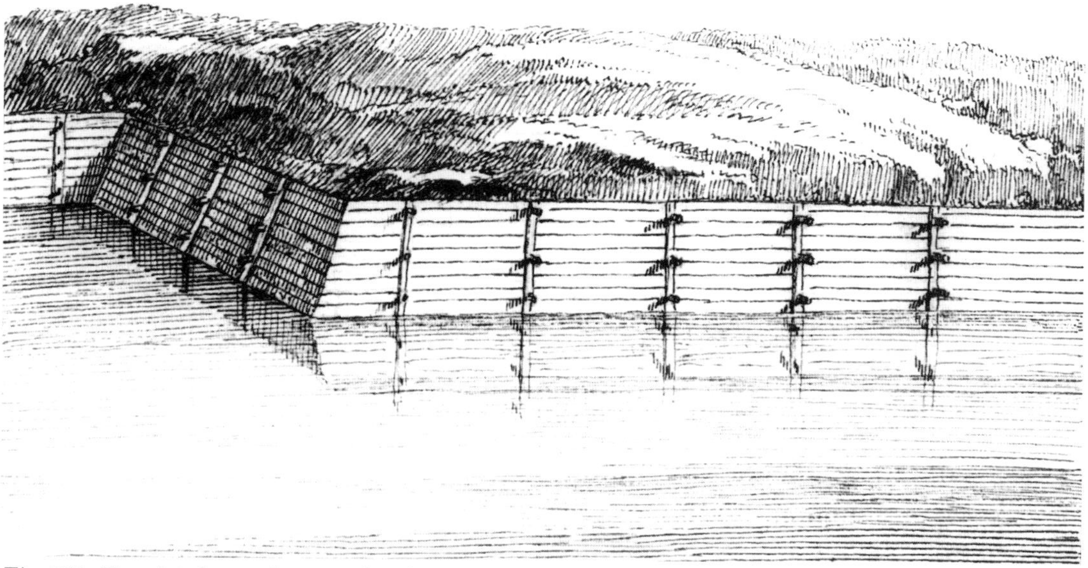

Fig. 181 Use of timber to shore up river banks

now full of farmers and their women, who danced and regaled themselves very well. I stayed there a few hours and took part in their pleasure but, lacking a bed and good fodder for the horse, I continued my journey to the next
19 'Wash', which I succeeded in passing between two and three o'clock in the morning. On the other side I found an inn that gave me a welcome rest, although otherwise it was rather poor.

The town of Boston

Boston lies near the sea, and has some shipping for the account of Lincoln.

The town of Sleaford

Otherwise there is no town worth mentioning in this low-lying, flat district except Sleaford, which has a large church and some beautiful houses, but no manufactories.

Sources of livelihood [from manufacture] in Lincolnshire

These are uncommon everywhere in Lincolnshire because the inhabitants of this county mostly make their living by farming and animal husbandry and, in the towns, by trade with the surrounding countryside.

The nature of the land between Sleaford and Newark

The distance between Sleaford and Newark is said to be 14 miles, but it is actually a good 20 miles.[15] The country now became higher and I travelled over a fairly elevated heath belonging to Lord....,[16] where a large number of rabbits
had their warrens. At regular intervals there 20
were huts for the keepers, who made sure that the rabbits were not disturbed by strangers.

From the flat and treeless heath, I descended to a fertile valley, the greater part of which was sown with beans. I was told that the sowing was carried out in the same way as for wheat and barley.

The town of Newark and its horse market

Newark is a small town with quite a few beautiful houses. It also has a church in the gothic style, with a large stone tower, in accordance with the custom of the country. There is a horse market held here six times a year and, as it happened, the day of my arrival coincided with the largest and best-attended of these, with people coming from far and wide. In addition to the best of the horses bred in the county itself, there were also large numbers from Yorkshire, which county has the same reputation for horse trading as the province of
Västergötland in Sweden. For this reason 21
Yorkshire is called 'Whipshire'. A horse that in Sweden could be bought for 200 daler silvercoin would here cost 400 or more.

The consumption of iron

The iron consumed in the inland towns in the district is mainly used for horseshoes, tyres and

Fig. 182 The city of Nottingham and its castle

other household articles. It is sold in the shops for £19.10s to £20 per ton, the Swedish being made into horseshoes and the Russian into tyres. However, at this time there was no Russian iron available. Some of the merchants in these towns get their iron from Hull and others from Lynn Regis, the result being that the price of iron is lower than might be expected in a town located inland and where there are no ironworks.

The navigable River Trent

2 August. The road from Newark to Nottingham is reckoned to be 19½ miles long, and is very pleasantly located by the bank of the River Trent, which is navigable up to Burton in
22 Staffordshire, also to Derby, which gives this part of the country undeniably great advantages.

The town of Nottingham and its stocking factories

Nottingham was originally built on a small rock but, owing to the large manufacture of hosiery, it has latterly grown so much that it now has a similar number of inhabitants to Birmingham, Exeter, Cambridge and other towns that can be classified as coming in the third group after London in this respect [see Fig. 182].

In Nottingham and the surrounding countryside it is estimated that there are 3,000 to 4,000 stocking frames in operation, producing more than 20,000 pairs of stockings a week, of every kind and quality that one could possibly imagine. The thumping and squeaking of the stocking frames can be heard all the time, encouraging the people to be diligent and industrious. This music is so common in these parts that a house from which it was missing
might be thought empty and deserted. 23

Stocking frames and needles

The stocking frames and all their accessories are also made in Nottingham. There are 14 workshops where frames are made and 60 making needles, of which there are 20 different types, for use in wool, cotton and silk stockings. The largest are used for wool and are called '10 course'.

Stocking needles are made from iron wire, cut first to the length required for each type. The blanks are then clamped in a vice with jaws extending upwards to form a sort of hopper. A notch is made in the wire by means of a cold chisel, as shown by the letters 'a' and 'b' in the drawing. The point is made by filing, and then the needle is polished. Next, it is placed in a hole made in an iron bar and bent and adjusted with a pair of round tongs. Finally, the other end, which will be tinned, is flattened with a hammer [see Fig. 183].[17]

In addition to the workshops making frames there are a number dealing with the brasswork.
Assembly of the frames is also a specialised 24
trade, and this was said to be so lucrative that a man could earn a guinea a week in this

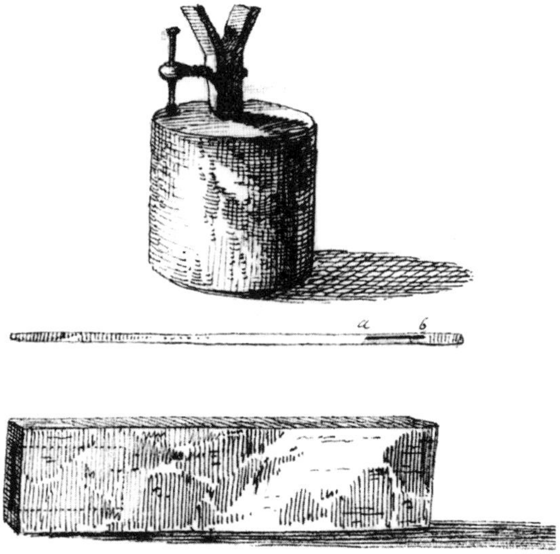

Fig. 183 Stocking Needle manufacture

occupation, whereas frame-makers have to be satisfied with 8 to 10 shillings. The actual knitting process is no different from that used in France and other places, but I found the price of silk stockings much higher here. I was asked 14 shillings for a pair of the best quality, which I bought in Montpellier for 12, and the latter were much more even, both in respect of the knitting and of the silk, being free from streaks caused by poor-quality silk. Prices for woollen stockings appear to be rather more reasonable, and the same can be said for cotton, although there is a large difference between retail and
25 wholesale prices.

Spinning, twinning and stocking-knitting

There are a number of machines here for twisting wool, which are nearly the same as those for twisting silk. I saw blue wool being spun on a wheel that had two spindles, keeping both hands busy. It was designed in the same way as the famous Mr Hedman's machine in Sweden, which has been common for many years. The wheel must be twice as wide as usual in order to carry the two cords. The pulleys are placed above the wheel, one on each side, and the wool flock, well carded and slightly oiled, is supported by a board on top [Fig. 184].

Bleaching mill at Bulwell

Four miles from the town, at Bulwell, there is a bleaching mill constructed in the Dutch way, for linen and cotton stockings and thread bonnets.[18] Scouring is mostly carried out with fuller's earth. Soap is expensive owing to the high Excise Duty that has been imposed in order to
encourage the linen factories in Scotland. 26
Between the bleaching processes, the linen or cotton cloth is placed in barrels with sour milk, after which it is scoured in fulling stocks and again bleached to a fairly good whiteness. The acid in the milk has a good influence on the bleaching. In Haarlem in Holland, acid and stagnant water have the same effect.

Bulwell forge

Bulwell forge, located a short distance from the bleaching mill and belonging to Lord Middleton, has two finery hearths and one chafery hearth. Production is only four tons per week, but five

Fig. 184 Double spinning wheel

tons in wintertime when there is more water available. The pig iron comes from Wingerworth furnace in Derbyshire. Consumption of charcoal in the finery hearths is two to two-and-a-half loads per ton, at a cost of 20 shillings per load. It is obtained 4 miles from here. The chafery hearth uses 11 hundredweight of pitcoal per ton, costing 4½ pence per hundredweight. The wages are as usual, 10 shillings per ton in
27 the finery and 9 shillings in the chafery.

Calculation of the cost of the iron per ton of bar iron:

Pig iron, 1½ ton at £7.15s	£9.4s.0d
Charcoal, 2½ loads at £1	£2.10s.0d
Pitcoal, 11 cwt at 4½d	4s.1d
Wages	19s.0d
Total	£13.7s.1d

To this figure must be added cost of buildings, manager's salary, rents, interest on working capital etc, estimated to amount to a total of	£2.0s.0d.
The selling price at the forge is now	£20 per ton.

Basford, a village with factories for red and white lead and lead shot

On the way home I passed Basford, a church village, and viewed there a works for red lead, established by Mr Wright, an ironmonger from Nottingham, together with a foundry for lead shot and a factory for making white lead. The latter is considered to be the best in England as far as the whiteness of the product is concerned. In Nottingham there are several more similar factories.

The furnace for the red lead is 6 feet wide, 28
7 feet long and has two fireplaces, shown by letters **a** and **b** in figure no. 185.

Progress of roasting is observed by the development of the colour, and the time taken varies, but is generally 24 hours.

Two fothers a week can be produced, each estimated to weigh 2,256 lb. For each roasting operation, 18 cwt of lead is charged into the furnace. A fother increases in weight to 20 cwt during roasting. At Holywell, a charge of 13 cwt increases to 14 cwt.

The lead is bought for 17 shillings per fother and the red lead sells for 18 shillings per cwt or 112 lb.

Limestone quarry and lime-burning

One-and-a-half miles away there is a limestone quarry with stone of a special type that looks like brownish sandstone, although on close inspection one finds in it shining crystals of calcite. The stone occurs in horizontal layers of
varying thickness, generally separated from one 29
another by fine blue or red clay.

At the coal mines, situated a mile away, I was told that the limestone strata continue to a depth of 24 feet, and that the stone becomes

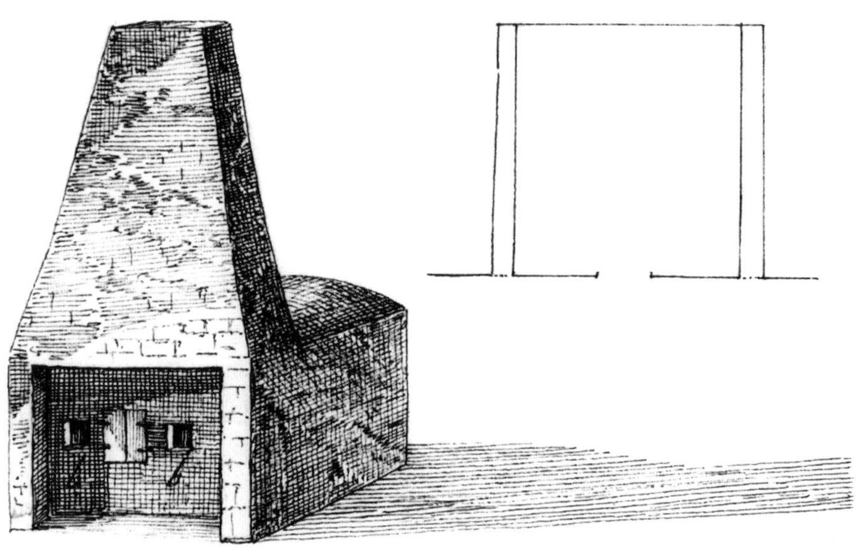

Fig. 185 Furnace for red lead

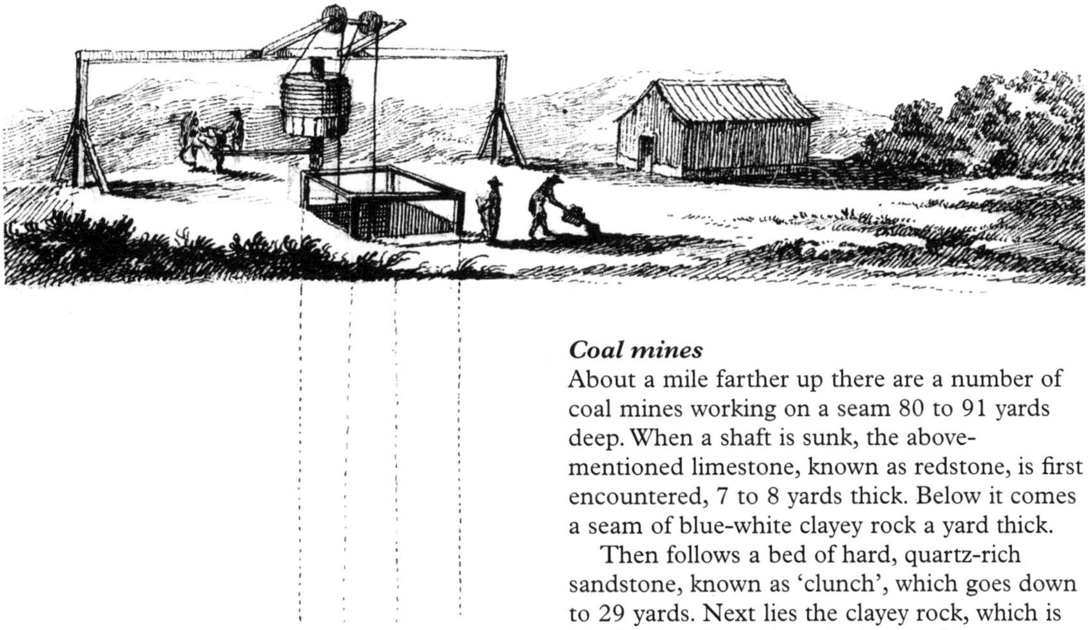

Fig. 186 [reference placed here in text, but does not seem relevant, showing a mine shaft and horse gin]

denser and harder the farther down it is found. This I could also confirm by my own observations at the quarry. Here I noted, furthermore, that the top layer was very soft. Immediately below the soil that covered it, the stone had so little cohesion that it was gradually absorbed by the soil, and at this point the beginning of the crystallisation could be seen.

For the lime burning, a kiln hewn out of the rock itself is used. It is filled with alternate layers of coal and limestone. A kiln is charged with three score or 60 quarters of limestone, each quarter being equal to eight stricken bushels.

Lime for fertilising of fields

To the three score quarters of limestone, four
30 score cwt of coal are added, costing 4 pence per cwt. Eight bushels, or one quarter, of burnt lime are sold for 12 pence and are mainly used in the surrounding countryside for fertilising fields, alternating with dung or soil. The fields are left fallow every third year and during this time are fertilised, first with dung and then with lime, the latter being spread on top of the former, whereupon both are ploughed in whilst the weather is fine, because it is said that rain kills the lime. Afterwards, at Michaelmas time, the field is sown with wheat, which gives an abundant crop.

Coal mines

About a mile farther up there are a number of coal mines working on a seam 80 to 91 yards deep. When a shaft is sunk, the above-mentioned limestone, known as redstone, is first
encountered, 7 to 8 yards thick. Below it comes 31
a seam of blue-white clayey rock a yard thick.

Then follows a bed of hard, quartz-rich sandstone, known as 'clunch', which goes down to 29 yards. Next lies the clayey rock, which is black where it touches the first coal seam. This seam is 3 feet thick, but consists of such poor and soft coal that it is not considered worth working. Below this seam follows a clayey rock known as 'meanstone', then half a yard of the clunch mentioned above and, next to it, the coal seam resting on clayey rock.

The coal seam is 4 to 5 feet thick at this point and consists of denser coal than that described above, although at the top there is a good deal of charcoal dust separating the coal into layers.

Nottingham Castle

Before I left Nottingham I looked at the castle, which is the property of the Duke of Newcastle [see Fig. 187]. It is a splendid building of
dressed stone, situated on a rock with an 32
excellent view of the town and the surrounding plain. The rock consists of a soft sandstone of the same kind as is found in the town of Nottingham itself, into which its famous cellars are cut. From the top of the rock on which the castle is built a tunnel has been cut through the rock down to a little river that runs past the foot of the cliff. Without doubt, this tunnel was made in the days when this was a fortification, in order to secure the supply of water during a siege.

The iron trade in Nottingham

The iron trade in Nottingham is mainly in the hands of a Mr Wright, who is fairly wealthy and

Fig. 187 Nottingham Castle

buys 300 tons of Swedish iron and 1200 tons of Russian iron per year. The latter is chiefly used for tyres.

Iron with the stamp ***HG*** from Gävle,[19] in the
33 form of $1\frac{1}{2}$-inch to 3-inch-wide flat bars, was formerly much sought after and was mostly used for looms. Last year it was rather red-short and since then there has been no demand for it.

The stamp known as ***Burning Mountain***[20] is considered very good. The following stamps from Gävle are reasonably good: ***B***, ***XX*** , ***xx/xx***.[21] ***X/L***, good.[22] ***RF***, ***Anchor***, ***E crowned***, ***EW***, acceptable.[23]
The following stamps from Gothenburg are also acceptable: ***:)(:***, ***Cl***[24]

The iron can be shipped on the River Trent up to a place $1\frac{1}{2}$ miles from Nottingham for 13 shillings per ton,[25] and to 'Bart'[26] in Staffordshire for 17 shillings. At the present
34 time the iron is sold in Nottingham for 20 shillings per cwt with three months' credit.

Lord Middleton's palace

On 4 August in the afternoon, I went from Nottingham to Lord Middleton's house, which lies 3 miles from the town in a very beautiful park.[27] At some distance away it looks like two palaces, consisting of a tall house on the inside with a lower one built around it in the form of a square. When one enters it becomes apparent that it is all one building, in the centre of which is a large hall lit from above through large windows. Not many of the other rooms could be viewed because His Lordship himself was in residence. Next to the house there is a garden with terraces and, beyond it, a spacious park with long avenues radiating from the corners of the building, so that there is an unobstructed
view of the park and the faraway fields that 35
surround it [Fig. 188].

The stables are on the western side and, on the other side, in the garden, are corresponding buildings consisting of two squares surrounded by stables and houses for the servants.
The stables are provided with roomy stalls, but only along one side. On the other side there are large windows opposite each stall. In addition, the walls are whitewashed which makes the room very light and pleasant. Down in the park a small lake has been excavated in order to improve the view. In the avenues there are gazebos built of the same dressed stone as the remainder of the buildings, with the exception of the stables, which are of brick, with stone only on the front.

The character of the countryside and the agriculture

On the way to Derby the country was fertile and mostly planted with peas. Large quantities

Fig. 188 Wollaton Hall

of unslaked lime had been carted to the fields,
36 which were lying fallow, as happens every third year in this district, and placed in heaps beside them, waiting for fine weather. As soon as this arrives, the lime is spread out and ploughed in. Wheat is sown at Michaelmas time. A field to be sown with two bushels of seed requires a load of lime containing 12 quarters, each of eight stricken, or level, bushels, costing 12 shillings. In addition, some dung has to be added and this is spread on the field beforehand. It was said that in a good year for corn, a piece of land treated in this way can produce 40 bushels from two bushels of seed. Although not by any means a rare occurrence, this does not happen every year.

The town of Derby

The journey now went so quickly, in the company of a good-natured farmer, that I came upon Derby unexpectedly, although I was not all dissatisfied to see such a pleasant and well-situated town. The River Derwent, which after a
37 roundabout way of several miles falls into the River Trent, almost surrounds this town because of its dams and canals, on which there are many well-designed water-driven mills.

Silk-making machinery in Derby

Amongst these, the first that one notices is the silk mill which has been so magnificently built and equipped by Mr 'Beredt'.[28] Here one single main waterwheel sets 97,000 [sic] machines in motion and provides employment for many people.[29] This type of manufacture and machinery have been described previously in connection with my journey in Italy.

Factory for china or porcelain in Derby

Three years ago, two factories were established here, one for china or porcelain, and the other for flint or white-ware. The first-mentioned originated from the Chelsea factory near London, and the second from Newcastle in Staffordshire [Fig. 189].

The paste for the china is made up from white quartz sand, obtained from the neighbourhood of Lynn, which is calcined, ground and washed. Bone ash, prepared in the same way, is added before mixing with water to the consistency of gruel. Finally, this mixture is poured into a tank made of brick, under which 38
a fire is made for the purpose of drying it. It is taken up when sufficiently thick for throwing. For modelling, the mixture is of a consistency that can be poured into the plaster moulds. If the figure is to be hollow, some of it is allowed to run out again. Head, arms, feet etc of a figure are moulded separately and subsequently stuck together after being softened with water and a brush. This porcelain is very fragile before firing has taken place. This is carried out in a large muffle, built of bricks and a clay obtained nearby, which is said to be more resistant to heat than Stourbridge clay.

Only 40 people were employed at this factory, and nowadays only figures and flowers are made, sold at a price 25 per cent less than 39
that of Chelsea figures. They are also considering installing equipment for throwing of bowls and plates etc, in which case another kiln will be built, of the same type as that at Chelsea.

White-ware factory at Derby

The white-ware factory[30] is a much larger establishment than the one described above, and has two large kilns of the Chelsea type.

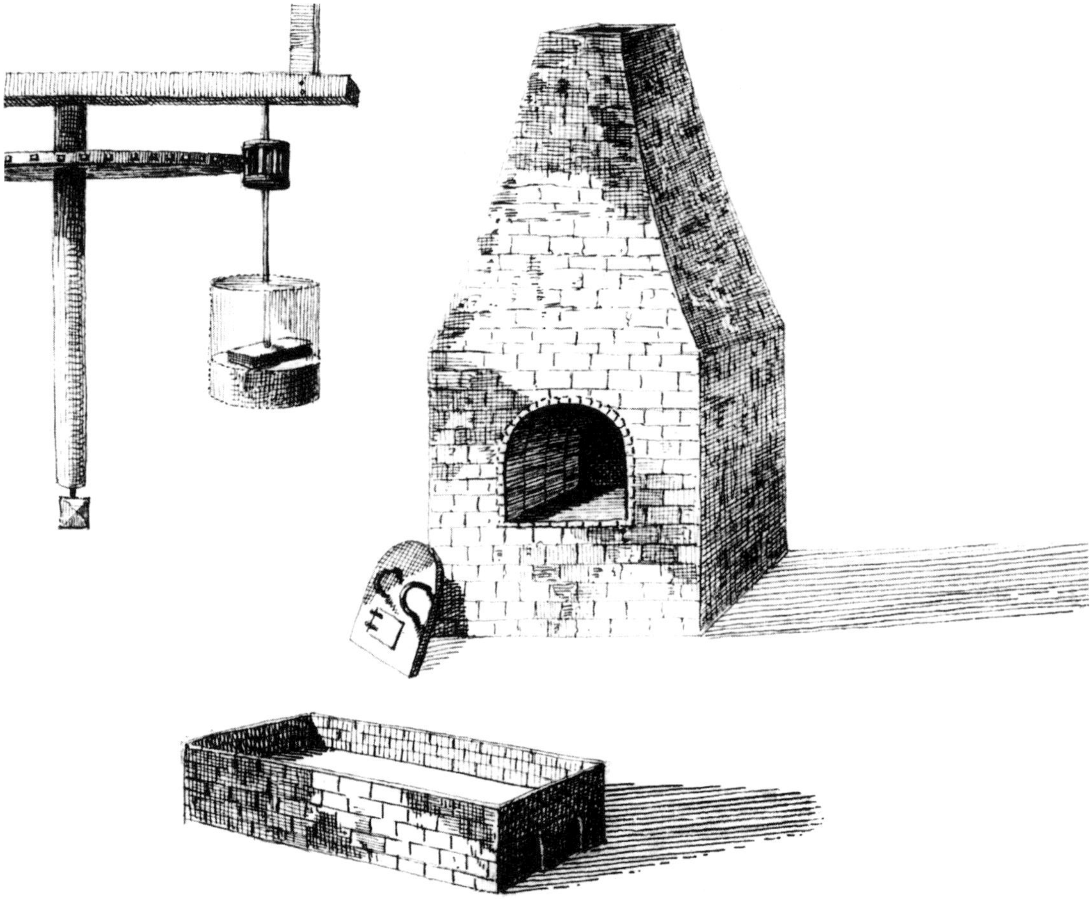

Fig. 189 Mixing equipment, drying tank and muffle

The body consists of half 'dutch pipe-clay' and half calcined and ground black flint, a material which is not found in this place, and has to come by water from other provinces in England. The clay also has to be calcined and ground before mixing with the flint, which takes place in two boxes, one above the other, through which the slurry of water and ground material flows and is blended. Subsequently it is placed in a tank made of brick heated by a fire underneath, where it is dried to a consistency convenient for throwing or modelling.

In order to make the handles they have a machine (letter **d**, Fig. 190) through which the body is forced by means of a screw.[31] In this way any grooves or indentations required can be made.

When blue colour is required on the white-ware, they draw on the vessels and then strew smalt or cobalt into the hollows. The salt vapours which are used for the glaze then melt the smalt to a blue glass which adheres to the pattern, although not very uniformly.[32]

Prices of white-ware from Mr 'Rolf Steen'

Ordinary plates, per dozen	2s.0d
Ditto, with modelled roses, per dozen	2s.6d
Dish for serving puddings	2s.0d
Tea cups, with handles, per dozen of 36	1s.6d
Half pint, per dozen of 24	1s.6d
One pint, per dozen of 12	1s.6d
Two pint, per dozen of six	1s.6d
Cheese plates, each	1s.4d
Bowls, 6 inches diameter, per dozen of 24	1s.6d
Breadbaskets, nine inches diameter, each	2s.0d
Chamber pots, each	1s.6d
Sugar bowls or caskets, per dozen of 18	1s.6d
Sugar-cups, per dozen of 24	1s.0d
Teapots, holding more than 1 pint, per dozen of eight	1s.6d
Large chamber-pots, per dozen of four	1s.6d

Fig. 190 Kiln, mixing tanks, extrusion press and drying tank

Everything that is not of first class quality is sold for 12 pence per dozen, each dozen calculated as above. For breakages in transport there is a breakage allowance of 1 shilling in the pound.

When the vessels are to be fired, they are placed in specially-made pots of fireclay, which are stacked on top of one another until the whole kiln is full. These pots must be provided with holes in the sides to permit the entry of the salt-vapours that take the place of glaze. Firing requires three days and two nights, and towards the end the salt is thrown into the kiln through openings at the top.

Slitting and rolling mill at Derby

Close by the white-ware factory there is a slitting and rolling mill belonging to Mr Evans
and Mr Storrer, ironmongers, of Derby.[33] 42
It was not in operation at the time, owing to a shortage of the Russian iron that is used for rolling-hoop iron. The consumption of iron for this purpose amounts to about 150 tons per annum.

Besides the rolling of hoop iron, the mill is also employed in slitting English and Swedish iron, forged to suitable dimensions, namely two-and-three-quarters to $3\frac{1}{2}$ inches wide and $\frac{1}{2}$ inch thick, to produce nail rods. These are sold in the neighbourhood, particularly a few miles away in 'Billport'.[34] The total quantity is nearly 100 tons per annum.

At this time in the slitting mill, they were occupied with turning the rolls, using the same method as described at Birmingham and Pontypool, with the exceptions that here they employed both small and large pieces of steel ground along the length and that, finally, a bar of the same length as the roll-face was wedged against it, thus finishing the whole face in one
43 operation.

Under the roll there was a piece of cast-iron on which the steel was placed. Wedges driven in between iron bars, hooked to the uprights of the roll stand and the roll itself, press the steel against the roll face.

Fig. 191 Roll-base plate and wobbler boxes

Sometimes copper sheets are also rolled at this mill, the bars being obtained from a copper smelter 9 miles away. The roll stand was so designed that three types of roll, differing in length, could be placed in it, namely: 14 inches, 18 inches and 30 inches long. No complicated design was needed for this, simply a base plate long enough to accommodate extra sets of holes for the uprights, as shown in the attached drawing no. 191, as well as couplers or wobbler boxes of three different lengths to fit the varying distance between the end of the waterwheel shaft and the wobbler on the roll.

Two furnaces are available for the heating, one in operation and the other being repaired, as previously described at Pontypool.

Various makes of iron and the iron trade in Derby

The following Swedish iron stamps are common
in Derby:[35] 44

Gothenburg

:)(: OK	These are used for slitting; bars $2\frac{1}{2}$ inches to $3\frac{1}{2}$ inches wide and $\frac{1}{2}$ inch thick.

Gävle

HG	This stamp was very red-short last year, but an improvement has now been promised.
	Burning Mountain, said to be fine for any use.
ø	A good middle-quality stamp, of which Mr Storrer has recently received a small consignment, for which he is said to have paid £16 per ton. Carriage to Derby for 60 bars was 20 shillings.
xxBxx	A middle-quality stamp.
AF	This stamp was said to be Swedish but was very badly forged. It was intended for slitting.

There are two ironmongers in Derby, who get their iron from Hull and together consume 160 to 180 tons of Swedish iron and 150 tons of Russian iron per annum. The Russian iron is
mostly used for hoops, with a little used for 45
nails. It was said that the price in Petersburg for the brands 'Sable' and 'Gouvernmentz' was now fixed at 75 kopeck per pud, and that it was expected that it would be sold in Hull, free of all charges, for £5.10s per ton. The last consignment sold for £5.15s.

Russian iron is also used for wheel-rims. The Swedish iron is employed by blacksmiths to make horseshoes and for other similar purposes, and it now costs £20 per ton, with four to six months' credit.

Consumption of iron in Burton

In Burton, which lies on the River Trent 8 miles from Derby, the total consumption of Swedish and Muscovy iron is nearly 300 tons, and it is sold by Mr Master of Hull, and by Mr Williamson's warehouse.

Burton beer

Large quantities of ale, known as Burton beer, are exported from this place.

Silk-stocking factories at Derby

In Derby, as well as the manufactories mentioned above, there are a number of stocking-knitters, particularly for silk stockings,
46 owing to the proximity of the silk mill.

Hall, Sir Nath Courser's palace

From Derby I took the road to Hall, the estate of Sir Nath Courser.[36] This is famous in the area for its grottoes, designed by his Lady, situated by Little Eaton, which lies in a corner of the park. One of the grottoes is decorated with all kinds of slag, crystals, shells, corals etc; another with roots of trees and fine woodwork. The third is full of bones, skulls and antlers of the deer that are so abundant in the park. A small stream flows through the park and forms a number of small waterfalls. Below the houses it drives three waterwheels that set four pairs of millstones in motion, also a sieving mill and a water-pump for the house and garden, which are situated above the stream. In the park there is a mineral spring that smells of sulphur from a short way away. The water from it deposits a white sludge on the sides and bottom
47 of the runnel. It tastes like water in which eggs have been boiled. It is used both for drinking, and for bathing against scurvy and eczema. The arrangements made at the spring are convenient for these purposes, and a woman waits upon those who visit it.

Newmille blast furnace

Four miles from here lies Marmey forge, also called Newmille, owned nowadays by Mr Madder. Here there are two forges, with two finery hearths and one chafery hearth, lying side-by-side by the River 'Darr'.[37] These were not in operation for the time being, owing to a shortage of pig iron. They use both their own iron, from the Wingswart furnace, and American iron. The latter is mixed with the former to make the wrought iron useable, because their own iron is full of impurities
48 causing the wrought iron to be cold-short.

Slitting and rolling mill

The iron that is made here, about 300 tons per annum, is all used at the slitting mill, and sold to the nailers in the neighbourhood for 10s.9d per bundle, 60 lb in weight.

As well as the iron for nails slit in the slitting-mill, they also roll hoop-iron for export. This is shipped to Hull by water and sold there at a guinea for 120 lbs. In addition, large plates are rolled and sent to Birmingham. These are 3 feet long and 1 foot 3 inches wide, and sell for 30 shillings per cwt. For this purpose, Russian iron is mostly used, when it is available, and also Swedish, which is approximately 3 inches wide and ½ inch thick. Owing to a lack of both kinds of iron, the mill was not working. The rolling of plates consumes up to 100 tons per annum of Russian or Swedish iron and, when there is a good supply of these kinds of iron in convenient widths, they also roll sheets for 49
tinning, for which a special workshop has been established at the mill.

Just before I arrived they had been slitting iron of their own manufacture for the requirements of the nailers. This was so red-short that when cut off in the hot state, it broke in two or three places.

The rolls used here for preparing iron for slitting are sufficiently wide that they can also be used for both hoops and wide plates.

The furnace for re-heating was constructed in the same way as described previously, that is, with air-holes in the bottom, on which the coal was placed inside the furnace itself, with the iron on top.

The pitcoal used at the slitting-mill and in the chafery hearth is bought for 3½d per cwt. The charcoal costs 28 to 30s a load, and a cord costs 11 to 12s, 5 or 6 miles away. A load of charcoal amounts to two to two-and-a-half 50
cords, according to circumstances.

The town of Belper with nail-forging and coal mines in the neighbourhood

The town of Belper lies 2 miles from the mill, and has many coal pits in the neighbourhood, as well as a large number of nailers, who together produce three or four tons of nails per week. Prices of nails are given in the table below.

Current price at Belper:

Small hobnails, 1½ lb per 1000, which is 1200 [sic]	8d, wages 4d
Hobnails, 2–2½ lb	12d, wages 6d
Two penny, 2 lb	12½d
Three, 4 lb	17d
Four, 6 lb	23d
Six, 8 lb	29d
Eight, 12 lb	42d
Ten, 18 lb	54d
12, 20 lb	60d

Larger nails are sold at 3½d per pound.

At these prices the nails are delivered to the
51 merchant 'Joh Thondells', and subsequently sold by him. A bundle of 60 slit iron bars, weighing 60 lb is sold for 10s.9d.

Denby copper-smelting works

Denby copper-smelting works is located 4 miles from Belper and is owned by Mr Low.
The copper ore comes partly from their own mines in North Derbyshire, and partly from the York and Richmond copper mines. Brass was formerly made at this works and the calamine for it was obtained from the lead mines in Derbyshire. This production has now ceased and the calamine is sent to the Cheadle brass works in Staffordshire.

Coal mines at Belper

The coal seams in the mines near Belper all contain layers of charcoal or charcoal dust. These layers are spread fairly uniformly over the thickness of the seams although they are somewhat more frequent at the middle. The seams dip to the north, and in other places to the east and west.

The lead mines and limestone quarries of 'Craitz'[38]

Crich is a small town 4 miles from Belper.
52 Here there are some lead mines in operation, situated in a limestone hill lying between strata of quartz sand. This hill is about 1 mile long and half a mile wide. On the surface of the hill there are a number of quarries and limekilns, where large quantities of lime are burnt for the requirements of the surrounding area, both for agricultural purposes and for masonry.
The stone is greenish with shining flat spots and particles. It contains many shells, mussels, belemnites and other fossils, and it smells of 'orsten'[39] when scratched. On the surface one can still see, in some places, flint mixed in with petrifactions, and it thus appears probable that the entire hill formerly consisted of clay, flint and chalk, all during their own particular epochs, now finally transformed into limestone.

The ore lodes, which have been worked for a very long time, were discovered during
53 quarrying for limestone.

They strike partly south-east and north-west, and partly east and west, and are mostly perpendicular. The main lode strikes south-east and north-west and varies in thickness from 1½ feet to 4 feet. The other lodes, crossing the main lode, are sometimes 1 inch to 12 inches and 1½ feet thick, thinner rather than thicker at the conjunction with the main lode.

When the shafts are sunk, the ordinary limestone is found down to a depth of 36 to 40 fathoms, and below it there occurs a greenish clay with green marble crystals, generally 2 yards thick. It should be pointed out that these strata of clay and marble contain no
veins of lead, although the lead ore does 54
sometimes penetrate the clay or marble up to a few inches. Under this clay lies a layer of grey limestone eight fathoms thick containing the lead lode which was originally worked here. Then follows a 9-inch seam of clay, and under it the limestone and the lode again. This limestone is interrupted by a thin layer of clay, and finally the limestone with the lode is encountered again.

The miners are generally paid according to the amount of ore produced, and claim to be able to earn 10 shillings a week when on shift work. Wages and overheads for a load of lead ore amount to nine, 19, 20 or 35 shillings at different times. A load contains nine dishes, and a dish is 2 gallons or one peck. A load of ore is sold to the smelter for 40 to 50 shillings. A few years ago a fother of lead, weighing 22½ cwt,
sold for £11, but the price has now risen to 55
£19.19. In London, a fother weighs 19½ cwt.

East of the limestone hill, one of the cross lodes has been explored down to a depth of 40 fathoms, where a seam of clay 9 inches thick was found. Below it there was no green marble, and the limestone with the lode lay directly beneath. The lode was one hand thick and did not improve, as is usually the case, when the clay seam was passed. In the large shaft on the western side the green marble was found between the clay seams, but 2 yards away it petered out.

From the west an adit, or so-called 'sough', has been driven at the 30-fathom level of the shaft, the total depth of which is now 53 fathoms. During the driving of the sough under the western part of the hill, which consists of gritstone, a quartzy sandstone, the limestone rock was encountered.

Three years ago, work was started on a new 56
adit to the north, 1½ miles from the mine. The purpose of this was to reach deeper levels and to cut through the cross-lodes. This adit was started in a clunch or black shale, and has now reached the gritstone or sandstone

Fig. 192a [not referred to in text, but probably a drawing of the clay mine]

underneath which they are expecting to find the limestone.

Clay mine and pottery factory

Half a mile to the west on the other side of the gritstone hill, there are clay mines that yield a clay which is even more fire-resistant than Stourbridge clay. When the shafts are sunk, usually to a depth of 17 yards, clunch or black shale is first encountered. Then there is a black, coal-like rock half a yard thick, and under this the clay seam, half a yard to 1 yard thick.
57 This clay seam is like a fairly hard kind of rock when quarried, similar to the iron ore at Wednesbury mined in association with coal seams, though not as dense. When this rock is allowed to lie in the open for some time, in some cases as long as two to three years, it dissolves to a fine clay. This is dried, ground, sieved and made into a dough which is moulded, nearby, into furnace bricks and all kinds of pots for roasting and boiling, and for many other purposes.

The kiln in which these clay vessels are fired is constructed as shown in Fig. 192b, with five arched trays, made of clay, resting on ledges on the sides of the kiln, which can be removed and replaced as required.

According to Mr Da Costa's notes,[40] this clay, which is hard as stone, should be mixed with one-fifth part of Northampton clay, though the proportion can be greater or smaller as
58 circumstances dictate.

Northampton clay is completely black but becomes white when fired, and is used at the pipe factories in the neighbourhood. When this clay is mixed with the other type, the body becomes tougher and easier to work. Firing must be carried out with pitcoal, which burns well, and it generally takes forty hours. Towards the end, the vessels are glazed by means of salt, which is thrown in through holes at the top of

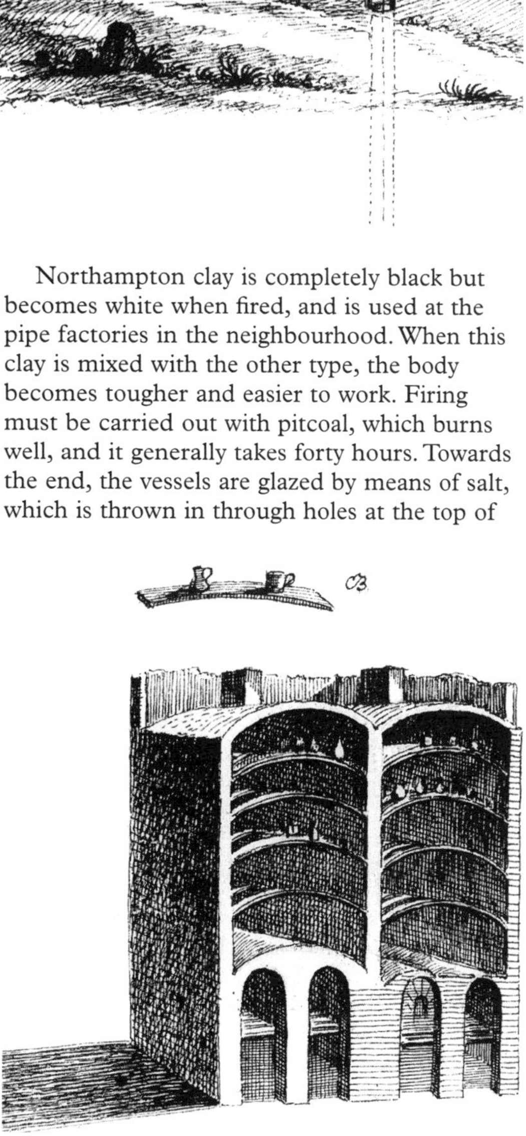

Fig. 192b Pottery kiln and trays

the kiln. The factory has three kilns, and the owner, a Mr Dadd, ascertains with the aid of a thermometer when it is time to throw the salt in. However, he would not disclose the procedure, and it was not permitted to enter the factory during the firing. People living in the area told me that they can see the smoke from the salt, white as snow, three or four times towards the end of the firing, and that the interval between smoke emissions is an hour or
59 a little over.

The vessels fired and glazed in this way acquire a coffee-brown colour and look rather well. The prices are as follows:

'Frosted' half pints per dozen of 24, sold at	16d
Plain, ditto	12d
Plates per dozen of 12	18d

and so on, always 6 pence less than white-ware in Derby.[41]

When the stone-like consistency of the clay has finally disintegrated, it is squeezed together into lumps and piled up as shown in drawing no. 193. Pitcoal is also placed in the piles and ignited in order to dry the clay. Afterwards it is ground by means of a perpendicular millstone, also shown in drawing no. 193,[42] and finely sieved, dispersed in water and finally dried in a tank, as described at Derby.[43]

Fig. 193 Edge runner mill, clay-drying and salt-glaze mugs

Lead-smelting furnaces

Two miles from Crich, on the way to Matlock Bath, I viewed the lead-smelting furnaces, of which two were now in operation. These are of the type called 'cupolas', heated on the reverberatory principle, as described at Hotwell
and Bristol. There was only a minor difference in 60
design, namely that the ones illustrated in Fig. 194a have an adjacent storehouse for the ore, and a chimney to take away the fumes from the slag that falls down from the grate. The furnace is charged with one ton of galena, previously mixed in the ore store with pitcoal and limestone. Smelting takes nine hours. The wages for the workers at the furnace are 8 shillings per week.

A little farther down there was another furnace in operation, blown by bellows approximately 2 feet square and long, provided with a crucible at the front to receive the molten lead and slag. The of type coal used here is known as coke or coked pitcoal. Slag from the reverberatory furnaces was being smelted [Fig. 194b].

Closer to Matlock Bath there were three
furnaces smelting galena, which is the old way 61
of smelting in this province. The furnace for the smelting of the lead ore is built in the old way and is described later on.

Lead mines on Cromford Moor

On Cromford Moor there were innumerable shafts of lead mines to be seen, some of which had been sunk to depths of more than 600 feet. The veins mostly strike east and west and are parallel, as is shown by the great number of shafts that were sunk throughout the field, simplifying the raising of the ore and providing ventilation. One of the shafts was sunk in a gritstone that only went down for a few fathoms before meeting black shale continuing for about 480 feet down until the limestone with the vein is reached. The clay mentioned at Crich as being encountered during sinking of lead shafts
also occurs in this neighbourhood, but of 62
varying thickness, sometimes five to ten fathoms, and it can then happen that the lead vein is forced out of its perpendicular position by 3 to 7 yards, each yard equal to 1½ aln.[44]

Fig. 194a Lead works at Crich

Calamine in the lead veins

In the surrounding district there are considerable quantities of calamine or gallmey in the lead veins, but it is noticeable that the content of lead ore decreases with increasing content of calamine and vice versa. The calamine does, however, contain some galena.

Roasting is carried out here in a reverberatory furnace constructed with three doors, similar to an iron-melting furnace at the iron foundries in London and Bristol and in Amsterdam and Rotterdam, however, with the difference that at this place the furnace has a flat, horizontal bottom, whereas at the other places it is hollowed out in front of the outlet to create a reservoir for the iron. Calamine is placed in the furnace in bowls, just as it is mined, about half-a-ton at a time, and roasted until it is white, which takes four to five hours [Fig. 194c].

63 Matlock Bath lies 2 miles along the River Derwent, which at this point cuts deep into the limestone hills, so that the view is similar to that at Hotwells near Bristol. Here there are two separate baths, situated a little way from one another, but otherwise like that at Hotwells, though not as warm.

Proof that the water contains lime is provided by the small knob of rock below the springs, which has been formed entirely by deposition. Even though there is plenty of water in the streams running down the rock, it must have taken thousands of years for this knob to have grown.

In order to encourage people to believe that the water is warm, the baths are housed in vaulted buildings. Large numbers of people

Fig. 194b [not referred to in text, probably the second lead furnace near Crich]

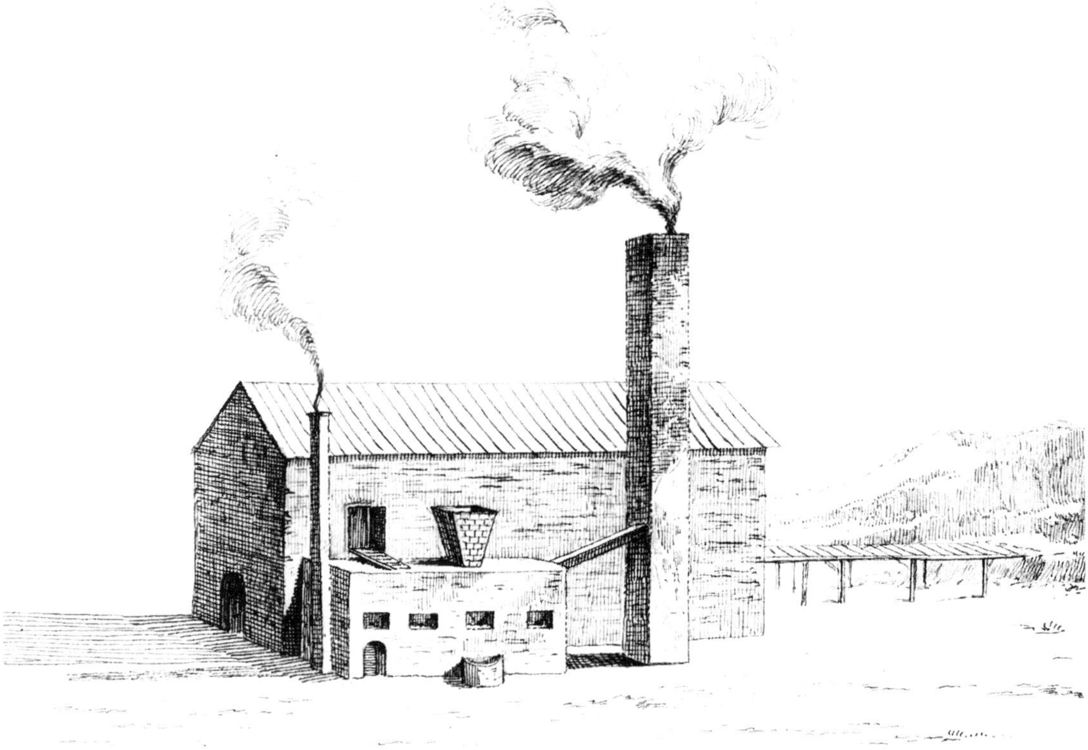

Fig. 194c [not referred to in text, probably the roasting furnace near Matlock]

come here in July and August, at times more
64 than can be accommodated.

Lead and calamine mines

The lead deposits are located in a limestone hill, which is covered with gritstone on the south-east side. At both ends of this mine area there are so-called 'Rackwork' or vertical deposits, which strike north-west and south-east, whereas all the others which lie in the mile in between are horizontal, or so-called 'Pipework', and dip to the east. They are close to breaking through to the Portway deposit, which is also horizontal, and to a Rackwork deposit which is expected to give a rich return. This latter will not be driven very deep as it is water-logged, and in the course of work many years ago reached through to the horizontal Portway deposit.

There are so many mines and workings in this area for many miles around that it is
65 impossible to count them all.

However, no metals other than lead and calamine are known here, and they are extracted from the same deposits. In some mines there is little or no calamine, whilst in others there is plenty of calamine and lead is absent.

Winster, a mining town with lead mines in the neighbourhood

Winster, which lies 12 miles from Crich and 8 miles from Matlock Bath, is a mining town which has been renowned for its rich lead mines for many centuries. They are worked on the same conditions and liberty as apply to calamine and zinc ore, which is extracted to excess.

Here I went down into one of the principal lead mines now in operation. Never before have I been so worn-out and tired as on this occasion, since the way down at this place, as is the case in most lead mines in England, is by climbing down on the cross-beams with which the shaft is timbered. One stands with a foot on
a beam on one side of the shaft, supporting 66
oneself with an elbow on a beam on the opposite side, changing position step-by-step down the whole shaft. In this deposit the shaft was 100 fathoms deep, with at least 1½ feet between each beam on which one had to climb down, and later on up again. The lead deposit was a vein that sloped sharply to the west, located in clay of an orange colour. In some places the clay was so water-soaked that one had to wade through mud at times up to the knees. The lead ore lies in the form of nests or clumps in this

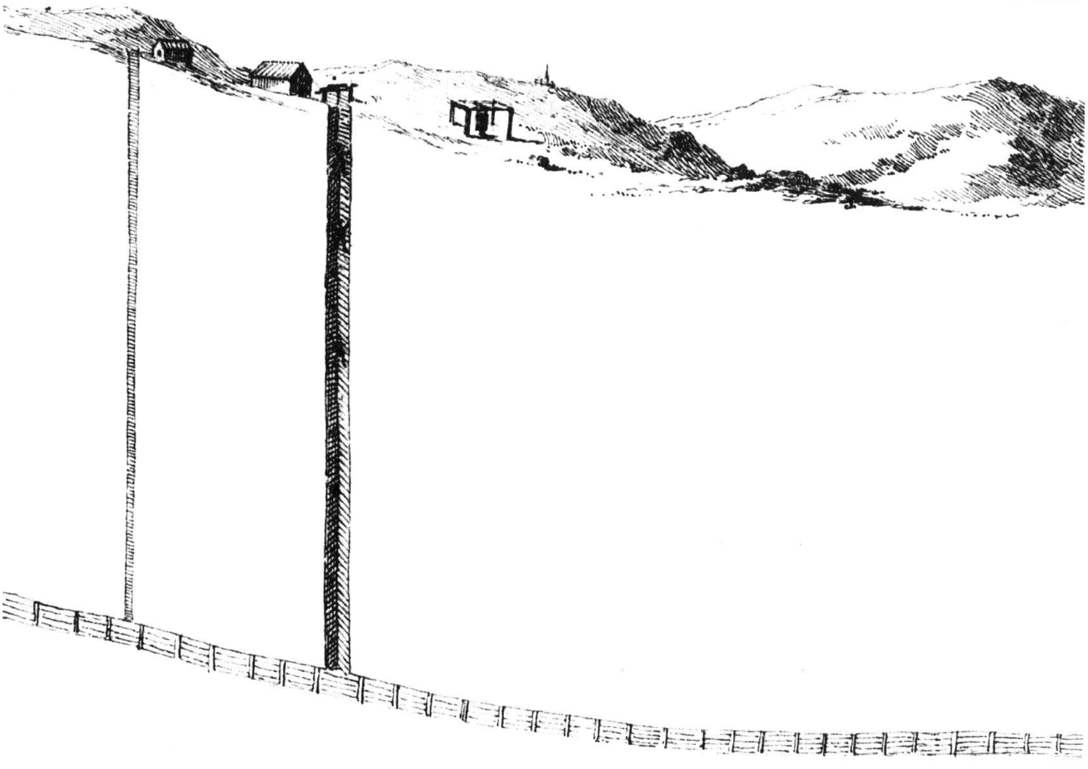

Fig. 195 [not referred to in text, but may be a drawing of the lead mine described to the left]

clay seam, sometimes in greater, sometimes in lesser quantities [Fig. 195].

On the way to Chatsworth, a magnificent house belonging to the Duke of Devonshire, there are a number of lead-smelting ovens of the type usual in this area, in which chopped-up and
67 dried wood is used instead of coke [Fig. 196].

Only a few pieces of wood are loaded at a time, together with two shovels-full either of ore or of unsmelted material taken out from the bottom of the oven for recirculation. The oven is built of granite and is 24 inches high, of which the upper hearth, [tapping arch], from **a** to **b** in the drawing, measures only 16 inches, and the opening **b–c**, from which the unsmelted ore is removed, 8 inches. Some of the molten lead also runs out at this point, down in the crucible **p**. Beneath the opening **b–c** there is a further hearth 60 inches deep which has no outlet and is always kept full of lead. The length of the oven from **a** to **e** is 21 inches, and the width in to the tuyere, 11 inches. The tuyere opening is by the upper hearth. When the lead runs down to the container 'a' from the deeper inner hearth, it is
68 ladled into cast iron measure **f**.[45]

This method of smelting could be much improved if the oven were built a little higher, so that the ore would have melted by the time it came down to the hearth, where there is virtually no heat left. The reason for this is partly the large opening at the bottom, and partly the unsuitable position and height of the tuyere. To this the smelters retorted that the waterfall for the bellows wheel is too low for a higher oven, and that the hole needs to be large in order to get the unsmelted lumps out at all. These answers showed the extent of their insight into the smelting process, and required no further comment. In any case, the ore in this area is so easily smelted that they obtain the metal regardless of how they proceed. They are able in this way, if the ore is rich, to smelt one ton, that is, seven-and-a-half skeppund, of lead
in a day. 69

The furnace operators maintain that this method of smelting, regardless of how impractical it seemed to me, is superior to that used in cupola furnaces or so-called reverberatory furnaces. In addition, the price of lead produced in their furnaces is always 5 shillings per ton higher because of the purity of the metal.

In this county there are 12 cupola furnaces as well as innumerable other furnaces. It is said

Fig. 196 Lead-smelting oven fuelled with wood

that the annual production in Staffordshire is between 5000 and 6000 foder of $22\frac{1}{2}$ cwt, where each one hundred weight is equal to 112 English pounds.

Chatsworth is a palace or castle, which belongs to the Duke of Devonshire, built at the beginning of the eighteenth century with all magnificence that can be imagined.

Notwithstanding that the Duke was at this time in residence, the greater part of the house was open to visitors, with its fine furniture,
70 tapestries, paintings, statues, tables, doorways and stairs of Italian marble. The house is built of sandstone blocks, very well worked, and all the windowpanes, of which there are a great number, are of polished mirror glass.

The garden is very spacious and has many fine water effects and basins, including a cascade so remarkable that it hardly has its match at Winter Garten in Hessen-Cassell or at Marly near Versailles in France, though this last is no longer in operation.

There was also a tree made of lead, most true to nature and not so small, the leaves of which sprayed water, as did the bushes in the area, so that the innocent had difficulty avoiding becoming soaked if that was the wish
71 of the master of the water effects and the ruler of the garden. A duck quacked and a high fountain gave the sounds of pistol shots, as well as many other remarkable and curious inventions.

One could also visit the stables, where there were a number of fine hunters, including a Hungarian horse, a present from the Empress.

The park is situated above the Castle, full of red deer and partridges, and in the garden there are many hares. On an outcrop of rock there is a pleasure house which looks like a fortress.

Bakewell is situated nearby, and here a stone known as 'Rottenstone' is quarried, used for metal polishing and at Wolverhampton for steel polishing.

Chesterfield is a market town and, like most of the towns in this county, has a number of
stocking looms. There are also three works 72
producing so-called Nottingham ware, the kiln and production process for which has already been described under Crich.

I arrived at one of the kilns during firing, which was said to continue for two days and one night. At this point it had been going on for 24 hours and they had already been throwing in salt, which was said to occur many times during firing.

On the way to Sheffield, which lies 12 miles from Chesterfield, I passed a number of coal mines, all seam-works of greater or lesser depth according to the height at which the shaft was located, from eight to 60 yards.

At all of these places there were remains of charcoal in the coal with the sap rings still visible, from which one can see that both deciduous and evergreen woods grew in this area in prehistoric times before the Great Flood.

In the towns and villages through which we travelled, some of the inhabitants made nails, some scythes and some sickles.

The price of nails was the same as I
73 mentioned at Belper, but here they have a
constant price for slitting iron, 10 shillings for a bundle weighting 60 lb, in good times and bad.

Scythes are worked piecewise at 1½ to 2 shillings, with a length of .... [missing]

Files were of two types, sold for 2 to 3½ shillings per dozen, cut on one side and flat on the other. They are cut on one side and ground on the other [sic].

Folding knives	[production costs]
Forging blades	from 2d to 8d
Grinding blades	2d to 8d per dozen
Making haft	from 6d to 6s per dozen 74
Scales[46]	from 6d to 2s.6d per dozen
Springs	from 3d to 12d per dozen

Since the blade is made longer towards the back, a small anvil is bound over the larger one to make the work easier. The blades are scored
with a chisel to make the lock. 75

If the hollow piece which is at the corner of folding knives is to be decorated, use is made of a hollow cut in a small anvil which is either hammered firmly into the block or bound in place with steel wire as mentioned above.

The situation of the manufacturing town Sheffield is shown in the drawing below.[47]

Notes and references

1 The Bow factory was established in about 1749 and continued in operation until 1776.

2 This drawing is difficult to interpret. RRA's description seems to suggest that the pumps were set about 10 feet above the surface of the water to be pumped, and that the pumps were force or jack-head pumps that raised it another 50 feet or so. Wooden water pipes were more usually made of elm.

3 A reference to pargeting work.

4 'Bishopswood' must be Bishop's Stortford, and 'Acrell', Hockerill.

5 The chapel of King's College.

6 The Great Ouse.

7 An important firm of merchants and iron masters in Stockholm.

8 Presumably one of the two Bedford rivers.

9 More likely to have been herons. *Lloyd's Natural History*, ed. E Bowdler Sharpe, published 1896, states: 'there is evidence that until the year 1590 [the crane] continued to breed in the fens and swamps of the eastern counties, whilst its visits in winter continued with regularity to a later period, though they gradually diminished.' RRA was, of course, in the area in the summer.

10 Tod, a unit of weight formerly used in the wool trade.

11 The distance is in fact 11 miles.

12 A prominent Gothenburg merchant.

13 Probably 'Fowler'.

14 The Great Ouse.

15 The present road is 18 miles long.

16 Name omitted in MS.

17 These are 'bearded' needles, the end of which is recurved and lies over a groove in the shank into which it can be depressed so that a stitch further down the shank can be slid over it. It is this groove that is made by the chisel cut. The shanks are tinned because the needles are put in groups into a die in which they are fixed together by casting a strip of alloy around their shanks, and these strips are in turn clamped into the frame, so presenting a straight row of equally-spaced needles.

18 Thread bonnets—literal translation. Presumably lace bonnets.

19 The stamp ***HG*** was from the Hofors group of ironworks in the province of Gästrikland. Hofors itself was founded in the seventeenth century and is still in operation.

20 Tolvfors (Gästrikland).

21 Wall (Gästrikland), not known.

22 Norrby (Närke).

23 Frotuna (Närke), Iggesund (Hälsingland), not known, not known.

24 Nolby (Värmlamd), Älvsbacka (Värmland).

25 Probably charges for shipping from the Humber.

26 'Bart' must be Burton on Trent.

27 Wollaton Hall.

28 This name – possibly Barrett – is not familiar. The mill was established by the half-brothers Thomas and John Lombe.
29 This surprisingly high figure may refer to the number of individual moving parts.
30 The composition of the body shows that the factory made white earthenware.
31 This machine appears to have been a hand-driven extrusion press.
32 This appears to be a description of the scratch blue process, as used in Staffordshire salt-glaze ware.
33 Thomas Evans and William Storrer.
34 From what follows, it is clear that RRA refers to Belper.
35 Nolby (Värmland); Mölnbacka (Värmland); Hofors (Gästrikland); Tolvfors (Gästrikland); possibly Bofors (Närke); not identified; not identified.
36 It has not been possible to identify this estate.
37 River Derwent.
38 Crich.
39 'Orsten' is the Swedish name for a limestone occurring in Sweden that contains small quantities of bituminous matter.
40 No further information is given about Mr Da Costa and his notes.
41 See Vol. 2 pp.40–41.
42 A primitive form of edge runner mill.
43 See Vol. 2 p.38.
44 Aln, an old Swedish unit of length equal to two old Swedish feet or 59.4 cm.
45 The letters referred to in the text are missing from the drawing.
46 The covers on the sides of the haft or handle.
47 There is no such drawing.

Journey 6b Sheffield to Newcastle

Sheffield, Chapeltown, Barnsley, Clifton, Wortley, Wakefield, Leeds, York, Beverley, Hull, Beverley, Scarborough, Irton, Osgodby, Whitby, Sandsend, Staithes, Guisborough, Stockton, Darlington, Middleton Tyas, Durham, Sunderland, Shields, Tynemouth, Newcastle.

Fig. 197 The Marquess of Rockingham's mansion at Wentworth

On 15 August I travelled from Sheffield to Wentworth House, which is a very large and splendid building, belonging to the Marquess of Rockingham [Fig. 197]. Most of the interior is still not quite finished. At the ground-floor entrance to the house, there is a beautiful group of figures in marble of more than human size, representing three stages of Samson's fight with the aid of the jawbone of an ass. There are also many statues of plaster standing in niches.
In the rooms there are mainly family portraits, except in one that is filled with miniatures. There are very many books, beautifully bound, in the library and also costly astronomical instruments. The walls of the halls and corridors are covered with a great number of plans of
76 cities and other engravings.

The Marquess has recently returned from his travels and is 24 years old. He is married to the daughter of a rich gentleman and is now said to have revenue of £25,000. One of his ancestors was beheaded for being an adherent of Charles I.[48]

At the exit from the house to the park there are four obelisks standing on a level lawn and on another side there is a beautiful dome on columns. On a high hill a mile away a pyramid of considerable size can be seen.

Chapeltown blast furnace

Chapeltown furnace, belonging to the Duke of Norfolk, lies 3 miles from Wentworth but was not in blast at this time [Fig. 198]. At the furnace there was a stack of coal in the open, looking like a house. The forest from which the charcoal is made consists mainly of oak, but there is also hazel, ash, alder and birch. These English names are the same as the Swedish.[50]

Fig. 198 Chapeltown blast furnace[49]

77 Wood is paid for by the cord, which costs no more than 8s to 10s. One-and-a-half to two cords yield one dozen seams[51] of charcoal, one seam being equal to a quarter or eight bushels. Twelve seams are sold for 21s. The furnace holds five to six dozen and is estimated to use six dozen each 24 hours of the campaign or 40 loads per week.[52]

The iron ore is mined in the neighbourhood, not more than 1 or 2 miles away, and is found below and between the coal seams. It is generally full of small seashells, as shown by drawing no. 199. The weekly production of pig iron amounts to 13 to 14 tons, when all goes well. The furnace was 24 feet high and square as shown by the drawing, because the fireplace[53] had been taken out. Large bellows of leather were used that had to be dismantled and repaired after each campaign.

Mining of iron ore

I visited the ironstone mines a mile away and found that the ore lies at depths of 60 to

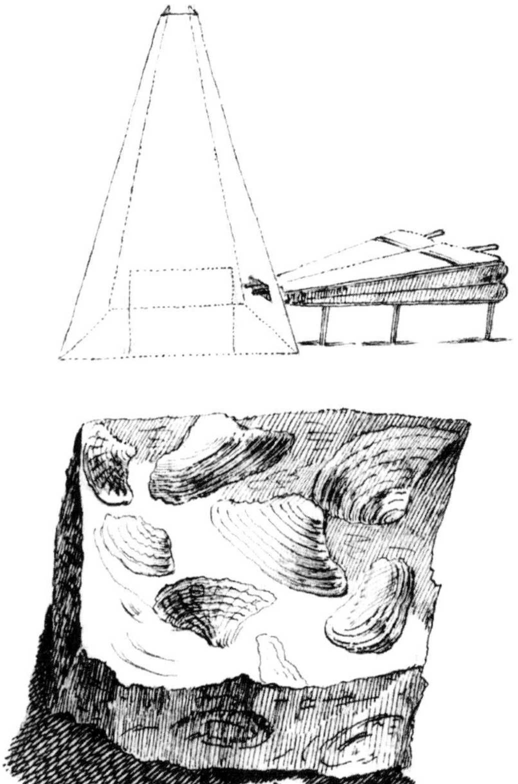

Fig. 199 Bellows and ore containing shells

90 feet. Above it there is first a sandy mica-schist 78
that continues down to a depth of 30 feet to 36 feet and then 'binds'[54] which, further down, softens to a clay and below it coal, ore, various kinds of rocks and again at greater depth, a coal-seam that is worked in some places.

Lord Strafford's mansion

A mile from Barnsley stands Lord Strafford's Mansion,[55] which is large and impressive. Below it there is an obelisk on a plain. To enhance the prospect over the house from half a mile away, a large rock has been left in a large stone-quarry and on top of this the lord has built a ruin that also can be seen from Barnsley on the other side of the hill. On the opposite side of the house, a considerable edifice looking like a fortress and an obelisk have been erected on a hill, and on yet another side there is an open temple with a colonnade.

Sandstone quarry with impressions of plants

At the quarry mentioned above it was observed that in a quartz-like sandstone there were impressions of plants, of the same kind as those I had seen previously at Wednesbury in Staffordshire in the iron ore mined there below 79
the coal seam. Here I found these impressions 9 inches wide and 3 feet long, and generally flat. When the stone is quarried, one generally sees behind the impressions a cavity filled with a very dark, black-brown flour, which is undoubtedly a residue of the vegetable matter that made the impression in the sand.

Here, there are also imprints of a striped wood or perhaps more likely a reed, as shown by drawing no. 200. There are also large, wide marks of a leaf, or perhaps bark, covered by needles, that appear to be lying irregularly on top of each other, although in some places the imprints look more like the first figure.
The quarry workings are located at the top of a hill which, according to English ideas, would be considered fairly high. 80

The town of Barnsley and its wire-drawing works

Barnsley is a medium-sized town, where a large number of workers are occupied with the drawing of wire,[56] partly made of English iron, but mostly of the so-called 'Dans-iron', that comes from Sheffield and is the best of the Öregrund-iron and costs 24 shillings to

Fig. 200 Sandstone with plant fossils

25 shillings a hundred-weight. It arrives cut to lengths of 3 feet, so that the grain of the fractures can easily be studied.

In Barnsley it is first taken to the 'Nakins' forges, of which there are ten in the town [Fig. 201a]. In each of these three men are employed, who first draw the iron down to a ½ inch square cross-section and 18 feet to 21 feet length[57] by forging. During this operation two or more bars are often welded together to produce the required length. The bars are finally drawn through four holes before it is ready for the wire-drawers, drawn by a horse-driven winch. See Fig. 201b.

They [the men in the Nakins forges] accept the bars at a weight of 14 lb per stone and deliver it back, drawn four times to 0 gauge, at 13 lb per stone.[58] The wages are 3s.3d for each one-and-a-half stone, which are divided amongst the men in such a way that the master gets 15d and the other two get 12d each. If the iron is drawn down under a tilt hammer it does not perform so well in subsequent operations as when forged by hand. The cause of this is thought to be less heating. Pitcoal is used for the reheating. The drawing dies are made of double refined blister steel from Sheffield, which costs 4d a pound.

After the forge men are finished with it, the iron is drawn six times through dies by means of a horse-driven capstan. The payment for this work is 2s for each one-and-a-half stone. Subsequently the wire is drawn by hand.
The Dans-iron must be annealed between every two draws but the English iron can stand being drawn four times between annealings. 82

When the wire has been annealed and cooled by itself,[59] it must be scoured before it is ready to be passed through the drawing dies again. For this purpose forge cinder and woollen cloths are used, and the work is accomplished by pulling the wire by hand through cinder held in a cloth, after which the wire is wound onto wooden pegs, knocked into the wall.

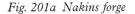

Fig. 201a Nakins forge

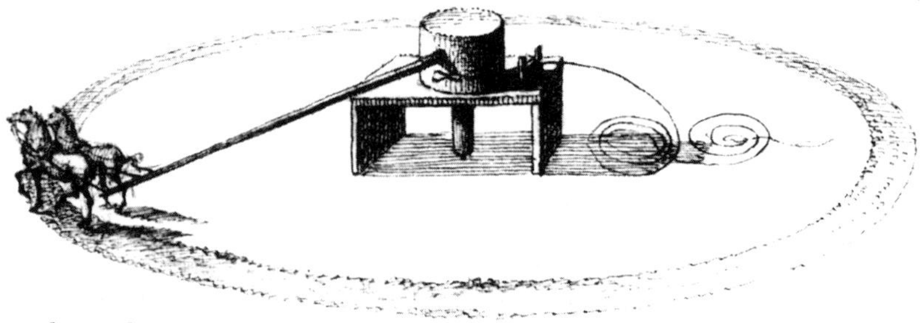

Fig. 201b Horse-drawn drawing winch

The wire was now transferred to a third workshop for further processing and drawing by manpower. To begin with this was done by means of a capstan, the man walking around it in a circle in the same way as the horse did according to the description in the foregoing. When the wire gets still finer it is wound onto a
83 horizontal drum turned by hand [Fig. 202].

Gauge	*Price, pence per lb.*	
	English Iron	Dans Iron
1–4	12	15
6 and 7	16	20
8	16	24 seldom made
9	18	–
10	20	–
11	22	–
12	28	–

There are eight Wire Masters here who employ many workers, namely, Fisher, 'Radi', Tompson, two Clarks, Oddy, 'Reussen', 'Tors', Ellis. The price of wire nowadays is as shown. The greatest consumption of Numbers 5, 6, 7 and 8 Dans wire is for the stocking weaving frames in Nottingham and Derbyshire. Number 9 and 10 wire of English iron is mainly used for carding combs. Numbers 1, 2, 3 and 4 wire of Dans iron is mostly sent to London, and is undoubtedly used for weaving velvet and carpets.

Wages

For drawing from gauge no. to no.

From	To	Pence per lb.	Cumulative per lb.
1	4	1½	1½d
4	7	1½	3d
7	9	2	5d
9	12	5	10d

Fig. 202 Man-drawn winch

84 ### *Iron and steel-wire drawing works at Clifton*

In Clifton, 12 miles from Barnsley on the road to Halifax, considerable quantities of fine wire are made, but the heavier wire is bought from Barnsley.[60]

In addition to the consumption of iron for wire in Barnsley, about 40 tons a year of Gothenburg iron is used for horse shoes and other purposes. Of this iron the stamp ***)(*** [61] is good enough for wire.

	Gauge	*Price per stone of 13 lb.*	
	1	10s	
	2	10s	
	3	10s	
	4	10s	
	5	10s.6d	
	6	10s.6d	These sizes of English
	7	11s	iron are used for rivets by the cutlers of Sheffield
	8	11s	do.
	9	12s	do.
	10	12s	do.
	11	12s	do.
	12	13s	do.
85	13	13s	do.
	14	14s	For stocking needles
	15	18s	do.
	16	18s	do.
	17	18s	do.
	18	18s	do.
	19	20s	do.
	20	20s	do.
	21	20s	do.
	22	22s	For carding combs
	23	23s	do.
	NachZeif	18s	do.
	24	30s	Of good iron
	25	30s	
	26	30s	
	27	30s.6d	
	28	30s.6d	
	29	30s.9d	
	30	3s	
	31	31s.2d	
	32	31s.5d	
	33	32s	

English wire, or in other words wire made of
86 English iron, is sold for 1½d less than the above listed prices and generally for carding-combs and similar uses that do not require such soft and uniform wire. Wire of steel is made here to order, the steel being procured from a tilt hammer in Sheffield.

Wortley bar-iron forge

Wortley forge lies 6 miles from Barnsley and belongs to Mr 'Lochshett' and 'Forgeland' in Sheffield.[62] There are two workshops here, one with two hearths or fineries where three-and-a-half to four tons a week can be fired and forged to anconies, using charcoal, costing 22s a dozen. A ton of iron requires three-and-a-half dozen. The wages are 10s [a ton] the same as is common in other places.

As far as the hearths and the hammer were concerned, there was nothing remarkable here that had not already been observed quite often
in England, except that the paddles of the 87
waterwheels driving the hammers were made of sheet-iron, each one being fixed to two iron brackets, and that the wheels themselves were provided with three stout iron hoops as shown by the annexed drawing no. 203.[63]

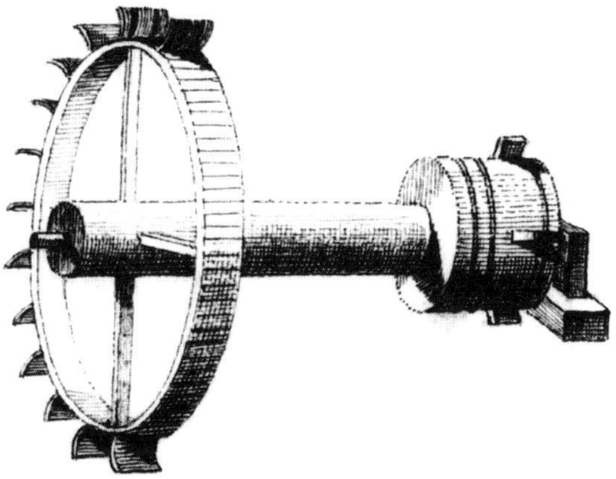

Fig. 203 Waterwheel with iron paddles

At the lower forge[64] there were three hearths, of which only one was in operation, melting down old iron scrap. When there is an abundance of water, one of the other two is used for firing pig iron and the remaining one for chafing. Both the latter two hearths got their blast from two bellows through long pipes made of sheet-iron that also conveyed air to a furnace on the other side of the forge that was said to have been used for welding together lumps of iron. The whole arrangement was so involved and ill-contrived that it does not deserve further mention.[65]

Wire-drawing mill for iron and steel wire at Wortley

In a couple of valleys, extending to the west and
88 south of the forges mentioned above,[66] another two works had been established, one a wire-drawing mill and the other a rolling and tinning mill for tinplate. The wire mill consisted of three separate workshops.[67]

There was a tilting hammer for drawing down the bars to a thickness suitable for the wire-drawing operation. The wire mills themselves were built according to the pattern commonly used in Wales, whence wire drawing by waterpower was introduced into this neighbourhood, not so long ago. Here, as in Wales, the forged iron is coiled after annealing, and scoured with slag in cylindrical, hollow drums and then allowed to lie in water, as it was said, to soften. Four scouring drums were driven by one waterwheel and six cast
89 gearwheels [Fig. 204].

When the wire has been drawn through the holes in the draw-plate a few times and annealed and scoured again, it is placed in an acid lees contained in stone troughs located above the heating furnaces. This is said to shorten the whole process, because a couple of hours in the lees correspond to a couple of days in water, but I cannot say which way can be considered the best. Wire is made here at two wire mills, producing up to 2 tons a week between them, which comes to nearly 100 tons a year, provided that there is enough water, which was not the case at the time of my visit.

Comparisons between wire of Swedish iron and wire of English iron

The workers were not able to tell me anything about the prices, but in Barnsley I heard that the iron wire made here [in Wortley] of ordinary kinds of iron was sold for considerably less than the hand-worked wire made there [in Barnsley] either from Dans-iron or English iron. The latter is only used in Barnsley. Although many of the people in this part of the country are concerned 90
with wire-drawing, it is, nevertheless, not possible to find anybody who really understands it and can explain the difference in quality between Dans wire, drawn of Öregrund iron, and English wire made of English iron. The people in Barnsley say that Dans wire is the best, but the Wortley people claim the same for their product. Dans wire is used for needles for the stocking-frames in Nottingham and the surrounding country, because it is considered more springy, but English wire, on the other hand, is used for carding-combs, because it is alleged to be softer. Just the same, the carding-comb makers claim, and not without reason, that the English wire is harder because it is brittle, but the stocking-needle makers say that it is both soft and brittle.

The wire made from Swedish iron was consequently not given absolute precedence and there were several opinions about the reasons for this. The workers in Barnsley were convinced that Dans wire would be useless if it were drawn down by a water-driven tilt 91
hammer. Others do maintain, and quite rightly so, that both the intrinsic quality of the iron and

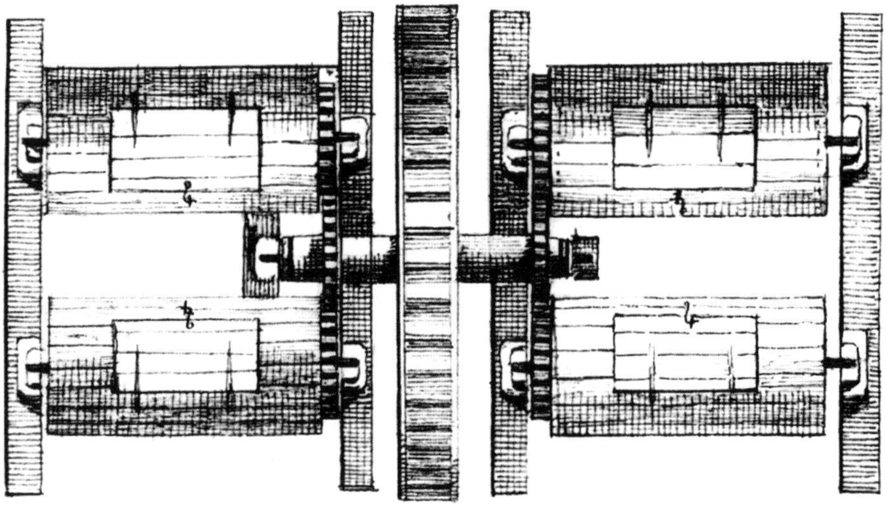

Fig. 204 Water-driven scouring drums

the way it is worked contribute to making the wire good and serviceable.

Iron-sheet rolling and timing at Wortley

The tinplate works is located 1 mile from the forges and 2 miles from the wire mill.
It consisted of a rolling mill with its reheating furnaces, a workshop for annealing and removing of scale, a workshop for pickling and scouring and another one with three pots for tinning, polishing and removal of the thick tin on the lower edge. In the rolling mill there were two separate stands of rolls with their reheating furnaces. The first stand rolled sheets for tinning and was provided with rolls 12 inches long and 11 inches in diameter and was otherwise designed in the same way as the mills at Pontypool from where the art of making tinplate was stolen. The reheating furnace was of the same size as the ones described at this
92 place, but designed as a reverberatory furnace and fired with pitcoal, which was also the case at one of the rolling-mills in Pontypool.

Double sheets rolled here are $16\frac{1}{2}$ inches long and $12\frac{1}{2}$ inches wide, English measurement, and 100 sheets go into each box. Single sheets are $13\frac{1}{2}$ inches long and $10\frac{1}{2}$ inches wide, and packed 225 to a box. Eight of these sheets are rolled from one piece of iron, 4 inches wide, $10\frac{1}{2}$ inches long and $\frac{1}{2}$ inch thick or 16 of the thinnest, that are used in Manchester for making tags for shoelaces. Although they are paper-thin these sheets are sold at the same price as the double sheets and a box holds 100.

The second stand of rolls is designed to roll larger, black sheets, and the rolls are 30 inches long and have a diameter of 12 inches, with
93 other parts of the stand in proportion.

The furnace for this stand of rolls was larger inside than the one previously mentioned and was fired with pit-coal that was thrown into it. The largest sheets that could be rolled were 28 inches wide and 5 feet to 10 feet long. The sheet-bars, which were forged quite wide and thick, were first rolled broadside-on to 28 inches in length, then rolled lengthwise in further heats. When the sheet reached 5 feet in length it had to be doubled because the furnace did not hold greater lengths and also because of the difficulty of handling long sheets and their rapid cooling when thin and single.

Besides these stands of rolls, there were two additional ones used for the turning of rolls and for flattening the sheets, by cold rolling after annealing and removal of the cinder or scale by rubbing. At the roll-turning machine it was
observed that a long but defective roll was made 94
into a shorter [but sound] one by turning a new neck where a blow-hole had been found in the surface. In order to facilitate the turning of the necks, the posts of roll-housings were longer than usual.

A new method had been invented here to remove the cinder that forms on the surface during rolling and annealing. This consisted of removing the sheets from the furnace with tongs as soon as they had become red-hot and throwing them into a water-trough hewn out of sandstone, plentiful in this neighbourhood. In the trough there was a grid of iron that could be raised by a winch, thus removing all the sheets from the hot water in one operation. In spite of this invention the sheets had to be scrutinised very carefully in order to ensure that
all cinder or scale was removed that might 95
prevent the functioning of the pickling process and consequently also the tinning itself. When this has been carried out properly the plates are rolled flat in the mill already mentioned and are subsequently taken to the pickling room, which is built above the furnaces, in order to heat the pickle made up of wheat-bran and water and give it acidity. Then follows the scouring after which the plates are submerged in water to prevent rusting, whilst they are waiting to be placed in the tin-pot. When I asked if the water in which the plates were protected from corrosion had not been mixed with some other substance, the answer was no. Just the same, it appears probable that some lime had been added as this material is known to be corrosive.[68]

During tinning, tallow, whale-oil and resin
are used, mixed together. The plates are first 96
boiled in one cell and then dipped consecutively into a second and a third pot, which gives the tin more lustre. Afterwards the plates are scoured with wheat-bran and the tin on the lower edge melted off in a trough.

The single plates, whether thick or thin, are packed 225 to a box, that sells for 53s.6d, of the double 100 are packed in a box selling at the same price.

On the way back we passed the stream that drives these mills and it had a footbridge built across it consisting of single upright stones as shown by drawing no. 205. The dam in the river

Fig. 205 Stone bridge and dam

was made of slabs of stone on edge so that the water can run freely between them and over them when there is a flood, which strengthens the dam rather than the opposite.

Coal seams

97 There are coal seams in many places around here, of which the top ones generally contain so much fine charcoal powder that the coal is either thrown away as being of no use or left as a roof above the workings.

Bullfighting and other amusements

At the end of the park that surrounds Lord Strafford's house, baiting of bulls by dogs and sack races had been arranged for the amusement of the gentry, and I saw these as I went past.

In Barnsley, preparations were being made for a yearly festival, that was going to be held two days later and the actors had already arrived and the same evening were going to perform the tragedy Romeo and Juliet in a small barn. Posters were up advertising a concert by a blind violinist and the comedy [sic] was to be performed for nothing because theatre performances for payment are not permitted in the provinces.

[Fig. 206 missing, no reference in text]

The nature of the country

The distance from Barnsley to Leeds is considered to be 14 miles, which equals 20 English.[69] The soil between the two towns is 98
mostly sandy, due to a sandy type of rock with impressions of vegetable matter, already described on the journey to Barnsley. This was also seen in some stone-quarries encountered during the trip to Leeds.

The town of Wakefield and its woollen manufactures

Wakefield is an attractive and populous town that has factories for woollen cloth and other woollen manufactures and a navigable river to Hull, called the Calder, which makes commerce so much easier. Rhenish millstones, quarried in the vicinity of Coblenz, are used here in the flourmills that are located beside the stone quarry.

Oat bread

Between Wakefield and Leeds it is 6 of the long miles,[70] and along this road it was noticed at a flourmill that the people were busy drying and

milling oatmeal, which in Yorkshire is much used for bread, baked into thin cakes. These are also eaten by the better classes with butter for
99 breakfast and with tea.

The oats were dried in a kiln constructed of perforated iron sheets above a furnace fired with coke of pitcoal, here called cinder, but in other places called coke or culm.

Pitcoal quarries, fire engines and glass-furnace coking of pitcoal

A mile from Leeds there were two fire engines at the pitcoal quarries[71] and also a short distance away a glass furnace for bottles. The small coal that cannot conveniently be loaded onto wagons is here coked in kilns and used for the drying of malt and oats. As soon as the coal has been ignited and heated right through, it is raked out of the kiln and strewn around the field for the fire to go out by itself. Through this firing the coal loses most of the sulphurous smoke and becomes more suitable for drying malt than it was before.

The town of Leeds and its woollen manufactures and market

Leeds is a considerable and populous town situated on a navigable river called the Aire,
100 which also produces plenty of water power. As a result this place has risen to become the main centre for all woollen manufactures in England. Its large amount of commerce and profitable trade can best be judged by the fact that on a single market day, the turnover in cloth is said to amount to as much as £20,000. Saturdays and Tuesdays are market days throughout the year and it was noted as peculiar that all the people concerned with the trading were so quiet that they whispered into each other's ears. This considerable market only lasts for one hour, which is between 6 and 7 in the morning. The largest amount of trade takes place on Tuesdays, because on Saturdays there is not such a large influx of buyers and sellers from the surrounding country and small towns. It is estimated that in Leeds and its vicinity up to 3000 pieces of cloth are made each week.

Freight wagons with wide wheels

On the road to York, which is 24 miles from 101
Leeds, I met some heavy wagons with the newly-developed wheels of 9 inches width, which have been prescribed by an Act of Parliament. They were not quite as high as usual, but appeared to have a fairly good effect on the road, because they served to level out the road in practically the same way as a roller [Fig. 207].

Burning of lime and fertilising the fields.

The farm workers were now employed in carting of lime for dumping on the fields that were lying fallow, instead of dung. The lime was subsequently spread out with a spade and rolled down. The lime is made here by burning a chalk somewhat harder and more like stone than usual and several quarries for this material were seen along the road. The soft chalk is burnt in heaps built on the ground of alternate layers of stone and pitcoal. A hole is left at the centre,

Fig. 208 Lime kiln

Fig. 207 Freight wagons with wide wheels

through which the coal is lit and the heap is then burnt like a charcoal stack, although it is
102 not covered with turf or earth [Fig. 208].

Pottery

I also visited a pottery, 5 miles from Leeds, but not far off the road. The clay was said to be refractory and was mined at a depth of 60 feet, just below the coal seam that is being worked in this district. The coal here was 3 feet thick and the clay $1\frac{1}{2}$ feet to 2 feet thick. The vessels produced were well made and were fired in porcelain kilns, of the type that has been described several times before, but the method of glazing with salt was not known. Instead, the commonly used lead glazing was employed, making the vessels more expensive and less valuable. The clay is dispersed in water and then dried in a brick basin, in the same way as in Derby at the white-wares factory.

Horse-racing at York

I have seldom had so much company on the road as this time, because the whole population of the country around here was setting out and heading for York to attend the horse-racing
103 starting on that day, 19 August at half past four in the afternoon. I too made my appearance there to see the great concourse of people and was surprised when I found that there was hardly room for me out by the race-course and even less in the town, which otherwise is large enough and, except for the horse-racing, not overflowing with people. Mr Tenwick's bay mare Duchess, Mr Hassel's grey horse Smuggler and Mr Swinburn's chestnut horse Dicky Dickinson raced today for the King's Plate, which amounted to 100 guineas in hard cash. The last-mentioned took the prize, although the betting most everywhere was six to four in favour of Duchess winning. Besides these horses there were two others, that raced for a private bet between the owners themselves. The strongest of the horses, which was favoured seven to three by the betting, collapsed during the race leaving the course free and open for the other one right up to the winning-posts. Jockey and saddle are
104 weighed both before and after the race and the horses should be of the same height, which is carefully measured. A four-year-old horse should carry 8 stone, a five-year-old 9 stone, a six-year-old 10 stone. If the horse is more than five years old it carries $10\frac{1}{2}$ stone, each stone being equal to 14 lb.

The course is generally staked out to a distance of 2 miles, which has to be run twice for the King's Plate, or even three times if the first two did not give a decisive result.
The horses rest for a little while between races and are then led around and some water is poured into their mouths from a bottle. If the jockey and the saddle do not weigh as much as the horse should carry according to his age, a belt is tied around it, in which lead weights are placed, that have been carefully weighed and adjusted.

The horse race in York is considered the second most important [in the country] after
Newmarket and goes on for eight days. Each 105
day there is one particularly large and important race. Many of the foremost aristocrats in England attend this race meeting and the most distinguished amongst those present now were the Duke of Hamilton and the Earl of Coventry with their beautiful consorts and also the Marquis of Rockingham with his Marchioness and large staff of attendants. The expenses that these horse races cost the English noblesse can be inferred when one knows that rooms for a week cost 20 to 30 guineas and that a gentleman and his family might bring, perhaps, 20 to 30 horses with them and their suite. Six would be for the carriage in which the wife and her ladies travelled, four for the husband's post-chaise or phaeton and 12, 15 and up to 20 for the livery servants and other attendants riding behind the carriages.

The bets are already made for the next year's meeting and rooms booked, because a much greater gathering of distinguished people is
expected than usual, due to the presence of the 106
Duke of Cumberland, which has been promised. He can hardly back out now, unless death intervenes, which so often prevents these important appointments.

The town of York and its large cathedral.

York is a large town located on the river Ouse, which is navigable from here to Hull [Fig. 209a]. It has many beautiful buildings but the Cathedral, here called the Minster, which can be seen from far away with its three towers, dominates all the others. It is a magnificent edifice, even if it is built in the Gothic style. It is 400 feet long and 200 feet wide at the transepts. The central tower has large windows on the sides and is open from the floor of the church

Fig. 209a York

to the ceiling, just like any other cathedral, which viewed from the inside looks very agreeable.

The journey to Hull and the character of the country between York and Hull

On the way to Hull, I travelled across many
107 large fields and wild places until I finally came across an innkeeper, who also was a farmer and even here I had trouble enough persuading him to take me in for the night. In this place I had to sleep in a cheese-store, and was nearly eaten by mosquitoes, which I had not seen before during my English journey, but I was now right out in the countryside and on the banks of a stream. The milk from 14 milch-cows here was made every morning into a cheese weighing about 20 lb. It was first poured into large pans of lead with outlet holes at the bottom through which it was drained leaving the cream, which was churned [to butter] twice a week. The whey from the cheese-making was fed to the pigs, as is customary all over England.

In the morning I continued my journey to Beverley, 30 miles from York and 9 from Hull. The country along the road was alternately fertile fields and meadows and large tracts of
108 waste land used for the rearing of cattle and sheep. In some places there were also warrens or plantations for breeding rabbits.

The town of Beverley and its business

Beverley is a long town, with two large churches, one of which is beautiful and built in the gothic style. Amongst other epitaphs I noticed a very old painting representing a king and a bishop giving benediction and underneath it was written: 'As free make I thee, as heart may think and eyes may see.'

The town does not have any special manufactories, except a few looms for serges. Many people are also occupied with the preparation of flax and the spinning and weaving of linens. The flax is procured from Hull, but is imported. Tanning of leather and malting of barley is also carried out here.

The sale of iron is very small because the blacksmiths buy what they need for horseshoes,
wheel-tyres and other household requirements 109
from Hull. Other iron manufactures, made in Sheffield and Birmingham, are sold in the local shops.

The character of the countryside

The country between Beverley and Hull is rather low-lying and, where it is cultivated, there are a number of windmills to pump the water from the lowest parts. Peat for fuel is cut in the ditches and it shines rather white and clay-like.[72] The road is well built and provided with milestones that on one side have steps hewn into them in order to make it convenient for the women to mount their horses.

Haymaking

On this day, 20 August, the haymaking[73] had not yet been completed in this vicinity. The usual long scythes – 3 feet to 3 feet 6 inches – are used here and during the entire harvest they are not removed from the stock and are not sharpened more than, perhaps,
twice except with sticks of oak coated with fat 110
and sand or otherwise with sandy whetstones. The stock should be bent upwards so that the mower does not have to bend down as far and, therefore, would not have to complain so much

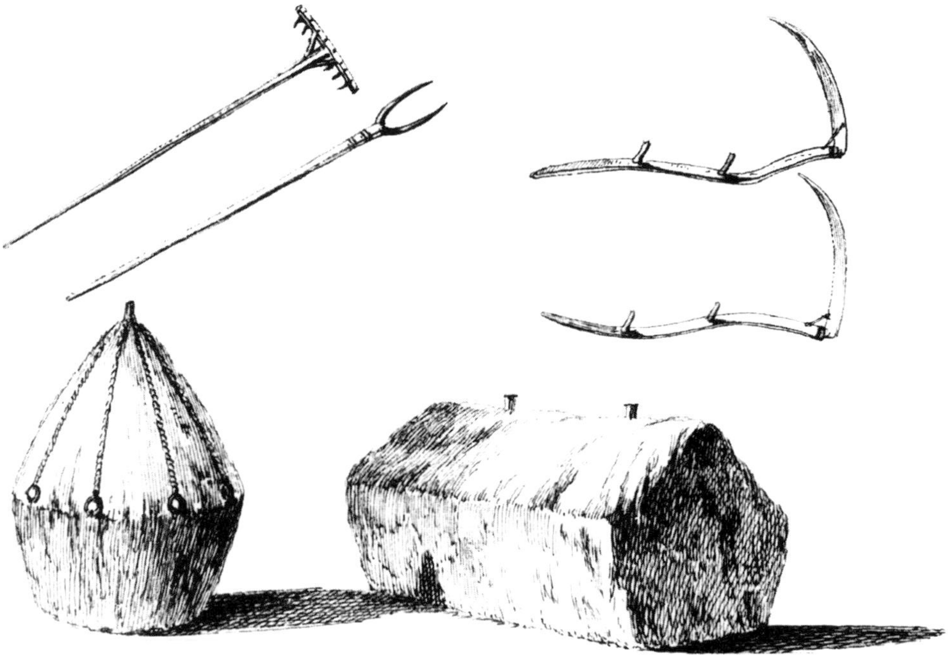

Fig. 209b Haymaking

about backache as he would do in Sweden. The scythe is fixed to the stock by means of a ring and a wedge, both made of iron, and two pieces of leather are placed under the wedge to fasten it firmly. The little hasp in 'b' in Fig. 209b,[74] serves only to prevent grass from getting stuck in the angle between scythe and stock. The pitchfork 'c' is used to lift the hay on to the wagon or up on to the haystacks but never for throwing, which requires more effort and causes much hay to be lost. When the hay is being drawn into rows one hay maker generally goes ahead with a fork followed by another with a rake, who takes care of any hay left by the fork. The hay is then allowed to lie in rows for a few days until it has dried and can be stacked,
111 because otherwise it is feared that it might start burning in the stacks. Occasionally, if the weather is bad, a hole is made in the stacks with barrels that serve as air ducts or chimneys.

The town of Hull and its location and trade

Hull lies on the River Humber, where a number of other rivers from the country around it meet, particularly the Trent and the Ouse which, with their many small tributaries and canals, facilitate transport from Hull to places far inland. This and the convenient harbour that Hull possesses has made the town into one of the largest ports for foreign trade in England and the inhabitants have also won for themselves considerable riches and a strong trading position. The ships that come here to the harbour go into a little river called the Hull, on the banks of which the merchants in the town have their warehouses in the same way as in Bristol or London [Fig. 210].

The town was formerly strongly fortified with walls and towers, but these are no longer being maintained, except the fort on the other side of the little river, where there is still a small 112
garrison of four companies of old soldiers, no longer fit for [active] service. During the last war[75] French prisoners of war – up to 1,500 men, not counting the officers – were interned here. The most unusual thing to be seen in this place was a cistern, constructed in the basement of one of the towers. There was no inflow of water except from the leaden roof of the tower, where it collects in rainy weather and subsequently runs down to the cistern through pipes made of lead. The bottom and sides of the cistern itself are lined with lead. In spite of this, it was said that pure water never was short, either summer or winter, and not even during the time when so many French prisoners had to be supplied with it.

The Church [in Hull] is large and, in its Gothic fashion, fairly beautiful, although it has a wooden vault in the manner of the country. 113

114

Fig. 210 Hull

In the market place stands an equestrian statue of William III, made of gilded lead and cast in the same way as the statue of Marcus Aurelius on the Capitol in Rome. The inscription reads as follows:

'This statue was erected 1734 to the memory of King William III our great deliverer'

Notes on the trade in iron and the consumption of iron in Hull

Gothenburg iron, 2½ inches to 3 inches wide and ½ inch to 1 inch thick, has recently gone up in price from 53 to 57 daler coppercoin per skeppund, due to the high price of Russian iron, formerly used for wheel-tyres in this vicinity. About 21,000 tons of first and second grade Öregrund iron is imported [a year], which is mainly sent to Sheffield for cementing to steel. Freight by water and carriage by land from Hull to Sheffield now costs 17 shillings a ton, and the price of Stockholm iron is now 53 daler in Stockholm. Öregrund iron is contracted and is sold here for £20.10s.0d a ton, but only to a few of the steelworks owners in Sheffield. 'Sabel' iron, which belongs to the Demidhoff
114 family in Russia, is also good enough for steel making but not so reliable as Öregrund iron. It now sells for 80 kopeck per pud @ 40 lb (63 pud makes one English ton)[76] and 'Government iron' costs 75 kopeck. German steel is sold for £50 a ton and goes to Sheffield for making razors. The merchants in Hull always keep up to 300 ton Öregrund iron in stock, in case of war or in case transport should fail. The 'Burning Mountain' stamp is considered to be the best from Gävle, but this year it cost 3 shillings per cwt more in Amsterdam.

Ordinary iron now sells in Hull for £16.0s.0d to £16.10s.0d a ton. The freight costs 15s from Stockholm and 10s from Gothenburg. The customs duty is £2.8s.8d if the iron arrives on an English ship, but £2.17s.9½d if the ship is Swedish, which amounts to £0.9s.4½d more. The best Russian iron sells for 75 kopeck per pud in St Petersburg.

When 75 kopeck per pud is paid for Russian iron at St Petersburg, the price here with
freight, duty and other taxes comes to £15 per 115
ton. The freight is only 5 shillings per ton as it serves as ballast for hemp.

Duty amounts to 3 guineas per ton including the increase and everything else.[77]

Freight to Sheffield by water to Tinsley Common with duty and land carriage, 17s 6d per ton

Ditto to Birmingham

To Nottingham, 4s 6d

To Leeds, duty of 1½d is payable for each bar of iron; since 60 bars of iron are usually reckoned to amount to a ton, the duty is thus 7s.6d per ton of bar iron.

Ditto freight or carriage from Hull to Leeds, 1d per bar, which makes 5s and the total costs 12s.6d.

At Hull some American 'Rock' iron used to be imported, but none has arrived for several years now.

The same is true of Spanish iron, which has not been imported for many years.

Most of the nails which come from Sheffield,
and also from Birmingham to Hull, are shipped 116
thence to London; this is not included in the export tallies for Hull.

Iron which is smaller than ¾ inch square attracts duty at £8.10s.9d. Leeds lies on the River Aire, which is leased out with its locks at £4,400 per annum. York on the River Ouse. Hull on the River or Bar, which is called the Humber and the little River Hull.

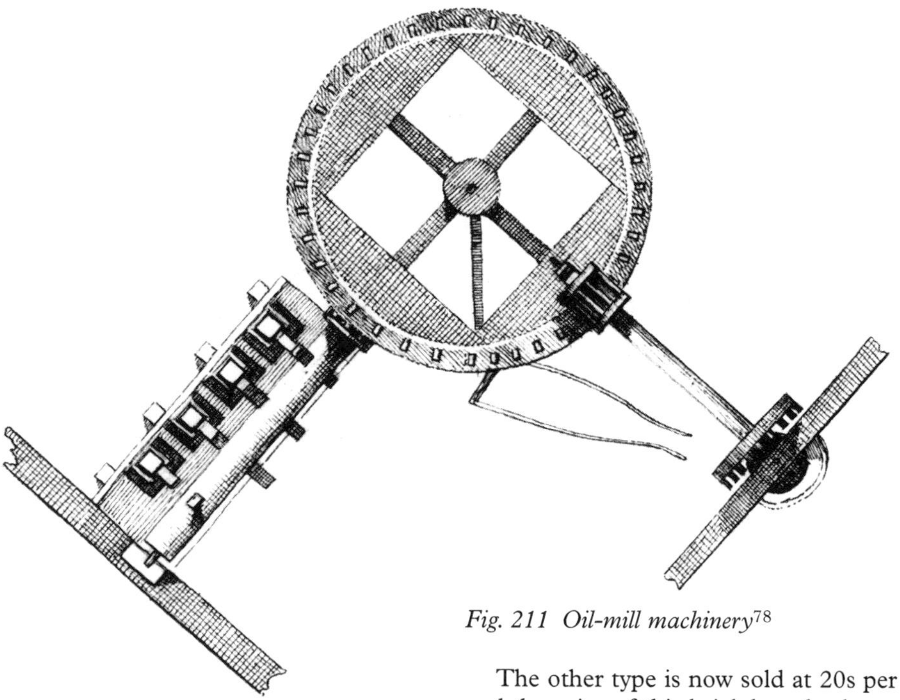

Fig. 211 Oil-mill machinery[78]

The principal industry of Hull, apart from extensive home and foreign trade, can be said to be the maltings, which here produce for export. In and around Hull there are 13 oil mills, some driven by horses and some by sails, most set up
117 in the Dutch manner with perpendicular mill-stones and stamps, with boiler and stirrer etc. [Fig. 211].

Rapeseed oil sells now for £22 per ton or 2s per gallon. Linseed ditto at £30 or 3s per gallon The seed cakes which remain after pressing are sold, in the case of rape-seed, at 45s per ton; they are used instead of manure. Linseed is sold at 45s per ton and is used as cattle feed and is also sold to Holland.

There are also a number of limekilns and brickworks here, working continuously; they produce both for the country's own needs and for shipment to foreign parts.

The lime is burnt here in ovens of the same type as I have already described at Bristol and London. The stone is a hard chalk, which is brought by boat down the rivers from inland areas. The price for lime is...[79]

Two types of brick are produced here, notably the usual sort, known as water bricks,
118 sold at 8 to 10s per thousand. Because of the fire at Gothenburg,[80] the price has been increased by 2s above the usual price, which was 8s per thousand.

The other type is now sold at 20s per 1,000, and the price of this brick has also been increased, from 13s. The difference between the two types of brick is that the former type is made of wet clay, which has not been kneaded and, instead of sand, which is usually spread underneath, the table is wetted with water. The roller, which is used to level the upper surface of the brick, is dipped in water. As a result, the clay is wetter and cracks both during drying and burning.

The other type, called stock brick, is made of a kneaded clay as stiff as can be worked. Sand is strewn on the table underneath and the top is levelled with a dry roller.

Fig. 212 [no reference in text, but probably a drawing of the brick kiln described opposite]

Fig. 213 Scarborough

The kilns for brick firing are built after the Dutch model, with small draught ovens fired
119 partly with coal and partly with peat. Firing continues for five to six or eight or more days according to the size of the kiln and weather conditions [Fig. 212].

The kiln workers earn 16d for 12 hours and the others get $2\frac{1}{2}$ shillings per 1,000 bricks.

Roof tiles are also produced here and are sold at 33s per 1000. They are $14\frac{1}{2}$ inches long and $9\frac{1}{2}$ inches wide across the curve.

A great deal of gypsum, here called plaster, is consumed in Hull and is used for floors in houses, something I also observed at various places in Staffordshire and on the journey through York. The gypsum comes from Staffordshire down the River Aire and usually resembles a blue clay mixed with narrow needles of gypsum. Sometimes one finds larger
120 pieces of gypsum crystal.

The gypsum stone costs 3s.6d at the quarry and, to this is added freight down the river, so that it becomes rather expensive at Hull.

At Hull there is also a sugar refinery located outside the town on the River Hull. Close by there is also a shipyard, supplied with timber from Lithuania and Pomerania.

On 25 August after dinner I left Hull, and headed for Scarborough but, because of wet weather, could not get further than Beverley, only 9 miles, which I had earlier passed on the journey from York to Hull.

Between Beverley and Scarborough, a distance of 35 miles, lie the villages of Molescroft, Leconfield, Dreffield, Langtoft and Seamer, where huge numbers of sheep graze on the large waste areas in this neighbourhood known as Commons.

A sheep that grazes on these Commons, which are dry with thin vegetation, only
produces 3 lb of wool, or three sheep to a stone, 121
which is 15 lb of wool.[81] The wool sells for 6d per lb. On the other hand, sheep which graze further inland on low-lying land with better grazing produce 10 lb of wool per annum, which sells for 9d per lb.

A shepherd looks after from three to 500 sheep and is paid from £7 to £10 in addition to his food.

The Commons, which this area consists of, resemble the plains around Salisbury. The rock here is also a kind of limestone, and one sees a number of tumuli on the hills, although there is no Stonehenge nor anything that could be a place of sacrifice.

When we were 5 or 6 miles from Scarborough we saw a low-lying cultivated area between the hills. After that came sand-dunes nearer the sea, stretching in towards the land on the north side but going out towards the sea in a wedge on the south side, where the limestone hills fade away.

Scarborough lies in a small bay by a steep cliff. Earlier there was a fortress at the end of
the hill but now there are only ruins [Fig. 213]. 122

Scarborough town, its harbour and activity

The harbour has a stone jetty or mole, now reinforced by a breakwater.

The town was in its heyday during the war years because of the many ships built here and the capital raised through freight. Now there is little employment apart from what can be gained from freight between Newcastle and London, as well as minor trade with Spain in fish, caught here in the bay and dried in the sun.

Fig. 214 Bathing houses on the shore at Scarborough [another version of Fig. 213]

The fish are 'shotfish', 'thornbacks', 'white torses' etc.[82]

When there was more seafaring activity here, up to 200 tons per annum of Swedish iron was used for anchors, bolts and other marine applications. Then, as now, iron was obtained from Hull merchants, although consumption now is hardly a quarter of what it was.
In addition about 150 tons of American pig iron was imported and converted at Mr 'Kochschet's' Seamer's Forge.[83] This iron sells for £17.10s though it is not well suited for maritime applications.

Bathing at Scarborough, and the spa water drunk here, are now the principal sources of income for the inhabitants. Large numbers of Gentry, or the well-off in society in the country, come here for the sake of their health, though even greater numbers come to enjoy themselves or to seek an advantageous marriage. Bathing is done in the cold, salt seawater; the beach is sandy and gently sloping, well suited to bathing. For the greater convenience of the bathers, more
123 than 30 wooden bathing houses have been built.

These are mounted on four wheels and can be drawn out into the water by a horse as far as required.

Women are dressed in a blue shift and accompanied by a married lady. But men usually enter the water naked, and those who wish to boast of their manliness only allow themselves to be driven a short distance out, so that they have the opportunity to show off their well-built bodies that much longer in front of the women bathing nearby.

Bathing is usually done before midday, or when it is high water, in order to gain the benefit of the fine sandy bottom.

There are many people who also drink the salt water. There is also an acidic water spring near the sea shore which many guests use for water drinking. This spring water contains minerals and iron and is called Spa water. *12*

Scarborough town: shipping, maltings, trade, iron consumption

From the castle I counted 120 ships that could be seen with the naked eye. It is said that more than 150 vessels belong here, most of which nowadays ship coal from Newcastle to London. There are also some which go whaling and others employed in shipping fish to Spain and Portugal.

There are a number of maltings at Scarborough, none in operation at present.

The principal businessmen in the town are Mr Blond, Messrs 'Bade', Joh. and Richard, and Mr Tailor.

Messrs Mould and Williamson in Hull supply Scarborough with iron, and this, according to the smiths, is sold at £16½ to 17 per ton in Hull, which rises to £17 to 17½
with freight. *12*

From the iron they forge anchors and other items for ships, for which 28 shillings per ton is paid.[84] Bolts are forged from iron from Seamer's Forge, which is supplied as 1-inch-square bar, subsequently rounded by the smiths.

The price at the forge was said to be 11s; after it was rounded to bolts it was sold for 28s per cwt or £28 per ton.

Comments on the seashore and worms

During my visit to Scarborough, which was a most enjoyable whole day, I walked along the shore to study the curious strata in the cliff,

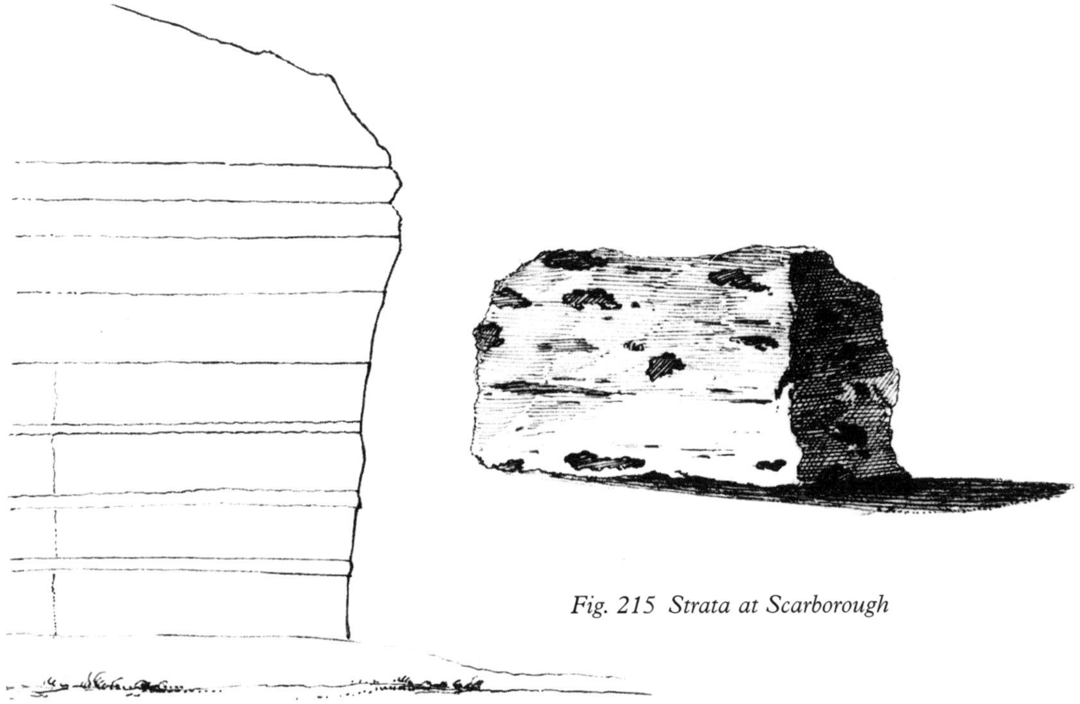

Fig. 215 Strata at Scarborough

which consisted mainly of quartzy sandstone. There were also layers of bluish clay under which there was a coal seam, although the coal was much spread out in the sandstone, as can
126 be seen in the drawing [Fig. 215].

During the afternoon, when the tide went out, I became aware of large numbers of people on the beach digging in the sand. I hurried over to them to find out what they were doing and discovered that they were looking for worms to use as bait. These worms dug themselves down in the sand both to retain moisture and to escape being caught by birds and other creatures.

Those looking for worms had certain signs to guide them. As the worms dig down in the sand they take in their own volume of sand which then goes out of the other or rear end. In this way it leaves as much sand on the surface, in the form of a worm, as its own size. And this is the sign that the fishermen look for when they
127 are hunting for worms.

Epitaph

On a gravestone at Scarborough I read the following inscription:

'This world is a City full of crooked streets
Death is the market place, where all men meet.
If life were merchandise that men could buy
Rich men would live and poor men die.'

Window tax in England

Window tax all over England is regulated in the following way by Act of Parliament:

If a house has only nine windows, 2s is paid. For a house with ten windows, one pays 6d for each window and 2s for the house, together 7s. A 14-window house is 9s and one with 15 windows, 9d from the first to the last, together with 2s for the house. A house with more than
20 windows pays 1s for each window as well as 128
2s for the house.

Irton, a small town

From Scarborough I went 4 miles westwards to a little town called Irton. Seamer's Forge, mentioned earlier, lies 1 mile from here.

Woods

Here there is a small river which has plenty of water, and in the valley there has been sufficient timber to have operated two refinery hearths and production of 150 tons for 24 years, with enough to last a good few years more.

At the chafery hearth, which is the third under one roof, Newcastle coal is used, for which they pay here 30s per cauldron. A cauldron contains 16 measures; a measure is two pecks, and a peck two bushels. The smiths said that they use
⅔ ton coal at a cost of 20s to 1 ton of iron. 129

The price of charcoal varies according to quality, from 5s to 8s per load containing 1 quarter or 8 bushels, which should be sufficient for a ton of iron; the cost is then 40s.

The annual production amounts to 150 tons; wages are the same as usual at other places, 19½s per ton. The works were at a standstill partly because of repair work and partly because of a lack of coal. There was little or no coal in sight.

As far as the buildings were concerned, I noted that the ponds and forge were constructed of worked stone, and that Mr Cockshutt, who had the works built, had placed the bellows up in the roof of the forge, whence the blast was led in tinned iron pipes to the hearths. I had observed this earlier at his ironworks at Wortley: it is an invention of remarkably little utility if there is in any case
130 space for the bellows. One advantage could be, however, that the leather bellows are placed somewhat further from the hearths and can therefore better tolerate the heat and need less frequent lubrication.

The pig iron used at these works comes from America and is bought in London. The price last year was £6½ to £7 per ton. Freight and transport to the works is estimated at 15s, so that the iron at the works costs about £7.15s per ton. The mark on this pig iron, said to be the best from America, is 'Nottingham', Bush River Company.

From Seamer's Forge I went 3 miles through the wooded valley to Osgodby where I had the iron produced at Seamer's Forge tested by a blacksmith. I found it to be 'flaky' and unsuitable for horseshoe nails, and worse than Gothenburg
131 iron and the mark ***A crowned***.[85] The smith told me that it always had this disadvantage and was of the opinion that it 'works hollow'.[86]

[This page of the MS has only four lines of text.]

Commons or waste land with ancient remains

26 August. From Osgodby to Whitby it is 30 miles and the countryside is mostly plains
132 and bare, extensive hills, in this area called Commons. The journey was nonetheless pleasant, as on the one side there was a view of the sea and many ships sailing out there and, on the other, the land side, one could see many tumuli which appeared to be older than any similar remains I had seen.

There were also standing stones similar to Hurling Stones in Cornwall and Devonshire or Stonehenge near Salisbury, although the latter exceeds the former in size to the same degree as St Peters and St Pauls churches do those at Vaksala and Läby.[87]

The first I encountered lies about 6 miles north-west of Scarborough on a hill from which one had a view over both the sea and a great part of the landscape or wastelands. The remains
consisted of ten upright stones which formed 13
somewhat more than a semicircle, of which the largest and best-preserved stone was 2 alns high.[88] The others were fallen and very worn and damaged. In the centre of the circle were traces of three or four stones which presumably were the base of the altar, if this can be considered to be a place of sacrifice, as is usually believed to be the case with this type of stone circle in England. The actual circle was 15 alns in diameter and was placed a little to the west of the highest point of the hill. About 30 alns distant there was yet another stone heap, though very low and fallen down, which may have either been a house for those who carried out
the sacrifices or only a shelter against the 13
weather from the north.

About 100 alns to the east of the above-mentioned stone heap, at the highest point of the flat moorland, was a tumulus consisting of a quantity of round grey stones worn by the passage of time, grown over with turf and heather, called 'ling' in English, found everywhere in these wastelands.

Some miles to the north-west I came upon yet another stone circle, but this had only three stones in position, placed in a triangle, as seen in Fig. 216, north, south and west. The distance, however, between the western and southern stones was larger than the other two spaces, which were 10 alns wide.

From here one could see a ruined barrow not far away to the north-west, and much farther away two much smaller ones, undoubtedly set up for the same purpose.

These extensive Commons, which as far as one can tell were once cultivated, are now of no other use to mankind than as a source of turf to the peasants who have settled in the valleys and come up here in the summer to cut it for fuel.

Turf-cutting on the Commons 13

The turves are stacked in heaps with the underside uppermost to dry in the sun whilst

Fig. 216 Moorland with standing stones

the underside, usually overgrown with heather, has to dry against the ground.

In the valleys there is also turf, 6 to 8 feet deep which, at the diggings, resembles turf in Holland. Sometimes they come across large fallen trees with branches and roots, which are hard and black. These rot quickly when exposed to the air.

Here and there on these Commons there are also sheep grazing, but they are small and thin, as their fodder is meagre.

Sheep pasture

Towards midday I sighted the ruins of the wonderful Abbey Church, which is situated on
136 the heights above Whitby, today an excellent seamark – see drawing no. 217.

Close by the church there is a fine house built from the ruins of the Abbey, owned by Esquire Cumbler, Lord of the Manor of Whitby County.

Whitby town: seafaring, fishing and trade

The town lies deep down in the valley between two hills, which form an excellent harbour, though generally dry at low tide.

By Act of Parliament, two moles have been built here, going out to sea at the harbour entrance. Lanterns are lit on these at night to guide seafarers. The expenses for these breakwaters are taken from those who ship Newcastle coal, now the chief activity of the place, since in peace time there is nothing else for their ships to do. These ships are now said to number 450.

Fig. 217 Whitby town and Abbey

The 'encouragement' of 40s per ton of freight which Parliament gives Greenland traffic has also caused some from this place to dare to take the long and uncertain voyage. This year
137 four ships have brought no fewer than 11 whales here, pure profit, as the costs of the journey are usually covered by the 40s per ton.

The iron trade here is dead, as is everything else in time of peace, as no ships are being built. During the French war as many as 15 were launched in some years.

The little iron trade for the town's needs and for the few inhabitants inland is handled by Mr Linshill, who sometimes orders his iron from Stockholm, Messrs Finlay and Jennings, but this year from Gothenburg, Mr Gerhard. Consumption in wartime could reach 100 tons or above, but now it is no more than 40 tons. The iron is sold to the smiths at £18 to
138 £19 per ton.

From Drammen, Christiania and Frederikshald, ships arrive every year with timber and tar. Ships from the last-named place often bring iron as ballast, which is said to be Swedish.

I visited Captain Wilkinson who travels to Stockholm and there met the son of the late Assessor Uhrlander, who is here at Mr Finlay's expense to learn the English language. He had learnt it so well that he had almost forgotten his mother tongue.

Derelict alum works at Whitby

A little way from Whitby by the seashore there used to be an alum works. This was operated by Mr 'Chumbler' but he has now closed it because the alum shale dug out by the shore became too expensive to recover. The cause was the thick clay and soil with which it was covered.

Remarks on the alum shale

During a walk along the shore, which is very pleasant at low water but flooded when the tide is high, I found quantities of *Cornu ammonis*, belemnites and mussels in the alum shale which
139 projected everywhere, not only in the cliff, but also on the shore where there is no sand cover. It was nonetheless difficult to get them out as the inner part was hard and sat fast in the shale, whilst the outer part was loose and weathered by the action of air and the alum salt, so that it usually broke before one could succeed in removing it. The alum shale, see drawing no. 218, is here 10 to 12 fathoms high. It is covered with a reddish clay and above this alternate layers of sandy stone strata, clay and earth. Also in these layers there were minor seams of coal, with signs in it of small plants, creeping heather and other bushes with which this area was covered before it was flooded at this
height.[89] 14

Sandsend alum works

From Whitby the journey continued 3 miles to the Sandsend alum works which is situated by the sea and is seen in drawing no. 219. These works are the largest in England and belonged to the late Duke of Buckingham. Since he died without heirs, it fell to the Crown, but later it was passed on to his mother against a certain payment. On her death the lease, which includes substantial other property, went to Mr. 'Fibs', a natural son of the duchess in question.

Earlier, 12 to 16 pans had been in operation here, but now it has been reduced to eight pans. This is partly because the price of alum has dropped since a number of alum works have been set up in the area, and partly because the alum shale is becoming more difficult to extract. The further inland the quarry advances, the
thicker becomes the overburden. 14

They have a particular way of working the shale quarry here which is a mixture of 'stross' work and 'furstenverk'.[90] Their 'strosser' lie to the side, as the drawing shows, but the actual work is carried out from below upwards.

The shale here suitable for alum extraction has a perpendicular height of 15 yards, but it is worked on a slope so that a man can stand at the side and hack away the shale and the pieces roll down.

About 80 persons worked at the quarry, see drawing no. 220, and they usually begin work at 5 o'clock in the morning, finishing at 11 o'clock midday, after which, at this time of year, they go home to their domestic chores. The work is paid according to regulation, and for 4 square yards or 6 alns square they get 4 pence, equivalent to 8 styver.[91] The shale is so loose and the work
therefore so easy that a fit man can make 14
16 pence, that is 3 daler kopparmynt. Regardless of whether they are working at 'Rich' or 'Rubbish' (the alum shale or the earth which covers it) they receive the same wages. Those who deal with 'Dogger' are paid in a different way, as this is a hard layer of sandstone just above the shale, which often has to be blasted.

Fig. 218 Alum shale in cliffs at Whitby

As soon as the alum shale has been hacked out, it is driven in a wheelbarrow over a bridge to the roasting oven in order to maintain height with the least effort.

At the bottom of the oven twigs are laid to a height of 1 aln, and then small wood to a quarter[92] and then again twigs to the same height as before. On top of this, shale is gradually stacked to 12 to 15 alns high, in
143 places where the oven is well alight. An alum oven of this kind can be left glowing or burning for six months before they take the roasted material out and place it in the leaching pans. They then begin to prepare and fill a new oven charge straight away. The pans in which the roasted shale is leached out are 1½ yards deep, 2½ yards wide and 5½ yards long. They are filled with shale and then fresh water is added. This is allowed to stand for a day and a night, when the liquid is run off to a container close by in which the alum boiling takes place. As soon as this first liquid has run off, fresh water is again added, and later this is repeated for a third time.

The first boiling takes place in the so-called sludge pan, which is cooled during the night and run off into a container so that the sludge can be removed from the bottom of the boiling
pan. It would melt if it were not emptied. 144
This is because the pans are made of lead, and the material that sinks to the bottom during the first boiling is stony and it stops water reaching the lead and cooling it. There are two of these pans always in operation, changing over each

Fig. 219 Sandsend alum works

day, so that on one day they are used for sludging and on the next for 'drawing'.

Draw pans are the pans in which boiling is carried out after the brine has gone through the sludge pan, and into which the brine left over after crystallisation is pumped. At Sandsend there are now six such pans in operation, and they are tapped and filled with fresh brine every morning.

Apart from those already mentioned, there is yet another alum pan in operation, called 'driver'. This boils at least as long as the others, usually 48 hours, and serves to strengthen the
second extract from the draw pans. For every 14
four pans there is one 'settler', which is a reservoir lined with 'kalkband'.[93] The alum brine from the two draw pans and the driver pan is run into the reservoir and mixed with a

Fig. 220 Alum Quarry

kelp lye, in proportion according to the strength of the brine which is checked very carefully with a balance by the boiling master every morning. During running off, I observed that at least one-fifth of the kelp lye ran into the alum pan, which was then mixed in the settler by stirring. This alum brine mixed with kelp lye is left to clarify in the settler reservoir for four hours and is then run off into wooden vessels for crystallisation.

At this stage the alum brine is mixed with urine, ten horse-loads per day for three pans,
146 roughly two-and-a-half barrels.

Note: Urine from country areas is considered best, especially from farm girls who drink much milk. It costs 1s per horse-load or about 4s per barrel.

The kelp which is leached and used in the running off from the boiling pans costs 45s per ton, although the Scottish variety costs 50s and somewhat more. The method of preparing the kelp is described later on. The brine is left in the wooden crystallisation vessels for 24 hours before it is pumped out and boiled once more. Alum salt, which has settled on the sides and bottom of the vessels, is shovelled up, rinsed in fresh water and thrown into one of the draw pans into which a little water has been sprinkled to dissolve the salt. It is then run into a large chest or tray, where it stands for two weeks to
147 crystallise again and cool down. The curious thing is that the brine that runs out of the chest when it is opened after two weeks is still rather warm. The alum salt, which has settled in large crystals, is broken up and stacked in the store before being sent to London.

List of alum works in England

		Mr. Fibs
Sandsend	8 pans, producing	600 Tons
Kettle Ness	3	200 ditto
Boulby	4	250
Lingbury	4 (3 in operation)	290
[missing]	4	200
Timmelby	2	100
Peck	6	260
Stowpeck	4	200
Littlepeck	4	200
		2,300 Tons

A quantity of iron is used at the alum works, partly for grates under the coal and partly for support of the pans, which are made of lead,
2½ alns wide, 5 alns long and 1 deep. Under 148
the pans there are cast-iron straps everywhere to hold them up, but they do not last long because of the heat.

Some of the bar iron that is used is 1½ to 2 inches square and some is flat, and comes from the towns Whitby and Stockton, and even some from Hull and Newcastle. I was told that the price now was £17 per ton plus freight and cartage. The cast iron comes from Newcastle and costs £10 per ton.

The workers who look after boiling are paid 2s for 30 working hours.

For four pans, production is 5½ to 6 tons per week, which at Sandsend means 12 tons; the annual production is thus 600 tons.

The price for alum in London is now £17 per ton, and freight to London costs 10s per
ton. Production costs at Sandsend are said not 149
to exceed £9 to £10 per ton.

The alum master at Sandsend wishes to travel to Norway or some other country to teach the art of making white alum, and he thought that he ought to be able to earn £500 for this secret. His name is Rodger Stonehouse and he is manager for Mr Linshill at Whitby, who has already encouraged him to travel to Christiania.

Guisborough, Kettle Ness and Boulby alum works

In the course of the journey from Sandsend on the way to Guisborough, I visited Kettle Ness, Boulby and Lingbury alum works, all situated by the seashore and operated in the same way as described at Sandsend. None of these, however, have so much good alum shale: they all have higher 'Rubbish' and lower strata, so costs are higher.

Kelp burning at Staithes

The best time to burn kelp is from 15 April to the end of August.

Staithes is a small fishing port, lying 7 miles from Sandsend and 5 from Guisborough, where a great deal of kelp is burnt. This is used in
precipitation of alum brine. This kelp is burnt 150
from a plant which grows on rocks by the sea, underwater at high tide but easily accessible when the tide is low. The leaves of the plant are thick, bulbous and very large, and the plant is firmly attached to the rock. It is cut, laid on the beach to dry and burnt in a small oven ½ aln high, built of loose stones in a circle of 5 quarters in diameter or thereabouts.

Fig. 221 Kelp-burning at Staithes

Children and old women are employed in burning fern ash, as I described at Worcester. Having regard to its high salt content, this could also be used for precipitation in alum boiling, but it would be dearer here than kelp. Kelp burning can be seen in drawing no. 221

Burnt kelp from Staithes is sold from £33 to £45 per ton. The reason for the low price
151 compared with the Scottish product is that in Scotland they are able to burn the kelp on rocks. Here at Staithes it must be burnt on the ground where sand and other contaminants get into it.

Fishing off Staithes

Fish caught off Staithes is dried in the sun and sold for £14 per ton. It is then exported by ship to Spain and Portugal.

Guisborough, as can be seen from drawing no. 222, formerly had a very well-known Abbey and a large Catholic church, of which one gable is still standing. The majority of all the other buildings, including gravestones and lead coffins, has been used later for house building in the town, especially on Esq. 'Kellnes' Estate, of which he is Lord of the Manor or landlord.

Abandoned alum works

A mile outside the town there is a high hill in the cliffs of which there was formerly an alum works, the first in England. This has now been abandoned in favour of the quarries down near
152 the sea. In blacksmiths' shops in Guisborough it was said that the iron price in Stockton was now £19 per ton.

Durham, a beautiful county

Yorkshire came to an end at the edge of a hill from which one could look out over the beautiful countryside in which the bishopric of Durham is situated, and it was as if one looked out over a new world, cultivated everywhere and without waste lands.

Stockton, town, its iron and other trade, and factories

At Stockton, Mr 'Keeds', a rich and prosperous man, said that there was little that could be done for iron trade there as long as the merchants in Hull and Newcastle can sell iron at the same price as the cost price of imports to Stockton, even in small parcels. This year he will bring in 200 tons from Vincent & Beckman in Gothenburg. He considered that total imports to Stockton these days could not exceed 300
tons. This could be doubled if everyone in the 15
surrounding area were to rely on Stockton. ***CI***, ***SF*** and ***OPS*** are regarded as good and respectable stamps.[94]

Lead export from 1,500 to 2,000 tons, copper 150 to 200 tons, which go to London and Bristol. Lead is sold per cask of 2200 weight[95] at £18.15s.

Stockton is 6 miles from the sea on the River Tees, which is navigable to Yarm and a further

Fig. 222 Guisborough town

6 miles higher up. From all the new houses and the very broad main street, it is clear that the town has been laid out in recent times and continues to grow all the time. This is partly because of the copious supply of lead from the upper part of Yorkshire, and also because of the exceptionally rich copper mine discovered 13 years ago at Middleton Tyas, 12 miles from here. Ever since then this mine has been worked
154 very profitably.

Shipping is the principal economic activity here, apart from a sugar refinery set up by Mr Sutton and Company and some looms for sailcloth. The sugar sells for 9d to 12d per pound, and is reckoned to be as good as London sugar; the workers come, moreover, from London.

The warp for the sailcloth was so taut that the man who was weaving had to stand on the pedals and bang three times for every insert with all the power he had. The reeds were made of iron rod and made in London.

When I asked for import and export lists at the customs house, I was given for answer that I might see them as soon as I showed an order from London.

Stamps from Gothenburg:

DS and ***CS*** regarded as good,[96] sold for £18 per ton cash. The price for this iron was said to be 54½ daler Kopparmynt per skeppund at 155
Gothenburg.

V[97] 6 inches wide and 1 inch thick, for ploughshares; ditto 1 inch square, for wheel nails; ditto 3½ inches square, for shovels.

HK[98] 2½ wide, ½ to 1 inch thick, for wheel rims. The price of this was said to have risen to 57 daler in Gothenburg since the Russian iron has become so expensive.

W[99] ½ inch square for wheel nails and grilles etc; ditto 1½ inches wide is in demand and used for all kinds of smaller blacksmiths' work, such as horse shoes, hinges etc; ditto 2 inches square for axles; ditto 1½ for grilles to support coal in 'wind furnaces'.[100]

This year, 80 tons have come from Gothenburg and the remaining consumption here is taken from Mr Sykes in Hull.

Blister steel costs in Newcastle: ton	£26
Ditto German steel	£50½ 156

At Stockton there are two merchants who import and trade in iron, Mr 'Sleen' and Messrs 'Nabien' & Watson. The former imports up to 200 tons from Vincent & Beckman in Gothenburg; the latter 100 to 120 from K Arfwedson in the same place. Both maintain that the iron from there is better and trading conditions better than in Stockholm or any other place. When they have insufficient iron

they buy iron from Hull, usually at the same price as the Gothenburg iron. The reason for this is said to be that merchants send iron over on commission for a better price than they would get in Gothenburg. Moreover, by loading the higher-quality iron uppermost in the ships they have got away with paying only two-thirds of the customs duty. Customs are trying to prevent this by weighing the whole cargo rather
157 than simply counting bars.

Iron is sold now in Stockholm for £18 ready money or £19 with six months' credit. Here in Stockton it is customary to give a rebate of 6d per £1 sterling if the customer pays cash immediately.

NB: Cast iron from Västmanland costs £12 per ton. There is a good deal of such iron here, in the form of pans for bread-baking, or rather, small ovens, flat irons, door knockers, ornaments for grilles etc.

Darlington, a small town, its activities

Darlington is a small town 6 miles west of Stockton, very well located, by a little river. In this river, the Skerne, grow the green, round reeds found in all Swedish lakes, which they use here to make mats, chair bottoms and bed bases.

There is also a stamp mill for softening the flax that comes from Holland, and is used in large quantities here for linen manufacture. At the weaving mills there are large numbers of looms, producing cloth for women's petticoats, for sheets and for tablecloths, as well as coarse cloth or unbleached cloth and men's waistcoats.

158 No damask or drill after the German manner is made here: all is woven simply, but still commands good prices.

The soil in this area is said to be unsuitable for growing flax, but this is not a problem as long as the raw material for the looms is available from Holland. Apart from this, the profit from farming here is an excellent source of income as long as large export subsidies for the products are obtained.

In Darlington there are ironmongers, but there is no other source of supply apart from Hull and Newcastle, as that from Stockton is dearer.

Mr Thornhill, who owns a large smith shop, both for black and white smithing, mainly grilles and fittings for stoves, was willing to open correspondence with Sweden and I gave him names of some merchants both in
159 Stockholm and Gothenburg.

Middleton Tyas, its copper mines and washing and smelting works

Middleton Tyas is 6 miles from Darlington and was formerly a place that lived only on lime burning. But 13 years ago copper ore was discovered in a limestone quarry close to the town. During the following years even more important discoveries were made, and now these works can with justification be reckoned amongst the richest in England. And bearing in mind the large quantity of rich copper ore which is extracted here, it can be counted as the noblest of its type in the whole of Europe.

But here, just as at other similar places, the local inhabitants are still just as poor as ever, in spite of having riches just within their grasp. Powerful and rich people have put everything
under their control. Truly, here it is as the 160
Prophet says: to the rich it shall be given, and from the poor it shall be taken away. Sometimes this happens as a result of the greater ability of the rich, sometimes through cunning, and sometimes through power and violence.

There are now four companies which operate these mines: the Yorks Interests, Mr. 'Skitlorts'[101] and Capt Paul, as well as the Derbyshire Companies, which have reached an agreement on the 'parson's rights' or 10 per cent.[102]

Here no mining concessions nor special staking out of the area in which one must operate are used: everyone works his own property, and the hedges or stone walls which separate the fields are the borders for each person's mining activities. One understands what riches are to be had in this copper area when one hears that the Derbyshire Company offered Mr. Northby £15,000 for a small field within the area, about 100 alns square. He has
not accepted the offer. 161

There are three ore bodies, of which two are vertical and are called 'pipes'; the third, the richest, is horizontal and is described as a seam, see drawing no. 223.

The pipes consist of black and clayey shale pressed together with malachite and lazurite. Both strike east and west and lie 200 alns apart.

The seam is south of the pipes and falls to the south-east. It consists of a reddish clay $1\frac{1}{2}$ to 2 and $2\frac{1}{2}$ alns wide, in which lie clumps of malachite and lazurite, more or less rich, both in width and thickness.

On the church's property there is a steam engine with a cylinder 54 inches in diameter.

Fig. 223 Copper workings at Middleton Tyas

Mr. Hartley has the field above and expects to be free from water at no cost to himself. Otherwise he is prepared to build a steam engine, but for the moment he makes use of a
162 horse wind. The coal used for the steam engine is bought 10 miles from here.

In the most recently dug shafts – they lie just below the church and are 16 to 17 yards deep – the following strata and types of rock have been found: first a little crust of shale, then a quarter of earth, then limestone 10 yards, then the upper copper seam, then a little over a yard of clay which divides to the south-east in two veins, then limestone 3 yards and, underneath, once again a copper seam, 2 yards thick, richer in copper than the other. At the bottom there is a sandstone called 'grit stone'.

Further up the hill there is a thicker crust of shale covering the limestone and, at the bottom of the valley, which is not particularly deep, there is none of any of this.

In the course of one summer 400 tons of copper ore were brought out and sold for £52 per ton. At the start, the same type of ore was sold to the Bristol and Wales Copper
163 Companies for £13 to £14 per ton.

There are now three smelting furnaces here, all built like those in Bristol, with reverberatory heating. A fourth is under construction.

During smelting I observed that they tapped every fourth hour, when they get copper for the first time. Then they charge more stones over the copper roofs[103] with a mixture of old copper slag taken from an abandoned copper works 1½ miles away.

When there is much malachite green in the charge, they mix in crushed coal to promote metallisation as there is altogether too little phlogiston in the ore.

The copper green, which is not solid, but spread about in the clay, is washed out and mixed with the other ore.

Washing is carried out in two ways. The first is in a washing gallery, letter **a**, which is built as
in Fig. 224 where the clay is put in a container 164
to be washed down by a thin stream of water. **b** is a deeper box, which the washer rakes continuously in order to stir up the clay and the finer sand. The coarser ore remains lying on the bottom. **c** is a box of the same depth where the ore, which is the heaviest, remains on the first third of the box and is taken out for smelting. The next third is washed again on the usual type of table, though rather small; and the remaining third is thrown away as unusable, even though there is a good deal of copper in it.

All of the limestone in the shafts or the quarries is full of shells which they call 'screws', because they resemble woodscrews. These are most apparent when the limestone has weathered for a time in the open air. Then the screws can be seen better, as they are solid and calcareous and changed into crystals, projecting from the partly dissolved limestone. In the quarry itself they cannot be seen so clearly – see drawing no. 225.

All of the mining work here is done in shafts, 165
and these are dug at short distance from one another. Because of changes in the weather, wind-traps are built at the top of the shafts, similar to those I described in Cornwall.

The ore is raised by means of hand winches and the way down is by means of crosspieces on all four sides of the shaft, exactly as I described in the lead mines in Derby.

Fig. 224 Copper ore washing

The work is very wet and difficult because of the clay, but the ore, which lies in lumps in the clay, is easy to get out.

On the journey to Durham, which lies 24 miles from Middleton Tyas, I passed Darlington for the second time and came up onto a Turnpike Road or metalled main road, on which one had to pay 3 pence or 16 öre kopparmynt for a horse for every Swedish mile or every 6 English miles. During the journey I fell in with a landlord or farmer who told me that this charge would continue indefinitely. This is because those who have loaned money
166 for the repair of the road are not keen to be repaid as long as they enjoy 5 per cent interest, an unusually high figure for this area, and wish to see the repairs continue as long as possible.

Durham city and bishopric

Durham is very well situated, surrounded by the River Wear. The land round about consists of woods, fields and meadows, giving a pleasing prospect. The best view is from the tower of the cathedral or Minster, which is 320 steps high.

The church lies at the end of the peninsula and is large but very coarsely built, as the builders did not know how thick the pillars and walls needed to be to support a stone vault, unusual in England.

Close to the church is the castle of the bishop who, with the cathedral chapter, has all the revenues from this province. This income is reckoned to amount to between £30,000 and £40,000 and is said to be divided up amongst
the clerics so that the bishop enjoys £12,000, 167
the Dean £2,500, and 12 Provosts £1,500 each, as well as canons, singers etc.

To the question of what trade is carried on in the city, the answer is 'Law and Gospel', as the great majority of the population consists of lawyers and priests.

Those who do not enjoy any of the ample profits regard these people as a plague, as there are too many of them.

Durham's factories and iron trade

On the outskirts of the city there are several weavers making Etamine.[104] There are also a number of blacksmiths' shops producing all sorts of articles for household use.

Messrs 'Dutsh' and Appleby sell iron retail, obtaining it from Newcastle at a better price than they believe they could achieve importing small lots from Gothenburg.

Owners of large smithies also fetch their iron from Newcastle, where they pay at present £17 per ton cash and 6 pence more per
hundredweight if taken on credit. 168

Fig. 225 Fossils in limestone

Sunderland, its iron trade and other activities

Sunderland, as shown in Fig. 226, lies on the coast at the mouth of the River Wear, 12 miles from Durham. The principal business is shipping as well as trade in coal. A number of coal mines were seen here in the course of my journey.

I observed that on the hillsides hereabouts where coal seams were being worked, there were outcrops of rock suitable for lime burning, and this is not allowed to go to waste in this part of the country. At the coal mines, however, lying at a distance in between, there is never limestone, and at times the coal seam lies 30 to 40 fathoms deep, in this case in sandstone, blue clayey rock with layers of clay in between, several times repeated.

Mr Russel is the only importer of iron in Sunderland, corresponding with Mr Gerhard in Gothenburg. This year he expects 64 tons in partnership with Mr 'Linschi' at Whitby who will bring in a similar quantity in his own ship
169 for himself.

Additional quantities that can be sold here – 40 to 50 tons – he obtains from Mr Williamson in Hull.

There is the same complaint in Sunderland about trade in iron and the relationship with Newcastle, as was formerly the case in Italy with regard to Cremona, described by Virgil in the following words: *Vae tibi tantum Vindiciarum Cramona.*[105]

All who have some small business and consumption of iron take their supplies from Newcastle, and the large turnover which the dealers there have from the surrounding districts means that they can be satisfied with a smaller profit margin than those who have lower turnover.

A further contribution is that shipbuilding has ceased, after which freight movements have become few and small compared with the time of war when many ships were fitted out here,
providing ordinary people with significant 170
employment and income.

There are a number of smiths' shops in Sunderland, some making anchors and other articles for ships, some making nails, and some making fittings for stoves and other household equipment.

These days, only anchors of the smaller sort, for fishing boats, are made here, and these are sold at 33 shillings per 100 wt, that is 112 English pounds.

Mr Thornhill, Ironmonger, has a smithy here of the same sort as his uncle in Darlington, producing both white and blacksmiths' work. He buys his iron from Newcastle and pays £17 per ton ready money. He had Hollands wire on trial at his shop, bought from Holland at 4 pence per pound. For English wire from
Barnstaple he has to pay 8 pence per pound, 171
although this is said to be much stronger and less brittle.

Fig. 226 Sunderland and the mouth of the River Wear

171 A number of shiploads of boards and timber come to Sunderland, mostly from Norway. 'Common Deals' are the most usual type of boards, 1½ inches thick, sold now for £3.10s per hundred.

'Gothenborough Boards', 2½ inches thick, are in demand here as each can be sawn into two or three boards. They have now become rare.

In Sunderland there are seven iron saltpans, in which salt is boiled from seawater using coal. Each week 21 tons or 157½ skeppund salt is produced, amounting to 8,190 skp per annum. Since the salt is consumed locally, duty is payable to the Crown: 3s.2d per bushel holding ½ cwt, or £6.3s.4d per ton. For the annual production of 1,092 tons this comes to £7,079.16s or, in Swedish money, 283,192 Dal kopparmynt. More details on this subject can be found under Shields, where salt-boiling is much
172 more important than here at Sunderland.

At the mouth of the River Wear, a strong and substantial mole has recently been built in order to protect ships lying in the harbour during stormy weather. At low water the river was so shallow at its mouth that women picking up coal on the shore could wade across. Now, however, work is going on to deepen the river using dredging barges.

Sir Richard Hilton's Castle

Three miles from the town Sir Rich. Hilton's Castle was seen, Fig. 227, an ancient gothic building.[106] Recently a pair of wings has been added in the same style, giving it a pretty appearance. Nearby is a small park planted with pine trees, most unusual in England. Just above are several large limestone quarries with
associated limekilns. 173

Shields town and saltworks in the area

Shields, which lies at the mouth of Newcastle River,[107] is 4 miles from here and 5 from Sunderland. One became aware of this place from far away because of the black coal smoke rising from the saltpans, of which on this side of the River Tyne and the north side there are 28, though not all were in operation at this time. This was the result of lack of demand for salt since a large number of saltpans had been set up at Lymington in Hampshire, supplied with impure rock salt from Liverpool.

A saltpan, see Fig. 228, is normally 22 feet long, 12 feet wide and a little more than ½ foot deep, constructed of 3 lin:[108] thick iron plate. Under the bottom of the saltpan are nine thick pieces of iron known as 'backs', which serve to support the bottom. These are made of four bars welded together, each 4 inches wide

Fig. 227a Hylton Castle

174 and 1 inch thick, 6 alns long, weighing $3\frac{1}{2}$ to 4 cwt.

For one saltpan, 125 iron plates are used, and the total weight of iron amounts to between 6 and 7 tons. It then lasts for 12 to 15 years with necessary repairs and patching.

A saltpan of this kind cannot be made, with all accessories, for less than £100 sterling.

Under one roof there are usually two saltpans operated by four women and one man, the saltmaster. Together they have wages of 16s per week, of which only 14s is paid out, the balance remaining as savings distributed once a year.

Beside the saltpan there is generally a reservoir containing salt seawater, which is filled when the water in the river is found to be sufficiently clean and salty.

From this reservoir the saltpan is pumped full of salt seawater, repeated nine times before

Fig. 227b [no reference in text, but probably a drawing of smoke rising from saltpans]

Fig. 228 Saltworks at Shields: saltpan and saltworks building

they can take out, or 'draw', the quantity of salt
175 required.

At the fifth filling a little ox blood is added to the pan, which is then stirred and the scum taken off during boiling. The same is done at the ninth filling, and each time a little under 1 quart of blood is added. They said that egg white has the same effect during refining as ox blood.

If the saltpan is new and in good order, they can draw salt three times per week, but normally they obtain five draws per fortnight.

Each drawing should amount to 1½ tons of salt, that is 60 bushels or 30 'Bowls'.[109]

Customs duty is 3s.1d per bushel of salt, weighing 56 lb, which gives £6.3s.4d per ton. But if the salt is to be transported 20 miles
176 away, the duty is only £5.14s.1d per ton.

When the salt is exported only 9d per bushel is paid in duty, but if it is sold to someone in England 3s.10d is paid for the same volume and weight, and for small quantities the cost is 4s or more per bushel.

At Shields there are 144 saltpans on the south side of the river, but no more than 80 are in operation at present. On the north side there are 24 saltpans, only 17 in operation.

Annual production of salt is said to be between 9,000 and 10,000 tons, of which 1,500 to 2000 tons is exported to Emden, Bremen, Holstein, Denmark, Holland and Gothenburg.

The Crown receives between £40,000 and £50,000 per annum from the duties on these saltpans.

Salt for export has to be at least three months old, and all the saltpans sell their salt in turn, one after the other, and only when the
Crown has received its portion. 177

Sixteen cauldrons of coal are consumed by a saltpan in one week, at a cost of 9s per cauldron, although most of the saltmasters have their own coal mines, so coal is not expensive for them. One cauldron of coal weighs 2½ tons.

Coal exported from Newcastle, 8 miles from Shields, comes down the River Tyne in barges, as the water is too low for large ships with cargo to sail to and from Newcastle. However, a ship drawing 12 feet can sail in at high water.

Coal is sold by the cauldron, weighing $2\frac{1}{2}$ tons or somewhat over.

The best-quality coal sells at 14s per cauldron, poorer quality at 9s, most of which goes for export.

A cauldron of coal exported on an English ship attracts 6s customs duty; on a foreign ship
78 the duty is 17s.

A large merchant ship carries 200 cauldrons of coal, which is 200 tons weight.

I went out on the harbour wall to see a vessel invented by Mr Lidell for disposal at sea of ballast from ships' loading cargo at Shields (Fig. 229) for which he has been granted a royal Letter Patent for 14 years.

The vessel has a hold amidships into which the ballast is loaded through hatches on deck. It then sails out to sea until it reaches water with a depth of 18 fathoms, when two hatches in the bottom are opened by means of chains and the ballast runs out. The hatches are drawn up again by the chains, whereupon they sail back, ready to take on a new load.

Fig. 229 Invention for disposal of ships' ballast

The fore and after parts as well as the sides of this vessel have double bottoms which keep it afloat and prevent more water coming in 179
through the bottom hatches than that taken in after dropping the ballast, when it is without load.

This type of vessel is called a Hopper, and the ballast which it transports is paid for by the ton. The weight is obtained by measuring how much the emptied ship rises and how much the Hopper sinks.

At South Shields there are four Glasshouses,[110] see drawing no. 230. Two of these make window glass, another both window glass and mirror glass, a third, common glass for inns and the fourth, bottle glass. All are owned by Mr...[111]

The process for manufacture of window glass is the same as described at Bristol, both for Crown glass and the simpler sort of Crown glass, which is 48 inches in diameter and is sold for 50s per dozen. A dozen is reckoned to be 12
round disks or 24 halves. 180

The lower-quality glass is sold by the...[112] Ditto cut panes ...[113] foot square are sold at 10d each.

Mirror glass is made by blowing, in the same way as at Vauxhall in London, little different from the Venetian method.

Firstly, molten glass is taken from the top of the crucible, when it is absolutely ready.[114] At this point a customs official measures the crucible and calculates how many hundred-weight of molten glass it contains: 9s.4d has to be paid to the Crown in duty for each cwt.

After this the glass-blowing begins: glass is added successively until there is enough to
make the bubble $\frac{1}{2}$ an inch thick. 181

Sizes can be made from very small up to 50 inches long by 36 inches wide.

When, as a result of blowing and swinging, the bubble has become long enough for the type of mirror glass it is intended for, it is heated in the oven, opened at the end and broadened out into a cylinder with the aid of a pair of shears in the usual way for fabrication of glass objects, see drawing no. 231 letter **a**.

Then the glass is heated again and a man runs up steps while another stands below and cuts off half of the glass with shears, as can be seen at letter **b**.

The glass is then broken away from the pipe and fastened at the other end to another pipe

Fig. 230 Glassworks at South Shields

which has a hot, square lump of glass at its end – letter **c**.

The glass is heated again and spread out at the end, as described. It is then heated yet
182 again, and the other end cut as described.

It is then spread out and laid in a hot semicircular scoop and carried to the cooling oven, which is sufficiently warm on the side nearest the hearth that the glass can be made absolutely flat with the help of an iron spade – letter **d**. It is then moved from this oven to another to cool further through a low opening – letter **e**.

The mirror glass made here is sent to London for polishing and silvering.

A newly-discovered coal seam

About 200 alns from the cliff by the river mouth at Shields, work is proceeding on two shafts down to a coal seam discovered by boring.

Fig. 231 Glass manufacture at South Shields

Fig. 232a Shields

This is said to be 9 feet thick. The depth from the top of the rock in which the shaft is being sunk down to the water in the basin or the sea, which lies close by, is between 17 and 20 fathoms, and the seam is even deeper, up to 30 fathoms under sea level – see drawing 232a.

In the one shaft, where a fire engine[115] is to be placed, they have already advanced 20
83 fathoms through a blue clay, here and there mixed with cobblestones and small pieces of coal. Under the clay they have come upon a sandstone said to continue to the coal seam.

Mr 'Challat', who lives in London, has taken on this work for his own account: it will cost him many thousands of pounds before he reaches the coal seam.

Tynemouth town, new and old fortress

The new fortress at Tynemouth is close to the northern part of Shields. It is not a massive structure, but well equipped with cannons.

The old fortress, which is a romantic ruin, lies half a mile out on the headland. There are ruins there of a fine church, built later, in the neighbourhood of which is the churchyard and burial ground, still used by the little town.

There is also a lighthouse, fired with coal. From the previous drawing one can see the situation of the fortress and that of the bathing beach below, formerly a small harbour.

At Tynemouth Baths and also at Shields and the surroundings, there are linen-weaving mills for coarse cloth for local use. The flax is obtained from Holland.

Fig. 232b Fortress at Tynemouth

Notes and references

48 Thomas Wentworth, first Earl of Strafford, Charles I's minister, beheaded 1641.
49 The Swedish word 'malm' on the stack in the foreground means 'ore'.
50 Similar: 'hassel', 'ask', 'al', and 'björk'.
51 Seam: an old word for a horse-load, usually equivalent to eight bushels in volume.
52 This corresponds to roughly two tons of charcoal per ton of iron produced.
53 RRA may refer to the inner lining of the furnace, removal of which might well leave the inside of the furnace square in horizontal section and wide at the bottom, as shown.
54 Indurated clay.
55 Wentworth Castle, at that time owned by the fourth Earl of Strafford. The distance from the centre of Barnsley is about two-and-a-half miles.
56 RRA refers to the drawing of 'Weyer eller staltråd', which means wire or steel-wire. 'Weyer' is undoubtedly simply his version of wire and although 'staltråd' literally means steel-wire, it is used in Swedish for both iron- and steel-wire. The correct translation of 'staltråd' is 'wire'.
57 Assuming that no welding was required, the original Dans-iron bars would have been between $^5/_8$ inches and $^3/_4$ inches square.
58 In other words, the hammermen of the Nakins forges received 14 lb of raw material and had to deliver back 13 lb drawn down to a smaller size. The difference of 7.3 per cent of the original weight was an allowance for scale-loss, scrap, etc.
59 'Cooled by itself' is a literal translation of RRA's notes, no doubt meaning that the wire was not quenched but allowed to cool in the air.
60 RRA probably means that heavy-gauge wire was bought as raw material for further processing at Clifton.
61 The stamp of Borgriks Forge in the province of Värmland.
62 John Cockshutt (the Elder) was the most prominent member of the Wortley partnership at this time, and owned Huthwaite Hall at Thurgoland nearby. This should probably therefore read '...Mr Cockshutt of Thurgoland near Sheffield'. See C R Andrews, *The Story of Wortley Ironworks,* 2nd edition (Milward, 1956).
63 This drawing may not be quite right, as the hoops are not shown on the waterwheel but on a drum with cams for lifting the hammer.
64 As the lower forge is referred to here, the information on the preceding page must refer to the top forge.
65 Robsahm, who visited Wortley in July 1761, expresses his surprise at RRA's statement, and says that he did not find anything unusual except that two sets of bellows [or four altogether] were driven by one shaft and that one set was placed above the other. Pipes of sheet-iron conveyed the air from the top set of bellows to a little hearth, placed at the opposite end of the same building, used for heating old scrap-iron for welding under the hammer. Sheet-iron pipes also led from the bottom of the lower set of bellows, which was placed a fair distance above the ground, through a number of bends to the large hearth.
This arrangement was used so that the heat transmitted by the metal of the pipes would not burn the leather of the bellows. See J L Robsahm, *Dagbok över en Resa i England,* MS M260, Kungliga Biblioteket, Stockholm, p.89.
66 The valley of the river Don in which Wortley iron-works were located runs approximately west above the works, but below them its general direction is to the south, although there are many twists and turns. RRA actually says that the two valleys stretched west and north but the latter is definitely a mistake and another example of the uncertainty he sometimes displays about the points of the compass.
67 Presumably the Old Wire Mill, the New Wire Mill and the Tile Mill mentioned by C R Andrews, *op. cit.*, p.48.
68 This is obviously wrong, probably due to a mistake by the transcriber. It should read, 'this material is known to inhibit corrosion'.
69 The actual distance from Barnsley to Leeds is about 18 miles in modern terms. What is implied by '14 miles' is uncertain: the Swedish mile is about 6 English miles.
70 Approximately 8 normal miles.
71 RRA uses the Swedish word, which means quarry, not mine.
72 To write of shining, white and clay-like peat sounds somewhat strange, but this is a literal translation.
73 At this late date, this must have been a second harvest.
74 'Hasp' appears to refer to a thin bar or wire across the corner of stock and blade. The letters are missing from the drawing.
75 Presumably the war of the Austrian Succession 1741–48.
76 In fact, 1 pud equals 16.38 kilograms, so RRA's figure is too high, even for long tons.

77 It is not clear what is meant by 'the increase ...', etc.
78 The drawing shows a schematic representation of a horse engine in the centre, driving stamps to the left and, to the right, what is probably the drive to a stirrer because it runs at relatively high speed.
79 Missing.
80 In 1746.
81 Should probably be 5 sheep to a stone.
82 RRA's versions of English names.
83 'Kochschet' is RRA's version of Cockshutt, the name of the family which participated in the partnership that owned the Wortley mills at this time.
84 This should probably be £28 per ton for the finished products, as 28s in wages alone seems too little.
85 Svartå (Närke).
86 RRA reports the English expression, which means that it is unsound.
87 Villages near Uppsala.
88 About 4 feet.
89 RRA probably refers to the biblical Flood.
90 'Strossverk' is 'stoping', but 'furstenverk' has not been identified.
91 Styver, a Swedish 1 öre coin.
92 If this is the English 'quarter', a layer of only 9 inches thick seems rather little.
93 Kalkband – meaning uncertain, but probably a lime compound with which the tanks are plastered.
94 Älvsbacka (Värmland), Stjärnfors (Närke), Björneborg (Gästrikland).
95 No unit given, presumably pounds.
96 Åbyhammar, Fellingsbro (Närke), Forsbacka (Värmland).
97 Upperud (Värmland).
98 Ransäter (Värmland).
99 Lesjöfors (Värmland).
100 Literal translation of 'vindugnar', furnaces working with natural draught, therefore needing grate bars.
101 'Skitlorts' may be a reflection of RRA's views in the previous paragraph, as his version of an English name in this case means 'excrement' in Swedish.
102 Presumably tithes.
103 Meaning unclear.
104 A loose canvas used as a base for embroidery.
105 RRA appears to misquote Virgil, Eclogues 9, line 28 which reads: 'Mantua vae miserae nimium vicina Cremonae' – 'Woe to you Mantua, too close to poor Cremona.'
106 Hylton Castle.
107 The River Tyne.
108 'Lin' is probably the English line, equivalent to the French 'ligne', the twelfth part of an inch, which would make the plates a reasonable ¼ inch thick.
109 'Bowls' written out in English in MS.
110 RRA uses the English word, meaning in this case 'glass factories'.
111 Name missing.
112 Missing.
113 Missing.
114 The word 'klar' means ready, but might also be translated as 'clear'.
115 RRA writes 'feuer inchen' which is not Swedish, but is obviously an attempt at phonetic rendering of 'fire engine', i.e. steam pumping engine.

Journey 6c Newcastle to Carlisle

Newcastle, Teams, Swalwell, Winlaton, Blackhall Mill, Shotley Bridge, Chopwell, Derwentcote, Gibside, Benton, Newburn, Hexham, Carlisle.

Fig. 233 Newcastle, town and situation, coal trade and manufactories

Newcastle, see drawing no. 233, lies 8 miles from Shields by the banks of the River Tyne. Small ships can reach here if they do not draw more than 12 feet and it is high water.

The town is built on both sides of the river, linked by a stone bridge. The quay, where ships lie, is on the north side of the river, which is Newcastle proper and stretches 2 miles along the river.

Above the bridge the river is shallower but coal can still be fetched several miles from here in large barges, in which it is taken down to
185 Shields and loaded onto ships.

The coal trade is the principal source of income in this place. And just the quantity sent to English ports is so large that the tax of 1s per cauldron, allowed by Parliament to the Duke of Richmond – and in existence since the time of Charles II – amounts to £12,000 to £15,000.

In Newcastle there are five churches, of which St Nicholas – see drawing no. 234 – is remarkable for the appearance of its tower, which has open arches at the top. Also the library, recently built nearby.

The finest part of the town is enclosed by old-fashioned city walls, along which one can walk beside the quay, where ships lie in the same way as in Genoa.

At the top of the hill, where part of the town is situated, there is still an old tower and other
remains of a fortress, from which 120 steps lead *18*
down to the river in two places.

Just outside the town there are various factories: glass works, silver extraction, mirror foundries, iron foundries, steel furnace and shops for hoes and American pickaxes, as well as a number of lime kilns.

In Newcastle there are only two glass works which, with those situated along the road to Shields, number 13. They make bottles, common window glass, table glass, Crown glass and white glass or crystal, for wine and spirit decanters. Glassworks of all these types have previously been described at Bristol.

Mr Joh Churchson now owns most of the glass-works hereabouts.

Silver extraction works near Newcastle

Half a mile outside the town is a smelting house where silver is extracted from lead brought down from the interior, belonging to Messrs
Blenkinsop, Church and Wilkinson. There are in *18*
addition four similar furnaces at Blaydon and more at Egelson,[116] belonging partly to Messrs Sowald and Blacket and partly to the Quaker Company. At these around 5000 tons of lead are treated annually, then sent to Newcastle for shipment.

Cupellation takes place in a reverberatory furnace – see drawing no. 235 – which is coal-

Fig. 234 The church of St Nicholas at Newcastle

fired. The test stands in the middle between the fire-hole and the chimney, just where the flame comes out, and is $1\frac{1}{2}$ alns long and 1 aln wide, mounted in an iron ring by which it can be drawn out and put in place again.

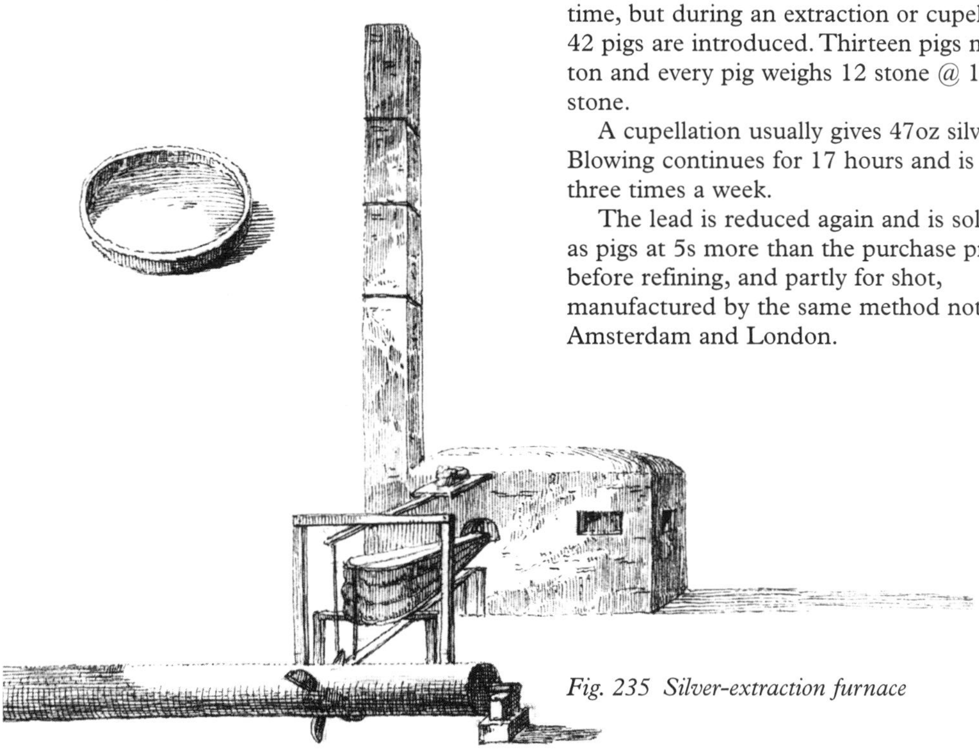

Fig. 235 Silver-extraction furnace

The litharge is driven off by a blast from double bellows set behind the test, and goes out through an opening on the other side, through which the lead is also added.

The test can contain $3\frac{1}{2}$ pigs of lead at a time, but during an extraction or cupellation
42 pigs are introduced. Thirteen pigs make one *188*
ton and every pig weighs 12 stone @ 16 lb per stone.

A cupellation usually gives 47oz silver. Blowing continues for 17 hours and is done three times a week.

The lead is reduced again and is sold partly as pigs at 5s more than the purchase price before refining, and partly for shot, manufactured by the same method noted in Amsterdam and London.

Current prices for lead and silver:
Refined lead sells for £17.15s per ton
On export 1s per cwt is paid in duty: this gives 20s or £1 per ton.
Silver is at present...[117]
Shot...[118]
Litharge...£19.10s per ton
Export of lead from Newcastle amounts
189 annually to 4000 tons.

For iron founding there are here six reverberatory furnaces, as already described at London and Bristol.

These manufacture cauldrons, pans, frying pans, flatirons, rings for wheel hubs, ploughs, baking ovens, rollers, kettles, cylinders and pump bodies, wheels for coal wagons and many other things too numerous to mention.

All of this is cast in sand, except large cylinders and pipes, where the mould is made of clay.

In order to keep water away from the moulds, which are dug deep down in the earth, they put in place a large container of welded lead plates.

When a large casting is to be made, the iron is allowed to run into the mould of its own accord, but for cauldrons and smaller castings, the iron is poured in with ladles.

One man can prepare the mould for a large cauldron in less than a quarter of an hour and,
190 with sufficient help, they can cast 50 cauldrons per day together with a quantity of smaller articles – see drawing no. 236.

The pig iron is partly obtained from London and partly from Holland. The former is American and costs in London £5½ or £6 to £6½ per ton. The latter consists of old ...[119] which here cost £6½ to £7 per ton.

Cementation furnace near Newcastle

The cementation furnace, located by Newcastle, belongs to Mr Hall and Co, who also has another cementation furnace and a forge for 'German steel' at Blackhall Mill, 10 miles up along the river Derwent. The furnace is charged with 10 tons of Öregrund iron at a time.

The material in which it is packed is charcoal 'dust' or breeze, and it has been found that coal made from juniper wood is the best. Next best is birch-wood coal, of which there is a fair supply in this neighbourhood. Alder coal is preferred to coal made of oak and beech.

When both pots – or chests – have been filled, the coal breeze on top is covered with

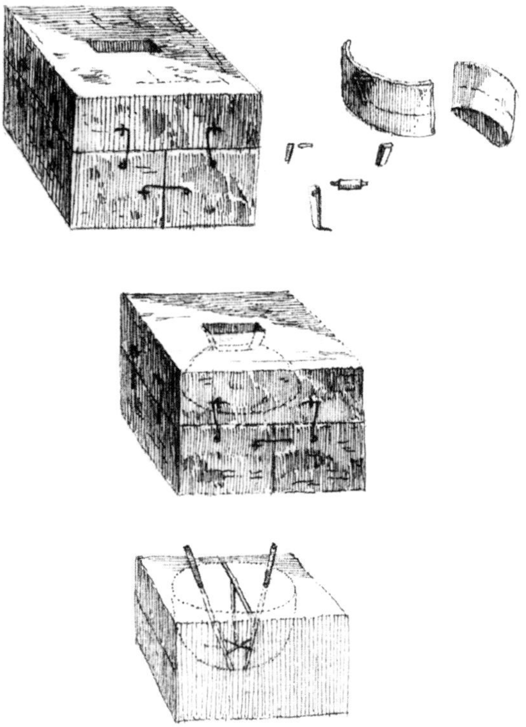

Fig. 236 Details of moulds for iron cauldrons

4 inches to 5 inches of fine sand. The purpose
of this is simply to prevent the fire from coming 19
into contact with the coal breeze and with the iron that is to be converted.

Firing goes on for 6 to 7 days, and cooling down for 10 to 12 days in wintertime and 16 to 20 days in the summer.

During the firing, 40 shillings worth of coal is burnt up, which corresponds to 12 fother or 4 chaldrons.

There are two workers, paid 7 shillings and 6 pence per ton of 2160 lb or 120 lb per hundredweight.

The stamps ***L OO W crowned PL crowned***[120] are considered the best iron for steel and nowadays cost £21 per ton.

The consumption of iron at the two cementation furnaces belonging to Mr Hall and Co. is estimated to reach an amount of 150 tons a year. Formerly, this was purchased directly from Messrs Finlay and Jennings in Stockholm, but is now procured in Hull, at a better price, it is said.

The best steel is now sold for £26 per ton of 21½ hundredweight or 20 hundredweight of
120 lb [sic].[121] 19

192 ***Heavy iron manufactures near Newcastle***

Henry 'Corlton' was previously for many years employed by Mr Crowley at Swalwell, but has recently started a works for his own account just outside Newcastle, where he, in addition to himself, employs four workers, who make hoes, spades and machetes for the plantations in America.

Fig. 237 Agricultural tools

The spades are split from the top and for some distance down. First, two blanks of 2½ inches Gothenburg iron are forged to a length of 9 inches and to the shape shown by the drawing no. 237. These blanks are then put on top of each other, with a piece of steel in between them, heated and welded together.

It should, however, be noted that the welding only extends as far as the steel. Subsequently the spade is forged to shape, particularly at the lower end where it is steeled. The upper end is trimmed by cutting. Then the socket is formed and holes punched in it, and finally the wooden
193 handle is fitted and secured with nails.

Price list

Spades, steeled and half tinned,[122]	per dozen, from
No. 1	26s
No. 2	30s
No. 3	33s

The grinding wheel is driven by a horse as shown by drawing no. 238.

Coal-storage houses, roads and coal transport at Newcastle

By the River Tyne and above the Newcastle quay there are a number of so-called staithes,[123] see drawing no. 239, which are coal-houses or storage places for coal. From these the coal is collected in due course by boats and then put on board the ships either at Newcastle or Shields, 8 to 10 miles further downstream.

The transportation from the mines to the aforementioned staithes is carried out by so-called wagons, provided with a door in the bottom to discharge the coal when they arrive in the staithes. The wagons run on four solid
wheels, either turned from a single piece of oak 194
or cast in iron, although the latter cause too much wear on the roads, which are built up to 8 or 10 miles from here. The roads are provided with wooden rails on both sides to ease the movement of the wheels. On downward slopes the horses are uncoupled and tied behind the wagon, and the driver sits on the end of a bar, resting on one of the rear wheels, in order to keep down the speed [Fig. 240]. In wet weather this is not always sufficient, and the wagons may run away in spite of the braking, turn over, hit

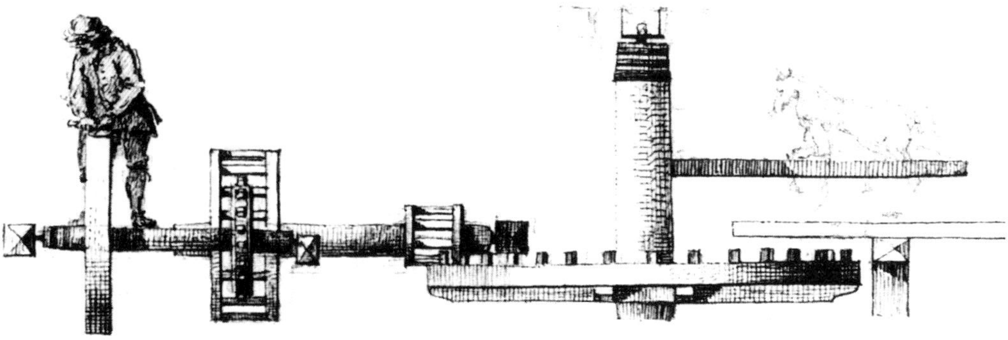

Fig. 238 Horse-driven grinding wheel

Fig. 239 Coal staithe at Newcastle

other wagons and break them in pieces. Sometimes people and horses are unfortunately also injured. To prevent this inconvenience, a large number of people are employed in wet weather putting ashes on the tracks or rails where there are hills.

This staithe, the one nearest to Newcastle, belongs to Lord Ravensworth, who also owns
195 'Southmore' colliery, from which every day 21 keels[124] of coal arrive, which is equal to 189 wagons. Nine wagons contain eight caldrons. The sales price is 14 shillings a cauldron.

The staithe or coal-house is built of planks and is 300 yards long. It slopes towards both ends so that the heavy coal wagons can run by gravity, without horse- or manpower the entire length on either side as shown by drawing no. 239. When they arrive at the turning point, generally at the middle of the building, there is a section of the rails that can be turned around a centre to the side where one wishes the wagon to go. When it arrives at the place where it is to be discharged, a door between the rails and also the door in the bottom of the wagon are opened and the coal falls down into the coal house.

When a boat is to be loaded, the coal is allowed to run into a chute that conveys it directly down into the boat.

Fig. 240 Coal wagon on downward slope

196 As soon as the wagon is empty it rolls out through another door. Subsequently the horse is hitched to it and pulls it back to the mine to be filled with coal again.

The wheels used under the coal wagons are generally cast of iron and come from Clifton in Cumberland. However, they are no longer considered the most suitable, particularly where the road is hilly, because they make the wagons heavy and make them almost impossible to stop when it is raining. It is, therefore, becoming very common to use iron wheels in front and wooden wheels, sawn from one piece, at the back.

The wheel axles are 3 inches square, and those that are welded together of $1\frac{1}{2}$ inches square Swedish iron are considered to be the strongest. Such a steel [sic] axle costs $3\frac{1}{2}$ shillings.

The wheels are 3 feet 6 inches in diameter and 6 inches wide.

Ironmongers in Newcastle

The following are ironmongers in Newcastle:
Messrs 'Whilchisson', 'Potts', 'Gerhard', who sell 200–250 tons a year.
Messrs 'Mancaster',
197 'Potts', 'Gerhard' 180–200 tons a year.
Messrs 'Pool', 'Potts' and Hall 60–80 tons.
Messrs Hall, 'Chaxon' and Comp.,
Öregrund Messrs 'Jen' and Hull 150 tons
Mr John 'Hodger' from Hull 80–100 tons
At Crowley's works, 750 tons are produced, but several thousand tons are consumed in addition.
'Peterbro.' 80 tons
Scotland ....

Factories in Newcastle

There is a sugar refinery in Newcastle, but they had to admit that they have by no means reached the state of perfection found in London. Likewise, there is a manufactory for cloth on the side of the river that is in the diocese of the Bishop of Durham. 'Brownwares' are also made here, but do not in any way look like the similar ware made in Staffordshire and Derbyshire.

Strings are also produced here from intestines of sheep, for braiding to horse-whips or for the thicker strings of violins and double-bass violins. The intestines first lie three days in
water and are then scraped and scoured on the 198
inside. Old hags and other poor women are employed in this work and sell the strings when dry for 1 shilling a gross. A gross is 12 dozen and each string, of which there are 12 in a dozen, is $8\frac{1}{2}$ yards long [Fig. 241].

Dressed lambskin, for fine gloves, sells for £3 per six score of 20 each [sic]. The same kind is also sold at the same price for 6 score of $16\frac{2}{3}$ each.

Flour mill at Newcastle

A mile outside Newcastle on the so-called Town Moor, a flour and sifting mill was built at the expense of Mr Hall and Co. some years ago, driven by water power. In view of its very practical design, it is in the district considered a masterpiece, although there are several mills of similar kind, both around London and in other places in England, although less money may have been spent in building them. This
particular one is supposed to have cost £1,400 199

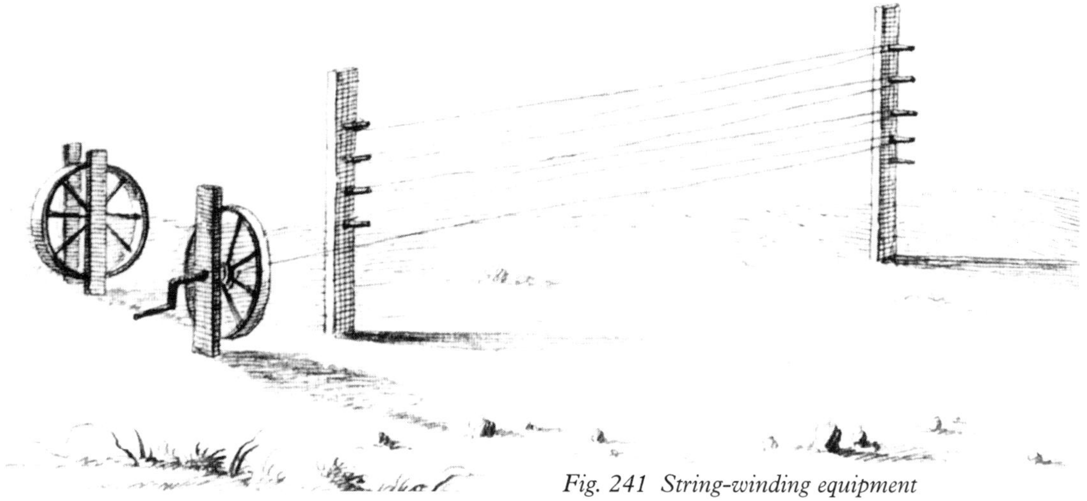

Fig. 241 String-winding equipment

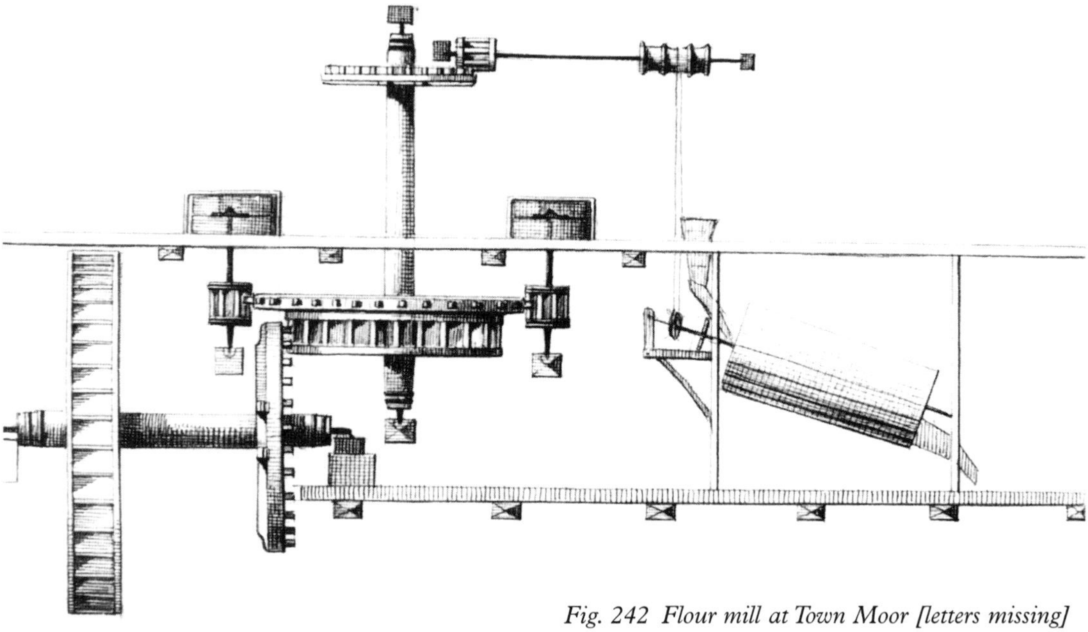

Fig. 242 Flour mill at Town Moor [letters missing]

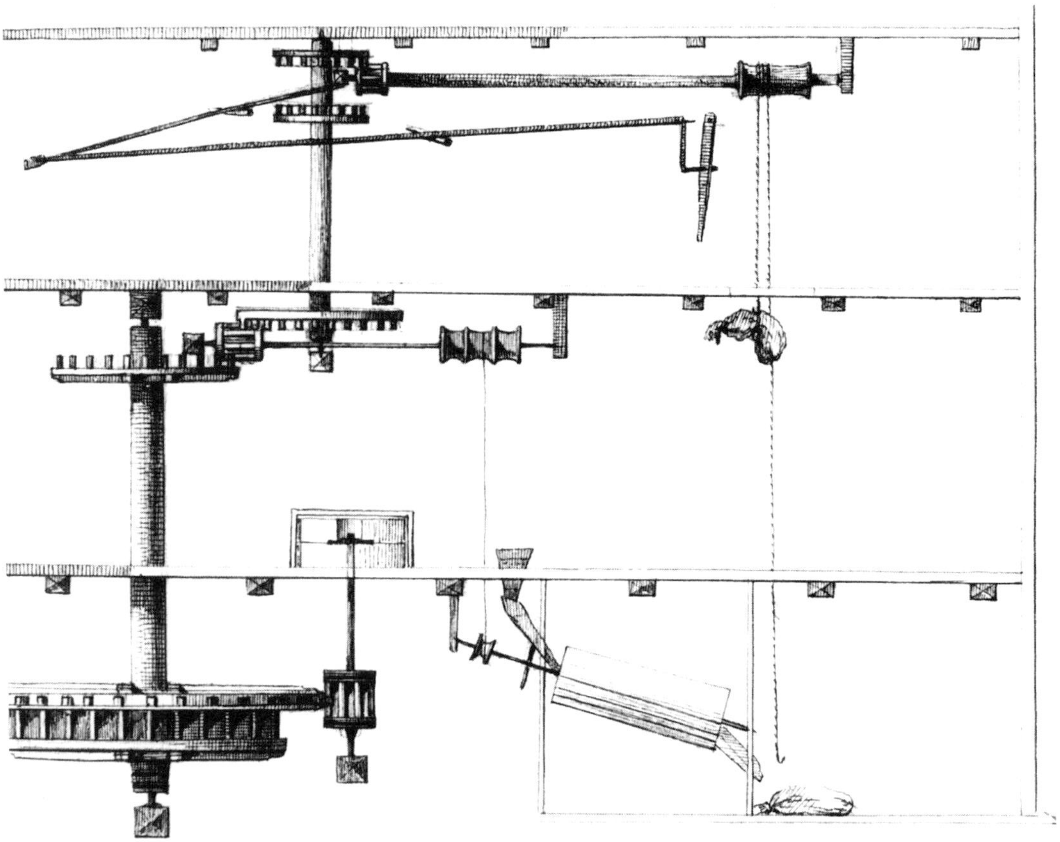

Fig. 243 Flour mill, showing winch details

or 48,000 daler coppercoin owing to the expensive dam and water channel, which are still inadequate. The mill consists of two pairs of stones, two sifting machines, a machine to hoist the sacks to the third floor, a lever hoist to lift the sacks when they are filled with flour and, finally, a barrow to convey the sacks from one part of the mill to another. All of this will be described in turn in the following remarks:

The stones are driven by an overshot waterwheel with deep buckets which is 18 feet in diameter. On the wheelshaft, but in another room, a trundlewheel of about 12 feet diameter and with 88 teeth is mounted, and this drives a horizontal lantern pinion 8 feet in diameter with 36 pins [Fig. 243].[125]

Above this lantern pinion and on the same shaft there is the great spur wheel with 84 teeth, driving the two stone nuts located under the millstones and with 11 teeth each. Consequently the stones make 10 revolutions for each revolution of the waterwheel on the
200 first gearwheel.

The sieving machine is shown in Fig. no. 242 and is driven by a rope running over pulleys.

The flour falls from the upper floor through a hopper, 'f', in which a rope is placed, which is pulled up by the weight of the flour but falls back when the hopper becomes empty.
It touches one of the pulleys causing a little bell to ring, which signals that the machine is empty.

The sifting cloths, which are fitted around a number of slats forming a cylinder (letter 'u') 6 feet long and 2 feet 6 inches in diameter, are made in Birmingham and have various degrees of fineness. The flour chest, located under the sieving machine, is divided into two compartments, namely letter 'Ÿ', where the finest flour collects and 'Z', for the coarser, which is subsequently sifted again. At the outlet end of the sifting machine there is a hopper, into which the coarsest part of the wheat runs
and which on the drawing is marked 's'. 201

The lever to lift the sacks with is shown by the attached drawing no. 244; also the barrow for transporting the sacks from one part of the mill to another, so that the miller's labourers do not have to lift them, which would make their work so much harder.

A short distance away from this water mill stands a windmill, which many people around Newcastle use, particularly in the summer, when the water is hardly sufficient to drive the sieving machine in the water mill.

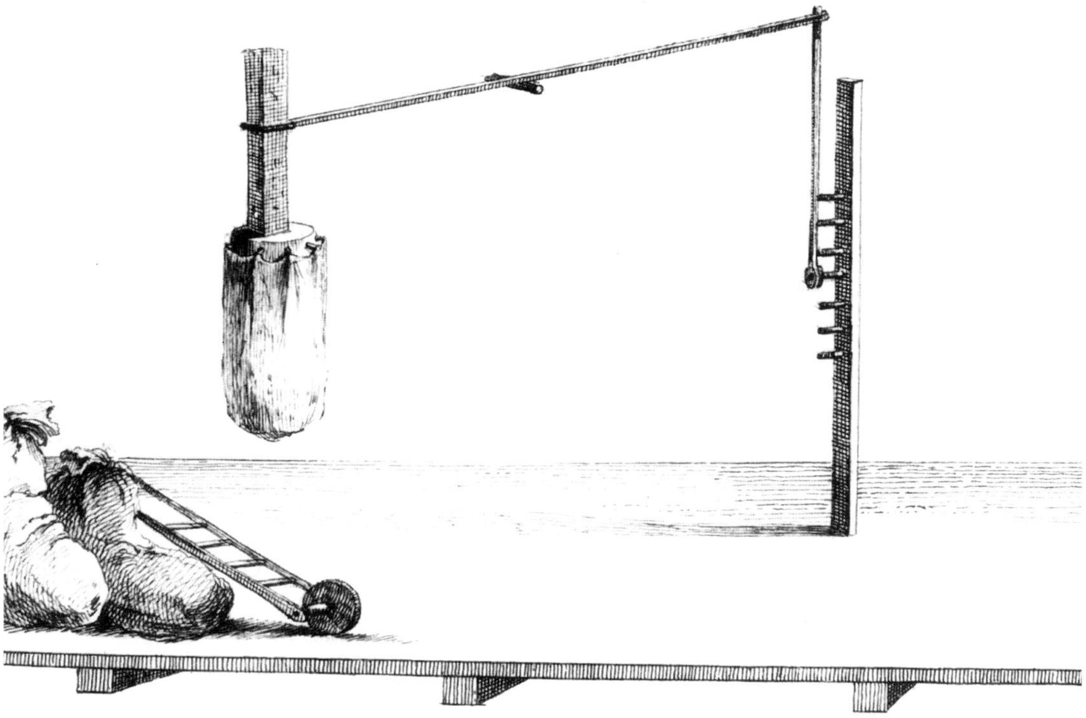

Fig. 244 Sack-lifting lever and barrow

Fig. 245 Kiln for drying oats

Further down there are also both wind- and water mills now occupied with grinding of oats both for bread and for gruel.

Oats to be ground first have to be dried on top of a kiln covered with iron plates according to the appended drawing [Fig. 245]. The oats are at 'a' and 'b' and are continuously raked so 202
that they are not burnt by the hot iron plates. When the grain begins to throw out sparks and smoke, it is dry enough to be taken to the mill for grinding. This is done by raising the runner so that it barely touches the oats. Afterwards the grain is taken out into the wind so that the husks blow away, after which it is ground in the usual way.

Four miles from Newcastle, at Marmille, there is a flour and bolting mill, built in the same way as Mr Hall's, and it has plenty of water so that it can always be in operation. The flour is sent to Scotland, and is sometimes also exported to foreign parts.

Mr Crowley's iron works called Teams

Teams is an iron works that has been established by Mr Crowley, 2½ miles from Newcastle on a little river that falls into the Tyne. The works consist of a steel forge with two hearths, where 203
mainly steel is drawn down to bars.

These are made into faggots of ½cwt or 1 cwt of 100 English lb in weight.

This steel is stamped ***JC3D3*** and ***D3***, which indicates the kind of iron of which the blister steel has been made: the first part [***JC3***] means the Öregrund ***L***[126] stamp. [The stamps] ***PL crowned***[127], ***D3, oo, W crowned***[128], and ***CDG***[129] and other Öregrund stamps that are known as 'Second Öregrund' [sic] ditto ***D3*** are bars drawn down from blister steel converted from Siberia iron, which was said to be the best for steel, although it seems more likely that they were referring to 'Sable' iron.[130]

Fig. 246 Tyne valley and windmills

The last-mentioned type of steel is mixed with the rest without affecting sales, I was told, although the hammerman said that steel made from the brand 'Sabel' does not have the same strength as that made of Öregrund iron.

Besides the above-mentioned faggot steel, a few tons a year of 'German Steel' are also made here by other smiths who have run away from
204 Mr Bertram at Blackhall Mill.

The process of manufacture is the following: Good blister-steel made from iron of the stamps ***L*** and ***PL crowned***[131] is descaled and drawn to a smaller size and charged into the steel furnace and converted a second time. It is then descaled again and drawn down to a slightly smaller dimension and placed in the furnace for the third time, to be subjected to a third conversion after which it is forged to 3 inches by 1 inch and stamped ***No. 1 boxed IC heart***.[132] Finally, it is packed in chests 4 feet long weighing 100 lb.

Charcoal is used to reheat this steel for forging, but for the ordinary faggot steel, pitcoal [is used]. The former kind is sold in London to be made into razors and other fine-edge tools, for 10 pence per pound, just over £93 per ton.

The last-mentioned kind is most in demand, and the East India Company dispatches it with their ships to a number of ports in East India. Each fleet is estimated to carry the best part of 300 tons.

German steel is sold for 6 shillings per
205 pound.

The charge for drawing down 'common' steel is 11 shillings and 8 pence a ton.

At Swalwell a Steel Master is in charge of all the cementation furnaces and is paid 12 shillings a week plus a bonus of 6 pence per ton.

The smiths are paid 2 shillings and 6 pence per ton for forging sheets for frying pans and shovels. These are then made in two smithies, with three smiths in each one.

The rolling mill is designed both for slitting and for the rolling of hoops. It is made in the same way as the ordinary slitting mills at Birmingham, except that when hoops are rolled, a piece of iron with holes in it is placed in front of the rolls. This iron is provided with a number
206 of holes, dimensioned according to the width of the hoops. The rods slit for rolling to hoops are 4 feet long and of varying thickness depending on the desired width of the finished hoops. After heating they are inserted between the rolls through the appropriate holes in rotation to

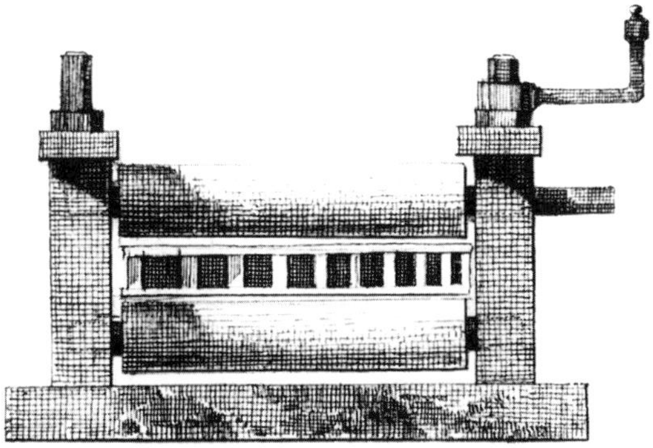

Fig. 247 Rolling mill at Swalwell

prevent uneven wear of the rolls. The procedure is to use the first hole on the left-hand side for the first pass after the initial heating, the hole next to it for the second pass after the second heating and so on. The hoops only pass through the rolls once [Fig. 247].

The workers are paid by the week and, when there is a surplus of water, two shifts are worked so that the mill can be kept in production day and night. Each shift consists of four people, namely: one who heats and removes the rods from the furnace, another who puts them through the rolls, another who receives them when they have passed through the rolls, and another who puts them down to cool and finally bundles them up. 207

The 'headman' at the slitting mill is paid per week	12s
Another next to him	10s
The third	8s
The fourth	8s

Besides these mills, there are six workshops at Teams for hoes that are used in America at the tobacco plantations. Each workshop houses three workers. The wages for making hoes per dozen and the iron and steel required are...[133]

There are also two workshops for frying pans and shovels, with three workers in each. The latter work according to weight and are paid, per cwt, 7 shillings, but for the smaller sizes 9 to 11 shillings per cwt. For shovels 8 shillings per dozen is paid.

In the grinding mill the workers are paid by 208
the dozen, namely: for grinding hoes, $1\frac{1}{2}$ to $2\frac{1}{2}$ pence a dozen. For spades, 9 pence per dozen. For anvils, 6 pence each if they weigh less than 1 cwt but, for 2 cwt and more, 9 pence to a shilling is paid.

Mr Crowley's bar-iron forges and iron-fabricating works called Swalwell

Swalwell is located by the river Derwent, where it flows out into the Tyne, so that above it there are waterfalls that provide power and below there is a channel that is navigable when the tide is high. The ships that come from Newcastle and Shields, the former 3 miles away and the latter 11 miles, can discharge their cargo inside the storehouse and load up again at the works.

This works belongs to Mr Crowley, who also owns Teams, which already has been mentioned, and Winlaton and Winlaton Mill that will be described later.

The Swalwell works comprises a bar-iron forge with two hearths, a plating forge making
209 various sheets for pans, a slitting mill, two steel furnaces, a foundry with two furnaces and a grinding mill with three stores. There are also 22 workshops for the forging of hoes for the West Indian tobacco plantations, with three workmen in each; three anchor forges with six workmen in each; three shops for screws and rods for beds; one shop for iron for bolts and screwbars, etc; three shops with three people in each for harpoons and other equipment for catching whales; one shop for balances and lifting jacks; two for machetes or fascine knives to cut sugar canes; two for fire-irons, consisting of pokers, fire-tongs and shovels; three for 'Capucher' for sugar mills or the gudgeons for sugar crushing rolls; one shop for braziers to place on the table and other such articles; two for ships' nails; ten for smaller nails and also many for hammers and other blacksmiths' tools.

The bar-iron forge consists of two hearths 210
and its yearly production amounts to 150 tons.

The pig iron came from London and was partly American and partly English. Charcoal was used in the finery hearth and pitcoal for chafing.

The hearths and the hammer were constructed in the usual way, but the bellows [sic][134] for one of them was made of cast iron in the shape of a cylinder, as shown by the attached drawing. I was told that this machine had already been in use for seven years and that it had performed very well [Fig. 248].

The cast-iron cylinders were 4 feet 6 inches long and 2 feet 3 inches in diameter.[135]

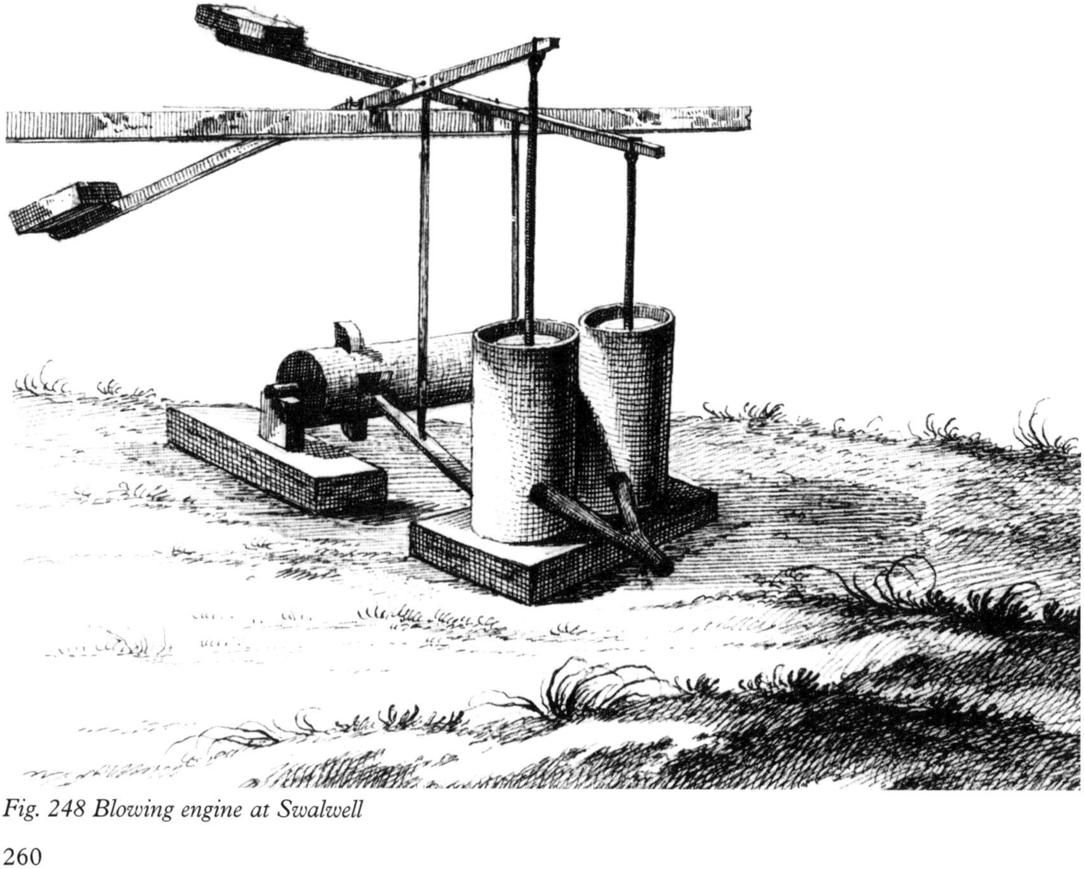

Fig. 248 Blowing engine at Swalwell

For one charge melted down in the finery it was stated that 40 seams of charcoal were used, carriage and wages for the colliers amounting to 14 pence each. This figure did not include the cost of the wood, which sometimes was purchased from places 20 miles away. Pitcoal can be bought very cheaply here as there are coal mines all around.

211 Cost of producing one ton of iron at Swalwell

Pig iron, including freight and all other costs	£7.5s
Charcoal	£3.15s
Pitcoal for the chafery hearth	7s
Wages for both hearths	£1.2s
Salary of the manager	6s
Rent for the land occupied by the forge and belonging to 'My Lord'	£1.5s
Total including cost of buildings, maintenance and repairs[136]	£14.0s

The plating forge sometimes makes sheets for pans and occasionally draws down small sizes of iron bars and also from time to time steel bars, for which at the moment there is such a large order from the East India Company, that all forges at Crowley's works are occupied with it.

The slitting mill[137] is used partly for rolling heavy sheets[138] and partly for slitting nailrods. The former are mainly used at the workshops for various purposes, but some small part is sold in London and the surrounding country. The nailrods are consumed at Swalwell,
212 Winlaton and in the neighbourhood, where there are more than 100 nailers.[139]

There are three steel furnaces in operation, one of which can convert 14, and the other two, 10 to 12 tons at a time. Their consumption of iron for steel-making is nearly 400 tons per annum. Of this more than 2/3 is Öregrund iron and a little less than 1/3 Russian or 'Sabel' iron, which latter is mixed in during the drawing down to faggot steel and also when steel is made for certain purposes in the fabricating works.

The iron foundry is occupied with all kinds of small castings such as bushes for wheel hubs, flat irons, pots, pans and kettles, door knockers, hammers and anvils, etc.

The cast iron used for this purpose comes from London and consists mostly of old cannon and other old iron. It is purchased in Holland and can occasionally include old Swedish guns.

The grinding mill has six stones and here files, axes, flat irons, hoes, mattocks and all kinds of carpenter's and shipwright's tools are ground. 213

In the anchor forges, of which there are three at Swalwell, all work is done by hand, and there are generally six to seven sturdy men in each forge, who are either paid by the day, when they earn 9 to 12, 12 to 14 shillings a week, or by the cwt or £3 per ton, when the anchors are smaller.

Anchors of every size are made, from 1 cwt to 74 cwt in weight. The latter is 3 tons and 14 cwt or just over 26 'skeppund'.[140]

The three anchor forges together use 6 to 7 tons Swedish iron per week from Gothenburg or ordinary stamps from Stockholm, considered the best for this purpose. I was told that anchors weighing 5 tons are only made for naval ships in wartime.

Three kinds of hoes are made, larger and smaller, which are shipped to America and used there at the tobacco and sugar plantations.

At Swalwell, there are 22 shops for the making of hoes and each has three workers. 214

For the bending of the handle into which the shaft is to be inserted, use is made of a hollow in an anvil, Letters 'a' and 'b' [Fig. 249].

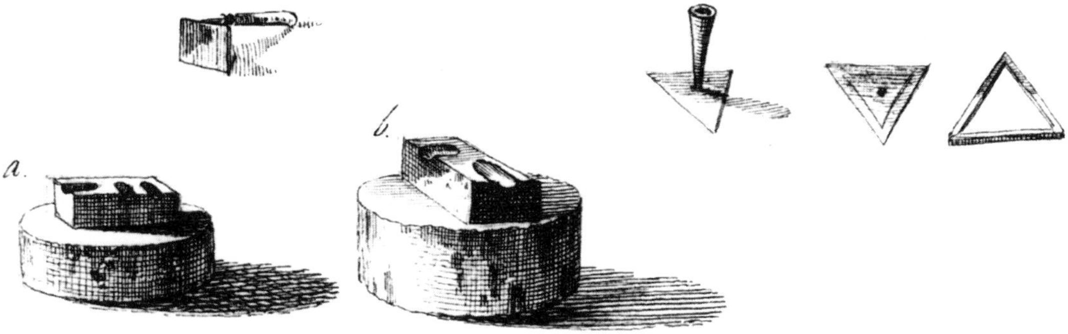

Fig. 249 with 250 Hoes and moulds

The lower part of the above-mentioned hoes is steeled with a piece of steel 4 inches square, forged to size in another workshop. This procedure is followed for all other work that is steeled and consequently a number of workshops were fully occupied in forging and preparing pieces of steel for steeling.
The workers in these shops are paid by the dozen for the pieces of steel that are made and the rate is set according to how thin they are forged to suit the particular purpose for which they are intended. For example, ships' scrapers require three pieces of steel, 3 inches to 4 inches long that first are welded together to form a triangle and then welded to the iron plate with the socket, which is placed in the centre as shown by the attached drawing.

The wages for making the pieces of steel for the scrapers are 2 pence a dozen. The making of the scrapers is also paid for by the dozen. Three smiths can forge two-and-a-half dozen hoes a day
215 and are paid 2, $2\frac{1}{2}$ and 3 shillings per dozen.

Iron rolled to strip is used for hinges, both large and small, and sold to the smiths at 22 shillings a cwt or £22 a ton.[141]

The finished hinges are sold back to the factory for 7 pence a pound, but it should be noted that if the smiths work in the 'Square' or factory compound, they pay back 2 pence out of each shilling [to the management], for which they obtain tools and coal. Those who work outside the square must pay for these items themselves [Fig. 251].

Knives for the cutting of sugar cane, which otherwise are known as 'Bils Tachen plain',[142] and generally are about 12 inches long with both the edge proper and the back steeled and sharpened and provided with a socket, are made for 1 shilling and 10 pence a dozen in wages. For this sum the smiths are provided with steel, iron and coal which subsequently are paid off at the rate of 2 pence a shilling.

216 Steel blanks for sugar-cane knives are made for $1\frac{1}{2}$ pence per dozen in wages. The grinding costs 8 pence per dozen. The wages for steeled iron shovels, described at Newcastle[143] are 7 to 8 shillings per dozen. The ordinary workers, who are paid by the day, do not get more than 14 to 15 pence[144] from the master and to him alone belongs what is left over of the profits.

The wages for fire shovels for London, weighing 8 lb a dozen, are 4 pence per pound and the iron used for them is bought for 2 pence per pound.

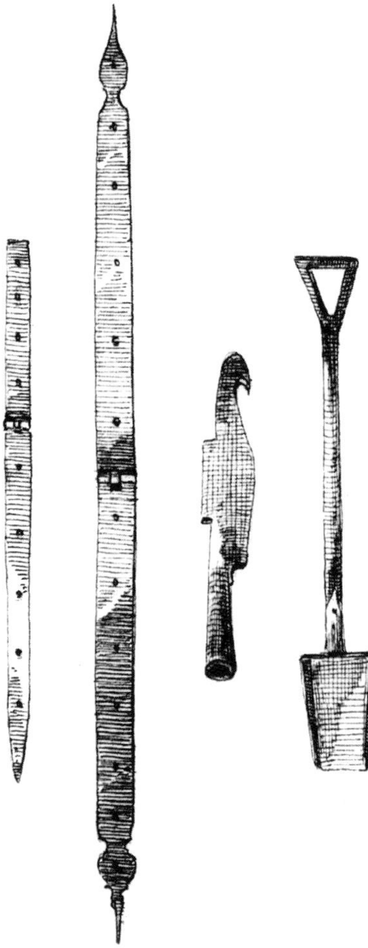

Fig. 251 Hinges, machete and shovel

Gudgeons or pivots for sugar mills [Fig. 252a, **b** and **c**] are steeled at the end and are 4 inches long. They look like a top and support the large cast-iron rolls for crushing sugar cane, which I am sure must be standing
on end, because otherwise they would be rather 217
too heavy.[145]

Harpoons for whale fishing, 12 inches to 18 inches long [Fig. 252a, **d**] cost 20 to 22 shillings a dozen in wages.

The wages for making braziers of various shapes and sizes [Fig. 252a, **e**] for warming plates and dishes, are 20 shillings a dozen.

Hammers and other similar articles cost $3\frac{1}{2}$ pence per pound in wages and the iron required costs 2 pence per pound. Iron for bolts is forged of $\frac{3}{4}$ inch, 1 inch and $1\frac{1}{2}$ inches square Swedish iron, and the wages are paid by the cwt.

In the town of Swalwell there are a number of smiths who make ship's nails. The raw

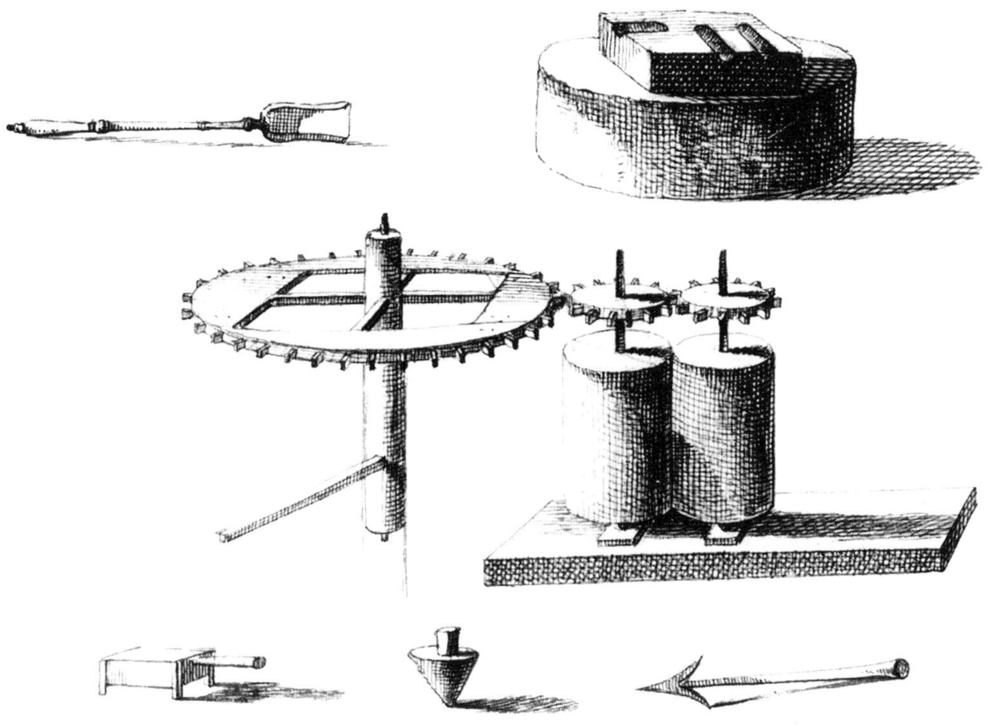

Fig. 252a Shovel and mould, sugar mill and gudgeon pin, harpoon and brazier (letters missing)

material for these is heavy, slit iron, dimensioned to suit each size of nail. The iron costs 20½ shillings per cwt at the factory, and is paid for by deliveries of iron, worked up to ship's nails at 25 shillings per cwt.

218 With decreasing size of the nails the payment per cwt increases to 26, 27, 28, 30 to 33 shillings.

For the forging of files the wages are 5 pence per dozen; for grinding …;[146] for cutting, 20 pence; and for hardening, 3 pence.

6 inches	1½d
8½ inches	2½d
9½ inches	3½d
11 inches	5d

8 inches per dozen	2s
9 inches "	3s
10 inches "	4s
11 inches "	6s

The sales prices for files are kept more or less in line with those current in Sheffield.

I have already mentioned that the workers living in the 'Square' or the factory compound pay 2 pence a week of each shilling for coal and tools and 8 pence a week for lodgings. Besides these amounts, they also pay ¼ pence of each shilling for the support of widows, children and the poor and this latter charge has to be paid by everybody working at Crowley's factories. 219
The chaplain and the schoolmaster at Swalwell, Winlaton and Winlaton Mill are paid by Crowley himself for his own account.

At Swalwell, Mr Sommerland is nowadays 'Head surveyor', and is paid a salary of £150 per annum. Under him there are 12 clerks, some paid 12 and others 18 shillings a week, and Mr Walter, who is inspector, 16 shillings.

The 'headman' over all the officials lives at the warehouse in Greenwich and is said to have a salary of £500 a year.

Winlaton Mill forge and iron-fabricating works belonging to Mr Crowley

Winlaton Mill is located a mile from Swalwell up the river Derwent and consists of: a bar-iron forge with three hearths; forges for plating and saw blades and for the drawing down of steel; a slitting and rolling mill designed for making nailrods as well as for rolling sheets; and a grinding mill with six stones.

The production consists of edge tools of every kind, axes of many types, carpenter's tools

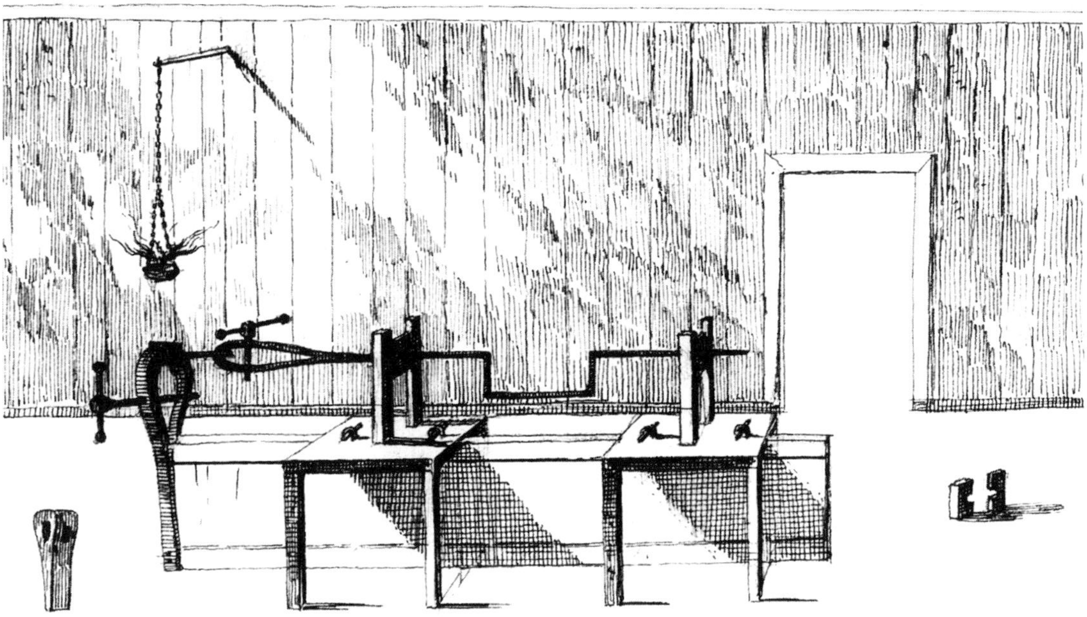

Fig. 252b [no reference in text, but may relate to Winlaton, especially since an axe head is shown; appears to be a machine for making screws]

and plane-irons, cooper's tools, trowels for
220 builders etc.

There is only one workshop for the making of saw-blades and it contains four hearths and uses the same kind of punching machine that was described at Wednesbury.[147]

Forging and cutting of files is carried out in three workshops with a total of 35 hearths and they are always busy.

The bar-iron forge can produce 250 tons a year, using English and American pig iron, but the slitting mill has a capacity of 500 tons of iron per year, provided that there is no shortage of water. However, the water supply appeared rather scanty just now. Hoes and axes are paid by the dozen and, for medium sizes, the wages are 2 shillings and 4 pence and, for grinding, 6 pence per dozen.

Three dozen per day can be made, which gives the master a profit of 4 shillings and he pays his hammermen 15 pence a day. Larger types of axes cost 3, 4 to 5 shillings in wages.

A certain kind of axe 1 inch long, ground and polished all over is made here. The edge is
221 not ground really sharp but left dull and, after grinding, they are thrown into a slurry of slaked lime and water that protects them from rusting. It is said that the Indians decorate their rooms with these axes.

Some axes and other edge tools are first ground and then blackened by smoke, after which the edge only is cleaned on the stone. The same procedure is used for various kinds of carpenter's tools that are coated with a black paint.

At Winlaton there are two workshops for axes. A smith is paid 4 pence a dozen for forging file blanks of 1 lb in weight or thereabouts.

Hoes are forged at 26 hearths, each serving three workers, who also are experienced in other types of work, for example shovels, pans, etc, for which some or all of them may be employed when there is a large demand. This happens every ten weeks, when a new list of fabricated articles comes from the main warehouse at
Greenwich as well as detailed stocklists of all 22
items made and information regarding the progress of the work at the various factories and regarding the state of their affairs.

At the forges of Winlaton Mill there was nothing special to be seen that had not previously been observed and reported at other similar mills. The only unusual feature was that the man who had built them claimed them to be the best-arranged works in England, but this was not visible to my eyes.

Because of shortage of water, the bar-iron forge was not in operation. The plating forge was drawing down blister steel to be made into bundles for the cargo of the East India ships, for which purpose the bar-iron forge also will be employed, as soon as there is enough water.

The slitting-mill was producing nailrods of Russian iron, due to lack of Swedish. Large quantities of these rods are consumed at Winlaton and Winlaton Mill, where more than 300 nailers always are at work. At the water-
223 driven works, both here and at Teams and Swalwell, the workers employed are paid 5 shillings a week when they are standing still due to alterations, repairs or lack of water or materials.

I was told that when Mr Crowley was here two years ago he had offered these workers 8 shillings a week for undertaking other work whilst idling away their time but they did not accept this offer, preferring their old freedom.

Winlaton Mill has six clerks who are paid 12 shillings a week, with exception of the chief clerk who has 16 shillings. Most of these clerks have nothing else to do than to make sure that no stranger enters the works without their knowledge and starts talking to the workers.

224 The wages are paid out every Saturday and the required cash is collected from the Royal Treasury in Newcastle. If some worker or one of the officials should wish to collect their daily wages earlier, this is not denied them. They must, however, show the cashier an authorisation note from the bookkeeper, showing what completed work they have turned in and what money might be due to them after deductions for rent, tools, coal, iron, the poor box, etc. To pay out money in advance for work to be done is neither usual in these works nor permitted.

Decorations on fire tongs and pokers are produced by means of dies as shown by the attached drawing [Fig. 253].

Winlaton iron-fabricating works belonging to Mr Crowley

Winlaton is a small town, located on a hill amongst the coal mines, $1\frac{1}{2}$ miles from Swalwell and 1 mile from Winlaton Mill. Mr Crowley has also placed an iron manufactory here, comprising the making of nails, patten-rings, hinges, chains of all kinds, large and small, bellows, fire-tongs, etc. 225

Patten-rings are used under a type of wooden shoe that women put on to walk in the dirt on the floor. The wages for making them are 8 pence a dozen and smiths who are experienced in this trade can make themselves a pretty penny.

Chains are made for wages of 4 to $4\frac{1}{2}$ pence a pound, the iron being debited to the smiths at $2\frac{1}{4}$ pence. They are also debited for the coal.

Fig. 253 Decoration of fire tongs and pokers

Bass bands are twisted chains to hang over saddles for horses. The smiths are paid 4½ pence per pound for making them. 'Pelhuys'[148] are three iron hoops and a handle bundled together in a set, used in London for water buckets. The smiths make them of their own iron for 7 shillings per dozen. The iron costs 20½ shillings and is rolled specially for this purpose. Pokers of an inferior kind are made for
226 12 shillings per dozen.

One dozen weighs 2⅓ to 3 lb and the iron costs 2 pence per pound.

Nails are of many different kinds and mostly made outside the factory square. The payment for ship's nails 16 inches to 10 inches is 25 shillings per cwt. Iron is bought for 20½ shillings. Eight-inch nails fetch 25 shillings and 6 pence, 6-inch nails 25 shillings and 10 pence and 4-inch nails 20 shilling ½ pence. 'Cachers' nails are 28 shilling per cwt. 'Billbords' without heads, weighing 18 lb per 1,000, cost 4 shillings 10½ pence. Hooks for curtains are 2 shillings per gross of 144 and the iron costs 20 shillings 6½ pence a cwt, but the smiths supply the coal themselves.

At the factory in Winlaton there are six clerks, of whom the chief clerk gets 16 shillings and the other 12 shillings weekly salary.

It was noted that the same system of paying for work done and paying wages was used here as at Swalwell and Winlaton Mill. There was here, as well as at the former places, a
227 warehouse with all kinds of goods needed by the workers. These are sold at the same prices as elsewhere. There is also in this place a store of coal, because the mines in the neighbourhood do not work in winter, and therefore they have to make sure that there were sufficient stores in the winter.

The goods fabricated here and for which the smiths have been paid are sent to Swalwell to be recorded and transported to London. Three ships are continuously occupied with these cargoes. They collect iron and other supplies from London and return with the fabricated wares. If there should sometimes be a scarcity of such freight it is easy to find cargoes of coal as this district furnishes virtually all coal used in London.

The consumption of iron at Mr Crowley's works

The following is an approximate summary of
228 the requirements of iron at Mr Crowley's Works:

For two slitting mills, one at Swalwell and one at Winlaton.	Tons
Note: Mostly for nails	800
For Teams, slitting and rolling mill for hoops and sheets	300
For three steel furnaces	400
For three anchor forges	350
For two forges for bolt iron and other heavy ship's forgings	150
For hoes, shovels, axes, pans and the like	250
For chains, patten rings and parts for kitchen ranges	60
For sugar-cane knives, curtain rods, bed screws, etc.	40

The requirements of iron for saw-blades, files and other articles of steel have already been included in the amount used by the steel furnaces and iron for nails is included in the amount used by the slitting mills.

The total annual consumption is thus at least	2,350
The most that is produced in the bar iron forges at Swalwell and Winlaton is	400 22
Consequently, Crowley's works purchase and consume every year of Swedish and Russian iron	1,950

This is mostly purchased in London.

It is not possible to obtain a record of the amount of iron consumed at these works, because most of it comes from London, where the customs duty already has been paid. However, the above rough estimate, which is not on the high side, shows that at Swalwell, Teams, Winlaton and Winlaton Mill, the total yearly consumption is at least 2,700 tons of bar iron, of which only 450 tons are made locally. The consumption of foreign iron is consequently about 2,250 tons which is divided between Sweden and Russia in such a way that three tons of Swedish iron are used for every ton of Russian.[149]

The profit made by the owner of the works, from the working up of such a large quantity of
iron, can be inferred from the knowledge that 23
the sale of this iron alone to the factories gives him a profit of £6,000 per year, without taking into consideration the profit made on the fabricated goods. The latter, when all costs have been deducted, are probably not so high, but nevertheless at least £5,000, which makes a total of £11,000 or 44,000 daler coppercoin.

Fig. 254a Blackhall Mill

Coal mines around Winlaton

There are three coal seams in the coal mines around Winlaton, of which the first one lies at a depth of 228 feet and is 28 inches thick, the second at 252 feet with a thickness of 34 inches and the third at 324 feet with a thickness of 54 inches.

The seams dip south-east, which is the case practically everywhere in the Newcastle area.

The stone that one has to go through before the coal seams are reached consists partly of sandstone or freestone, partly of a blue clay-like
231 stone, and partly of a black slate.[150]

Charcoal can plainly be seen in all the seams, lying in layers with bitumen and crystals of iron pyrites and quartz and sometimes interspersed with some clay-like and black slate.

Various coal mines by the River Tyne

At Stella, about 4 miles to the north-west,[151] there are a number of coal mines by the River Tyne that belong to mine owners in the neighbourhood.

'Raismore' coal pit is 4 miles higher up and 14 miles from Newcastle.[152]

When a shaft is sunk, the first seam of coal is found at a depth of 120 feet and it has a thickness of 90 inches. Twenty-four feet further down there is another seam 10 inches thick and 156 feet below it yet another seam 72 inches thick. The seams dip south, 3 feet in 120 feet or a little more.[153]

In another coal mine, 1,200 feet further to the north-west, the same seams are found except that the quartz has run out. In the steep slope of the hill to the north-west, an adit has been driven to the top coal seam, through which horses can be 232
brought into the mine. In this mine there is a fault,[154] the eastern part of the hill and the coal seams have at the same time been cut off and displaced 72 feet downwards. The hollow created by this sinking has been filled by a dark, smooth or slate-like rock [Fig. 254b].

In all the coal seams there are layers or traces of charcoal. Small pieces of charcoal are also mixed with the sandstone beds and this is every-where in coal-mining districts a sure sign that the coal seams are not far away. But, for me, it serves to prove that the sandstone beds and clay seams have grown faster than the coal seam and have actually split it in several seams. The fault mentioned above appears to have been caused by the elevation of the western part of the hill rather than by the sinking of the eastern. I will comment on this more extensively in the proper place. 233

On the western side of the fault, no shaft has been sunk to the aforementioned 6-foot seam, but it has been found east of it, and there is no doubt that the same seam does exist, 72 feet higher up, west of the fault.

Blackhall mill steelworks, established by Mr Bertram

Three miles further on to the south-west, and 13 miles from Newcastle, lies Blackhall Mill,[155] which in England is so renowned for its manufacture of German steel established there

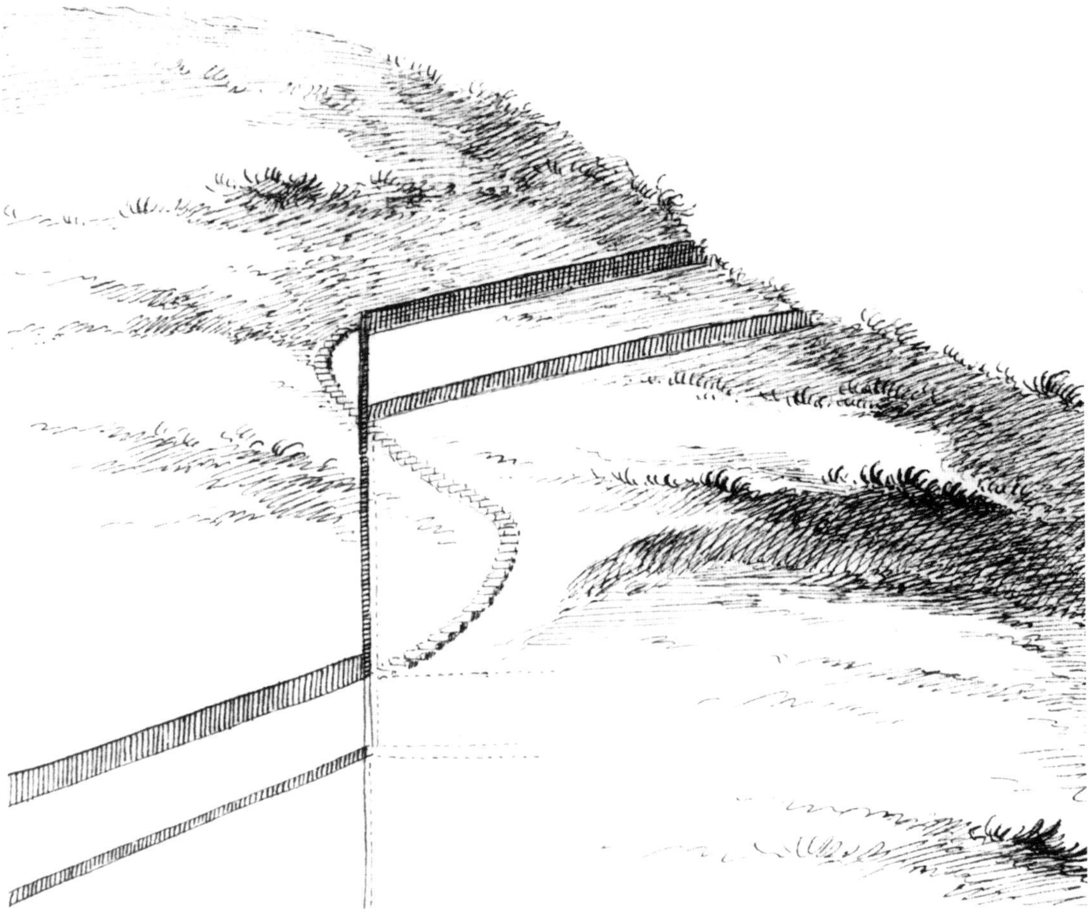

Fig. 254b Displacement of Coal Seams

by Mr Bertram, a native of Remscheid. About 60 years ago, he stayed for some time in Sweden and Stockholm, and there married the daughter of a goldsmith by the name of Israel. On the way home, bad weather forced the ship off its course and it landed at Shields. Here he was given employment by Mr ...[156] and was employed in setting up the steelworks, which now is leased to Mr Hall and Co.

At Blackhall Mill there is a steel forge with three hearths, and a medium-sized helve
234 hammer [Fig. 254a].

One hearth is used for making the German steel and this manufacture has been carried on by the son of the above mentioned Bertram, since his father died about 12 years ago.

The second hearth is used for chafing, and the third is also used for the chafing of blister steel, when there is plenty of water.

Just by the side of the forge, a steel furnace has been built in which Öregrund iron is converted to blister steel. Five kinds of German steel are nowadays made at the steelworks, namely in order of hardness:

1st which is the hardest, is called Double Spur, Double Star
2nd is next in hardness and called Double Spur, Single Star
3rd in order of hardness is Double Spur
4th is Double Cloth shear
5th is Single Cloth shear[157]

Besides these kinds there are two others under the heading German steel and they are: Bar steel,
in bundles or faggots, which is simply blister steel 235
drawn down under the hammer. Blister steel, as it comes out of the cementation furnace. All of these kinds of steel with their stamps and prices are recorded here [Fig. 255].[158]

The process differs from the one used for the production of steel in Germany, because here the steel is prepared from 'artificial blister steel',[159] produced by heating and cementing

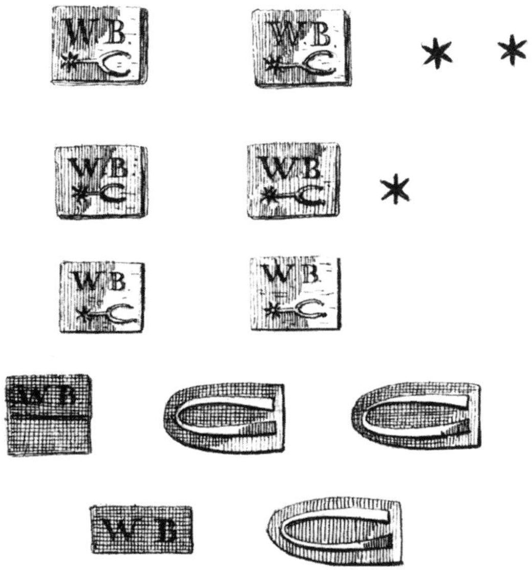

Fig. 255 Blackhall steel stamps

Öregrund iron with charcoal breeze. In making the German steel, on the other hand, pig iron or steel-iron[160] is first fired, then reheated, drawn down and sheared in the way which in Sweden is common for 'Styria' steel.

The most important skill required for this steel making is the ability to distinguish the harder blister steel from the less hard, and to place each piece of steel, according to hardness, into its proper classification and allocate to it the corresponding stamp. However, after careful observation, I found that they did not always
236 succeed in this.

If steel of the same stamp and quality as regards hardness as that obtained by cementation should be selected from the blister steel then it follows that, according to the nature of the steel, the last and softest sort should require more heating, working and hammering than the first, which should be the hardest. But, if the blister steel is too weak for this purpose from the start, less work is required to bring out its hard character and it will need greater skill to give the first sort sufficient hardness, since it in any case never matches the German 'Double Spur' and 'Double Star' steel.

It is said that when these works were started, old Bertram had considerable difficulties in developing the above-mentioned grades, particularly Double Spur and Double Star, which are the hardest, to approximately the
237 same level of quality as the genuine German or Remscheid steel, and he would perhaps never have succeeded if he had not been a German and if the English had not persuaded themselves to believe that he used the same raw materials and methods of production as common in Remscheid.

Amongst the many experiments made, both then and later, they also tried shearing the blister steel and drawing it down to smaller size, followed by placing it in the steel furnace to be cemented again in the same way as is done at Teams, as has already been reported and still is done by Crowley. Nevertheless, Mr Bertram acknowledged quite openly what he, through much trouble and effort, had learnt, namely that a good Öregrund iron properly converted to steel by cementation can never be further perfected by repeated processes of cementation and shearing. It is likely to lose in quality by such treatment and finally disintegrate like a slag without substance or life.

Bertram's main secret is thus to adopt the air 238
of a reliable and honest German steel worker. This gives him a good living, and his wages for converting and forging amount to £225 or 9,000 daler coppercoin per annum.

Furthermore, he has learned to seek out the best steel iron, from which he subsequently selects his raw material, usually ***L*, *PL crowned*, *W crowned*, *oo*,**[161] which converts well to No 1 and No 2 German steel. The softer iron is used for the other stamps. All of them are sheared[162] and drawn down under the hammer to ¾-inch-square bars. The bars really ought to be forged to thinner, flat bars, but the heavy hammer does not permit this. In any case this does not make any difference, since the steel has achieved a good reputation and sells well. After three apprentices had run away from his father, Bertram has not wished to engage anybody else to be taught the German steel process and the grading of the steel, but works alone, until his son has grown up. Note: the 239
hearth is 9 inches deep.

L*, *PL crowned*, *oo and ***W crowned***[163] were now said to fetch £21 a ton, and at these works a little more than 100 tons per year of these stamps is consumed. Thirty tons and perhaps a little more are made into German Steel, the rest is sold as blister steel and drawn down to bars for the East India trade.

The wages paid for German steel are £7.10s per ton and, for the drawing down of blister steel, 12 shillings per ton. Mr Bertram also provides housing and coal, and 5 shillings per day is paid when the hammer is shut down owing to lack of water or for repairs.

Shotley Bridge forge for sword blades and scythes

Mr Bertram took me 4 miles further up in the country to a place called Shotley Bridge, where 60 years ago a sword-blade factory was established by a company in London[164] that managed to spirit away just over 30 workers from Solingen. But since the laziness and arrogance of the Germans grew in proportion to the profits, which to begin with are reported to have been considerable, it was not long before they with presumptuous importunity revolted against their superiors. In addition they quarrelled amongst themselves about who should be considered the foremost of them and this dispersed the greatest part of the community.

Mr 'Blanchischep'[165] nowadays runs the factory from Newcastle. There are only eight workers left, of the most stupid kind of Germans, who are employed partly forging sword blades, mainly of the three-cornered kind, and partly making scythes for the demands of the surrounding countryside, and with grinding.

The steel that is used is obtained from Blackhall Mill and the yearly consumption does not exceed $\frac{3}{4}$ ton or 13 to 14 cwt.

For one dozen blades the wages are $7\frac{1}{3}$ shillings. The wages for grinding are 3 shillings per dozen. The blades are sold for 18 shillings per dozen. 241

Drawing and etching the decorations is also paid by the dozen. The surface is first covered with varnish on which the design is drawn and then many dozens of blades at a time are placed in a tub containing the etching solution prepared with sulphuric acid and Spanish Green.

The grinding stone used for the grinding of hollow blades is turned with a piece of iron that

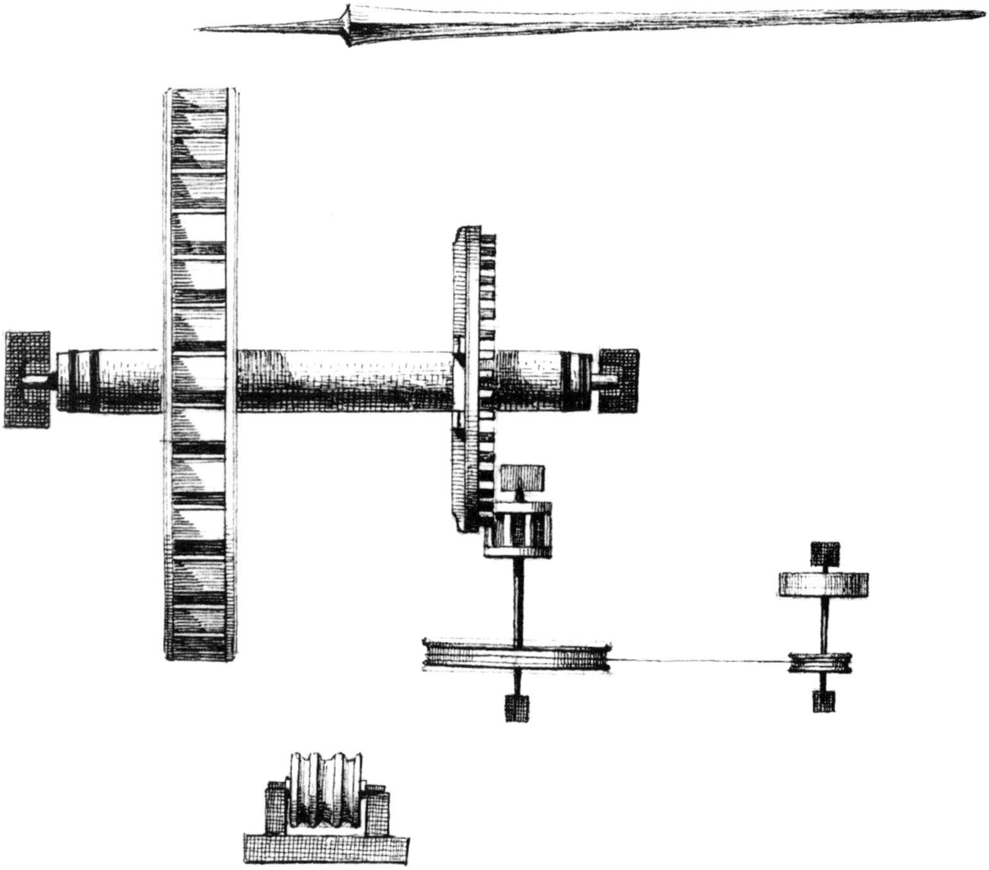

Fig. 256 Sword blade, grinding train and grinding stone

produces a number of ridges, and the blades are ground dry, without any water touching the stone. For the forging of the blades, the anvil was cut to form dies, and specially made stamps were used to make the blades hollow after they had been forged roughly to size. The haft and the heaviest part of the blade is of iron and Figure 256 shows the rough blank.

The wages for 100 scythes are £3, sharpening of 100 costs 15 to 16 shillings, namely, 'Graindins' 8 shillings, 'Oversatdins' 4s, 'Berdins' 4s.[166] Finally, they are placed in lime-water to be preserved against rusting in storage.

Scythes 3 feet 9 inches to 4 feet long are sold for 26 shillings per dozen and 4 feet 3 inches
242 long cost 30 shillings.

Five-foot scythes sell for 48 shillings per dozen and these are the ones mainly used in this country. Otherwise, shorter scythes are also made and sell for 15 to 20 shillings.

Bertram, the master steel-maker and his family

On the way back from Shotley Bridge, we visited Mr Bertram's two sisters, who are married to thriving and well-to-do farmers, who live well like their brother and have many kinds of wine in their cellars, some bought and some home-made.

Steel furnaces and cementation

After having been well entertained and lodged at Mr Bertram's house, I saw the steel furnace in the morning before departing [Fig. 257a].

The outside walls are, as usual in this part of the country, built of dressed sandstone with a large and wide chimney.

The furnace is fired from both ends and the flames play around the pots, and finally go up through a number of holes in the vault and into the chimney stack.

243 There are two pots or chests for the iron, one on each side of the fire-grate. They are 11 feet long, 22 inches wide and 32 inches high. The iron is packed in crushed birch charcoal which, next after charcoal from oak, has been found the best for cementation of iron. One must make sure that no bar of iron touches any other bar and that charcoal is evenly and firmly packed at the sides of, as well as below and above, the bars. On top, a 4-inch layer of fine sand is placed, which sinks down with the coal when it is partly consumed during the heating. The furnace is charged with 10 tons of iron at a time. It is fired for six days, but the cooling takes 11, 12, 14 and, in summer, up to 18 days.

One horse-load of birch charcoal, which contains ten bushels, costs 4 shillings and 6 pence, but any coal left from one campaign is used for the next, with addition of new coal to
replace that used up during the firing. 244

Two steel makers are paid 9 shillings each per week. The steel, as it leaves the furnace, is sold for £26 per ton. When it is drawn down to bars of the ordinary grade for the East India Trade, the price is £30 to £32 per ton. Of this amount Mr Bertram is paid 12 shillings a ton for the forging and the iron costs £21 a ton.

Summary of the cost of making the steel	
10 tons of iron @ £21 per ton	£210.00s
160 lb ditto [presumably for test bars]	£1.10s
Coal	£1.10s
Wages for 3 weeks @ 18 shillings	£2.14s
Total	£215.14s
To the above should be added:	
Clerk's salary	12s
Interest on building cost of £200, 1/12 of 5 per cent	17s
Carriage to Newcastle, etc	5s
Grand Total[167]	£217.8s

The sales price of the steel is £26 per ton
which, for 10 tons, amounts to £260. If the cost 245
of £217.18s is deducted from this sum, we arrive at a profit per campaign of £42.2s which, multiplied by 12, gives us the yearly profit of a steel furnace or £505.4s.

However, a steel furnace can hardly last more than 10 or 12 years, and consequently the loss of the capital used for the building of the furnace is £20 a year. £10 a year will be required for furnace repairs and, if these two sums are deducted from the profit as calculated above, we arrive at a final profit figure of £475.5s.

Chopwell paper mill

On the journey from Blackhall Hill I travelled down the river Derwent, where the water was rather low, and came across Chopwell paper mill, belonging to Richard Clark. Only coarse paper was made here, because the water, which comes partly from the coal mines, contains iron and is not suitable for better paper.

Fig. 257a Steel furnace at Blackhall Mill

The mill is water-driven and built according
246 to Dutch design, with knives.[168]

Price of Paper
'Demies for Printers Rime',[169] 4 shillings per pound
'Contishap' brown large ditto 5 shillings
Grey paper for the use of shops costs 2 shillings 4 pence

Derwentcote forge and steel furnace

Derwentcote forge belongs to Mr 'Hodgen' in Newcastle and consists of a hammer with two hearths with a yearly production of 150 tons of bar iron.

The pig iron comes from London and some of it is American and some English. The price is supposed to be at the present time £7.10s per ton, free Newcastle.

The charcoal used for the firing is collected from many miles away, and the wood for it has to be bought in advance, and is subsequently made into charcoal and carried to the works. It was said that a horse load of 10 bushels cost 4 shillings and 6 pence.

Pitcoal can be bought cheaply in the neighbourhood and is, therefore, used in the chafery hearth.

247 The firers are paid $10\frac{1}{2}$ shillings and the smiths at the chafery hearth $9\frac{1}{2}$ shillings a ton.

The bar iron is consumed in the district, and used for the fire grates of steam engines, for axles of coal wagons and for other similar purposes that do not require the highest quality iron.

A steel furnace and a hammer for drawing out the steel also belong to this works.
The furnace is of the same design as the one described at Blackhall Mill.

The pots are charged with 10 to 11 tons of Öregrund iron at a time and the heating takes 6 to 7 days, and the cooling 12 to 18 days, 40 shillings worth of coal is used,[170] of which some subsequently can be used again.

There are two workers, who are paid 8 shillings [per week] and 2 pence each per ton of steel, each ton being equal to 2160 lb English weight.

The man in charge of the steel forging was an apprentice of old Bertram's and he also makes a few tons a year of the so-called
German Steel, but the main work carried out 248
here is plain drawing out of blister steel to 1-inch and $\frac{3}{4}$-inch-square bars that are collected together into bundles of half a hundredweight and despatched to London for the East India Company.

The price of the steel has already been recorded at Teams and Blackhall Mill.
The production here amounts to a little more than 100 tons, but they would like to increase it if it only were possible to find a source of more Öregrund iron at a reasonable price.

At Lintz Green there were nailers working for Crowley's factory. They would be glad to find another buyer, because they believe that their nail-master at the factory is making too much profit out of their work [Fig. 257b].

Prices of nails:

Single and double tacks, per cwt	35s
7-inch nails	32s
14-inch and 15-inch nails	27 to 28s

249

2 lb of nails or 3-penny nails sell for $2\frac{1}{2}$ shillings per 1000

4-penny nails, 3 shillings per 1000

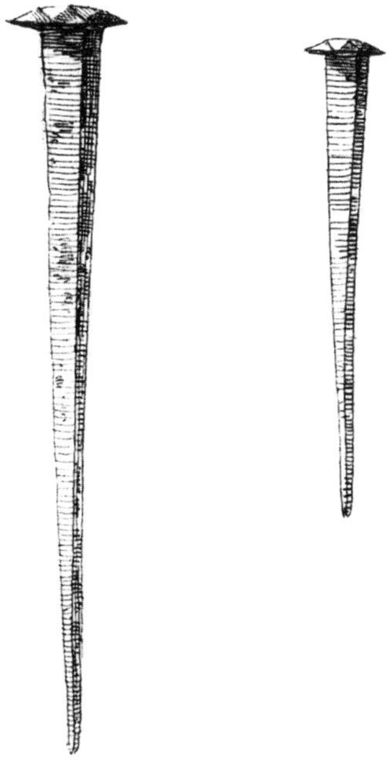

Fig. 257b Nails

The coal roads

On this road one is plagued by the coal wagons described at Newcastle, because it is really built for the wagons and so narrow that it is difficult to get past them, whether one takes the way leading to the coal seam or the one in the opposite direction.[171]

Owing to rain the road was now rather dangerous, because the wheels of the wagons slipped on the wooden rails laid on either side of the road, so that from time to time a wagon would run downhill out of control, and be smashed against other wagons that it hit. This happened in spite of the tiller brakes and in spite of the people specially employed to put hot ashes on the rails.

Gibside, the Estate of Mr Bowes

Gibside is the estate of Mr Bowes Esq., and is located a short way from the road and about 1½ miles from Winlaton Mill and 6 miles from Newcastle. The river Derwent flows past it.
250 We really deserved a better day for viewing such a splendid park with its green pathways, the beautiful garden and the magnificent buildings, which, according to English custom, are spread about the park. They consist of a summer-house located on a hillock and built in the gothic style, lovely and pleasant, a pool according to the Greek taste, adorned with a number of statues and a column, now being erected, which is to be dedicated to Minerva. The pedestal is 20 feet 1 inch in diameter and the height of the column itself will be 150 feet, not counting the statue, which will be 14 feet high [Fig. 258].[172]

This building project alone is supposed to cost £4,000, but such an outlay is small for a man who has an income of £22,000 a year from his estates and properties.

The hall itself is old but spacious and built in the Gothic style of dressed stone, as are all the other buildings.

When one walks in the avenues along the river one may unexpectedly catch sight of a
gunner taking aim. He looks very natural, but is 251
cast of lead and painted.

In addition to everything else, there is also a paper mill to be seen, which has the same trouble with rusty water as the mill at Lintz Green. In another place a brook runs down over a cliff, depositing a white cement on the bottom, but in the rain I could not investigate it.

There are many hares in the park. Amongst many kinds of trees growing there, I also saw spruce trees, here called spruce-fir, which are very rare in England.

Benton coal mine

After my return to Newcastle, I went 4 miles along the way to Shields to view the Benton coal mine, belonging to Lord Ravensworth and Mr 'Monichoa', and said to be the best in the neighbourhood. The mine is located on a flat field 1½ miles from the River Tyne, and between 54 feet and 72 feet higher than the water level in the river when the tide is out.

From the surface to the first coal seam,
which is 2 feet 6 inches thick, the depth is 180 252
feet and 90 feet. Further down there is another seam 7 feet in thickness. The latter is now being worked to great advantage, although two fire engines have to be kept going to keep the mine drained.

The seams dip south-east, as is generally the case in this neighbourhood of Newcastle. The coal mined here is mixed with layers of charcoal, but some parts of the seam have more of these and some less. Generally, most of the charcoal occurs where the seam divides into several strata.

Most of the coal in which the charcoal is found is separated from the solid coal when brought to the surface and used for the fire engine, otherwise it would be broken down to

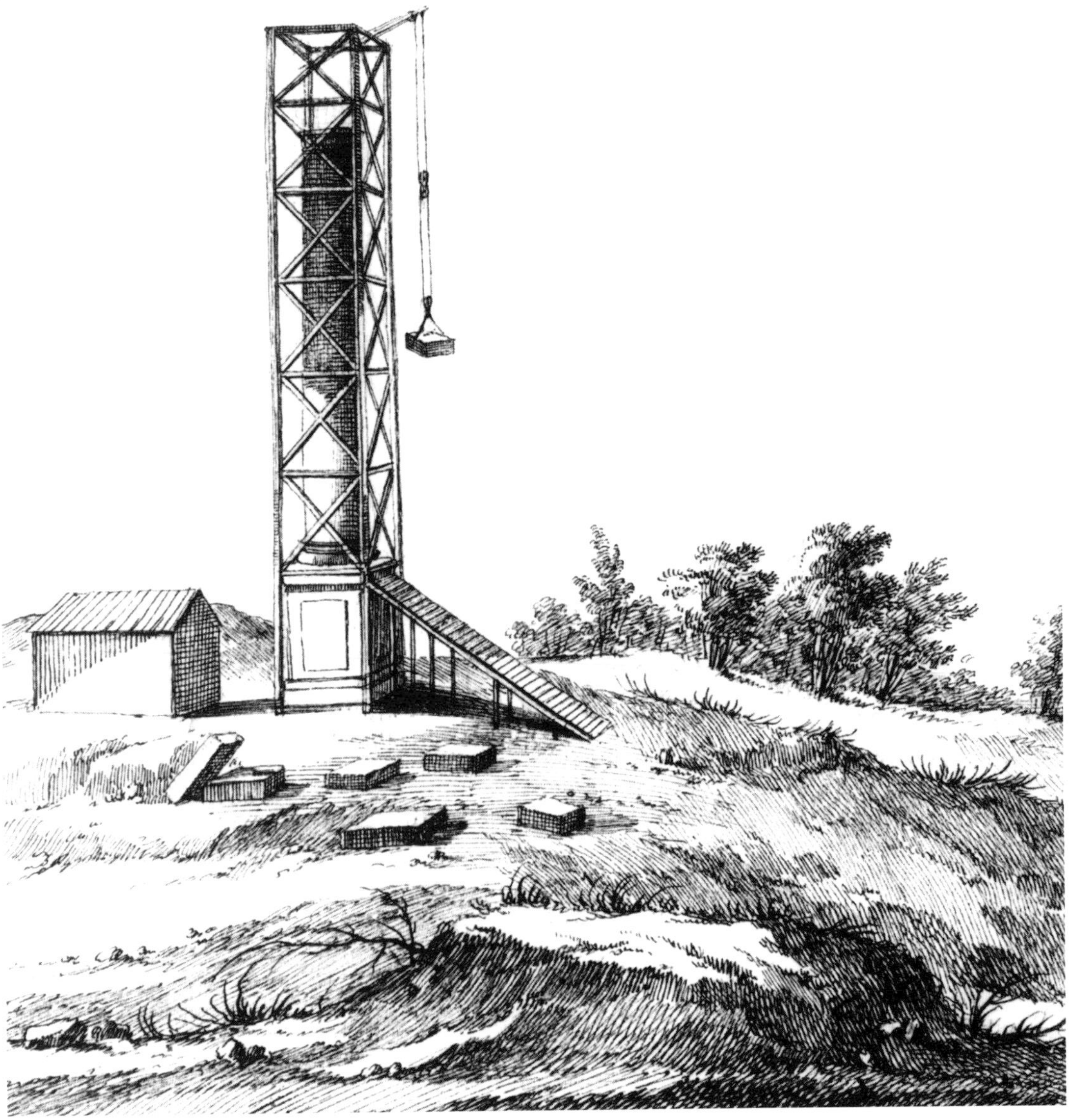

Fig. 258 Erection of column at Gibside

dust during the loading and unloading of the ships, which would greatly inconvenience the workers.

'Newmore' coal mine

'Newmore'[173] coal mine, belonging to Mr 'Habel' is located 3 miles west of Newcastle
253 on the River Tyne, where the tide is still 4 feet high and more when the Moon is full.

The coal seams are all mixed with charcoal in the same way as described above, and they dip south-east 6 feet and 120 feet, more or less. Here there is only one fault or 'trouble' where the coal seams have been displaced in such a way that the western part is higher and the eastern part is 3 feet lower [Fig. 259].

Newburn, Mr Hall's Estate

During my journey from Newcastle and on the way to Carlisle, I visited Mr Hall, at his country house called Newburn, which stands by the River Tyne, 4 miles from Newcastle.

The fruit in the gardens here was not ripening very fast although it was located in a fairly sunny position. There was no hope that the peaches, of which there were considerable quantities, would become usable this year, except, perhaps, for boiling for pie fillings.

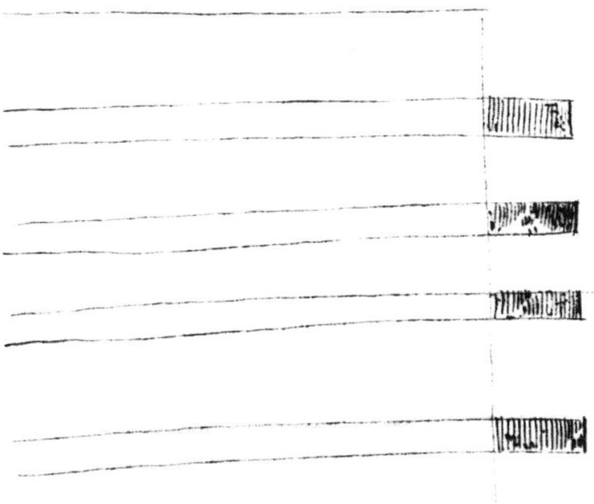

Fig. 259 Coal seams at 'Newmore'[174]

254 Three-year-old hay was now being bought for 20 shillings per ton. I was told that about every third year, when there is a bad harvest, the price generally is 30, 40 shillings and even more.

Coal seams and fire engines

On the way to Hexham, which mainly follows the River Tyne, work was proceeding on a fire engine and two shafts for a coal mine, where the seams have already been discovered through boring. The first lies at a depth of 156 feet and is 3 feet 9 inches thick and 18 feet below it there is another seam of 3 feet thickness.

This place is called Wylam and belongs to Mr 'Blachet',[175] who in this part of the country has scraped together a large fortune, mainly from lead mines. His estate lies 8 miles from here and is reportedly one of the most beautiful in this neighbourhood.

Ovingham and Corbridge, two small towns

Ovingham and Corbridge are small towns, well located by the River Tyne, the one 10 and the other 16 miles from Newcastle, but otherwise there is nothing to see except fields and
255 meadows.

Lime is here used as fertiliser. I met a number of horses loaded with potatoes which were being taken to the market in Newcastle, where they are sold by the bushel.

At Corbridge there is a factory for Berlin or Prussian Blue, established by a German a few years ago.

Hexham, town with a woollen mill

16 September. Hexham is located 23 miles from Newcastle and has a factory making clothes for soldiers and also a number of tanners and glove-makers. The church is large and consists of the surviving parts of an Abbey, which still is partly maintained by Mr ...[176]

The journey continued to Brampton, 25 miles from Hexham. The countryside between them consists mainly of hills and wasteland.

The Roman Wall

I passed two places by the so-called Roman Wall, erected by Roman Emperors during antiquity as
a defence against the Scots and the Picts. 256

Very little of it remains today. In a few places there is a short piece of a solid wall with a deep trench on the northern side.

New road between Newcastle and Carlisle

A new road between Newcastle and Carlisle is now being built that will be 57 miles long. It will mostly follow the above-mentioned Roman Wall, which in olden times stretched right across the country. The building of this road was ordained by an Act of Parliament, and its real purpose is to facilitate the transport of guns etc in case of a rebellion in Scotland and it is, therefore, called the Military Road. It is 21 feet wide.

Potato farms

In several places here the road will go through tracts of wasteland. Building of houses and cultivation of the soil has already begun and it is particularly potatoes that are planted.
Note: lime is not suitable for manuring potatoes. Dung should be used in preference, if it can be obtained.

Shipbuilding

In the depth of the countryside where there was
no water to be found, I caught sight of a 257
shipbuilding yard, which I found rather peculiar. However, it did not seem so absurd after I had been told that this establishment is used for cutting and prefabricating ship's timbers, which makes the transport in wagons to Liverpool and other ports much easier.

Coal mines and lime-burning

Not far from Brampton there are some coal mines between the hills that contribute towards giving the surrounding countryside a more pleasant appearance, because the coal can be used for burning lime to fertilise fields and meadows. No limekilns of the kind previously described at several places are used here. Instead, limestone and coal in alternate layers are built up to the same shape as a charcoal-burning heap, then covered with turf and lit at the centre.

I have also previously seen lime burnt in this way around Swalwell, and it was mostly carried out on the field itself so that the lime and the 25
ashes of the coal and the turf were utilised as efficiently as possible.

Notes and references

116 Egelson – not identified.

117 Price missing.

118 Price missing.

119 Something has been left out here, but RRA is probably referring to old cannon as he has done at various other places during his journey.

120 Leufsta, Österbybruk, Västland, Åkerby (all Uppland).

121 RRA points out here that steel was reckoned by the 'long ton'.

122 It is unusual to hear of a spade being tinned, but RRA describes the spade as half tinned. Perhaps the upper part was tinned as protection against corrosion, but it would not serve any purpose to tin the lower part, since the tin would soon wear off.

123 RRA calls these structures 'stitz'.

124 According to R E Jupko, a keel was a measure for coal equal to 8 Newcastle caldrons, equal to 21 ton 4 cwt, equal to 424 cwt [of 112 lb]. Twenty-one keels consequently equalled 445 tons 4 cwt. Assuming 300 working days per year, the yearly shipment from the staithes would amount to 133,560 tons and be worth £93,492. The capacity of each wagon would have been 2.36 tons.

125 The diameters and counts given yield wheels of very different pitches, which must be wrong in some respect.

126 Leufsta – subsidiary? (Uppland).

127 Åkerby (Uppland).

128 Österby, Västland (both Uppland).

129 Karlholm (Uppland).

130 This paragraph does not seem to make much sense but is a literal translation. The first sentence mentions four well-known Swedish iron stamps but includes 'D3' not, as far as is known, an iron stamp, but an element of the steel stamp described in the previous sentence. It is possible that the copyist had difficulty here in deciphering RRA's notes, and may even have omitted a whole line.

131 Leufsta – subsidiary?, Åkerby (both Uppland).

132 Blackhall Mill steel stamp.

133 Left blank in MS.

134 This is a very early mention of an iron blowing tub, so it is not perhaps surprising that RRA used the Swedish word for bellows.

135 RRA's colleague Samuel Schröderstierna, who visited Crowley's works in 1749, also saw the blowing engine in operation. According to him the cylinders were 4 feet by 2 feet and he adds that the pistons were provided with leather packings. It is possible that the smaller dimensions he gives are bore and stroke rather than outside measurements.

136 No separate amounts for the buildings and repairs are shown. It is possible that they are included in the £1.5s which is paid to 'My Lord', which would otherwise appear inexplicably high.

137 The slitting mill must have been combined with a rolling mill, although this appears to have been provided with rolls long enough for rolling sheets.

138 What was meant by 'heavy sheets' can only be speculated. Sheets for frying pans and the like were probably at least $^{1}/_{16}$ inch thick and possibly more. 'Heavy sheets' might have been anything up to $^{1}/_{4}$ inch, which was generally the thickness used for saltpans.

139 It is not quite clear if these 100 nailers were employed by Crowley's as outworkers or independent workers.

140 This is correct for 'skeppund uppstadsvikt'.

141 This figure corresponds to 2.36 pence per pound.

142 This sounds as if it were taken from a price-list or catalogue. 'Bils' is probably short for billhook and 'Tachen' probably means fork or a faggot of brushwood or the like. According to *The Technological Dictionary – English – German – French*, edited by E V Hoyer and F Kreyter, (Wiesbaden: 1903) a billhook is a

'Faschinessmesser' in German. It seems reasonable to assume that fascine knives could be used for both faggots and sugar cane.

143 See p.192.

144 his corresponds to 7 to 7/6 per 6-day week.

145 What RRA means is obviously that conical gudgeons would not be very suitable for supporting heavy rolls in a horizontal position and in this he is undoubtedly correct.

146 No figure given in MS.

147 See Vol 1 p.51.

148 Probably 'pail hoops'.

149 The figures stated in this paragraph do not agree with the estimate above it. RRA probably had second thoughts after having made the original estimate, but never got around to changing it. In any case, the difference between the two figures for the consumption of foreign iron, namely 1950 tons and 2250 tons, is certainly not more than the uncertainty inherent in his estimates.

150 The Swedish word for slate used by RRA can also mean shale.

151 The distance between Winlaton and Stella is more like 1 mile.

152 It has not been possible to find this coal mine on any of the Ordnance Survey maps. However, travelling 4 miles up the river from Stella, one reaches just above Wylam, whereas 14 miles from Newcastle would be near Riding Mill.

153 This corresponds to 1° 26 minutes.

154 RRA actually uses the word 'trouble', which is probably a local word for fault.

155 RRA and also other Swedish travellers call it Blackermille, which may be the way Blackhall Mill was pronounced locally. Although the distances from Newcastle and Winlaton to Blackhall Mill are not given correctly by RRA – they are more like 10 miles and 5 miles – there are other references that show beyond doubt that Blackhall Mill and Blackermille are the same place. It should also be remembered that RRA was by no means always correct when he quoted distances.

156 Name missing from MS.

157 These steel grades are given by RRA in approximations to English, and the stamps in Fig. 255 show the spur, star and shear devices.

158 No prices are given.

159 The word 'artificial' used for blister steel has not been encountered anywhere else. However, steel produced directly from manganese-bearing iron ore was in the past called 'natural' steel and this technique was particularly well developed in Austria and Germany, from which countries there was a considerable export of the resulting product. It would appear that RRA used the expression 'artificial' blister steel to mark the contrast between it and the so-called 'natural' steel.

160 Steel iron was pig iron made from high manganese ores, otherwise free from undesirable impurities such as phosphorus, sulphur and arsenic and, therefore, suitable for steel making.

161 Leufsta, Åkerby, Västland, Österbybruk (all Uppland).

162 After cementation.

163 Leufsta, Åkerby, Österby, Västland (all Uppland).

164 The Hollow Sword-Blade Company.

165 Probably 'Blenkinsop'.

166 These are obviously RRA's interpretations of English terms. 'Graindins' must be grinding; 'Oversatdins' remains obscure; 'Berdins' may be burnishing.

167 RRA has made some small mistakes in his calculations, which have been corrected. His grand total came to £216.16s

168 A Hollander beater.

169 These terms are given in English.

170 This figure appears to have included both pitcoal for firing and charcoal for packing the bars. It was the charcoal that could be reused to some extent.

171 RRA's comments show that there was much traffic of coal wagons, that the road was a double track and, finally, that it was also used by ordinary travellers. We do not know how RRA travelled in this part of the country but it seems likely that he was on horseback. The road that he refers to must have been the one from Pontop to Blaydon Staiths. See Charles E Lee, 'The world's oldest railway', *Transactions Newcomen Society,* (1946), map on p.150.

172 According to *Country Life*, (27 September 1973), pp. 150–151 the column is still standing. It is 140 feet high and surmounted by a figure of Liberty. Much of the Hall is in ruins. The owner of Gibside at the time of RRA's visit was Mr George Bowes, who is said to have erected the column to celebrate his election to Parliament.

173 It has not been possible to find 'Newmore' on any of the 1-inch Ordnance Survey maps. RRA might mean Newburn, in which case Mr 'Habels' would be Mr Hall.

174 Incomplete and not very informative.

175 Probably 'Blackett'.

176 Name missing.

Journey 6d Carlisle to Liverpool

Carlisle, Maryport, Workington, Clifton, Whitehaven, Egremont, Borrowdale, Ulverston, Penny Bridge, Spark Bridge, Garstang, Poulton le Fylde, Preston, Wigan, Chowbent, Prescot, Liverpool.

Fig. 260 Carlisle

The town of Carlisle and its business

Carlisle is the capital of Cumberland and it stands at the confluence of the three rivers Eden, Caldone and Petteril.[177] The Castle and the fortifications are not very well maintained and for this reason it was immediately surrendered to the Pretender during the last Rebellion. The trade of this place is feeble and of little importance, and there is no manufacture of anything except riding-whips and fish hooks, well liked by coachmen and anglers [Fig. 260].

The iron consumed here comes from Mr 'Poal' of Newcastle, 'Elizab: Rossaide' in Liverpool and Mr 'Hone' in Whitehaven. All told, it amounts to 50 or 60 tons a year, which is retailed by Mr 'Marwite', Mr 'Spedin' and 'Johna Robinson White-smidt'.[178]

In Newcastle the price of ordinary iron was now reported to be £17.10s., but 'slender' or
259 1-inch-square bars were £18 a ton.

Carriage from Newcastle cost 35 shillings a ton, from Liverpool the carriage by sea costs 5 shillings a ton, and by land 3 shillings and 4 pence,[179] or a total of 8 shillings and 4 pence. The stamp ***H.***[180] from Gothenburg is considered good.

On the way to Workington we passed the small towns Wigton and Horby, where hemp and flax were spun. The raw material is obtained from Whitehaven and Carlisle where the finished product is sold. Otherwise fishing is the livelihood of these towns. By the seacoast some salt pans were seen, but they were no longer in use.

Maryport, a small town

Ellenfoot, now called Maryport, lies by the outlet of a little river only 2 miles from Workington and two years ago there was nothing here except a fisherman's cottage. Now it is a small town with a harbour and ships, which is due to the discovery of some coal mines and the building of a blast furnace and a glassworks.

Blast Furnace

The furnace was in blast and operated 26
by Mr 'Hortle' of Whitehaven.[181] The coal comes from Scotland by ship and costs 4 shillings a sack. Ore of the red kind is also shipped in by sea from Ulverston and other places in Westmoreland, as well as a grey kind that grows [sic] below the coal seams and is found by the shore of the sea. The red ore, which is the principal one, costs 14 shillings per ton and the iron made from it fetches £7.10s per ton. The furnace is 22 feet high and smelts 16 tons a week [Fig. 261].

Each charge contains seven measures of coal, 3 feet long and 1 foot 9 inches wide. Fourteen charges are made every 24 hours. The wages are 11 and 8 shillings a week.

Fig. 261 Blast furnace at Maryport

Summary of costs at Ellenfoot	
Coal 28 loads per week	
@ 18 shillings per load	£67.4s
Ore of the red kind, 18 tons	
@ 14 shillings	£12.12s
Ore of the grey kind, 20 tons	
@ 8 shillings	£8.0s
Limestone for fluxing, 3 tons	
@ 5 shillings	15s
2 furnace keepers	
61 @ 11 shillings a week each	£1.2s
2 fillers @ 8 shillings per week each	16s
Rent for the land on which the furnace stands, building costs, salary of the manager, etc.	£5.10s
Total	£95.19s
The 16 tons of pig iron produced per week sell for £7.10s per ton	£120.0s

The cost of blowing in the furnace should be deducted from the £120 and the production should, therefore, be considered to be 14 tons instead of 16.

14 tons of pig iron @ £7.10s per ton	£105.0s
Profit	£15.0s

[This profit amounts to £0 18s 9d per ton if split over 16 tons.]

Workington

Workington, also located by a small river, provides a convenient entrance for ships, of which a number were now lying idle in the harbour. The shipping of coal to Ireland is the main business here and the supplies are fairly plentiful and the coal mines are very near.

Coal mines

The shafts of the coal mines are 180 feet to 210 feet deep and they are located about 72 feet above seal level. Next to the coal seams there is generally a black shale, which has many
beautiful impressions of vegetable matter. 262
The waste heaps were searched for samples of these, but they were brittle and weathered.

Messrs 'Walcher', 'Parchen' and 'Rodders' are retailers of iron for the requirements of this place. It is fetched from the forges in Lancashire, from Whitehaven and from Dumfries in Scotland. The total consumption is not estimated to exceed 50 tons [per year].

Clifton blast-furnace and foundry

Clifton furnace is located 8 miles from Workington and 6 from Whitehaven[182] and belongs to Messrs. 'Chux and Co.' in Newcastle. The furnace is built in the usual manner, but nothing but pit coal is used for the smelting. This has first been placed in heaps, covered with ashes and soil, and coked just like a

Fig. 262 Clifton furnace and coking stacks

charcoal-burning stack, only in much shorter time [Fig. 262].

The ore comes from Westmoreland, but is also mixed with some ore from the coal seams or sea coal[183] as mentioned previously. Some limestone is also included in each charge of ore.

263 The iron made here is used for castings either directly from the furnace or later on, after remelting in a reverberatory furnace located nearby, for pots and other small items.

The process is kept so secret, particularly as far as their own countrymen are concerned, that one of the partners, who was in charge of the works, as soon as he caught sight of me, gave me a polite *consilium abeundi*[184] and told me that the same thing had happened to him at Coalbrookdale. At this works there is, according to him, not only a similar foundry for pots, etc, but also a forge where bar iron is made from pig iron smelted with coke.

During my visit to Coalbrookdale I did find the same smelting process used for producing pig iron for castings, but no bar iron was made from it. However, many experiments had been made with coke pig iron, but so far it had never
264 been possible to bring the product to the same perfection as bar iron made from other pig iron smelted according to the old method with charcoal.

Nevertheless, it is not considered impossible to make ductile wrought iron of pig iron that has been smelted with coke. The very poor results achieved by the experiments made with coke iron are ascribed to the ignorance shown by the firers and hammermen as soon as they are compelled to deviate from their old habits.

Whitehaven town, its harbour, industry and trade

Sir James Lowther, to whom this town belonged, died in London on 1 January 1755. According to the newspapers, he left estates and cash to a total amount of £600,000, which he had willed to his relations because he died a bachelor, in his 79th year. Two years ago he had one leg sawn off because of gangrene caused by gout and was on that occasion happily rescued from the onslaught of death.

This town is the largest of the towns on the Cumberland coast, and has a well-situated dry 26
harbour surrounded by stone piers. During spring tide there is water to a depth of 14 feet, 16 feet and 18 feet, but ships are left dry on the sandy bottom when the tide goes out.

The town has a large number of ships and a large trade with America, particularly in tobacco leaves and raw sugar. Factories for working up these raw materials into rolls of tobacco, snuff

Fig. 263 Burning spoilt tobacco

and sugar tops have been established here. The master sugar refiner comes from Hamburg and knows his job well. Nevertheless, sugar is much more expensive here than in Hamburg, and when it costs $9\frac{1}{2}$ pence a pound there, it cannot be sold in Whitehaven for less than 12 pence. To a great extent this difference is caused by the customs duty on the raw sugar, which amounts to 4 shillings and 9 pence per hundredweight. Sugar that is exported to Ireland is given a drawback of 9 shillings per
266 hundredweight.

For tobacco that is imported, a duty of $5\frac{3}{4}$ pence is paid but, if it is spoilt, it is burnt in a building with two high chimneys, located at some distance from the town. The stacks disperse the harmful smoke and the owner of the tobacco is paid $1\frac{1}{2}$ pence[185] by the Government. The ashes are subsequently used for bleaching flax, for which purpose they are supposed to be very suitable [Fig. 263].

Coal mines at Whitehaven

The considerable coal mines, located close to the harbour and which used to belong to Sir James Lowther, are one of the several reasons for the great shipping and trading of Whitehaven. Sir James was the Lord of the Manor here and also owned the 'royalty' estimated to the worth £1,000,000 in cash and property, which is 40 million in Swedish money.[186] His yearly income from the coal mines alone was said to amount to £12,000 to £14,000 [Fig.264].

2,500 tons of coal are raised each week, or 267
833 wagons each holding 3 tons. The sales price is 3 shillings and 4 pence per ton. The duty paid is 5 shillings per ton on coal for the home market, for France, 3 shillings and for Ireland, 1 shilling.

The miners work in three shifts, day and night, and the pay is 6 to 14 pence per ton, depending on the travelling distance underground and the danger involved. In these

Fig. 264 Coal transport and harbour at Whitehaven

mines a great number of miners have been suffocated by the inflammable gas found in some parts and not long ago 22 people lost their lives all at once in this way.

At the mines nearest to the harbour there are two fire engines consuming 50 tons of coal a week. Each engine raises 52 gallons a stroke and makes 13 strokes a minute.[187] Each gallon holds four bottles.

268 When the deepest shaft, which lies right by the seashore, was sunk, no fewer than 13 separate seams of coal were found. In the following section detailed information is given about the way of working and the rock formations [Fig. 265].

All the seams dip south-west and appear to be directed more or less towards the sea. The degree of dip is generally such that an advance of 6 feet in depth corresponds to a horizontal advance of 60 feet.[188]

Just outside the town, a new adit has been driven into the lowest coal seam and its outlet is in a steep slope of the cliff. This adit is generally 24 feet wide [sic][189] and it is designed to be convenient for the horses entering and leaving the mine, where they are used for transporting coal underground. After proceeding for a mile through the adit, the shaft which is furthest to the south-west is reached. It has a depth of

269 63 feet to the lowest coal seam.

Below this, the shaft has been sunk a further 90 feet to 108 feet. The total depth is estimated to be 648 feet of which 630 feet are below sea level. When this depth below the surface of the sea is reached, it was customary to toast Sir James in wine, and we were also provided with the required beverage on this occasion.

Of the above-mentioned coal seams, only three are being worked nowadays, namely the first, which is 3 feet 10 inches thick and mined to supply the two 'fire-engines'. The second is 3 feet 6 inches thick, and lies next to the third, which is 6 feet thick.

On the way down from the surface through the adit already mentioned, we travelled across a number of so-called troubles or faults, always downcast on the south-western side or upcast on the north-eastern. At the last trouble the down-throw was 60 feet, all at once. The troubles occur similarly in all the coal seams. 27

In the roof of the adit and in other places where the coal seam had been removed it was possible to see in the black shale distinct impressions of large trees with branches and sometimes even with roots. All the coal seams are mixed with layers of charcoal and this admixture, when substantial, divides the coal seam itself into distinct separate layers.

To safeguard the security of the mine in the future, the work is organised so that parts of the coal seam 12 yards square are removed, whilst adjoining parts are left standing as 12-yard-square pillars. In this way the mining is continued as far as the seam extends [Fig. 266a].

Inflammable air in the coal mines

In some places where the so-called foul air occurs, the miners dare not approach with any
'71 light or other flaming fire. Instead they manage to work by the light from sparks of fire produced by a machine consisting of a rotating steel wheel with a piece of flint held against it [Fig. 266b].[190] In a few places in this mine, the fumes of foul air have been seen streaming out of cracks in the coal seam and it has been possible to feel plainly the raw and chilly blast, as if it came from a small pair of bellows. This caused Sir James to brick up and completely enclose these places from the rest of the mine workings, and to convey the inflammable air generated by the fissured coal through pipes and up a shaft to the surface. There it bursts into flames as soon as a candle or other flaming material gets within 4 feet to 6 feet distance of the pipe, from which
it is blown out as from a pair of bellows. 272

When this air, which contains no visible fuel, has been ignited in the way described, it burns forever, unless it is deliberately extinguished by closing the pipes. However, it is always kept burning, because it is considered that this improves the draught and the exhalation of the aforementioned foul and inflammable air.

This air can be contained in bladders of oxen or pigs and retains its inflammable nature even after having been carried many hundreds of miles away, as evidenced by tests made for the Academies of Science in London[191] and Saint Petersburg. Of three bladders sent to London, two were leaky and had collapsed, but the third was tried four months later, and the air that was pressed out of it caught fire when brought near a candle. If one pours sulphuric acid on iron

Fig. 265 Coal workings

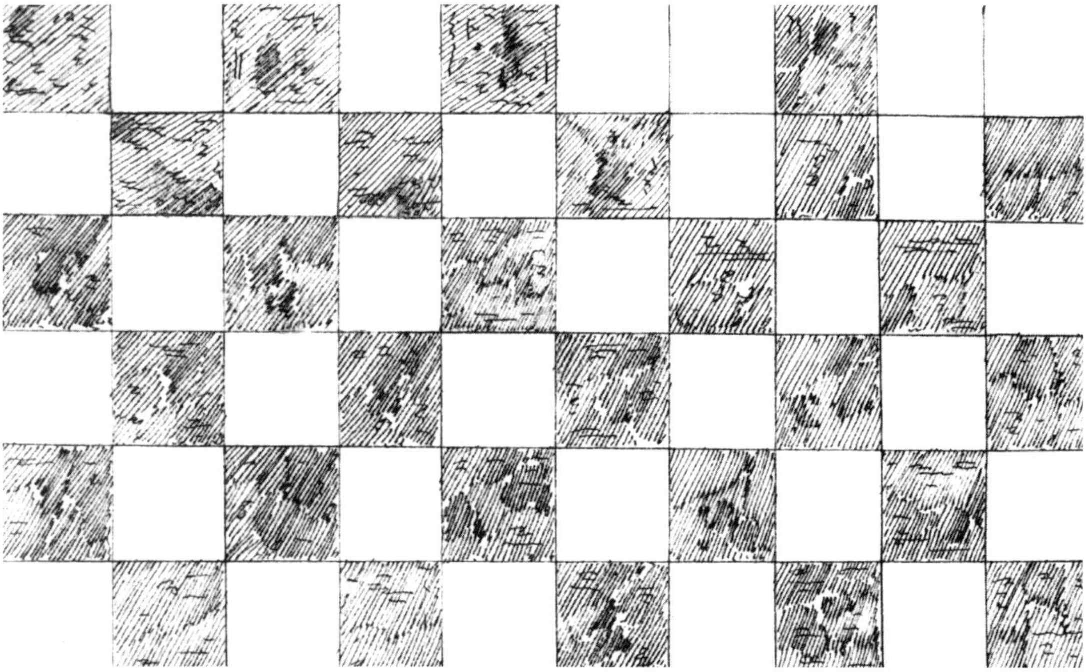

Fig. 266a Plan of mine workings

filings, a kind of air is produced that burns in the way described and can be collected in
273 bladders as shown by drawing no. 267.

A man or any other animal can breathe in this air without any ill effects as far as their health is concerned, except if it catches fire, when everybody present is instantly killed. Those who very occasionally recover say that they were completely unconscious and felt no pain when the fire occurred.

How little harm this air does to the lungs is shown by the miners who breathe it in for amusement. When exhaled it catches fire when a candle is placed nearby. They also test places

Fig. 266b Spark machine

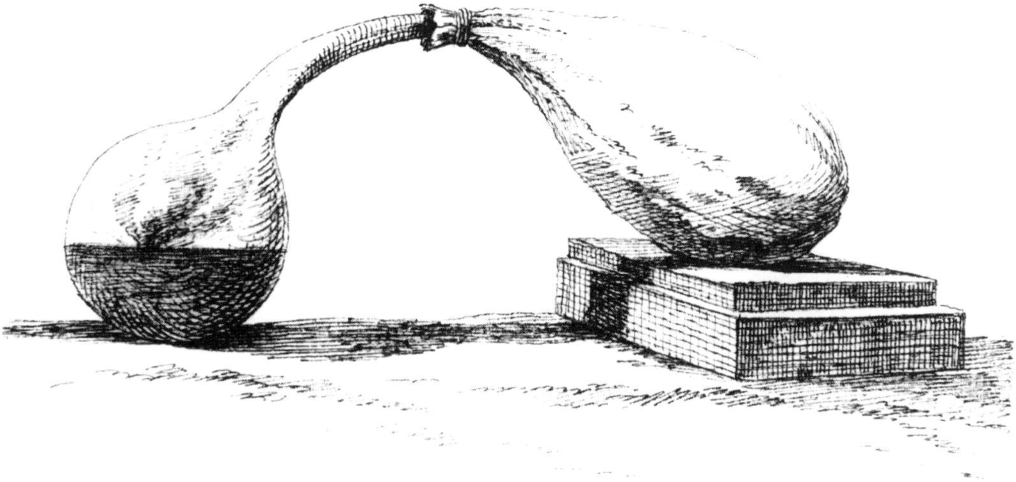

Fig. 267 Experiment to produce inflammable air

about which they are uncertain by breathing in the air there and then breathing it out into an ox bladder, which is taken to the surface. When the air, on being pressed out of the bladder, ignites immediately, it is dangerous and contaminated by the aforementioned inflammable air. 274

I have myself tried the air above the pipe, but found only a cool breeze and a bituminous but not unpleasant odour.

Vitriol works at Whitehaven

The iron pyrites, which is occasionally found in the coal here, is sold to a vitriol works situated near Whitehaven. The price is the same as that for coal, 3s.4d per ton. The pyrites is laid out in rows on a piece of ground that has been walled in. The vitriol is leached out gradually, depending on how much rain falls, and is led to a cistern. From here it is pumped up into the lead vessel where iron scrap is added in a certain proportion. Otherwise the boiling process is the same as already described at

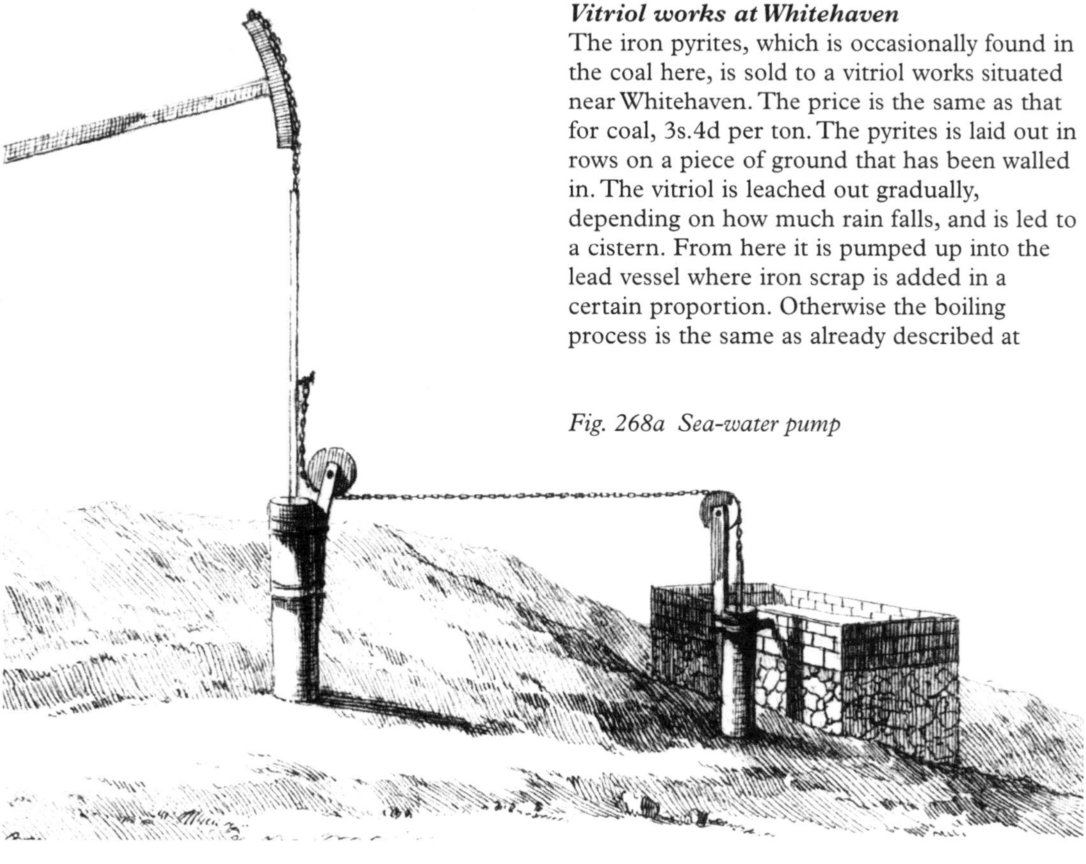

Fig. 268a Sea-water pump

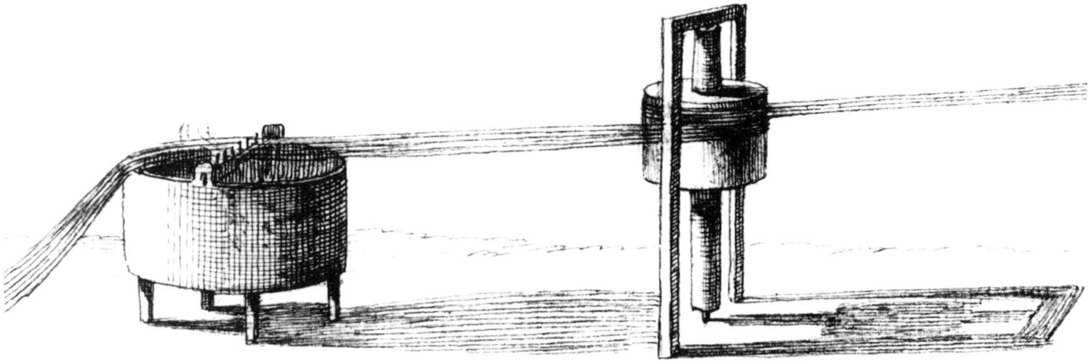

Fig. 268b Yarn tarring

Mr Zeel's works in London.[192] In this way 3 tons of vitriol can be boiled here per week, for which ½ ton of scrap iron is used. [Gap in MS here.]
275 The vitriol is sold to Ireland for £9 per ton.

The duty is ....[193] Scrap iron is bought in Holland for this purpose and costs ....[194]

Salt-boiling works at Whitehaven

Near the two fire engines located by the seashore, Mr James has two saltpans. The brine is pumped from the sea by a pump connected to one of the engines by means of a chain as shown by drawing no. 268a. It is subsequently boiled in iron pans constructed in the same way as described in Shields. For salt consumed in the neighbourhood, duty of 3 shillings and 4 pence a bushel is charged, and it is sold for 4 shillings and 1 pence.

In Whitehaven there are also two rope-walks, where spun hemp yarn is pulled through a kettle of boiled tar by winches as shown by drawing no. 268b.

The iron trade in Whitehaven

Mr How is the only person in Whitehaven who imports iron from foreign places and he also has
276 an iron works of his own at Egremont.

From St Petersburg, 200 tons per year of Siberian iron are imported. Mr How uses this partly for slitting and hoop iron, and partly for the requirements of iron for wheel tyres etc of the surrounding countryside. From Gothenburg in Sweden he takes 30 tons, of which some that is square is used for wheel nails[195] and some that is flat, for horseshoes. His correspondent in Gothenburg is Mr Gerhard and in St Petersburg, Baron Woolf.

The iron made by Mr How at Lower Mill near Egremont, 6 miles from Whitehaven, is used for nailrods, wheel-axles, ploughs, flukes for anchors, etc. According to his own statement, the yearly production amounts to 200 tons.

Besides Mr How, there are also Mr Fisher and Mr 'Schain', who trade in iron but they only procure small lots from Dumfries and Liverpool. Mr Spedding,[196] who is Sir James's
steward at the coal mines, uses 20 to 30 tons of 277
iron per year, which he buys partly from Mr How and partly from various places nearby. Iron bought in Dumfries costs £17 and sells for £18 and 19 a ton.

Various Gothenburg stamps of iron are bought for £16 and 15 shillings a ton and sold at £19. The English iron for £19 a ton. It is believed that the merchants in Dumfries smuggle in a good deal of iron and thus can sell it cheaper than anybody else.

Lingonberries and their use

On the so-called 'moors' on the uninhabited plains in Cumberland, and particularly on those in the neighbourhood of Whitehaven, a kind of 'lingon'[197] berry grows, here called Cranberries or Thorberries, but they never reach the same ripeness and perfection as in Sweden.
They are preserved for salads and pies in three different ways, namely:

1. Cooked with sugar to jam, in the Swedish way.

2. Cooked until they disintegrate, then strained and cooked again with sugar to the consistency
of a jelly. 278

3. Dried and bottled, so that they can be kept for several years. However, it should be noted that in this case most of the berries are unripe and completely dry.

Iron-ore mine with very rich ore

On the way from Whitehaven to Egremont I passed an iron-ore mine, where formerly the best iron ore in England is said to have been found. They can continue to boast about this, since nearby another find of ore has been made, which is as good as any in the country.

The ore mined here is of the red kind with a tinge of violet and it occurs in seams below the limestone. In some places, however, there is an accumulation of seams that have burst through the limestone crust, which in such locations is no more than 12 feet to 18 feet thick.

This kind of ore is generally so soft that one can write with it, which I had already observed
279 in ore shipped to Bristol from Lancashire and also in that from Biscay, although the latter is lighter in colour. The ore here shows varying fracture, in some places it is finer and more fully developed, and I have rarely seen any better ore as far as density and weight are concerned.

Depending on the circumstances, the ore is sold for 11, 12 and up to 13 shillings a ton. There was a more than considerable stockpile at the new mine, which is only 18 feet deep.

Egremont, a little town

Egremont is a small town that lies 6 miles from Whitehaven and has a dilapidated castle belonging to the Earl of Egremont.
The inhabitants of the town are occupied with the weaving of linen and tanning of hides.
The women spin for their keep. A short distance below the town there is a paper mill that has its market in Ireland, although otherwise there is
280 nothing special to be seen there.

Lower Mill iron works

Two miles further down lies 'Laër Mill'[198] belonging to Mr How and Co. in Whitehaven, which already has been mentioned.[199] There are three forges and a slitting mill here. In the first forge there are three hearths, namely two for firing and a third for chafing. Charcoal is used in all of them. Some of it comes from distances of many miles away in the surrounding countryside and some by sea from Scotland. A horse load of the former costs 4 shillings and 4 pence and of the latter 4 shillings.

For the chafing, breeze and small coal is mainly used but these cannot be used for the firing. This causes the chafing to slow down, though the iron is softer and of better quality when heated with charcoal than when pitcoal is employed in the chafery hearth.

The pig iron fired here is partly English and
partly from Virginia and now costs £$7\frac{1}{2}$ to £8 281
per ton.

At the second forge belonging to Lower Mill there is only a chafery hearth in which iron, welded together from old iron scrap in a wind furnace, is heated for drawing down under the hammer.

Summary of iron-making costs at Lower Mill

Pig iron, $1\frac{1}{4}$ ton @ £7.15s[200]	£9.13s.9d
Coal $2\frac{1}{2}$ dozen @ 4 shillings 2 pence	£6.5s.0d
Wages for firing and chafing	£1.0s.0d
Ground rent, building costs	£1.10s.0d
Total [per ton][201]	£18.8s.9d

Scrap iron made usable

The scrap is mainly purchased in London and comes from Holland packed in barrels and consists of old nails, locks, keys and all kinds of rusty iron.

To make it more suitable for welding together there is a machine, similar to the one employed by the wire mill in Wales, for

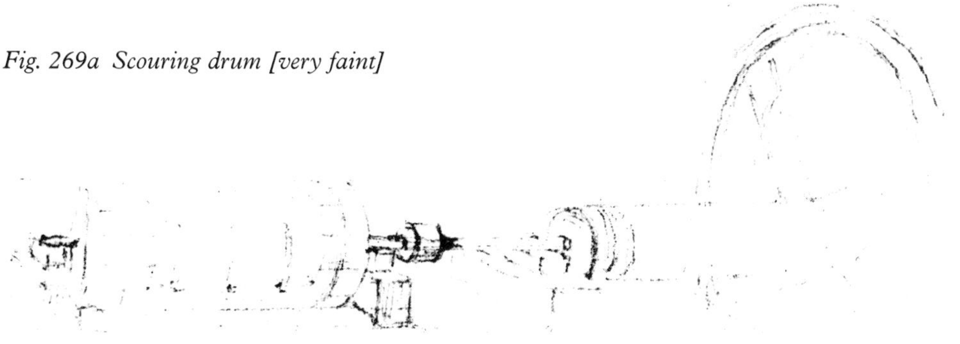

Fig. 269a Scouring drum [very faint]

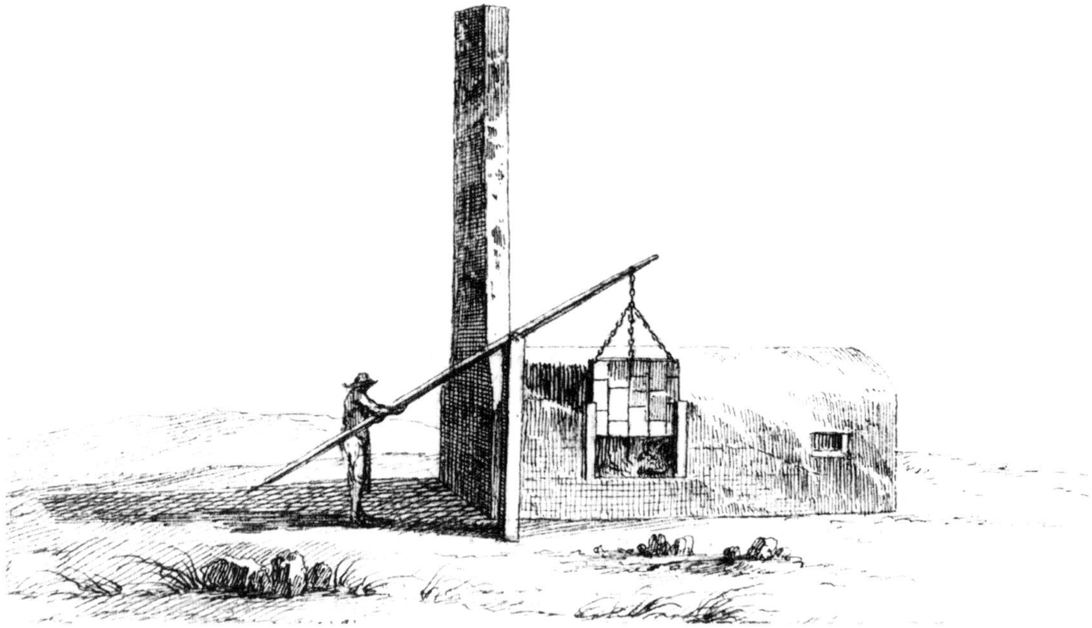

Fig. 269b Scrap-iron furnace

removing the rust by scouring. The scrap is placed in it and the machine is then rotated. See
282 drawing no. 269a.

After scouring, the iron scrap is placed in specially thrown clay pots, 12 inches high and 8 inches in diameter, which are carefully closed at the top. After they are thoroughly dry they are placed in the wind furnace, which is designed in the same way as the furnaces used for copper smelting. See Fig. 269b.

When the pot and its contents have been properly heated right through, it is taken out, the top opened and a red-hot iron bar stuck into the scrap. With the aid of the bar the contents, now welded together, are removed to the hammer and forged into a solid lump which, after reheating in the chafery hearth, is drawn down to bars. If sufficient quantities of scrap were available, it would be possible to weld together in this way 6 to 7 tons a week, but lack of raw material slows down the production of this forge so that it does not amount to more than 40 to 50 tons a year.
283 The wages are 12 shillings per ton, but in addition a man is paid 2 shillings a week for keeping the fires burning and for throwing the pots, which cannot be used more than once.[202]

A new iron-smelting process

To increase production at this forge, Mr Charles Wood, who is a partner in the works and also the manager, has been considering a new method of smelting iron ore in an air furnace to make it malleable and suitable for forging in the same furnace. Experiments with this method are said to have been made some 20 years ago, and Mr Assessor Swedenborg[203] is supposed to have come here to see them, armed with a recommendation from 'Mr Mondell', who now is Consul at Cagliari and works the lead mines on Sardinia.

The furnace was now being built and the design the same as that of the copper-smelting furnaces commonly used at Bristol and in Wales,
as shown by the attached drawing no. 270. 284

Mr Wood told me that neither natives nor foreigners will have access to the new works when it starts operating, and that Mr Assessor Swedenborg also failed in his endeavour to find out about it, in spite of the great efforts that he made.

As far as I am concerned, I do not doubt that such a smelting process could work if only a suitable [source of] phlogiston[204] and sufficient lime are charged together with the ore, which for this process must be roasted. The ore must be of a quality that lends itself to the production of a good and malleable iron.

Slitting mill at Lower Mill

Besides the two forges already mentioned, a slitting mill also belongs to this works but it was

not in operation. Generally it is fairly busy slitting nail rods for the requirements of the neighbourhood and rolling hoop-iron. English iron is used for the former but the latter is made
285 of Siberia iron, imported by Mr How in his own ships, which go to collect hemp and flax, and take the iron as ballast.

The graphite mines of Borrowdale

A few miles further inland from the seashore there are many bare and high mountains, mainly consisting of a light grey slate and a darker kind of the same rock. In this place, Borrowdale near Keswick, the famous 'blacklead' or graphite mines are also located. They were not being worked now, because in one summer enough graphite can be mined to satisfy the small demand in England for several years.

These mines belong to an Irish Gentleman by the name of Shepherd, who has obtained the promise of high penalties for anybody breaking into them and carrying on trade in graphite without his knowledge, which previously has been common practice.

In this place the graphite is known as 'wadd' and is sold for 5, 10, 15 to 20 shillings,
depending on the quality and purity. 286

Slate, lead and copper mines

Slate is also quarried and mined[205] in this neighbourhood and shipped to Ireland and to many places in England. Further north there are also lead and copper mines, particularly on the southern side of the River Derwent. In this country there is an old saying that the River Derwent and the Derwent Falls are worth all England etc, which I cannot properly explain, because every place in England is so richly blessed with metals and other gifts of nature that I can hardly give any one province preference over another.

Iron-ore mines at Ulverston

Five miles from Ulverston I again came across a large number of fairly rich iron mines. They completely filled a tract of land with a circumference [sic] of half a mile. All of them worked one and the same seam, which in some places lies at a depth of 120 feet and in others at 180 feet to 210 feet, depending on how the rock rises or falls.

The tract is called Whitrigg Hill and Whitrigg bottom[206] and the mines are worked [sic] by
'Lord Montichao',[207] 'Mr Schow', 'Mr Sowent' 287
and other gentlemen interested in this sort of thing.

Fig. 270 Furnace under construction

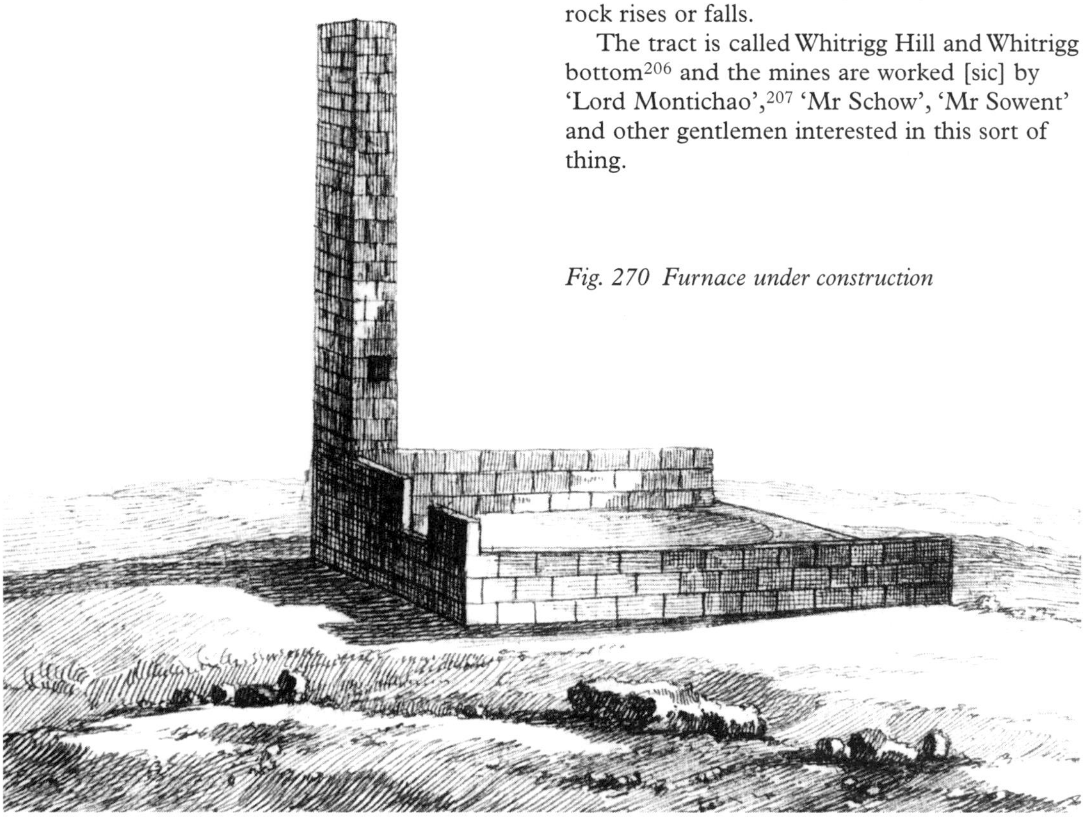

Fig. 271 [no reference in text; water and hills, possibly location of Penny Bridge]

The seam being worked is not thicker than 9 feet to 12 feet and the middle part of it, that is richest, is removed and sold for 10, 12, to 14 shillings a ton.

I had now, when the tide was out, passed two bays of the ocean,[208] each crossing being about 1½ miles long, but two more[209] remained. These had deeper water and were 4 miles across. The Government keeps pilots there to show travellers the road across the water.

Whilst I waited in Ulverston – a small market town – for low water to enable me to pass the sands, I went to see the iron works located in the neighbourhood, within 5 or 6 miles from the town.

The Newland blast furnace

The Newland blast furnace,[210] belonging to Mr Ford, was in full blast. It was designed in the
288 usual way described so many times before. However, the overseer of the furnace stated that it was 26 feet high from the hearth to the throat, where the charging takes place. At other furnaces I have been told that they were 22 feet to 24 feet.

The furnace is charged 18 times a day, each charge containing 6 bushels or baskets of coal that are 3 feet long and 1 foot 9 inches wide. Of the bushels there are 48 to a dozen [sic]. On top of this charcoal, 5 hundredweight of ore is charged, which is equal to 560 lb, besides limestone, which is added in accordance with the operational requirements of the furnace. The red ore is not roasted or calcined, but the ore mixed below the coal seams has to be lightly roasted. This ore constitutes about one sixth of the total quantity of ore used.

The furnace is tapped twice a day and the production amounts to 15 to 16 tons a week, if all goes well. The coal is purchased from many miles away in the surrounding countryside and a dozen, which is 12 sacks or horse loads, now costs 37 shillings. The daily consumption
amounts to four dozen. 289

The ore is obtained in the neighbourhood and the red kind costs from 11 to 14 shillings a ton. The grey ore, which lies below the coal seams, costs 8 to 9 shillings, but is generally red-short and of poor quality.

The overseer gets 12 shillings, and the helpers 8 to 9 shillings a week. The former told me that at some blast furnaces 14 to 16 shillings a week is paid, particularly when castings also are made, which was not the case at Newland during this campaign. A campaign generally lasts 5 to 6 months, longer or shorter, depending on how much coal it has been possible to procure, but this commodity is now becoming both scarce and expensive.

Penny Bridge blast furnace and foundry

Penny Bridge furnace lies 2 miles further up between the mountains, by a little river that has sufficient water. The campaign here had just begun and the bellows had not been started yet.

At this furnace all kinds of heavy castings are made for chemical works and also Guinea
290 kettles [Fig. 272].

The sales price of these heavy castings was said to be £11, but for smaller ones £12, £13 to £14 per ton.

Other blast furnaces in the district

List of blast furnaces[211]

Within 8 to 9 miles of Ulverston:

1. Newland
2. Penny Bridge
3. Duddon Bridge
4. Nibthwaite
5. Low Wood
6. Backbarrow
7. Gunsey

The above are all in Westmoreland and on the other side of the sands in Lancashire are:

8. Leighton
9. Halton, 2 miles from Lancaster.

Those marked with an X[212] have been built within the last 12 years, which has caused the price of coal to rise from 25 to 31 shillings a dozen. In Scotland, not far from Inverness, a new blast furnace has recently been built and blown in, which takes its ore from this part of the country.

Spark Bridge forge

Spark Bridge forge lies two miles above the Penny Bridge furnace and comprises two hearths, namely a fining hearth and a chafery hearth, in which it would be possible to fire and draw down $2\frac{1}{2}$ tons a week, with three workers for each hearth working night and day. At the time of my visit they could hardly produce as
much as 2 tons a week due to lack of coal and 291
only two hands or people were working 16 hours a day. Each charge consists of 70 lb pig iron, and when the work goes on night and day, 17 to 18 a day can be made.

At the finery hearth two dozen of coal are allowed per ton of bar iron and at the chafery hearth one dozen, but since mainly breeze and small coal are used in the latter, the actual consumption generally exceeds one dozen. One dozen coal now cost 37 shillings, whereas 12 years ago the cost was 24 [shillings]. The wages per ton are 12 shillings for fining and 10 shillings for chafing or drawing to ordinary flat sizes. The iron is sold for £20 a ton and there are 40 bars per ton.

Summary of costs at Spark Bridge Forge[213]

$1\frac{1}{4}$ ton pig iron @ £7.10s.0d	£9.7s.6d	
Coal, $2\frac{1}{3}$ loads @ 46 shillings	£5.7s.4d	
Wages for firing and chafing	£1.2s.0d	
Ground rent, building costs, etc.	£1.5s.0d	
Total	£17.1s.10d	292

The master chafer at Spark Bridge previously worked in Staffordshire for 'Mr Morgtrey', who

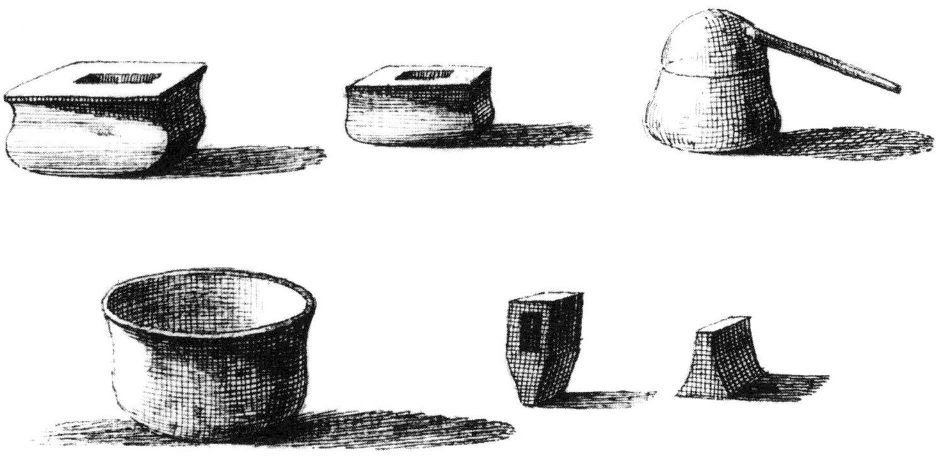

Fig. 272 Castings at Penny Bridge

Fig. 273 Lancaster

had made two trips to Sweden to study the making of iron and steel. When he returned he praised the Swedish industry highly and said that old crones in Sweden could draw down the iron more efficiently and to a better finish than the best chafery smiths in England ever could.

Other forges in the neighbourhood

List of bar iron forges in the neighbourhood

Spark Bridge, 'Mr Kendel'[214]	2 hearths
Nibthwaite	3 hearths
Backbarrow	4 hearths
Gunsey	2 hearths
'Chetton', 'Mr Ralisson and Co.'[215]	2 hearths

Two miles from Lancaster lies 'Chetton'[216] forge belonging to Mr Rawlinson and Co.,
293 which can produce $2\frac{1}{2}$ tons a week, when there is water enough, but just now the forge was shut down for lack of both water and coal.

Pine plantation and lime burning

On the return trip from the iron-works I saw in a number of places how pine trees had been planted on the hills and seemed to grow vigorously. Lime for the fertilising of fields and meadows in this district was burnt in lime kilns, as described at Bristol.

The burning is carried out in the same way as there, by charging the kilns with alternate layers of peat and limestone crushed to the size of a closed fist.

The water in the inlet from the sea was low between one and two o'clock and more than 30 horses passed across it without any mishap, although in some places there was so much water that they barely could stay on their feet. A contributory factor was the current caused by the incoming tide.

The town of Lancaster and its shipping, trade and manufactories

Lancaster is located on the River Lune, which is navigable for 15 miles from the sea to the Stone
Quarry. They have considerable trade with 29
America, whence they generally import raw sugar, rum, tar, pitch, resin etc, and to which they export manufactured iron in form of hoes, spades, nails and axes, cotton and linen cloth, large quantities of candles, Delft ware, Manchester ware and other goods [Fig. 273].

As far as factories are concerned, there are here a sugar refinery and a porcelain factory where Delft ware[217] is made from Irish clay. The recently built kilns are designed in the Delft fashion and fired with peat. The iron merchant here is Mr Butterfield who usually imports 30 tons from Mr Gerhard in Gothenburg with ships that subsequently go to Norway to complete their cargo with timber. Last year, 30 tons of small-size iron bars came from Rotterdam for the Guinea trade, and 'Mr Richard Tomson' has received 20 tons of Muscovy iron as ballast in a ship with a cargo of

95 flax and hemp. Muscovy iron is used for wheel tyres, the Swedish for horse shoes and horse-shoe nails and the English for nails.

Fields fertilised with marl

On the way to Preston I saw people occupied with the ploughing of the fields, using four horses pulling one plough, harnessed one in front of the other. In this district the fields are fertilised with marl, and a large number of marl pits could be seen from the road. These were generally 12 feet to 18 feet deep and some contained red marl, others, blue and others, a mixture of red, blue and brown-coloured marl. In some places the red is preferred, in others the blue or the brown are commended. Which one is the best depends on the quarry from which the marl is extracted and on the land to which it is applied. The marl can be quite hard, but in the air it falls apart. However, it is supposed to be best when it is already soft as quarried.

Marl is distinguished from clay both by its colour and by the fact that it falls apart into many particles of cubical shape. The month of April is said to be the best time to marl the fields.

96 The marl then disintegrates during the summer and has time to attract the salts[218] from the air, which, no doubt, are mainly responsible for the beneficial effects of marling as well as liming on the fertility of the soil.

£6 to 7 is the usual cost of having a field fertilised with marl. In the part of the country the size of a field is 160 square 'ruths' , and each 'ruth' is ...[missing] square yards or 4 square fathoms.[219] Such a marling lasts for 20 years and more and produces good growths of both corn and hay.

The town of Garstang and forge shops

Garstang is a market town located 10 miles from Lancaster and 10 from Preston.
The inhabitants are occupied with the spinning of flax, the product being sold in Preston.
The flax is originally bought from Latvia.
There were some workshops here for the forging of iron shovels, axes and spades for the India trade. These are sold to merchants both in
297 Lancaster and Preston. Axes are sold for 6 pence a pound, spades from 24 to 30 shillings a dozen and iron shovels for the same amount.

Poulton-le-Fylde, a small town

West of Garstang towards the sea coast lies a small town called Poulton-le-Fylde and 2 miles from there at Wardleys,[220] there is a warehouse with iron, hemp, boards etc, imported by Mr Shepherd and 'Mr Harnb.' from St. Petersburg, Latvia, Norway and Gothenburg. Every Tuesday they come here to sell their stock to those who wish to buy. The buyers come both from Preston and Lancaster as well as from the surrounding countryside and the prices are said to be more favourable here than in the towns nearby, which gives them a much larger turnover.

Bloomery

Six miles west of Garstang lies a bloomery, which now was not in operation but which can produce 2 hundredweight a day or 12 per week. A few miles away is yet another bloomery called 'Mihltarp'.[221] The two bloomeries together can produce 60 tons a year. The bloomery hearth 298
shown by the drawing is 2 feet wide and 2 feet deep.

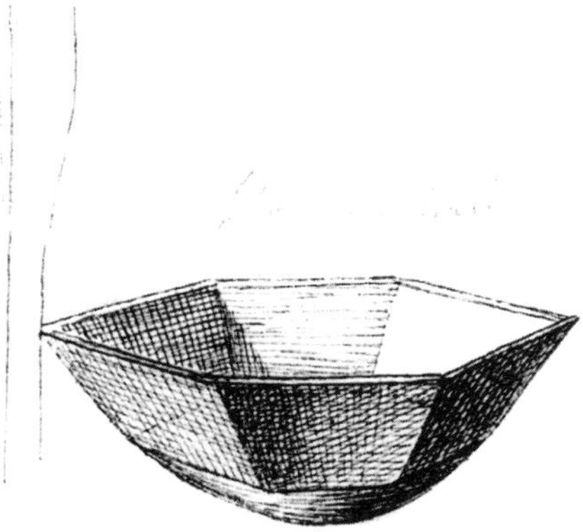

Fig. 274 [does not seem to be relevant, drawing of a hexagonal bowl, probably incomplete]

Iron prices at Wardleys

The iron sales at Wardleys are said to amount to between 200 and 300 tons. These quantities are claimed to include English, Russian and Swedish iron. The Swedish is sold at £17 'ready money' and the Russian fetches £16.15s.
The English, which in the rolling and slitting mill has been converted to nail rods or made suitable for plough shares or similar requirements, costs £19 to £20.10s or £21 a ton.

The nature of the country and its cultivation

When one crosses the sands above Lancaster the country begins to look less mountainous than in Westmoreland, and the further one

Fig. 275a Reservoir

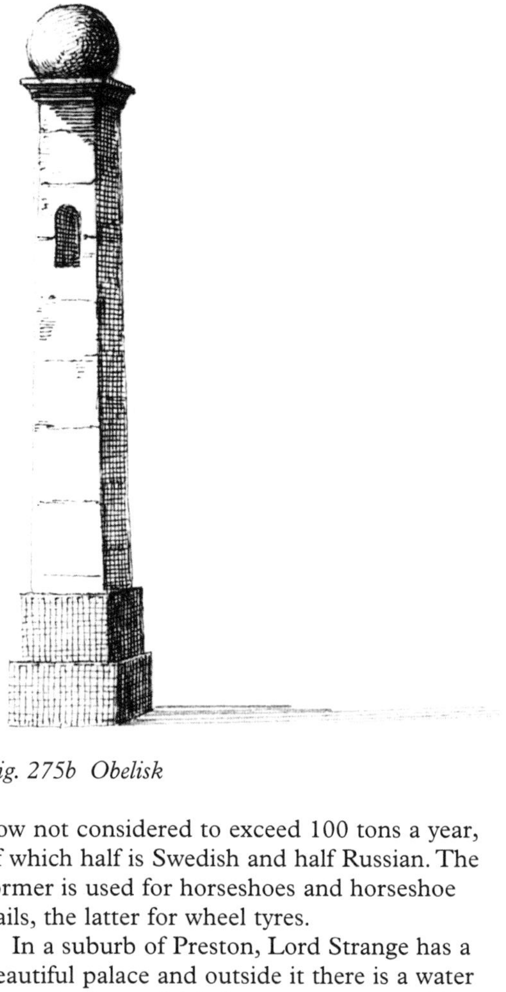

Fig. 275b Obelisk

advances toward Preston, the flatter and better cultivated it becomes. That marl occurs most everywhere makes a contribution to the cultivation that is not inconsiderable. The marl benefits the meadows just as much as the fields, but it has to be ploughed in and corn grown a few times on the land before it can be laid
299 fallow. It is claimed in this locality that marl is much more beneficial to agriculture than lime, but in other places, where lime is being used as fertiliser, it is claimed that nothing can surpass it. One does hear the same sort of talk from those accustomed to fertilising their fields and meadows with manure.

Manure obtained in this part of the country is used for fertilising meadows and is spread out thinly just after the haymaking.

The town of Preston, its location and trade

Preston stands on a hill, located in a pleasant plain not far from a navigable river recently provided with a beautiful stone bridge consisting of five arches. Cotton and linen mills provide the main occupation in this populous town. They give many merchants plenty to do, with the importation of raw materials as well as
300 with the exports of manufactured goods, mainly to Russia and America.

The ships that bring timber and boards from Norway also load some Gothenburg iron. Some Russian iron comes in ships carrying hemp and flax from St Petersburg for the account of 'Mr Th. and Madame Meijer'. Nevertheless, the sale of iron in this locality has decreased since Mr Shepherd of Kirkham and others have established a warehouse at Wardleys on the peninsula that juts forth between Lancaster and Preston. The total sales of iron in Preston are now not considered to exceed 100 tons a year, of which half is Swedish and half Russian. The former is used for horseshoes and horseshoe nails, the latter for wheel tyres.

In a suburb of Preston, Lord Strange has a beautiful palace and outside it there is a water reservoir, from which the water is pumped into the town through pipes. The pump is driven by a horse wheel that also supplies power to a roller mill for malt [Fig. 275].

The recently planted avenue and the beautiful view of the new bridge and the
01 surrounding countryside is noteworthy.

As well as the textile mills, there is a sugar refinery in the town, and also a melting furnace in a foundry making many kinds of castings, but I was there on a Sunday and it was not working.

Wigan, a small town with coal mines producing cannel coal

Wigan is a small town and market place, renowned for its coal mines, in which cannel coal is mined. This type of coal is different from all other coal found in England or elsewhere, because it is completely compact and dense, without any layers or visible crystals, let alone the veins of charcoal that usually appear in the ordinary mineral coal. The price of this coal is 3 pence a hundredweight and thus twice that of other coal used in the district. The cannel coal burns with a bright flame and is excellent in the winter, when the days are dark and short, because it makes a room nearly as bright and cheerful as a log fire.

02 A man skilled in turning has recently settled in this place with the idea of making from cannel coal all kinds of small articles, such as inkpots, salt cellars, pepper-pots, candlesticks etc, and it is very probable that he could make money in this way, because the work can be done quickly and the finished goods are as sought after as they are rare. However, he has acquired a taste for dogs and for hunting[222] with the gentry, which in ordinary circumstances he would not dare to do, because he is a Roman Catholic and not very rich. The result is that he never has anything ready for visitors when they wish to buy something from him.

According to the Laws of England, no Catholic is allowed to possess a gun or to go hunting and the same applies to members of the Church of England unless they own a rent-roll amounting to at least £100 a year.

Factories in Wigan

In Wigan there are non-ferrous metal foundries for small bells, candlesticks and other household goods. There are also large numbers of women and children occupied with the spinning of
03 cotton.

A gunsmith who moved to this neighbourhood has achieved a great reputation, particularly for his steel bows of which he makes three different kinds. They can shoot balls and cost from 35 shillings to 2½ guineas. He also assembles guns, which are sold for 5 guineas, decorated with silver mountings. He buys the barrels from Birmingham.

There is little trade in iron here, because the consumers who live here have many opportunities to obtain it from Liverpool and other towns nearby with the coal wagons that come and go every day.

'Brackmill' and 'Barth' forge, iron manufactories

Brockmill[223] is located a mile from Wigan and 4 miles further on towards Preston lies Backaker or Barthforge. The latter comprises two hearths for fining pig iron and chafing the wrought iron, and the annual production is 80 tons, whereas Brockmill makes no more than
30 tons. 304

At Birkacre there is also a slitting mill that supplies some of the nailers in the neighbourhood of Chowbent,[224] 6 miles from here, where there are up to 300 of them. At Chowbent, Öregrund iron is used for horseshoes and horseshoe nails and it costs £22 to 23 per ton.

Brockmill has a wind furnace for melting down scrap, some of which is purchased in London and some from foundries in the neighbourhood that specialise in the casting of pots. The latter consists of castings that have become malleable iron during remelting. The former kind of iron melted down from scrap iron is the best, and used for making hoes, shovels and sugar-cane knives. The latter, on the other hand, is used for the core of forge anvils[225] and for other heavy forgings.

In the smithy there are five hearths, where ten people are occupied making hoes and other goods, all of which are sold in Liverpool for the
West India trade. 305

At one of the hearths, where they reheat the scrap iron for drawing down under the hammer, I saw a peculiar kind of tuyere, the design of which I waited in vain to have explained to me, because its advantages as well as the benefits derived from other inventions made at these works are kept secret. The tuyere is forged of wrought iron, which is common in bar-iron forges, although cast iron tuyeres are used for blacksmiths' hearths [Fig. 276].

A small lead pipe enters one side of the forged tuyere and on the opposite side a short piece of this pipe emerges, from which water runs into a trough used for cooling the tongs.

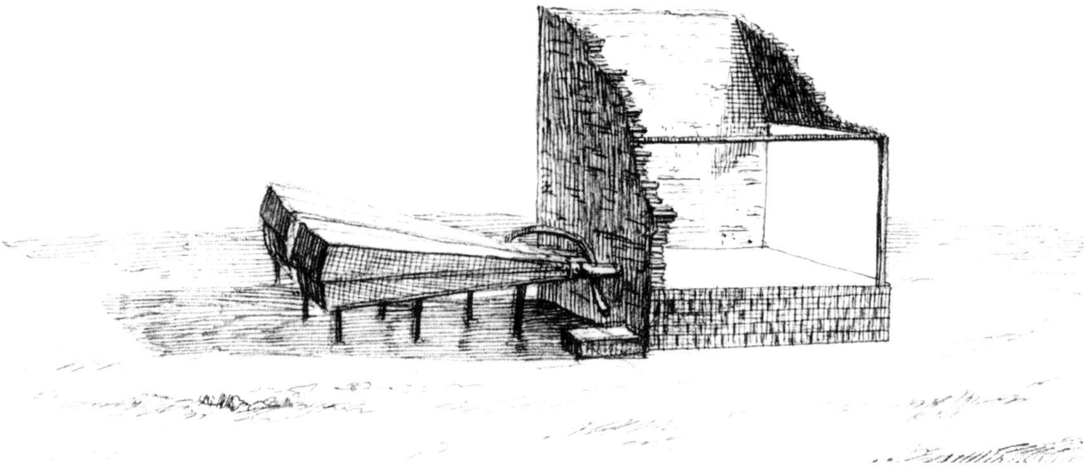

Fig. 276 Bellows and tuyere at Brockmill

The advantage of this arrangement is that the water cools the tuyere, which undoubtedly was made hollow at the outlet. I am quite certain of this, because I noticed that the water had become warm during its passage through the
306 tuyere.

For hoes, two pieces of iron are selected, 4 inches or 5 inches long depending on the size of the finished article, and in between them at one end a piece of steel is placed, whereupon the sandwich is welded together. One end, destined to become the socket, is forged down thin and cut. It is then bent and formed into a socket over an anvil. The other end is drawn down to a sheet of suitable thickness for the blade of the hoe and then forged and bent to shape in a die cut into the anvil. Finally, the hoe is trimmed even with a shear and hardened and ground. Two hands can forge two dozen hoes a day and, if they have been partly fabricated beforehand with the socket etc, they can make three dozen.

The wages are 9, 10 to 12 pence per dozen according to size. Sugar knives, which are called 'Sucherbis', cost 10 pence per dozen for one
307 kind and 12 pence per dozen for another type. Anvils for smithies are sold for 6 pence a pound, but the work is carried out at day rates.

Machine for making screws

Another machine for the cutting of all kinds of screws is locked in a cellar, where the work also is done. The method used is supposed to be very ingenious and is kept very secret.

In the absence of Mr 'Thornis', to whom the works belongs, I tried to bribe the workers to show me the machine, but they told me that it was locked in and that they had sworn to keep the invention secret, so that not even 100 guineas could induce them to reveal it. Subsequently I found out that the works formerly had been the property of an expert mechanic who had made himself poor through experimenting, and now lived a few miles away in a little town called 'Holland'.[226] I was also told that he there had built a very peculiar
windmill to his own designs and ideas. 30

I therefore went to Up-Holland, both to see the windmill and to find out what I could about the screw machine.

By telling that I had already seen such a machine and by asking questions, to which the answers could only be yes or no, I found out that the main secret is a very accurate master screw and nut controlling the dimensions of the screws and nuts that are made. The master screw is forge-welded[227] to the blanks for the former. Blanks, both for screws and nuts must be very accurately and finely turned. The piece of steel that performs the cutting must be very carefully fitted to the master screw and it is necessary to have several on hand to replace tools that become dull. The tool is placed in a hole made for the screw in a sleeve, and for the nuts it is fitted to a round bar of iron of a diameter proportioned to the size of the sleeve. The depth of each cut is 1 'lineas'[228] and, before the next cut, a piece of iron was placed
in the hole raising the steel. 30

The rotation was said to be achieved by a mechanism with cogwheels meshing with another wheel at the end of the screw machine.[229] A screw of 3 inches to 4 inches or up to 6 inches diameter can be made by this method within 4 to 5 hours. The price of the screws is 12 pence per pound.

Invention for putting bellows in motion

In addition to this invention, the above-mentioned man, whose name is Melin, had at Brockmill made a contrivance to drive five pairs of bellows from one waterwheel by means of flat rods. The workmen at each hearth could stop the bellows as often as they wished by pulling up a weight, and start them again as soon as the weight was released. The flat rods leading to one particular hearth were linked to another set of rods connected to a crank on the waterwheel shaft and so on. This involves a number of triangles and supports arranged in various ways. A neater and better construction could have been achieved if only triangles had been designed according to the change in the
direction of the bars. The English have so far 310
not had the right knowledge of these problems, which are so important in all design of power transmission equipment [Fig. 277].

Windmill invented by Mr Melin

The windmill, invented by the above-mentioned Mr Melin, is no longer kept secret either in England or in Holland, because he has obtained exclusive rights for 14 years in both places. He has already sold the rights to build his design of mill to two people living in the neighbourhood. One of them is Sir Rodger Brock, who already has used such a mill for several years for pumping water from one of his coal mines. The other person uses the design for a flourmill located some miles from here.

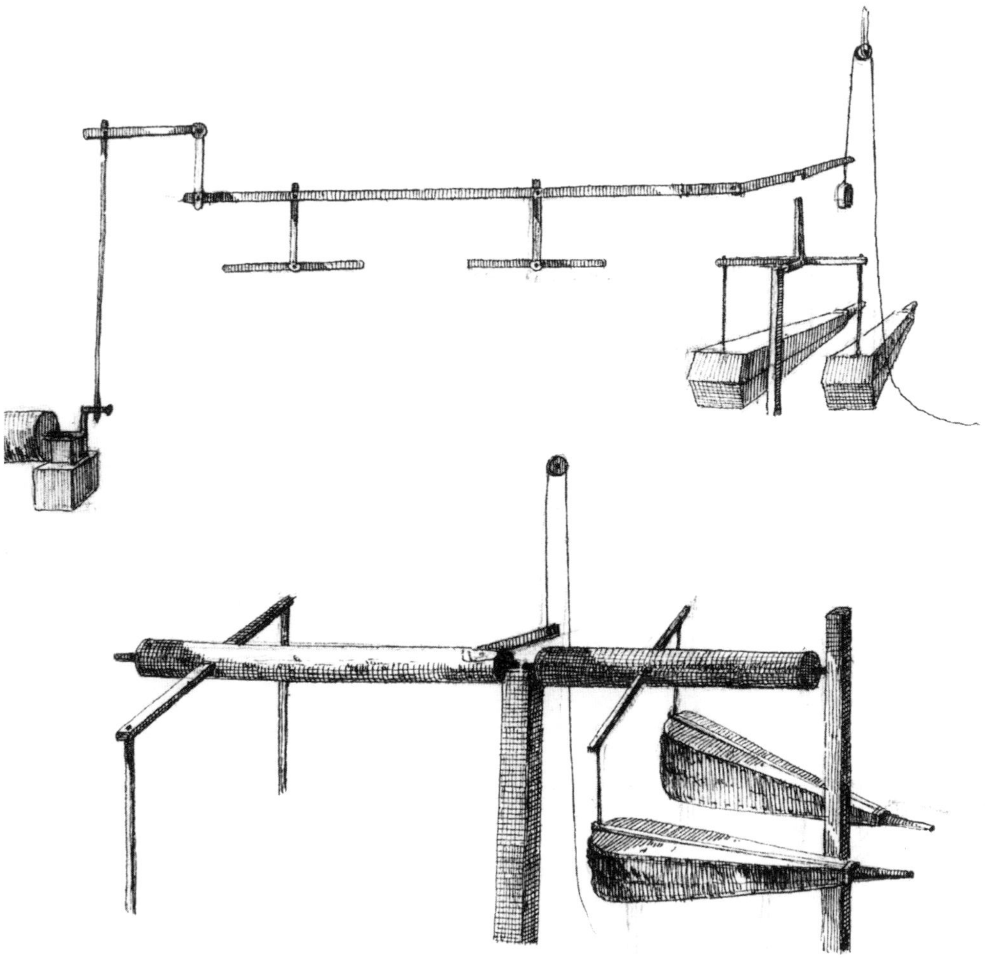

Fig. 277 Bellows-driving train

Fig. 278 Mr Melin's windmill

Each of them paid the inventor 20 guineas. The main part of the invention consists of a regulator, which not only causes the mill to turn into the wind, but also keeps the speed uniform both in strong and moderate winds.

The mill has eight sails as shown by the
311 appended drawing [Fig. 278].

Each sail is provided with at least eight panels made of thin boards, which can be closed by iron bars with weights hanging from them, but opened by stronger wind.

All the rods reach to the wind-shaft where they are attached to a rod, by means of chains running over pulleys, which can move lengthwise inside the hollow wind-shaft. The opposite end of the latter rod is connected to a chain by means of a swivel, the other end of which is wound around a horizontal drum mounted on gudgeon pins. A quadrant fitted to the drum carries another chain with the weight on the end, as shown by drawing no. 279a.

The governor, which controls the position of the sails in relation to the direction of the wind, is a set of smaller sails that rotate on a shaft at right angles to the wind shaft proper. The fantail, or wheel with small sails, can move in either direction and its movement is by means of gears that transfer the movement to a track wheel,
which can operate backwards or forwards and is 31
fitted to the poles that move the cap.

As long as there is a good wind for the sails, the fantail stands behind the mill in the lee of the tower but, as the wind turns, it starts rotating and winds the sails back into the wind.

The mill built by the coal mine only had four sails. As the crank for the flat rods prevented the striking rod from passing out through a hollow gudgeon pin at the end of the wind shaft, holes had been made in the shaft, through which bars fixed to the rod projected. These bars supported an iron ring pressing against a hinged frame of iron, which supported the weight as shown by drawing no. 279b. This arrangement could be simplified by placing the crank on a separate shaft geared to the wind shaft. The driving gear on the wind shaft as well as the gudgeon would have to be provided with holes at the centre to let the striking bar through. Another way to simplify the design would be to use springs mounted inside the hollow wind shaft instead of
313 a weight.

Description of the coal seams at Wigan and discussion regarding their genesis, etc

During my stay in Wigan I went to see the so-called cannel pits that are located about a mile away, but were formerly also worked in the town itself. The properties of this cannel coal and the difference between it and ordinary mineral coal have already been mentioned, but here there is still space to add that both originated from trees and forests which, during some change in the position of the Poles of the Earth, were flooded by the sea and then buried in sand and clay, which both are products of the sea. Many aeons and eras then passed before the wood reached the point where it could decay, ferment and catch fire under the water [sic], after which it gained the nature of bituminous and mineral-containing vapour able to attract similar or different matter occurring in nature.

The same is true for the various layers of 314
different kinds of stone that separate the coal seams to a greater or lesser extent. A small grain of sand has been sufficient to start a seam of quartz many fathoms thick. Similarly, a thin film of clay or soil will have been the germ and origin of strata of clay and soil, which, under the influence of pervading mineral vapours, have gradually been made hard and stone-like.

There is no better proof of what has been said above than the charcoal found in many seams of mineral coal and the evenly distributed

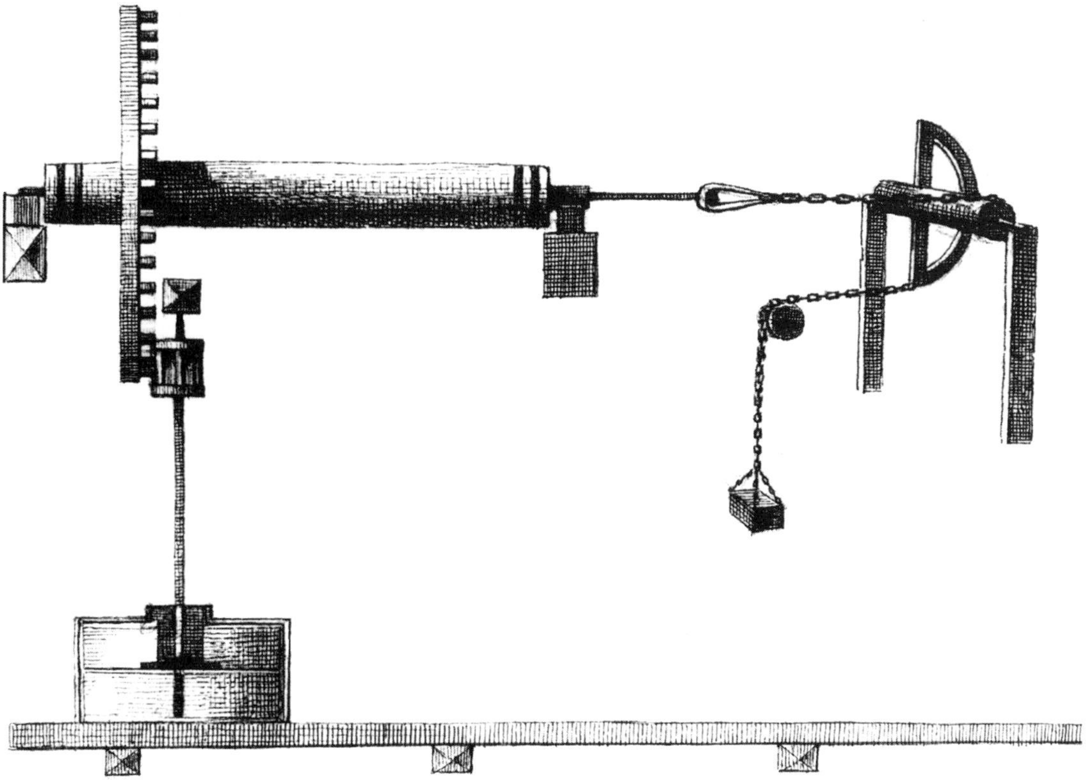

Fig. 279a Details of sail-adjusting mechanism

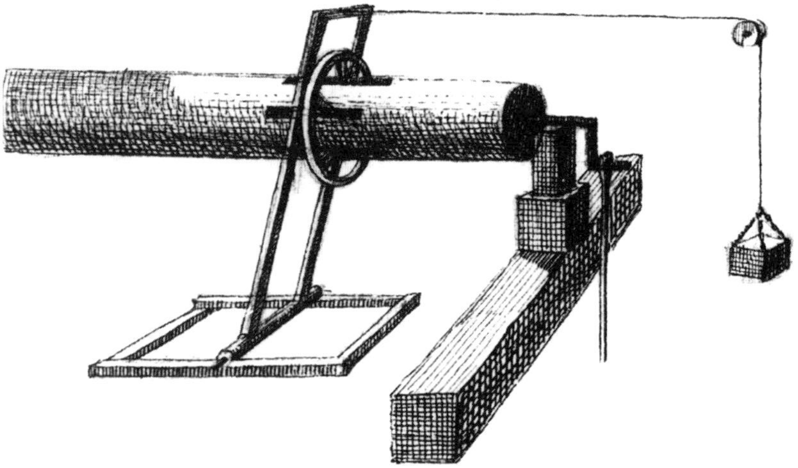

Fig. 279b Details of striking gear

veins of stone that lie between them, in spite of the fact that the mines in which they are observed may be separated by several miles.

… or the black shale which carries imprints of twigs, roots, trees and many kinds of flower.

… or the clay-coloured iron ore, impregnated with fine mussel shells and vegetable matter that is sometimes found broken into pieces and upended to a height of several fathoms, without the existence of any disturbance of the younger
315 strata and seams.

… or the many fractures and disturbances that occur in the bowels of the Earth, whilst the position of the coal seams in relation to each other and to the rock strata that divide them remains unchanged.

… or cracks and crevices, caused by disturbances, but later filled and grown over, not by earth or extraneous types of stone, but with the material which grows and dominates in the surrounding rock.

The sum of all of this, and each paragraph considered separately, shows clearly how rocks, minerals and fossils have originated and the consequence thereof, namely the growth and increase of the Earth, and neither Pythagoreans nor others with their fairy-tales can obscure the light it throws.

In the beginning of this section it was mentioned that cannel coal has its origin in charred forests that, during some flood, were immersed and buried below the surface of the earth, but it is difficult to find anything to prove
316 this contention when the cannel coal is studied in isolation, without considering the overlying types of rock strata and coal seams, because the cannel coal shows no traces of charcoal and there are no imprints of vegetable matter near the seams. To show this more clearly, I wish to note down all the different types of rocks that occur on the way down to a cannel seam [Fig. 280].

As far as the thickness of the overlying top soil and marl is concerned, it depends both on the type of soil that occurs and on how many alterations it has been subjected to due to floods, agriculture, drainage and other activities of both man and beast. Letter **B** is a hard, sand-like rock, which I call the old because, like the topsoil and marl, it does not have a uniform thickness but has most likely been thrown up by
the waves of the sea. 317

Letters **C** and **D** are both uniform and their thickness varies very little in distances of a mile or more. Letter **E**, or the so-called blackbast, is a type of rock consisting of mixed clay and sand, impregnated with a finely distributed bituminous vapour, originating partly from the adjoining coal seam and partly from other bituminous substances.

F is a thin coal seam that is assumed to have been attached to the coal seam letter **L**, which in its turn has adjoined the seams **O**, **Z** and **S**.

The reasons why I believe this are:

1) A number of coal mines at Newcastle, with cannel and ordinary mineral coal mixed.
2) The clay-like seams of iron ore impregnated with seashells, that often are fractured and raised on end together with the growing strata of sand, earth or coal.
3) The uniform bands of these seams continue from **B**, which is the rock crust, to the furthest

Fig. 280 Cannel-coal pit, shaft and rock strata [letters missing]

318 depth that so far has been reached in a coal mine. This could never have originated from sedimentation and cementation in the sea, because many marine plants would then be found in it, occasionally found in the top rock crust and also in the scattered seams of iron ore. It is also impossible that a surging sea could have deposited such uniformly parallel layers of many kinds of rock, and even less possible that a deluge or a sudden flood of water could have been the cause. That which is done with violence and surprise could never result in such a regular and orderly product, neither amongst the living nor amongst the dead materials of nature. Doctor Woodward's thoughts regarding the disintegration of the earth during the great flood and the conservation of sea shells and other fossils that could impregnate the rocks when they solidified
again, are ridiculous, and only show the effect 319
of straining infallible natural history to the utmost in order to make it conform to the Scriptures and to the unfounded fancies of man.

4) I also adduce, as proof, that the strata of rock lying between the coal seams were still growing

and increasing; the sticky material that exists between each section or band of a coal seam; the soft, recently crystallised, grains of sand or quartz crystals; the parallel bands and streaks of different colours that occur in every seam etc, all of which makes one understand that this formation of crystals has taken place over many aeons and changes of weather. This has caused the crystallising liquid to be affected by the mineralised vapours present from time to time.

How the crystallisation can take place in the rock as well as in the cannel seams, under the weight of the overlying rocks many fathoms
320 high, or even miles high, can be explained by hydrostatic and pneumatic instruments. They show that the smallest tube of water that reaches any appreciable depth and then spreads out horizontally, is strong enough to shift mountains and that a gentle breeze working according to the same principle can lift a weight that manpower could not move.

That such veins of water do exist deep down, is well known to our colliers and miners, who must spend much money in drawing it up as otherwise it would submerge their place of working. They also know that the profound depths themselves produce vapour and gas, that could have the same and even a far worse result, as the miners at Whitehaven and Wigan, who so often experience its immense power when set alight and the deplorable effect it has on the weak human body, do not doubt.

5) In the same category belong 'Blackhaft' and
321 'Rooft', which are shown under Letters **e**, **h**, **n**, **p**, **r** and **t**. These types of rock are subject to being hardened to rock as well as containing inflammable material, because these two substances mix if the finely dispersed vapour of pitch, which originates at the surface of the coal seam **F**, and the concentrated mineral solution about to crystallise on the surface of the quartz vein **D**, are adjacent to one another.

6) The coal seams **F** and **D**, that everywhere are found to be impregnated with charcoal, are thinner than the cannel seam **f**, because the first deposit of pitch, attracted or generated when the charcoal first started to form, occurred at the bottom of the coal seam **I** but, as it subsequently became more solid than the charcoal, the bituminous substances have, according to the usual laws of attraction, collected in greater quantity at this location, which in due course has been separated from its
322 originators due to the intrusion of another stone-like material, creating the strata **k**, **l**, **m**, **n**.

7) Yet another cause of the growth of mineral coal and other types of stratified rocks that occur in between, as well as below and above the coal seams, can be deduced from the fact that when the old rock, Letter **B**, occasionally increases to a considerable thickness, resulting in a greater pressure on the growing coal seams and strata of stone, these are generally found to be thinner in proportion to the increase of the pressure.

What greater and more unequivocal proof of the growth of the above-mentioned types of coal and rock can one demand? If these seams and rocks had been the result of a hurried piece of work (and it does not appear that the Eternal Being had any particular reason for hurrying) and had been roughly fashioned and then put in their place, what power would subsequently 323
have been able to force them away from there or press them to a thinner shape? But, as they now are a creation of time, begotten and hatched by nature itself, we cannot only find the reason for it, but also venture to state that anything that does not agree with the course of nature is also incompatible with infinite wisdom of the laws of the Almighty.

There is so much more reason to believe that there are further coal seams below the cannel coal if only the colliers would try to go deeper, as these seams at Wigan, including the Blackbast and Rooft, all told do not reach to more than 21 feet in thickness, although at Wednesbury there is a seam 33 feet thick and in addition another seam above it 6 feet to 7 feet thick.

At the entrance to Sir Roger Brock's cannel pit, which lies further down than those mentioned above and about ½ mile away from 324
them, I enquired about the types of rock found there during the sinking of the shaft and found that they were practically the same as the ones described, only with the exception that Letter **B**, which I called the old rock, had run out at this place and also the soft kind of rock Letter **C**, so that shaft at the first went through top soil mixed with clay and some marl with a total thickness of about 12 feet. Below it the grit-stone, marked **D**, took over and here was said to be 45 feet thick, then followed 'blackbast', a little coal, 'whitlord', etc all the way down to the cannel in the order shown by the list. However, it was explained that here all the strata and seams of coal, stone and cannel coal, were a little thicker than at the previous place.

325 All the strata dip slightly south-east, about one in twenty. The dip is here called ebb. Fractures are often found as well as troubles or faults of $^{1}/_{2}$ yard, 1 yard and slightly more during the working of the cannel seam and in such cases all the overlying strata have sunk to the same extent. At the St Thomas cannel pit, the whole of the western side is said to have sunk down no less than 150 feet, here called fall.

Practically everywhere in this neighbourhood it was observed that the rock and coal strata, locally known as metals, from and including the old rock Letter **B** to the cannel seam Letter **f**, did not total more than 144 feet in thickness. To the north, where the top crust of stone for some reason increases to considerable heights, the thickness of the other strata decreases and the stone compresses to a few yards.

Chowbent, a small town and its nail trade

Four miles from Wigan lies a small town called Chowbent, which has considerable trade in nails
326 with Liverpool and in the town and its
surroundings there are estimated to be 300 nailers.

Most of the iron consumed comes down the river Irwell to Warrington. Mr Willington of Chowbent has a warehouse in Wigan, open every Friday. Iron for small and large nails is cut in a shear and sold for 19s.6d to 20s per cwt. A certain amount of Öregrund iron is also used here, essentially for horseshoe nails, for which the price is £22.10s per ton cut to size. According to Mr Collier, this amounts to 40 to 50 tons [per annum]. For his part, Mr Collier takes 10 [tons] and apart from him there are a number of others who deal in nails and supply iron to the smiths. One thousand horseshoe nails of English iron are sold for 2s while those of Öregrund iron fetch 3s.6d.

At [Up-] Holland and in various places along the way to Prescot and Liverpool, smiths were employed in making chains for slaves, sold from
$3^{1}/_{2}$d to $3^{3}/_{4}$d per pound. 327

For this purpose Swedish iron costing £18.10s to £19 is used. At Chowbent there are also a number of blacksmiths making hinges and chains or hoops for tubs.

Prescot, a small town, and its factories for pots and vessels and other wares

Prescot is a small market town 10 miles from Liverpool, which is noted mainly for its two potteries making mugs for drinking and for two others making larger earthenware pots and sugar moulds.

In the vicinity there are three kinds of clay, one bluish, which is refractory, one brownish red and a third more or less white. For drinking mugs, which here are thrown very thin, all three types of clay are mixed together, because the refractory kind is too brittle to be worked by itself [Fig. 281].

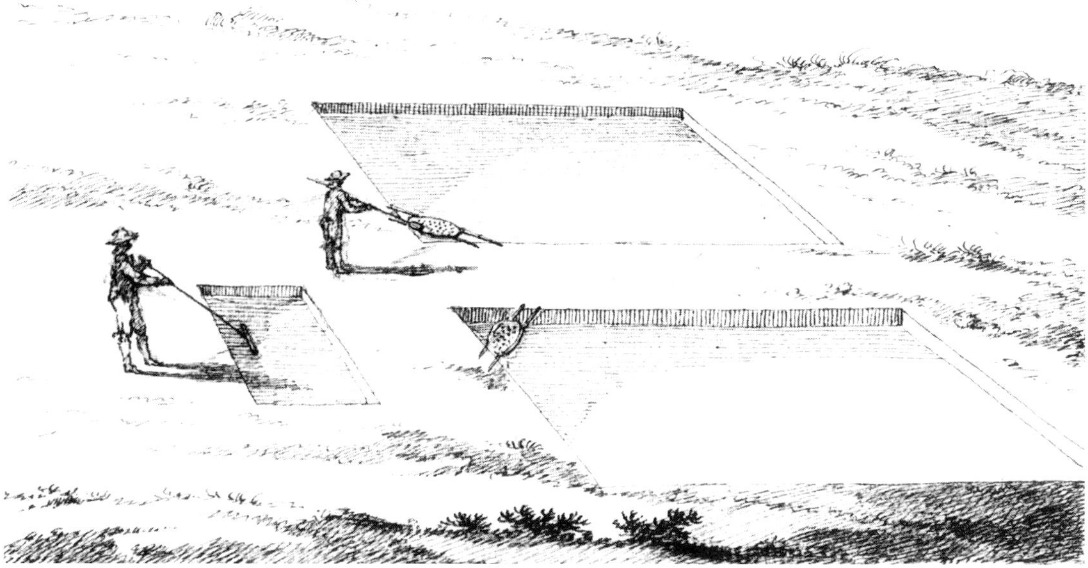

Fig. 281 Clay-mixing pits

The clays are first placed in a pit and stirred
328 up with water by means of a rake until they are dispersed. The clay water is then scooped out with a ladle and emptied into a large pond and at the same time sieved through a hair cloth. It remains in the pond for a few days until it is sufficiently dry to be suitable for throwing. The clay that has been prepared in this way dries very quickly, so that the thrower must have a boy helper who, with the aid of a pulley and cord, sets the potter's wheel in motion by cranking. Otherwise the wheel is constructed in the usual way [Fig. 283].

Quart mugs, holding a little more than a 'stop',[230] sell for 5 pence per half dozen; pint mugs sell for 9 pence per dozen; bottles sell for 9 pence per dozen; chamber pots sell for 9 pence per dozen.

The drinking mugs are brown and glazed with a mixture of galena and clay water.

Fig. 282 Pottery kiln at Prescot

The bottles are black to look like glass and are glazed with galena, magnesia and clay water.

The kilns for firing these products are constructed in the same way as the ones at
Chelsea and Bow, but here pit coal is used as 329
fuel and the firing continues for two days and two nights. All the pottery fired in this furnace is placed in 'Chapsels' or clay dishes that are then stacked one on top of the other until the furnace is full [Fig. 282].

In the pottery making the sugar moulds, the furnace is built in the same way as mentioned, but no 'Chapsels' were used for the firing of the larger-size earthenware vessels. The brownish red clay is used for this purpose and is well mixed and kneaded but it is neither dispersed in water nor sieved through hair cloth. During the throwing of the large vessels a boy is also employed to furnish the motive power by winding a crank. A sugar mould, 2 feet 3 inches in height and with a capacity of 10 gallons, sells for 7 pence. A smaller one, 1 foot 6 inches in height and 9 inches in diameter at the large end, is sold for 3 pence and one of 1 feet 3 inches in height for $2\frac{1}{2}$ pence. There are workers here who put hoops of hazel around them as soon as they come out from the kiln.
They are paid separately and get 3 pence per 330
dozen.

Moulds for sugar 'Candy' are made in the same way, but are closed at the top and have small holes at the sides. They are sold at the same price as the sugar moulds.

Tobacco pipes are also made at Prescot, of clay imported from Ireland. Pipes 1 foot 6 inches long sell for 2 shillings a gross. There is also a glass house here, specially equipped for window-glass and drinking glasses, but it is leased by the Stourbridge Company for £50 a year, only to prevent glass from being made. Otherwise the business in Prescot consists of cotton-spinning and stocking-weaving.

Most of the iron used here is forged to picks for the coal mines in the neighbourhood. For this purpose $1\frac{1}{4}$-inch square bars are the most suitable. They come from Liverpool and are mostly Swedish iron. The steeling is carried out with blister-steel.

The prices of iron were here:

Swedish	18–19s per 100 lb.	
English	$19\frac{1}{2}$–20s per 100 lb.	
Slit iron	21s per 100 lb.	331

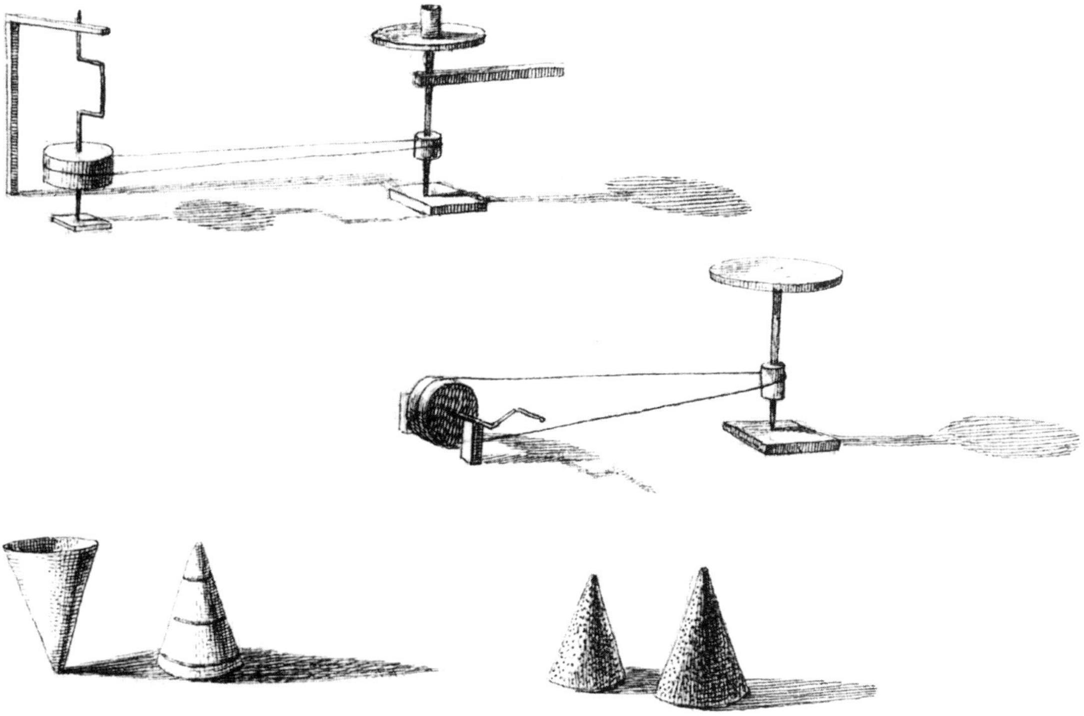

Fig. 283 Pottery wheels and sugar moulds

Burning of lime

At a number of places along the road there were kilns for burning lime. The limestone comes from a place several miles away by a canal that is dammed up. In the raw condition it is sold for 5 shillings a ton. With one load of coal, costing 2½ shillings in this district, it is possible to produce 40 measures, of which three make a horse load, weighing 180 lb and selling for 18 pence. Twelve score measures costing £6 are required for a field of 160 square 'Roots', where a 'Root' is 8 yards and a yard is 1½ alns and 3 'lineer'.[231]

Notes and references

177 This is not quite correct. The Petteril joins the Eden on the eastern outskirts of Carlisle whereas the Caldone does not join the Eden until about a mile further down the river as the crow flies.

178 The last two names are probably 'Spedding' and 'Jonah Robinson, Whitesmith', i.e. tinsmith.

179 In RRA's time ships could not reach Carlisle but had to dock and unload their cargo at Port Carlisle on the Solway Firth about 11 miles from the centre of the town. A canal from the port to Carlisle was built in 1823.

180 The stamp of the Rådenefors forge, located about 60 miles north of Gothenburg in the province of Älvsborg. It was established in 1725 and in operation until about 1880.

181 Thomas Hartley of Whitehaven.

182 According to J D Marshall and M Davies-Shiel, *The Industrial Archaeology of the Lake Counties* (Newton Abbot: David & Charles, 1969), pp.41, 250, 251, the furnace was located on the river Marron, ¾ mile south of the village of Little Clifton. It was established in 1723 and abandoned in 1781. The distances given by

RRA are not correct. They should be 4 miles and 13 miles respectively.

183 Sea coal would here not mean sea borne coal, but coal washed up on the shore from seams cropping out under the sea.

184 Advice to leave.

185 Presumably 1½ pence per lb.

186 £1 equalled 40 daler coppercoin.

187 This corresponds to 676 gallons per minute per engine or 340,560 gallons per hour.

188 This corresponds to 5° 40'.

189 The MS clearly gives '12 alns', equivalent to 24 feet, but this would be impossibly wide. Two alns or 4 feet would be more likely.

190 The steel mill shown by Fig. 266 appears to be a rather larger machine than others described in contemporary reports, although it still has the single wheel with a pinion to raise the speed familiar from the small portable ones.

191 No doubt RRA means the Royal Society.

192 This is one of RRA's London visits which does not appear in the fair copy MS.

193 Figure missing.

194 Figure missing.

195 These were large nails, known as strake nails, used to fix strake tyres to wooden wheels. Strake tyres were made in sections and not welded together to form a complete circle.

196 The Speddings were a well-known family of land and mining agents who served the Lowthers for several generations. The Spedding referred to here was probably Carlisle Spedding, 1695–1755.

197 *Vaccinium vitis-idaea.*

198 Lower Mill. On the modern 1-inch Ordnance Survey map there is such a place on the River Eden about 2 miles south of Egremont, and it is assumed that this is RRA's Lower Mill. So far no reference has been found to the iron mill here in the extensive literature on Lakeland industrial history.

199 See p.276.

200 Should be £9.14s.3d.

201 In view of this high cost it is surprising that the mill could be kept in operation.

202 A workman could not exist on 2 shillings a week, so the job appears to have been a part-time one. The requirements of pots would have been fairly substantial, however, because nearly 2000 pots with 63 lb in each would be needed for the indicated production of 40 tons a year.

203 Emanuel Swedenborg, born in Sweden 1688, died in London 1772, Swedish metallurgist, Government Official and founder of Swedenborgianism, a religious sect. He was a member of the Swedish Ministry of Mining and Metallurgy and held a fairly high position as indicated by his title Assessor. He describes a process, similar to the one mentioned above in his work *Opera Philosophica et Mineralia,* Swedish translation by Hjalmar Sjögren (1923), p.191.

204 I.e. a suitable reducing agent.

205 RRA here uses a Swedish word which means both quarrying and mining.

206 According to the modern 1-inch Ordnance Survey map, Whitrigg is located 3½ miles south-west of Ulverston, as the crow flies. By road the distance may well have been 5 miles in RRA's day.

207 Possibly Lord Montague.

208 The estuaries of the rivers Esk and Duddon.

209 This must refer to Morecambe Bay.

210 According to Schubert, *op. cit.*, p.382, the furnace was in operation 1747–1891.

211 The only one of the nine furnaces located in Westmoreland was Duddon Bridge; all the others were in Lancashire, unless the border between these counties has been altered since 1754. The first seven furnaces were within 8 to 9 miles of Ulverston, except Gunsey which is nearly 12 miles away.

212 The mark X has been left out, perhaps by the transcriber, but H R Schubert, *op.cit.*, gives the following information about the years when these furnaces were established and shut down:

	Established	*Shut Down*
1. Newland*	1747	1891
2. Penny Bridge*	1748	1780
3. Duddon Bridge	1736	1866
4. Nibthwaite	1736	*c.*1855
5. Low Wood*	1748	1798
6. Backbarrow	1711	196?
7. Gunsey	1711	1750
8. Leighton	1713	1806
9. Halton*	1756	1790

Those marked with * have been established within 12 years of RRA's visit in 1754. Halton furnace must have been established earlier than stated by Schubert.

213 Two small mistakes in the calculation of items 1 and 2 have been corrected – cost of pig iron and cost of coal. However, it is somewhat peculiar that the figure of 46 shillings a load or dozen has been used as the unit cost of the charcoal. This figure is similar to the unit cost paid at Maryport blast furnace, whereas RRA, only just above the summary of costs at Spark

Bridge, on p.290 has quoted 31 shillings and on p.291 37 shillings. If we assume that the unit cost of the charcoal is 37 shillings a dozen, then the coal cost per ton of bar iron will be £4.6s.4d instead of £5.7s.4d and the total cost per ton £16.0s.10d, instead of £17.1s.10d.

214 This is most likely one of the members of the Kendall family, which stemmed from Stourbridge. According to Alfred Fell, in *The Early Iron Industry of Furness and District* (reprint 1968), pp. 265–266, this family was connected with various iron works in the district, for example Gunsey and Duddon. However, Fell does not mention them in connection with Spark Bridge.

215 'Mr Ralisson' was probably one of the members of the Rawlinson family which, according to Schubert, was prominent in the iron industry of the Furness District during the sixteenth and seventeenth centuries.

216 'Chetton' might be a misspelling of Caton, 4 miles north-north-west of Lancaster and 2 miles east of Halton, where there was a blast furnace. See p.290.

217 Delft ware is, of course, not porcelain but earthenware. However, in Swedish, all ceramic ware is called porcelain.

218 It is not clear what salts RRA expected to be extracted from the atmosphere.

219 Ruth must be RRA's version of 'rood', 5½ yards, though how this could be related to 4 square fathoms is not clear.

220 According to J J Bagley, *Lancashire* (Batsford, 1972), p.180, 'At Wardleys, near Hambleton on the north bank of the Nyre, there can still be seen remnants of quays and of the large and commodious warehouse which, according to Edward Baines's Directory of 1825, the principal manufacturers of Kirkham kept for the reception of flax and tallow from the Baltic. Wardleys, like Skippool, was part of Poulton but, from the first years of Victoria's reign, both have been completely overshadowed by Fleetwood, a nineteenth-century new town.'

221 It has not been possible to trace this name on the Ordnance Survey map.

222 The Swedish word used by RRA can mean either going shooting or riding to hounds. It is assumed that he is referring to the latter.

223 RRA spells Brockmill 'Brackmill' and Birkacre 'Backaker', but there can be no doubt about their identity. Brockmill can be found on the original 1-inch Ordnance Survey map on the River Douglas. Birkacre is shown on the River Yarrow, about 2 miles south-west of Chorley, both on the original and on the latest edition of the 1-inch OS map. The two forges are mentioned by Owen Ashmore in *The Industrial Archaeology of Lancaster* (1969), and he also mentions a Burgh forge near Birkacre, which might be RRA's Barth forge. Alan Birch in his article, 'The Haigh Iron Works, 1789–1856', *The Bulletin of the John Rylands Library*, Vol. 35 (1952), pp. 316–333, states that the Brock Mill forge became part of an integrated concern called the Haig Iron Works, when it was formed in 1789.

224 Chowbent, formerly a separate village, has long since been swallowed up by Atherton, east of Wigan.

225 The use of different makes of wrought iron for different parts of heavy forgings was well known. RRA gives several examples.

226 Up-Holland, about 6 miles west of Wigan.

227 It appears unlikely that forge welding could have been used, because serious distortion problems would have been encountered.

228 1/12 inch (see note 108), implying that the machine was for cutting large screws.

229 RRA saw similar machines in operation later on during his journey and found that couplings were employed. See Vol. 2 pp. 403–406. No mention is made of the motive power.

230 RRA probably means a Swedish 'stop', which was equal to 1.3 litres. An English stop could be a gill, pint or quart, the last mentioned equal to 1.13 litres.

231 'Roots' must be rods, although a rod is usually 5½ yards. There are indeed just over 1½ Swedish alns to a yard, although the difference is a little more than the 3 'lineer' or ½ inch mentioned.

Journey 6e Liverpool to London

Liverpool, Warrington, Northwich, Chester, Holywell, Wrexham, Ellesmere, Shrewsbury, Coalbrookdale, Newport, Eccleshall, Newcastle under Lyme, Bilston, Wednesbury, Stowe, Winslow, Wendover, London.

Liverpool seaport, its factories, trade and shipping

Liverpool is located in Lancashire on the east side of the river Mersey, only 3 miles from the sea. It is one of the most flourishing ports in England, and trades particularly with West India and with the African coasts. Sugar, muscovado or raw sugar, tobacco, tar, pig iron, etc, are imported from various ports in America, and generally paid for by deliveries of English
332 manufactures.

20,000 to 30,000 slaves are brought from Africa[232] and some gold. These imports are paid for with East Indian cloth, thin English cotton and linen products, hats, Venetian glass pearls, voyage iron,[233] brass-dishes and kettles, guns, gunpowder, swords and knives. The slaves are, in due course, sold in America, mostly for cash.

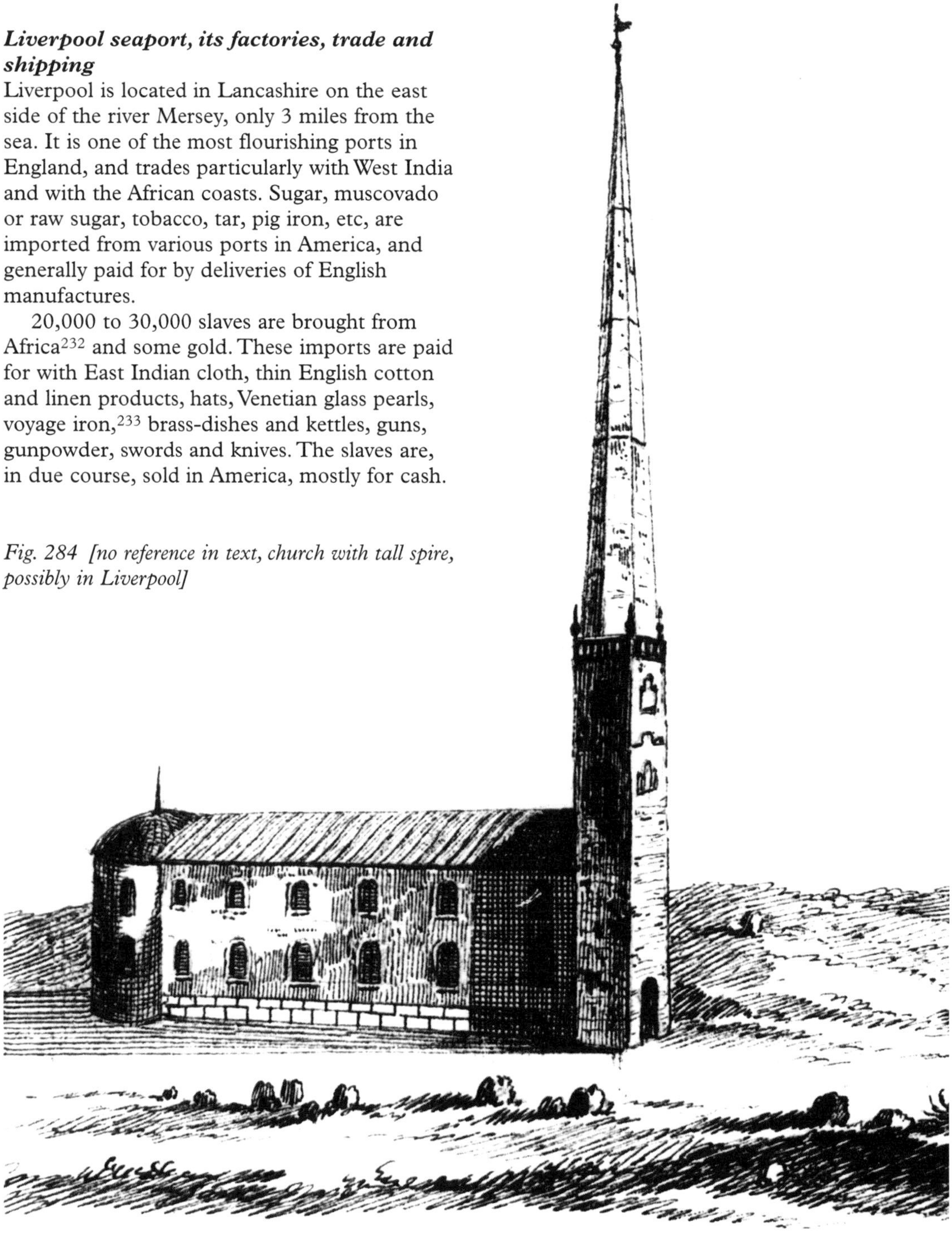

Fig. 284 [no reference in text, church with tall spire, possibly in Liverpool]

Some ships also sail to Livorno and other Italian ports and to Russia, where manufactured goods are exchanged for hemp, iron and timber.

Ships are sent to Sweden to fetch iron. Voyage iron, used for the African trade, is most in demand and nowadays costs £20.0s.0d, £20.10s.0d to £21.10s.0d, depending on the supplies available when the ships for Africa are loading their cargo. This iron comes in 5½-foot lengths and is 1½ inches wide and about 2½ 'lin.'[234] thick and there are about 350 bars to a ton. Of other ordinary iron there are 40 bars to
33 a ton, of narrow flats 50 bars to a ton.[235] The latter is used for wheel tyres and for horseshoes and other small forgings and now sells for £17.10s.0d to £18.0s.0d a ton.

Messrs Cunliffe and Sons are nowadays the largest merchants here, and import iron both from Stockholm and Gothenburg. In the former town they deal with Messrs Finlay and Jennings and in the latter with Mr Gerhard.

The customs duty on foreign iron amounts to 48 shillings and 6 pence[236] and 10 shillings more if it arrives in a foreign ship or a total of £2.18s.6d. If the iron is exported again the exporter receives a drawback of the duty paid less 3 shillings and 6 pence, which is half of the so-called subsidy.

'Mr Frahtard' trades with Messrs Vincent and Beckman in Gothenburg and has recently received 20 tons of iron on consignment from Mr Hoppenstedt in Kalmar.[237] This iron is cold short and sells for £17.0s.0d per ton.

34 In this place the iron from Gothenberg is considered better than that from Stockholm.[238] The latter is mostly cold short, whereas the former is soft and dense.

An account of goods imported to Liverpool from 10 October, 1753 to 10 October, 1754

Iron from	No. of bars	Ton[239]
Sweden	59,184	955
Russia	17,132	379
Spain	1,025	30
Total		1364

Iron exported from Liverpool in the same year

To	Ton
Africa, bar iron	329
Africa, wrought iron	160
To America, wrought iron	77
Total	566

Diversified goods exported from Liverpool in the same year

To	Ton	
Africa, pewter	19	
Wrought brass	15	
Wrought copper	15	
Lead	3	
America, wrought copper	4	335
Wrought pewter	5	
Wrought tin	1	
Wrought brass	3	
Lead	10	
Portugal, wrought lead	242	
Holland, wrought lead	175	
Italy, wrought lead	137	
Sweden, wrought lead	21	

There are in Liverpool five sugar factories, ten potteries for earthenware or so-called Delft ware, six factories for tobacco pipes, four glass-houses, of which only three were in operation, ten tobacco factories making roll tobacco and 'Cardus',[240] four salt pans, two anchor forges, a sail-cloth factory and a large number of saddlers and shoemakers working on goods for export. For all leather goods worked up for export the Government pays a bounty of 1½ pence for 336 each £ paid out for leather. There are also several distilleries for spirits and breweries as well as tar distilleries, stocking looms, silk-mills, gunsmiths and 'Pingon Vine draver' [sic].[241]

The sugar that is refined is not only for sale within the country but also for export to America.

Earthenware factory in Liverpool

The Delft or earthenware potteries sell most of their production for export to America [Fig. 285]. Ordinary plates sell for 3 shillings a dozen, and similar plates of somewhat better quality and painted for 5 shillings. Samples of these and other products of this factory were purchased.

Prices of Delft ware

	Shillings per dozen
Chocolate cups	1s.6d
Saucers for the above	1s.6d
Ornamental tiles for ovens, etc, 5 inches square, according to painting	from 1½ to 3½
Plates	3 and 5

There is a discount of 5 per cent for cash payment. There is no drawback or customs duty when these wares are exported. 337

Fig. 285 Pottery kiln at Liverpool

The raw material for this earthenware is clay of two different kinds: one that is white and comes from Ireland, and another reddish one, found a few miles from Liverpool. The two kinds are mixed in equal proportions and placed in a large vat where they are stirred and dispersed in water. The slurry is subsequently scooped up, sieved through hair cloth and emptied into shallow ponds in the same way as described at Prescot. The kiln is constructed according to the method used at Delft. It is fired both with wood and peat. The former is mainly birch and costs 10 shillings a cord, the latter is purchased by volume and costs 6 pence for half a bucket. Several of these potteries have attempted to make porcelain using white quartz and pipe clay as raw materials, but without success. However, one of the workers has recently found a way of glazing the so-called white ware, which one pottery intends putting into production.

White ware is made in Staffordshire, the raw material consisting of half pipe clay and half flint, but there it is glazed with salt which is difficult and cannot be painted. 33

The tobacco factories at Liverpool

At the tobacco factories they spin Virginia leaf after the normal fashion, but somewhat thinner and in large rolls. And at the rolling stage they add a 'sauce', consisting of ....[242] to prevent rotting. When the rolls are put in the press they are wrapped in sackcloth and sail twine and placed on end. All nuts and bolts in the presses are made of iron. The price for tobacco is $3\frac{1}{2}$ to 4d per pound, and for cartridges 4d to $4\frac{1}{2}$d per pound.

For slicing cartridge tobacco a machine is used, as shown in the drawing, operated by a

Fig. 286 Tobacco-slicing machine

Fig. 287 Glass furnace with calcining oven; Pipe kiln; Press for pipe moulds [letters missing]

strong man. Every time the knife is raised the leaves, pressed together in a box, are moved 2 to 3 'linar'[243] further in under the knife [Fig 286].

Glass-houses at Liverpool

Of the 4 glass-houses existing in Liverpool only two are in operation and they make bottles and drinking glasses. The design of the furnaces and
339 the way of working, the composition of the glass, the prices etc were discussed previously at Bristol. The only difference here is that the cooling oven is attached to the glass furnace itself, which is common in Sweden, but the flame does not enter it. Instead it is heated from a calcining furnace built underneath it. See drawing no. 287, letters a, b.

Pipe factories in Liverpool

There are six factories for tobacco pipes in Liverpool, obtaining their clay from Bettisford and Poole in the south of England. Pipe clay is also said to be found on the Isle of Wight. The pipes are sold for 9 pence to 30 pence per gross. The wages are also paid per gross and amount to 4 to 12 pence. In addition the kiln master gets 1 penny per gross.

The kiln is built in accordance with the attached drawing no. 287 and can hold 40 gross at a time. It is fired with pit coal in six little fireplaces around the periphery and the firing is carried on for 24 hours.

As far as the shaping of the pipes is
concerned, nothing special was noted, except 340
that the mould was split into two parts and when these were screwed together the bowl was also pressed. See Fig. 287. It should, however, be noted that the outlet hole at the bottom of the bowl was made by hand. The moulds for the pipes are made in Chester of iron and cost 18 to 20 shillings for the two halves.

Salt-boiling in Liverpool

The salt pans in Liverpool are constructed in the same way as at the Droitwich salt wells in the neighbourhood of Worcester, with the chimney going through the drying room horizontally before it turns up vertically to take away the smoke.

The pans are 16 feet long, 10 feet wide and 12 inches deep. They are not stayed with thick iron bars as noted at Shields and Whitehaven, but the plates overlap and are very well riveted. The firing is carried out with pit coal and 12 pans per week are evaporated producing all together $8\frac{1}{2}$ to 9 tons of salt.

A bushel of salt, which is 56 lb, is charged with excise duty of 3 shillings and 2 pence in Shields, but here the excise is 3 shillings and 2 pence for 68 lb rock salt, payable as soon as it 34
is dispatched from the salt mines at Northwich and Winsford, that lie 30 miles further up in the country, but can send the salt down the river to Liverpool.

At each salt pan there are two salt boilers, who are paid 7 shillings a week as well as 12 lb 'overweight' which the Crown allows for impurities contained in the salt which are lost during refining. One bushel of refined salt is sold for 3 shillings and 6 pence, but to strangers for 4 pence only, although it was said that the price for strangers now had been raised to 5 pence and that the largest consumption of salt is in Ireland followed by 'Narven' and Russia.

The refining of salt at Liverpool consists of dissolving the rock salt in tanks, emptying the solution into other tanks where it is clarified and finally pumping it to the salt pans for the boiling.

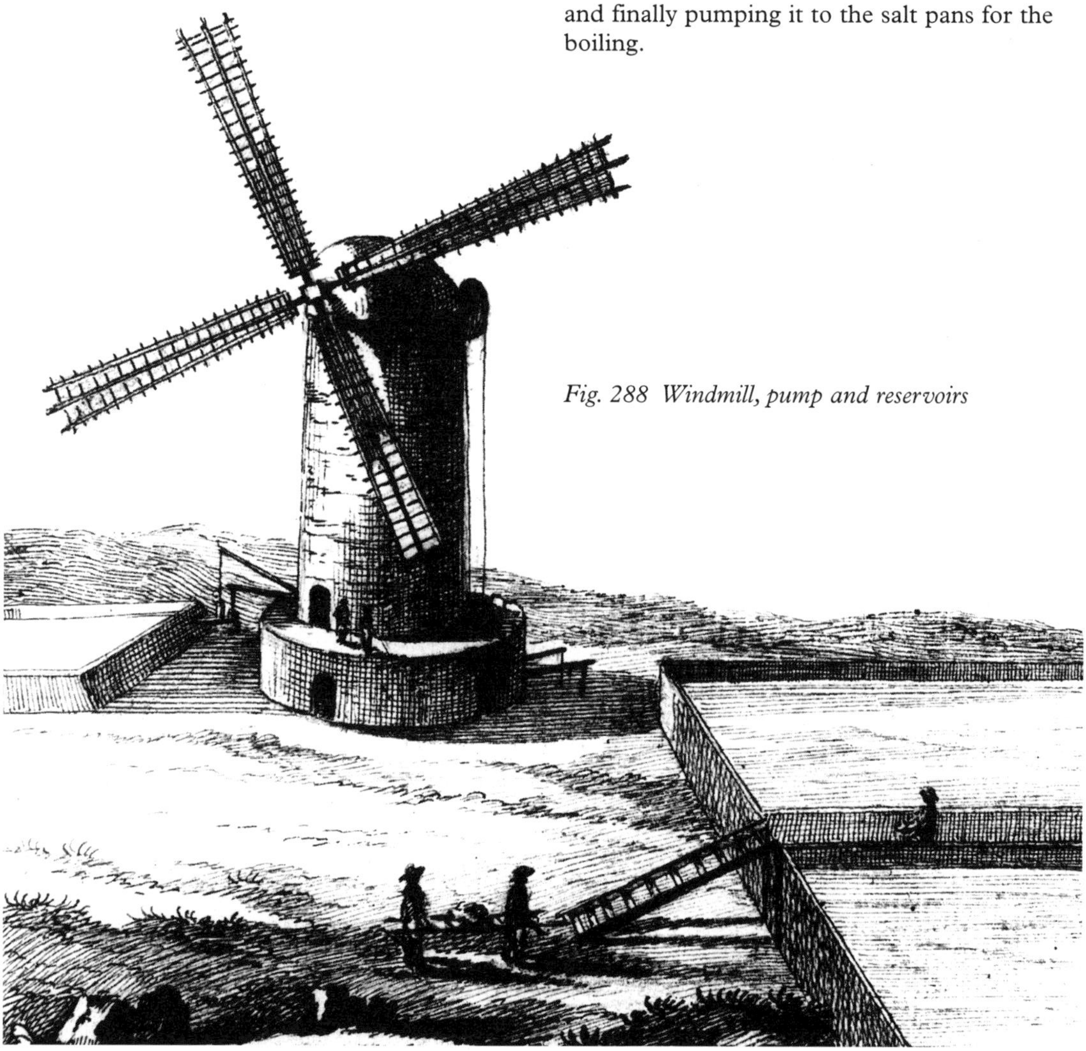

Fig. 288 Windmill, pump and reservoirs

42 The salt is removed from the pans as it crystallises during the boiling. When larger crystals are to be made, the temperature is lowered towards the end to cut down the rate of evaporation. Ox blood is added to the salt solution at the beginning of each boiling, but the workers said they can also make fine white salt without the blood.

The salt pans belonged to Mr 'Blechford', who has had a windmill built just beside them that grinds and sieves flour, and also pumps water up into the high reservoirs when required. A vertical shaft reaches right down to the bottom of the mill above the water pumps by means of gearing. A screw moved the gear wheel on the crankshaft back and forth to engage or disengage the wheel on the vertical shaft [Fig. 288].

The forging of anchors in Liverpool

Gothenburg iron is used in the anchor forges, except for the flukes, which are purchased roughly forged to shape from English mills. Finished anchors are sold by the hundredweight. The price is 30 shillings and 4 pence,
43 and lower for smaller ones.

Tar distillation in Liverpool

Amongst the distilleries, of which there are many that work for the American and African markets, there is also one that distils various liquids and oils from tar. These products are sold in half quart[244] bottles and are labelled with name and price. To sell the bottles faster, a printed piece of paper is pasted on each one stating the properties of the contents and extolling their medicinal virtues. The latter had most likely been dreamt up by the manufacturer himself. I purchased double samples of these products and had them packed in a box and sent to London.

The work of the gunsmiths consists mainly of fitting butts to and finishing guns, as has already been noted at Bristol. From Bristol samples of guns with their prices were sent to Stockholm. Gun barrels, locks and other parts come from Birmingham. 344

Factory for watchmaker's tools in Liverpool

Mr Dan. Mather, pinion wire drawer,[245] lives in the park a mile from Liverpool. He makes all kinds of steel hardware required for a watchmaker's shop and particularly a kind of grooved steel wire for pinions in small pocket watches. This pinion wire is from No. 1 gauge down to No. 4 gauge in diameter. It is grooved in a number of different patterns with 5 to 12 grooves and sold by the foot.

The raw material for the pinion wire is Mr Bertram's Double Shear Steel costing 6

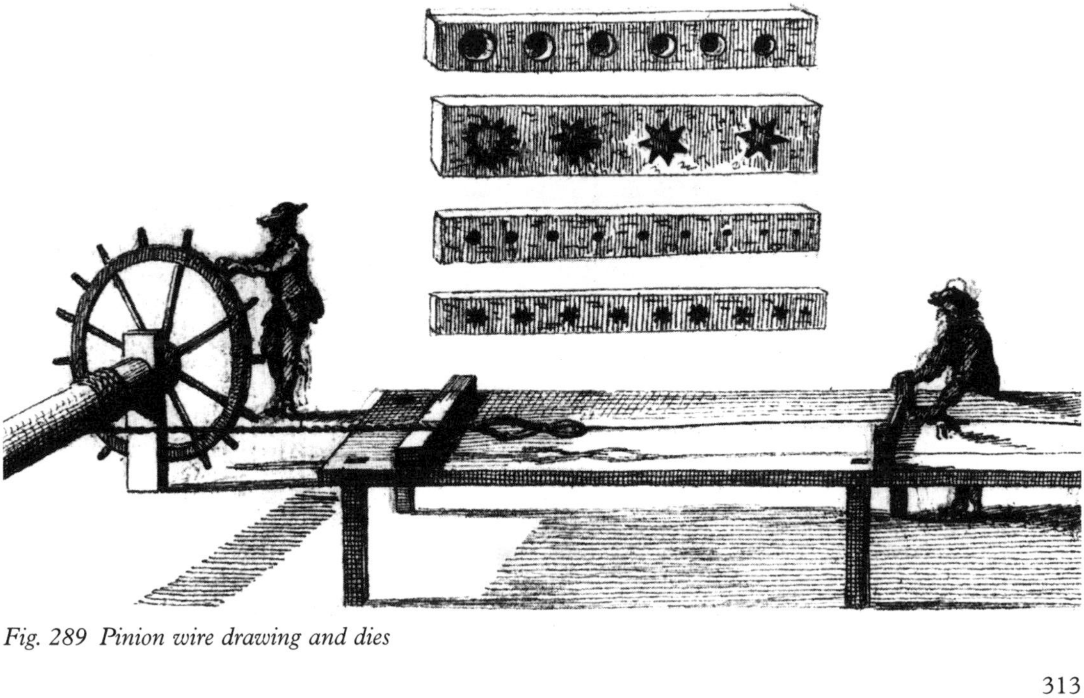

Fig. 289 Pinion wire drawing and dies

pence a lb. However, the whole consumption does not exceed 10 to 12 hundredweight a year or a little more than half a ton. The steel is first drawn down under the hammer to thin bars that are subsequently cold-drawn to round wires of the diameter required for the pinion-wire that is to be made.

Drawing is then continued through dies with shallow grooves and through further dies with grooves of increasing depth until the wire is finished. During drawing, which is carried out by the machine shown by drawing no. 289, the wire is well lubricated with oil and when completed is scoured with finely crushed forge
345 cinder and woollen and linen rags. Finally it is cut by filing into lengths of 1 foot and 1 feet 6 inches and 3 feet.

The same Mr Mather also has workers making tongs, pliers, wires, small hammers and other tools for watchmakers, which he claims to be the best in England. Samples and prices have been sent to London.

Information regarding American iron-works

During my stay in Liverpool I obtained some information about American Ironworks from 'Mr Frastard', who recently was there and saw the Potaxan works in Maryland, owned by Mr Richard Smoyden. At this place there are two smelting furnaces and three forges and the ore is obtained in the neighbourhood. The forests of oak and fir are abundant and the work is carried out by 120 Negroes, supervised by a few Europeans. A good slave costs 30 to 40 guineas.

The works lies 10 miles from a navigable river called the Potaxan. Some of the pig iron is sent to Liverpool where it is sold for £6.10s.0d
to £7.0s.0d per ton. 34

In Pennsylvania, which is said to be a magnificent and fertile country, it is mainly Germans who work the mines, the blast furnaces and the forges. The production of both pig iron and bar iron is greater than in Maryland, but the forests are not so large because more of the land is cultivated.

Botanical remarks about water lilies

On the way to Warrington, which is located on the same river as Liverpool, but 18 miles higher up, it was observed that water lilies grew in a 10 or 12 year old clay or marl pit and it is questionable if this plant is found anywhere else in the whole of England. One must, therefore, ask from whence the water lilies have come, because it is well known that they do not grow on dry land and thus have not spread from the surrounding meadows.

The old tale that birds have brought seeds from Sweden or from some other country must also be treated with suspicion. However, it is

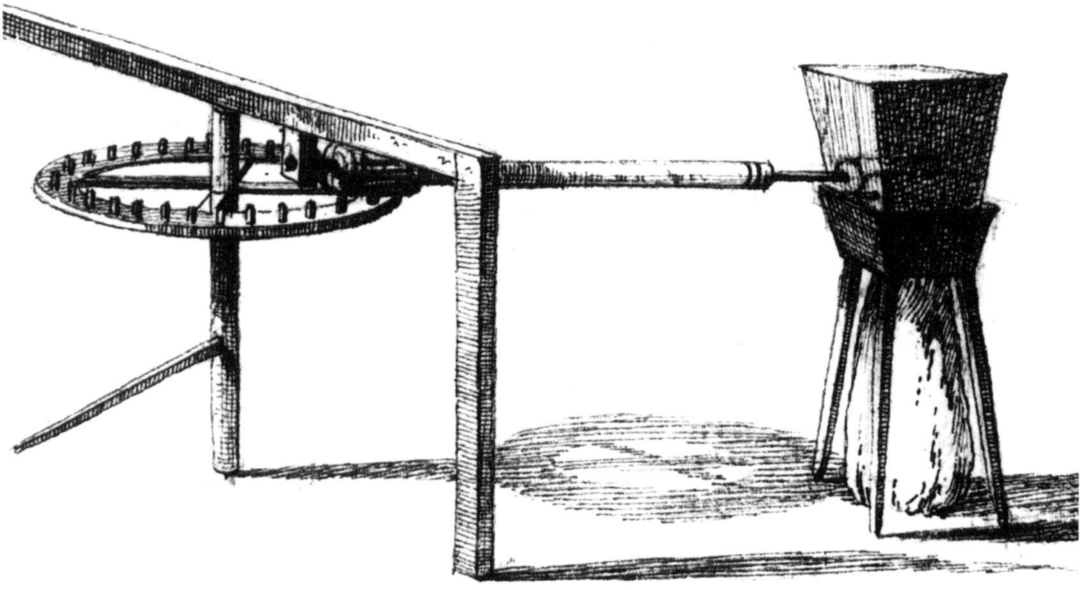

35

Fig. 290 Machine for rolling malt

nowadays more fashionable to hold somewhat
347 absurd ideas, than to believe that which experience clearly appears to show, namely that nature possesses an active power, not only to reproduce life and substances already known, but to create infinite numbers of new plants, animals and minerals, each in accordance with the various influences to which she has been subjected during the aeons of time when the earth has been moving nearer to or further away from the sun.

Sowing of wheat

The farmers in the district were now busy sowing wheat. The soil is made into beds, 4 feet wide and 1 feet 6 inches high, although the land otherwise is even and horizontal. Just before the sowing, the wheat is mixed with a few handfuls of lime in the same way as in Limousin in France, in order to prevent the black mould that otherwise might spoil much of the crop. Opinion here agrees that marl is better as fertiliser than lime, because it lasts much longer, but it does not produce as good yields as lime
348 can do on suitable soil. Around Liverpool the fields were fertilised with lime and ash from soap boiling in Ireland.

Rolling of malt

The machine, shown by drawing no. 290, for rolling malt, was seen at an Inn by the roadside. I was told that the work can be done faster with it, and costs less, and that the malt releases more of its flavour, than when the old type of malt-mill with grooves, which looks like a coffee-grinder, is used.

Coal mine

The Tarbock coal pit, belonging to Lord 'Minnelye', lies 2 miles from Prescot and has two coal seams, the first 12 feet thick at a depth of 162 feet, and the other one 17 feet 6 inches thick and at a depth of 225 feet. The seams dip south-east or as the miners there say, 11 o'clock. Waterwheels are used for drawing up the water, which runs off underground through adits. The coal is sold for 3 pence per hundredweight and is mixed
349 up with charcoal, which occasionally makes it soft and fragile.

The table below, listing the rock strata from the top to the lowest coal seam, shows that they are very similar to the ones found in the cannel pits at Wigan 13 or 14 miles away.

	Thickness in feet
Gritstone rock	18
Blue Flag, which has several thin seams of iron ore	144
Coal	12
Blue Flag	51
Blackbast	1½
Coal	5½

Gritstone is a light grey, sandstone-like rock and Blue flag is a bluish grey and clayey rock, containing some mica.

The town of Warrington its factories and trade in iron

Warrington is a fairly large commercial town that gets it supplies shipped up the river from Liverpool in shallow draught boats. Recently a sugar refinery has also been built here. The main industry is the manufacture of pins, which 350
keeps 10 workshops busy. The brass wire comes from Bristol and the price of the pins that are made is shown in the table below:

	Price of pins
Nr.99	20 pence a lb
88	20 pence a lb
1313	20 pence a lb
131313	20 pence a lb

Fig. 291 Wide wheel, showing double tyres

Fig. 292 Edge runner crusher for copper ore

Small pins, stuck on paper, are sold for 3 pence a paper. There are also a number of weavers producing sail-cloth and linen. Foreign iron for the requirements of the town and the surrounding countryside these days comes mainly from the merchants in Liverpool, and the consumption amounts to 250 tons a year. Some is also imported directly from Messrs. Arfridsson[246] and Gerhard in Gothenberg by Mr Barthon and Mr Worst.

Mr Tittly owns a slitting-mill, located 6 miles from the town, where mainly Russian iron is rolled and slit, when it can be had at a reasonable price, but this year it has been too
351 expensive and also in short supply.

Consumption of iron

Mr Barthon	80 ton
Mr Worst	60 ton
Mr Tittly for slitting	100 ton
Total	240 ton

Wheel-tyre iron $2\frac{3}{4}$ inches wide and $\frac{7}{8}$ inches thick, and for wide wheels $4\frac{1}{2}$ inches wide and $\frac{3}{8}$ inches thick is in demand and the sales are good in this town as well as almost everywhere else in England.

Of the latter size of iron, two bars side by side are used for the wide wheels, a total width of 9 inches. If the iron is slightly narrower than $4\frac{1}{2}$ inches, a small gap is left in the middle of the wheel between the two bars as shown by drawing no. 291. $2\frac{1}{2}$ inches wide iron is used for horseshoes and is slit in two for this purpose to $\frac{7}{8}$ inches and 1 inch square. $1\frac{1}{4}$ inches square is used for large nails to keep strake tyres in place and for fireplaces and grills in buildings and houses. $1\frac{1}{2}$ inches to 2 inches square is suitable for the picks used in the coal mines.

Tyre iron for sale in Lancashire should be $2\frac{3}{4}$ inches wide, $\frac{3}{4}$ inches thick and 9 feet long
or a little more. This iron costs 21 shillings per 352
hundredweight.

A wheelwright told me that his work would be much easier if he could obtain iron 9 inches wide and $\frac{1}{2}$ inch thick for the wide wheels. He was now trying to increase the width of Russian iron for this purpose.

In addition to the above mentioned merchants who sell iron in Warrington there is also a 'Mr Ask' from Chowbent, who keeps a stock of bar iron here and comes once a week to weigh out iron particularly for the nailers around Chowbent. He also sells 10 to 15 tons
of Öregrund iron, which he has had slit to thin 354
rods for horseshoe nails. It is supposed to cost £28 a ton when purchased from Mr Spooner in Birmingham.[247] The slit iron is sold for 23 to $23\frac{1}{2}$ shillings per hundredweight.

The Öregrund iron is said to be much in demand and the best possible raw material for horseshoe nails. The consumption could be far larger if the price were not so excessively high.

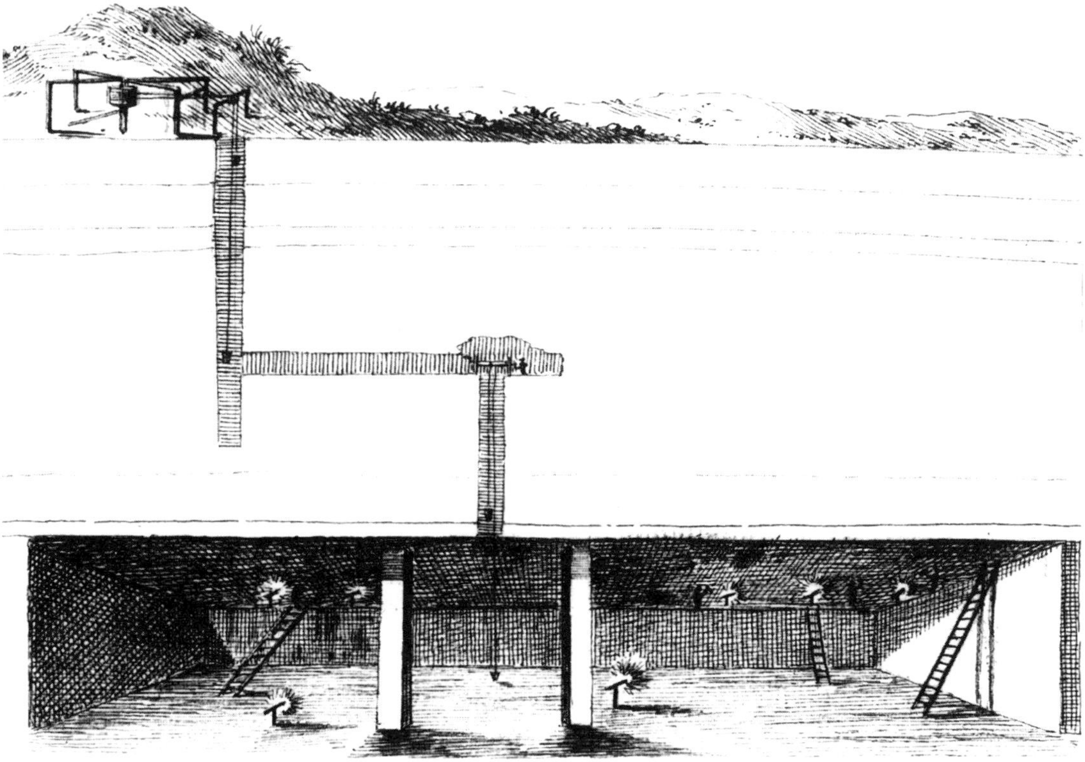

Fig. 294 Rock-salt mine at Northwich

Price of iron in Warrington

	Price per ton
English	£20.10s.0d
Russian	£21.0s.0d
Swedish, ordinary	£21.0s.0d
Swedish, Öregrund	£23.0s.0d

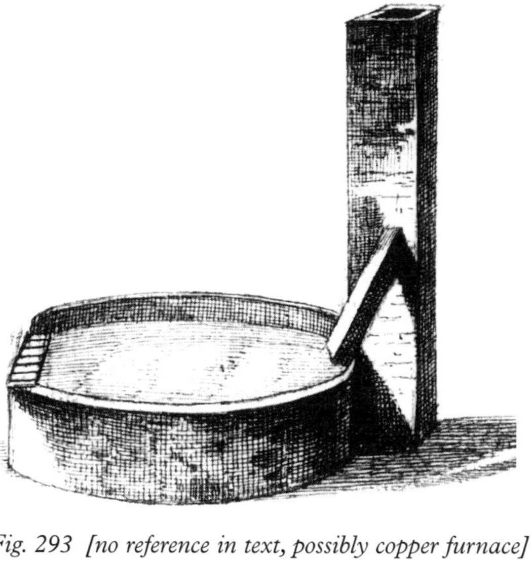

Fig. 293 [no reference in text, possibly copper furnace]

Cash payment is made immediately, but known and reliable customers are given 6 months credit.

Mr Patten's copperworks at Warrington

Just outside Warrington by the harbour there is a copperworks belonging to Mr Patten who has recently built a wonderful mansion nearby.[248] The smelting works consists of 12 wind furnaces, of which generally half are in operation. The ore comes from Cornwall, by the sea. Before the ore is charged into the furnaces it must be roasted or calcined, which, depending on the sulphur content, takes a longer or shorter time. The most common kind of ore, which costs
from £8 to £10 a ton to buy in Cornwall, is *354*
roasted for 12 hours before smelting, then crushed under a large stone, as shown by Fig. 292[249] and again roasted, this time for 18 hours. If the copper has not separated out, the sequence of roasting and smelting is repeated. The process does not in any way differ from that noted both in Bristol and Wales.[250] The refining is carried out by placing charcoal on the molten material in the wind furnace, as was observed previously at Vauxhall in London.[251]

The copper from here is sent to the brass mill at Cheadle in Staffordshire, which also belongs to Mr Patten and Co.[252]

The town of Northwich and salt mines

From Warrington our travels continued to Northwich, 16 miles away, where the famous rock-salt mines are located. Nine mines are now being worked on the same seam. I went down into the pit owned by Mr Antrobus, which is
355 189 feet deep, and found it very similar to the mines at Wieliczka in Poland, except that in Northwich the workings are less extensive and the miners not so numerous. A salt seam the depth of which so far is unknown is being mined here. Although in most places tunnels 9 fathoms or 18 yards high have been driven into the salt, the bottom has not been seen. Above the tunnels 12 feet to 15 feet of salt was left in place to support the overlying rock [see Fig. 294].

I was told that in one mine a hole had been bored to 60 feet below the present working floor, without exposing anything but the pure rock salt. There were 16 miners in this pit who hewed the salt from the walls with hacks and were paid 2 shillings and 6 pence a ton. When the salt has been raised to the surface it is sold at the shaft for 12 shillings a ton to those
356 who subsequently refine it. For this purpose about 63 salt pans have been installed.

The refiners pay the government 3 shillings and 2 pence for each 68 lb rock salt, which amounts to a large sum of money over a year. To make sure that no salt is removed from the mine without the duty being paid, a number of customs officers are stationed here. Anybody found with salt in his possession on which duty has not been paid, is fined £20 or given a corresponding gaol sentence, even if no more than a single pound of salt is involved.

A salt pan can boil 12 charges a week, each producing about 2¼ tons of salt. A bushel, which weighs 56 lb is sold for 2 shillings, but to foreigners for export, the price is only 7 pence.

Due to poor ventilation, the candles used by the miners to light their place of work can only burn when they are tilted over at an angle. There are always workers on the ground above who blow down air through wooden tubes by means of bellows.

The salt that is mined is generally reddish in
357 colour and mixed with clay, and it must, therefore, be refined before it is fit to use. Nevertheless, it does contain some lumps that are as clear and pure as the Polish rock salt.

Although this bed of salt now forms one solid mass, it is, nonetheless, possible to detect in it strata, that differ from each other in both colour and the amount of clay mixed in. It should also be mentioned that during the sinking of the shafts through the overlying blackbast rock, horizontal veins of salt are found. If these are studied in conjunction with the strata of the main salt-bed, they show quite unmistakably how it has grown over time from infiltration of salt and its crystallisation.

The salt pans around here do not refine rock salt in the way it is done in Liverpool and Droitwich, but boil salt solutions that are pumped from the shafts or from mines that have become flooded.

One bushel of salt is sold for 1 shilling 11
pence and is exported at a price of 7 pence a 358
bushel of 56 lb. in weight.

A method of salting hams

One way to salt a ham so that it keeps well and tastes well is to first cover it with muscovado sugar. One half to three quarters of a pound of this sugar is required for one ham, which is left in it for 24 hours, after which time the ham with the sugar is placed in a bag and a quarter pound of saltpetre added. Subsequently it is thoroughly rubbed with common salt and allowed to lie in it for 14 days. After this treatment it is hung up and will keep for several years, and both looks and tastes very appetising. If the ham can finally be smoked it tastes even better.

Farm management

The road from Northwich to Chester passed across several plains and uninhabited stretches of land used mainly for grazing of cattle, but in some places rabbits had been introduced and were looked after by the gentry in the neighbourhood.

I stayed overnight in a small town that had been burnt down a couple of years ago, but now had been pretty well rebuilt.

The farmer in this part of the country
fertilises and improves his fields and meadows 359
with marl, which is considered to have a more lasting effect than lime. Soil that has been well marled can grow corn for several years, and then be used as a meadow or for grazing cattle for the next 12 to 15 years. A farm hand is paid £5 a year, which is increased by £1 every year,

Fig. 295 Chester

as long as he works well, until £10 is reached. A boy who just has started to serve is paid 25 shillings and his food.

The town of Chester, its factories and trade

Chester is a very ancient town, which flourished in the days of the Romans and was strongly fortified. The town walls are still kept in repair and serve as pleasant promenades, from which there are glorious views up country as well as down the river towards the sea, 20 miles away. The surroundings show that Chester was formerly located by a wide bay of the sea, navigable right up to the walls of the town, but owing to the changes to which the earth is subjected from time to time, it is now very
360 difficult to sail up the river, even for small ships. However, a company has now undertaken to remedy this situation by dredging when the water is low. Almost all of the streets in the town have arcades and promenades as is usual in Padua and other Italian cities. The difference is that here the promenades are one storey up, while in Italy they are at street level. The latter gives the inhabitants the possibility of having their shops and stores in the promenades, which are called ...[253] [Fig. 295].

The main trade in this town is in cheese and lead, the latter made in Wales. At this time there was a market to which strangers could bring all kinds of goods free of duty. A glove hangs outside to signify that the market is free, but when it is taken in, strangers are no longer allowed to trade. Formerly this freedom lasted for 30 days, but now it barely lasts 14 days, and
for hats and gloves, that also are made here, the 361
market is only free for two days.

In Chester there are only two importers of iron, namely Mr Prescot and 'Mr Perchin', who with their ship loads of hemp and timber from Riga, Reval and St Petersburg generally also bring in 10 tons of Russian iron, which this year has been both scarce and expensive.
Mr Prescot, in addition, procures 40 to 50 tons of iron from Mr Gerhard in Gothenburg. The rest of the iron consumed in this district, not counting English iron, comes from Liverpool, but I was told that no more than 160 tons of foreign iron a year arrives in this town. This year only 20 tons of Russian iron has been received and no Swedish iron at all.

Price of iron in Chester 362

	Price per hundredweight
Swedish	21s
Russian	21s
English	20s

Six months' credit is given to known customers or otherwise a discount of 10 shillings a ton.

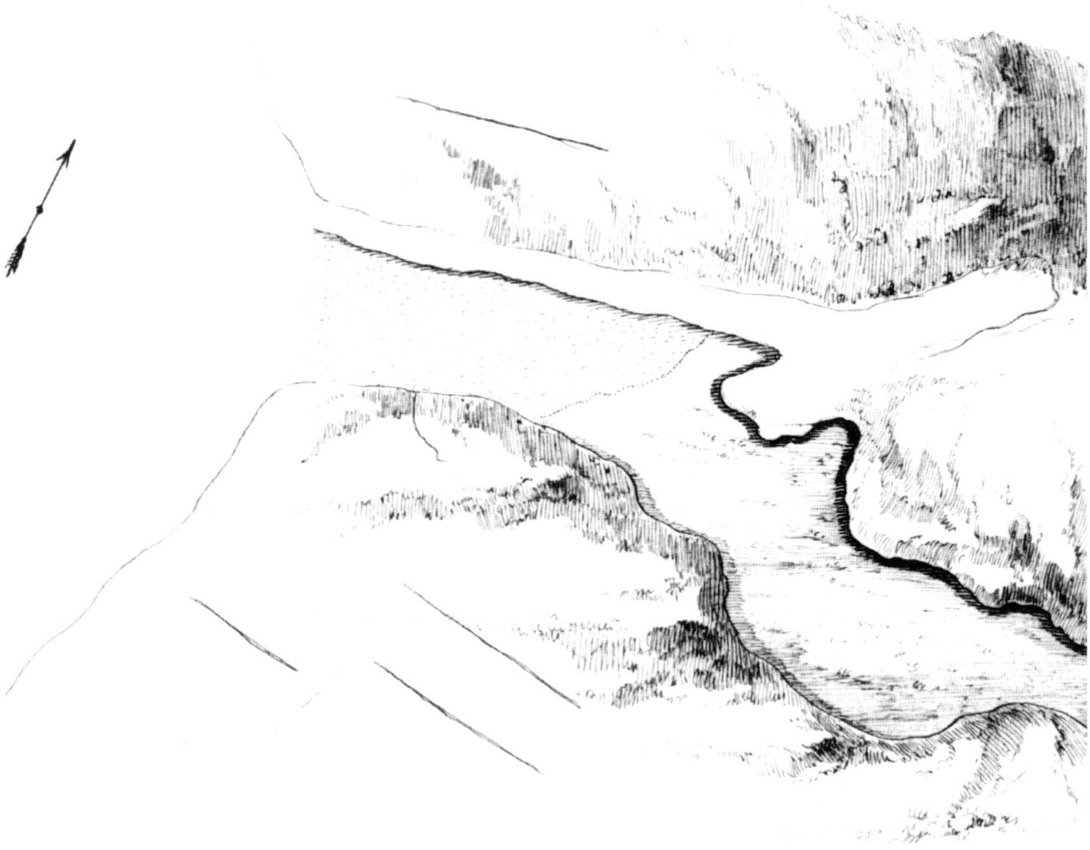

Fig. 296 The flood plain of the River Dee

Price of Lead
One fother of lead weights 21 hundredweight, 1 quarter and 20 pounds or 2148 pounds English weight and is sold in Chester for £17-10-0.

Export from	*Tons*
Chester	6000
Newcastle	3000
Hull	3000
Stockton	2000
Bristol and South Wales ...[254]	

There are here three ships engaged in the African trade, and their loads include voyage iron from Liverpool.

During my stay in Chester, I went to a gunsmith just outside town, who also made
363 moulds for pipes, costing 12, 15 to 20 shillings, cheese-presses and other things, but he had nothing ready for sale, as he will not produce anything except against an order. In London I was told that the same articles are made there and can be had with engraved legends and crests.

A gun, for which he asked 4 guineas, was well made but unembellished. Barrels are produced from scrap iron or Swedish iron. The ones manufactured in Birmingham with English iron as raw material are considered to be rather unreliable and only suitable for the
Guinea trade. 364

17 October 1754, I travelled from Chester to Holywell in Flintshire, which is considered to cover a distance of 14 miles, but actually is just over 20 English miles.

Note on the growth of the land
We rode on our horses across a smooth plain, through which the River Dee flows, and which is said to be flooded in winter. The location of the plain between Wales, Cheshire and the ancient town of Chester and the flooding, by

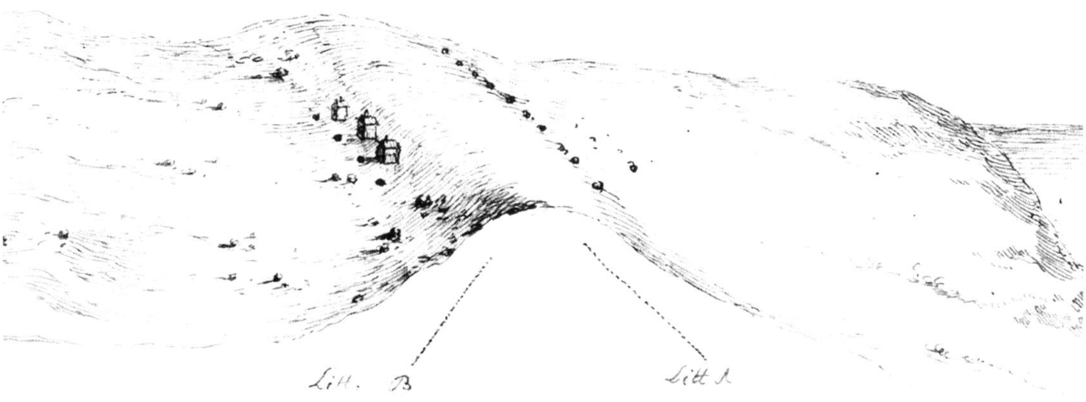

Fig. 297 Ridge with mineral workings

the sea, of the banks of the river Dee nearer to its outlet, 20 miles from here, demonstrate that the plain was once a navigable bay of the ocean. The fact that the seawater has receded is not due to a lowering of its level, but to the growth of the earth and the raising of the bedrock itself, of which there are many proofs to be found in the surrounding coal mines [Fig. 296].

Fertilising of the fields

In Flintshire, where the land was partly flat and low lying and partly hilly, it was observed in several places that the farmers were occupied
365 with ploughing and fertilising fields that earlier in the year had been sown with wheat.

The fertiliser was dung, but in some places in this county they have also started to mix it with lime, which has proved advantageous.

Coal seams and veins of lead and calamine

The coal seams that are being worked here are located in the north-western part towards the seashore or the river and are covered by a number of strata consisting of sandy or hard and dense rocks. Further up the country, towards the south-east, a limestone ridge, full of veins of lead and zinc, rises below the above mentioned strata. A number of these veins were worked in ancient times and are still being worked.

Due to its rise, the limestone ridge has caused the coal seams and the mineral veins to dip north-west, and has also pushed the river Dee to the north-western side of the sands as shown by Fig. 296. There are here two main veins of lead and calamine that run along the ridge, one on each side. They are 8 to 16 or
366 20 feet thick. The veins dip 60 degrees and on the northern side the dip is north, on the southern side south, as shown by drawing no. 297. There are also within a couple of miles a number of transverse veins of lesser thickness that have been opened up and consist partly of galena or a green and whitish congelation of lead minerals and partly of yellowish calamine mixed with other zinc bearing minerals.

The main vein on the northern side is believed to have been worked in the time of the Romans, but it has also yielded large quantities of lead ore in later years. The miners still work there every day extracting calamine, which the ancients did not know how to use. The southern vein, marked **b** in the drawing, was found some years ago as a result of a trial pit sunk by Mr Smedley and is now worked in a number of places with great success and yields mainly lead
ore. The transverse veins are not so rich in ore, 366A
but when they cross the main veins at an acute angle, there is a concentration of ore, though this does not occur when the angle approaches 90 degrees.

Smelting of galena

It was observed that burnt lime was added during the smelting of the galena. The green and white lead ore found around here also requires a small addition of crushed pit coal which supplies phlogiston. The smelting sometimes takes nine hours and other times 12 hours, and is carried out in reverberatory furnaces as described at Bristol and Derby. In these furnaces pit coal was used as fuel. The slag hearths are also built according to the Derby design, but instead of wood, culm or charred pitcoal is used. The hearth is 3 inches higher and it is blown by double bellows, driven

by tramping, because both smelting furnaces and slag hearths are located near the sea shore
367 to facilitate shipment. In this neighbourhood there are eight smelting furnaces for lead and four slag hearths and also three wind furnaces for the cupellation of silver, which is carried out by the same method as already described at Newcastle [Fig. 299].

In the county of Flintshire and the surrounding parts of the country, the yearly production of lead amounts to 6,000 tons, not counting the galena sold to potteries and for other purposes, which in this country amounts to a large consumption. It was stated that from the above mentioned 6,000 tons of lead, all of which is cupellated, 4,000 marker silver a year is extracted.[255]

The galena is sold to the smelting furnaces for £10 to £11 a ton and the cupellated lead is
368 sold for £17.10s.0d a ton.

Approximate figures for the production of lead in England [sic]

	Tons per year
County of Flintshire	6,000
South Wales	2,000
Counties of Somerset and Bristol	2,000
Derbyshire	9,000
Yorkshire and Durham	2,600
County of Cumberland	500
Scotland	[missing]
The amount of silver extracted is	
Wales	4,000 marker
Yorkshire	4,000 marker

One ton of lead equals 21 hundredweight and 60 lb or 2,410 lb.

Production of white and red lead

There is also a white-lead factory being built here and a red lead works that is already in operation. These belong to Mr Smedley, who nowadays is the most prominent operator of mines and smelting works in the district.
The raw material for the manufacture of the red lead is litharge from the cupellation furnace, ground to a fine powder and sieved before being placed in the calcining kiln. Thirteen

Fig. 299 Calamine calcining kiln

Fig. 298 Litharge calcining kiln

hundredweight at a time is charged, which in three days, through moderate heating, steady firing and continuous stirring, is converted into a beautiful red paint pigment, so called red
369 lead, of which great quantities are used by the English glass-works.

A peculiar thing about the process is that when 13 hundredweight of litharge is charged into the kiln, 14 hundredweight is taken out. It is impossible to understand from where the added weight comes and it disappears if the red lead is melted again.

One ton of red lead, which equals no more than 20 hundredweight, is sold for £18, or for £19.10s.0d if it is of better quality. The calcining kiln is constructed in the same way as the ones described in London and Derby and is fired with pit coal [Fig. 298].

Calcining of calamine

The calcining of the calamine in this neighbourhood is also carried out in the same way as described in Derbyshire. The difference here is that the ore is first crushed and impurities removed by hand picking, after which it is pulverised under large millstones that roll around in a vertical position and then sieved.

370 When this process has been duly completed, the calamine is charged into the calcining kiln, which is constructed in accordance with drawing no. 299. The calcining takes 10 to 11 hours, and I was told that the charge weighs one ton, but it did not appear to be that much. Pitcoal was used for the firing. The workers at the kiln were paid 16 pence for 12 hours. The calamine is purchased for £3.0s.0d to £3.10s.0d to £4.0s.0d a ton, in accordance with the quality and is sold after roasting for £9.0s.0d a ton. It was said that the loss of weight during the calcining amounted to between 20 and 30 per cent.[256]

The town of Holywell and its holy well

Holywell is a small town, which in Catholic times was supported by large numbers of pilgrims who came to this place to bathe in a spring dedicated to St. Winefride. It is supposed to have burst forth at the spot where a tyrannical lover struck the head off this saint, who was restored to life by a monk capable of performing miracles and living in the neighbourhood. The spring water contains some lime and the volume of water amounts to a
371 hudred barrels[257] a minute, or so I was told.

Above the spring a beautiful Gothic colonnade has been built, which in Cromwell's time was damaged by the destruction of its images and ornaments. It has now been fairly well restored, the cost being defrayed by money subscribed by the local gentry. In front of the colonnade there is a basin for bathing and inside a smaller one for better class people.

Many crutches hang from the ceiling, as testimonials of the cures accomplished here. An account made by a Catholic priest states that St. Winefride still performs miracles for the faithful and devout souls. On top of the cliff stands a chapel where services are held when there is an influx of spa visitors, although there are not so many now as in former times.

The water from the holy well drives a number of flourmills and other works, amongst
them mills for snuff, paper and wires, and a 372
copper-mill comprising a hammer and a rolling-mill.

The snuff is ground with stones, in the same way as flour, but that mill was not in operation.

Paper mill at Holywell

At the paper mill, grey paper is made from coarse linen and woollen rags. The cutting up of the rags is carried out in the Dutch way, using a water driven roll bristling with knives at the periphery, as is also the vat in which the roll is placed. The rotation of the roll forces the rags, which are suspended in the water that fills the vat, in between the knives again and again until they have been cut so fine that they form a slurry with water. The slurry is subsequently heated by addition of hot water and the fibres taken up on a sieve made of brass wire. The paper thus formed is dried and put into piles containing definite numbers of sheets, ready for sale. The process, although for a
different kind of paper, was seen in Holland and 373
described with a drawing of the machinery.

Wire drawing at Holywell

The wire mill belongs to Mr John 'Parcher' in 'Brinmade' and operates according to the method used in Pontypool, as already noted. The difference was that after annealing, the wire in Pontypool was placed in ponds filled with water to soften, or as it is called here, to take the fire out of it. Here in Holywell, it is piled up under a leaking water trough, so that the water constantly drips onto it. This is supposed to dissolve the iron faster, and cause rust on the

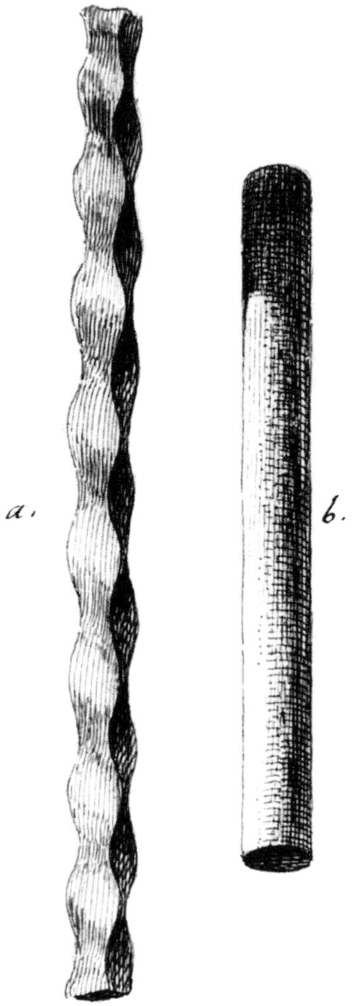

Fig. 300 a & b Copper rods

surface with the assistance of the air, than if it were completely submerged in the water. It was also noted that the scouring took place in specially constructed wooden cylinders rotated by a water wheel, which also drove the draw benches, as previously described. The iron used for the wire comes partly from Pontypool and partly from the neighbourhood, where it is made from pig iron smelted in Lancashire.
374 To make it more suitable for wire drawing, it is drawn down by a trip hammer to long and thin rods.

The price was said to be £22 per ton in Pontypool. Sixteen different sizes of wire are made here and sold for 20 to 40 shillings a bundle, each containing 6 rings and weighing 62¼ lb. For each finer gauge the price increases by 1 shilling, but below no. 14 gauge the increase is 2 shillings.[258] Production amounts to 1,000 bundles a year.

Copper hammer and rolling mill and making of rods at Holywell

The copper used is smelted at Mr Patten's works in Warrington. The copper mill at Holywell consists of a large hammer for drawing down the copper until it is of suitable size for rolling. Forging and rolling are conducted under the same roof, but neither the hammer nor the rolling mill were in operation because the workers were busy drawing down copper to rods for the Guinea trade.

The work was carried out with the aid of a small trip hammer and the copper was first forged into rods looking like wreath-iron[259] as shown by Fig. 300a and then made into rods 375
with circular cross-section as shown by Fig. 300b, using rounded dies both in hammer head and anvil. The production would take much less time if the rods were drawn through holes in an iron plate, as is done with heavy brass wire, but I was told that this way of processing would not give the copper the same degree of ductility that it gets from the forging which is required for this particular operation. The Negroes in Guinea use the rods as ornaments and wind them around arms and legs.

Forty tons of copper a year are worked up at this mill, mostly for the Guinea trade. The coal pit belonging to the Quaker Co. lies by the shore of the bay of the ocean that stretches up towards Chester and is worked to a depth of 376
150 feet below sea level.

Coal seams and notes on them

A number of coal seams have been found here, when a shaft was sunk to 261 feet, as shown by figure No. 301. All the seams, except the lowest one, which is marked **d**, contain an abundance of charcoal. In the iron ore that accompanies the coal seams and also in some of the other coal seams, impressions of straw, twigs and other vegetable matter are found. In some places faults occur in the coal seams, which cause them to fracture and sink 3 feet to 4 feet 6 inches and it was noticed that if one seam has faulted all the others fault to the same extent.

The clay that lies between the coal seams **c** and **d** is peculiar, because it swells up, which causes much work and expense when it is removed. It does not appear difficult to

Fig. 301 The Quaker Co. coal mine

77 conclude that this clay is a new intrusion which has placed itself between the two coal seams just mentioned and which as yet has not had time to harden to a firm consistency, and even less to acquire a similarity to the rock overlying the other coal seams.

Bychton coal pit lies 5 miles further west towards the sea and belongs to Mr Pennant.

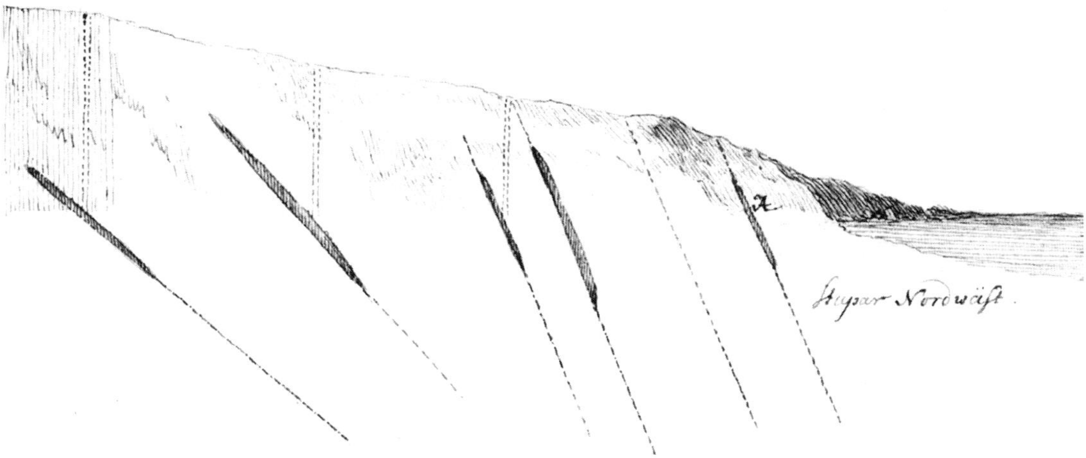

Fig. 302 Coal seams at Bychton

The following strata were observed when descending a shaft 120 feet deep:

	Thickness
Clay	24 feet
Sandy	18 feet
Hard sandstone	24 feet
Blue, stone-like clay	24 feet
Black shale	24 feet
Coal	6 feet
Total	120 feet

The coal seam dips north-west, 1 foot in 5 feet,[260] but further on towards the sea the seams dip much more, as shown by Fig. no. 302, which was made when an adit was
378 driven 40 years ago.

It does not appear that the steep dips can have been caused by anything else than the growth of the limestone ridge and its consequent rise in the south-east, combined with the scouring action of the sea in the bay to the north-east of the coal seams, which has prevented the crystallisation of the rock to the thickness it has reached further inland.

With Mr Pennant, who has a fine collection of fossils, I took a walk along the seashore, where one of the steep coal seams cropped out in many places. The overlying rock consisted of a soft, clay-like shale, which was grey and glistening, and in some places was beautifully ornamented with impressions of grass and other vegetable matter. On this occasion, however, implements for breaking them loose were not at hand. These fossils indicated that the coal seam had originated in a swampy tract of land covered with grass and brushwood rather than from large trees growing in a large forest.
The charcoal that could be seen in the mineral 37
coal was also in the form of small and thin pieces compared with what is found in the coal mines at Wednesbury and other parts of England.

In some places, where the coal seam cropped out in the cliffs by the seashore, it had caught fire and caused the surrounding rocks to conglomerate into a most peculiar looking mass, as shown by Fig. 303.

Pattferry forge

Six miles from Holywell lies a forge, called Pattferry Forge, where 150 tons of bar iron a year are produced. The pig iron comes from Dalcowen Furnace located in Wales 14 miles away and the ore is shipped in from Cumberland.

Fig. 303 Cliffs with coal outcrops

Summary of cost per ton of bar iron made at Pattferry.

	Pig iron, 1¼ ton @ £7	£8.15s.0d
	Coal, 2½ to 2¾ dozen @ £2.10s	£6.11s.6d
	Wages, finery 15 and chafery 10 shillings	£1.5s.0d
	Rent for the works, building costs, interest etc.	£1.5s.0d
380	Total	£17.16s.6d

There are no trees in this part of the country except the ones that grow in the hedges serving as enclosures for fields and meadows. However, it was said that there are some parks further up in Wales and also some forests in the valleys. The trees that do grow in this country are mainly oak, aspen, birch and other broadleaf trees. Amongst them are also sometimes pine trees planted in avenues, although they really are indigenous in Scotland.

Reasons for the lack of forests in England

I have observed that the lack of timber and charcoal in Wales as well as in other parts of England is not so much due to a shortage of forests as to unsatisfactory forestry. If the people in this place would cultivate the trees growing in the hedgerows, in the same way as the Biscayans
381 in Spain look after theirs, namely by not letting the trunk grow taller than 12 feet and by sawing off all the branches growing on it every three or four years, I venture to say that more firewood and charcoal would be produced than the inhabitants require for their ordinary consumption. After all, pitcoal supplies all the necessary fuel in most localities. If the inhabitants became so thrifty that they would plant new trees wherever an old one had been felled, and replenish the hedgerows with fast-growing trees, there would be good reason to believe that there would be no more complaints about lack of charcoal for the blast furnaces and forges in England.

Lead mines

On the road to Wrexham I passed several lead mines working in the limestone ridge east of Holywell that I have already mentioned.

The character of the countryside around Wrexham

Near Wrexham the land flattens out and there is not so much uncultivated common land to be seen as further up in Wales. The hedgerows around the fields and meadows were fairly 382
closely planted with deciduous trees, and some small forests were seen briefly in passing several gentlemen's seats or manor houses.

Bersham blast furnace

Three miles from the above mentioned town lies Bersham blast furnace, which gets its ore partly from Cumberland and partly from some coal mines in Flintshire. The iron is smelted with charcoal, and used for casting kettles, pots, flatirons, wheel hubs and other small hardware, here as well as at the Pont-y-blew forge, which is located 7 miles further on along the road to Shrewsbury. This forge produces 150 tons of bar iron a year, sold in the district. The selling price is now £20 to £21 a ton.

The wages at the forge are the same as at Coalbrookdale, namely 11 shillings in the finery and 10 in the chafery, but the coal is here somewhat cheaper, because a cord of wood, 8 feet long, 4 feet high and 4 feet wide, can be bought in the vicinity for 8 to 9 shillings, whereas it costs 10, 12 to 14 shillings in the last 383
mentioned place.

Wrexham forge

Wrexham or Abenbury forge lies only 2 miles from the town. It gets its pig iron from Backbarrow blast furnace in Westmoreland and the production amounts to over 60 tons a year.

Summary of cost per ton of bar iron at Pont-y-blew

Pig iron, 1¼ ton @ £6.10s	£8.2s.6d
Charcoal, 2½ to 3 dozen @ £2.13s	£7.0s.0d
Wages for finery and chafery	£1.5s.0d
Rent for the works, buildings cost, transport, etc.	£1.5s.0d
Total	£17.12s.6d

Summary of cost per ton of bar iron at Abenbury

Pig iron, 1¼ ton from Backbarrow @ £7.10s	£9.7s.6d
Charcoal, 2½ dozen @ £2.10s	£6.5s.0d
Wages for finery and chafery	£1.5s.0d
Freight and carriage charges for pig iron	£0.12s.6d
Rent for the works, building costs, etc.	£1.10s.0d
Total	£19.0s.0d

The town of Wrexham

384 Wrexham is the county town of Denbighshire and has a fine church with a tower, but otherwise not worthy of note except possibly for its agriculture. Dung is used as manure both for the fields and also spread thinly on the meadows in the autumn.

Ellesmere, a small town

Ellesmere is a small town in Shropshire, just across the border from Denbighshire. Formerly there was a castle here and the location is very attractive due to several small lakes in the vicinity, very seldom found in England. Not far away the river Dee flows through a valley covered with broadleaf trees and joins the Severn which is navigable right down to Chester and Bristol.[261]

Shrewsbury and Upton and Tern Forges

Close by Shrewsbury lies a forge belonging to Mr Harvey, a Quaker. It consists of three hearths and produces 5 tons a week or 250 tons a year. The wages per ton are 12 shillings in the finery and 10 in the chafery. Pig iron from Leighton blast furnace costs £6.6s.5d and the
385 carriage 5 shillings.

A few miles from Shrewsbury on the way to Coalbrookdale there is another forge called Upton, which belongs to Mr Blunt and produces 140 tons a year. Another one at Tern, belonging to Mr Gee, produces 120 tons. 27 hundredweight of pig iron are allowed per ton of bar iron, and 70 lbs. are melted down to produce a bloom of which 16 to 17 can be made per day, when the finery is working flat out. The blooms are drawn down to anconies in two heats and then taken to the chafery to be drawn down further to bars in another two heats, although sometimes three heats might be required. The finery is allowed 1¾ loads or dozen of charcoal per ton of wrought iron and the coal costs 50 to 52 shillings a dozen in this locality. Pitcoal is used in the chafery, although small charcoal is employed when dense or soft iron is made. The wages are 12 shillings a ton in the finery and 10 in the chafery.

The Town of Shrewsbury and its trade

Shrewsbury, formerly called Salop, is a considerable town, which was fortified in earlier times and still retains its walls. There is no
386 industry worth mentioning, but nevertheless the trade is considerable, because the town is

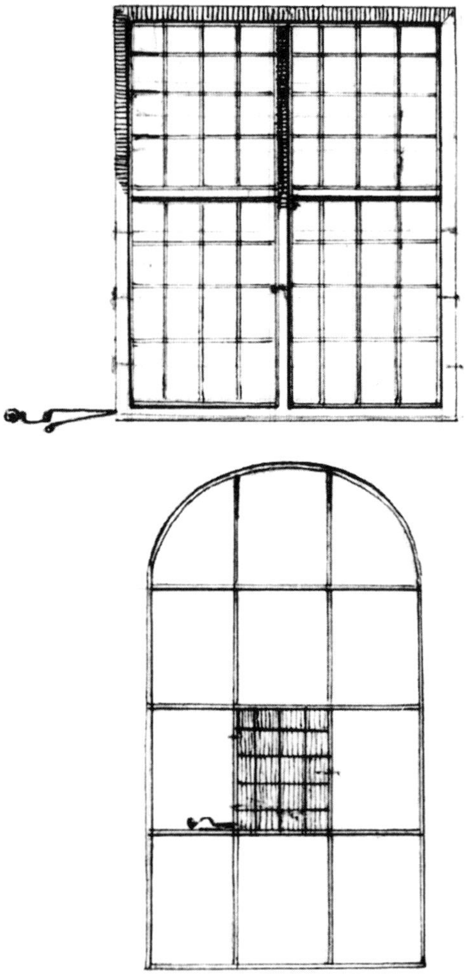

Fig. 304 House and church windows of iron

situated on the river Severn, which is navigable to a point, between twenty and thirty miles upstream and downstream to its outlet at Bristol, ...[262] miles away. This makes it possible for the inhabitants of the town to buy various products of the land as well as manufactured goods from the central parts of Wales, particularly coarse, undyed cloth and also to procure from Bristol and supply to adjoining districts all sorts of necessities. In Shrewsbury there are three iron merchants, who are mainly concerned with the sale of English iron, except for 50 or 60 tons of Russian and Swedish stamps used for wheel-tyres and horseshoes, which can be sold every year. It is bought in Bristol and the price of Russian and Gothenburg iron is £21.10s.0d to £22.0s.0d a ton, whereas the English costs £20 a ton.

Window-frames of iron

In addition to the usual consumption of iron by households that is found all over England, the
387 people of this province use window-frames of iron. These are welded at the corners and then riveted together with a thin piece of sheet-iron, to make them safer for the window-glass panes. For high windows, espagnolettes are also used in order to make it possible to close them tightly and uniformly both at the top and the bottom. On the outside there is a spring that supports the weight of the window when it is opened, and which also is provided with a catch to hold the window in position. I have also seen this arrangement in other places in England on church windows with iron frames that could be opened [Fig. 304].

Transport of charcoal on the River Severn

At Shrewsbury there are two stone bridges across the River Severn, and the ships that pass beneath them are built so that they can lower their masts. I saw a number of large ships coming down the river loaded with charcoal,
388 destined for …[263] that lies 8 miles below Bewdley, for the account of Mr Knight, who in the vicinity on the river Stour owns a number of forges, as I have mentioned previously on my trip from Pontypool to Birmingham. The bulk of this charcoal is made 15 to 20 miles further up in the country by Mr Knight's men, from wood purchased by them in advance. However, some of the coal is delivered to …,[264] at a price of £3 a dozen, which is equal to 12 horse loads. One horse load of charcoal is a sack of coal, 6 feet long and 3 feet 5 inches wide, and is said to weigh 2 hundredweight when the coal is dry, otherwise more. The charges for carrying the coal down the Severn were from 7 to 10 shillings a dozen, according to the distance. In addition it costs 18 pence a dozen for carriage by land to the forge.

Summary of production costs per ton at
389 *Mr Knight's forges in Staffordshire*

Pig iron	£7.10s.0d
Charcoal	£7.10s.0d
Wages	£1.0s.0d
Overheads, such as rent and building costs	…[265]

The iron is sold for £22 per ton long weight.[266]

Various forges and blast furnaces

There are no fewer than 16 forges and 4 blast furnaces in this county and I visited a number of them but found nothing special that I have not already remarked upon elsewhere, except at Coalbrookdale, which is located 12 miles below Shrewsbury near the river Severn [Fig. 313]. This iron works belongs to a company in which Mr 'Edw. Pohn', Mr Champion, Mr 'Ragers,' Mr Ford and Mr Darby now are the principal share-holders.[267] The three latter live at the works as well. The main industry here is the
foundries, supplied with iron for large castings 390
by two blast furnaces. For pots and other small odds and ends, 2, 3 and up to 5 reverberatory furnaces are used according to demand. Smelting in the blast furnaces is carried out with charred pitcoal, which I observed before at the Clifton furnace in Cumberland. The construction of the blast furnaces is the same as that of other British furnaces and the stone for the hearths is procured from the Forest of Dean, where it is dressed to the desired dimensions. A complete set of stones for a hearth costs £10. In other places, where this kind of stone is not available, Stourbridge brick is used instead, but it only lasts about 3 months, whereas the stone stands up for 2 years or more, if raw materials and water do not give out. In England it is now known that when such shortages occur, the furnace can be damped down, which preserves the heat in the furnace with very little fire for
several consecutive weeks, so that the campaign 391
can be restarted without renewing the furnace lining and with a smaller expense for blowing-in, particularly when charcoal is used for smelting. The hearths of the reverberatory furnaces are made of ordinary dry sand to the volume required for the iron that is to be melted and then covered with a 3 to 4 inches thick layer of another kind of sand that is more refractory and hardens more readily. This is rammed down hard and renewed every 8 days.

The furnace is charged 12 times per 24 hours in the following way: first, nine baskets of coal, 1 foot 6 inches in diameter and 2 feet 9 inches deep, are dumped into the furnace. On top of this, and right at the centre of the throat, the ironstone is placed. It consists of 45 bushels, 9 inches wide and 18 inches deep, each holding about 50 lb. ore or more. In addition two bushels of limestone are added, but at the beginning, and also towards the end of the campaign, less ore is charged.

When the furnace is in full production, no more than 12 to 13 tons can be made with coke, although it is possible to reach 18 to
392 19 tons a week with charcoal. The iron produced with coke is considered the best for castings, but not fit for making bar iron, although a number of attempts have been made. It sells for £7 in form of sows, whereas the iron smelted with charcoal at other blast furnaces fetches £6.15s.

Willey and Leighton blast furnaces

Willey and Leighton blast furnaces are located 3 or 4 miles from Coalbrookdale, and also belong to the same partnership. Here the smelting is carried out with charcoal and the ore is obtained from the local coal mines. It is mainly of the same kind as that used for making foundry iron at Coalbrookdale. The production amounts to 600 tons [a year] at each furnace.

Summary of costs, per week for pig iron smelted in the two furnaces

	Cost per week
Charcoal, 30 dozen @ 54 shillings	£81.0s.0d
Ore 40 ton @ 7 shillings	£14.0s.0d
Limestone	15s.0d
Wages for 2 people down below and 2 fillers	
392	£2.0s.0d
Maintenance costs etc., estimated	£3.0s.0d
Total	£100.15s.0d

The weekly production is generally 17½ tons, which sells for £6.11s.0d per ton or £117.12s.6d per week. Sometimes it is possible to get a price of £7 a ton, which makes the profit that much larger.

The ore is mined at a number of coal pits, where it is found in certain strata and contains many impressions of plants.

Prices of Castings	£ per ton
Kettles weighing 7 hundredweight, with a capacity of 1150 gallons, each gallon equal to 3 bottles	£12.0s.0d
Ditto for cooking on board the ships in the Guinea trade with lock on top	£16.0s.0d
Pots	£13.0s.0d
Ditto, delivered in Bristol	£14.0s.0d
Flat-irons with handles	£24.0s.0d
394 Cylinders for fire-engines, turned	£32.0s.0d
Grills and gates	£14.0s.0d

Note: For cylinders £2 per ton is obtained, calculated on the basis of weight before boring, and for boring £5 per ton.[268]

Casting of various kinds of goods

For the heaviest castings moulds of loam are used. The main parts of these are built in bricks as already described in London. For drying the moulds, ovens have been built of appropriate sizes for the various moulds and provided with a number of grates in tiers above each other as shown by drawing no. 305. On the grates, fires are made with coke.

The mould for a large pot or cauldron is constructed of bricks on a fixed base, and the sweep is hooked onto a vertical spindle of iron that stands in the centre of the mould. Fires are
kindled inside the mould as the laying of the 39.
bricks and the application of the loam take place. See drawing no. 305, letter **c**. Oval pots are shaped by moving the sweep against two oval rings fixed one above the other.

Moulds for pots and pans, flat irons, bushes for wheel hubs, lattice-work, gates with their posts and other accessories are all cast in sand moulds made in flasks, as I have already so often described in London, Bristol, Newcastle etc., and also in Amsterdam and Rotterdam in Holland.

A post for a large garden gate had acquired some holes during casting, which were filled with copper, because it was said that if they were filled with cast iron, it would become so hard that no file would be able to make it smooth. If the people here had understood the reason for this, they could have saved their copper and accomplished the same thing with the cast iron, which in this neighbourhood has a
steely nature, if a small coal fire had been made 39
on top of the iron after it had been poured into the holes. This would have kept it hot longer and prevented the hardening.

Two gates 8 feet high and 4 feet wide were being cast. In the bars **a-a** [letters missing], there were holes for the cast vertical rods that had conical ends at the bottom. The holes at the top were lined with lead [Fig. 306].

Casting of iron rolls

Rolls for rolling silver, copper or iron sheets are cast in moulds of iron, made by casting in loam moulds, followed by accurate turning. The iron moulds consisted of three pieces as shown in Fig. 306. Letter **a** is the mould for the body of the roll. Letter **b** designates the moulds for the

Fig. 305 Mould preparation

roll-necks and square wobblers, which are
inserted into the ends of **a**. The whole mould
assembly is shown by letter **c**. The molten iron
is poured into the cavity from the top as shown
by letter **d**, after the different parts of the mould
397 have been securely tied together, so that the
fluid power of the iron cannot part them. It may
seem strange that iron can be cast into iron
moulds that still can be taken apart without
anything being damaged, and this in spite of the
fact that no paint is used inside the mould to
facilitate the separation of the casting.

The reason why this is possible is the expansion
of the iron when it is hot and liquid and its
contraction when it starts to cool off. A roll cast
in this way will always be found to have a
smaller volume when cold than the mould itself,
so that it can readily be shaken out. The rolls
founded by this method are much harder than
those cast in loam or sand, and can therefore
not be turned in the usual way, but are ground
with sand. A machine for this purpose was
described in Birmingham. 398

Rolls of this kind are particularly used for
rolling silver and other metal for coins, which
must be fairly accurate. For the rolling of iron
sheets, the rolls are generally founded in loam
or sand and then turned in the ordinary way as
described at Pontypool.

The hardness of the rolls is not so much
caused by the method of casting, but rather
more by the process of melting. Long
experience has shown that pig iron smelted with
coke becomes harder and whiter in the fracture
when it is re-melted the second time in the air
furnace, and even harder after the third re-
melting. Thus this type is used for the above
mentioned rolls only when it has been melted
several times. When the iron runs out from the
blast furnace, the fracture appears uniformly
grey, but after the first re-melting one finds grey 399
and white grains mixed in the fracture, and after

Fig. 306 Cast iron gates; iron rolls

the second it is uniformly white and looks like frozen glass that has been quenched in water, about which more will be said in another context.

Iron castings for parts of steam engines

Coalbrookdale has recently started to cast in iron all parts required for fire engines that when the engines were first developed were cast of non-ferrous metal, for example the main cylinders, with pipes and pump-barrels etc. Others, such as the boiler with its cover were forged of copper, but later made of lead plates. In accordance with their new ideas, Coalbrookdale now makes use of nothing but cast iron, which is much lower in price, and does anything that could be achieved with the other metals.

The cylinder for the great fire engine at Redruth in Cornwall was cast here. Its diameter
400 is so large that a man can ride through it without bending down[269] and its total weight was ... [missing].

Also made here are kettles, or so-called boilers, for fire engines and recently some have been made that weighed 7,100 and ¼ lb. [sic]. The lid that covers them is not much smaller, and is bolted to the boiler proper in the same way as has been used for water pump cylinders for a long time. In order to avoid increasing the size of the boiler in proportion to the size of the cylinder, one fire engine has been provided with three boilers, two of which supply steam to the third one, which is placed directly underneath the cylinder. This arrangement works admirably.

Fig. 307 Large kettle [no reference in text]

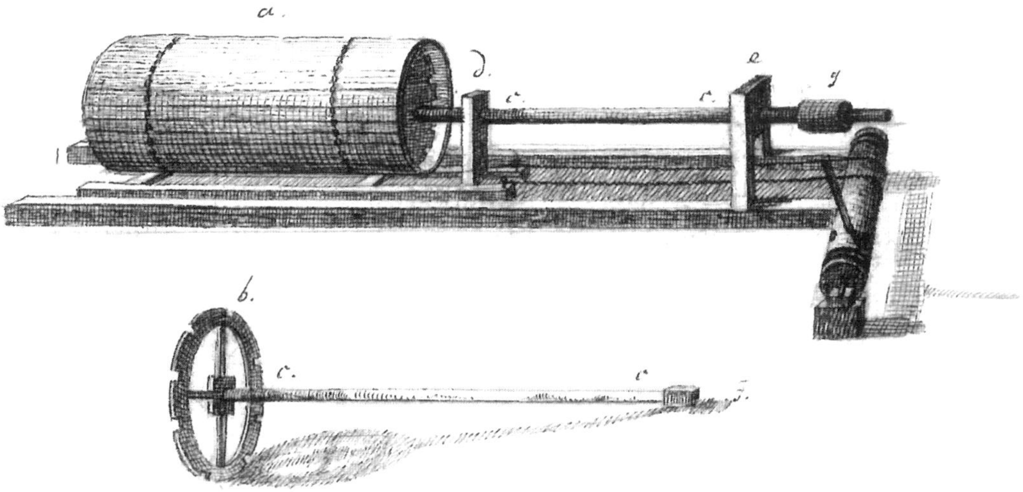

Fig. 308 Machine for boring cylinders

Turning of cylinders for fire engines[270]

401 If one had not seen how such a large and heavy object as the cylinder of a steam engine is turned smooth inside, one would find it very difficult to understand how it is done, but relatively speaking it can be carried out just as easily as a turner hollows out a tobacco pipe or some other small tube. The method is the same, the only difference being that the size of the tools and equipment and the driving power have to be proportional to the weight, hardness and size of the object that is to be worked [Fig. 308].

The cylinder **a** is placed in a horizontal position on a carriage that travels on a track specially made for this purpose. The carriage can be moved inwards or outwards, as required, by means of chains or ropes that are wound around the drum of a windlass. A wheel **b**, cast to suit the diameter of the cylinder, is provided with a number of holes around the periphery into which pieces of steel are inserted.
The wheel is securely fastened to an accurately turned bar **c** that is placed in supports, of which **d**, the one nearest to the cylinder is moveable,[271] whilst the other one **e** is fixed to
402 the beams that make up the track or the bed of the lathe. The cutting wheel with its pieces of steel is inserted in the cylinder and the square end of the bar **c** is connected to the waterwheel by means of a cast iron sleeve **g** and the boring commences. A cylinder of this kind has to be turned several times,[272] because to begin with it is not possible to take very heavy cuts. Nevertheless, the boring of a cylinder can be carried out in 8 to 14 days by one man.

Previously, forged bars were used for the boring, but it has now been found that bars cast of iron are far better, as long as they have been turned all over.

Various inventions at the iron foundries

It is amazing how far the art of casting iron has been developed in this place and I do not have time on this occasion to enumerate everything
that is accomplished here by the easiest and 403
most ingenious methods. Just the same, I must mention the invention of a method of cutting holes in boilers or other vessels, if so desired, without going to any extra trouble in making the mould and also the method of casting and turning screws, which has been brought to a high degree of perfection [Fig. 309].

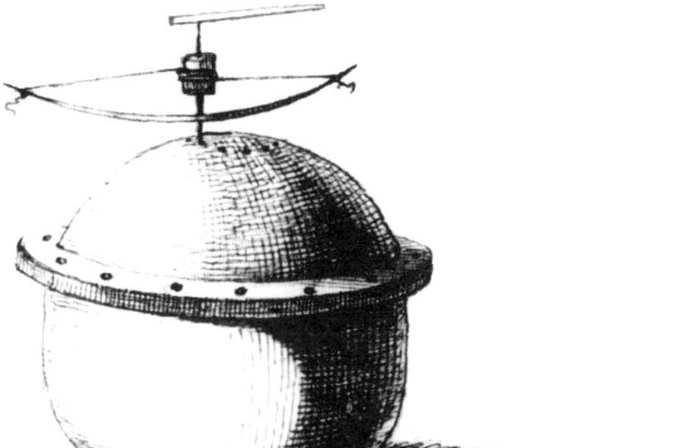

Fig. 309 Method of cutting holes in boilers

The former idea is carried out by drilling small holes along an outline drawing of the hole that is to be made. The piece inside the small holes can then easily be knocked out and the edges trimmed with a cold chisel.

The castings for the latter idea [i.e. for screws] are, as usual, made in sand moulds in flasks or, if screws of unusually large size are required, in loam moulds. In either case the castings must be provided with gudgeon pins at both ends to make it easy to place them in a set of roll housings, to be turned smooth all over.

There is a set of housings especially for such turning operations, designed so that the posts with their chocks can be moved further away
404 from each other or closer together as circumstances dictate and as is shown in further detail in drawing no. 310A.[273]

As soon as the screw blanks have been turned accurately all over, they are placed in a lathe, designed for screw cutting, in which they are connected to a master screw that moves in its nut. This screw is called the regulator because it regulates and controls the cutting of the screw as further shown by drawing no. 310B.[274]

If the nut for the regulator and the cutting tool were placed on a carriage moved back and forth by the regulator, it would be unnecessary to have such a long lathe bench with many supports for tools, sleeves and nuts. It would be sufficient to have the equipment shown in drawing no. 311, where the regulator is located
between coupling sleeves **a** and **b**, and its nut in 405
support **c**. The cutting tool is located at **d**. The screw blank is **e**, **a** and **f**, **g**, **d**, **c** designates the sliding carriage, which is moved backwards and forwards by the regulator **a**, **b** and its nut during the screw cutting.[275]

The screw cutting lathe could be driven by a waterwheel as shown by drawing no. 312, the power being transmitted through two large spur wheels, one on the water wheel shaft and the other on the lathe and two by shafts with pinions that could be engaged or disengaged as required.[276] The price of these screws made of cast iron is 6 pence per lb., but forged ones cost
10 pence a lb. 406

At each of the two blast furnaces there are boring mills or 'turning machines' for cylinders and pump barrels, as already described, and the

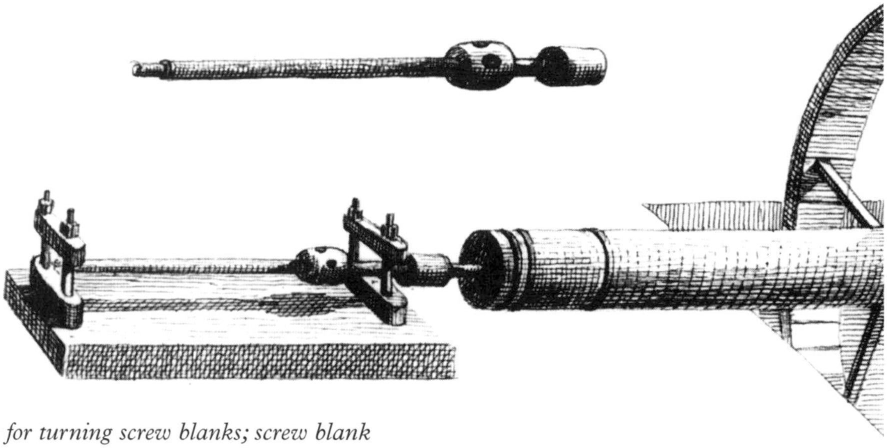

Fig. 310a Machine for turning screw blanks; screw blank

Fig. 310b Machine for turning screws

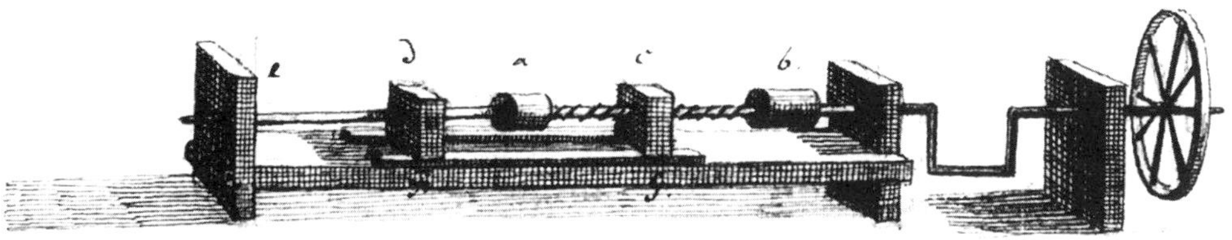

Fig. 311 Machine for turning screws, RRA's modification

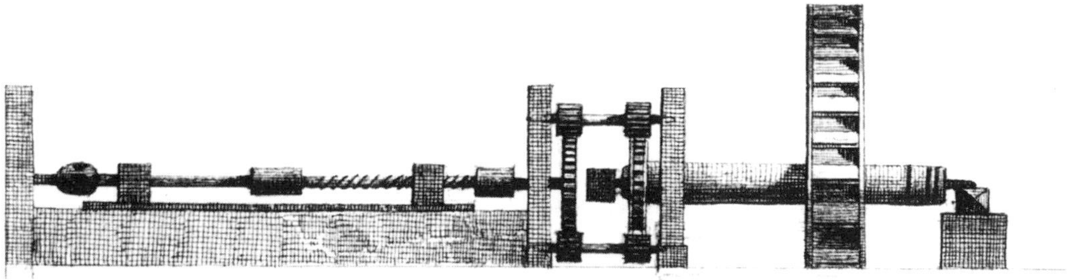

Fig. 312 Water-driven lathe

water that drives all the wheels is pumped back to the mill-pond again by a fire engine, located not far from the lower furnace.

Bar-iron forge

A short distance further down there is a bar iron forge with three hearths that produces 130 to 150 tons of bars a year. The pig iron comes from Willey and Leighton furnaces, located two or three miles from here, where the ore is smelted with charcoal, each furnace producing 600 tons a year. For one ton of bar iron the finers are allowed 2 dozen charcoal, but they admitted that they could manage with 1¾ dozen if the quality was very good. It was also said that at the chafery not more than
407 1 dozen is used.

One dozen of coal contains 12 sacks or pony loads, which in this neighbourhood cost 54 shillings and more. A cord of wood, 8 feet long, 4 feet high and 4 feet wide costs 10 to 14 shillings.

The finers are paid 15 shillings a ton and the chafers or hammer men 10 shillings, but they are not paid anything extra for over-iron or over-coal, nor are they paid their usual wages if the forge is shut down for lack of water, but must then do other work at day rate.

Summary of cost per ton of bar iron at Coalbrookdale

Pig iron, 1¼ ton, @ £6 15s	£8.9s.0d
Charcoal, 2½ dozen @ £2 17s	£7.2s.6d
Wages	£1.5s.0d
Rent for the works, interest on capital employed, maintenance and staff salaries	£1.4s.0d
Total	£18.0s.6d

If the profit included in the sales price of the pig iron, which amounts to something like 408
£1.10s or £1.15s is deducted from the above stated costs of the bar-iron, the total cost of the two operations will here be £16.5s to £16.10s a ton, whereas the sales price at the works is £21 to £22 a ton.

Forge for fabricated goods

By the same little stream, but down by the river Severn, there is yet another forge belonging to the Coalbrookdale Co., but now let to Mr 'Hollen'[277] who has established there a manufactory of sheets and various goods fabricated from sheets, which occupies a number of workshops in the vicinity.[278] The workers who make the pans are paid 9 shillings a hundredweight if they are without handles, but only 6 shillings with long handles and 7 with shorter ones.[279] Such pans are in due course sold for 5 to 6 pence per lb.

Cover dishes, plate warmers sell for 24 shillings a dozen. Most of these fabricated goods are sent to Bristol, but a large part goes
to the surrounding district and to Wales. 409

Fig. 313 Coalbrookdale works, fire engine and mill-pond

Lead-smelting works

Some years ago Mr Gee established a nail forge here, comprising several workshops, but since the price of iron started to increase so much it has been shut down. In its stead, a smelting works for galena was built by the Salop Company. The ore for it comes down the Severn from the mines of Lord 'Pauves' in Wales and from the Pannels[280] lead mine in Shropshire. It costs £13.10s a ton and the lead sells for £17.10s. The production amounts to 60 tons per year and good ore yields 8 tons of lead per week.

Limestone Quarry and Lime-burning

Amongst the other wonders of this neighbourhood, the limestone quarries and the 'coal and iron pits' should not be passed over. The former work a number of limestone beds that by some subterranean force have been
410 upended by just over 60 degrees, or as it is generally expressed here, they dip south-east 1½ fathoms in 2.[281] In the limestone there are many kinds of mussel-shells. The burning is carried out with pitcoal, which in places is in alternate layers with the crushed limestone. When the limekiln is full, the limestone itself is built up to 2 feet above the throat and covered with clay to keep the heat in.

The burnt lime, which is produced here in great quantities, is shipped both up and down the Severn and is mainly used on the farms.

Notes on the coal seams

The proximity of the coal seam and the limestone quarry in this place was rather curious, because there were coal pits every 180 feet to 240 feet[282] and the seam was not more than 36–45 feet from the surface, dipping south-east although not so steeply as the limestone beds below it. These would soon be found if somebody would take the trouble of
extending the coal shafts downwards. 411

The coal seam becomes almost horizontal as it stretches towards the south-east, and a mile away it divides into three seams, all of which are mixed with charcoal and undoubtedly all caused by the same flood.

The list below enumerates the different strata found in the Dingle coal pit at Coalbrookdale:

	Thickness, feet
Clay	18
Gritstone or sandy, grey stone	12–18
Clunch, a kind of soft, black shale	15
Coal	2¼
Many layers of stone	120
Coal	2¼
Clunch	21–24
Coal	'binstes'
White stone	15
Coal	2¼–3
Total[283]	227¾–237¾

A little further on towards the south-east, the
412 depth to the lowest coal seam is 264 feet.

On the way to Newport, to the north-east, I obtained information about the kinds of rock penetrated during the sinking of New pit, but the list, shown below, is not reliable, as it does not agree with the depth of the shaft. However, it is very difficult, or practically impossible, to produce an accurate and detailed account of all the different kinds of rock in a coal mine, unless one happens to present in person either during the boring or during the sinking of the shaft.

New pit coal mine	Thickness, feet
Clay	10
Measures (hard blue clay)	2½
White baying	
Wiga rock	
Coal	2½
Tuffet rock	21
White rock	1½
Linxed Great	2
413 Ponistone, hard stone 4 inches	⅓
White Lad	
Coal	3
Black staff 1 inch	
Coal	3
Clath coal	2½
Pimple measures	4½
Iron stone	1½
Bortsh White stone	7
Flint Coal	2½
Total	55

The mine was now said to be 180 feet deep and consequently either a number of coal seams have been left out, or the thicknesses of the seams enumerated above have been understated.

Owing to the convenient transport of coal on the river Severn, this commodity costs [no]
more here than at Wednesbury in Staffordshire. 414

Transport of coal in wagons

The wagons in which the coal was transported from the mines to the ships on the river, are built in the same way as in Newcastle and Whitehaven, although the iron wheels under them are not so large. When the wagons approach the river Severn, they are hooked on to an iron chain that is wound on a drum provided with spikes[284] and in this way very slowly lowered down the steep slope, whilst an empty wagon is pulled up, as shown by drawing no. 315. If the wagons start going too fast the winding man has a brake in the form of a wooden lever that is pressed against the drum to slow them down. However, when I was viewing the operation of the incline he let the speed get out of hand and the loaded wagon accelerated so fast that the chain broke and the wagons ran down the hill out of control and were smashed to bits. It was fortunate that the people were able to get out of the way so that no further
damage was caused.[285] 415

Newport and Eccleshall, small towns

23 October, 1754, I left Coalbrookdale to continue my journey to Newcastle in Staffordshire, which lies 30 miles further up the

Fig. 314 Limestone quarry and kilns

Fig. 315 Coal wagon way

country, in order to seek information about the production of the beautiful white ware and other porcelain and earthenware that is carried out there.

On the way I passed through Newport and Eccleshall, which deserve nothing more than having their names mentioned, although I happened to visit them on their market days. The surrounding country is flat and well cultivated, particularly where there is access to lime for fertilising. The lime is mixed with the dung and is transported on horseback for many miles, where the roads are so deep in mud that they are impassable for wagons and carts.

Lord Gower's House, Trentham Hall

A few miles from Newcastle I passed 'Trenton Seat', belonging to Lord 'Gar'[286] which has a beautiful mansion with fish ponds and a large park for deer, surrounded by a 10 foot high
416 brick wall.

Manufacture of pots and pans

At Newcastle there was a maker of pots and pans, who procured his sheet-iron from the Lea and Warringham Forges in Cheshire for 28 shillings a hundredweight. Frying pans with short handles sell for $5\frac{1}{2}$ pence per lb. and pans with long handles for $4\frac{1}{2}$ pence.

Swedish iron is used for horseshoes in Newcastle and costs 22 to 23 shillings a hundredweight.

Newcastle, town in Staffordshire

Newcastle [under Lyme] in Staffordshire is renowned for the large amount of crockery made in the vicinity, and also for its manufacture of hats, which has been brought to a high degree of perfection.

Earthenware factories at Newcastle

There is also an earthenware factory established by Mr Wilson, where so called 'Bost' ware or fine pots of light yellow colour are made. The raw material is pipe-clay, which comes from Purbeck near Poole in Dorset and the
glazing is carried out with litharge. 417

The factories for earthenwares and white wares in Burslem

Burslem lies 4 miles away and has no fewer than 30 factories and kilns for white ware,

tortoise-shell, 'bost', black and red ware and each kiln occupied 12, 16 to 20 people.
The composition of white ware is one part pipe clay and $5\frac{1}{2}$ parts of flint. Before mixing, both must be reduced to the finest possible size.
The pipe clay is dispersed in water and sieved through hair-cloth. The flint is calcined and crushed by a large edge runner mill, see drawing no. 316-I. After sieving it is ground by horizontal stones working in water as already noted at Bristol and Hotwell and shown by drawing no. 316-II.

The flint flour produced in this way is sold for 1 shilling per 16 pints. The raw flint, as it comes from Liverpool, Chester and other seaports, costs 20 shillings, pipe clay 35 shillings a ton, coal for the calcining 5 pence a hundredweight and Plaster of Paris from

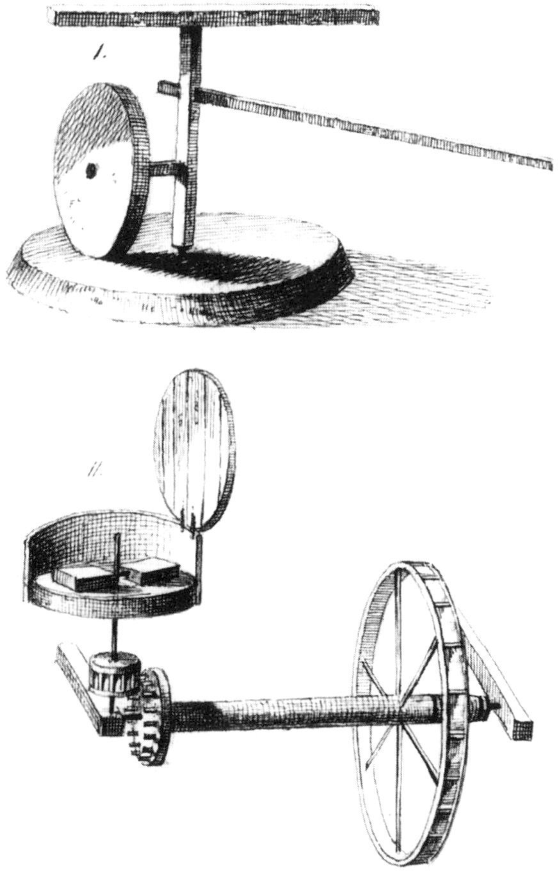

Fig. 316 Edge runner and horizontal mills at Burslem

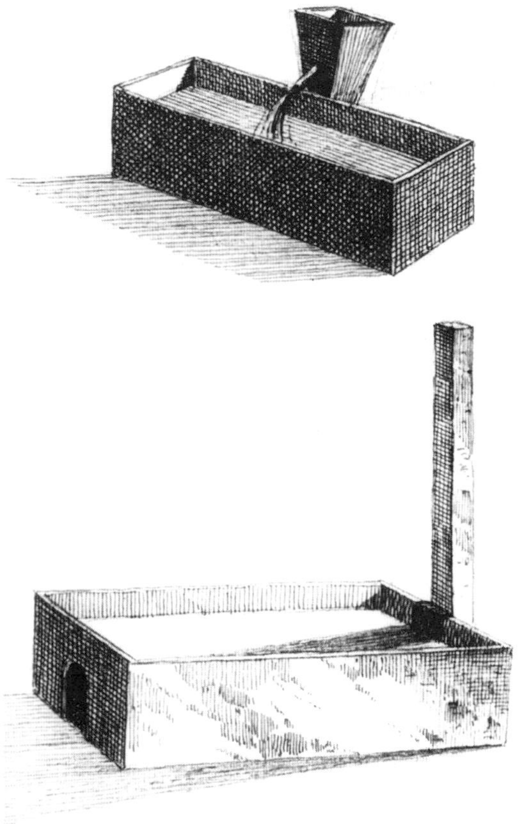

Fig. 317 Slip-mixing tanks

Derbyshire for the moulds 18 pence a hundredweight. The mixing takes place in a tank placed 418
in an elevated position, and the slip is run off into another tank and finally into a third, which is built of thick bricks and provided with a fire grate underneath, where coal is burnt to dry the slip to a suitable consistency for throwing or moulding. See drawing no. 317.

When the vessels are completed, they are dried and then placed in saggers,[287] which are stacked one on top of the other in the kiln. After the access opening has been bricked up, the firing starts and continues for 38 to 40 hours. The kiln should then have reached its highest temperature and the crockery should be thoroughly heated right through, which is 419
ascertained by taking out small sample cups with an iron bar and breaking them. The glazing then commences and is carried out by throwing common salt into the kiln with a small iron scoop, through little holes in the roof. About half a bushel or 28 lb. salt is thrown in through all the holes together and the process is repeated each half hour for six hours. The total

time for the firing is thus 44 to 46 hours. A total of 6 bushels of salt is used, each bushel costing 3 shillings and 7 pence or for 6 bushels 21 shillings and 6 pence. The consumption of coal per kiln and firing is [left out].

Prices of various kinds of crockery

Sales Prices of embossed and tortoise-shell ware

	Shillings per dozen
Tea pots, 12, 18 and 24 in a dozen	4s.6d
Plates, 12 in a dozen	4s
Tea pots from Joh. 'Worverton'. Each dozen consists of 12, 18 or 24 according to size.	
Tea pots, white ware	1s.6d
Cream colour ware with lead glazing	6s
420 Bush grey colour with lead glazing	6s
Orange colour with lead glazing	6s
Red china, not glazed	5s
Agate colour, lead glazed	6s
White ware, enamelled	8–12s

I ordered samples of these wares, to be delivered by common carrier to the Castle Inn, Wood Street, London.

The watchman[288] is paid 16 pence for 12 hours.

The potteries in Hanley for earthenware and so-called white ware

In Hanley[289] there are also nearly 430 makers of white ware and other pottery. The kilns are everywhere in this district built as shown in drawing no. 318. For the firing of white ware the same method is used as the one just described, except that the coal may be a little better in one place than in another, which sometimes causes 2 to 3 hours difference in the time taken. 421

When using salt for glazing some manufacturers are rather parsimonious due to the high price of the commodity, whereas others are fairly liberal, which makes the glazing more even and smooth. At some kilns I was told that

Fig. 318 Pottery kiln at Hanley

Fig. 319a I: Machine for extruding handles etc; II: Drive for potters wheel

a satisfactory glaze could not be obtained unless 7 to 8 bushels of salt were used.

As soon as salt had been thrown in through a hole it was covered with a brick. This was done at all holes, both the ones on top and the ones around the sides, in order to prevent the fumes from the salt from escaping, because it is these fumes that adhere to the pottery and produce the glaze. Here I was also told that the proportions of pipe clay to flint flour were $5\frac{1}{2}$ to 1.

For making handles and small vines to place on the outside of teapots, etc. they had a machine that pressed the clay out through a hole, giving it the same shape as the hole. See drawing no. 319a, I.

Flowers and leaves that were placed on 422
teapots were also pressed, but in moulds, and generally of whiter material than the grey base. See drawing no. 319B, III. Plates and dishes that are embossed are first formed roughly to shape, then allowed to dry somewhat in front of a fire before pressing. See drawing no. 319b, IIII.

A potter's wheel is used for throwing, but it is always turned by a boy to increase the speed. See drawing 319a, II. In order to make the grey or so called embossed crockery, a grey flour is mixed in. In this way it is also possible to make marbled crockery by mixing grey clay with white. That which is grey or decorated with
other colours, must be fired twice, namely once 423
for the ordinary glazing with salt, and a second time for the blue colour or enamel, which, as I was told, is mixed with clay. Crockery with a

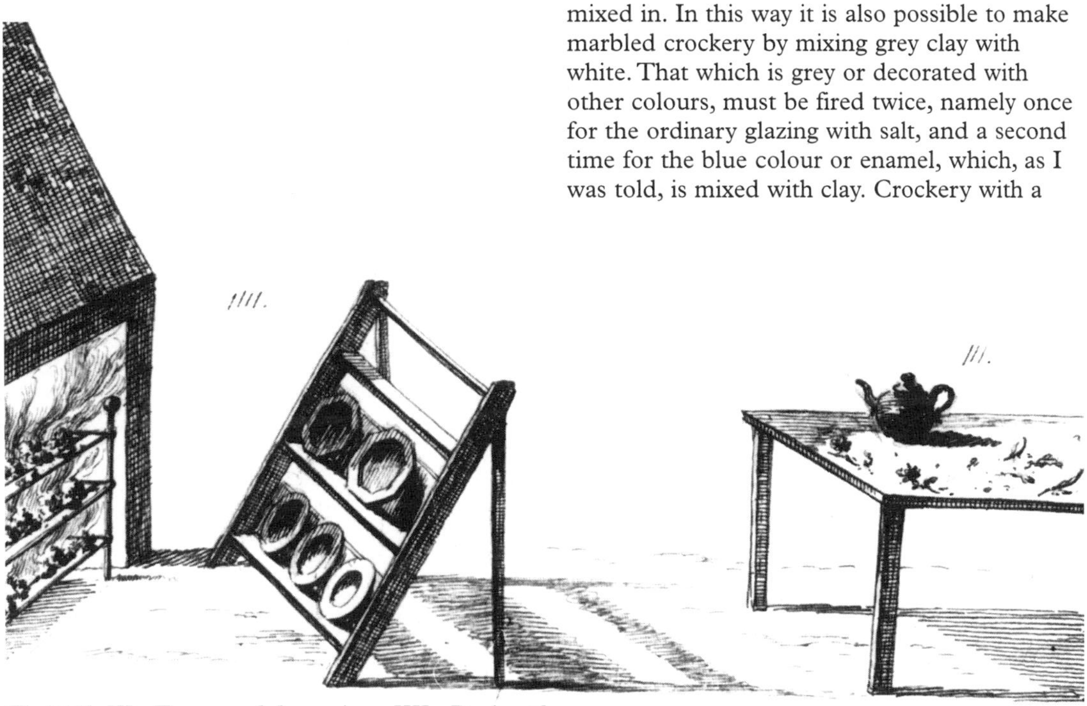

Fig.319b III: Teapot and decorations; IIII: Drying plates

blue linear pattern, which can be finished in a single firing is also made but is seldom very even. This is carried out by sprinkling the blue pigment or smalt powder along lines drawn on the surface of the crockery or in score marks made with the point of a sharp knife.

Prices of various Kinds of Crockery

	Shillings a dozen
Red china tea pots,	
6, 12, 18 to 24 a dozen	4s.6d.
Ditto, but glazed with lead	5s
Black painted tea pots	8s.6d
Ditto, not painted	2s.6d
Enamelled, white ware tea pots	10s
Ash colour tea pots with white flowers and glazed with lead	5s
Ditto, marbled with various colours and glazed with lead	6s
Ditto, blue and white 'Rond', salt glazed and enamelled	6s
Ditto, white ware, fancy patterns, 424 3, 4 to 6 in a dozen	1s.6d
Tortoiseshell tea pots, glazed with lead	4s.6d

Various kinds of crockery

None the various kinds of clay found in this place are suitable for salt glazing. Instead, the crockery is given a yellow, brown, speckled or black glaze with litharge, red lead, white lead, galena and magnesia that are mixed in various proportions, according to the colour desired. This gives the vessels a good appearance, but due to the glaze they do not last well even though they cost more.

There is here a red clay of the same colour as the iron ore in Cumberland, and from this unglazed tea-pots are made that are called 'red china'. Red clay mixed with blue and whitish produce a marbled and speckled colour that must be glazed with lead.

Pots with a black under-glaze and painted, gilded or silvered, must be fired three times, the first for the clay itself, the second for the under-
425 glaze and the third for the painting.

Other potteries in the same neighbourhood

In addition to the potteries in the towns already mentioned, there are also large numbers in Stoke, etc., where mostly the same kind of ware as that already enumerated is made and also some simpler crockery. When, as it sometimes happens, many kilns are glazing with salt at the same time, there is such a thick smoke of salt in these manufacturing towns, that people in the streets cannot see 6 feet ahead, which, however, does not cause any difficulties. On the contrary, the smoke is considered so healthy that people who are ill come here from far away to breathe it.

Valley of crockery

The crockery produced is mainly sent to London and other seaports, from which much of it is exported to America and many other foreign countries. The potteries are said to
employ many thousands of people, but it 426
is rather peculiar that this district has been selected by the industry since the main raw materials, pipe-clay and flint, are lacking and must be fetched from far away.

Porcelain factory at Longton

Longton Hall is a gentleman's mansion where a porcelain factory was established a few years ago. So far it has not progressed further than to the making of figures after patterns from Saxony, which have not been equalled, either in respect of body, modelling or painting. Nevertheless, they were afraid of showing what they were doing, as if they were the foremost porcelain factory in existence and the only one with complete knowledge of the art, which, however, is now widely spread around the whole of Europe.

List of porcelain factories in Europe

In England there are no fewer than six porcelain factories, namely: Chelsea, Bow, Worcester, Derby, Longton and the one just started at Vauxhall. In addition there are two in Italy, namely: Naples and Florence, two in France at
Paris and also one in Flanders and one in 427
Berlin.[290]

Coal mines at Hanley

24 October. There were a number of coal mines in Hanley and in the neighbourhood that supply the many potteries in the district with fuel. The kinds of earth and rock that the shafts pass through before they reach the top coal seam and also between the seams is shown by drawing no. 320, and are pretty much the same throughout the district. The strata dip north-west 3 feet in 9 feet. In this place, as well as in most other localities in England, there are ore troubles in the coal seams, which have been fractured and displaced upwards or downwards as shown by the drawing.[291]

Fig. 320 Mines and kilns

The clay found next to the coal seams is to some extent worked up at the potteries to crockery, which is glazed with litharge and galena. This type of glaze is not as strong as the
428 salt-glaze which requires a much higher heat.

The character of the countryside in Staffordshire

The country between Newcastle and Wolverhampton in Staffordshire consists of low hills with well-cultivated fields and meadows, hedges and flourishing woods of broadleaf trees. Dung and lime mixed together are used as fertiliser.

Hunting and shooting

I stopped for a little while to look at the dangerous and breakneck hare hunt that some gentlemen were amusing themselves with.
A number of sets of hunting dogs were let loose to start the hare, which during the day hides in the hedges that serve as fences around fields and meadows. As soon as this dumb animal has been frightened and tries to save its life by running away, the fun starts and dogs, horses and men all vie with each other in attempting to be nearest to the poor beast when it finally expires of exhaustion. However, it is not a rare occurrence that both horses and riders come to

Fig. 321 [apparently another version of Fig. 320]

grief when jumping over hedges and ditches and
429 thus perish before the hare.

Another kind of hunt, or coursing with large greyhounds, is not so dangerous, because when the hare has been started it is not long before it is caught and killed, particularly if there is plenty of space in the field where the coursing takes place. A third kind of hunt that is common here and in most parts of England, is the hunting of grouse, partridges, pheasants and woodcocks, either with guns, after the dogs have found their hiding places and made them fly, or with nets specially made for the purpose.

No Englishman dares to pass the time in this way unless he has an income of £100 a year and he must not enter anybody else's property, unless he has very kind and well disposed neighbours.

In addition to the types of hunting already mentioned, there is yet another one, namely the hunting of red deer and roe-deer which is
430 reserved for the rich gentry. It is conducted on horse-back as described above in the case of the hares, but requires much more space, people, hounds and horses.

Stone, a small town and its iron trade

Stone is a small town that derives its income from agriculture and country trade but has no industry. The iron used here for horseshoes and wheel tyres is Swedish and comes from Burton, 18 miles away.[292] It comes to Burton up the river Trent from Hull. The carriage by land costs 12 pence a hundredweight and the price of Swedish iron in Stone is £22 per ton, whereas English costs £20. Well-known buyers are given 6 months credit.

The town of Stafford and its consumption of iron

Stafford is the capital of Staffordshire, but otherwise not noteworthy for industry or for any kind of trade. Iron costs the same here as in Stone and there are 3 or 4 ironmongers, but the consumption of Swedish iron does not exceed
20 tons a year. 431

Blanks or billets for ploughshares, iron axles and other similar heavy forgings are purchased from the forges at the 'iron ports' that are located further down the country near Stourbridge and Birmingham.

Horse-race

During my short stay in this place, a kind of delirium, in England called horse-racing, raged amongst the people in the same ways as previously described at Huntingdon and York. Everybody living in the county who has any money to fritter away in his trouser-pocket purse appears here at the appointed time and place to see some horses running and to provide some money for publicans and rascals to exist on during the coming year. This goes on for quite a time, depending on the extent to which the county is blessed with rich inhabitants. Here a meeting generally lasted for three days.

Wolverhampton, a manufacturing town

Wolverhampton is one of the three towns in England famous for fabrication of iron and steel-ware. It is particularly renowned for all kinds of polished articles, such as buckles, watch-chains, candle-snuffers, etc., as described
432 during my previous trip from London to Birmingham and Wolverhampton.

Coal mines at Wolverhampton

The coal mines near Wolverhampton do not have such thick seams as those at Wednesbury 4 miles away, but they are still rich, and supply an abundance of coal, giving the industries in the town and the neighbourhood great satisfaction and a price advantage over other manufactories. Just the same, many provinces in Sweden where the people are industrious and where timber is in good supply, both should, and surely would, undercut the manufacturers in Wolverhampton, as far as price is concerned, as well as those in other English towns and in Continental towns, provided, of course, that the proper arrangements for the desired type of production were made.

Bilston town with iron and metal-working factories

On the way to Wednesbury and Birmingham I went through Bilston, which manufactures many kinds of wares in non-ferrous metals such as pinchbeck, as well as engraved and turned
433 mother-of-pearl for boxes and watch-chains, buttons and all sorts of similar small articles. Here are also workshops for enamelled boxes made of copper sheets, which are stamped in dies of various shapes. Lacquered boxes of iron sheets are also made around here. All these wares are sold at high prices, the actual figures depending on the pattern and the novelty-value of inventiveness displayed by the painting, enamelling or lacquering.

Coal-mines at Bilston

A coal mine in the vicinity that I visited was working the seams shown in drawing no. 322, which dipped very little. Two quite thick seams were being mined and a fire engine had been installed to keep the water out.

The coal mined here has a rather high content of charcoal, which forms layers together
with the other bituminous material that has 434
grown on to it, as is generally the case in all coal mines in England with exception of the Cannel coal mines at Wigan. The interspersed layers of charcoal make the work of the miners infinitely easier because the coal splits very readily into pieces along the layers, which saves much effort.

Wednesbury town and coal mines

Wednesbury is perhaps the most famous place in the world for its tremendously thick seams of coal that measure 30, 33, 36 and 39 feet in height. A result of this abundance of coal is that the mines nowhere else are worked so carelessly and with such prodigality as here, where the miners can see quite plainly that the coal cannot come to an end in their lifetime [Fig. 323].

The coal mine that I saw during my last trip to this place had now fallen in and the depression and holes that resulted could be seen from the surface. It was very strange that all this happened in the evening when all the miners
had gone home so that no further harm was 435
done, although no work could be carried out in the mine for a time.

In the area around Wednesbury, as at many other places, it sometimes happens that the coal seam suddenly comes to an end and drops 30 to 40 yards. There appears to be no reason why the lower section of the coal seam and its surrounding rocks should have sunk down. It seems rather than the rocks which have penetrated above and below the coal seam at some places have had more nourishment above, and in other places greater quantities of clayey material, together with the consolidating material below the coal seam. This becomes easier to understand when it is appreciated that the soil is higher in those places where the seam lies deeper, and is lower again where the seam is encountered at a depth of 4 yards, or even, at
times, appears at the surface. 436

Fig. 322 Coal mine and fire engine

An example of what has just been cited can be seen in drawing no. 324.

Coal seam **A** appears to have been broken off and fallen away from seam **B** with all the rocks lying underneath, marked **C**, **D**. But how can a fall of this kind occur when the side of rock **E** slopes down under the side of rock A, and thus, according to the laws of nature, should support rocks **A C D**, even if so much was dug away that a drop of 20 fathoms could take place?

If rock **E**, which lies under seam **B**, had not, through stronger layers of clay and stone strata, separated seam **A** from seam **B**, the result would have been a different inclination between the two seams. This has not occurred, neither here nor elsewhere.

The same applies to the inclination that is observed in the fault between **E** and **A**, i.e. the
437 relationship is always the same.

Here there is a general rule of thumb amongst the Colliers or those who work in the mines: when they lose the coal seam, they look for it by following the fault in question. This is done in the following way: if the fault falls out of the perpendicular away from them upwards, they know that they will find the seam [in that direction]. Similarly, if the fault in question falls away from them downwards, they always find the lost seam that way.

At the coal mines a mile further east there are the following rocks:

'Clair'
'Roschtk', consisting of a stony clay which lies in thin strata
Thin Coal, only 1 yard
Hard 'Bott' and Iron Stone
Hard 'Klunst' and 'Rach' to the mean
Coal, 6 to 7 yards deep

Fig. 323a Wednesbury and coal mines

Fig.323b The same, with thick coal seams

Fig. 324 Faults in coal strata

N.B. Clean Coal is the name given to the best
438 and strongest seams

Everywhere the coal is mixed in distinct layers with charcoal.

Note: The best and thickest seam is called the 'main coal'.

Brass mill and iron-fabricating works at Wednesbury

A brass mill has recently been established in Wednesbury by Mr Wood. He obtains his copper from Bristol and the calamine from Derbyshire.

Mr Wood also owns a forge for plating and for making saw blades and carriage springs and another forge where 'old bushel iron' is melted and drawn down. All of this was mentioned during my first trip to this vicinity, as well as the gun locks that are made in the neighbourhood.

This time I arrived in Birmingham late on Saturday night and left again on Sunday morning, travelling to Stowe, belonging to Lord
439 Cobham.

Stowe and its gardens

It is visible for miles around, with its beautiful monuments and other excellent splendid structures, mainly columns and temples, that are more than royal and have been described previously.

Limestone quarry and Lime-burning at Winslow

Near Winslow there was a limestone hill, consisting of a number of beds in which petrified snails and mussels could be seen. The kiln, located just outside the town, was vaulted and provided with chimneys, as shown by drawing No. 326, in order to save fuel, which is expensive in this district where there are no coal mines. For the firing of both lime- and brick-kilns, twigs and branches from the hedgerows are used, as well as peat cut on low-lying tracts of land. The hedgerows around the fields and meadows consist mainly of bushes that bear various kinds of berries, both red and blue as well as black, some of which are used
for making preserves and wine. 440

Also in this district, the fields are divided into strips 24 feet to 30 feet wide and slightly raised at the centre, which serves the same purpose as ditches without any loss of land. As fertiliser, dung, lime and some earth mixed together are used, the earth being taken from ditches or from the roads.

Sowing of turnips and grazing for sheep

Turnips sown after midsummer can be taken up in October and the field ploughed and sown again with turnip seed. This provides grazing for

Fig. 325 [hilly landscape with villages, associated in the text with Stowe though relevance is not obvious]

the sheep during the winter and also fertiliser for next year's barley, as the sheep leave much rich dung behind both in the sheepfolds and on the fields. As soon as the leaves have been eaten, the farmers start taking the turnips up with the aid of hoes, because it is not only the sheep here that like them, but the people thrive and grow fat on them. However, it is said that this is not true of the north of England and Scotland, and perhaps applies even less to sheep that live in a
441 different climate.

Pickling of cucumbers

When cucumbers are to be pickled, a brine, strong enough to float on egg, is prepared and the cucumbers are allowed to soak in it for 6 to 7 days. For 400 cucumbers, 1 ounce of white ginger and ½ ounce of pepper are boiled with beer vinegar, and the resulting liquid is poured hot on the cucumbers that have previously been removed from the brine. Next morning, the liquid is heated up and again poured over the cucumbers and the process is repeated 9 days in succession until the cucumbers have taken on a bright green colour and the pickling is complete.

Agriculture

In many places in Buckinghamshire the people were busy sowing wheat. Two ploughs were being used for this purpose, one to make the furrows and another to turn them over after the wheat has been sown, thus ploughing the seed in. Subsequently the field is smoothed out and harrowed.

A few miles past Wendover on the way to
London, the fields are no longer made into 442
beds, as at Winslow, which is unnecessary, because the land has a natural slope, so that excess water can run off. All soil is not equally suitable for the same kind of cultivation.
A clayey soil requires ditching or making up into beds, because otherwise it is difficult for the water to drain away and penetrate this sticky and impermeable earth. A sandy or chalky soil, on the other hand, seldom or never gets too much water because it is thirsty and the water readily runs through it. In such place too much run-off of water must be prevented, and it is rather more important to make sure that the supply of water is sufficient.

The ploughs are provided with small wheels underneath and the tyres and spokes are forged

Fig. 326 Lime kiln at Winslow

of iron, but the hubs are made of wood and
have a cast iron bush inside. Such a plough is
443 pulled by 3 or 4 horses, although the soil does
not look hard, but soft and friable.

Preparing wheat for sowing

Before the wheat is sown, it is soaked for 4 to 5 hours in a brine so strong that an egg can float in it. When the brine has been drained off, lime is strewn over the wheat and mixed thoroughly with it, so that the wheat grains are uniformly covered, after which they are ready for sowing. I was told that this method not only rids the grain of mites, but also produces stronger roots and more plentiful growth.

The character of the countryside

Here I travelled several miles through a very pleasant valley which had soil containing much flint and was told that little fertilising is required, because the flint dissolves into a chalky earth that is very fertile, as already remarked during my French trip.

The trip to London

The nearer we got to London the more 444
carriages and the more travellers were seen on
the highway. The latter were generally anxious
to find some company in view of the danger of
being robbed by highwaymen, as so often is
reported in the London Gazettes. Many
reminders of this were seen hanging in gallows
along the highway. 445

Notes and references

232 The slaves were not actually brought to England, but taken directly from Africa to America.

233 Voyage iron, according to Sven Rinman, was generally $1\frac{1}{2}$ inches wide, $\frac{3}{8}$ inch thick and 10 feet long. This does not agree with the dimensions given by RRA, but it should be remembered that there were no rigidly standardised sizes in those days. However, Rinman's dimensions do correspond to 118 bars per 2240 lb whereas RRA's would give 350. In any case, voyage iron had to be fairly thin because it was intended to be bent and folded into a small package at its port of destination, for further transport by horse or mule. See Rinman, S, *Bergverks-lexicon*, 2 vols. (Stockholm: 1788–9), Vol. I p.205.

234 7/32 inch.

235 By ordinary iron, RRA probably meant square bars. Common sizes were 1 inch square by 14 feet long, corresponding to 46 bars per 2240 lb and $1\frac{1}{8}$ inch square by 14 feet long corresponding to 37 bars per 2240 lb. Narrow flats were $1\frac{1}{2}$ inches wide, $\frac{3}{8}$ inch thick and up to 17 feet long, equal to 69 bars a ton. The dimensions only differ from Rinman's voyage iron as far the length is concerned.

236 Per ton.

237 Mr Hoppenstedt was a member of the family who were partners in the Hershopp forge, established 1725 and in operation until about 1860.

238 According to Heckscher, *Sveriges Ekonomiska Historia*, Part II p.100, the total export of bar iron from Sweden during the period 1751–55 was 42,922 tons a year on average. Of this quantity 59 per cent went via the port of Stockholm and 26.9 per cent via Gothenburg. The rest, or 14.1 per cent, was handled by several small ports.

239 The figures have been rounded up or down to the nearest ton.

240 'Cardus' may be how RRA heard the word 'cartridges' as these appear in a later description.

241 Pinion wire drawer.

242 Recipe missing.

243 $\frac{1}{6}$ to $\frac{1}{2}$ inch.

244 It is difficult to understand why RRA talks about half quarts instead of pints. However, he might mean half a Swedish quarter which was equal to about $\frac{1}{3}$ of a pint.

245 Pinion wire is steel or brass wire drawn to the section of a pinion. It was particularly used for making pinions for watches.

246 Kristian Arfridsson, 1717–1799.
247 A mistake has obviously been made here. The slit iron must have cost £28 a ton and the bar iron from Öregrund £23–23½. See also the table below.
248 According to the *Victoria History of the County of Lancaster*, Vol. III p.321, the mansion was erected by Thomas Patten, a prosperous merchant, in 1750. For many years it was the seat of the Patten family, but is now the town hall of Warrington.
249 The figure shows an edge runner mill.
250 The copper smelting at Bristol was described on pages 271 to 274 and 279, but RRA does not describe any copper smelting works in Wales. He does mention Redbrook copper works, but it is actually in Gloucestershire, although Wales is just across the River Wye.
251 This part of the Diary is missing.
252 RRA states that the copper was sent to the brass works in Derby, but this must be a mistake, because there was no brass works in Derby, or in Derbyshire. On the other hand, Thomas Patten and some of his partners at Warrington did own a brass works at Cheadle and this is, no doubt, where the copper went.
253 Missing, should be 'rows'.
254 Missing.
255 1 marker 'bergsvikt' = 374 g.
256 The theoretical loss from pure zinc carbonate to pure zinc oxide would be 35%.
257 Assuming 1 barrel equal to 36 gallons the flow would amount to 3600 gallons per hour.
258 i.e. there were 12 gauges costing 1 shilling and four costing 2 shillings.
259 RRA mentions wreath iron in Vol. 1 p.308 and shown in drawing no. 159, but it looks rather different from the copper leaves mentioned above, illustrated by drawing no. 300a.
260 A dip of 1' in 5' equals 11° 20'.
261 The Dee, in fact, does not join the Severn. In going from Wrexham to Shrewsbury, a total distance of 28 miles, RRA would have crossed the Dee after travelling about 4 miles, but would not have encountered the Severn until just before Shrewsbury. Nevertheless, the distance between the two rivers is not very great, and this, no doubt, caused the confusion.
262 Distance missing, should be about 95 miles.
263 The name has been left out in the MS.
264 Here again the name has been left out.
265 Table incomplete in MS.
266 A ton long weight was 20 cwt @ 120 lb or 2400 lb. According to R Q Nott, *The Coalbrookdale Group, Horsehay Works*, pig iron was sold by long weight and melting iron by short weight (1 cwt @ 112 lb).
267 The names Champion, Ford and Darby are all known at Coalbrookdale at this time. 'Ragers' should perhaps be Reynolds, but the name 'Pohn' is entirely unfamiliar. See Raistrick, *Dynasty of Iron Founders* (David & Charles, 1970).
268 The meaning of this note is not clear, as £2 per ton for casting seems too little, though £5 for boring may be correct.
269 It appears that the men at Coalbrookdale were having a joke at RRA's expense: the largest cylinder noted by Farey in his historical review in 1827 was 75 inches bore.
270 This is believed to be the earliest description and drawing of a boring mill for engine cylinders.
271 The drawing shows it fitted to the travelling carriage.
272 i.e. the boring process has to be repeated.
273 RRA is describing the means of making large press screws with capstan heads. The screw blank, cast with journals and some sort of tit-end to insert into a coupling box or an integral coupling, as shown separately above, is turned in a heavy lathe built like a set of roll housings and driven by a water wheel. The slots or holes for shifting the heads, described in the text, are not shown.
274 In this machine there is a guide screw working through a screwed hole in a poppit. The blank, coupled to the master screw, works through another poppit in which there is an adjustable cutter rather like that in a screw box. This drawing seems to show the workpiece coupled to the master screw by the end opposite to the capstan head, not by the head end as shown (much more clearly) in Fig. 310a, with the former journal and coupling piece (to be cut off later) running off to the left of the picture. The arrangement as shown has been garbled, probably by the copyist. Note that the plain turning, which goes on with rotation all in one sense, is done by water power, while for the screwing, which requires repeated reversals of motion, the lathe is driven by a labourer.
275 In RRA's design, the master screw, workpiece and driving crank no longer traverse, so the machine can be shorter by the length of the screw, although problems associated with friction of the carriage on the bed and with adjusting the cutter might well outweigh the advantages.

276 RRA deserves credit for seeing that his arrangement might more readily be driven by millwork. However, the proportions of the drawing are questionable, another arbour would be needed to reverse the motion and there should also be some form of clutch.

277 This is probably Cornelius Hallam, who, according to Arthur Raistrick, *op.cit.*, p.115, had a forge in the Dale in the 1730s. He could still have been active during RRA's visit or might have been succeeded by a son.

278 This appears to show that much of the production was carried out by out-workers.

279 These figures show that the high cost was in the making of the pans themselves, not in any handle that might be fitted.

280 Probably the Pennerly mine in the South Shropshire field, 12 miles south-west of Shrewsbury, the only source of lead-ore in the county.

281 This corresponds to 37°, and the upending would, therefore, have been 53°.

282 These pits are probably what is marked b in Fig. 314.

283 RRA gives 222½.

284 Although RRA does not mention it, the links of the chain no doubt meshed with the spikes.

285 Although it may appear that one wagon is passing over another in the drawing, it is more likely that it shows a passing place with the two tracks at the same level, with two flat switches which could be automatic.

286 Trentham Hall, the seat of Lord Gower.

287 Protective casings of fireproof clay. RRA uses the word 'Chapsel'.

288 It is not clear what the watchman actually did, but probably he looked after the kiln and its firing.

289 RRA calls it 'Hendelsgreen' and the *Victoria County History of Staffordshire* confirms that 'Hanley Green as an alternative to Hanley was in use by the end of the 16th century and its use still lingered on in the middle of the 19th century'.

290 RRA has left out Meissen in Saxony, although he mentions patterns from this area in the preceding paragraph.

291 This information is not on the drawing.

292 The distance between Stone and Burton is 23 miles as the crow flies and considerably more by river.

Journey 7 London to Dover

23 January 1755. London, Crayford, Dartford, Rochester, Canterbury, Dover (29 January).

The journey from London to Dover and Flanders

On 23 January 1755 I set out on my journey from London to Dover and Flanders and on the way, 12 miles from London, I viewed an iron works at Crayford where iron is slit and rolled to hoops.

Rolling- and slitting-mill at Crayford

This works belongs to an ironmonger in London by the name of Fuchs, who uses between 600 and 700 tons of iron a year, most of which is Russian, which now costs as much as Stockholm iron, or £16 to £17 a ton. The finished hoops are sold for £21 to £22 a ton and are tied together to bundles, 20 hoops in each. Hoops for export to Portugal and Spain are rolled to a width of 1 inch to $1\frac{3}{4}$ inches and a length of 7 feet 6 inches to 15 feet or 20 feet.[293] The weight of a 10 feet hoop is $2\frac{1}{4}$ lbs. or 5 hundredweight for a double bundle which consists of 4 single bundles.[294]

The following iron stamps:

1752	***1752***	***1752***	***Sabel***
ΠXS	***BxS***	***HTS***	***CNL***
			NPL

446

are all Russian, and had recently been received from London to be rolled to hoops. The Sabel stamp is considered the best and the Government iron next best.

In an emergency, Gothenburg iron is used, but it loses more in weight due to scale, and is less suitable for rolling, because it is drawn down to thinner and narrower dimensions than the Russian.

The bars to be rolled are cut to length by a large shear. The actual length of the bar stumps depends on the length and width of the finished hoops, which is adjusted according to weight. The next operation to which the iron is subjected is heating in the reverberatory furnace, and then follows rolling and slitting into rods and the final rolling to hoops. The mill
447 can roll and slit 3 tons of iron in 12 hours, but when hoops are being rolled, no more than $1\frac{1}{2}$ tons is produced in the same time [Fig. 327].

Four workers are employed at the rolling- and slitting-mill, not counting those who straighten the hoops and tie them into bundles. The 'headman', or the one who makes the slitting rolls and assembles the stands of rolls, is paid 16 shillings a week and also gets free housing. The 'heater' is paid 10/6 a week and the two other men 8 to 9 shillings.

The furnace is 9 feet long, 3 feet wide and 1 foot 6 inches high, but the height gradually decreases towards the chimney, in order to force the flame down onto the iron, which lies on the bottom. Letter A [missing in Fig. 327] is the handle of a damper that shuts off the draught when the iron has been heated and the rolling begins. It is possible to heat 16 to 20 hundredweight of sheared iron stumps at a 448
time, but not more than 6 to 8 hundredweight of slit rods for the rolling of hoops.

Fig. 327 Furnace at Crayford; rolls

Summary of Costs of Rolling Hoops

During two days 6 ton iron @ £17 a ton is rolled and slit	£102.0s.0d
During four days 6 ton iron is rolled to hoops with 5% scaling loss	£5.2s.0d
Coal consumed during 2 days rolling and slitting 24 bushels @ 1 shilling	£1.4s.0d
Coal consumed during 4 days rolling of hoops 32 bushels @ 1 shilling	£1.12s.0d
Weekly wages for the headman	16s.0d
Weekly wages for the heater	10s.6d
Weekly wages for two labourers	17s.0d
Wages for straightening and bundling the hoop-iron, 4 shillings a ton	£1.10s.0d
Installation and maintenance costs, and the manager's salary	£2.0s.0d
Total:	£115.11s.6d

449

Taking all the different sizes of hoops into consideration, their average sales price is £21.10s.0d a ton, which for 6 tons amounts to £129.0s.0d Deducting the production costs from this figure, we arrive at a profit of £13.8s.6d per 6 ton.

The consumption of pitcoal for [rolling and] slitting amounts to 12 bushels a day, but for the rolling of the hoops only 8 bushels a day are used. The coal costs 1 shilling a bushel but when bought in large quantities it is possible to negotiate a lower price, not least as this mill is located down the river Thames from London.

The town of Dartford and a rolling- and slitting-mill nearby

Another 3 miles from London lies Dartford, and nearby a rolling- and slitting mill where hoop-iron is made from Russian iron. This mill belongs to Messrs. Melcher and Wild, two merchants in London. The supply of water here is not so good as at Crayford and therefore the production does not amount to more than 400 tons a year.

The length of the body of the rolls used at 450
this mill was only 9 inches, not counting necks and wobblers. The diameter of the bottom roll was between 11 inches and 12 inches, but top roll was ¼ smaller,[295] which stretches the iron better lengthways during the rolling. If the rolls were of the same diameter the iron would spread more laterally instead [Fig. 328].[296]

At this mill it was observed that the cutting- 451
discs were only steeled at the periphery, because the cutting is performed by the edges. For the

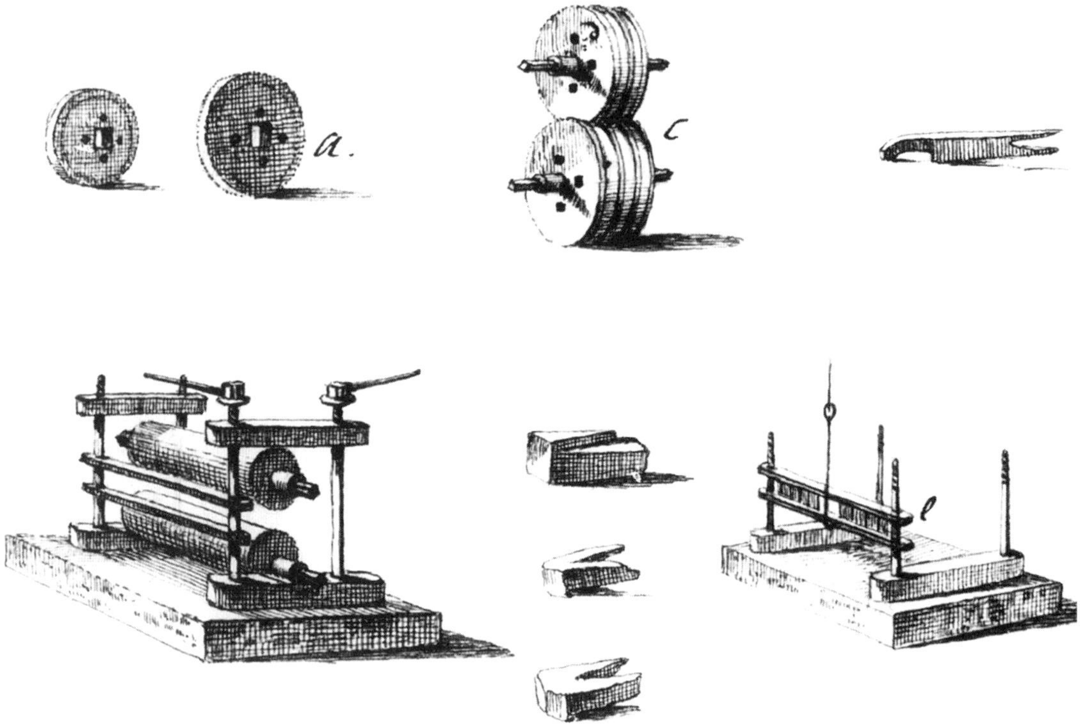

Fig. 328 Rolls and slitting discs at Dartford

same reason the two outside discs are only
452 steeled on the inner edges, as shown by letter **a** on the drawing.

When the discs have been assembled in the roll-housings, a bar of iron as shown by letter **b** is placed in each groove which guides the slit bars so that they do not bend, neither up nor down, but pass straight out from the back of the rolls. The actual diameter of the cutting discs does not matter, but it is highly necessary that all of them have exactly the same diameter. The cutting edges are not sharpened in any way except by the hammer during forging. For the hardening, the discs are heated in the reverberatory mill furnace. When assembled, the discs do not overlap by more than $\frac{1}{2}$ inch or less as indicated by letter **c**. When the discs are assembled on their shafts, smaller iron discs or rings are placed between them to keep them at equal distance from each
453 other. Finally they are secured by two screws as shown by letter **d**. When the slitting- and rolling-mill has been working for some time, it is cooled down by letting water from a lead pipe run over it.

During the rolling of hoops, it was observed that it was necessary to change from one end of the rolls to the other in order to ensure a more even wear of the roll surface. At this works a number of pieces of iron are used for this purpose, and placed between two horizontal iron bars, letter **e**, fitted to the posts of the mill. Between them only sufficient room for the iron bar being rolled to hoops is left. The above mentioned pieces of iron fill the space between the two horizontal bars that support them, and are fastened by means of a hook to the top one, but in such a way that they can be readily
450 removed or slid from side to side.

The towns of Rochester, Strood and Chatham

28 January (1755). The town of Rochester is located by the River Medway, 30 miles from London in the county of Kent. Very close to Rochester are Strood and Chatham, two small towns, the latter being noteworthy for its Royal Shipyard and Docks. Here I counted between 40 and 50 warships lying in the river. The yard was busily engaged with the rigging out of ships intended for the defence of the American Colonies against the French and it was, therefore, forbidden to view either the shipyard
451 or the dock at close quarters.

Messrs 'Machy' and 'Muilman' have contracted to supply the Government with all the iron consumed here for the account of the Admiralty. In Rochester and Strood there are also some blacksmiths who make ships bolts, small anchors for fishing-boats and the like, but the iron used for these purposes, as well as for wheel-tyres, gratings, horseshoes and other work is obtained from Messrs. Morgan, Mister and Raby, Ironmongers of London, and costs £18 a ton, excluding carriage which the buyer must pay himself.

Not counting the iron used by the shipyard, the consumption of Swedish iron in these towns may amount to between 70 and 80 tons per
annum. 453

Straw chopping box at Rochester

The appended drawing no. 329 shows the design of a straw chopping box in use at
Rochester. Letter **A** is the trough in which the 454
straw, hay or sainfoin is placed. **B** is a piece of board, connected to a pedal by cords **c-c**, which pushes the hay together under the knife during cutting. **F** is the chopping knife, connected with the pedal **gg** and the cross-rail **h**, so that both are lifted with the knife. **I** is a bar which is fixed over the pedal to make it easier to support the foot and at the same time to press the hay together during cutting. **K** is a fork that draws the hay forward every time the foot is lifted.

Drawing no. 330 shows the method used for cutting hay from a stack. The cutting-knife is only sharpened on one side, the blade being 1 foot 3 inches long. The man who does the cutting holds the handle with both hands as the
drawing demonstrates. 456

Canterbury town, Bishop's Seat and factories

Canterbury, located in Kent 27 miles from Rochester and 53 miles from London, is the seat of an Archbishop. The town is of considerable size and has 14 churches in addition to the Cathedral, which is a vast edifice in the Gothic style.

There is here a factory for the weaving of brocade, silk stockings and Turkish carpets. Of the carpets, two kinds are made. 'Tapis de Bruxelles' is woven on a loom called 'Lisse Basse'.[297] Some looms of this type are also found at Les Gobelins in Paris [Fig. 331].

The other kind is called 'Tapis de Châlons- 457
sur-Marne', after the place where they

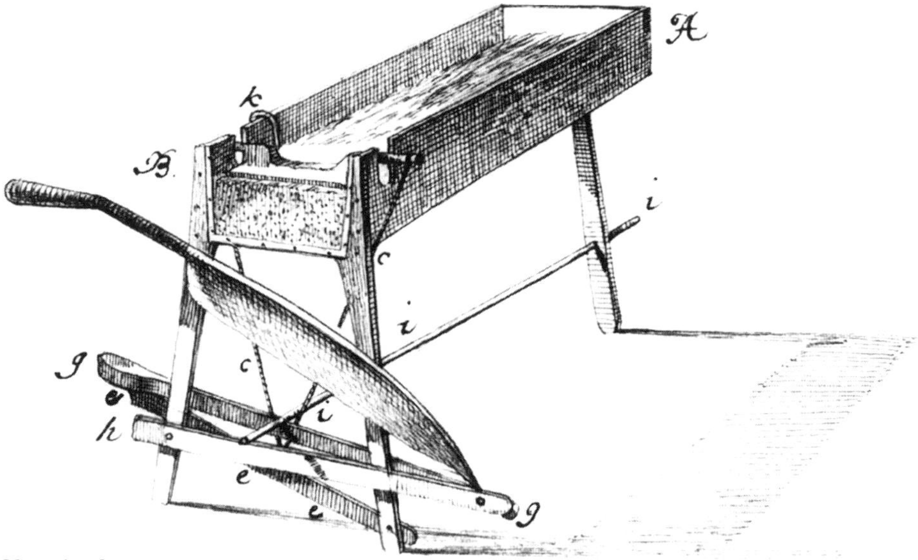

Fig. 329 Chopping box

Fig. 330 Cutting hay from a stack

Fig. 331 Lisse Basse

[originated]. This is made by weaving on a loom called 'Lisse Haute', the design of which is shown by drawing No. 332.

At Gobelins, carpets are made on the same type of loom, the only difference being that there they are smooth, and here they are stitched in the same way as velvet.

For this purpose only worsted is used, wound onto wooden pegs that look like distaffs, as shown in Fig. 332, letter **a**. Each colour has to be tied separately into tufts, which are subsequently cut with scissors. If a small piece with the same colour is made, the tufts are placed over an iron rod with a knife at one end, which cuts off the tufts, letter **b**. As soon as the tufts are tied they are pushed together with an iron comb.[298]

I was told that a fire screen that was being made during my visit would cost 16 guineas.

NB Four miles from London near Chelsea, at a place called Fulham, there is also a factory for tapestries of this kind, run by a French merchant. The Duke of Cumberland brought the workers from Paris.[299]

The consumption of iron in Canterbury 458

Most of the iron consumed in Canterbury is handled by Mr Creed, an ironmonger, who buys it from Mr Wordsworth in London. The greater part of it is used for wheel-tyres and horseshoes, but a little is for grilles and fire-grates. The dimensions of the bars are $1\frac{3}{4}$ inches × $\frac{3}{8}$ inches, $2\frac{1}{2}$ inches × $\frac{7}{8}$ inches and intermediate sizes of square bars from $\frac{3}{8}$ inches to 1 inch and $1\frac{1}{2}$ inches.

The stamps ***)(*** and ***)-(***[300] from Stockholm and ***HOS***[301] from Gothenburg are in demand here. The iron is bought in London for £17 to

Fig. 332 Lisse Haute [letters missing]

Fig. 333 Stacks of hop poles

£17.5.0 and sold in Canterbury for £18.10 a ton. Blanks for ploughshares come from Sussex, where they cost £16.10.0 to £17.0.0 a ton; also heavy square bars for grates under brewing coppers, which, however, are of poor quality iron.

Hop-gardens

29 January. The country around Canterbury is quite fertile and particularly suitable for growing hops, and one could see here whole
459 fields full of stacks of hop poles, which from a far distance looked like tents in a camp for a large army [Fig. 333].

The hop-mounds were now all spread out evenly and will not be made up again until the hop-shoots start appearing in the spring. Last year the hops were sold for 35 to 40 shillings a hundredweight, mostly to buyers in London.

The soil in the province of Kent

Below the soil itself in the whole of this district for miles around and right down to the sea there is nothing but chalk, which here and there contains a few layers of flint. To increase the amount of fertiliser available, chalk is burnt to lime and mixed with dung and earth that are allowed to rot together. The thickness of the soil above the chalk is generally no more than a foot. The brownish soil itself originated from
dissolved and decayed chalk. 454

The town of Dover and the packet-boats that go between Dover and Calais

Dover is located by the sea 16 miles from Canterbury and is the harbour for travelling to France. 4 packet-boats and 8 other ships are maintained here for this purpose. To hire a ship
sailing across to Calais, a distance of 22 miles, 455

Fig. 334 Dover, harbour and cliffs

costs 3 guineas in the summer, but 5 guineas in the winter. Of this amount, the ship must pay £12.10s.0d [sic] on arrival in Calais. If one happens to arrive in Dover when the packet-boat is ready to sail, one can travel in it for no more than half a guinea a passenger. If one should wait a day or two for the departure, the intended saving is soon eaten up because the keepers of the Inns here are past masters of the art of fleecing their customers. In addition to what they make from the passenger traffic, the inhabitants of this town also derive some income from trading in coin and contraband.

The nature of the English coast 456

The whole of this seacoast, as well as the country for some distance inland, consists of chalk hills that shine forth for miles out to sea. In clear weather the coasts on both sides of the Channel can be seen, the French coast also consisting of chalk hills. When the wind is favourable, as it was on this occasion, the ships sail from Dover to Calais in less than 3 hours.

I sailed on the packet-boat across the 460
Channel to Calais. Drawing No. 334 shows a view of Dover and its castle, including part of the town and its castle and the chalk cliffs.

Notes and references

293 RRA has left out the thickness, but it is known that hoop iron generally was made $^1/_8$ inch, $^1/_4$ inch and $^5/_{16}$ inch thick.

294 There are several inconsistencies in this sentence. If we assume that the bars were of the smallest section indicated, namely 1 inch × $^1/_8$ inch, the weight of a 10 feet length would still be 4.3 lb and not 2.25 lb. Since the total weight of 4 single bundles or 80 bars is stated to be 5 hundredweight or 560 lb, each bar would weigh 7 lb, which is the weight of a bar $1^5/_8$ inch × $^1/_8$ inch × 10 feet.

295 In other words, if the bottom roll was 12 inches in diameter, the top one would be 9 inches.

296 Part of pages 450 and 451 are taken up by remarks about Rochester, Chatham and Strood, whereupon RRA returns to the rolling and slitting mill at Dartford.
To get this text placed in its right context the part about the three towns has been moved backwards in order to unite the two sections about the Dartford Mill.

297 Lisse basse, low warp loom; lisse haute, high warp loom.

298 RRA's original sketch, in one of the surviving notebooks, shows more detail, including drawings of the bobbins, the rods with knives and the iron comb.

299 This paragraph comes from the notebook, not included in the fair copy.

300 Nolby, Geijersholm (both Värmland).

301 Gravendal (Dalarna).

Appendices

Appendix 1 Source materials

The documents used for this translation are listed below.

Library at Jernkontoret, Stockholm

The Angerstein Travel Diaries and Commentaries
Eight volumes in full morocco bindings, gilded spines with red labels, approximately 230 × 270 mm. These are hand-written fair copies of Angerstein's notebooks in a German gothic cursive script (*tysk slängstil*). At least two different hands are identifiable. Foreign words and subject headings are written in English copperplate. See illustration on p.xxi. Fair copies in pencil of Angerstein's sketches are bound in with the text.

The two volumes covering Angerstein's visit to Britain are:

'II. Bandet: Dagbok öfver Resan genom England åren 1753, 1754 och 1755, af R. R. Angerstein, förra delen' (456 pp., 185 illustrations)

'III. Bandet: Dagbok öfver Resan genom England åren 1753, 1754 och 1755, af R. R. Angerstein, senare delen' (471 pp., 169 illustrations).

Riksarkivet (Swedish State Archives), Stockholm

'Jernkontorets Fullmäktiges Arkiv' F IIa: 4
This folder contains original notebooks and working papers.

1 Notebook with soft marbled covers, approximately 165 × 195 mm. 'No. 2' is written on the front. Diary for the period 25 October to 16 December 1753, written in a transitional hand. Wide margins used for ink sketches and subject headings. See illustration on p.xx (page for 3 December 1753). Note: this notebook and the one in F IIa: 5 are the only surviving notebooks of the 20 which Angerstein filled during his travels in England and Wales.

2 Similar notebook entitled 'Collectanea under Resan i Ängland' ('Notes from Journey in England'), with 'Af intet värde och kommer ej att utskrifvas' ('of no value, not to be copied') written in another hand. Various subjects, including: blast furnaces in North America; iron mines in England; forests in England; Bromford Forge; forests – lecture by Mr King; iron stamps and prices (transcribed in Vol. 1, pp. 120–4).

3 Notebook with soft marbled covers, approximately 170 × 105 mm. Rough notes and sketches, mostly in pencil. Some names written out in English hands, e.g. 'Hanbury, Roberts & Allen, Merchants in Bristol'.

4 Bundle of folios, approximately 200 × 310 mm, written in a gothic hand with corrections in another hand. Transcription of the diaries for 15 September 1753 to 29 January 1755, i.e. the whole of the journeys in England and Wales, apart from the first section of Vol. 1, which has Latin pagination. This appears to be an intermediate transcription, and the corrections seem to be in Angerstein's own hand. The folios are numbered to correspond with notebooks 1 to 19, plus the final one which also covers Ghent, most of which do not survive. There are no illustrations.

'Jernkontorets Fullmäktiges Arkiv' F IIa: 5
This folder contains an unbroken series of diary notebooks, starting in London on 27 January 1755 and continuing with Angerstein's journey to the Low Countries. One is of interest here:

Notebook with soft marbled covers, approximately 120 × 175 mm, entitled 'London & Gand No.1'. Diary and sketches for 27–29 January 1755 and beyond.

Appendix 2 Iron and steel stamps

The stamps that Angerstein encountered in his travels provided a valuable source of commercial and technical intelligence, and he took pains to copy them into his notebooks, together with comments about performance and price.

Most of the stamps in the table below are Swedish iron stamps. In the year 1600, the Swedish government ordained that each forge should mark every bar that it made with a distinguishing mark. This enabled the government to safeguard the quality of the iron and to keep track of its passage through government weigh-houses and bonded stores on the way to export. It also ensured that the forges did not exceed their quota.

By Angerstein's time there were several hundred of these stamps in the official records, including drawings of each stamp, with the name, location and ownership of the forge and its annual production quota.

The principal sources for identification of the stamps in the diary have been the stamp books held in the archives of Jernkontoret. The better-known stamps, such as Österby (Österbybruk) and Leufsta (Lövstabruk), presented little difficulty and we can be sure of the attribution. Others have been more of a problem, not least because the drawings in the manuscript are often sketchy and have probably lost detail in the copying process; some have proved impossible to place. The attributions given represent our best effort at identification at this stage, though further research might reveal different answers.

Reference symbols have been used in the main text. These are given in the table, together with copies of the drawings in the manuscript.

Manuscript page	Location	Symbol used in text	Stamp in manuscript	Attribution
Volume 1				
XVI	London	***Crown***		London weigh house stamp
Facing *XVII* (Fig. 25)	Snowhill	… …		Not identified (Öregrund) Not identified (Öregrund)
77	On way to Salisbury	***RD***		Rottnedal (Värmland)
78	Plymouth	***EL***		Didrikshammare
		M+		Åttersta (Gästrikland)
123	Exeter	***Lx***		Västanfors (Västmanland)
		oo		Österby (Uppland)
		EL		Didrikshammare
		W		Tunafors (Sörmland)
124	Exeter	***HOS***		Gravendal, Strömsdal (Dalarna)

Manuscript page	Location	Symbol used in text	Stamp in manuscript	Attribution
124	Exeter	***IS***		Krontorp (Värmland)
		IL		Bjurbäck, Storfors (Värmland)
		X		Smedjebacken (Värmland)
		GC		Molkom (Värmland)
		Stenback		Harg (Uppland)
		OPS		Gammal Kråppa, Björneborg (Värmland)

Volume 2

Manuscript page	Location	Symbol used in text	Stamp in manuscript	Attribution
32	Nottingham	***HG***	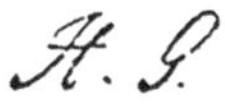	Hofors (Gästrikland)
33	Nottingham	***Burning Mountain***		Tolvfors (Gästrikland)
		B		Wall (Gästrikland)
		xx		Not identified
		xx/xx		Not identified
		X/L		Norrby (Närke)
		RF		Frötuna (Närke)
		Anchor		Iggesund (Hälsingland)
		E crowned		Not identified
		EW	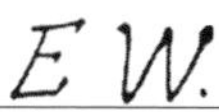	Not identified
		:)(:		Nolby, Borgvik (Värmland)
		CI		Älvsbacka (Värmland)
44	Derby	***:)(:***		Nolby, Borgvik (Värmland)
		OK		Mölnbacka (Värmland)
		HG	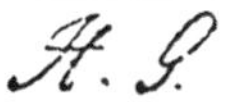	Hofors (Gästrikland)
		Burning Mountain		Tolvfors (Gästrikland)
		Ø		? Gyllenfors (Västergötland)

Manuscript page	Location	Symbol used in text	Stamp in manuscript	Attribution
44	Derby	***xxBxx***	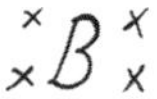	Not identified
		AF		Not identified
84	Cliston	***)(***		Borgvik (Värmland)
114	Hull	***Burning Mountain***		Tolvfors (Gästrikland)
131	Seamer	***A crowned***		Svartå (Närke)
153	Stockton	***CI***		Älvsbacka (Värmland)
		SF	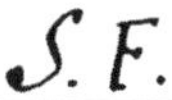	Stjärnfors (Närke)
		OPS		Björneborg (Gästrikland)
154	Stockton	***DS***		Åbyhammar, Fellingsbro (Närke)
		CS		Forsbacka (Värmland)
155	Stockton	***V***		Upperud (Värmland)
		HK		Ransäter (Värmland)
		W		Lesjöfors (Värmland)
191	Newcastle	***L***		Leufsta (Uppland)
		oo		Österby (Uppland)
		W crowned	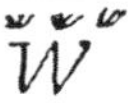	Västland, Strömsberg (Uppland)
		PL crowned		Åkerby (Uppland)
203	Teams	***JC3D3***	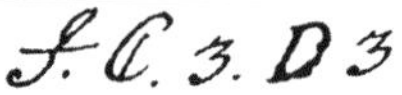	Crowley steel stamp
		D3	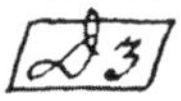	Crowley steel stamp
		L		Leufsta (Uppland)
		PL crowned		Åkerby (Uppland)
		oo		Österby (Uppland)
		W crowned	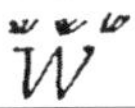	Västland, Strömsberg (Uppland)
		CDG		Karlholm (Uppland)
204	Teams	***L***		Leufsta (Uppland)

Manuscript page	Location	Symbol used in text	Stamp in manuscript	Attribution
204	Teams	***PL crowned***		Åkerby (Uppland)
		No. 1 boxed IC heart		Crowley steel stamp
238	Blackhall Mill	***L***		Leufsta (Uppland)
		PL crowned		Åkerby (Uppland)
		W crowned	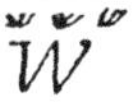	Västland, Strömsberg (Uppland)
239	Blackhall Mill	***oo***		Österby (Uppland)
		L		Leufsta (Uppland)
		PL crowned		Åkerby (Uppland)
		W crowned	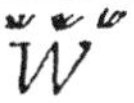	Västland, Strömsberg (Uppland)
259	Carlisle	***H***		Rådanefors (Västergötland)
445	Crayford	***1752*** П****S***	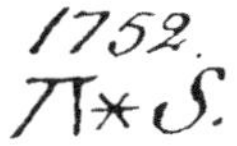	Russian iron stamp
		1752 BxS	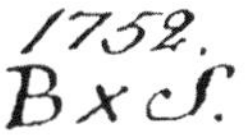	Russian iron stamp
		1752 HTS		Russian iron stamp
		Sabel CNL NPL		Russian iron stamp
458	Canterbury	***)(***		Borgvik (Värmland)
		)-(		Geijersholm (Värmland)
		HOS		Gravendal (Dalarna)

Appendix 3 Translation methods and conventions

Most of the translation was made directly from photocopies of the text of the bound fair copies of Angerstein's notes, held in the archives of Jernkontoret, though use was also made of the original notebooks where available. Mid-eighteenth century Swedish presented few problems that could not be solved with the help of contemporary and modern dictionaries, but the gothic handwriting of the copyists was a considerable palaeographic challenge. Marianne Fornander's transcript was a great help here in the later stages of the work. Ironically, Angerstein's own hand, of which little remains, is easily legible to the modern eye. Mistakes that appear to have crept in during the copying process – notebook, to intermediate copy, to fair copy – are noted, though passages where the sense is completely lost are few.

The translation has been kept as literal as possible; insertions necessary to make sense are indicated by square brackets.

Angerstein often has idiosyncratic spellings of English proper names and, unless the correct version is clear beyond doubt, his version is given in inverted commas – e.g. 'Acrell' – with an endnote giving possible interpretation (in this case, Hockerill). The same applies to trade terms and, if no clarification is available, there is no endnote.

The endnotes are intended to aid interpretation, but being based on the translators' own research, tend to reflect their own particular interests. Advice from specialists has been particularly helpful in this area.

The illustrations

The pen-and-ink sketches in Angerstein's surviving notebooks are clear, though small and fairly crude. In the few cases where it has been possible to compare the originals with the fair copies, it can be seen that the artist has improved perspective and added minor artistic flourishes, though significant detail is sometimes lost and there are some outright mistakes. Indicative letters referred to in the text are often absent.

Most of the drawings have a simple caption associated with the figure reference number in the margin of the fair copy. Occasionally there is a drawing lacking any reference in the text, though it has usually been possible to make a clear identification. A few near-duplicates appear for no obvious reason.

Weights, measures and currency

In the diary, English and Swedish units are used indiscriminately, and these have been carried through to the translation, though an endnote has been added where necessary for the sake of clarity. The following conversions may be useful, though the figures were subject to local variation and should be treated with caution:

1 famn = 3 alnar = 178 cm
1 aln = 2 fot = 59 cm
1 Swedish mile = *c.* 6 English miles
1 English mile = 1.6 km

1 skeppund (viktualievikt) = 20 lispund = 170 kg
1 lispund = 20 skålpund = 8.5 kg

1 tunna = 2 spann = 147 litre (stricken measure)
1 kanna = 2 stop = 4 kvarter = 1.3 litre

1 daler kopparmynt = 4 mark = 32 öre
£1 sterling = *c.* 40 daler kopparmynt
£1 sterling = 20s = 240d
1s = 12d.

Bibliography

All published books referred to in the main text and in the notes are listed below, together with a few books of more general interest.

Althin, T, 'Eric Geisler och hans utländska resa', *Med Hammare och Fackla*, 26 (1971).

Andrews, C R, *The Story of Wortley Ironworks*, 2nd edn (Nottingham: Milward, 1956).

Baxter, B, *Stone Blocks and Iron Rails* (Newton Abbot: David & Charles, 1966).

Boyer, C S, *Early Forges and Furnaces in New Jersey* (London: OUP, 1931).

Bowden, M (ed.), *Furness Iron* (English Heritage, 2000).

Broling, G, *Anteckningar under en Resa i England 1797, 1798 och 1799 Vol. I–III* (Stockholm: Lindh, 1811).

Brook, F and Allbutt, M, *The Shropshire Lead Mines* (Leek: Moorland Publishing Co., 1973).

Buchanan, R A, *Industrial Archaeology in Britain* (Harmondsworth: Penguin, 1972).

Buchanan, R A and Cossons, N, *The Industrial Archaeology of the Bristol Region* (Newton Abbot: David & Charles, 1969).

Ferrner, B, Woolrich (ed.), *Journal 1759/1760, an Industrial Spy in Bath and Bristol* (Eindhoven: De Archaeologische Pers, 1987).

Flinn, M W, *Men of Iron, the Crowleys in the Early Iron Industry* (Edinburgh: The University Press, 1962).

Day, J, *Bristol Brass: the History of the Industry* (Newton Abbot: David & Charles, 1973).

Day, J and Tylecote, R F (eds.), *The Industrial Revolution in Metals* (London: Institute of Metals, 1991).

Ford, T D and Rieuwerts, J H (eds.), *Lead Mining in the Peak District* (Bakewell: Peak Park Planning Board, rev. edn 1970).

Gale, W K V, *The British Iron and Steel Industry* (Newton Abbot: David & Charles, 1967).

Gale, W K V, *Iron and Steel* (Hartington: Moorland Publishing Co., 1977).

Gale, W K V, *The Iron and Steel Industry, a Dictionary of Terms* (Newton Abbot: David & Charles, 1971).

Hart, C E, *The Industrial History of Dean* (Newton Abbot: David & Charles, 1971).

Heckscher, E F, trans. Ohlin, *An Economic History of Sweden* (Cambridge, MA: Harvard University Press, 1954).

Hildebrand, K-G, trans. Britton, A, *Swedish Iron in the Seventeenth Century* (Stockholm: Jernkontorets Bergshistoriska Utskott, 1992).

Hudson, K H, *The Industrial Archaeology of Southern England*, 2nd edn, (Newton Abbot: David & Charles, 1968).

Macfarlane, W, *Iron and Steel Manufacture*, 5th edn (London: Longman, Green, 1917).

Marshall, J D and Davies-Shiel, *The Industrial History of the Lake Counties*, 2nd edn (Cumbria: Bekermet Bookshop, 1977).

Raistrick, A R, *Dynasty of Iron Founders: the Darbys and Coalbrookdale* (Newton Abbot: David & Charles, 1970).

Rees, D M, *Mines, Mills and Furnaces: an Introduction to Industrial Archaeology in Wales* (London: HMSO, 1969).

Rees, W, *Industry before the Industrial Revolution* (Cardiff: University of Wales Press, 1968).

Reynolds, J, *Windmills and Watermills* (London, Hugh Evelyn, 1970).

Richardson, J B, *Metal Mining* (London: Allen Lane, 1974).

Riden, P, *A Gazetteer of Charcoal-fired Blast Furnaces in Great Britain in Use Since 1660*, 2nd edn (Cardiff: Merton Priory Press, 1993).

Rinman, S, *Försök till Järnets Historia* (Stockholm: 1782).

Rinman, S, trans. of *Allgemeine Bergverks Lexicon* (1808).

Rolt, L T C and Allen, J S, *The Steam Engine of Thomas Newcomen* (Hartington: Moorland Publishing Co., 1977).

Rydberg, S, *Svenska Studieresor till England under Frihetstiden* (Uppsala: 1951).

Savage, G, *Porcelain through the Ages*, 2nd edn (Harmondsworth: Penguin, 1963).

Schubert, H R, *History of the British Iron and Steel Industry* (London: Routledge & Kegan Paul, 1957).

Smith, D M, *The Industrial Archaeology of the East Midlands* (Dawlish: David & Charles, 1965).

Straker, E, *Wealden Iron* (Newton Abbot: David & Charles, 1969).

Svedenstierna, E T, trans. Dellow, *Svedenstierna's Tour of Great Britain 1802–3* (Newton Abbot: David & Charles, 1973).

Swedenborg, E, trans. Sjögren, *Opera Philosophica et Mineralia* (Stockholm: 1923).

Index

Names of individuals are only indexed if they are of wider significance; the many local merchants and ironmongers encountered along the way are not included.
Page numbers in *italics* refer to illustrations.